1993 CASE AND
STATUTORY SUPPLEMENT

to

PRODUCTS LIABILITY

AND

SAFETY

CASES AND MATERIALS

By

W. PAGE KEETON

W. Page Keeton Professor of Law of Torts
University of Texas

DAVID G. OWEN

Webster Professor of Tort Law
University of South Carolina

JOHN E. MONTGOMERY

Dean and Professor of Law
University of South Carolina

MICHAEL D. GREEN

Professor of Law
University of Iowa

SECOND EDITION

Westbury, New York
THE FOUNDATION PRESS, INC.
1993

COPYRIGHT © 1980, 1983, 1985, 1989 THE FOUNDATION PRESS, INC.

COPYRIGHT © 1993
By
THE FOUNDATION PRESS, INC.
All rights reserved

ISBN 1–56662–074–0

[No claim of copyright is made for official U.S. government statutes, rules or regulations.]

PRINTED ON 10% POST CONSUMER RECYCLED PAPER

K., O., M. & G. Prod. Liab. & Safety 2nd Ed. UCS
1993 Case & Stat. Supp.

PREFACE

The purpose of this supplement is to keep the student of products liability law current with developments that have occurred since 1989. We have included several recent cases that shed important new insights on this area of the law. State legislatures continue to enact products liability "reform" acts of various types, and a number of the more important statutes of this type are included for the first time in this supplement. At the federal level, bills continue to be filed, and Congress continues to debate whether and how to legislate on products liability law. We have included the last significant bill to be reported out of committee, S. 640, the Product Liability Fairness Act, which narrowly escaped passage in the Senate in 1992.

Other than substituting S. 640 for its predecessor Senate bill and report, we have retained the Restatement, Uniform Commercial Code, and legislative materials set out in the statutory supplement that accompanied the second edition of the casebook in 1989. In order to maximize the materials available to teachers and students, we have erred on the side of over-inclusion, so that we expect teachers to be selective in their assignments from this supplement.

From time to time we receive comments and suggestions for improvement from users of the book. We consider this information valuable in our ongoing effort to present teachers and students with the most useful and up-to-date materials on the law of products liability that we can possibly provide. With this in mind, we once again invite comments and criticisms on the materials in the hardback and this supplement alike.

DAVID G. OWEN
MICHAEL D. GREEN

June, 1993

*

ACKNOWLEDGMENTS

We are grateful for the diligent research and administrative assistance of Ted Olt and the secretarial and administrative assistance of Diana DeWalle and Jimmie Sneed.

We would also like to acknowledge the following publishers who permitted us to use the materials noted:

American Law Institute, Restatement of the Law, Torts, Second, selected sections. Copyright © 1965 by The American Law Institute. Reprinted with the permission of The American Law Institute.

Uniform Commercial Code, Official Text and Comments, selected sections. Copyright © 1987 by The American Law Institute and the National Conference of Commissioners on Uniform State Laws. Reprinted with permission of the Permanent Editorial Board for the Uniform Commercial Code.

Lurking in the background, as ever, remain our wives, Joan and Carol.

D.G.O.
M.D.G.

*

SUMMARY OF CONTENTS

	Page
PREFACE	iii
ACKNOWLEDGMENTS	v
TABLE OF CASES	xxi
CASES AND NOTES	1
RESTATEMENT (SECOND) OF TORTS (1965), SELECTED SECTIONS	219
UNIFORM COMMERCIAL CODE, SELECTED SECTIONS	297
SELECTED STATE PRODUCTS LIABILITY STATUTES	364
CONSUMER PRODUCT SAFETY ACT, AS AMENDED	440
MAGNUSON–MOSS WARRANTY ACT	501
MODEL UNIFORM PRODUCT LIABILITY ACT	517
S. 640, PRODUCT LIABILITY FAIRNESS ACT	615
COMMITTEE REPORT ON S. 640	630
EEC DIRECTIVE ON LIABILITY FOR DEFECTIVE PRODUCTS	734

TABLE OF CONTENTS

	Page
Preface	iii
Acknowledgments	v
Table of Cases	xxi

CASES AND NOTES

CHAPTER 2. THEORIES OF MANUFACTURER LIABILITY

SECTION 4. STRICT LIABILITY IN TORT

Casebook page		Supplement page
185	Note on Risk Spreading	1

CHAPTER 3. THE CONCEPT OF DEFECTIVENESS

SECTION 1. THEORIES AND TESTS OF DEFECTIVENESS

A. Consumer Expectations

194	Note on Children's Expectations	2
205	*Ewen v. McLean Trucking Co.*	2

B. Risk-Benefit Analysis

215	Note on What Counts as Risk	7
222	*Griggs v. BIC Corporation*	7

C. The Continuing Search for a Viable Test of "Defectiveness"

241	Note on Alternative Design Under Barker	18

SECTION 5. LIMITATIONS ON DEFECTIVENESS

D. Unavoidable Dangers and "State of the Art"

454	Note on Imputing Knowledge of Danger	19
455	*Snyder v. Mekhjian*	19

CHAPTER 4. CAUSATION

SECTION 1. CAUSE IN FACT: CONNECTING PLAINTIFF'S HARM TO DEFENDANT'S BREACH OF DUTY

B. Reliance on Warnings

489	Note on the Physician's Role in Causation	29

TABLE OF CONTENTS

CHAPTER 6. DAMAGES
SECTION 2. EMOTIONAL DISTRESS

Casebook page		Supplement page
585	*Khan v. Shiley Incorporated*	30

SECTION 4. PUNITIVE DAMAGES

629	Note on Introducing Evidence of Defendant's Wealth	37
631	*Pacific Mutual Life Insurance Co. v. Haslip*	37
	Note on *TXO*	63

CHAPTER 7. SPECIAL TYPES OF DEFENDANTS
SECTION 6. CERTIFIERS, ENDORSERS, AND PUBLISHERS

682	Note on Advertisers for Contract Killers	64

SECTION 9. ALLOCATING RESPONSIBILITY AND LOSS: CONTRIBUTION AND INDEMNITY

A. Loss Allocation Within the Distribution Chain

708	Note on *Promaulayko*	65

CHAPTER 8. SPECIAL TYPES OF PRODUCTS AND TRANSACTIONS
SECTION 5. DISPOSAL AND DESTRUCTION

782	*High v. Westinghouse Electric Corporation*	66

CHAPTER 9. SPECIAL ISSUES IN AUTOMOTIVE LITIGATION
SECTION 1. CRASHWORTHINESS

810	*Perry v. Mercedes Benz of North America, Inc.*	73

CHAPTER 10. SPECIAL ISSUES IN TOXIC SUBSTANCE LITIGATION
SECTION 1. LIABILITY STANDARDS AND PROBLEMS OF JUDICIAL ADMINISTRATION

A. In General

879	*Cimino v. Raymark Industries, Inc.*	86

B. Cigarette Litigation

880	*Cipollone v. Liggett Group, Inc.*	101
887	*Haines v. Liggett Group, Inc.*	124

TABLE OF CONTENTS

SECTION 2. CAUSATION

A. The Capacity of the Agent to Cause Plaintiff's Disease

Casebook page		Supplement page
922	*DeLuca v. Merrell Dow Pharmaceuticals, Inc.*	130
	Note on *Daubert*	149

B. Whether Plaintiff's Disease Was Caused by the Agent

936	Note on Fiber Drift Theory of Exposure	150
938	*Landrigan v. The Celotex Corporation*	150

C. Identifying the Party Responsible for the Agent

938	*Smith v. Eli Lilly & Company*	158

D. Apportioning Causation

952	*Dafler v. Raymark Industries, Inc.*	190

SECTION 3. STATUTES OF LIMITATIONS, RES JUDICATA AND DAMAGES

998	*Sullivan v. Combustion Engineering*	202

SECTION 4. INTERGENERATIONAL HARM

1003	*Grover v. Eli Lilly & Co.*	206

CHAPTER 11. "CRISIS" AND "REFORM"

SECTION 2. THE SECOND "CRISIS"—THE 1980s

1034	*Blankenship v. General Motors Corporation*	215

RESTATEMENT (SECOND) OF TORTS (1965) SELECTED SECTIONS

CHAPTER 14. LIABILITY OF PERSONS SUPPLYING CHATTELS FOR THE USE OF OTHERS

TOPIC 1. RULES APPLICABLE TO ALL SUPPLIERS

Section		Page
388.	Chattel Known to Be Dangerous for Intended Use	220
389.	Chattel Unlikely to Be Made Safe for Use	229
390.	Chattel for Use by Person Known to Be Incompetent	232

TABLE OF CONTENTS

TOPIC 2. PERSONS SUPPLYING CHATTELS TO BE USED FOR THEIR BUSINESS PURPOSES

Section		Page
391.	Chattel Known to Be Dangerous	235
392.	Chattel Dangerous for Intended Use	236
393.	Effect of Third Person's Duty to Inspect	239

TOPIC 3. MANUFACTURERS OF CHATTELS

394.	Chattel Known to Be Dangerous	240
395.	Negligent Manufacture of Chattel Dangerous Unless Carefully Made	241
396.	Effect of Third Person's Duty to Inspect	247
397.	Chattel Made Under Secret Formula	248
398.	Chattel Made Under Dangerous Plan or Design	250

TOPIC 4. SELLERS OF CHATTELS MANUFACTURED BY THIRD PERSONS

399.	Chattel Known to Be Dangerous	251
400.	Selling as Own Product Chattel Made by Another	251
401.	Chattel Likely to Be Dangerous	253
402.	Absence of Duty to Inspect Chattel	258

TOPIC 5. STRICT LIABILITY

402 A.	Special Liability of Seller of Product for Physical Harm to User or Consumer	260
402 B.	Misrepresentation by Seller of Chattels to Consumer	268

TOPIC 6. INDEPENDENT CONTRACTORS

403.	Chattel Known to Be Dangerous	273
404.	Negligence in Making, Rebuilding, or Repairing Chattel	274

TOPIC 7. DONORS, LENDERS, AND LESSORS OF CHATTELS

405.	Donors and Lenders of Chattels Known to Be Dangerous	275
406.	Manufacturer Giving or Lending Negligently Made Chattel	275
407.	Lessors of Chattels Known to Be Dangerous	275
408.	Lease of Chattel for Immediate Use	276

TABLE OF CONTENTS

CHAPTER 16. THE CAUSAL RELATION NECESSARY TO RESPONSIBILITY FOR NEGLIGENCE

TOPIC 1. CAUSAL RELATION NECESSARY TO THE EXISTENCE OF LIABILITY FOR ANOTHER'S HARM

TITLE A. GENERAL PRINCIPLES

Section		Page
433 A.	Apportionment of Harm to Causes	278
433 B.	Burden of Proof	284

TITLE C. SUPERSEDING CAUSE

440.	Superceding Cause Defined	289
441.	Intervening Force Defined	290
442.	Considerations Important in Determining Whether an Intervening Force Is a Superceding Cause	291
452.	Third Person's Failure to Prevent Harm	292

UNIFORM COMMERCIAL CODE, SELECTED SECTIONS

Table of Jurisdictions Adopting Code	299
Article 1. General Provisions	300

PART 1. SHORT TITLE, CONSTRUCTION, APPLICATION AND SUBJECT MATTER OF THE ACT

Section		
1–101.	Short Title	301
1–102.	Purposes; Rules of Construction; Variation by Agreement	301
1–103.	Supplementary General Principles of Law Applicable	301
1–104.	Construction Against Implicit Repeal	302
1–105.	Territorial Application of the Act; Parties' Power to Choose Applicable Law	302
1–106.	Remedies to Be Liberally Administered	303
1–107.	Waiver or Renunciation of Claim or Right After Breach	304

PART 2. GENERAL DEFINITIONS AND PRINCIPLES OF INTERPRETATION

1–201.	General Definitions	304
1–203.	Obligation of Good Faith	307
1–204.	Time; Reasonable Time; "Seasonably"	308
1–205.	Course of Dealing and Usage of Trade	308

TABLE OF CONTENTS

	Page
Article 2. Sales	311

PART 1. SHORT TITLE, GENERAL CONSTRUCTION AND SUBJECT MATTER

Section
- 2–101. Short Title — 311
- 2–102. Scope, Certain Security and Other Transactions Excluded From This Article — 311
- 2–103. Definitions and Index of Definitions — 311
- 2–104. Definitions: "Merchant"; "Between Merchants"; "Financing Agency" — 312
- 2–105. Definitions: Transferability; "Goods"; "Future" Goods; "Lot"; "Commercial Unit" — 313
- 2–106. Definitions: "Contract"; "Agreement"; "Contract for Sale"; "Sale"; "Present Sale"; "Conforming" to Contract; "Termination"; "Cancellation" — 314
- 2–107. Goods to Be Severed From Realty: Recording — 315

PART 2. FORM, FORMATION AND READJUSTMENT OF CONTRACT

- 2–201. Formal Requirements; Statute of Frauds — 316
- 2–202. Final Written Expression: Parol or Extrinsic Evidence — 318
- 2–204. Formation in General — 319
- 2–206. Offer and Acceptance in Formation of Contract — 319
- 2–207. Additional Terms in Acceptance or Confirmation — 320
- 2–208. Course of Performance or Practical Construction — 320
- 2–209. Modification, Rescission and Waiver — 321

PART 3. GENERAL OBLIGATION AND CONSTRUCTION OF CONTRACT

- 2–301. General Obligations of Parties — 323
- 2–302. Unconscionable Contract or Clause — 323
- 2–303. Allocation or Division of Risks — 325
- 2–312. Warranty of Title and Against Infringement; Buyer's Obligation Against Infringement — 325
- 2–313. Express Warranties by Affirmation, Promise, Description, Sample — 325
- 2–314. Implied Warranty: Merchantability; Usage of Trade — 328
- 2–315. Implied Warranty: Fitness for Particular Purpose — 331
- 2–316. Exclusion or Modification of Warranties — 332
- 2–317. Cumulation and Conflict of Warranties Express or Implied — 335
- 2–318. Third Party Beneficiaries of Warranties Express or Implied — 336
- 2–327. Special Incidents of Sale on Approval and Sale or Return — 337
- 2–328. Sale by Auction — 338

TABLE OF CONTENTS

Article 2. Sales—Continued

PART 5. PERFORMANCE

Section		Page
2–503.	Manner of Seller's Tender of Delivery	338
2–507.	Effect of Seller's Tender; Delivery of Condition	339
2–508.	Cure by Seller of Improper Tender or Delivery; Replacement	340
2–510.	Effect of Breach on Risk of Loss	341
2–511.	Tender of Payment by Buyer; Payment by Check	341
2–512.	Payment by Buyer Before Inspection	341
2–513.	Buyer's Right to Inspection of Goods	342
2–515.	Preserving Evidence of Goods in Dispute	344

PART 6. BREACH, REPUDIATION AND EXCUSE

2–601.	Buyer's Rights on Improper Delivery	346
2–602.	Manner and Effect of Rightful Rejection	347
2–605.	Waiver of Buyer's Objections by Failure to Particularize	348
2–606.	What Constitutes Acceptance of Goods	348
2–607.	Effect of Acceptance; Notice of Breach; Burden of Establishing Breach After Acceptance; Notice of Claim or Litigation to Person Answerable Over	350
2–608.	Revocation of Acceptance in Whole or in Part	352

PART 7. REMEDIES

2–711.	Buyer's Remedies in General; Buyer's Security Interest in Rejected Goods	354
2–714.	Buyer's Damages for Breach in Regard to Accepted Goods	355
2–715.	Buyer's Incidental and Consequential Damages	356
2–716.	Buyer's Right to Specific Performance or Replevin	358
2–717.	Deduction of Damages From the Price	358
2–718.	Liquidation or Limitation of Damages; Deposits	359
2–719.	Contractual Modification or Limitation of Remedy	360
2–720.	Effect of "Cancellation" or "Rescission" on Claims for Antecedent Breach	361
2–721.	Remedies for Fraud	362
2–725.	Statute of Limitations in Contracts for Sale	362

SELECTED STATE PRODUCTS LIABILITY STATUTES

Arizona Revised Statutes Annotated	364
California Health & Safety Code	368
Connecticut General Statutes	372
District of Columbia Code Annotated	379
Idaho Code	384

TABLE OF CONTENTS

	Page
Illinois Revised Statutes	391
Kansas Statutes Annotated	395
Louisiana Revised Statutes Annotated	400
General Laws of Mississippi	405
Missouri Revised Statutes	410
New Jersey Revised Statutes	413
Ohio Revised Code Annotated	417
Oregon Revised Statutes	426
South Carolina Code Annotated	429
Texas General Laws	430
Washington Revised Code Annotated	434

CONSUMER PRODUCT SAFETY ACT AS AMENDED

SELECTED SECTIONS

Section		
2051.	Congressional Findings and Declaration of Purpose	443
2052.	Definitions	444
2053.	Consumer Product Safety Commission	447
2054.	Product Safety Information and Research	450
2055.	Public Disclosure of Information	451
2056.	Consumer Product Safety Standards	455
2057.	Banned Hazardous Products	456
2058.	Procedure for Consumer Product Safety Rules	456
2060.	Judicial Review of Consumer Product Safety Rules	462
2061.	Imminent Hazards	464
2063.	Product Certification and Labeling	466
2064.	Substantial Product Hazards	467
2065.	Inspection and Recordkeeping	470
2066.	Imported Products	471
2067.	Exemption of Exports	473
2068.	Prohibited Acts	474
2069.	Civil Penalties	475
2070.	Criminal Penalties	476
2071.	Injunctive Enforcement and Seizure	476
2072.	Suits for Damages	477
2073.	Private Enforcement	478
2074.	Private Remedies	479
2075.	State Standards	479
2076.	Additional Functions of Consumer Product Safety Commission	481
2077.	Chronic Hazard Advisory Panels	485
2078.	Cooperation With States and Other Federal Agencies	487
2079.	Transfers of Functions	488
2080.	Limitations on Jurisdiction of Consumer Product Safety Commission	491
2081.	Authorization of Appropriations	492

TABLE OF CONTENTS

Section		Page
115.	Sanctions Against the Bringing of Frivolous Claims and Defenses	590
116.	Arbitration	592
117.	Expert Testimony	598
118.	Non-pecuniary Damages	602
119.	The Collateral Source Rule	605
120.	Punitive Damages	608
121.	Severance Clause	611
122.	Effective Date	612

S. 640, PRODUCT LIABILITY FAIRNESS ACT

TITLE—I

101.	Short Title	616
102.	Definitions	616
103.	Preemption	619
104.	Jurisdiction of Federal Courts	620
105.	Effective Date	620

TITLE—II

201.	Expedited Product Liability Settlements	620
202.	Alternative Dispute Resolution Procedures	621

TITLE—III

301.	Civil Actions	622
302.	Uniform Standards of Product Seller Liability	622
303.	Uniform Standards for Award of Punitive Damages	623
304.	Uniform Time Limitations on Liability	625
305.	Uniform Standards for Offset of Workers' Compensation Benefits	626
306.	Several Liability for Noneconomic Damages	628
307.	Defenses Involving Intoxicating Alcohol or Drugs	629

SENATE COMMERCE COMMITTEE REPORT ON S. 640

Purpose of Bill	631
Background and Need	632
Legislative History	650
Summary of Major Provisions	652
Estimated Costs	654
Regulatory Impact Statement	657
Section–by–Section Analysis	658
Rollcall Votes in Committee	696
Changes in Existing Law	697

TABLE OF CONTENTS

EEC DIRECTIVE ON LIABILITY FOR DEFECTIVE PRODUCTS [734]

*

TABLE OF CASES

Principal cases are in italic type. Non-principal cases are in roman type. References are to Pages.

Adams v. Murakami, 37
Anderson v. Owens–Corning Fiberglas Corp., 19

Barker v. Lull Engineering Co., Inc., 18
Bernal v. Richard Wolf Medical Instruments Corp., 18
Beshada v. Johns–Manville Products Corp., 19
Blankenship v. General Motors Corp., 215
Borel v. Fibreboard Paper Products Corp., 150
Braun v. Soldier of Fortune Magazine, Inc., 64
Brown v. Superior Court (Abbott Laboratories), 19

Cimino v. Raymark Industries, Inc., 86
Cipollone v. Liggett Group, Inc., 101, 124
Coburn v. Sun Chemical Corp., 72

Dafler v. Raymark Industries, Inc., 190
Daubert v. Merrell Dow Pharmaceuticals, Inc., 113 S.Ct. 320, p. 149
Daubert v. Merrell Dow Pharmaceuticals, Inc., 951 F.2d 1128, p. 149
DeLuca v. Merrell Dow Pharmaceuticals, Inc., 130, 149

Eimann v. Soldier of Fortune Magazine, Inc., 64
Ewen v. McLean Trucking Co., 2

Garside v. Osco Drug, Inc., 29
Griggs v. BIC Corp., 7
Grover v. Eli Lilly & Co., 206

Haines v. Liggett Group Inc., 975 F.2d 81, p. 130
Haines v. Liggett Group, Inc., 140 F.R.D. 681, p. *124*
High v. Westinghouse Elec. Corp., 66, 72

Irwin Yacht Sales, Inc. v. Carver Boat Corp., 65

Kalik v. Allis–Chalmers Corp., 72
Khan v. Shiley Inc., 30

Landrigan v. The Celotex Corp., 150
Lohrmann v. Pittsburgh Corning Corp., 150
Lykins v. Westinghouse Elec., 72

Pacific Mut. Life Ins. Co. v. Haslip, 37
Perry v. Mercedes Benz of North America, Inc., 73, 84
Pietrone v. American Honda Motor Co., Inc., 18
Promaulayko v. Johns Manville Sales Corp., 65

Robertson v. Allied Signal, Inc., 150

Smith v. Eli Lilly & Co., 158
Snyder v. Mekhjian, 593 A.2d 318, p. 28
Snyder v. Mekhjian, 582 A.2d 307, p. *119*
Sullivan v. Combustion Engineering, 202

Thacker v. UNR Industries, Inc., 150
Thompson v. Merrell Dow Pharmaceuticals, Inc., 152

Valenti v. Surgiteck–Flash Medical Engineering Corp., 7

Wood v. General Motors Corp., 84

TABLE OF CONTENTS

Section		Page
2082.	Interim Cellulose Insulation Safety Standard	494
2083.	Congressional Veto of Consumer Product Safety Rules	499

MAGNUSON–MOSS WARRANTY ACT

2301.	Definitions	502
2302.	Rules Governing Contents of Warranties	504
2303.	Designation of Written Warranties	506
2304.	Federal Minimum Standards for Warranties	507
2305.	Full and Limited Warranting of a Consumer Product	509
2306.	Service Contracts; Rules for Full, Clear and Conspicuous Disclosure of Terms and Conditions; Addition to or in Lieu of Written Warranty	510
2307.	Designation of Representatives by Warrantor to Perform Duties Under Written or Implied Warranty	510
2308.	Implied Warranties	510
2309.	Procedures Applicable to Promulgation of Rules by Commission; Rulemaking Proceeding for Warranty and Warranty Practices Involved in Sale of Used Motor Vehicles	511
2310.	Remedies in Consumer Disputes	511
2311.	Applicability of Provisions to Other Federal or State Laws and Requirements	515
2312.	Effective Dates; Time for Promulgation of Rules by Commission	516

MODEL UNIFORM PRODUCT LIABILITY ACT

Introduction		518
100.	Short Title	523
101.	Findings	523
102.	Definitions	525
103.	Scope of This Act	533
104.	Basic Standards of Responsibility for Manufacturers	535
105.	Basic Standards of Responsibility for Product Sellers Other Than Manufacturers	549
106.	Unavoidably Dangerous Aspects of Products	553
107.	Relevance of Industry Custom, Safety or Performance Standards and Practical Technological Feasibility	555
108.	Relevance of Legislative or Administrative Regulatory Standards and Mandatory Government Contract Specifications	560
109.	Notice of Possible Claim Required	563
110.	Length of Time Product Sellers are Subject to Liability	565
111.	Comparative Responsibility and Apportionment of Damages	571
112.	Conduct Affecting Comparative Responsibility	576
113.	Multiple Defendants: Contribution and Implied Indemnity	584
114.	Relationship Between Product Liability and Worker Compensation	586

1993 CASE AND
STATUTORY SUPPLEMENT

to

PRODUCTS LIABILITY

AND

SAFETY

CASES AND MATERIALS

*

Chapter 2

THEORIES OF MANUFACTURER LIABILITY

SECTION 4. STRICT LIABILITY IN TORT

ADD to page 185 at the end of note 3:

There is an increasing interest in the jurisprudence of products liability. See Attanasio, The Principle of Aggregate Autonomy and the Calabresian Approach to Products Liability, 74 Va. L. Rev. 677 (1988); Owen, Products Liability: Principles of Justice for the 21st Century, 11 Pace L. Rev. 63 (1990); Owen, The Moral Foundations of Products Liability Law: Toward First Principles, 68 Notre Dame L. Rev. 427, 430 (1993) ("At bottom, product accidents are moral—not technological—events.").

Chapter 3

THE CONCEPT OF DEFECTIVENESS

SECTION 1. THEORIES AND TESTS OF DEFECTIVENESS

A. CONSUMER EXPECTATIONS

ADD to page 194 after note 2:

2A. See April A. Caso, Note, Unreasonably Dangerous Products From a Child's Perspective: A Proposal for a Reasonable Child Consumer Expectation Test, 20 Rut. L.J. 433 (1989); Ark. Code § 16–116–102(7) (1987) ("as to a minor, 'unreasonably dangerous' means that a product is dangerous to an extent beyond that which would be contemplated by an ordinary and reasonably careful minor considering his age and intelligence.")

ADD to page 205 after note 12:

EWEN v. McLEAN TRUCKING CO.
Supreme Court of Oregon, 1985.
300 Or. 24, 706 P.2d 929.

LINDE, JUDGE.

Plaintiff is the guardian *ad litem* of Sophie S. Ewen, who was struck by a truck while crossing a street intersection. In addition to negligence actions against the trucking company and the driver, plaintiff brought a "product liability civil action," ORS 30.900, against International Harvester Company, the manufacturer of the truck, alleging that its defective design prevented the driver from seeing pedestrian traffic immediately in front and to the right of the truck. Plaintiff had judgment on a jury verdict against International Harvester, which was affirmed on appeal. *Ewen v. McLean*, 70 Or.App. 595, 689 P.2d 1309 (1984).

Defendant's petition for review brings before this court a single issue, whether the following instruction was reversible error:

"A product is dangerously defective when it is in a condition unreasonably dangerous to the user."

Ch. 3 THEORIES AND TESTS OF DEFECTIVENESS

"Unreasonably dangerous in this context means dangerous to an extent beyond that which would be contemplated by the ordinary purchaser of this type of product in the community. Purchaser and users is [sic] anyone who may reasonably be expected to be affected by the product, such as a pedestrian."

Defendant objected at trial and argued on appeal that the expectations of a pedestrian are not a test of dangerousness to a "user or consumer" within the meaning of the product liability law. The Court of Appeals noted that in *Phillips v. Kimwood Machine Co.*, 269 Or. 485, 525 P.2d 1033 (1974), this court had treated the test of reasonable consumer expectation as equivalent to a test whether a reasonable seller, with knowledge of the dangerous characteristic in question, would market the product. From this, the Court of Appeals inferred that in effect the jury is to evaluate the allegedly defective product from the perspective of a "reasonable person," and that "whether the jury is instructed to view the product from the perspective of the 'reasonable manufacturer' or the 'reasonable consumer' or the 'reasonable pedestrian' is of little moment." 70 Or.App. at 604 (footnote omitted). It therefore concluded that the quoted instruction was not erroneous. We reverse the decision of the Court of Appeals and remand the case to the circuit court.

ORS 30.920 provides:

"(1) One who sells or leases any product in a defective condition unreasonably dangerous to the user or consumer or to his property is subject to liability for physical harm or damage to property caused by that condition, if:

"(a) The seller or lessor is engaged in the business of selling or leasing such a product; and

"(b) The product is expected to and does reach the user or consumer without substantial change in the condition in which it is sold or leased.

"(2) The rule stated in subsection (1) of this section shall apply, even though:

"(a) The seller or lessor has exercised all possible care in the preparation and sale or lease of the product; and

"(b) The user, consumer or injured party has not purchased or leased the product from or entered into any contractual relations with the seller or lessor.

"(3) It is the intent of the Legislative Assembly that the rule stated in subsections (1) and (2) of this section shall be construed in accordance with the Restatement (Second) of Torts sec. 402A, Comments *a* to *m* (1965). All references in these comments to sale, sell, selling or seller shall be construed to include lease, leases, leasing and lessor.

"(4) Nothing in this section shall be construed to limit the rights and liabilities of sellers and lessors under principles of common law negligence or under ORS chapter 72."

As subsection (3) expressly states, the substantive formulas codified in subsections (1) and (2) are to be "construed in accordance with the Restatement (Second) of Torts sec. 402A, Comments *a* to *m* (1965)." The present issue concerns Comment *i*, which reads in part:

"The article sold must be dangerous to an extent beyond that which would be contemplated by the ordinary consumer who purchases it, with the ordinary knowledge common to the community as to its characteristics."

This is the standard for defects sometimes called the "consumer contemplation test." Defendant argues that even though a pedestrian may recover damages for injuries caused by a defective truck, the scope of the rule does not bring the pedestrian into the class of consumers who have purchased a product with ordinary knowledge of its characteristics and whose expectations determine whether the product is dangerously defective. Neither plaintiff nor the Court of Appeals squarely maintains the contrary, that a pedestrian is a "consumer" of trucks. Rather, plaintiff takes issue with some of the theoretical reasons defendant offers for the consumer expectations test, and the Court of Appeals, as quoted above, concluded that it was immaterial whether the jury was told to assume the perspective of a manufacturer, a consumer, or an injured pedestrian, because by the objective calculus employed by a hypothetical reasonable person, each should arrive at the same measure of an alleged defect.

As a prediction of jury behavior, that may or may not be true. Trial by jury rests on the assumption that jurors will do their best to follow the law as explained by the court and that accurate instructions matter. *Cf. Sandford v. Chev. Div. Gen. Motors*, 292 Or. 590, 603–04, 642 P.2d 624 (1982). Certainly counsel's battles over the supplemental instruction in this case suggest that trial lawyers thought it would matter to the jurors from which perspective they should evaluate the alleged defect. The question, in any event, is not what lawyers or judges may think on that subject, but what the legislators who proposed and enacted ORS 30.920 thought.

ORS 30.920 was enacted in 1979. * * *

* * *

The question that concerns us in the present case is what significance the legislators attached to the consumer contemplation test stated in the Restatement's Comment *i*, quoted above. Although Comment *i*, like the others, was not set out in the bill but was only incorporated by reference, its substance did not go unnoticed. In the Senate, the chief proponent of the proposal to codify Comments *a* to *m*

Ch. 3 THEORIES AND TESTS OF DEFECTIVENESS

spoke of the confusion created by courts in "moving away from the provisions of 402A." * * * A witness for the Portland Chamber of Commerce stated [in legislative hearings]:

> "The Oregon Supreme Court eroded away the rules when it refused to accept the consumer oriented rule anymore. Instead, it substituted what is called a seller oriented rule for the definition of unreasonably dangerous. The Supreme Court stated it is not what the consumer expects that is important; it is what a reasonably prudent manufacturer would do, knowing of the potential danger. Some people think that is a much more liberal rule. Some consumers think it is a much more restrictive rule, and not the rule they would like."

* * * The case to which the foregoing testimony referred was *Phillips v. Kimwood Machine Co., supra.* In *Phillips*, Justice Holman wrote for the court:

> "A dangerously defective article would be one which a reasonable person would not put into the stream of commerce *if he had knowledge of its harmful character.* The test, therefore, is whether the seller would be negligent if he sold the article *knowing of the risk involved.* Strict liability imposes what amounts to constructive knowledge of the condition of the product.
>
> "On the surface such a test would seem to be different than the test of 2 Restatement (Second) of Torts § 402A, Comment *i.*, of 'dangerous to an extent beyond that which would be contemplated by the ordinary consumer who purchases it.' This court has used this test in the past. * * * " (Footnotes omitted. Emphasis in original.)

269 Or. 492–93. The opinion asserted that the two statements of the test are "not necessarily different standards," quoting a federal court's opinion to the effect that they are "two sides of the same standard." *Id.* at 493, *quoting Welch v. Outboard Marine Corp.*, 481 F.2d 252, 254 (5th Cir.1973). * * *

* * *

In any event, the "consumer contemplation" test of Comment *i* was brought to the attention of the legislature, and it was enacted. It follows at least that a jury in a product defect case should receive some instruction phrased so as to focus on what extent of risk an ordinary consumer would contemplate when purchasing a product with the knowledge of its characteristics common to the relevant community. We do not prescribe the specific form of jury instructions. As we said in *Ireland v. Mitchell*, 226 Or. 286, 294, 359 P.2d 894 (1961), "A trial judge is not a mere automaton whose function is limited to reciting the words approved by statute or by the Supreme Court." The instruction can be given in different ways that are consistent with the statute. We

5

leave trial courts free to choose the words that they think will best explain the law to the jury that has heard the particular case before the court. Whether any role remains for the instruction approved in *Phillips v. Kimwood Machine Co., supra,* 269 Or. at 501 n.14, is not before us in this case because no such instruction was asked or given. Rather, we have reviewed the discussion before the legislature for the light it sheds on the assumption of the Court of Appeals that it is immaterial what perspective is chosen for evaluating an allegedly dangerous product because all "objective" tests ultimately reduce themselves to the perspective of a hypothetical "reasonable person." Whatever the jurisprudential merits of that view may be, it negates the importance that the proponents of ORS 30.920, rightly or wrongly, attached to the consumer contemplation test of Comment *i*.

An instruction based on Comment *i* was given in this case. The instruction left out some words that are used in the Comment and added other words that are not there. In referring to the extent of a product's danger that "would be contemplated by the ordinary purchaser of this type of product in the community," the instruction somewhat elliptically omitted reference to the consumer's knowledge of the characteristics of the product, an element that appears in Comment *i*; but that is secondary to defendant's criticism of the instruction. As we have said, the law does not oblige every judge to repeat the identical words of a prescribed formula in instructing every jury. The crux of defendant's objection, rather, is that the last sentence of the instruction extended the "consumer contemplation" test of Comment *i* to include the expectations of anyone who might reasonably be expected to be affected by the product, "including a pedestrian."

We conclude that the statement is too broad. The word "consumer," as used in Comment *i*, does not include everyone who might be affected by the product. If the reporters, advisers, consultants, and other experts who participate in the preparation of the Restatements want to invoke the general judgment of an ordinary reasonable person, they know how to say so. *See, e.g.,* Restatement, Second, Torts §§ 11, 12 (1965) (define "Reasonably Believes" and "Reason to Know"); § 283 ("Conduct of a Reasonable Man; The Standard"); and § 291 ("Unreasonableness; How Determined * * *"). ORS 30.920(2)(b) implicitly allows an "injured party" other than a user or consumer to recover if the product causing the injury is defective and unreasonably dangerous within the meaning of ORS 30.920(1), but we have seen no indication that the legislature meant this reference to the "injured party" to alter the test for defects stated in Comment *i*.

The instruction therefore was erroneous. We have given serious consideration to the question whether the error was so prejudicial as to require reversal. It can be argued that when the product is a vehicle to be used in traffic, the expectations of a driver and of a pedestrian as to the visibility of pedestrians from the driver's seat are unlikely to be so different as to lead a jury to a different result. If the instruction had only made a passing reference to the expectations of a pedestrian, submerged in otherwise correct instructions, perhaps it might be unlikely to have affected the outcome. See *Smith v. Holst*, 275 Or. 29, 549 P.2d 671 (1976). But here the erroneous proposition that a purchaser or user includes anyone expected to be affected by the product, "such as a pedestrian," was singled out for a supplemental instruction at plaintiff's request and over defendant's advance objection. Plaintiff stressed the expectation of an "ordinary pedestrian" beyond that of a purchaser or driver in closing argument. Plaintiff obviously regarded the point as important at trial. We are in no position to say that in fact it was unimportant.

The decision of the Court of Appeals is reversed and the case is remanded to the circuit court for further proceedings.

B. RISK–BENEFIT ANALYSIS

ADD to page 215 after note 1:

1A. In Valenti v. Surgiteck–Flash Medical Engineering Corp., 875 F.2d 466, 467–68 (5th Cir. 1989), the plaintiff appealed the trial court's that grant of judgment n.o.v., claiming the trial court had failed to weigh the danger of the product to plaintiff and compare it to the utility to plaintiff. The Fifth Circuit affirmed, rejecting plaintiff's argument:

> [The relevant precedent] requires that the danger in fact of the product to society as a whole be weighed against the utility of the product to society as a whole. If danger in fact and utility are balanced on an individual basis, plaintiffs would be able to recover whenever injured while using a product because their benefit from using the product will almost always be outweighed by the injury suffered.

ADD to page 222 after note 15:

GRIGGS v. BIC CORPORATION
United States Court of Appeals, Third Circuit, 1992.
981 F.2d 1429.

ROSENN, CIRCUIT JUDGE.

This diversity litigation arises out of serious injuries sustained by an infant as a result of a childplay fire ignited with a disposable butane cigarette lighter by his older half-brother. Two principal issues are raised on appeal, one of which the parties agree is an issue of first impression, namely, whether the lighter was defective under strict products liability law because it was not designed by the manufacturer to be "childproof."¹ The second issue is whether the manufacturer had a duty under negligence law to manufacture a childproof lighter when childplay lighter fires were foreseeable and a childproof safety design was feasible at the time. The district court granted the manufacturer's motion for summary judgment. *Griggs v. BIC Corp.*, 786 F.Supp. 1203 (M.D.Pa.1992). The court concluded that the manufacturer had no duty under strict liability law to manufacture a lighter resistant to child play and that BIC was entitled to summary judgment on the negligence claim as well. The plaintiffs timely appealed. We affirm on the issue of strict liability, but reverse on the issue of negligence.

I.

The material facts are not in dispute and can be stated briefly. On October 10, 1985, Zachary Griggs, then aged 11 months, sustained serious injuries in a fire at his Pennsylvania home that his three year old stepbrother, Kenneth Hempstead, ignited with a disposable butane cigarette lighter manufactured by the defendant BIC Corporation (BIC). Kenneth removed the lighter from his stepfather's pants pocket in the early hours of the morning and set fire with it to Zachary's bedding while the rest of the household slept. Two incidents within six months preceded this fire, in which Kenneth attempted to light either matches or a lighter, of which his parents were aware and for which they disciplined Kenneth. Prior to Zachary's injuries, his mother had seen warnings that BIC placed on the packaging of its lighters to keep them away from children. She was also independently aware that these lighters should be kept out of the reach of children.

Plaintiffs, Timothy W. Griggs and Catherine H. Griggs, individually and as parents and guardians of Zachary, sued BIC in the United States District Court for the Middle District of Pennsylvania alleging that BIC's failure to manufacture a childproof lighter constituted both defective and negligent design.

* * *

III.

In *Webb v. Zern*, 422 Pa. 424, 220 A.2d 853, 854 (1966), the Pennsylvania Supreme Court adopted section 402A of the Restatement (Second) of Torts (hereinafter Restatement) as the law of strict products liability in Pennsylvania. That court subsequently established that section 402A "imposes strict liability in tort not only for injuries caused by the defective *manufacture* of products, but also for injuries caused by

---

1. The term "childproof" is used in this opinion to refer to childproof and child resistant designs.

Ch. 3   THEORIES AND TESTS OF DEFECTIVENESS

defects in their *design.*" *Lewis v. Coffing Hoist Div., Duff–Norton Co.,* 515 Pa. 334, 528 A.2d 590, 592 (1987) (citations omitted).

A central goal of strict liability doctrine is to relieve the plaintiff of proof problems associated with negligence and warranty theories of liability. The Pennsylvania Supreme Court has stated that "[s]trict liability requires, in substance, only two elements of requisite proof: the need to prove that the product was defective, and the need to prove that the defect was a proximate cause of the plaintiff's injuries." *Berkebile v. Brantly Helicopter Corp.*, 462 Pa. 83, 337 A.2d 893, 898 (1975) (footnote omitted).[4] The Supreme Court of Pennsylvania adopted this goal on the principle that the realities of our economic society today compel "the conclusion that the risk of loss for injury resulting from defective products should be borne by the suppliers, principally because they are in a position to absorb the loss by distributing it as a cost of doing business." *Azzarello v. Black Bros. Co.*, 480 Pa. 547, 391 A.2d 1020, 1023 (1978).

Courts, keeping pace with the advances in our complex industrial and commercial world, have concluded that the doctrine of *caveat emptor*, which prevailed in the early nineteenth century marketplace to protect an emerging manufacturing industry, should give way to a concept more concerned with a helpless consumer who is vulnerable to the perils of such products because of the aggressive marketing and advertising tactics of today's commercial world.[5] Most courts have therefore adopted the concept that the suppliers of defective products should bear the risk of loss without regard to fault or privity of contract. *Id.* 391 A.2d at 1024.

The plaintiffs maintain, therefore, that under the strict products liability rule adopted by Pennsylvania, misuse or abuse of a product is not a defense to products liability claims. They argue that the Pennsylvania rule is that products "used in an unintended manner can be judged defective if the change, misuse, or abuse is foreseeable to the manufacturer." Thus, they do not claim the BIC lighter was defective because it failed to perform in the manner for which it was intended, but that it was defective because it was not childproof. They also make the expansive claim, citing *Azzarello* and *Berkebile*, that "[i]t has been determined that industry can and should pay for *all* injuries and deaths that are caused by defective or unsafe products." In other words, they

---

4. The section 402A(1) term "unreasonably dangerous" has no independent significance under Pennsylvania law; it "merely represent[s] a label to be used where it is determined that the risk of loss should be placed upon the supplier." *Azzarello v. Black Bros. Co.*, 480 Pa. 547, 391 A.2d 1020, 1025 (1978). The *Azzarello* court points out that the term presents a difficulty because it "tends to suggest considerations which are usually identified with the law of negligence." *Id.*

5. The enormous number of new products reaching just a part of the retail marketplace is reported in a recent article in the *New York Times*. "This year, 16,000 new products have arrived in supermarkets and drug stores." Trish Hall, *Telling the "Yeas" from the "Nays" in New Products*, N.Y. Times, Dec. 9, 1992, at C1.

assert that under current law the manufacturer is an insurer of injuries caused by defective or unsafe products.

* * *

In *Lewis*, the court described three alternative tests used by courts in various jurisdictions to determine whether the manufacturer should bear the risk of loss in a design defect case: the "consumer expectations test," the "risk-utility test," and its own test set forth in *Azzarello*.[6] 528 A.2d at 593. Under *Azzarello*, the existence of a defect is intimately related to the product's intended use because the product is defective only if it "left the supplier's control lacking any element necessary to make it safe for its intended use or possessing any feature that renders it unsafe for the intended use." *Azzarello*, 391 A.2d at 1027 (footnote omitted).

Based on the *Azzarello* standard, the trial court in this case concluded that "a product may not be deemed defective unless it is unreasonably dangerous to *intended users*." *Griggs*, 786 F.Supp. at 1205. Although the parties in this case apparently agree that BIC's lighters are not intended for use by unsupervised children, the plaintiffs maintain that the court erred when it substituted "intended user" for "intended use" in the *Azzarello* standard, thus limiting the safety inquiry to adults.[7] This is an illusory distinction, however, because the concept of intended use impliedly encompasses the participation of an intended user. Thus, because children are not intended users, BIC is not strictly liable.

Plaintiffs further alleged, however, that BIC is strictly liable under section 402A because it designed a lighter unreasonably dangerous to foreseeable users, young children. They contend that BIC knew that

---

6. The plaintiffs contend that Pennsylvania law dictates the use of a risk-utility analysis that takes foreseeability into account in order to make this threshold determination, rather than following the court's *Azzarello* approach. Although the supreme court has acknowledged the existence of a risk-utility approach to this question, Pennsylvania courts have declined to embrace it. *See, e.g., Lewis*, 528 A.2d at 592; *Dauphin Deposit Bank & Trust Co. v. Toyota Motor Corp.*, 408 Pa.Super. 256, 596 A.2d 845, 849 (1991); *Hite v. R.J. Reynolds Tobacco Co.*, 396 Pa.Super. 82, 578 A.2d 417, 421 (1990), *appeal denied*, 527 Pa. 666, 593 A.2d 842 (1991). Additionally, the supreme court has specifically stated that foreseeability "is a test of negligence.... [I]t is irrelevant in a strict liability case." *Berkebile*, 337 A.2d at 900. The Griggses' contention is therefore meritless under Pennsylvania law.

7. The Griggses seem to suggest that Kenneth did use the lighter for its intended use, i.e., to produce a flame, and so their case falls under and satisfies the *Azzarello* standard because, gauging by the results of Kenneth's "intended use," the product must be lacking an element necessary to make it safe for its intended use. This suggestion requires a convoluted reading of the standard that is nowhere suggested by the Pennsylvania courts' application.

Alternatively, the Griggses seem to be trying to equate "intended" use with "expected" use, which then allows them to connect children with lighters by using foreseeability evidence, where something that may be foreseeable is then expected. Foreseeability, however, plays no part in the initial determination of defect in strict liability. *Berkebile*, 337 A.2d at 900. This is therefore a futile line of reasoning.

Ch. 3   THEORIES AND TESTS OF DEFECTIVENESS

its disposable butane lighters were attractive to children, could be easily lit by children as young as age 3, "and that every year a substantial number of fires were in fact caused by young children who obtained and used BIC lighters." Plaintiffs also claim that they were prepared to prove that thousands of children have been killed or seriously injured with childplay fires over the past twenty years and that BIC knew or should have known that a much safer, child resistant lighter design was feasible at the time of the accident. The defendant accepted the plaintiffs' feasibility and foreseeability allegations for purposes of the summary judgment motion, but argued that the issue was restricted to whether it had a duty to make its lighter childproof, not whether it was feasible to do so, or whether the danger was foreseeable.

The plaintiffs rely heavily on *Suchomajcz v. Hummel Chemical Co.*, 524 F.2d 19 (3d Cir.1975), to support their strict liability claim. This case, however, is inapposite as to this specific claim. As BIC notes; *Suchomajcz* is not a products liability case, does not involve allegations of product defect, and predates *Azzarello*. Rather, it stated a negligence action, and we discuss it more fully later in this opinion in connection with the negligence issue raised by plaintiffs. The plaintiffs have cited numerous cases which we have reviewed. None of them supports the contention that in Pennsylvania a manufacturer has a duty in strict liability law to guard against foreseeable use by unintended users in the context of the initial determination of defect.

The district court noted in its opinion that defendant did not dispute the past injuries to children through use of butane lighters and that it was undisputed that the lighter in question was not actually defective in that it performed the function for which it was designed. Because the plaintiffs do not contend that the lighter was unsafe for its intended use, the trial court committed no error in holding that the lighter was not defective and that BIC as a matter of law should not bear the risk of loss. Accordingly, the trial court did not err in granting BIC's motion for summary judgment because of the alleged product defect.

IV.

We now turn to the second and more formidable of plaintiffs' claims: whether the manufacturer owed a duty to the injured victim under common law negligence which it violated, resulting in the injuries sustained. Pennsylvania courts have set forth the elements of negligence as follows:

   1) A duty or obligation recognized by the law, requiring the actor to conform to a certain standard of conduct for the protection of others against unreasonable risks;

   2) A failure to conform to the standard required;

3) A causal connection between the conduct and the resulting injury; and

4) Actual loss or damage resulting to the interests of another. *Morena v. South Hills Health Sys.*, 501 Pa. 634, 462 A.2d 680, 684 n. 5 (1983) (citing William L. Prosser, *Law of Torts* § 30, at 143 (4th ed. 1971)); *Fennell v. Nationwide Mut. Fire Ins. Co.*, 412 Pa.Super. 534, 603 A.2d 1064, 1066–67 (1992). At issue in this aspect of the present case is the element of duty. Normally, "[t]he determination of what duty, if any, a defendant owes to potential plaintiffs is a question of law." [Citations.]

Under Pennsylvania law, no tort liability may be imposed upon a defendant who does not owe a duty to the injured plaintiff. [Citations.] In properly determining that BIC's lighter was not defectively designed under strict liability law, the district court concluded that BIC had "no duty to childproof its lighters." *Griggs*, 786 F.Supp. at 1209. The district court relied on this conclusion in its strict products liability rationale to establish the absence of duty in negligence.[8] Thus, the immediate question is whether under Pennsylvania law the absence of "duty" to the unintended user in strict liability also is determinative of the absence of duty in negligence. As the Pennsylvania Supreme Court has not directly decided this subtle question, we must predict how it would resolve the issue if presented to it.

The Pennsylvania Supreme Court has attempted to insulate the concepts and vocabulary of negligence from those of strict liability. In *Azzarello*, the court pointed out that the "unreasonably dangerous" language of section 402A presents difficulty because it "tends to suggest considerations which are usually identified with the law of negligence." 391 A.2d at 1025. The court therefore stated that the words "'unreasonably dangerous' have no independent significance and merely represent a label to be used when it is determined that the risk of loss should be placed upon the supplier." *Id.* The court also has noted that foreseeability is a test of negligence that is irrelevant in the context of strict liability. *Berkebile*, 337 A.2d at 900. More recently, the court flatly stated that "negligence concepts have no place in a case based on strict liability." *Lewis*, 528 A.2d at 593.

Confusion has arisen because a number of courts have chosen the term "duty" as a shorthand for the threshold determination in strict liability that social policy supports placing the risk of loss in a given case on the seller. Duty is an historic concept closely identified with

---

8. BIC contends that the duty requirement is identical in strict liability and negligence claims. The only Pennsylvania Supreme Court decision cited for this proposition, *Azzarello*, 391 A.2d at 1020, does not support it. The Pennsylvania Superior Court case cited, *Dauphin*, 596 A.2d at 850–51, in turn accepts as persuasive a Texas Court of Appeals decision in a strict liability and negligence case based on failure to warn where the Texas court substituted "no duty" in strict liability for no duty in negligence in a conclusory way without analyzing whether the inquiries are coextensive.

Ch. 3   THEORIES AND TESTS OF DEFECTIVENESS

negligence, and a conclusion that a duty exists under negligence law expresses the existence of foreseeability of harm and serves as a predicate for fault, a highly important element of negligence liability. However, foreseeability and fault have no place in strict liability, and indeed, the district court's analysis of the strict liability claim properly did not incorporate either concept.

More than just highlighting the Pennsylvania Supreme Court's attempts to maintain strict liability and negligence as two independent grounds for a personal injury claim, these observations point to an important theoretical basis for such a separation: The underlying analyses necessary to reach each legal conclusion of duty are qualitatively different. As we observed earlier, foreseeability properly did not enter into the determination that yielded the "no duty" conclusion in strict liability. Foreseeability, however, is an integral part of a determination that a duty does exist in Pennsylvania negligence law. [Citation.] The Pennsylvania Supreme Court has stated that "[t]he test of negligence is whether the wrongdoer could have anticipated and foreseen the likelihood of harm to the injured person, resulting from his act.... 'The risk reasonably to be perceived defines the duty to be obeyed[.]'" *Dahlstrom v. Shrum*, 368 Pa. 423, 84 A.2d 289, 290–91 (1951) (quoting *Palsgraf v. Long Island R.R.*, 248 N.Y. 339, 162 N.E. 99, 100 (1928)); [citation].

Because foreseeability is an integral part of the duty analysis in negligence, and because the "duty" analysis in strict liability eschews foreseeability as an element, holding "no duty" in strict liability does not *per se* eliminate consideration of the duty factor in negligence law. We believe, therefore, based on its precedent that strives to maintain the difference between negligence and strict liability law, that the Pennsylvania Supreme Court would reject the proposition that the social policy determination as to product defect in strict liability is the equivalent of a determination of duty in negligence law.

Given that BIC conceded foreseeability for purposes of its summary judgment motion, a finding of duty in negligence would turn on the last remaining piece of the traditional duty puzzle: whether the foreseeable risks were unreasonable. The Pennsylvania Supreme Court has not decided this question and we must therefore predict how it would respond. The classic model for analyzing this aspect of negligence law is the risk-utility form of analysis, which balances "the risk, in the light of the social value of the interest threatened, and the probability and extent of the harm, against the value of the interest which the actor is seeking to protect, and the expedience of the course pursued." W. Page Keeton et al., *Prosser and Keeton on the Law of Torts* § 31, at 173 (5th ed. 1984) (footnotes omitted) (hereinafter *Prosser and Keeton*) [citations.] Restatement § 291–93.

As guidance for analyzing the probability and extent of the harm in the context of unreasonable risk, *Prosser and Keeton* states the following:

> No person can be expected to guard against harm from events which are not reasonably to be anticipated at all, or are so unlikely to occur that the risk, although recognizable, would commonly be disregarded.... On the other hand, if the risk is an appreciable one, and the possible consequences are serious, the question is not one of mathematical probability alone.... As the gravity of the possible harm increases, the apparent likelihood of its occurrence need be correspondingly less to generate a duty of precaution.

Prosser and Keeton § 31, at 170–71 (footnotes omitted).

Before analyzing and balancing these factors to determine if the foreseeable risk in this case is unreasonable, a review of the record evidence provides some statistical background. In an Advance Notice of Proposed Rulemaking published in the Federal Register by the Consumer Product Safety Commission, 53 Fed.Reg. 6833 (1988), the Commission computed national fire loss estimates for 1980 through 1985, inclusive. "Residential fires started by children playing with lighters are estimated to have taken an average of 120 lives each year.... [O]n average at least 750 persons were injured each year in residential fires started by children playing with lighters.... The annual cost of childplay lighter fires [is] $300–375 million or 60–75 cents per lighter sold."[9] *Id.* at 6836.

Based on the Commission's report, the gravity of the possible harm, in terms of both personal injury and property damage by childplay fires, is appreciable, recurring, and serious. The social value of the safety to be secured is indisputably high. These statistics suggest further that the likelihood of the occurrence of harm is sufficiently substantial to generate a duty of precaution, a conclusion which is reinforced by BIC's concession of foreseeability.

The factors to be considered when analyzing the utility of the conduct in question, i.e., the reason for the failure to childproof the lighter, must be balanced against the probability and gravity of the risk. *Id.* at 171; Restatement § 291–93. They are: (1) "the social value of the interest which the actor is seeking to advance"; and (2) "any alternative course open to the actor." *Prosser and Keeton* § 31, at 171–72; Restatement § 292. The only interest BIC can be seeking to advance by not childproofing its lighter is one of cost and its own economic health. A manufacturer's economic health is undeniably valuable to society for many reasons, including the bearing it has on the employment of workers, the payment of taxes, and the availability

---

9. "The average price for the product is less than one dollar." 53 Fed.Reg. at 6836. Thus, dollar for dollar, these lighters are involved in causing almost as much damage through childplay as they generate in sales at the retail level.

Ch. 3 THEORIES AND TESTS OF DEFECTIVENESS

of a socially useful product. Because BIC has also conceded the feasibility of childproofing the lighter for purposes of its summary judgment motion, it presumably had economic alternatives, unless childproofing the lighter would impair the lighter's usefulness or make it too expensive to maintain its marketability. Tying this conclusion to social value considerations, if the design change would not make the lighter too expensive to maintain its utility and marketability, then it is reasonable to expect that the consumer would still buy it with the cost of the design change incorporated.

On balance, the high social value placed on the safety of people and property threatened by childplay fires, the high gravity of risk, the considerable probability of risk, and the likelihood of a reasonably available alternative may outweigh BIC's interest in producing its lighters without childproofing features. In such circumstances, the risk of omission would be unreasonable.

In *Suchomajcz v. Hummel Chem. Co.*, we applied this risk-utility analysis in a case bearing similar issues to the present one. In *Suchomajcz*, two minor children were killed and four injured when a bottle abandoned by a minor child containing firecracker chemicals exploded when a third party threw a match into the bottle. The plaintiffs sued the chemical manufacturer who had sold the chemicals to a buyer that was known by the manufacturer to be selling firecracker kits illegally. The trial court granted the manufacturer's summary judgment motion on plaintiffs' negligence claim. 524 F.2d at 22–24.

We held that the alleged facts presented a jury question as to whether the manufacturer violated its duty to avoid conduct which might involve an unreasonable risk of harm through the foreseeable action of a third party. *Id.* at 29. We also pointed out in this case decided under Pennsylvania negligence law that the doctrine of intended use for the product "cannot shield a manufacturer from liability resulting from misuse of a product if that misuse is foreseeable." *Id.* at 28. We further noted that the principle making a manufacturer

> liable for a foreseeable misuse of his product is consistent with the more general Pennsylvania rule that the intervening negligent act of a third party does not constitute a superseding cause shielding a tortfeasor from liability unless the intervening act was unforeseeable, highly extraordinary, or extraordinarily negligent. [Citations.]

Id. at 28.

We therefore reversed the grant of summary judgment.

* * *

* * * Similarly, in the present case, the magnitude of the risk in selling lighters without childproof features to the public, when BIC knew the frequency with which they are ignited and used by children with access to them to set childplay fires, may have been considerable because of the significant possibility that the lighters would cause serious bodily harm to a number of people. The social utility of sales without childproof features may also be minimal.

As discussed *infra*, we noted in *Suchomajcz* that "Pennsylvania does impose liability upon a manufacturer for harm caused by misuse of its product, if that misuse was foreseeable." In the instant case, BIC apparently could foresee that children who had access to the lighters would misuse them in their current state. As we have observed, the social utility of selling lighters without a childproof design may be minimal; the social consequences of such sales may be catastrophic. *Suchomajcz*, 524 F.2d at 25. Thus, the risk of harm with respect to duty may indeed be unreasonable.

Recently, the Alabama Supreme Court resolved an issue very similar to the one we face in this case. In *Bean v. BIC Corp.*, 597 So.2d 1350 (Ala.1992), a four-year-old girl was killed in a childplay lighter fire set by the girl and her five-year-old brother. The girl's parents sued BIC, alleging, *inter alia*, negligent design based on the lack of features to make the lighter childproof. As in the present case, BIC conceded foreseeability and feasibility for purposes of its summary judgment motion, which the trial court granted.

On appeal, the Alabama Supreme Court alternatively formulated the principal issue as "whether a manufacturer will ever have a duty to make a product intended to be used by adults safer by designing and manufacturing the product to deter or discourage use by children unable to appreciate the risks involved in use of the product." 597 So.2d at 1352. The court "decline[d] to make the sweeping and decisive pronouncement that a manufacturer of a product that it intends to be used by adults never has a duty to make the product safer by making it child-resistant when the dangers are foreseeable and prevention of the danger is feasible." *Id.* The court observed that duty "remains a function of foreseeability of the harm tempered by a consideration of the feasibility of an alternative." *Id.* The court therefore found the grant of summary judgment to be improper.

A few final points must be addressed. First, BIC asserts the prevailing wisdom that strict liability is purportedly easier to prove than negligence, implying that the failure of a strict liability claim should automatically be fatal to a negligence claim based on the same nucleus of operative facts. This might be true if the negligence inquiry differed from the strict liability inquiry by simply requiring an additional element, e.g., defect and causation plus fault. See *Dambacher v. Mallis*, 336 Pa.Super. 22, 485 A.2d 408, 424 (1984) ("[I]n a negligence case the plaintiff must prove, not only that the defect caused his injury and that the product was defective, but in addition, that in manufactur-

Ch. 3   THEORIES AND TESTS OF DEFECTIVENESS

ing or supplying the product the defendant failed to exercise due care."), *appeal dismissed,* 508 Pa. 643, 500 A.2d 428 (1985).

Viewing the negligence claim as merely one step beyond strict liability, however, obscures the true difference between negligence and strict liability under Pennsylvania law. In strict liability, the focus is on a defect in the product, regardless of fault, *Lewis,* 528 A.2d at 593, and that defect is determined in relation to a particular subset of the general population: the intended user who puts the product to its intended use. In negligence the focus is on the reasonableness of a defendant's conduct, *id.,* and this reasonableness is determined in relation to a different subset of the general population, and one that is conceivably broader: anyone who foreseeably may be subject to an unreasonable risk of foreseeable harm.

Rather than looking at strict liability as an easier claim to prove, it is more fruitful to recognize that Pennsylvania law provides a trade-off between the two types of personal injury claims. In strict liability, the plaintiff need not show fault, but only prove a product defect. A product cannot be defective when its design and performance meet all of the requirements of the intended user, regardless of the foreseeability of misuse by unintended users. In negligence, the plaintiff must prove fault of the manufacturer, which is an element not required in strict liability law. The scope of inquiry, however, expands because of the duty to unintended but foreseeable users. Although the results may very well often be the same in strict liability and negligence under a given set of facts, the focus of each claim is different, and therefore proof of negligence may be possible without a finding of strict liability.

BIC points out that the Pennsylvania Superior Court in *Dambacher* introduced a product defect as an element of negligence, thereby short-circuiting the traditional negligence analysis. 485 A.2d at 424. We first note that it is just as unfortunate that courts deciding a negligence claim do so in strict liability language as it is that courts deciding a strict liability claim use the language of negligence. The conclusion in strict liability that a product is defective results from the same analysis that produced the conclusion that BIC had "no duty" to childproof the lighter. This analysis does not take into account factors that must be examined in negligence.

It is reasonable, therefore, to predict that the supreme court would reject the *Dambacher* elements in favor of the standard negligence formulation under Pennsylvania law because (1) the *Dambacher* formulation does not maintain the separation of concepts and vocabulary in strict liability and negligence analyses that the supreme court strives for, and more importantly, (2) it reflects a misunderstanding of the theoretical underpinnings of each claim. Thus, we predict that the Supreme Court of Pennsylvania would hold that if a manufacturer of cigarette lighters may reasonably foresee that they will fall into the hands of children, who, albeit unintended users, can ignite them with a probability of serious injury to themselves and others, and if childproofing the lighters is economically feasible, the manufacturer would have a duty to guard against the unreasonable risk of harm by designing the lighter to be childproof.

* * *

VI.

In summary, we conclude that the Pennsylvania Supreme Court would hold that the district court in this case did not err in holding that BIC's lighter was not defective under strict products liability law, but that it erred in entering summary judgment on the claim under negligence law. Accordingly, the summary judgment in favor of BIC on the strict liability claim will be affirmed. The summary judgment entered in favor of BIC on the negligence claim will be reversed and the case remanded for further proceedings on this issue consistent with this opinion. Each side to bear its own costs.

C. THE CONTINUING SEARCH FOR A VIABLE TEST OF "DEFECTIVENESS"

ADD to page 241 before note 1:

0. Three years after *Pietrone*, a different district of the California Court of Appeals addressed the same question, whether the plaintiff had the burden to prove an alternative feasible design as part of his prima facie case. Bernal v. Richard Wolf Medical Instruments Corp., 221 Cal. App.3d 1326, 272 Cal.Rptr. 41 (1990). During an operation, the arthroscopic scissors used by plaintiff's surgeon broke. The loose broken blade complicated the operation, resulting in deterioration of plaintiff's joint and the need for future surgery. Plaintiff's experts testified that several design choices, including the material used in the scissors, resulted in their fracturing. The trial judge had instructed the jury that "plaintiff must show by a preponderance of the evidence that a reasonable alternative design was possible." *Held*, judgment on verdict for defendant reversed, and remanded for retrial. The Court of Appeals concluded that plaintiff's evidence was sufficient to meet his burden of production and shift the burden to defendant under *Barker*.

SECTION 5. LIMITATIONS ON DEFECTIVENESS

D. UNAVOIDABLE DANGERS AND "STATE OF THE ART"

ADD to page 454 after note 2:

3. The California Supreme Court extended the knowledge-of-danger aspect of *Brown* in failure to warn cases to all products in Anderson v. Owens–Corning Fiberglas Corp., 53 Cal.3d 987, 281 Cal.Rptr. 528, 810 P.2d 549 (1991). Rejecting *Beshada* and the handful of other decisions that had imputed knowledge of danger, the court held that defendants in an asbestos case could introduce evidence that the dangers involved were neither known nor scientifically capable of being known at the time that defendants failed to issue a warning.

REPLACE McKee v. Miles Laboratories on pages 455–58 with:

SNYDER v. MEKHJIAN

Superior Court of New Jersey, Appellate Division, 1990.
244 N.J.Super. 281, 582 A.2d 307.

PRESSLER, JUDGE.

The fundamental issue raised by this action is whether liability attaches to anyone, and if so to whom and under what legal theory, when a surgical patient contracts Acquired Immune Deficiency Syndrome (AIDS) as a result of transfusion with contaminated blood supplied by a non-profit blood bank. We granted plaintiffs leave to appeal from the trial court's interlocutory order dismissing the strict liability counts against all defendants, and we now affirm that order. We also granted plaintiffs' motion for leave to appeal from the interlocutory order denying their motion for discovery from the blood bank of the infected donor's identity, medical records, and recollections of the screening process to which he was required to submit before his donation was accepted. We reverse the order denying discovery subject to the protective conditions hereafter described.

Plaintiff William Snyder, whose wife Roslyn sues *per quod*, underwent elective coronary artery by-pass surgery and an aortic valve replacement at St. Joseph's Hospital in Paterson on August 23, 1984. The surgery was performed by defendant Haroutune Mekhjian, assisted by defendants Youngick Lee and Wilmo Orejola. Some hours after the original surgery, a second surgical procedure was performed to repair a bleeding artery. During this procedure plaintiff was infused with among other blood products, a unit of platelets, identified as serial number 29F0784, which had been supplied to St. Joseph's by defendant Bergen Community Blood Center (BCBC), a nonprofit collector and distributor to hospitals of donated blood. Plaintiff's recuperation proceeded uneventfully, and he was discharged from the hospital several weeks later.

In April 1984 the HTLV–111 virus (HIV) was identified as the cause of AIDS. By March, 1985, tests were available which enabled the nation's blood banks to screen all donated blood for HIV antibodies. This screening process was attended by a nation-wide "Look Back" program by which the blood banks were able to determine whether a now-identifiable HIV-positive donor had given blood prior to March 1985 and, if so, to which hospital that donor's blood had been supplied. In October 1986, BCBC wrote to St. Joseph's to advise that unit number 29F0784, supplied by it to the hospital on August 23, 1984, had come from a donor now testing positive for HIV antibodies. The hospital, by review of its records, ascertained that plaintiff had received that unit, and in April, 1987, it so advised his physician, offering the hospital's resources should further testing of the patient and counselling services be required. According to the physician's note on the hospital's follow-up report, he determined that:

> Recipient [plaintiff] now lives in Florida. Prior to my notifying him he was tested in response to the CDC [Center for Disease Control] recommendation that all recipients be tested. His tests were positive. His wife and two sons were subsequently tested and found to be negative. He is being counselled by a physician in Florida. The recipient has no risk factors.

Plaintiff instituted this action in February 1989 against the hospital, the physicians involved in his diagnosis and treatment, BCBC, and the American Association of Blood Banks (AABB). AABB is a national non-profit association of non-profit blood banks, whose members, of which BCBC is one, collect about half of the country's donated blood. The American Red Cross collects the other half. As we understand the record, AABB collects and disseminates relevant scientific and administrative information to its thousands of members, prescribes standards for their operations, and speaks for them.

Plaintiff asserted a strict liability claim against all defendants, contending that at the time of his transfusion, laboratory tests as well as donor screening techniques were available which, had they been employed, would have screened out HIV-positive donors and rendered the supply of donated blood safe from AIDS contamination. AABB did not, however, recommend their use to its members, and BCBC did not use them. Plaintiff claims that since the blood he received from BCBC could have been made safe, all those in the chain of collection and

Ch. 3 *LIMITATIONS ON DEFECTIVENESS*

distribution of the infected blood he did receive should be held strictly liable for providing him with a defective product.

Plaintiff also asserted negligence claims against all defendants. His claims against the physicians are based on the assertion of professional negligence in not advising him of the risk of receiving contaminated blood and of the option either to collect his own blood for transfusion prior to the surgery (autologous transfusion) or to arrange to have blood available from family members or other known donors (direct donor transfusion). He also claimed that it was the negligence of Dr. Mekhjian and his assistants in failing to repair the bleeding artery during the original surgery which caused the necessity for the second surgery and the consequent contaminated transfusion.

Plaintiff's negligence complaint against the BCBC and AABB was based on the state of scientific knowledge respecting AIDS, its diagnosis and transmission at the time of his transfusion. He alleged that these defendants greatly enhanced his risk of receiving contaminated blood by failing to prescribe and implement available risk-reducing procedures in the blood-collection process. He also asserted that BCBC negligently failed to follow such screening procedures as it did then have in place, inadequate as they may have been. He claimed that but for that negligence, BCBC would have rejected the infected donor's blood. Plaintiff also asserted consumer fraud and punitive damages claims against these defendants based on their alleged knowing and irresponsible failure to protect the blood supply from AIDS contamination.

On summary judgment motions by defendants, the following dispositions ensued: 1) the consumer fraud and strict liability claims as against all defendants were dismissed; 2) all claims against St. Joseph's Hospital were dismissed; 3) the punitive damage claims against the physicians were dismissed. The claims which survived are the negligence claims against AABB, BCBC and the surgeons and the punitive damage claims against AABB and BCBC. In addition, the court ruled that BCBC was not entitled either to charitable immunity pursuant to *N.J.S.A.* 2A:53A–7 or to the $10,000 damages limitation of *N.J.S.A.* 2A:53A–8. Finally, by separate order, the court denied plaintiff's application for production by BCBC of its records of the still anonymous donor of unit number 29F0784.

Plaintiff sought leave to appeal only from the dismissal of the strict liability claims and the denial of the donor discovery motion. No defendant sought leave to appeal from any ruling adverse to it. Consequently strict liability and discovery of the donor records are the only issues now before us.

Consideration of the strict liability claims requires a brief foray into the relevant scientific facts as they were known in August 1984 and the manner in which they were responded to by the nation's blood-banking organizations. As appears from the experts' materials included in the record on the summary judgment motions, the critical period of AIDS contamination of the blood supply was from mid–1981, when the first AIDS cases were diagnosed, to March 1985, when the first test for HIV virus antibodies was developed and in place. According to the scientific data in the record, both the Center for Disease Control (CDC) and the Public Health Service Committee on Opportunistic Infections had, prior to the end of 1982, reported to the blood banking community the likelihood that AIDS was transmissible through blood products. It was also by then reported that the major risk groups for AIDS included homosexual males, intravenous drug users, recently emigrated Haitians and hemophiliacs. In early January 1983, CDC held a meeting attended by among others, representatives of the blood-banking industry, the National Gay Task Force and the National Hemophilia Foundation. Its summary report of the session noted the reluctance of "some participants ... to accept the hypothesis that AIDS has been transmitted by whole blood," but nevertheless reported a consensus "that it would be desirable to exclude high-risk donors to reduce the risk of AIDS transmission via blood and blood products."

CDC also reported the then availability of several surrogate laboratory tests for AIDS, including the Hepatitis B Core Antibody Test and the T–4, T–8 Ratio Test. As we understand the record, a surrogate test in this context is one which does not reveal the presence of HIV virus antibody itself but rather is based on the high statistical correlation between infection with the HIV virus and the presence of other physical manifestations for which there are tests. The theory is that laboratory verification of these other manifestations is a reliable indicator of AIDS infection. According to the CDC data assembled in December 1982, the various surrogate tests would correctly identify between 66% and 88% of AIDS-infected donors, the degree of correlation depending on the risk category to which they belonged. The tests, however, had about a 5% false positive rate, which would result in rejection of "safe" blood and hence in a diminution of the nation's blood supply. Moreover, the cost of the tests would add to the price of collection and distribution of blood products.

The report summarizing the January 1983 meeting observed that the various participants had "differing perceptions" regarding not only the risk of AIDS from blood donation but also "the best approach for establishing altered guidelines for blood donation donor screening or testing and donor restriction." But as information continued to be collected, the CDC became increasingly concerned about AIDS contamination of the blood supply. In March 1983, a recommendation was issued designed to keep members of high risk groups from donating blood, urging donor screening procedures which would include "specific laboratory tests as well as careful histories and physical examinations," and advising use of autologous transfusions where indicated. By January 12, 1984, according to one of plaintiff's experts who cited the issue of the *New England Journal of Medicine* of that date, "the national medical community officially recognized that which was generally known for well over a year," namely, that "AIDS was transmissible through blood and blood products." The virus was isolated several months later, testing began in March 1985, and it is apparently now believed in the scientific community that as a result of later test refinement, blood can now be made virtually 100% safe from AIDS contamination.

The controversy centers on the period from early 1983 to the inception of specific HIV antibody testing in March 1985. According to the record, the nation's commercial blood bankers had initiated surrogate testing and aggressive donor screening of high-risk groups starting in late 1982 when the hepatitis core antibody test was initially licensed by the FDA. The medical director of the Stanford University Blood Bank started surrogate test screening there in July 1983, and by June 1, 1984 such testing was routinely done by other non-profit blood banks throughout northern California. The American Red Cross and the AABB however, apparently because of their concern over maintaining the adequacy of the blood supply and containing the cost of its collection, continued to take the publicly expressed view, despite privately expressed reservations by some of its officials, that the risk of AIDS infection from blood transfusion was minimal (less than one in a million), that routine surrogate testing of blood was not advisable, and that aggressive interviewing to determine a donor's membership in a high-risk group was inappropriate. Instead, the AABB recommended educational campaigns for self-screening by high-risk donors, donor interviewing to elicit physical symptoms associated with AIDS, non-targeting of high-risk groups for donor recruitment, and use of autologous transfusion when appropriate. Consequently, most of AABB's members, including BCBC, did not perform any laboratory testing until the spring of 1985 and did not aggressively seek to exclude male homosexuals or members of other high-risk categories.[10]

10. The foregoing factual recitation is culled from documents in the record before us. The same chronology but without reference to such matters as surrogate testing and the response of the commercial blood banks and the northern California non-profit blood banks' activity is reviewed in *Kozup v. Georgetown University*, 663 F.Supp. 1048, 1051–1053, (D.D.C.1987), *affirmed in part* and *vacated in part* 851 F.2d 437 (D.C.Cir.1988). For recent discussion and analysis of the position of the American Red Cross and AABB from January 1983 to March 1985 on such matters as surrogate testing and aggressive donor interviewing. See Feldschuh and Weber, *Safe Blood* (Free Press, 1990); Rock, "Inside the Billion–Dollar Business of Blood," *Money Magazine*, (March 1986). Note further that on July 13, 1990, the Subcommittee on Oversight and Investigations of the U.S. House of Representatives Committee on Energy and Commerce conducted public hearings on the safety of the nation's blood supply. The opening statement of the Chairman, Congressman John D. Dingell, noted that the inquiry "has its roots in the early to mid 1980's, when the blood industry and the Government failed to prevent the transfusion of thousands of units of blood and blood products infected with the AIDS virus."

We address the strict liability claims against this factual background. The critical point which emerges from the foregoing recitation is that however safe from AIDS contamination donated blood may now be, the best that can be said for the blood supply in August 1984 is that the risk of contamination, while then subject to significant reduction, nevertheless remained appreciable. That is to say, if a blood bank had then employed all the laboratory testing and donor screening techniques available to it, it would nevertheless have missed, statistically, at least 12%, and perhaps as much as 33%, of all AIDS-infected blood. We are satisfied that aside from any other consideration, this margin of error rendered the blood supply unavoidably unsafe, precluding the application of strict liability principles to all of those in the chain of collection and distribution.

In *Brody v. Overlook Hospital*, 127 N.J.Super. 331, 317 A.2d 392 (App.Div.1974), aff'd, 66 N.J. 448, 332 A.2d 596 (1975), we reviewed the policy considerations which impelled our conclusion that strict liability cannot be imposed on a non-profit blood bank and its non-profit distributees in the case of hepatitis-contaminated blood. To be sure, at the time of the blood transfusion in *Brody*, there was apparently no available test at all for the serum hepatitis virus with which that plaintiff was infected. It was thus manifest that we were dealing with an unavoidably unsafe product having a high degree of public utility and social benefit which was therefore exempt from strict liability doctrines. *See generally Shackil v. Lederle Laboratories*, 116 N.J. 155, 561 A.2d 511 (1989); *Restatement (Second) Torts* § 402A comment k, (1965). [Citations.]

We appreciate the difference between having no test at all and having a test with a significant, if not perfect, degree of reliability. But even an 88% reliability factor is, in our view, insufficient to overcome the other policy reasons on which we relied in *Brody* in rejecting strict liability. In sum, considering the public health implications of blood collection and distribution and the non-profit status of that segment of the industry involved in *Brody*, we were there convinced that it would be inimical to the public interest to call upon the non-profit blood bank and those in its distributive chain to warrant a blood product whose safety was beyond their power to ensure. So here. In 1984, no matter how diligent and aggressive BCBC might have been in donor screening and laboratory testing, it would nevertheless necessarily have supplied some AIDS-contaminated blood. The unfortunate recipient of that blood would be in no different legal or equitable position than the plaintiff in *Brody*, nor would the blood bank. In short, product protection for the patient and legal protection for the blood bank remains the same—that is, that the blood bank is obliged to do everything it reasonably can do to ensure safety, but it cannot be responsible for what is not within its capacity to control. This rationale of *Brody* was forcefully reiterated by the Supreme Court in *Feldman v. Lederle Laboratories*, * * *.

We need not consider the question of whether strict liability principles could apply, at least to the blood bank, upon a showing, as we now understand could be made, that with proper testing techniques, blood can be made completely safe from AIDS contamination. We note only that New Jersey does not have any statutory inhibition to such a result[2] and that it might be cogently argued that the blood-banking industry's scientific capacity to warrant the freedom of blood from AIDS contamination should result in its legal obligation to so warrant.

Little need be said respecting the inapplicability of strict liability to defendants St. Joseph's, AABB, and the physicians. The physicians are clearly exempt under the holding and rationale of *Newmark v. Gimbel's, Inc.*, 54 N.J. 585, 258 A.2d 697 (1969). AABB is not itself a supplier or tester of blood. It itself does not deal in producing or distributing a product whether or not the blood bank itself does. As to St. Joseph's, we concur with the holding of *Johnson v. Mountainside Hosp.*, 239 N.J.Super. 312, 571 A.2d 318 (App.Div.1990), that for purposes of product liability law, a hospital cannot be held strictly liable for a latently defective product supplied to it by another for its use in rendering treatment.

What we have said respecting strict liability does not, of course, affect plaintiffs' remaining negligence causes of action against the remaining defendants. There is certainly enough in this record to raise a factual question as to the reasonableness of AABB's conduct in opting to forego guidelines which would have required its members to perform surrogate laboratory testing or more vigorous donor screening. There is also a factual question as to BCBC's conduct in collecting blood without these techniques, irrespective of AABB's guidelines.[3] If it were determined that the conduct of either BCBC or AABB, or both, unreasonably created an appreciable enhancement of plaintiff's risk and that the enhanced risk was a substantial factor in producing his injury, they would be liable to him in negligence even though he might have contracted AIDS even if they had taken every available precaution. *See Evers v. Dollinger*, 95 N.J. 399, 417, 471 A.2d 405 (1984). *See also Ayers v. Jackson Tp.*, 106 N.J. 557, 591–599, 525 A.2d 287 (1987). In addition, there is a more direct negligence claim against BCBC, namely the allegation that but for its unreasonable conduct in screening the donor of the contaminated blood, that infected unit would have been initially rejected.

2. Forty-eight states have statutory provisions exempting suppliers of contaminated blood from strict liability on various alternative bases. *See Roberts v. Suburban Hospital*, 73 Md.App. 1, 532 A.2d 1081, 1086, n. 3 (1987).

3. We point out that the northern California blood banks using surrogate testing in 1983 and 1984 were AABB members.

Finally we have no doubt that the viability of the negligence cause of action against the physicians has been adequately demonstrated. Aside from the issue of the unrepaired bleeder, there is record support for the proposition that a jury could find that in the case of elective surgery in August 1984, the physician's duty to inform the patient included advice as to the possibility of AIDS contamination and the availability of autologous and direct donor transfusion.

We now address the question of donor records. To begin with, we note that BCBC has already supplied plaintiffs with the registration form of the donor of unit number 29F0784 with his name and any other identifying information redacted. This form consists of a series of questions relating to medical history, previous blood donation and vital signs at the time of the donation. BCBC asserts that this information is adequate for plaintiff's purposes. It also asserts that any further information either identifying the donor or in any other way permitting plaintiff to penetrate the donor's anonymity or privacy would breach BCBC's obligation of confidentiality imposed both by considerations of public policy and by the dictates of *N.J.S.A.* 26:5C–5 to –14 (confidentiality of records of AIDS patients).

We consider first plaintiff's need for further information. He claims that he requires it for several reasons. First, none of the defendants is now willing to admit that unit number 29F0784 was contaminated. While there is no question that the donor of that unit tested positive for HIV antibodies in 1986, defendants apparently insist on putting plaintiff to his proof that the donor had been infected as far back as August 1984. It is certainly inferential from the circumstances that he was then infected, particularly in view of the medical assurance referred to *supra* that plaintiff had no other risk factor. But defendants' refusal to concede the point entitles plaintiff to seek direct proof that the donor was HIV-positive in 1984.

Beyond that causation issue, plaintiff cogently asserts a need in respect of the question of BCBC's negligence. Illustratively, it was known before August 1984 that early symptoms of AIDS infection include particular lymph-node swelling and skin disorders, and, in fact, by 1983 the commercial blood bankers were conducting routine physical examinations of donors to determine the presence of these symptoms. Did the donor here have those symptoms then? Was he asked about them? Was he physically examined in this respect? Was he given the appropriate high-risk group self-screening information? Was a reasonable effort made to determine if he was in a high-risk category? Were his responses to the medical history questions accurately recorded? Were the questions adequately explained to him? Would present screening requirements, short of laboratory testing, have revealed his AIDS infection? Undoubtedly other relevant lines of interrogation would suggest themselves. All of this information is, in our view, highly pertinent to the issue of BCBC and AABB negligence and is, moreover, to a large extent not available from any source other than the donor himself.

The question then is how to balance plaintiff's need to gain relevant information against the donor's right to privacy and the public's need to maintain confidentiality, which is said to be a cornerstone of the nation's blood donation program. We start with *N.J.S.A.* 26:5C–5 to –14, which is intended to protect the confidentiality of individual AIDS records while assuring their limited availability for essential health, scientific and other legitimate purposes. The statute stipulates that unless disclosure is expressly provided for by *N.J.S.A.* 26:5C–8, it may be obtained only by court order for good cause shown. *N.J.S.A.* 26:5C–9(a). In assessing good cause, moreover, the court is required to "weigh the public interest and need for disclosure against the injury to the person who is the subject of the record, to the physician-patient relationship, and to the services offered by the program [of diagnosis and treatment of AIDS and conditions related to HIV infection]." Moreover, if good cause is found, the court is required to determine the extent to which disclosure is necessary and to impose appropriate safeguards.

We are convinced that confidentiality of blood bank AIDS records rests upon significant public and private considerations and is ordinarily essential to assure the continued effectiveness of the screening process, the willingness of donors to continue to participate in blood collection efforts, and the general integrity of the nation's blood programs. Nevertheless where, as here, a litigant's discovery need cannot otherwise be met and it is possible to accommodate that need with limited and controlled intrusion, some access under careful court supervision is appropriate and justifiable. *See Belle Bonfils Mem. Blood Center v. District Court*, 763 P.2d 1003 (Sup.Ct.Colo.1988); *Tarrant County Hosp. Dist. v. Hughes*, 734 S.W.2d 675 (Ct.App.Tex.1987); *Stenger v. Lehigh Valley Hosp. Center*, 386 Pa.Super. 574, 563 A.2d 531 (1989); *Boutte v. Blood Systems, Inc.*, 127 F.R.D. 122 (W.D.La.1989); *Mason v. Regional Medical Center of Hopkins County*, 121 F.R.D. 300 (W.D.Ky.1988); *But see* contra *South Florida Blood Service v. Rasmussen*, 467 So.2d 798 (Fla.App.1985); *Krygier v. Airweld, Inc.*, 520 N.Y.S.2d 475, 137 Misc.2d 306 (Sup.Ct.1987); *Doe v. American Red Cross Blood Services*, 125 F.R.D. 646 (D.S.C.1989).

Plaintiff has not yet been able to determine if the donor is still alive. That is the first order of business for BCBC's disclosure. If he is not alive, the trial judge shall explore with counsel the possibility of obtaining information respecting the stage of his disease in 1984, his membership in a high-risk category, and any other relevant information from other sources. The donor's personal representative will, moreover, have to be noticed of these proceedings. If the donor is alive, the court shall determine procedures best calculated to provide plaintiff with the information he requires while giving maximum protection to

the donor. For example, the donor's name need not be supplied if his "veiled" deposition is permitted. If such a deposition were to be permitted, the court could appropriately limit in advance the areas of questioning and impose such other conditions as would insure the donor's anonymity. If, on the other hand, only a deposition on written questions pursuant to *R.* 4:15 were permitted, the court could rule on the list of questions prior to their submission and permit an alias identification and oath. It may also be that the donor would have no objection to providing, openly and frankly, the information plaintiff requires or he may authorize his physician to do so. Thus it may also be prudent for the court itself initially to communicate with the donor. In addition, it is likely that the parties themselves will be able to suggest to the court further limitations on the substance of the inquiry and the technique by which it is to be pursued that will afford plaintiff a reasonable discovery opportunity at the least possible cost to the confidentiality interests here implicated.

The ultimate point of course is that plaintiff has suffered a most grievous harm which was apparently inflicted upon him by this donor, whether unwittingly or not. He does not seek redress from the donor but rather from those defendants whose responsibility it was to stand protectively between them. The degree of plaintiff's injury, his right to redress from those who may have negligently failed to protect him, and his need for information which only the donor can provide if redress is to be obtained, all justify the limited disclosure we here sanction without unduly prejudicing the interests of the public and the donor's privacy rights.

The order appealed from is affirmed insofar as it dismissed all strict liability claims. It is reversed insofar as it denied all discovery of donor information, and we remand for further discovery proceedings consistent with this opinion and for trial of the negligence causes of action.

NOTE

1. The New Jersey Supreme Court permitted an interlocutory appeal on the question of further discovery about the donor of the blood. The court affirmed per curiam, but two lengthy opinions by Justice Pollock (concurring) and Justice Garibaldi (dissenting) thoroughly canvassed the issues bearing on the tensions among the plaintiffs' need to obtain additional information to prove their claim, the donor's privacy interests, and society's interest in ensuring a stable and adequate supply of blood. Snyder v. Mekhjian, 125 N.J. 328, 593 A.2d 318 (1991).

Chapter 4

CAUSATION

SECTION 1. CAUSE IN FACT: CONNECTING PLAINTIFF'S HARM TO DEFENDANT'S BREACH OF DUTY

B. RELIANCE ON WARNINGS

ADD to page 489 before Note 5:

4A. **Pharmaceuticals.** In a case where plaintiff alleges a failure to warn with regard to a prescription drug, what causal showing is required? Suppose that plaintiff's physician states that he does not warn his patients about the adverse effects suffered by plaintiff; should summary judgment be entered? In Garside v. Osco Drug, Inc., 976 F.2d 77 (1st Cir. 1992), plaintiff received an antibiotic and barbiturate, the combination of which resulted in such severe skin poisoning (known as "TEN") that she lost her sight, suffered severe hearing loss, and was left with extensive scarring. In response to her claim that the barbiturate manufacturer should have warned of the dangers of combining the barbiturate with penicillin, her doctor submitted an affidavit asserting that he was generally aware of TEN and that he did not warn his patients about it. The trial court entered summary judgment for the manufacturer, but the First Circuit reversed. Relying on comment j, the court held that once plaintiff proves that a drug manufacturer failed to warn of a nonobvious risk, a rebuttable presumption of causation arises. Defendant may then submit evidence to rebut the presumption, but to justify summary judgment the evidence must clearly show that the physician was fully aware of all information that would be required in an adequate warning and that the physician nevertheless prescribed the drug and did not inform the patient. Why would a physician ever admit to such facts?

Chapter 6

DAMAGES

SECTION 2. EMOTIONAL DISTRESS

ADD to page 585 after note 7:

KHAN v. SHILEY INCORPORATED
Court of Appeal, Fourth District, 1990.
217 Cal.App.3d 848, 266 Cal.Rptr. 106.

SONENSHINE, ASSOCIATE JUSTICE.

Plaintiffs appeal after the trial court granted summary judgment against them in their action involving an allegedly defective mechanical heart valve. They contend the court applied incorrect legal principles in concluding that in light of the fact the valve implanted in Judy Khan's heart had not yet malfunctioned, any grievances were speculative and their lawsuit premature.

I.

Judy Khan was 33 years old when, on July 29, 1983, a Bjork–Shiley convexo-concave valve was implanted in her heart to replace a diseased mitral valve. She had first learned about her condition six months earlier and was told she would die without the implant. Before the surgery, Khan had been experiencing fatigue, double vision, exhaustion, and shortness of breath. Within two months of the operation, her symptoms were gone and she was "feeling good about life."

Khan had been advised of the risks associated with mechanical heart valves including the potential for blood clots and the possibility the valve would be rejected by her body. She also knew she would always be a slave to blood thinner medication. She was not, however, told there was a risk the valve might fracture.

In November 1985, Khan's surgeon informed her Shiley had told him the implanted valve was within a group of valves being recalled due to a propensity to fracture.[4] He stated there had been numerous reports the valves were "falling apart and malfunctioning without notice resulting in death to the patients." According to information he received from Shiley, the risk of a second open-heart surgery was even higher than the risk of a malfunction. Further, because any malfunc-

---

4. Shiley's "Dear Doctor" letter dated October 14, 1985, indicates the valve in question had "a statistical fracture rate of 11 per 1,000 through three years of implantation."

tion could be fatal, she should go to the nearest hospital if her valve ceased to operate.⁵

Since learning of the recall, Khan's life has not been the same. Although she "made it through the surgery in excellent condition, [she] still face[s] the possibility of the valve falling apart inside of [her] heart and killing [her]. Knowing that [she] face[s] almost certain death without notice has made living a nightmare." She has been treated by three different mental health professionals for her emotional problems and has also experienced physical symptoms associated with her anxiety.⁶

In October 1986, Khan and her husband filed a lawsuit against Shiley Incorporated and its parent company, Pfizer, Inc. A second amended complaint for damages, filed May 10, 1988, sought both compensatory and punitive damages, and alleged eight causes of action, including negligence, fraud and misrepresentation, breach of warranty (express and implied), strict liability in tort, intentional infliction of emotional distress, and, as to Jan Khan, negligent infliction of emotional distress and loss of consortium. It alleged "an extraordinary number of the more than 80,000 c-c valves implanted to date have malfunctioned as a direct and proximate result of conduct of the defendants as alleged herein, causing death or other serious injury and damages to those persons in whom the c-c valves were implanted and their spouses." While the complaint acknowledged Khan's valve "has not yet malfunctioned", it alleged it "is defective and likely to malfunction at any moment because of the conduct of the defendant[s] as alleged herein, thereby exposing [Khan] to the constant threat of imminent death or other serious physical injury and the anxiety, fear and emotional distress that results therefrom."

The complaint also alleged, in its second cause of action for fraud and misrepresentation, "[d]efendants fraudulently, intentionally and negligently misrepresented the characteristics and safety of the c-c valve and fraudulently, intentionally and negligently concealed material, adverse information regarding the characteristics and safety of the c-c valve. Defendants made these representations and concealed adverse information at a time when defendants knew, or should have known, that the c-c valve had defects, dangers and characteristics and was other than defendants had represented to physicians and the consuming public, including plaintiffs." Examples of defendants' conduct included misrepresentation as to the valve's safety and propensity

---

5. Sometime in 1984, Khan had read a newspaper article regarding faulty heart valves manufactured by Shiley. She knew hers was a "Shiley valve," but did not ascertain whether it was one of the faulty ones. Although she was prompted to look at her "Implantation Data" card, she did not contact Shiley.

6. Khan's physical symptoms include an increased heart rate, abnormal heart rhythms and palpitations, increased blood pressure, stomach cramps and spasms, dizziness, headaches, hyperventilation, and lightheadedness.

to fail, failure to adequately test the valve, failure to provide adequate warnings which fairly reflected known risks, making of understatements in reports as to the failure rate when they knew the rate was much higher, and omission of material facts showing the valve had a history of strut fracture. Further, the complaint alleged defendants made these misrepresentations with the intention plaintiffs and their physicians would rely on them, thereby inducing selection of the Shiley valve.

On May 12th, defendants filed their motion for summary judgment. Supporting declarations alleged, among other things, all heart valves have an inherent risk of failure and all heart valve recipients always face a risk of death. Further, the risk Khan's valve would fail actually decreased over time; the risk of fracture in heart valve recipients in their sixth postoperative year, such as Khan, is approximately 0.225 percent per annum. In essence, it was defendants' position California law does not recognize plaintiffs' causes of action "based upon their purported emotional distress for an alleged fear of future malfunction." Relying on Khan's 1988 deposition testimony, they asserted the valve had not malfunctioned and, in fact, had "saved [her] life through its effective performance for nearly five years."

Plaintiffs opposed the motion, insisting they had a legitimate claim for all medically verified emotional and physical injuries sustained by Khan after she learned of her dilemma. They argued the valve was defective, had been declared by the Food and Drug Administration (FDA) to be "adulterated," [7] and, to date, had "killed and injured at least 243 people." [8]

* * *

The court announced its tentative ruling was to grant the motion, noting "while some valves of this type have failed, there's no indication this valve has failed or will fail." It found "[t]here's been nobody injured yet." And, just before uttering its final decision, it exclaimed: "We've been asked to speculate about something that may or may not happen, and there is no allegation, nothing that's been presented in the opposition papers, that show any basis now that there is a defect...."

---

7. Documents which plaintiffs obtained from the FDA disclosed that in December 1985, after Shiley voluntarily recalled the valves, the FDA notified Shiley the recall was classified as Class I. According to plaintiffs, this meant the FDA found the valve represented "a situation in which there is a reasonable probability that the use of, or exposure to, a violative product will cause serious adverse health consequences or death." An internal memorandum dated December 18, 1985, issued by the FDA's Recall and Notification Branch, Office of Compliance, stated: "We consider the product to be adulterated because the strut on the valves may fracture. The heart valves, if implanted, may malfunction and cause serious adverse health consequences or death as a result of strut fracture."

8. Of the approximately 81,000 valves implanted as of April 1988, Shiley had received reports of 243 fractures. Plaintiffs assert two-thirds of those implantees have died.

Ch. 6   EMOTIONAL DISTRESS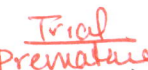

[I]t's premature on that basis." In response to plaintiffs' counsel's inquiry as to the basis of the court's ruling on each of the various theories of liability, the court said, "You're premature."

II.

* * *

Plaintiffs contend the trial court not only ignored uncontested material facts showing they have suffered injury and the valve is defective, but also failed to correctly apply settled principles of law. The gist of their argument is the court erred in acquiescing to defendants' argument that "malfunction" is an element in a products liability lawsuit. They insist the owner of a product, functioning as intended [9] but containing an inherent defect which may cause the product to fail in the future, has an action against the manufacturer. Plaintiffs are mistaken.

"Products liability is the name currently given to the area of the law involving the liability of those who supply goods or products for the use of others to purchasers, users, and bystanders for losses of various kinds *resulting from so-called defects in those products*." (Prosser & Keeton, Torts (5th ed. 1984) § 95, p. 677, italics added.) Possible theories of recovery include strict liability in tort, negligence (i.e., in creating or failing to discover a flaw, in failing to warn or failing adequately to warn, or in the sale of a defectively designed product), and breach of warranty (express and implied).

No matter which theory is utilized, however, where a plaintiff alleges a product is defective, proof that the product has malfunctioned is essential to establish liability for an injury *caused by the defect*. Indeed, as stated in *Greenman v. Yuba Power Products, Inc.* (1963) 59 Cal.2d 57, 27 Cal.Rptr. 697, 377 P.2d 897, "A manufacturer is strictly liable in tort when an article [it] places on the market, knowing that it is to be used without inspection for defects, proves to have a *defect that causes injury* to a human being." [Citations.]

This essential element of causation is missing here. Khan's alleged injury was not caused by any defect in the valve. Rather, it was caused, if at all, by the knowledge the valve may, at some future time,

---

9. Khan testified at her deposition the valve had "not yet" malfunctioned. She also responded affirmatively when asked if, to her knowledge, the valve has "worked properly" and has "done its job" since it was implanted in her heart.

Plaintiffs concede the valve "has not yet experienced complete structural disintegration due to strut fracture, with the resultant inevitable severe cardiac injury or death, that has plagued identical C–C valves." However, they insist the fact the group of valves which includes Khan's has been declared by the FDA to be "adulterated" establishes there is a design defect. They further assert defendants have not met their burden to establish the valve implanted in Khan's heart has not begun to fall apart. And they maintain there is a dispute as to whether the valve is "functioning as intended." Thus, if the valve is not functioning as intended, then it must be malfunctioning.

33

fracture. As counsel for defendants asserted at the hearing below: "The issue here is whether [the valve has] malfunctioned or not, and all the discovery in the world isn't going to shed any light on that. If her valve does malfunction, she will have a cause of action. [¶] She'll still have to prove it was a defective product, but that hasn't happened yet." [11]

III.

Plaintiffs contend the court's "greatest error" was in failing to recognize that their verified emotional injuries entitle them to a jury determination of their claims under *Molien v. Kaiser Foundation Hospitals* (1980) 27 Cal.3d 916, 167 Cal.Rptr. 831, 616 P.2d 813. Once again, they are confused.

Molien acknowledged that damages for emotional distress could be recovered, in the absence of physical injury, by an individual who is a direct victim of the defendant's negligent conduct and where it is foreseeable that serious emotional distress will result from such negligent conduct. Negligent infliction of emotional distress is *not*, however, an independent tort. (6 Witkin, *op. cit. supra*, Torts, § 838, p. 195.) As explained in *Marlene F. v. Affiliated Psychiatric Medical Clinic, Inc.* (1989) 48 Cal.3d 583, 257 Cal.Rptr. 98, "Damages for severe emotional distress ... are recoverable *in a negligence action* when they result from the breach of a duty owed the plaintiff that is assumed by the defendant or imposed on the defendant as a matter of law, or that arises out of a relationship between the two." (*Id.*, at p. 590, 257 Cal.Rptr. 98, italics added.)

Contrary to plaintiffs' assertion, Khan is not "the quintessential 'direct victim' as contemplated by *Molien* ...." Indeed, she has not yet been victimized. In the absence of product malfunction, Khan cannot establish defendants breached any duty owed to her.

Plaintiffs' reliance on *Barth v. Firestone Tire and Rubber Co.* (N.D.Cal.1987) 661 F.Supp. 193 for the proposition that California law permits recovery for emotional injury caused by the fear of contracting a disease in the future, is also misplaced. In that class action lawsuit, an employee exposed to industrial chemicals asserted claims of fraudulent active concealment and misrepresentation, battery, intentional

---

11. Judy Khan's lawsuit is not unique. Defendants have alerted us to a number of cases involving the same claims, including two unpublished United States Court of Appeal decisions and two rulings of the Los Angeles Superior Court. In three of them, summary judgment was granted in Shiley's favor. In one Los Angeles case, the trial judge found there was no viable cause of action in the absence of malfunction, stating "until [the valve] fails there is no proximate harm that I can see." In a fourth case, originating in the United States District Court for the District of Maryland, the plaintiff's claim was dismissed because Maryland law precludes recovery based on future harm unless the harm is more likely than not to occur.

The record reflects plaintiffs' attorneys have instituted virtually identical lawsuits against Shiley in Orange County Superior Court on behalf of 16 other valve recipients. At oral argument, Shiley's lawyer informed us 90 cases were pending.

infliction of emotional distress, and unfair and deceptive trade practices. He alleged he suffered two forms of injury: injury to his immune system rendering him more susceptible to developing various forms of cancer, and injury through the increased risk of cancer. The defendant moved to dismiss on the ground the plaintiff failed to allege a present injury. The court found the plaintiff's allegations of injury to his immune system and the presence of diseases in their latency stage were sufficient for that purpose.

The court also remarked, noting it was unconcerned with problems of proof at that stage of the proceeding: "The plaintiff also clearly asserts a claim for emotional distress. He alleges that he suffers from fear of contacting serious and/or lethal diseases as a result of his exposure to the toxic chemicals at the Firestone plant. These emotional injuries state a present injury upon which some claims for relief may be based." (*Id.*, at p.196.)

We reject plaintiffs' assertion the quoted language "undeniably establishes that the court expressly found that the present fear of potential future harm constitutes an actionable claim." The plaintiff in *Barth* had a "legally cognizable injury [in which he alleged] damage to his immune system and the presence of diseases in their latency period." (*Id.*, at p.197.) Thus, his emotional injuries constituted not a separate claim, but rather, an element of damages for the underlying legal injury. Here, Khan's alleged emotional injuries are not a basis for recovery absent a ground for imposing liability pursuant to a recognized cause of action. So long as the valve continues to function, no cause of action exists under any products liability theory.

IV.

Finally, plaintiffs contend even if product malfunction is a prerequisite in a strict liability context, it has no bearing on causes of action for negligence,[12] breach of warranty, or fraud. They are partly correct. A cause of action does not presently exist under any theory premised on the *risk* the valve *may* malfunction in the future. This includes negligence, i.e., failure to warn, and breach of warranty. Allegations of fraud, however, are in a class by themselves.[13]

---

12. Plaintiffs contend *Vanoni v. Western Airlines* (1967) 247 Cal.App.2d 793, 56 Cal.Rptr. 115 supports their position that product malfunction is not required to establish negligence. In *Vanoni*, the plaintiffs alleged they suffered shock to their nervous systems when they thought the airplane in which they were traveling was going to crash. The trial court sustained a demurrer without leave to amend and the appellate court reversed, noting allegations of shock to one's nervous system are sufficient to state a physical injury. The case does not, however, purport to hold that one's fear something may happen in the future is, without more, actionable.

13. We note that in only one of the cases referred to in footnote 11, *ante*, i.e., the Maryland case, did the complaint contain allegations of fraud. In affirming the lower court's dismissal of the lawsuit on the ground Maryland law precludes recovery unless there is a greater than 50 percent likelihood the injury will occur, the court did not separately address the claim of fraud.

For purposes of establishing fraud, it matters not that the valve implanted in Khan's heart is still functioning, arguably as intended. Unlike the other theories, in which the safety and efficacy of the *product* is assailed, the fraud claim impugns defendants' *conduct*.

* * *

Plaintiffs assert defendants misrepresented the characteristics and safety of the valve while concealing other material, adverse information. Specifically, they contend defendants misrepresented the valve's propensity to fail, and omitted material facts showing the product had a history of strut failure even before one was implanted into Khan's heart. And they did so with knowledge of the substantial risk of death and without providing adequate warnings which fairly reflected the known risks. Furthermore, defendants allegedly made these misrepresentations with the intention plaintiffs would rely on them in selecting the Shiley valve. Plaintiffs relied on and were induced by these representations in making their selection. They would not otherwise have selected the Shiley valve; indeed, at least six other mechanical heart valves were available at the time of Khan's surgery.

Plaintiffs' complaint contained allegations sufficient to state a cause of action for fraud. In moving for summary judgment, defendants essentially ignored plaintiffs' fraud theory, focusing instead on whether or not the valve had malfunctioned. In so doing, defendants failed to meet their burden to establish there was no triable issue of material fact with respect to the fraud claim. Thus, the motion was erroneously granted as to that cause of action and, accordingly, summary judgment was improper.

We reach this conclusion notwithstanding defendants' position that the unprecedented cause of action plaintiffs seek to establish is contrary to public policy. We recognize the role public policy has played, and continues to play, in the torts arena. However, our decision neither establishes a new cause of action nor drastically extends existing law.[14] It merely confirms that a manufacturer of a product may be liable for fraud when it conceals material product information from potential users. This is true whether the product is a mechanical heart valve or frozen yogurt.

[Reversed.]

---

14. Asserting the implanted valve has saved and, for more than five years, has sustained Khan's life, defendants maintain there are compelling reasons why a new cause of action should not be created. They contend if manufacturers faced liability to users of products based on product failures experienced by other users, "there would be no incentive to develop or manufacture heart valves or other critical medical devices and drugs. The consequences of such a drastic extension of existing law would be disastrous for health care in this country and would inundate the judicial system with an avalanche of premature and speculative claims." At oral argument, counsel for defendants exclaimed that allowing plaintiffs to proceed with their fraud theory would similarly have a chilling effect on the manufacture of critical medical devices.

Ch. 6   PUNITIVE DAMAGES

SECTION 4. PUNITIVE DAMAGES

ADD to page 629 before note 1:

0. Notwithstanding the decision in *Vossler* and the trend that it identified in other jurisdictions, the California Supreme Court decided that evidence of the financial condition of the defendant was required in a punitive damages case. Adams v. Murakami, 54 Cal.3d 105, 284 Cal.Rptr. 318, 813 P.2d 1348 (1991). The Court justified its ruling by characterizing financial condition as one of three prerequisites for the fact finder to determine the appropriate amount of money to punish the defendant. Such evidence is also required for judicial review of the appropriateness of the amount of any jury award of punitive damages. In part, the Court relied on the Supreme Court's decision in *Haslip*, infra, requiring some judicial review of punitive damages awards to satisfy due process. The *Adams* court also held that the plaintiff has the burden to introduce the financial condition evidence; otherwise defendant is put to the Hobson's choice of trying to deny its liability for punitive damages while at the same time providing evidence that bears on the appropriate amount of damages.

The Court did not decide what type of evidence of financial condition should be introduced. Should it be the total wealth of the defendant? The total revenues of the product that caused injury? The net profit to the defendant from engaging in the conduct that justified the award of punitive damages?

ADD to page 631 after note 6:

PACIFIC MUTUAL LIFE INSURANCE CO. v. HASLIP

Supreme Court of the United States, 1991.
___ U.S. ___, 111 S.Ct. 1032, 113 L.Ed. 2d 1.

JUSTICE BLACKMUN delivered the opinion of the Court.

This case is yet another that presents a challenge to a punitive damages award.

I

In 1981, Lemmie L. Ruffin, Jr., was an Alabama-licensed agent for petitioner Pacific Mutual Life Insurance Company. He also was a licensed agent for Union Fidelity Life Insurance Company. Pacific Mutual and Union are distinct and nonaffiliated entities. Union wrote group health insurance for municipalities. Pacific Mutual did not.

37

Respondents Cleopatra Haslip, Cynthia Craig, Alma M. Calhoun, and Eddie Hargrove were employees of Roosevelt City, an Alabama municipality. Ruffin, presenting himself as an agent of Pacific Mutual, solicited the city for both health and life insurance for its employees. The city was interested. Ruffin gave the city a single proposal for both coverages. The city approved and, in August 1981, Ruffin prepared separate applications for the city and its employees for group health with Union and for individual life policies with Pacific Mutual. This packaging of health insurance with life insurance, although from different and unrelated insurers, was not unusual. Indeed, it tended to boost life insurance sales by minimizing the loss of customers who wished to have both health and life protection. The initial premium payments were taken by Ruffin and submitted to the insurers with the applications. Thus far, nothing is claimed to have been out of line. Respondents were among those with the health coverage.

An arrangement was made for Union to send its billings for health premiums to Ruffin at Pacific Mutual's Birmingham office. Premium payments were to be effected through payroll deductions. The city clerk each month issued a check for those premiums. The check was sent to Ruffin or picked up by him. He, however, did not remit to Union the premium payments received from the city; instead, he misappropriated most of them. In late 1981, when Union did not receive payment, it sent notices of lapsed health coverage to respondents in care of Ruffin and Patrick Lupia, Pacific Mutual's agent-in-charge of its Birmingham office. Those notices were not forwarded to respondents. Although there is some evidence to the contrary, see Reply Brief for Petitioner B1–B4, the trial court found, App. to Pet. for Cert. A2, that respondents did not know that their health policies had been canceled.

II

Respondent Haslip was hospitalized on January 23, 1982. She incurred hospital and physician's charges. Because the hospital could not confirm health coverage, it required Haslip, upon her discharge, to make a payment upon her bill. Her physician, when he was not paid, placed her account with a collection agency. The agency obtained a judgment against Haslip and her credit was adversely affected.

In May 1982, respondents filed this suit, naming as defendants Pacific Mutual (but not Union) and Ruffin, individually and as a proprietorship, in the Circuit Court for Jefferson County, Ala. It was alleged that Ruffin collected premiums but failed to remit them to the insurers so that respondents' respective health insurance policies lapsed without their knowledge. Damages for fraud were claimed. The case against Pacific Mutual was submitted to the jury under a theory of *respondeat superior*.

Ch. 6   PUNITIVE DAMAGES

Following the trial court's charge on liability, the jury was instructed that if it determined there was liability for fraud, it could award punitive damages. That part of the instructions is set forth in the margin.[1] Pacific Mutual made no objection on the ground of lack of specificity in the instructions and it did not propose a more particularized charge. No evidence was introduced as to Pacific Mutual's financial worth. The jury returned general verdicts for respondents against Pacific Mutual and Ruffin in the following amounts:

Haslip:	$1,040,000[2]
Calhoun:	15,290
Craig:	12,400
Hargrove:	10,288

Judgments were entered accordingly.

On Pacific Mutual's appeal, the Supreme Court of Alabama, by a divided vote, affirmed. 553 So.2d 537 (1989). In addition to issues not now before us, the court ruled that, while punitive damages are not recoverable in Alabama for misrepresentation made innocently or by mistake, they are recoverable for deceit or willful fraud, and that on the evidence in this case a jury could not have concluded that Ruffin's misrepresentations were made either innocently or mistakenly. The majority then specifically upheld the punitive damages award.

One Justice concurred in the result without opinion. *Ibid.* Two Justices dissented in part on the ground that the award of punitive

---

1. "Now, if you find that fraud was perpetrated then in addition to compensatory damages you may in your discretion, when I use the word discretion, I say you don't have to even find fraud, you wouldn't have to, but you may, the law says you may award an amount of money known as punitive damages.

"This amount of money is awarded to the plaintiff but it is not to compensate the plaintiff for any injury. It is to punish the defendant. Punitive means to punish or it is also called exemplary damages, which means to make an example. So, if you feel or not feel, but if you are reasonably satisfied from the evidence that the plaintiff, whatever plaintiff you are talking about, has had a fraud perpetrated upon them and as a direct result they were injured and in addition to compensatory damages you may in your discretion award punitive damages.

"Now, the purpose of awarding punitive or exemplary damages is to allow money recovery to the plaintiffs, it does to the plaintiff, by way of punishment to the defendant and for the added purpose of protecting the public by detering [sic] the defendant and others from doing such wrong in the future. Imposition of punitive damages is entirely discretionary with the jury, that means you don't have to award it unless this jury feels that you should do so.

"Should you award punitive damages, in fixing the amount, you must take into consideration the character and the degree of the wrong as shown by the evidence and necessity of preventing similar wrong." App. 105–106.

2. Although there is controversy about the matter, it is probable that the general verdict for respondent Haslip contained a punitive damages component of not less than $840,000. In Haslip's counsel's argument to the jury, compensatory damages of $200,000 (including out-of-pocket expenditures of less than $4,000) and punitive damages of $3,000,000 were requested. Tr. 810–814. For present purposes, we accept this description of the verdict.

damages violated Pacific Mutual's due process rights under the Fourteenth Amendment. *Id.*, at 544–545.

Pacific Mutual, but not Ruffin, then brought the case here. It challenged punitive damages in Alabama as the product of unbridled jury discretion and as violative of its due process rights. We * * * granted certiorari, ___ U.S. ___ (1990), to review the punitive damages procedures and award in the light of the long-enduring debate about their propriety.[4]

III

This Court and individual Justices thereof on a number of occasions in recent years have expressed doubts about the constitutionality of certain punitive damages awards.

In *Browning–Ferris Industries of Vermont, Inc. v. Kelco Disposal, Inc.*, 492 U.S. 257 (1989), all nine participating Members of the Court noted concern. In that case, punitive damages awarded on a state-law

---

4. Compare, *e.g., Fay v. Parker*, 53 N.H. 342, 382 (1873) ("The idea is wrong. It is a monstrous heresy. It is an unsightly and an unhealthy excrescence, deforming the symmetry of the body of the law."), with *Luther v. Shaw*, 157 Wisc. 234, 238, 147 N.W. 18, 19–20 (1914) (Timlin, J., "Speaking for myself only in this paragraph.... The law giving exemplary damages is an outgrowth of the English love of liberty regulated by law. It tends to elevate the jury as a responsible instrument of government, discourage private reprisals, restrains the strong, influential, and unscrupulous, vindicates the right of the weak, and encourages recourse to and confidence in the courts of law by those wronged or oppressed by acts or practices not cognizable in or not sufficiently punished by the criminal law.").

This debate finds replication in the many *amicus* briefs filed here. See, *e.g.*, Brief for Alliance of American Insurers et al. 5 ("The Due Process Clause imposes substantive limits on the amounts of punitive damages that civil juries can award. This conclusion is evident from history."); * * * Brief for Business Roundtable et al. 2 ("An award that is not rationally related to the retributive and deterrent purposes of punitive damages is unconstitutionally excessive."); Brief for Defense Research Institute 2 ("No society concerned for fairness and regularity in the administration of justice can afford to tolerate an essentially lawless regime of punishment."); Brief for Pharmaceutical Manufacturers Association et al. 4 ("Any award of punitive damages for lawful conduct approved in advance by the [Food and Drug Administration] must be deemed arbitrary and excessive."); Brief for Aetna Life Insurance Company et al. 6 ("[A] State may impose punishment on its citizens only pursuant to standards established in advance."); Brief for Hospital Authority of Gwinnett County, Georgia, 2 ("In the absence of a statute ... an award of punitive damages ... violates the defendant's right to due process ... unless it is shown by clear and convincing evidence that the act constituted a crime.... Awards of punitive damages in excess of twice the amount of actual damages (that is, awards in excess of treble damages) ... violate ... due process...."); Brief for Mid–America Legal Foundation 8 ("System as applied today merely introduces a wild-card into the legal process...."); Brief for Association for California Tort Reform 2 ("Until state legislatures do their job and set maximum limits for punitive awards and establish meaningful criteria for juries to use, punitive damages are *per se* a violation of due process."); Brief for Association of Trial Lawyers of America 3 ("There is no 'explosion'.... Punitive damages neither deter innovation nor place American businesses at a competitive disadvantage...."); Brief for National Insurance Consumer Organization 3 ("Punitive damages have developed as the most effective means by which the states can protect their citizens against corporate misconduct."); Brief for Attorney Generals of Alabama et al. 1 ("The States—and not this Court—should decide how and when punitive damages may be assessed in civil cases between private litigants.").

claim were challenged under the Eighth and Fourteenth Amendments and on federal common-law grounds. The majority held that the Excessive Fines Clause of the Eighth Amendment did not apply to a punitive damages award in a civil case between private parties; that the claim of excessiveness under the Due Process Clause of the Fourteenth Amendment had not been raised in either the District Court or the Court of Appeals and therefore was not to be considered here; and that federal common law did not provide a basis for disturbing the jury's punitive damages award. The Court [in *Browning Ferris*] said:

> "The parties agree that due process imposes some limits on jury awards of punitive damages, and it is not disputed that a jury award may not be upheld if it was the product of bias or passion, or if it was reached in proceedings lacking the basic elements of fundamental fairness. But petitioners make no claim that the proceedings themselves were unfair, or that the jury was biased or blinded by emotion or prejudice. Instead, they seek further due process protections, addressed directly to the size of the damages award. There is some authority in our opinions for the view that the Due Process Clause places outer limits on the size of a civil damages award made pursuant to a statutory scheme ... but we have never addressed the precise question presented here: whether due process acts as a check on undue jury discretion to award punitive damages in the absence of any express statutory limit.... That inquiry must await another day." U.S., at ___ (slip op. 18).

* * *

JUSTICE O'CONNOR, joined by JUSTICE STEVENS, concurring in part and dissenting in part, observed:

"Awards of punitive damages are skyrocketing.

• • • • •

"I do ... agree with the Court that no due process claims—either procedural or substantive—are properly presented in this case, and that the award of punitive damages here should not be overturned as a matter of federal common law.... Moreover, I share Justice Brennan's view, ante, at 1–2, that nothing in the Court's opinion forecloses a due process challenge to awards of punitive damages or the method by which they are imposed...." *Id.*, at ___ (slip op. 1–2).

In *Bankers Life & Casualty Co. v. Crenshaw*, 486 U.S. 71 (1988), a challenge to a punitive damages award was made. The Court, however, refused to reach claims that the award violated the Due Process Clause and other provisions of the Federal Constitution since those claims had not been raised and passed upon in state court. *Id.*, at 76–80. JUSTICE

O'Connor, joined by Justice Scalia, concurring in part and concurring in the judgment, said:

> "Appellant has touched on a due process issue that I think is worthy of the Court's attention in an appropriate case. Mississippi law gives juries discretion to award any amount of punitive damages in any tort case in which a defendant acts with a certain mental state. In my view, because of the punitive character of such awards, there is reason to think that this may violate the Due Process Clause.

• • • • •

> "This due process question, serious as it is, should not be decided today.... I concur in the Court's judgment on this question and would leave for another day the consideration of these issues." *Id.*, at 87–89.

* * *

IV

Two preliminary and overlapping due process arguments raised by Pacific Mutual deserve attention before we reach the principal issue in controversy. Did Ruffin act within the scope of his apparent authority as an agent of Pacific Mutual? If so, may Pacific Mutual be held responsible for Ruffin's fraud on a theory of *respondeat superior*?

Pacific Mutual was held responsible for the acts of Ruffin. The insurer mounts a challenge to this result on substantive due process grounds, arguing that it was not shown that either it or its Birmingham manager was aware that Ruffin was collecting premiums contrary to his contract; that Pacific Mutual had no notice of the actions complained of prior to the filing of the complaint in this litigation; that it did not authorize or ratify Ruffin's conduct; that his contract with the company forbade his collecting any premium other than the initial one submitted with an application; and that Pacific Mutual was held liable and punished for unauthorized actions of its agent for acts performed on behalf of another company. Thus, it is said, when punitive damages were imposed on Pacific Mutual, the focus for determining the amount of those damages shifted from Ruffin, where it belonged, to Pacific Mutual, and obviously and unfairly contributed to the amount of the punitive damages and their disproportionality. Ruffin was acting not to benefit Pacific Mutual but for his own benefit, and to hold Pacific Mutual liable is "beyond the point of fundamental fairness," Brief for Petitioner 29, embodied in due process, *id.*, at 32. It is said that the burden of the liability comes to rest on Pacific Mutual's other policy holders.

The jury found that Ruffin was acting as an employee of Pacific Mutual when he defrauded respondents. The Supreme Court of Alabama did not disturb that finding. There is no occasion for us to question it, for it is amply supported by the record. Ruffin had actual authority to sell Pacific Mutual life insurance to respondents. The insurer derived economic benefit from those life insurance sales. Ruffin's defalcations related to the life premiums as well as to the health premiums. Thus, Pacific Mutual cannot plausibly claim that Ruffin was acting wholly as an agent of Union when he defrauded respondents.

The details of Ruffin's representation admit of no other conclusion. He gave respondents a single proposal—not multiple ones—for both life and health insurance. He used Pacific Mutual letterhead which he was authorized to use on Pacific Mutual business. There was, however, no indication that Union was a nonaffiliated company. The trial court found that Ruffin "spoke only of Pacific Mutual and indicated that Union Fidelity was a subsidiary of Pacific Mutual." App. to Pet. for Cert. A2. Pacific Mutual encouraged the packaging of life and health insurance. Ruffin worked exclusively out of a Pacific Mutual branch office. Each month he presented to the city clerk a single invoice on Pacific Mutual letterhead for both life and health premiums.

Before the frauds in this case were effectuated, Pacific Mutual had received notice that its agent Ruffin was engaged in a pattern of fraud identical to those perpetrated against respondents. There were complaints to the Birmingham office about the absence of coverage purchased through Ruffin. The Birmingham manager was also advised of Ruffin's receipt of non-initial premiums made payable to him, a practice in violation of company policy.

Alabama's common-law rule is that a corporation is liable for both compensatory and punitive damages for fraud of its employee effected within the scope of his employment. We cannot say that this does not rationally advance the State's interest in minimizing fraud. Alabama long has applied this rule in the insurance context, for it has determined that an insurer is more likely to prevent an agent's fraud if given sufficient financial incentive to do so. See *British General Ins. Co. v. Simpson Sales Co.*, 93 So.2d 763, 768 (Ala.1957).

Imposing exemplary damages on the corporation when its agent commits intentional fraud creates a strong incentive for vigilance by those in a position "to guard substantially against the evil to be prevented." *Louis Pizitz Dry Goods Co. v. Yeldell*, 274 U.S. 112, 116 (1927). If an insurer were liable for such damages only upon proof that it was at fault independently, it would have an incentive to minimize oversight of its agents. Imposing liability without independent fault deters fraud more than a less stringent rule. It therefore rationally advances the State's goal. We cannot say this is a violation of Fourteenth Amendment due process. See *American Society of Mechanical Engineers, Inc. v. Hydrolevel Corp.*, 454 U.S. 556 (1982); *Pizitz*, 274 U.S., at 115. These and other cases in a broad range of civil and criminal contexts make clear that imposing such liability is not fundamentally unfair and does not in itself violate the Due Process Clause. See *Shevlin–Carpenter Co. v. Minnesota*, 218 U.S. 57 (1910); *United States v. Balint*, 258 U.S. 250, 252 (1922); *United States v. Park*, 421 U.S. 658, 670 (1975).

We therefore readily conclude that Ruffin was acting as an employee of Pacific Mutual when he defrauded respondents, and that imposing liability upon Pacific Mutual for Ruffin's fraud under the doctrine of *respondeat superior* does not, on the facts here, violate Pacific Mutual's due process rights.

V

"Punitive damages have long been a part of traditional state tort law." *Silkwood v. Kerr–McGee Corp.*, 464 U.S. 238, 255 (1984). Blackstone appears to have noted their use. 3 W. Blackstone, Commentaries * 137–138. See also *Wilkes v. Wood*, 98 Eng. Rep. 489 (C. P. 1763) (The Lord Chief Justice validating exemplary damages as compensation, punishment, and deterrence). Among the first reported American cases are *Genay v. Norris*, 1 S.C.L. (1 Bay) 6 (1784), and *Coryell v. Colbaugh*, 1 N.J.L. 77 (1791).[5]

Under the traditional common-law approach, the amount of the punitive award is initially determined by a jury instructed to consider the gravity of the wrong and the need to deter similar wrongful conduct. The jury's determination is then reviewed by trial and appellate courts to ensure that it is reasonable.

This Court more than once has approved the common-law method for assessing punitive awards. In *Day v. Woodworth*, 13 How. 363 (1852), a case decided before the adoption of the Fourteenth Amendment, Justice Grier, writing for a unanimous Court, observed:

"It is a well-established principle of the common law, that in actions of trespass and all actions on the case for torts, a jury may inflict what are called exemplary, punitive, or vindictive damages upon a defendant, having in view the enormity of his offence rather than the measure of compensation to the plaintiff. We are aware that the propriety of this doctrine has been questioned by some writers; but if repeated judicial decisions for more than a century are to be received as the best exposition of what the law is, the question will not admit of argument. By the common as well as by statute law, men are often punished for aggravated misconduct or lawless acts, by means of a civil

---

5. For informative historical comment, see Owen, Punitive Damages in Products Liability Litigation, 74 Mich. L. Rev. 1257, 1262–1264, and nn. 17–23 (1976).

action, and the damages, inflicted by way of penalty or punishment, given to the party injured.

. . . . . .

".... This has been always left to the discretion of the jury, as the degree of punishment to be thus inflicted must depend on the peculiar circumstances of each case." *Id.*, at 371.

So far as we have been able to determine, every state and federal court that has considered the question has ruled that the common-law method for assessing punitive damages does not in itself violate due process. But see *New Orleans, J. & G. N. R. Co. v. Hurst*, 36 Miss. 660 (1859). In view of this consistent history, we cannot say that the common-law method for assessing punitive damages is so inherently unfair as to deny due process and be *per se* unconstitutional. "'If a thing has been practised for two hundred years by common consent, it will need a strong case for the Fourteenth Amendment to affect it.'" *Sun Oil Co. v. Wortman*, 486 U.S. 717, 730 (1988), quoting *Jackman v. Rosenbaum Co.*, 260 U.S. 22, 31 (1922). As the Court in *Day v. Woodworth* made clear, the common-law method for assessing punitive damages was well established before the Fourteenth Amendment was enacted. Nothing in that Amendment's text or history indicates an intention on the part of its drafters to overturn the prevailing method. See *Burnham v. Superior Court of Calif., Marin Cty.*, ___ U.S. ___ (1990); *Snyder v. Massachusetts*, 291 U.S. 97, 111 (1934) ("The Fourteenth Amendment has not displaced the procedure of the ages.").

This, however, is not the end of the matter. It would be just as inappropriate to say that, because punitive damages have been recognized for so long, their imposition is never unconstitutional. See *Williams v. Illinois*, 399 U.S. 235, 239 (1970) ("Neither the antiquity of a practice nor the fact of steadfast legislative and judicial adherence to it through the centuries insulates it from constitutional attack...."). We note once again our concern about punitive damages that "run wild." Having said that, we conclude that our task today is to determine whether the Due Process Clause renders the punitive damages award in this case constitutionally unacceptable.

VI

One must concede that unlimited jury discretion—or unlimited judicial discretion for that matter—in the fixing of punitive damages may invite extreme results that jar one's constitutional sensibilities. See *Waters–Pierce Oil Co. v. Texas (No. 1)*, 212 U.S. 86, 111 (1909).[8] We need not, and indeed we cannot, draw a mathematical bright line between the constitutionally acceptable and the constitutionally unac-

---

8. See also Owen, The Moral Foundations of Punitive Damages, 40 Ala. L. Rev. 705, 739 (1989) ("Yet punitive damages are a powerful remedy which itself may be abused, causing serious damage to public and private interests and moral values.").

ceptable that would fit every case. We can say, however, that general concerns of reasonableness and adequate guidance from the court when the case is tried to a jury properly enter into the constitutional calculus. With these concerns in mind, we review the constitutionality of the punitive damages awarded in this case.

We conclude that the punitive damages assessed by the jury against Pacific Mutual were not violative of the Due Process Clause of the Fourteenth Amendment. It is true, of course, that under Alabama law, as under the law of most States, punitive damages are imposed for purposes of retribution and deterrence. *Aetna Life Ins. Co. v. Lavoie,* 470 So.2d 1060, 1076 (Ala.1984). They have been described as quasi-criminal. See *Smith v. Wade,* 461 U.S. 30, 59 (1983) (REHNQUIST, J., dissenting). But this in itself does not provide the answer. We move, then, to the points of specific attack.

1. We have carefully reviewed the instructions to the jury. By these instructions, see n.1, *supra,* the trial court expressly described for the jury the purpose of punitive damages, namely, "not to compensate the plaintiff for any injury" but "to punish the defendant" and "for the added purpose of protecting the public by [deterring] the defendant and others from doing such wrong in the future." App. 105–106. Any evidence of Pacific Mutual's wealth was excluded from the trial in accord with Alabama law. See *Southern Life & Health Ins. Co. v. Whitman,* 358 So.2d 1025, 1026–1027 (Ala.1978).

To be sure, the instructions gave the jury significant discretion in its determination of punitive damages. But that discretion was not unlimited. It was confined to deterrence and retribution, the state policy concerns sought to be advanced. And if punitive damages were to be awarded, the jury "must take into consideration the character and the degree of the wrong as shown by the evidence and necessity of preventing similar wrong." App. 106. The instructions thus enlightened the jury as to the punitive damages' nature and purpose, identified the damages as punishment for civil wrongdoing of the kind involved, and explained that their imposition was not compulsory.

These instructions, we believe, reasonably accommodated Pacific Mutual's interest in rational decisionmaking and Alabama's interest in meaningful individualized assessment of appropriate deterrence and retribution. The discretion allowed under Alabama law in determining punitive damages is no greater than that pursued in many familiar areas of the law as, for example, deciding "the best interests of the child," or "reasonable care," or "due diligence," or appropriate compensation for pain and suffering or mental anguish. As long as the discretion is exercised within reasonable constraints, due process is satisfied. See, *e.g., Schall v. Martin,* 467 U.S. 253, 279 (1984); *Greenholtz v. Nebraska Penal Inmates,* 442 U.S. 1, 16 (1977). See also *McGautha v. California,* 402 U.S. 183, 207 (1971).

2. Before the trial in this case took place, the Supreme Court of Alabama had established post-trial procedures for scrutinizing punitive awards. In *Hammond v. City of Gadsden*, 493 So.2d 1374 (1986), it stated that trial courts are "to reflect in the record the reasons for interfering with a jury verdict, or refusing to do so, on grounds of excessiveness of the damages." *Id.*, at 1379. Among the factors deemed "appropriate for the trial court's consideration" are the "culpability of the defendant's conduct," the "desirability of discouraging others from similar conduct," the "impact upon the parties," and "other factors, such as the impact on innocent third parties." *Ibid.* The Hammond test ensures meaningful and adequate review by the trial court whenever a jury has fixed the punitive damages.

3. By its review of punitive awards, the Alabama Supreme Court provides an additional check on the jury's or trial court's discretion. It first undertakes a comparative analysis. See, *e.g., Aetna Life Ins. Co. v. Lavoie*, 505 So.2d 1050, 1053 (1987). It then applies the detailed substantive standards it has developed for evaluating punitive awards.[10] In particular, it makes its review to ensure that the award does "not exceed an amount that will accomplish society's goals of punishment and deterrence." *Green Oil Co. v. Hornsby*, 539 So.2d 218, 222 (1989); *Wilson v. Dukona Corp.*, 547 So.2d 70, 73 (1989). This appellate review makes certain that the punitive damages are reasonable in their amount and rational in light of their purpose to punish what has occurred and to deter its repetition.

Also before its ruling in the present case, the Supreme Court of Alabama had elaborated and refined the *Hammond* criteria for determining whether a punitive award is reasonably related to the goals of deterrence and retribution. *Hornsby*, 539 So.2d, at 223–224; *Central Alabama*, 546 So.2d, at 376–377. It was announced that the following could be taken into consideration in determining whether the award was excessive or inadequate: (a) whether there is a reasonable relationship between the punitive damages award and the harm likely to result from the defendant's conduct as well as the harm that actually has occurred; (b) the degree of reprehensibility of the defendant's conduct, the duration of that conduct, the defendant's awareness, any concealment, and the existence and frequency of similar past conduct; (c) the profitability to the defendant of the wrongful conduct and the desirability of removing that profit and of having the defendant also sustain a

---

10. See *Central Alabama Electric Cooperative v. Tapley*, 546 So.2d 371, 377–378 (Ala.1989). This, we feel, distinguishes Alabama's system from the Vermont and Mississippi schemes about which Justices expressed concern in *Browning–Ferris Industries of Vermont, Inc. v. Kelco Disposal, Inc.*, ___ U.S. ___ (1989), and in *Bankers Life & Casualty Co. v. Crenshaw*, 486 U.S. 71 (1988). In those respective schemes, an amount awarded would be set aside or modified only if it was "manifestly and grossly excessive," *Pezzano v. Bonneau*, 133 Vt. 88, 91, 329 A.2d 659, 661 (1974), or would be considered excessive when "it evinces passion, bias and prejudice on the part of the jury so as to shock the conscience," *Bankers Life & Casualty Co. v. Crenshaw*, 483 So.2d 254, 278 (Miss.1985).

loss; (d) the "financial position" of the defendant; (e) all the costs of litigation; (f) the imposition of criminal sanctions on the defendant for its conduct, these to be taken in mitigation; and (g) the existence of other civil awards against the defendant for the same conduct, these also to be taken in mitigation.

The application of these standards, we conclude, imposes a sufficiently definite and meaningful constraint on the discretion of Alabama fact finders in awarding punitive damages. The Alabama Supreme Court's post-verdict review ensures that punitive damages awards are not grossly out of proportion to the severity of the offense and have some understandable relationship to compensatory damages. While punitive damages in Alabama may embrace such factors as the heinousness of the civil wrong, its effect upon the victim, the likelihood of its recurrence, and the extent of defendant's wrongful gain, the fact finder must be guided by more than the defendant's net worth. Alabama plaintiffs do not enjoy a windfall because they have the good fortune to have a defendant with a deep pocket.

These standards have real effect when applied by the Alabama Supreme Court to jury awards. For examples of their application in trial practice, see *Hornsby*, 539 So.2d, at 219, and *Williams v. Ralph Collins Ford–Chrysler*, Inc., 551 So.2d 964, 966 (1989). And post-verdict review by the Alabama Supreme Court has resulted in reduction of punitive awards. See, *e.g.*, *Wilson v. Dukona Corp.*, 547 So.2d 70, 74 (1989); *United Services Automobile Assn. v. Wade*, 544 So.2d 906, 917 (1989). The standards provide for a rational relationship in determining whether a particular award is greater than reasonably necessary to punish and deter. They surely are as specific as those adopted legislatively in Ohio Rev. Code Ann. § 2307.80(B) (Supp. 1989) and in Mont. Code Ann. § 27–1–221 (1989).[11]

Pacific Mutual thus had the benefit of the full panoply of Alabama's procedural protections. The jury was adequately instructed. The trial court conducted a post-verdict hearing that conformed with *Hammond*. The trial court specifically found the conduct in question "evidenced intentional malicious, gross, or oppressive fraud," App. to Pet. for Cert. A14, and found the amount of the award to be reasonable in light of the importance of discouraging insurers from similar conduct, *id.*, at A15. Pacific Mutual also received the benefit of appropri-

---

11. We have considered the arguments raised by Pacific Mutual and some of its *amici* as to the constitutional necessity of imposing a standard of proof of punitive damages higher than "preponderance of the evidence." There is much to be said in favor of a State's requiring, as many do, see, *e.g.*, Ohio Rev. Code Ann. § 2307.80 (1989), a standard of "clear and convincing evidence" or, even, "beyond a reasonable doubt," see Colo. Rev. Stat. § 13–25–127(2) (Supp. 1979), as in the criminal context. We are not persuaded, however, that the Due Process Clause requires that much. We feel that the lesser standard prevailing in Alabama—"reasonably satisfied from the evidence"—when buttressed, as it is, by the procedural and substantive protections outlined above, is constitutionally sufficient.

ate review by the Supreme Court of Alabama. It applied the Hammond standards and approved the verdict thereunder. It brought to bear all relevant factors recited in *Hornsby.*

We are aware that the punitive damages award in this case is more than 4 times the amount of compensatory damages, is more than 200 times the out-of-pocket expenses of respondent Haslip, see n.2, *supra*, and, of course, is much in excess of the fine that could be imposed for insurance fraud under Ala. Code §§ 13A–5–11 and 13A–5–12(a) (1982), and §§ 27–1–12, 27–12–17, and 27–12–23 (1986). Imprisonment, however, could also be required of an individual in the criminal context. While the monetary comparisons are wide and, indeed, may be close to the line, the award here did not lack objective criteria. We conclude, after careful consideration, that in this case it does not cross the line into the area of constitutional impropriety. Accordingly, Pacific Mutual's due process challenge must be, and is, rejected.

The judgment of the Supreme Court of Alabama is affirmed.

JUSTICE SOUTER took no part in the consideration or decision of this case.

JUSTICE SCALIA, concurring in the judgment.

In *Browning–Ferris Industries v. Kelco Disposal, Inc.*, 492 U.S. 257 (1989), we rejected the argument that the Eighth Amendment limits punitive damages awards, but left for "another day" the question whether "undue jury discretion to award punitive damages" violates the Due Process Clause of the Fourteenth Amendment, *id.*, at 277. That day has come, the due process point has been thoroughly briefed and argued, but the Court chooses to decide only that the jury discretion in the present case was not undue. It says that Alabama's particular procedures (at least as applied here) are not so "unreasonable" as to "cross the line into the area of constitutional impropriety," *ante*, at 20. This jury-like verdict provides no guidance as to whether any *other* procedures are sufficiently "reasonable," and thus perpetuates the uncertainty that our grant of certiorari in this case was intended to resolve. Since it has been the traditional practice of American courts to leave punitive damages (where the evidence satisfies the legal requirements for imposing them) to the discretion of the jury; and since in my view a process that accords with such a tradition and does not violate the Bill of Rights necessarily constitutes "due" process; I would approve the procedure challenged here without further inquiry into its "fairness" or "reasonableness." I therefore concur only in the judgment of the Court.

I

As the Court notes, punitive or "exemplary" damages have long been a part of Anglo–American law. They have always been controversial. * * *

* * *

Even fierce opponents of the doctrine acknowledged that it was a firmly established feature of American law. Justice Foster of the New Hampshire Supreme Court, in a lengthy decision disallowing punitive damages, called them "a perversion of language and ideas so ancient and so common as seldom to attract attention," *Fay v. Parker*, 53 N.H. 342, 343 (1873). The opinion concluded, with more passion than even petitioners in the present case could muster:

> "Undoubtedly this pernicious doctrine has become so fixed in the law ... that it may be *difficult* to get rid of it. But it is the business of courts to deal with difficulties; and this heresy should be taken in hand without favor, firmly and fearlessly.... Not reluctantly should we apply the knife to this deformity, concerning which every true member of the sound and healthy body of the law may well exclaim—'I have no need of thee.'" *Id.*, at 397 (internal quotations omitted).

In 1868, therefore, when the Fourteenth Amendment was adopted, punitive damages were undoubtedly an established part of the American common law of torts. It is just as clear that no particular procedures were deemed necessary to circumscribe a jury's discretion regarding the award of such damages, or their amount. As this Court noted in *Barry v. Edmunds*, 116 U.S. 550, 565 (1886), "nothing is better settled than that, in cases such as the present, and other actions for torts where no precise rule of law fixes the recoverable damages, it is the peculiar function of the jury to determine the amount by their verdict." * * *

Although both the majority and the dissenting opinions today concede that the common-law system for awarding punitive damages is firmly rooted in our history, both reject the proposition that this is dispositive for due process purposes. *Ante*, at 14–15; *post*, at 18. I disagree. In my view, it is not for the Members of this Court to decide from time to time whether a process approved by the legal traditions of our people is "due" process, nor do I believe such a rootless analysis to be dictated by our precedents.

II

Determining whether common-law procedures for awarding punitive damages can deny "due process of law" requires some inquiry into the meaning of that majestic phrase. [Justice Scalia traced the intellectual roots of the due process clause to language in the Magna Charta. He then proceeded to trace its development in Supreme Court jurisprudence. He concluded that the due process clause does not and can not invalidate any procedure employed consistently since the adoption of the Bill of Rights. The due process clause might invalidate newly adopted procedures, but it has no application to "procedures of the ages."]

"The 'natural law' formula which the Court uses to reach its conclusion in this case should be abandoned as an incongruous excrescence on our Constitution. I believe that formula to be itself a violation of our Constitution, in that it subtly conveys to courts, at the expense of legislatures, ultimate power over public policies in fields where no specific provision of the Constitution limits legislative power." *Adamson, supra,* at 75 (Black, J., dissenting).

In any case, our due process opinions in recent decades have indiscriminately applied balancing analysis to determine "fundamental fairness," without regard to whether the procedure under challenge was (1) a traditional one, and if so (2) prohibited by the Bill of Rights. * * *

* * *

Let me be clear about the scope of the principle I am applying. It does not say that every practice sanctioned by history is constitutional. It does not call into question, for example, the case of *Williams v. Illinois,* 399 U.S. 235 (1970), relied upon by both the majority and the dissent, where we held unconstitutional the centuries-old practice of permitting convicted criminals to reduce their prison sentences by paying fines. The basis of that invalidation was not denial of due process but denial to indigent prisoners of equal protection of the laws. The Equal Protection Clause and other provisions of the Constitution, unlike the Due Process Clause, are not an explicit invocation of the "law of the land," and might be thought to have some counter-historical content. Moreover, the principle I apply today does not reject our cases holding that procedures demanded by the Bill of Rights—which extends against the States only *through* the Due Process Clause—must be provided despite historical practice to the contrary. Thus, it does not call into question the proposition that punitive damages, despite their historical sanction, can violate the First Amendment. *See, e.g., Gertz v. Robert Welch, Inc.,* 418 U.S. 323, 349–350 (1974) (First Amendment prohibits awards of punitive damages in certain defamation suits).

* * *

A harsh or unwise procedure is not necessarily unconstitutional, *Corn Exchange Bank,* 280 U.S., at 223, just as the most sensible of procedures may well violate the Constitution, see *Maryland v. Craig,* 497 U.S. ___, ___ (1990) (slip op., at 1–2) (SCALIA, J., dissenting). State legislatures and courts have the power to restrict or abolish the common-law practice of punitive damages, and in recent years have increasingly done so. See, *e.g.,* Alaska Stat. Ann. § 09.17.020 (Supp. 1990) (punitive damages must be supported by "clear and convincing evidence"); Fla. Stat. § 768.73(1)(a) (1989) (in specified classes of cases, punitive damages are limited to three times the amount of compensatory damages); Va. Code § 8.01–38.1 (Supp. 1990) (punitive damages limited to $350,000). It is through those means—State by State, and, at the federal level, by Congress—that the legal procedures affecting our citizens are improved. Perhaps, when the operation of that process has purged a historically approved practice from our national life, the Due Process Clause would permit this Court to announce that it is no longer in accord with the law of the land. But punitive damages assessed under common-law procedures are far from a fossil, or even an endangered species. They are (regrettably to many) vigorously alive. To effect their elimination may well be wise, but is not the role of the Due Process Clause. "Its function is negative, not affirmative, and it carries no mandate for particular measures of reform." *Ownbey*, 256 U.S., at 112.

We have expended much ink upon the due-process implications of punitive damages, and the fact-specific nature of the Court's opinion guarantees that we and other courts will expend much more in the years to come. Since jury-assessed punitive damages are a part of our living tradition that dates back prior to 1868, I would end the suspense and categorically affirm their validity.

JUSTICE KENNEDY, concurring in the judgment.

* * *

JUSTICE O'CONNOR, dissenting.

Punitive damages are a powerful weapon. Imposed wisely and with restraint, they have the potential to advance legitimate state interests. Imposed indiscriminately, however, they have a devastating potential for harm. Regrettably, common-law procedures for awarding punitive damages fall into the latter category. States routinely authorize civil juries to impose punitive damages without providing them any meaningful instructions on how to do so. Rarely is a jury told anything more specific than "do what you think best." See *Browning–Ferris Industries v. Kelco Disposal, Inc.*, 492 U.S. ___, ___ (1989) (slip op., at 2) (Brennan, J., concurring).

In my view, such instructions are so fraught with uncertainty that they defy rational implementation. Instead, they encourage inconsistent and unpredictable results by inviting juries to rely on private beliefs and personal predilections. Juries are permitted to target unpopular defendants, penalize unorthodox or controversial views, and redistribute wealth. Multimillion dollar losses are inflicted on a whim. While I do not question the general legitimacy of punitive damages, I see a strong need to provide juries with standards to constrain their discretion so that they may exercise their power wisely, not capriciously or maliciously. The Constitution requires as much.

The Court today acknowledges that dangers may lurk, but holds that they did not materialize in this case. See *ante*, at 15–20. They did materialize, however. They always do, because such dangers are part-

and-parcel of common-law punitive damages procedures. As is typical, the trial court's instructions in this case provided no meaningful standards to guide the jury's decision to impose punitive damages or to fix the amount. Accordingly, these instructions were void for vagueness. Even if the Court disagrees with me on this point, it should still find that Pacific Mutual was denied procedural due process. Whether or not the jury instructions were so vague as to be unconstitutional, they plainly offered less guidance than is required under the due process test set out in *Mathews v. Eldridge*, 424 U.S. 319, 335 (1976). The most modest of procedural safeguards would have made the process substantially more rational without impairing any legitimate governmental interest. The Court relies heavily on the State's mechanism for postverdict judicial review, *ante*, at 17–20, but this is incapable of curing a grant of standardless discretion to the jury. *Post hoc* review tests only the amount of the award, not the procedures by which that amount was determined. Alabama's common-law scheme is so lacking in fundamental fairness that the propriety of any specific award is irrelevant. *Any* award of punitive damages rendered under these procedures, no matter how small the amount, is constitutionally infirm.

Notwithstanding its recognition of serious due process concerns, the Court upholds Alabama's punitive damages scheme. Unfortunately, Alabama's punitive damages scheme is indistinguishable from the common-law schemes employed by many States. The Court's holding will therefore substantially impede punitive damages reforms. Because I am concerned that the Court today sends the wrong signal, I respectfully dissent.

I

Due process requires that a State provide meaningful standards to guide the application of its laws. See *Kolender v. Lawson*, 461 U.S. 352, 358 (1983). A state law that lacks such standards is void for vagueness. The void-for-vagueness doctrine applies not only to laws that proscribe conduct, but also to laws that vest standardless discretion in the jury to fix a penalty. See *United States v. Batchelder*, 442 U.S. 114, 123 (1979). I have no trouble concluding that Alabama's common-law scheme for imposing punitive damages is void for vagueness.

A

Alabama's punitive damages scheme requires a jury to make two decisions: (1) whether or not to impose punitive damages against the defendant, and (2) if so, in what amount. On the threshold question of whether or not to impose punitive damages, the trial court instructed the jury as follows: "Imposition of punitive damages is *entirely discretionary* with the jury, that means you don't have to award it unless this jury feels that you should do so." App. 105–106 (emphasis added).

This instruction is as vague as any I can imagine. It speaks of discretion, but suggests *no* criteria on which to base the exercise of that discretion. Instead of reminding the jury that its decision must rest on a factual or legal predicate, the instruction suggests that the jury may do whatever it "feels" like. It thus invites individual jurors to rely upon emotion, bias, and personal predilections of every sort. As I read the instruction, it as much permits a determination based upon the toss of a coin or the color of the defendant's skin as upon a reasoned analysis of the offensive conduct. This is not "discretion in the legal sense of that term, but ... mere will. It is purely arbitrary and acknowledges neither guidance nor restraint." *Yick Wo v. Hopkins*, 118 U.S. 356, 366–367 (1886).

* * *

Alabama's common-law punitive damages scheme * * * permits a jury to decide whether or not to impose punitive damages "without imposing a single condition, limitation or contingency" on the jury. *Ibid.* The State offers no principled basis for distinguishing those tortfeasors who should be liable for punitive damages from those who should not be liable. Instead, the State delegates this basic policy matter to individual juries "for resolution on an ad hoc and subjective basis, with the attendant dangers of arbitrary and discriminatory application." *Grayned v. City of Rockford*, 408 U.S. 104, 108–109 (1972).
* * *

The vagueness question is not even close. This is not a case where a State has ostensibly provided a standard to guide the jury's discretion. Alabama, making no pretensions whatsoever, gives civil juries complete, unfettered, and unchanneled discretion to determine whether or not to impose punitive damages. Not only that, the State *tells* the jury that it has complete discretion. This is a textbook example of the void-for-vagueness doctrine. Alabama's common-law scheme is unconstitutionally vague because the State entrusts the jury with "such broad and unlimited power ... that the jurors must make determinations of the crucial issue upon their notions of what the law should be instead of what it is." *Ibid.*

* * *

B

If an Alabama jury determines that punitive damages are appropriate in a particular case, it must then fix the amount. Here, the trial court instructed the jury: "Should you award punitive damages, in fixing the amount, you must take into consideration the character and the degree of the wrong as shown by the evidence and [the] necessity of preventing similar wrong." App. 106.

The Court concludes that this instruction sufficiently limited the jury's discretion, *ante*, at 16–17, but I cannot share this conclusion. Although the instruction ostensibly provided some guidance, this appearance is deceiving. As Justice Brennan said of a similar instruction: "Guidance like this is scarcely better than no guidance at all. I do not suggest that the instruction itself was in error; indeed, it appears to have been a correct statement of [state] law. The point is, rather, that the instruction reveals a deeper flaw: the fact that punitive damages are imposed by juries guided by little more than an admonition to do what they think is best." *Browning–Ferris, supra*, at ___ (slip op., at 2) (concurring opinion). I agree wholeheartedly. Vague references to "the character and the degree of the wrong" and the "necessity of preventing similar wrong" do not assist a jury in making a reasoned decision; they are too amorphous. They restate the overarching principles of punitive damages awards—to punish and deter—without adding meaning to these terms. For example, the trial court did not suggest what relation, if any, should exist between the harm caused and the size of the award, nor how to measure the deterrent effect of a particular award. It provided no information to the jury about criminal fines for comparable conduct or the range of punitive damages awards in similar cases. Nor did it identify the limitations dictated by retributive and deterrent principles, or advise the jury to refrain from awarding more than necessary to meet these objectives. In short, the trial court's instruction identified the ultimate destination, but did not tell the jury how to get there. Due process may not require a detailed roadmap, but it certainly requires directions of some sort.

* * *

Paraphrased slightly, the court's terse instruction told the jury: "Think about how much you hate what the defendants did and teach them a lesson." This is not the sort of instruction likely to produce a fair, dispassionate verdict. Like most common-law punitive damages instructions, this one has "an open-ended, anything-goes quality that can too easily stoke ... the vindictive or sympathetic passions of juries." P. Huber, Liability: The Legal Revolution and Its Consequences 118 (1988) (hereinafter Huber). Our cases attest to the wildly unpredictable results and glaring unfairness that characterize common-law punitive damages procedures. See *infra*, at 13–14.

One need not look far to see that these so-called standards provide no guidance to Alabama juries. Consider, for example, a recent Alabama case involving a collision between a train and a tractor-trailer truck, which resulted in the death of the driver of the tractor. Notwithstanding that the tractor pulled onto the tracks right in front of the train, thereby ignoring a stop sign, three warning signs, and five speed bumps, the administratrix of decedent's estate asked for $3 million in punitive damages. The jury, after receiving instructions no more vague than those at issue here, awarded her $15 million. *Whitt v. Burlington Northern R. Co.*, No. CV–85–311 (Cir. Ct. Ala. Aug. 23, 1988), aff'd conditionally, No. 88–376 (Ala. Sept. 21, 1990) (remitting award to $5 million), stay granted ___ U.S. ___ (Dec. 5, 1990) (Kennedy, J., Circuit Justice).

That Alabama's "standards" in fact provide no guidance whatsoever was illustrated quite dramatically by Alabama Supreme Court Justice Houston in his concurring opinion in *Charter Hospital of Mobile, Inc. v. Weinberg*, 558 So.2d 909, 916 (Ala.1990). He pointed to two cases involving substantially the same misconduct and jury instructions, but having very different results: *Washington Nat. Ins. Co. v. Strickland*, 491 So.2d 872 (Ala.1985), and *Land & Assocs., Inc. v. Simmons*, 562 So.2d 140 (Ala.1989). In both cases, an insurance agent misrepresented to a prospective insured that coverage would begin as soon as the insured paid the first premium when, in reality, the agent should have known that coverage was conditioned upon a medical examination that the insured was unlikely to pass. See *Strickland, supra,* at 873, 877; *Simmons, supra,* at 142. In one case, the jury handed down a punitive damages award of approximately $21,000—15 1/2 times the compensatory damages. See *Strickland, supra,* at 874. In the other case, the jury penalized substantially the same conduct with a punitive damages award of $2,490,000—249 times the compensatory award. See *Simmons, supra,* at 151 (Houston, J., concurring specially). These vastly disparate results demonstrate that, under Alabama's common-law scheme, any case-to-case consistency among verdicts is purely fortuitous.

This is not a case where more precise standards are either impossible or impractical. See *Kolender*, 461 U.S., at 361. Just the opposite. The Alabama Supreme Court has already formulated a list of seven factors that it considers relevant to the size of a punitive damages award:

" '(1) Punitive damages should bear a reasonable relationship to the harm that is likely to occur from the defendant's conduct as well as to the harm that actually has occurred. If the actual or likely harm is slight, the damages should be relatively small. If grievous, the damages should be much greater.

" '(2) The degree of reprehensibility of the defendant's conduct should be considered. The duration of this conduct, the degree of the defendant's awareness of any hazard which his conduct has caused or is likely to cause, and any concealment or "cover-up" of that hazard, and the existence and frequency of similar past conduct should all be relevant in determining this degree of reprehensibility.

" '(3) If the wrongful conduct was profitable to the defendant, the punitive damages should remove the profit and should be in excess of the profit, so that the defendant recognizes a loss.

" '(4) The financial position of the defendant would be relevant.

" '(5) All the costs of litigation should be included, so as to encourage plaintiffs to bring wrongdoers to trial.

" '(6) If criminal sanctions have been imposed on the defendant for his conduct, this should be taken into account in mitigation of the punitive damages award.

" '(7) If there have been other civil actions against the same defendant, based on the same conduct, this should be taken into account in mitigation of the punitive damages award.' " *Green Oil Co. v. Hornsby*, 539 So.2d 218, 223–224 (1989), quoting *Aetna Life Ins. Co. v. Lavoie*, 505 So.2d 1050, 1062 (Ala.1987) (Houston, J., concurring specially).

In my view, these standards—the "*Green Oil* factors"—could assist juries to make fair, rational decisions. Unfortunately, Alabama courts do not give the *Green Oil* factors to the jury. See 539 So.2d, at 224 (Maddox, J., concurring specially). Instead, the jury has standardless discretion to impose punitive damages whenever and in whatever amount it wants. The *Green Oil* factors play a role only *after* the jury has rendered its verdict. The trial court and other reviewing courts may—but are not required to—take these factors into consideration in determining whether a punitive damages award is excessive. *Id.*, at 223.

Obviously, this *post hoc* application of the *Green Oil* factors does not cure the vagueness of the jury instructions. Cf. *Baggett v. Bullitt*, 377 U.S. 360, 373 (1964) ("Judicial safeguards do not neutralize the vice of a vague law"). See also *Roberts v. United States Jaycees*, 468 U.S. 609, 629 (1984). As respondents candidly admit, judicial review in Alabama is limited to the *amount* of the award. The void-for-vagueness doctrine, on the other hand, is concerned with the *procedures* by which the amount is determined. After-the-fact review of the amount in no way diminishes the fact that the State entrusts its juries with standardless discretion. It thus does not matter that the amount settled upon by the jury might have been permissible under a rational system. Even a wholly irrational process may, on occasion, stumble upon a fair result. What is crucial is that the existing system is not rational. "Procedural due process rules are shaped by the risk of error inherent in the truth-finding process as applied to the generality of cases, not the rare exceptions." *Mathews v. Eldridge*, 424 U.S., at 344. The state court justice who devised the *Green Oil* factors, Justice Houston, has recognized this. Addressing a vagueness challenge to the State's punitive damages procedures, he wrote: "We have attempted to deal with the issue of the reliability of punitive damages assessments by post-trial review only. *That attempt does not really address the issue.*" *Charter Hospital*, 558 So.2d, at 915 (Houston, J., concurring specially) (emphasis added; citations omitted).

II

For the reasons stated above, I would hold that Alabama's common-law punitive damages scheme is void for vagueness. But the Court need not agree with me on this point in order to conclude that Pacific Mutual was denied procedural due process. Whether or not the Court agrees that the jury instructions were so vague as to be unconstitutional, there can be no doubt but that they offered substantially less guidance than is possible. Applying the test of procedural due process set out in *Mathews v. Eldridge, supra,* more guidance was required. Modest safeguards would make the process significantly more rational without impairing any legitimate governmental interest.

A

In *Mathews v. Eldridge, supra,* at 334, we recognized that " ' "due process," unlike some legal rules, is not a technical conception with a fixed content unrelated to time, place and circumstances. *Cafeteria Workers v. McElroy,* 367 U.S. 886, 895 (1961).' " "Due process is flexible and calls for such procedural protections as the particular situation demands." *Morrissey v. Brewer,* 408 U.S. 471, 481 (1972). Accordingly, *Mathews* described a sliding-scale test for determining whether a particular set of procedures was constitutionally adequate. We look at three factors: (1) the private interest at stake; (2) the risk that existing procedures will wrongly impair this private interest, and the likelihood that additional procedural safeguards can effect a cure; and (3) the governmental interest in avoiding these additional procedures. *Mathews, supra,* at 335.

Applying the *Mathews* test to Alabama's common-law punitive damages scheme, it is clear that the state procedures deprive defendants of property without due process of law. The private property interest at stake is enormous. Without imposing any legislative or common-law limits, Alabama authorizes juries to levy civil fines ranging from zero to tens of millions of dollars. Indeed, a jury would not exceed its discretion under state law by imposing an award of punitive damages that was deliberately calculated to bankrupt the defendant. Unlike compensatory damages, which are tied to an actual injury, there is no objective standard that limits the amount of punitive damages. Consequently, " 'the impact of these windfall recoveries is unpredictable and potentially substantial.' " *Bankers Life & Casualty Co. v. Crenshaw,* 486 U.S. 71, 87 (1988) (opinion concurring in part and concurring in judgment), quoting *Electrical Workers v. Foust,* 442 U.S. 42, 50 (1979).

Compounding the problem, punitive damages are quasi-criminal punishment. Unlike compensatory damages, which serve to allocate an existing loss between two parties, punitive damages are specifically designed to exact punishment in excess of actual harm to make clear that the defendant's misconduct was especially reprehensible. Hence, there is a stigma attached to an award of punitive damages that does not accompany a purely compensatory award. The punitive character of punitive damages means that there is more than just money at stake. This factor militates in favor of strong procedural safeguards.

* * *

Crucial to *Mathews'* second prong, the procedural infirmities here are easily remedied. The Alabama Supreme Court has already given its approval to the *Green Oil* factors. By giving these factors to juries, the State would be providing them with some specific standards to guide their discretion. This would substantially enhance the fairness and rationality of the State's punitive damages system. Other procedural safeguards might prove equally effective. For example, state legislatures could establish fixed monetary limits for awards of punitive damages for particular kinds of conduct. So long as the legislatively determined ranges are sufficiently narrow, they could function as meaningful constraints on jury discretion while at the same time permitting juries to render individualized verdicts.

Another possibility advocated by several commentators, see *ante*, at 1046, n.11; Wheeler 300–301, is that States could bifurcate trials into liability and punitive damages stages. At the punitive damages stage, clear and convincing evidence that the defendant acted with the requisite culpability would be required. This would serve two goals. On a practical level, the clear-and-convincing-evidence requirement would constrain the jury's discretion, limiting punitive damages to the more egregious cases. This would also permit closer scrutiny of the evidence by trial judges and reviewing courts. See Ellis, Punitive Damages, Due Process, and the Jury, 40 Ala. L. Rev. 975, 995–996 (1989). On a symbolic level, the higher evidentiary standard would signal to the jury that it should have a high level of confidence in its factual findings before imposing punitive damages. *Id.*, at 995; Wheeler 297–298. Any of these rudimentary modifications would afford more meaningful guidance to juries, thereby lessening the chance of arbitrary and discriminatory awards, without impairing the State's legitimate interests in punishment and deterrence. Given the existence of several equally acceptable methods, concerns of federalism and judicial restraint counsel that this Court should not legislate to the States which particular method to adopt. I would thus leave it to individual States to decide what method is most consistent with their objectives.

The final *Mathews* factor asks whether the State has a legitimate interest in preserving standardless jury discretion that is so compelling as to render even modest procedural reforms unduly burdensome. The Court effectively answered this question in *Gertz*, 418 U.S., at 349, announcing that "the States have *no substantial interest* in securing for plaintiffs ... gratuitous awards of money damages far in excess of actual injury" (emphasis added).

Respondents do not give up easily. They point out that the State has a substantial interest in deterring wrongful conduct and draw from this a peculiar argument. They contend that, by making jury awards more predictable, procedural safeguards will tend to diminish the deterrent effect of punitive damages. If award amounts are predictable, they argue, corporations will not avoid wrongdoing; instead, they will merely calculate the probability of a punitive damages award and factor it in as a cost of doing business. Accordingly, to best advance the State's interest in deterrence, juries must be given unbridled discretion to render awards that are wildly unpredictable.

This argument goes too far. While the State has a legitimate interest in avoiding rigid strictures so that a jury may tailor its award to specific facts, the Due Process Clause does not permit a State to classify arbitrariness as a virtue. Indeed, the point of due process—of the law in general—is to allow citizens to order their behavior. A State can have no legitimate interest in deliberately making the law so arbitrary that citizens will be unable to avoid punishment based solely upon bias or whim. The procedural reforms suggested here in no way intrude on the jury's ability to exercise reasoned discretion, nor do they preclude flexible decisionmaking. Due process requires only that a jury be given a measurable degree of guidance, not that it be straight-jacketed into performing a particular calculus.

Similarly, the suggested procedural safeguards do not impair the State's punishment objectives. Admittedly, the State has a strong interest in punishing wrongdoers, but it has no legitimate interest in maintaining in pristine form a common-law system that imposes disproportionate punishment and that subjects defendants guilty of similar misconduct to wholly different punishments. Due process requires, at some level, that punishment be commensurate with the wrongful conduct. See *Solem v. Helm*, 463 U.S. 277, 284–290 (1983); *id.*, at 311, n.3 (Burger, C.J., dissenting). The State can therefore have no valid objection to procedural measures that merely ensure that punitive damages awards are based on some factual or legal predicate, rather than the personal predilections and whims of individual jurors.

B

In his concurrence, Justice Scalia offers a very different notion of what due process requires. He argues that a practice with a long historical pedigree is immune to reexamination. *Ante*, at 15. The Court properly rejects this argument. *Ante*, at 14–15. A static notion of due process is flatly inconsistent with *Mathews*, 424 U.S., at 334–335, in which this Court announced that the requirements of the Due Process Clause are " 'flexible' " and may vary with " 'time, place and circumstances.' " We have repeatedly relied on the *Mathews* analysis, and our recent cases leave no doubt as to its continued vitality. See, *e.g., Washington v. Harper*, 494 U.S. ___, ___ (1990) (slip op., at 17);

Brock v. Roadway Express, Inc., 481 U.S. 252, 261–262 (1987); Walters v. National Assn. of Radiation Survivors, 473 U.S. 305, 320–321 (1985); Cleveland Bd. of Education v. Loudermill, 470 U.S. 532, 542–543 (1985); Ake v. Oklahoma, 470 U.S. 68, 77 (1985); Schall v. Martin, 467 U.S. 253, 274 (1984).

* * *

Punitive damages are * * * ripe for reevaluation. In the past, such awards "merited scant attention" because they were "rarely assessed and likely to be small in amount." Ellis, Fairness and Efficiency in the Law of Punitive Damages, 56 S. Cal. L. Rev. 1, 2 (1982). When awarded, they were reserved for the most reprehensible, outrageous, or insulting acts. See F. Pollock, Law of Torts (1887); Huber 119. Even then, they came at a time when compensatory damages were not available for pain, humiliation, and other forms of intangible injury. Punitive damages filled this gap. See K. Redden, Punitive Damages § 2.3(A) (1980); Note, Exemplary Damages in the Law of Torts, 70 Harv. L. Rev. 517, 519–520 (1957).

Recent years, however, have witnessed an explosion in the frequency and size of punitive damages awards. See RAND Institute for Civil Justice, M. Peterson, S. Sarma, & M. Shanley, Punitive Damages— Empirical Findings iii (1987) (hereinafter RAND). A recent study by the RAND Corporation found that punitive damages were assessed against one of every ten defendants who were found liable for compensatory damages in California. Id., at viii. The amounts can be staggering. Within nine months of our decision in Browning–Ferris, there were no fewer than six punitive damages awards of more than $20 million. Crovitz, Absurd Punitive Damages Also "Mock" Due Process, Wall St. Journal, March 14, 1990, p. A19, col. 3. Medians as well as averages are skyrocketing, meaning that even routine awards are growing in size. RAND vi, ix, 65. The amounts "seem to be limited only by the ability of lawyers to string zeros together in drafting a complaint." Oki America, Inc. v. Microtech Int'l, Inc., 872 F.2d 312, 315 (CA9 1989) (Kozinski, J., concurring).

Much of this is attributable to changes in the law. For 200 years, recovery for breach of contract has been limited to compensatory damages. In recent years, however, a growing number of States have permitted recovery of punitive damages where a contract is breached or repudiated in bad faith. See, e.g., Seaman's Direct Buying Serv., Inc. v. Standard Oil Co., 36 Cal.3d 752, 686 P.2d 1158 (1984). Unheard of only 30 years ago, bad faith contract actions now account for a substantial percentage of all punitive damages awards. See RAND iv. Other significant legal developments include the advent of product liability and mass tort litigation. "As recently as a decade ago, the largest award of punitive damages affirmed by an appellate court in a products liability case was $250,000.... Since then, awards more than 30 times as high have been sustained on appeal." *Browning–Ferris*, 492 U.S., at ___ (slip op., at 1) (opinion concurring in part and dissenting in part). "Today, hardly a month goes by without a multimillion-dollar punitive damages verdict in a product liability case." Wheeler, A Proposal for Further Common Law Development of the Use of Punitive Damages in Modern Product Liability Litigation, 40 Ala. L. Rev. 919 (1989).

* * *

III

"'The touchstone of due process is protection of the individual against arbitrary action of government.'" *Daniels v. Williams*, 474 U.S. 327, 331 (1986), quoting *Dent v. West Virginia*, 129 U.S. 114, 123 (1889). Alabama's common-law scheme for awarding punitive damages provides a jury with "such skeletal guidance," *Browning–Ferris, supra*, at ___ (slip op., at 2) (BRENNAN, J., concurring), that it invites—even requires—arbitrary results. It gives free reign to the biases and prejudices of individual jurors, allowing them to target unpopular defendants and punish selectively. In short, it is the antithesis of due process. It does not matter that the system has been around for a long time, or that the result in this particular case may not seem glaringly unfair. The common-law scheme yields unfair and inconsistent results "in so many instances that it should be held violative of due process in every case." *Burnham*, 495 U.S., at ___ (slip op., at 1) (WHITE, J., concurring in part and concurring in judgment).

I would require Alabama to adopt some method, either through its legislature or its courts, to constrain the discretion of juries in deciding whether or not to impose punitive damages and in fixing the amount of such awards. As a number of effective procedural safeguards are available, we need not dictate to the States the precise manner in which they must address the problem. We should permit the States to experiment with different methods and to adjust these methods over time.

This conclusion is neither ground-breaking nor remarkable. It reflects merely a straightforward application of our Due Process Clause jurisprudence. Given our statements in recent cases such as *Browning–Ferris, supra*, and *Bankers Life, supra*, the parties had every reason to expect that this would be the Court's holding. Why, then, is it consigned to a dissent rather than a majority opinion? It may be that the Court is reluctant to afford procedural due process to Pacific Mutual because it perceives that such a ruling would force us to evaluate the constitutionality of every State's punitive damages scheme. I am confident, though, that if we announce what the Constitution requires and allow the States sufficient flexibility to respond, the constitutional problems will be resolved in time without any undue burden on the federal courts. Indeed, it may have been our hesitation that has inspired a flood of petitions for certiorari. For more than 20 years, this Court has criticized common-law punitive damages procedures, see *supra*, at 1062–63, but has shied away from its duty to step in, hoping that the problems would go away. It is now clear that the problems are getting worse, and that the time has come to address them squarely. The Court does address them today. In my view, however, it offers an incorrect answer.

NOTE

In TXO Production Corp. v. Alliance Resources Corp., ___ U.S. ___, ___ S.Ct. ___, ___ L.Ed.2d ___, 1993 WL 220266 (1993), the Court again revisited the due process issue in punitive damages litigation. TXO was found to have knowingly instituted a frivolous declaratory judgment action based on concocted evidence against Alliance for the purpose of cheating Alliance out of oil and gas rights possibly worth millions of dollars. The West Virginia Supreme Court of Appeals affirmed jury awards of $19,000 in actual damages, based on Alliance's cost of defending the declaratory judgment action, and $10 million in punitive damages, some 526 times the amount of the compensatory award. The Supreme Court affirmed. Writing for a plurality of 3½ justices, Justice Stevens reaffirmed *Haslip*'s grounding of the Constitutionality of such awards in terms of reasonableness, and its commensurate refusal to adopt a mathematical bright-line test:

> In sum, we do not consider the dramatic disparity between the actual damages and the punitive award controlling in a case of this character [involving] malicious and fraudulent [conduct]. The punitive damages award in this case is certainly large, but in light of the amount of money potentially at stake, the bad faith of petitioner, the fact that the scheme employed in this case was part of a larger pattern of fraud, trickery and deceit, and petitioner's wealth, we are not persuaded that the award was so "grossly excessive" as to be beyond the power of the State to allow.

Concurring in the judgment, Justice Scalia (joined by Thomas, J.) concluded that the defendant had been accorded procedural due process because the jury had been instructed on the purposes of punitive damages and the award had been reviewed for reasonableness by the trial court and the state supreme court. Dissenting, Justice O'Connor (joined by White, J., and partially by Souter, J.) argued that both the size of the verdict and the lack of an adequate post-verdict review conflicted with *Haslip*'s "promise that punitive damages awards would receive sufficient constitutional scrutiny to restore fairness in what is rapidly becoming an arbitrary and oppressive system."

Chapter 7

SPECIAL TYPES OF DEFENDANTS

SECTION 6. CERTIFIERS, ENDORSERS, AND PUBLISHERS

REPLACE note 6 on page 682 with:

6. Compare Braun v. Soldier of Fortune Magazine, Inc., 968 F.2d 1110 (11th Cir.1992), cert. denied ___ U.S. ___, 113 S.Ct. 1028, 122 L.Ed.2d 173 (1993), in which plaintiffs sued the magazine for negligence in publishing the following classified advertisement:

> **GUN FOR HIRE:** 37 year old professional mercenary desires jobs. Vietnam Veteran. Discrete [sic] and very private. Body guard, courier, and other special skills. All jobs considered. Phone (615) 436–9785 (days) or (615) 436–4335 (nights), or write: Rt. 2, Box 682 Village Loop Road, Gatlinburg, TN 37738.

Plaintiffs' decedent was murdered in a contract killing by the individual (and two others) who placed the ad. The jury awarded the plaintiff-children of the decedent $2.375 million in compensatory damages and $10 million in punitive damages, the latter of which was reduced to $2 million by remittitur. *Held*, a publisher can be found liable for negligence where it publishes an advertisement that "contains a clearly identifiable unreasonable risk, that the offer in the ad is one to commit a serious violent crime, including murder."

Addressing the first amendment claims of the defendant, the court observed that the first amendment does not afford protection for speech that proposes criminal or illegal activity. Nevertheless, because of expressed concerns about chilling effects (and presumably the less–than–100–percent certainty that the ad was offering illegal activity), the court went on to analogize the situation to the defamation area, where First Amendment limitations on state tort law have been imposed by the Supreme Court. The court concluded that the enhanced negligence standard imposed by the trial court's instructions were consistent with First Amendment protection for this commercial speech.

The court distinguished Eimann v. Soldier of Fortune Magazine, Inc., 880 F.2d 830 (5th Cir.1989), cert. denied 493 U.S. 1024, 110 S.Ct. 729, 107 L.Ed.2d 748 (1990), in which the court of appeals reversed a multi-million dollar jury verdict in a case involving a similar contract killing. The *Eimann* decision was based solely on tort principles. The court of appeals found that the advertisement involved (which differed modestly from the *Braun* ad) was too ambiguous to impose a duty on the publisher to screen and reject it.

See generally Michael I. Meyerson, This Gun for Hire: Dancing in the Dark of the First Amendment, 47 Wash. & Lee L. Rev. 267 (1990); Note, Publishers' Liability for Commercial Advertisements: Testing the Limits of

SECTION 9. ALLOCATING RESPONSIBILITY AND LOSS: CONTRIBUTION AND INDEMNITY

A. LOSS ALLOCATION WITHIN THE DISTRIBUTION CHAIN

ADD to page 708 after the *Promaulayko* opinion:

0. The New Jersey Supreme Court reversed. Promaulayko v. Johns Manville Sales Corp., 116 N.J. 505, 562 A.2d 202 (1989). The court provided the additional facts that Amtorg is a corporation founded to promote trade between the former Soviet Union and the United States and employs Soviet citizens, who are on leave from the Soviet Ministry of Foreign Trade. Amtorg was involved in over 80 percent of Soviet exports to the United States. Buck is a broker of mineral products, whose asbestos sales were less than one percent of its business. Relying on the general principle that ordinarily distributors higher in the chain of distribution are better able to spread the costs of liability and the obvious connection between Amtorg and the Russian suppliers of asbestos, the court held that Buck was entitled to indemnification from Amtorg. The court discounted the jury's apportioning of fault as a "sterile" assignment not based on active fault, but based on their location in the distribution chain and proximity to decedent's employer. See also Irwin Yacht Sales, Inc. v. Carver Boat Corp., 98 Or.App. 195, 778 P.2d 982 (1989) (retailer assigned 40 percent of "fault" could still maintain indemnity claim against manufacturer, because finding of fault did not indicate whether it was passive or active negligence).

Is there any vitality left to the opinion of the Superior Court? Should there be?

Chapter 8

SPECIAL TYPES OF PRODUCTS AND TRANSACTIONS

SECTION 5. DISPOSAL AND DESTRUCTION

REPLACE Kalik v. Allis–Chalmers Corp. and notes 1–3 on pages 782–87 with:

HIGH v. WESTINGHOUSE ELECTRIC CORPORATION
Supreme Court of Florida, 1992.
610 So.2d 1259.

OVERTON, JUDGE.

We have for review *High v. Westinghouse Electric Corp.*, 559 So.2d 227 (Fla. 3d DCA 1989), in which the district court affirmed the trial court summary judgment, holding that Westinghouse, as the manufacturer of electrical transformers, is not liable to an employee of a scrap metal salvage business for injuries allegedly sustained from a hazardous fluid that was released in dismantling transformers in the scrapping process. The district court then certified that "the within question passes upon one of great public importance within the meaning of article V, section 3(b)(4), Florida Constitution." *Id.* at 229 n.2. While we approve the district court's decision on the question of strict liability, we find that there remains an issue of fact on the question of negligence. Consequently, we quash in part the decision of the district court of appeal and remand this case for further proceedings.

The relevant facts in the record are as follows. Westinghouse manufactured electrical transformers and sold them to Florida Power and Light Company (FPL). From 1967 to 1983, FPL sold its electrical transformers for junk to Pepper's Steel and Alloys (Pepper's), a scrap metal salvage business. To manufacture the electrical transformers sold to FPL, Westinghouse purchased products from Monsanto, a manufacturer of polychlorinated bithenyls (PCBs). In a January 15, 1972, letter and indemnification agreement from Westinghouse to Monsanto, Westinghouse acknowledged that Monsanto had notified Westinghouse that the PCBs used in its products tended to persist in the environment; that care was required in their handling, possession, use, and disposition; and that tolerance limits had been or were being established for PCBs in various food products.[2] In 1976, Westinghouse wrote a letter

---

2. In the letter and indemnity agreement, Westinghouse agreed to indemnify and hold harmless Monsanto from Westinghouse's use of PCBs purchased from Monsanto. * * *

to its utility company customers, including FPL, disclosing the potential existence of PCBs in their transformers. In that letter, Westinghouse informed them that some oil-filled transformers had been contaminated with PCBs in the manufacturing process. Westinghouse's letter suggested that when performing repairs, routine maintenance, or disposal, all oil-filled transformers should be checked for the presence of PCBs.

Studies of humans exposed to PCBs have shown numerous adverse effects, including but not limited to chloracne and other epidermal disorders, digestive disturbances, jaundice, impotence, throat and respiratory irritations, and severe headaches. It is undisputed that none of the junk transformers that FPL sold to Pepper's contained any labels, markings, or warnings of any kind that the transformers contained PCBs or that the contents might be hazardous to human health.

Willie J. High was the main truck driver for Pepper's from 1965 to 1983. As part of his duties, he picked up aluminum wire, cable, and other scrap metal. He also picked up transformers from FPL in Miami and other cities around Florida. As part of his job, High loaded and unloaded the transformers onto Pepper's truck with a forklift. Specifically, he hooked and unhooked the forklift cables. During this process, he came into contact with the PCB-contaminated transformer oil.

In 1975, the Dade County Department of Environmental Resource Management (DERM) cited Pepper's for a number of environmental ordinance violations. In 1983, DERM, the State of Florida Environmental Regulation Department, and the Environmental Protection Agency (EPA) determined that Pepper's property was sufficiently contaminated with oil containing PCBs to justify commencement of federal, state, and county legal actions against FPL, Pepper's, and the owners of adjacent properties for violating county, state, and federal ordinances and laws and to demand a cleanup of the site by FPL. As a result of the media coverage given the DERM and EPA actions, High became aware that he had been exposed to PCBs while employed at Pepper's and that some of his physical and mental problems might be attributed to this exposure. Consequently, on July 9, 1983, High brought this action under strict liability and negligence theories.

The trial court granted Westinghouse's motion for summary judgment, holding as a matter of law that the ultimate disposal of the transformer was not foreseeable to the manufacturer as a reasonably intended "use." On appeal, the district court of appeal, in a split decision, affirmed. In explaining why strict liability under section 402A of the *Restatement (Second) of Torts* (1965) is not applicable, the district court stated:

> The dismantling and recycling of products after they have been destroyed have been held to be product uses not reasonably foreseeable to manufacturers....
>
> ... Westinghouse's transformers were destroyed prior to the alleged injuries. While the transformers were sealed and intact there was no harm. Rather, the alleged damage occurred after the contents of the devices were exposed through the dismantling process. Westinghouse's product as it had originally been sold to FP & L, for practical purposes, had ceased to exist at the time the alleged injuries occurred.
>
> Here, the determination of no liability is based upon a substantial change in the product from the time it left the manufacturer's control to the time of the subject incident; this change negates the manufacturer's liability for any alleged defect under 402A....
>
> Where it is undisputed that a product defect has been created by subsequent alteration (i.e., destruction) and not by the actions of the manufacturer, the manufacturer is properly exonerated of liability as a matter of law.

559 So.2d at 228. The district court concluded that

> the actual products supplied by Westinghouse were the electrical transformers, not the contaminated dielectric fluid. As a matter of law, the unsealing, stripping, and dumping of the contents of Westinghouse's product in order to salvage junk components were not reasonably foreseeable "uses" of the product nor was Willie High an intended "user" within the meaning of section 402A.

Id. at 229.

There are two questions we must address. The first is whether strict liability applies under section 402A of the *Restatement (Second) of Torts* for injuries that occur in dismantling an item. The second is whether the manufacturer, Westinghouse, in this instance was negligent in failing to timely warn of dangerous contents in its product that could cause injuries in its alteration and dismantling.

While these are questions of first impression in this state, other courts have addressed similar issues. In *Kalik v. Allis–Chalmers Corp.,* 658 F.Supp. 631 (W.D.Pa.1987), the owners of a scrap metal business that had been contaminated by PCBs sued the manufacturers and suppliers of the products containing the PCBs to recover cleanup costs and damages incurred under the Comprehensive Environmental Response Compensation and Liability Act of 1980. In that case, the scrap metal business had purchased junk electrical components as scrap. The electrical components contained, as they did in this instance, PCBs. During the course of dismantling, handling, and storing the junk electrical components, PCB-contaminated oil leaked or spilled onto the site. A furnace used in dismantling and processing the components caused PCBs in the components to allegedly produce dioxins, which also polluted the site. Plaintiff's damage claims were based upon a negligent failure to warn and strict liability in tort. The United States District Court in Pennsylvania considered whether plaintiff's use of the product was reasonably foreseeable to the manufacturer. Although the court agreed that this was ordinarily a question of fact, it held as a matter of law that the recycling of a product after it had been destroyed and the destruction of a product were not reasonably foreseeable uses to the manufacturer.

In *Wingett v. Teledyne Industries, Inc.*, 479 N.E.2d 51 (Ind.1985), *overruled on other grounds by Douglass v. Irvin*, 549 N.E.2d 368 (Ind. 1990), an employee of an independent contractor hired to remove ductwork in a foundry was injured when a connection between two segments of ductwork failed and a portion of the ductwork fell to the floor as the employee cut the support hangers. The employee sued the foundry owners and the manufacturer and the installer of the ductwork. The employee claimed that the connection between the segments of ductwork that failed, consisting of a sheet metal band, screws, and clamps instead of an iron collar and bolts found on the other segments, caused his injury. The Indiana Supreme Court affirmed the summary judgement in favor of the manufacturer, holding as a matter of law that the dismantling and demolishing of the ductwork was not a reasonably foreseeable "use" of the product.

Finally, in *Johnson v. Murph Metals, Inc.*, 562 F.Supp. 246 (N.D.Tex.1983), a United States District Court in Texas granted a summary judgment and held that fumes and particulates from smelting lead from scrap batteries were not created from a "use" of the batteries. In that case, the employees of various lead-smelting companies who had sued certain automotive battery manufacturers stipulated that their injuries did not result from working with intact batteries or from the destruction of batteries to obtain the lead for smelting. The lead fumes and dust that allegedly injured them were created only after the lead was extracted from the destroyed batteries and used in the smelting process. In determining that the plaintiffs were not "users" of defendants' products, the court held that "the defendants' product had ceased to exist." *Id.* at 249.

With regard to the first question and the applicability of strict liability under section 402A of the *Restatement (Second) of Torts,* we find that strict liability is not applicable. * * * In order for strict liability to apply to the manufacturer, the transformers in this instance must have been used for the purpose intended. In the instant case, High's injury resulted from dismantling the transformers and coming into contact with the PCBs as a result of this process. We agree with the district court that section 402A does not apply because of the substantial alteration of the product when High came into contact with the contaminated oil. Secondly, section 402A applies to intended uses of products for which they were produced. When an injury occurs under those circumstances, the manufacturer is strictly liable. We find, under the circumstances in the instant case, that dismantling a product is not an intended use as prescribed by section 402A. Therefore, we find, under these facts, that strict liability does not apply.

The second question we must address concerns liability based on negligence. We find that a manufacturer has a duty to warn of dangerous contents in its product which could damage or injure even when the product is not used for its intended purpose. This issue, which is not directly addressed by the district court of appeal, is whether Westinghouse was negligent in warning FPL of the possible danger of PCB contamination.

We find that Westinghouse had a duty to timely notify the entity to whom it sold the electrical transformers, FPL in the instant case, once it was advised of the PCB contamination. The record reflects that Monsanto, the PCB manufacturer, notified Westinghouse sometime between 1970 and 1972, of the dangerous toxic propensities of PCBs used by Westinghouse. We find that Westinghouse's November 22, 1976, letter to its utility customers, including FPL, relaying PCB information was adequate notice. However, whether or not the letter was timely is a question of fact that has not been resolved by this record. As stated earlier, Monsanto informed Westinghouse sometime between 1970 and 1972 of the dangers regarding PCB contamination, and in 1976, Westinghouse informed FPL that some products were contaminated. If Westinghouse knew or should have known from its early 1970s communications with Monsanto that some mineral oil transformers contained PCBs, then it is clear from the record that Westinghouse delayed in warning FPL of the contamination of these transformers. Although we hold that Westinghouse's letter to FPL was adequate notice, we find that Westinghouse had a duty to timely notify FPL so that FPL could timely notify Pepper's of the possible danger that could occur in dismantling the transformers so that it could proceed in the prescribed manner. If this notice was not timely, then the next question is whether the lack of timely notice by Westinghouse was the proximate cause of High's injury. Given the circumstances, we find the knowledge by Westinghouse of the PCB contamination in its transformers and the timeliness of Westinghouse's notice to FPL of that contamination are issues of fact that must be resolved in this case and are not proper for summary judgment.

For the reasons expressed, we approve in part and quash in part the decision of the district court of appeal and remand for further proceedings consistent with this opinion.

It is so ordered.

KOGAN, J., concurring in part, dissenting in part.

The central premise underlying the law of strict liability is that a for-profit enterprise is better able to shoulder, and therefore must assume strict liability for, the dangerous products it creates:

> The courts [in strict liability cases] have tended to lay stress upon the fact that the defendant is acting for his own purposes, and is seeking a benefit or a profit from such activities, and that he is in a better position to administer the unusual risk by passing it on to the public than is the innocent victim.

W. Page Keeton et al., *Prosser and Keeton on the Law of Torts* § 75, at 537 (5th ed. 1984). In other words, the "little man" should not be made to suffer when the for-profit enterprise that released a dangerous product into commerce can absorb the loss.

I see no reason why this principle should not be applied here. The facts disclose that Westinghouse released into commerce a product containing the highly dangerous chemicals called PCBs. While these chemicals were sealed inside transformers, surely Westinghouse cannot now contend that it was "unforeseeable" these transformers would some day be breached and would release their PCBs. It is obvious and foreseeable that whatever is sealed inside a container some day is likely to be released again. If people are injured by that release, then strict liability should exist.

This case is only little different from a toy manufacturer constructing a rubber ball inflated with a poisonous liquid. Obviously, the toy manufacturer does not intend for the liquid to be released; but if a child chews through the rubber coating and is poisoned by the liquid inside, I certainly believe any court in this state would hold the manufacturer strictly liable. We would not resolve such a case, as the majority does here, simply by noting that the manufacturer did not intend its product to be dismantled in this particular manner. * * *

While I agree with the majority on the duty-to-warn issue, I believe the present case also presents a valid claim for strict liability. Here, transformers were created by a for-profit enterprise. Inside these transformers was a dangerous liquid. This plaintiff has alleged that he was injured when that liquid was released again into the environment. In such an instance, any injury that has resulted should be borne by the party best able to absorb the loss—the manufacturer. Accordingly, I would allow the case to proceed on an alternative theory of strict liability.

NOTES

1. Aside from private tort actions, the primary control for improper disposal of hazardous waste is the Comprehensive Environmental Response, Compensation and Liability Act (CERCLA), 42 U.S.C.A. §§ 9601–75, a regulatory statute designed to clean up the legacy of decades of haphazard hazardous waste disposal and to provide funds to pay for the clean up costs. One provision of CERCLA

permits suits for "necessary costs of response" incurred by a private party against a class of persons that CERCLA deems responsible for cleaning up a waste site. Personal injuries such as Mr. High's are not recoverable under CERCLA. A few courts have suggested that medical monitoring costs for those exposed to hazardous waste may be recoverable under CERCLA. Compare Lykins v. Westinghouse Electric Corp., 27 Env't Rep. Cas. (BNA) 1590 (E.D.Ky.1988) (medical testing expenses recoverable when incurred in conjunction with a hazardous waste site cleanup) with Coburn v. Sun Chemical Corp., 28 Env't Rep. Cas. (BNA) 1665 (E.D.Pa.1988) (medical monitoring costs not recoverable under CERCLA).

In the *Kalik* case, cited in *High*, plaintiffs brought suit under CERCLA to recover the costs of cleaning up a site that was contaminated by PCBs that had leaked from junked electrical products manufactured by defendant.

2. How persuasive is the *High* court's holding that strict liability does not apply because dismantling of the transformers is not an intended use? Does the court correctly apply the misuse doctrine? The substantial change doctrine?

3. While the disposal problem is most severe for toxic substances, it exists as well for durable goods. Should General Electric be liable for the suffocation of a child playing in a dump who climbs inside a long-abandoned G.E. refrigerator, manufactured with a latching mechanism in the 1940s, who cannot get out when the door swings shut?

Chapter 9

SPECIAL ISSUES IN AUTOMOTIVE LITIGATION

SECTION 1. CRASHWORTHINESS

REPLACE Vanover v. Ford Motor Company and notes 1–2 on pages 810–14 with:

PERRY v. MERCEDES BENZ OF NORTH AMERICA, INC.
United States Court of Appeals, Fifth Circuit, 1992.
957 F.2d 1257.

REAVLEY, CIRCUIT JUDGE:

Lynda D. Perry contends that Mercedes Benz of North America (MBNA) defectively designed or defectively constructed the air bag system that was installed in Perry's automobile. The district court granted summary judgment for MBNA, 761 F.Supp. 437, holding that federal law preempts Perry's defective design claim and that Perry's evidence raised no genuine issues of material fact to support her claim of defective construction. We decide that summary judgment was proper on the defective construction claim. But we hold that federal law does not preempt Perry's design claim, and we remand the case for further proceedings.

I. BACKGROUND

Perry was injured in East Baton Rouge Parish, Louisiana, on March 4, 1986, when she lost control of her 1986 Mercedes Benz 190E and drove it into a ditch. Perry initially failed to notice a stop sign where the street that she was on dead-ended into another street, forming a "T" intersection. Once she saw the stop sign, Perry noticed a car approaching the intersection from her right. Thinking that she would not be able to stop in time to avoid the oncoming car, Perry decided to proceed through the intersection. The driver of the other car, deputy sheriff James Todd Morris, was able to avoid Perry's car, but Perry continued through the intersection and into the ditch on the other side. Perry's Mercedes was equipped with a driver's side air bag, but the air bag did not inflate on impact. Perry, who was not wearing a seat belt, struck the steering wheel or windshield and received facial lacerations and damage to her teeth and mouth. The parties dispute how fast Perry's car was traveling at the time of impact.

On February 27, 1987, Perry filed this suit against MBNA in Louisiana state court, alleging that the failure of the air bag to inflate caused Perry $500,000 in damages. MBNA removed this diversity case and moved for summary judgment. The district court granted MBNA's motion and held that: (1) federal law preempts Perry's defective design claim, and (2) Perry failed to raise an issue to support her claim of defective construction.

II. DISCUSSION

A. FEDERAL PREEMPTION OF THE DEFECTIVE DESIGN CLAIM

As the basis for her defective design claim, Perry alleges that MBNA designed its air bag systems with an unreasonably dangerous "deceleration velocity deployment threshold."[1] Under Louisiana products liability law as it existed when Perry filed this suit, a product is considered unreasonably dangerous in design if the "danger-in-fact" of the product outweighs the utility of the product, or if the product could have been designed or replaced with an alternative product with less risk of harmful consequences. *See Halphen v. Johns–Manville Sales Corp.*, 484 So.2d 110, 115 (La.1986). Essentially, Perry claims that MBNA is liable for her damages because it should have designed the air bag system to deploy upon the type of impact that Perry's vehicle sustained. MBNA argued, and the district court agreed, that federal regulations promulgated under the National Traffic and Motor Vehicle Safety Act of 1966 (the Safety Act or the Act), 15 U.S.C. §§ 1381–1431, preempt Perry's state law defective design claim.

1. *The Safety Act and the Regulatory Scheme.*

Congress' express purpose for enacting the Safety Act over twenty-five years ago was "to reduce traffic accidents and deaths and injuries to persons resulting from traffic accidents." 15 U.S.C. § 1381. To achieve this purpose, the Act delegates to the Secretary of Transportation the authority to establish "motor vehicle safety standards" (MVSS) that provide practical and objective minimum standards for the performance of motor vehicles and their equipment. *Id.* §§ 1391(2), 1392(a). The Secretary, in turn, delegated this duty to the National Highway Transportation Safety Administration (NHTSA). See 49 C.F.R. § 501.2. The NHTSA fulfilled its responsibility by promulgating the MVSS published at 49 C.F.R. §§ 571.1–.302.

The MVSS that is relevant to this case is 49 C.F.R. § 571.208 (Standard 208), which is entitled "Occupant Crash Protection." In Standard 208, the NHTSA set forth mandatory minimum "performance

---

1. The airbag system's "deceleration velocity deployment threshold" determines the force that must be caused by the vehicle's sudden deceleration to trigger inflation of the airbag. MBNA designed the system in Perry's vehicle with a minimum threshold of twelve miles per hour against a rigid barrier.

requirements" for automobile crash protection systems, without requiring the use of any single particular system or design. The NHTSA has considered requiring the installation of air bags and the use of particular designs in all vehicles, but has chosen not to do so. *See* 49 Fed.Reg. 28,982, 29,001 (1984). Instead, Congress and the NHTSA sought to ensure the minimum protection of occupants while allowing manufacturers to develop better systems through competition in the automobile industry. *See* S.REP. No. 1301, 89th Cong., 2d Sess. 1, 4 (1966), *reprinted in* 1966 U.S.C.C.A.N. 2709, 2712.

To meet the performance requirements of Standard 208, a manufacturer may choose from options that include both manual restraints (which require the occupant to act in some way to receive the protection) and passive restraints (which require no action by the occupant). Air bags and automatic seat belts are the most common forms of passive restraints. Standard 208 S4.1.2, which applies to the vehicle that Perry was driving, requires the manufacturer to choose one of three occupant restraint systems: (1) a complete passive protection system for frontal and lateral crashes (e.g., automatic seat belts with or without air bags); (2) passive protection for frontal crashes (e.g., an air bag) plus lap belts for lateral crashes and rollovers with a seat belt warning system; or (3) manual lap and shoulder belts with a seat belt warning system. *See Kitts v. General Motors Corp.*, 875 F.2d 787, 788 n. 2 (10th Cir.1989), *cert. denied*, 494 U.S. 1065, 110 S.Ct. 1781, 108 L.Ed. 2d 783 (1990). If a manufacturer chooses an option that includes the use of air bags or other passive restraints, the vehicle must meet the protection requirements set forth in Standard 208 S5.1–.3 for frontal, lateral, and rollover crashes. These requirements mandate that, following an "impact ... up to and including 30 mph, into a fixed collision barrier," an anthropomorphic test dummy must meet or exceed certain "Injury Criteria" specified in Standard 208 S6.

The system that MBNA chose to install in the vehicle that Perry was driving included both an air bag and a lap and shoulder seat belt. Thus, federal law required MBNA to design the system to meet the protection requirements and injury criteria of Standard 208 S5 and S6. Perry does not allege that the vehicle she was driving failed to meet these requirements. Instead, she claims that the vehicle was defectively designed because the likelihood of the injuries that she suffered outweighed the burden that adopting a safer system would place on the manufacturer, and thus it was unreasonably dangerous under Louisiana products liability law.

The Safety Act includes two sections that are particularly important to our determination of whether the Act and its regulations preempt Perry's state law design claim. The first is the "Preemption Clause," which provides:

> Whenever a Federal motor vehicle safety standard established under this subchapter is in effect, *no State or political subdivision of a State* shall have any authority either to establish, or to continue in effect, with respect to any motor vehicle or item of motor vehicle equipment any safety standard applicable to the same aspect of performance of such vehicle or item of equipment which is not identical to the Federal standard.

15 U.S.C. § 1392(d) (emphasis added). The second important section is the "Savings Clause," which states:

> Compliance with any Federal motor vehicle safety standard issued under this subchapter *does not exempt* any person from any *liability under common law.*

Id. § 1397(k) (emphasis added). We must determine whether the Preemption Clause prohibits Perry's claim or the Savings Clause allows it.

2. *The Federal Preemption Doctrine.*

The Supreme Court has "held repeatedly that state laws can be pre-empted by federal regulations as well as by federal statutes." *Hillsborough County v. Automated Medical Lab., Inc.*, 471 U.S. 707, 713, 105 S.Ct. 2371, 2375, 85 L.Ed.2d 714 (1985). The question of whether federal statutes or regulations preempt state law under the Supremacy Clause of the Constitution is essentially a question of congressional intent. *California Fed. Sav. and Loan Ass'n v. Guerra*, 479 U.S. 272, 280, 107 S.Ct. 683, 689, 93 L.Ed.2d 613 (1987). The Court in Guerra summarized the three ways that Congress may express its intent to preempt state law:

> First, when acting within constitutional limits, Congress is empowered to pre-empt state law by so stating in *express terms*. Second, congressional intent to pre-empt state law in a particular area may be *inferred* where the scheme of federal regulation is sufficiently comprehensive to make reasonable the inference that Congress "left no room" for supplementary state regulation.... As a third alternative, in those areas where Congress has not completely displaced state regulation, federal law may nonetheless pre-empt state law to the extent it actually *conflicts* with federal law. Such a conflict occurs either because "compliance with both federal and state regulations is a physical impossibility," or because the state law stands "as an obstacle to the accomplishment and execution of the full purposes and objectives of Congress."

Id. at 280–81, 107 S.Ct. at 689 (citations omitted, emphasis added); *see also Schneidewind v. ANR Pipeline Co.*, 485 U.S. 293, 300, 108 S.Ct. 1145, 1150–51, 99 L.Ed.2d 316 (1988). Thus, federal law may give rise to *express, implied* (or *inferred*), or *conflict* preemption of state law.

We do not hesitate to find preemption when Congress has *expressly* stated its intent. But we have a general hesitancy to *infer* a preemptive intent. Especially as to state regulation of matters of health and safety, "we start with the assumption that the historic police powers of the States were not to be superseded by the [federal law] unless that was the clear and manifest purpose of Congress." *Hillsborough County*, 471 U.S. at 715, 105 S.Ct. at 2376 (quoting *Rice v. Santa Fe Elevator Corp.*, 331 U.S. 218, 230, 67 S.Ct. 1146, 1152, 91 L.Ed. 1447 (1947)). Finally, we do not begin with an assumption against *conflict* preemption, for " '[t]he relative importance to the State of its own law is not material when there is a conflict with a valid federal law,' for 'any state law, however clearly within a State's acknowledged power, which interferes with or is contrary to federal law, must yield.' " *Felder v. Casey*, 487 U.S. 131, 138, 108 S.Ct. 2302, 2307, 101 L.Ed.2d 123 (1988) (quoting *Free v. Bland*, 369 U.S. 663, 666, 82 S.Ct. 1089, 1092, 8 L.Ed.2d 180 (1962)).

3. *Related Case Law.*

No court has addressed the particular issue in this case. Several courts, including four federal circuits, have considered the related question of whether the Safety Act and its regulations preempt a state tort action that is based on a manufacturer's failure to install an air bag system in its cars. This case takes us a step beyond those by asking whether tort liability is preempted when a plaintiff alleges that the air bag system that a manufacturer chose to install is defectively designed under state law. Nevertheless, we find guidance in the failure-to-install cases.

The First Circuit was the first circuit to consider the issue, in *Wood v. General Motors Corp.*, 865 F.2d 395 (1st Cir.1988). Patricia Wood was rendered quadriplegic in an accident involving a Chevrolet Blazer. The Blazer was equipped with seat belts and complied with all MVSS, but Wood was not wearing a belt at the time of the accident. Wood claimed that General Motors was liable for her injuries because it defectively designed the Blazer by equipping it with seat belts instead of air bags. The First Circuit rejected General Motors' argument that the Safety Act *expressly* preempted Wood's claim, but agreed with General Motors that Wood's claim was preempted because, if successful, it would *conflict* with "Congress' chosen method of increasing automobile safety." *Id.* at 412 (emphasis omitted).

In rejecting the express preemption argument, the court noted that the Preemption Clause prevents a State or political subdivision from establishing non-identical safety standards pertaining to the "same aspect of performance," but the Savings Clause appears to allow common law actions that would have the same effect. *Id.* at 403–07. The court believed that this created an ambiguity that resulted from the fact that, when it passed the Act, "Congress ... did not contemplate the likelihood that there would be a state tort action that would effectively create a state design standard conflicting with a federal safety stan-

Cases: don't expressly preempt but

All believe Fed. to preempt b/c st. law would conflict w/ Fed.

dard." *Id.* at 403. Because both Clauses, and the relationship between the two, were ambiguous in the context of a state tort standard not identical to the federal standards but pertaining to the same aspect of performance, the court "devine[d] [sic] no specific congressional intent in section 1392(d) *expressly* to preempt an action of the present type." *Id.* at 407 (emphasis added).

But the court held that Wood's state law claim was preempted because it would "stand as an obstacle" to—and thus *conflict* with—the Safety Act and its underlying regulations. *Id.* at 408. The court reasoned that: (1) section 1392(d) would expressly preempt a state regulation that required passive restraints, because such a regulation would be applicable to the same aspect of performance as, but not identical to, the federal standard; (2) Wood's state law tort action would have the regulatory effect of requiring passive restraints; and, therefore, (3) because Wood's action "would have the same effect as an impermissible state regulation, it is preempted because it stands as an obstacle to Congress's chosen method for achieving auto safety." *Id.* The court rejected Wood's argument that the Savings Clause foreclosed the possibility of conflict preemption because it found that Supreme Court cases support the view that "general savings clauses may not be read literally to permit common law actions that contradict and subvert a [federal] scheme." *Id.* at 415 (citing *International Paper Co. v. Ouellette*, 479 U.S. 481, 494, 107 S.Ct. 805, 812, 93 L.Ed.2d 883 (1987), and *Texas & Pacific Railway v. Abilene Cotton Oil Co.*, 204 U.S. 426, 436, 27 S.Ct. 350, 353, 51 L.Ed. 553 (1907)).

The Tenth Circuit was next to address the failure-to-install issue in *Kitts v. General Motors Corp.*, 875 F.2d 787 (10th Cir.1989). With little discussion, the Tenth Circuit followed *Wood*, stating: "Because we believe *Wood* directly addresses and correctly resolves the issue before us, we follow the general principles articulated in *Wood* and adopt the implied preemption rule of the First Circuit." *Id.* at 789.

One month later, the Eleventh Circuit faced the same issue in *Taylor v. General Motors Corp.*, 875 F.2d 816 (11th Cir.1989). Like the First and Tenth Circuits, the *Taylor* court found that the Safety Act does not expressly preempt a state tort action based on a manufacturer's failure to install an air bag. *Id.* at 825. But the *Taylor* court also agreed that the tort action is impliedly preempted because it would conflict with the federal regulatory scheme. Citing the Supreme Court's holding in *Fidelity Fed. Sav. & Loan Ass'n v. de la Cuesta*, 458 U.S. 141, 155, 102 S.Ct. 3014, 3023, 73 L.Ed.2d 664 (1982), that "a state common law rule cannot take away the flexibility provided by a federal regulation, and cannot prohibit the exercise of a federally granted option," the *Taylor* court held that Taylor's state tort claim was preempted because "a state common law rule that would, in effect, remove the element of choice authorized in Safety Standard 208 would frustrate the federal regulatory scheme." *Id.* at 827. Finally, the

Eleventh Circuit agreed with *Wood*'s determination that "a 'general' savings clause, such as that contained in the Safety Act, does not preclude a finding of implied preemption." *Id.* at 827–28 n. 20.

The Third Circuit has issued the latest opinion on the failure-to-install issue. In *Pokorny v. Ford Motor Co.*, 902 F.2d 1116 (3rd Cir.), *cert. denied*, ___ U.S. ___, 111 S.Ct. 147, 112 L.Ed.2d 113 (1990), the plaintiff claimed that Ford defectively designed its Econoline van because it failed to equip the van with air bags, automatic seat belts, or protective netting on the windows. *Id.* at 1117. Like the other circuits, the Third Circuit found that: (1) the Safety Act did not *expressly* preempt Pokorny's state tort claim, *id.* at 1121; (2) the claim that Ford is liable because it failed to install air bags is impliedly preempted because such a state standard would conflict with "the regulatory methods chosen by the federal government to achieve the Safety Act's stated goals," *id.* at 1123; and (3) the Safety Act's general savings clause does not preclude preemption of a state common law standard that conflicts with the federal scheme. *Id.* at 1125 & n. 10. But the Third Circuit emphasized that Pokorny's air bag claim was preempted not simply because federal safety standards have been established to govern the use of air bags, *id.* at 1121, but because Pokorny's air bag claim "presents an actual, clear conflict with federal regulation." *Id.* at 1123. Thus, the Safety Act preempted Pokorny's claims that were based on Ford's failure to install air bags or automatic seat belts, because they would create a state standard that conflicts with the choice that the regulations provide. *Id.* But the court held that the Act did not preempt Pokorny's claim to the extent that it was based on Ford's failure to install protective window netting, because a state standard requiring such netting would not prohibit an option that Standard 208 provides. *Id.* at 1125–26.

4. *Preemption in the Present Case.*

The district court in this case held that, although the Safety Act and its regulations do not *expressly* preempt Perry's defective design claim,[6] they implicitly preempt it because the claim would create a state common law design standard for air bag systems and thereby *conflict* with Standard 208's performance standards and the overall federal scheme. We begin our analysis by stating our agreement with the district court that Perry's defective design claim is not *expressly* preempted. In the Preemption Clause, Congress unambiguously expressed its intent to preempt all regulations *by a State or political subdivision of a State* that are applicable to the same aspect of performance as the federal standards but not identical to them. 15 U.S.C. § 1392(d). But Congress was just as unambiguous when it expressed its intent in the Savings Clause not to exempt any person from any

---

6. MBNA does not contest the district court's decision that Perry's design claim is not expressly preempted.

liability under common law. Id. § 1397(k). So Congress did not expressly preempt Perry's claim that MBNA's air bag system was unreasonably dangerous and thus defectively designed under Louisiana law.

Nor do we find that Congress has created a "scheme of federal regulation [that] is sufficiently comprehensive to make reasonable the inference that Congress 'left no room' for" Perry's tort claim. *Guerra,* 479 U.S. at 280, 107 S.Ct. at 689. Nothing in the Safety Act or its regulations reveals "the clear and manifest purpose of Congress" to take from the States the power to allow tort liability for unreasonably dangerous air bag systems. *Hillsborough County,* 471 U.S. at 715, 105 S.Ct. at 2376. In fact, the Savings Clause reveals that Congress had the opposite intent.

So we are left with the question of whether the imposition of state-law tort liability for the defective design of an air bag system would *conflict* with federal law. We think it obvious that there is no conflict in the sense that "compliance with both federal and state regulations is a physical impossibility." *Guerra,* 479 U.S. at 281, 107 S.Ct. at 689. Federal Standard 208 S4.1.2 provides that, if a manufacturer chooses to install an air bag system, that system must provide a level of protection that meets the *minimum* performance standards specified in S5 and S6. If a manufacturer is held liable in tort for not designing its system to provide protection greater than that required by the federal standard, the manufacturer can still comply with both the federal standard and the state tort standard by designing its system to meet the latter.

Thus, we are left with the question of whether state tort liability would *conflict* with federal law by standing "as an obstacle to the accomplishment and execution of the full purposes and objectives of Congress." *Id.* This is the form of preemption that the other circuits found in the failure-to-install cases, based on their belief that tort liability in those cases would interfere with "Congress's chosen *method* as well as ... the ultimate goal of the statute." *Wood,* 865 F.2d at 408 (emphasis added). But we find that it would not conflict with Congress' objectives and methods if MBNA were found *liable in tort* for failing to design its air bags to perform in a manner that effectively exceeds the federal minimum standards. The landmark for our analysis of this question is the Savings Clause, in which Congress expressly preserved common law liability *even if* the manufacturer complies with the federal standards. Perry contends that the legislative history of the Safety Act and its Savings Clause discloses Congress' intent that the federal scheme *never* preempt common law liability. We need not recite that history here, although we find it supportive of Perry's argument, because we find that the Savings Clause itself unambiguously reveals Congress' intent to preserve common law liability.

We are in agreement with the conclusion of the other circuits that the Savings Clause does not preserve common law actions that would *actually conflict with*, or "subvert," the objectives and methods of the federal scheme. *See Pokorny*, 902 F.2d at 1125 ("it is well-established that a savings clause like § 1397(k) does not 'save' common law actions that would subvert a federal statutory or regulatory scheme"); *Taylor*, 875 F.2d at 827–28 n. 20 ("a 'general' savings clause, such as that contained in the Safety Act, does not preclude a finding of implied preemption"); *Wood*, 865 F.2d at 415–16 (discussing the "general reluctance ... to follow a savings clause if state law will actually conflict with a federal regulatory scheme"). In reaching this conclusion, those courts found, first, that the imposition of common law liability for the "defect" urged by those plaintiffs would have a regulatory effect not unlike that of any state law or regulation, *see, e.g., Taylor*, 875 F.2d at 824 n. 16, 827; *Wood*, 865 F.2d at 410–12, and, second, that that effect would create an actual conflict with the federal scheme.

We agree with their findings that state damages awards based on tort liability can have a regulatory effect. But we find that liability for the defective design *of an air bag system* would not necessarily conflict with the objectives of the Safety Act or the methods that have been chosen to fulfill those objectives. The other circuits found an actual conflict in the failure-to-install cases because the tort claims sought to impose liability on the manufacturer for choosing an option that the federal scheme expressly granted them the right to choose. Thus, the Third Circuit concluded that "Pokorny's action does present an actual conflict with the Safety Act and Standard 208 to the extent that it alleges liability for Ford's failure to include air bags or automatic seat belts" because such liability "undermines the *flexibility* that Congress and the Department of Transportation intended to give to automobile manufacturers in this area." *Pokorny*, 902 F.2d at 1123 (emphasis added). But Pokorny's claim, to the extent it asserted liability for Ford's failure to install window netting, "presents no direct, actual conflict because it does not take away the *flexibility* established by the federal scheme, and it does not have the effect of prohibiting an *option* granted by Congress or the Department of Transportation." *Id.* at 1126 (emphasis added). And the Eleventh Circuit concluded that Taylor's failure-to-install claim "would frustrate the federal regulatory scheme" because it "would, in effect remove the *element of choice* authorized in Safety Standard 208." *Taylor*, 875 F.2d at 827 (emphasis added).

We need not decide today whether we agree with the conclusion that the other circuits reached on the failure-to-install issue. Although we have stated our agreement with much of their reasoning, we will wait to decide that issue if and when we face it. But even if we assume that allowing liability for a manufacturer's failure to install an air bag would conflict with Congress' chosen method by removing or requiring one of the manufacturer's choices, Perry's claim presents a different scenario. Once the manufacturer chooses an option that includes an air bag system, Standard 208 S5–S6 merely set forth *minimum* performance requirements for that system. To allow tort liability for the design of that system would not remove or require any particular choice, or otherwise frustrate "flexibility" that the federal scheme provides. We recognize that the manufacturer who chooses to meet only the bare minimum performance requirements will be burdened with the potential for tort liability, but this is the exact burden that Congress preserved in the Savings Clause, when it stated that "compliance with any Federal motor vehicle safety standard ... does not exempt any person from any liability under common law." Congress sought to meet its goal of minimizing the number of deaths and injuries caused by auto accidents by setting forth minimum standards and leaving common law liability in place.

MBNA contends that allowing common law liability for the defective design of an air bag system would conflict with another goal of the Safety Act, that "motor vehicle safety standards be not only strong and adequately enforced, but that they be uniform throughout the country." S.REP. No. 1301 at 12, *reprinted in* 1966 U.S.C.C.A.N. at 2720. To allow tort liability under state law, MBNA contends, would subvert this goal by allowing the development of a different standard in each State. But whether the need for uniform standards justifies the preemption of common law liability is a legislative question. Our role is to determine the intent of Congress as expressed by federal statutes and regulations. And the method that Congress chose for meeting its goal of uniformity is revealed in the Preemption Clause: *no State or political subdivision* shall establish any non-identical standards. As the Third Circuit explained in *Pokorny*,

> uniformity was not Congress's primary goal in enacting the Safety Act. In 15 U.S.C.A. § 1381, Congress declared that the Safety Act's purpose was "to reduce traffic accidents and deaths and injuries to persons resulting from traffic accidents." Congress evidently thought that preserving common law liability would further the goal of motor vehicle safety, since § 1397(k) was included as part of the Act. In the face of this clear declaration of congressional purpose, we are unwilling to accept an overly broad notion of preemption based on uniformity that could have the effect of undercutting Congress's concern for safety.

902 F.2d at 1122 (citations omitted).

We agree with the Third Circuit, and refuse to reject the Savings Clause in favor of Congress' secondary goal of uniformity. We thus find that Perry's state law claim for defective design of an air bag system does not create an actual conflict with the Safety Act and its underlying regulatory scheme. As a result, we cannot ignore the Savings Clause or find preemption in this case.

Ch. 9 CRASHWORTHINESS

5. *Evidence to Support the Defective Design Claim.*

MBNA contends that, even if Perry's defective design claim is not preempted, summary judgment was proper on this claim because Perry failed to adduce any competent evidence that the design of the air bag system was unreasonably dangerous. MBNA raised this argument before the district court, but that court based the summary judgment only on the preemption argument. We may affirm a district court's judgment on grounds other than those on which it was based. *See Lavespere v. Niagara Machine & Tool Works, Inc.*, 920 F.2d 259, 262 (5th Cir.1990) ("Our affirmance of the district court may rest on reasons not advanced by that court, although reversal may not be."). But we decline MBNA's invitation to do so in this case, and prefer, instead, to allow the district court to consider the issue first.

B. THE DEFECTIVE CONSTRUCTION CLAIM

Perry alleges that, even if MBNA did not defectively design its air bag systems, the particular system installed in her vehicle deviated from its design and thus was unreasonably dangerous under Louisiana law. Essentially, Perry contends that an air bag that was properly constructed to MBNA's standards would have inflated in this accident. The district court granted summary judgment for MBNA on this claim because it found that, based on the evidence provided, a reasonable juror could not find that Perry's vehicle sustained the type of impact required to deploy the air bag under MBNA's design specifications.[11]

When reviewing a summary judgment, we consider the record *de novo* and are guided by the same standards that guided the district court. *GATX Aircraft Corp. v. M/V Courtney Leigh*, 768 F.2d 711, 714 (5th Cir.1985). MBNA is entitled to summary judgment if it demonstrates by pleadings, depositions, answers to interrogatories, admissions, and affidavits, that there is no genuine issue of material fact and that it is entitled to a judgment as a matter of law. FED.R.CIV.P. 56(c). In response to this showing by MBNA, Perry may not rest on mere allegations or denials, but in the same manner must demonstrate facts that show that a genuine and material issue remains for trial. FED. R.CIV.P. 56(e). Perry's evidence must be both significant and probative. *State Farm Life Ins. Co. v. Gutterman*, 896 F.2d 116, 118 (5th Cir.1990).

Perry bears the burden of proving the elements of her claim. *See* LA.REV.STAT.ANN. § 9:2800.54. In essence, Perry must prove both the type of impact that is necessary to deploy the air bag according to MBNA's design, and that her vehicle sustained that type of impact. Axle Stehle, MBNA's expert, testified in his deposition that MBNA designed the system so that the air bag would deploy upon an impact equal to or greater than twelve miles per hour against a rigid barrier.

---

11. The district court also held, and we agree, that the Safety Act does not preempt claims that are based on the allegation that a vehicle was not constructed according to its design.

But because Perry's vehicle collided with an earthen embankment rather than a rigid barrier, this standard must be translated into terms that are applicable to this particular accident. Stehle testified to two separate methods for determining whether Perry's vehicle struck the ditch with the force equivalent to twelve miles per hour against a rigid barrier. First, Stehle testified that, based on his evaluation of the accident and the ditch, Perry would have had to have been traveling around forty to fifty miles per hour to trigger the air bag in this accident. Second, Stehle testified that a vehicle that sustains an impact equivalent to twelve miles per hour against a rigid barrier will suffer damage to its structural members, so we can determine whether Perry's air bag should have deployed by looking for structural damage to the vehicle. Perry offered no evidence to supplement or contradict Stehle's testimony on this point.

If Perry's speed at impact were the only material fact, we would agree with Perry that the existence of a genuine issue prevents summary judgment. But we must also consider Stehle's testimony that an impact that is sufficient to trigger the air bag would cause structural damage to the vehicle. While we might doubt that this would be true in every case, Perry offered no evidence to contest the validity of this standard, and thus we accept it as fact. Perry has offered no evidence that her vehicle suffered structural damage in this accident. In fact, the vehicle's repair records show only repairs to external parts and replacement of the steering wheel. And Stehle, who inspected the vehicle after it had been repaired, testified that he found no evidence that the vehicle had ever suffered structural damage. Because Perry offered no evidence to create a factual issue of whether an impact sufficient to deploy the air bag would cause structural damage to the vehicle, or whether her vehicle sustained structural damage, we agree with the district court that MBNA is entitled to summary judgment on Perry's defective construction claim.

We REVERSE the district court's judgment and REMAND this case for further proceedings on Perry's defective design claim.

NOTES

1. How should the burden of proof be allocated in *Perry* on the enhanced injury question? Does the *Sumnicht* opinion adequately deal with the situation in *Perry*? What impact should the plaintiff's failure to use her seat belt have on the analysis? See Lowe v. Estate Motors, infra, page 815 of the text.

2. Consider how *Perry* and the cases it cites, holding that airbag claims are preempted, are affected by the Supreme Court's subsequent decision in Cipollone v. Liggett Group, Inc., infra, Chapter 10.

3. As *Perry* states, four other courts of appeals found failure-to-employ airbag design defect claims preempted by the National Traffic and Motor Vehicle Safety Act, albeit on a variety of theories. In Wood v. General Motors Corp., 865 F.2d 395, 419–20 (1st Cir.1988), Judge Selya remarked in a dissent:

My brethren today espouse a vision of preemption that I find needlessly wide and a conception of the common law that seemingly misperceives tort as a regulatory system. What is more, this espousal occurs in an arena fraught with political drama—automobile safety regulation—where we should be especially reluctant to insulate administrative decisions from the prophylaxis of the civil jury, thereby placing common law protections beyond the reach of the motoring public. I am not so naive as to question that Congress may, if it chooses, shield its legislative product from unwanted state-law infringement. Short of that, however, the regulatory schematas of administrative agencies should be no less subject to the full panoply of democratic institutions than are the overt acts of other governmental instrumentalities.

While jury verdicts have an admittedly anecdotal quality, they are a core ingredient of our representative democracy, signifying the considered judgment of citizens forced to confront and define the scope of law in action. Because I can discern neither a clear expression that this tort action has been preempted nor any sufficient reason to imply so drastic a result, I would answer the certified question in the negative and affirm the decision below.

Chapter 10

SPECIAL ISSUES IN TOXIC SUBSTANCE LITIGATION

SECTION 1. LIABILITY STANDARDS AND PROBLEMS OF JUDICIAL ADMINISTRATION

A. IN GENERAL

ADD to page 879, after the notes:

CIMINO v. RAYMARK INDUSTRIES, INC.
United States District Court, Eastern District of Texas, 1990.
751 F.Supp. 649.

PARKER, CHIEF JUDGE.

The odyssey of asbestos litigation in the Eastern District of Texas has now entered its third decade. The trek started by Clarence Borel and Claude Tomplait has been marked by aimless wandering through the legal wilderness. The journey has taken its predicted toll. Raymark, Forty-Eight Insulations, Unarco, Standard Asbestos, Johns-Manville, Eagle-Picher, and now Celotex are bankrupt. Other defendants are clearly in the twilight of their participation. Four hundred and forty-eight members of the class have died waiting for their cases to be heard. The departed companies and plaintiffs have all been victims of a system that has seen a substantial majority of the compensation dollar go to witnesses and lawyers in the form of transaction costs. Transaction costs consumed $.61 of each asbestos-litigation dollar with $.37 going to defendants litigation costs; the plaintiffs receive only $.39 from each litigation dollar. Institute for Civil Justice, *Annual Report*, April 1, 1990–March 31, 1991 (RAND). The remaining parties have also been victimized by the same costs and the inability of the courts to provide a forum to the litigants.

A review of this litigation with the perspective of hindsight reveals many mistakes and missed opportunities by both this Court and the Court of Appeals. In 1981, Forty-Eight Insulations sought to conduct discovery in preparation for asserting a district wide market share determination among the defendants in order to reduce the costs of continuing expensive, individual discovery and trial on the exposure question, and to more accurately establish apportionment of causation among the defendants. Forty–Eight Insulations abandoned its motion because of pressure from co-defendants. In retrospect, this Court could have saved millions of dollars in unnecessary transaction costs by forcing the issue. Also, in 1981 in an attempt to reduce costs by avoiding repetitive identical trials, the Court by way of issue preclusion found asbestos containing products defective and unreasonably dangerous as a matter of law and further precluded plaintiffs from seeking punitive damages. The Court of Appeals in *Hardy v. Johns–Manville Sales Corp.*, 681 F.2d 334 (5th Cir.1982), rejected the approach. Again in retrospect, this Court should have recognized the fact that there was a disparity of appreciation for the magnitude of the problem between the trial court and the Court of Appeals. The disparity resulted from the trial court's daily involvement with asbestos litigation and the Court of Appeals' exposure being limited to infrequent appeals. Instead of blindly following *Hardy* for eight years, this Court should have caused thirty to forty identical appeals to have been processed in order to enhance the awareness level of the Court of Appeals. The defendants' victory in *Hardy* has cost over four hundred million dollars in increased and unnecessary transaction costs and has preserved for defendants the right to be subjected to punitive damages.

Yet another approach was the Court's establishment of a voluntary ADR program for asbestos cases filed after the cutoff date in *Jenkins v. Raymark Industries Inc.*, 782 F.2d 468 (5th Cir.1986). Most, but not all, defendants elected to participate. The ADR program provided many partial settlements before it was set aside by the Eastern District Court sitting en banc. The ADR program was flawed in three respects. First, under existing law it could not be binding or mandatory. Second, some plaintiffs' counsel were uncooperative and the defendants made it largely ineffective by delay tactics; and third, the defendants' inability to agree among themselves on apportionment of damages doomed the plan.

The Court was then back to the *Jenkins* procedure. However, *Jenkins* also was flawed in that it could not accommodate the large number of cases that had accumulated on the Court's docket.

The Court has now witnessed an evolution in defense strategy employed by Pittsburgh–Corning, Fibreboard and Celotex. Early on these defendants typically settled their cases. Pittsburgh–Corning was a prime mover in getting *Jenkins* settled. A new strategy has now been adopted. Pittsburgh–Corning, Fibreboard and Celotex have adopted a "fortress mentality" and are attempting to avoid liability by obstructing the Court's ability to provide a forum in these cases. It is a strategy that is not unique to East Texas, but is one that is being utilized all across the country. They assert a right to individual trials in each case and assert the right to repeatedly contest in each case every contestable issue involving the same products, the same warnings, and the same conduct. The strategy is a sound one; the defendants know that if the procedure in *Cimino* is not affirmed, these cases will never be tried.

If the Court could somehow close thirty cases a month, it would take six and one-half years to try these cases and there would be pending over 5,000 untouched cases at the present rate of filing. Transaction costs would be astronomical.

The great challenge presented to the Court by this litigation is to provide a fair and cost effective means of trying large numbers of asbestos cases. It is not enough to chronicle the existence of this problem and to lament congressional inaction. The litigants and the public rightfully expect the courts to be problem solvers.

THE REAL WORLD

In the real world, the scientific community long ago resolved the issues that continue to be litigated by the courts. Every institution, apart from the courts, that has investigated this remarkable natural mineral has concluded that it is inherently dangerous. The asbestos fibers themselves are invisible. They are easily dispersed into the air when asbestos containing products are handled, such as in application or removal. The scientific community agrees that:

1. There is no safe level of exposure.
2. There is a dose/response relationship that manifests itself in either the type disease that one may contract or the length of latency period between exposure and disease manifestation.
3. Asbestos is a competent producing cause of the diseases of mesothelioma, asbestosis, lung cancer, and pleural disease. Unanimity of opinion is not yet achieved regarding gastrointestinal tract cancers although the evidence has satisfied the Surgeon General.
4. Mesothelioma is an untreatable terminal cancer.
5. Asbestosis is a progressive untreatable disease of the lung.

Asbestos has either been banned or declared hazardous by the Occupational Safety and Health Administration, the National Institute for Occupational Safety and Health, the Environmental Protection Agency and the Surgeon General. These agencies have further concluded that all asbestos fiber types pose similar risks, therefore all fiber types are regulated equally.

During the course of the *Cimino* trial while the question of whether asbestos products were unreasonably dangerous was being litigated once again in Beaumont, the federal courtroom in Tyler was being used by the State Court of Appeals Judges because men in spacesuits were removing asbestos from their chambers.

THE PLAN

The plan is a simple one and reflects this Court's agreement with the comments of Professor Charles Alan Wright:

"I was an ex-officio member of the Advisory Committee on Civil Rules when Rule 23 was amended, which came out with an advisory committee note saying that mass torts are inappropriate for class certification. I thought then that was true. I am profoundly convinced now that that is untrue. Unless we can use the class action and devices built on the class action, our judicial system is not going to be able to cope with the challenges of the mass repetitive wrong."

See H. Newberg, *Newberg on Class Actions* § 17.06, at 373 (2d ed. 1985).

On February 19, 1990, this Court certified a class under Fed. R.Civ.P. 23(b)(3) consisting of 3,031 plaintiffs with existing cases in the Eastern District of Texas, all claiming an asbestos related injury or disease resulting from exposure to defendants' asbestos containing insulation products. Seven hundred thirty three cases were removed as a result of being dismissed, severed or settled. The class consisting of 2,298 plaintiffs went to trial against Pittsburgh–Corning, Fibreboard, Celotex, Carey–Canada, and ACL.

PHASE I

Phase I utilized the same procedures approved in *Jenkins v. Raymark Industries, Inc. supra*, to resolve all common issues. The issues were whether each asbestos containing insulation product manufactured by each defendant, settling and non-settling, was defective and unreasonably dangerous, the adequacy of warnings, the state of the art defense and the fiber type defense. The question of punitive damages in the entire case of the 2,298 class representatives was also submitted for jury determination.

PHASE II

Phase II required a jury finding for each of nineteen worksites during certain time periods regarding which asbestos containing insulation products were used, which crafts were sufficiently exposed to asbestos fibers from those products for such exposure to be a producing cause of an asbestos-related injury or disease and an apportionment of causation among defendants, settling and non-settling.

In other words, the exposure questions to be submitted would be specific as to time, place, craft, and amounts of exposure.

PHASE III

Phase III is the damage issue. The 2,298 class members were divided into five disease categories based on the plaintiff's injury claims. The Court selected a random sample from each disease category as follows:

	SAMPLE SIZE	DISEASE CATEGORY POPULATION
Mesothelioma	15	32
Lung Cancer	25	186
Other Cancer	20	58
Asbestosis	50	1,050
Pleural Disease	50	972
TOTAL	160	2,298

The damage case of each trial sample class member randomly drawn was then submitted to a jury. Each plaintiff whose damage case was submitted to the jury is to be awarded his individual verdict and the average verdict for each disease category will constitute the damage award for each non-sample class member.

Plaintiffs have agreed to the procedure, thereby waiving their rights to individual damage determinations.

THE TRIAL

Phase I began with jury selection on February 6, 1990 and the verdict was returned March 29, 1990. The Court then granted the parties' request for additional preparation time between Phase I and Phases II and III. Two juries were selected on July 3, 1990. The juries sat together for the first five trial days which were devoted to general medical testimony. The juries were then divided and began hearing testimony on groups of plaintiffs and returning damage verdicts. The last verdict for the 160 individual damages cases was received October 5, 1990.

In all, the trial consumed 133 days of trial time and produced 25,348 pages of transcript prepared as daily copy. The docket sheet in the Clerk's office is 529 pages long. The Court has entered 373 Signed Orders.

Prior to trial 1,885 sets of interrogatories were answered by the parties and 2,354 depositions were taken, with an additional 800 being taken during trial. Independent medical examinations were conducted of 1,400 plaintiffs.

During the course of the trial, 271 expert witnesses and 292 fact witnesses testified, 6,176 exhibits were received in evidence constituting 577,000 pages of documents. Fifty-eight individual lawyers participated in the in-court presentation of this case which was presided over in varying degrees by four district judges and three magistrates.

If all that is accomplished by this is the closing of 169 cases, then it was not worth the effort and will not be repeated.

PHASE II—STIPULATION

Phase II of the trial was designed to resolve the issue of the plaintiffs' exposure to the defendants' products on a class wide basis. The Court's goal in this respect was facilitated by the homogeneous nature of these particular plaintiffs' work histories.

The Court first compiled a list of worksites, various locations consisting mostly of oil and chemical refineries, where the majority of the plaintiffs allegedly were occupationally exposed to asbestos in the course of their employment. The Court next compiled a list of job classifications, or crafts, which the plaintiffs worked in during their employment at the worksites. It was contemplated that any plaintiff whose work history did not include a threshold amount of time in any of the worksites would have the exposure issue tried in an individual mini-trial.

Prior to the Court drafting a verdict form for Phase II, the parties agreed to stipulate as to what the jury findings would have been had Phase II been tried to a jury. The parties stipulated that the jury would have apportioned causation among the defendants in the amounts of 10% causation for each of the non-settling defendants and 13% causation for the settling defendant Johns–Manville Corporation.

The verdict form for Phase II would have been worksites. For each worksite there would have been two interrogatories. The first interrogatory would have asked whether or not each of the various crafts at a worksite was sufficiently exposed to asbestos for that exposure to be a producing cause of the disease of asbestosis [1] during successive time periods. The second interrogatory then would have requested the jury to determine, for each craft and each time period answered affirmatively in the first interrogatory, the percentage of comparative causation, if any, that each defendant's products contributed to the exposure.

CAUSATION

In order to recover under Texas law, a plaintiff must prove that a defendant's unreasonably dangerous product was a producing cause of a plaintiff's injury or disease. *Hartzell Propeller Co. v. Alexander*, 485 S.W.2d 943, 946 (Tex. Civ. App.—Waco 1972, writ ref. n.r.e.). A producing cause is defined as an efficient, exciting, or contributing cause which in a natural sequence of events produces an injury or disease. *Rourke v. Garza*, 530 S.W.2d 794, 800 (Tex.1975). There may be more than one producing cause of an injury or disease. *Id.*

A plaintiff in an asbestos suit need not show that exposure to a defendant's product was the sole cause of the asbestos-related injury or

---

1. Asbestosis was used as the threshold of exposure because both parties' experts agreed on the record that if an individual had sufficient exposure to asbestos to cause asbestosis, there was a sufficient level of exposure to cause any other asbestos-related disease.

disease. If exposure to the defendant's product combined with other causes to concurrently produce a single injury, the plaintiff may recover from the defendant for the entire injury. *Shipp v. General Motors Corporation*, 750 F.2d 418, 425–26 (5th Cir.1985). The plaintiff need only show that exposure to a defendant's product was a substantial factor in causing the plaintiff's injury. *Gideon v. Johns–Manville Sales Corporation*, 761 F.2d 1129, 1145 (5th Cir.1985).

* * *

REMITTITUR AND NEW TRIALS

The Court has examined the verdicts in the cases of the nine class representatives and the 160 trial sample plaintiffs and has ordered remittiturs in 34 of the pulmonary and pleural cases and in one mesothelioma case. The Court has granted a new trial in one mesothelioma case.

The usual remittitur analysis was conducted by the Court. However, in these cases the Court was required also to examine the medical evidence to determine which cases had progressed medically. The Court noted that many cases that earlier on had diagnosis of pleural disease or pulmonary asbestosis with limited fibrotic development had markedly changed as a result of disease progression by the time the cases actually went to trial.

PUNITIVE DAMAGES

In Phase I of this trial, the jury found the non-settling Defendants grossly negligent and held them liable for punitive damages. In response to Interrogatory VII of the Phase I verdict form, the jury assessed a punitive damages multiplier "for each $1.00 of actual damages" in the following amounts:

Carey-Canada	$1.50
Celotex	$2.00
Fibreboard	$1.50
Pittsburgh-Corning	$3.00

This use of a punitive damage multiplier was suggested in *Jenkins v. Raymark Industries, Inc.*, 782 F.2d 468, 474 (5th Cir.1986).

A plaintiff is entitled to recover punitive damages under Texas law if the evidence supports a jury finding of gross negligence on behalf of the defendant. "The critical issue in Texas punitive damages law is excessiveness or 'reasonable proportionality.'" *Jenkins v. Raymark Industries*, Inc., 782 F.2d 468, 474 (5th Cir.1986). Exemplary damages must be reasonably proportioned to actual damages. *Alamo Nat'l Bank v. Kraus*, 616 S.W.2d 908, 910 (Tex.1981). This court does not find the amount of the multipliers to be excessive as to suggest that passion rather than reason motivated the jury. *See Edwards v. Armstrong World Industries, Inc.*, 911 F.2d 1151, 1154 (5th Cir.1990).

* * *

STATISTICS

Phase III of the plan utilizes the science of statistics, or more specifically, inferential statistics. Aristotle is generally credited with launching the science of collection of comparative information by gathering data on 158 different city-states as set out in his *Politeiai* in the 4th century B.C.[2] During the Renaissance, the Germans refined the methodology of information gathering on the resources of states and gave it the name, "Staatenkunde." By 1660, it was incorporated into curriculum in German universities. Gottfried Achenwall, at the University of Gottingen, first used the word "statistics" in print in 1749. The British redefined the term to incorporate what had been called "political arithmetic." John Graunt's attempt to draw inferences from mortality data accumulated in London was hampered by the lack of a probability theory, but it was sufficient to gain him entrance into the Royal Society of London. His landmark treatise in 1662, "National and Political Observations Upon the Bills of Mortality," resulted in his being considered the world's first statistician. Edmund Halley, of "Halley's comet" fame, subsequently published a book which laid the foundation for the theory of annuities and the creation of mortality tables.

It was the French, however, who added the missing link—a comprehensive theory or calculus of probability. The basic principles of the theory of probability evolved from the correspondence between Blaise Pascal and another distinguished French mathematician, Pierre Fermat, concerning a gambling question posed to Pascal by a French nobleman. The first bell-shaped curve appeared in 1733, and with the publication of *Theorie Analytique des Probabilities* by Laplace in 1812, statistics came of age.

The science of statistics is now universally accepted, exerting the most profound influence on our daily lives. "The objective of statistics is to make an inference about a population of interest based on information obtained from a sample of measurements from that population." For example, statistical sampling plays a critical role in medical and pharmaceutical research. In 1954, a sample of 400,000 children was used to measure the effectiveness of the Salk vaccine for polio. Similar testing of new drug products has increased in recent years due to the stringent requirements of the Food and Drug Administration, aiding in the development of birth control pills, rubella vaccines,

2. The following brief summary of the history of statistics draws heavily on R. Larson and M. Marx, *Statistics*, 13–18 (1990).

Ch. 10 LIABILITY STANDARDS & JUDICIAL ADMINISTRATION

63 (5th Cir.1974), a Title VII case, the court made the following observation:

> However, when the class size or the ambiguity of promotion or hiring practices or the multiple effects of discriminatory practices or the illegal practices continued over an extended period of time calls forth the quagmire of hypothetical judgment discussed earlier, a class-wide approach to the measure of back pay is necessitated. It should be emphasized that this is not a choice between one approach more precise than another. Any method is simply a process of conjectures. (footnote omitted)

Pettway, 494 F.2d at 261.

The *Pettway* Court followed with several suggestions for computing approximate pay rates and pay periods using a class-wide approach. One suggested method involved the averaging of five pay rates, awarding each claimant back pay based on the average rate multiplied by years of employment. *Id.* at 262. Another suggested approach involved the use of a comparability formula in which earnings of a group of employees not injured by discrimination, comparable to the class according to specific relevant variables, are approximated and applied to the class. *Id.* at 263. On appeal after remand, the Court reiterated its approval of the above mentioned class-wide remedies. *Pettway v. American Cast Iron Pipe Co.*, 576 F.2d 1157, 1222 (5th Cir.1978), *cert. denied*, 439 U.S. 1115 (1979). The court also concluded that "*as a last resort* the [trial] court may utilize the individual-by-individual approach...." (emphasis added by court). *Id.*

The Court does not perceive the method of extrapolation used herein to be substantially dissimilar to the methods advocated in *Pettway*. As in *Pettway*, the desirability of proceeding on a class-wide, rather than individual basis, is readily apparent.

Against this backdrop, defendants assert that statistical methodology is somehow inappropriate for mass tort cases. This contention fails when examined under the same microscope used in other cases. The method incorporated into Phase III produces a level of economy in terms of both judicial resources and transaction cost that needs no elaboration. Moreover, defendants cannot possibly suggest that no form of statistical evidence is appropriate in this case. They frequently used statistics during this trial. At the outset, Owens–Illinois submitted a statistical analysis of a telephone survey conducted by Jury Analyst, Inc. on a sample of 500 people from each division in this district in support of its Motion to Transfer Venue. Defendants Fibreboard and Pittsburgh–Corning subsequently adopted that motion. The voluminous medical literature offered by both sides contains innumerable examples of statistical surveys and analysis.

Defendant Pittsburgh–Corning relied upon the testimony of Dr. Thomas Robert Savings to estimate the percentage of Pittsburgh–

Corning products in the Golden Triangle area. Dr. Savings made an extensive statistical analysis to compute the estimated market share for Pittsburgh–Corning which was then extrapolated to the chemical plants in the area. The Court is of the opinion that defendants' extensive reliance upon statistical analysis and extrapolation considerably weakens their argument against the use of the same by the Court. However, the question of whether the damage phase methodology of this trial is sufficiently accurate requires further examination.

When *Cimino* was certified, the Court had two options regarding damages—a lump sum award or the utilization of a random sample. The lump sum approach was rejected in *In re Fibreboard Corp.*, 893 F.2d 706 (5th Cir.1990). There appears to have been some confusion regarding the use of illustrative plaintiffs in the first plan with the utilization of random sampling techniques in the second plan. The original plan would have produced a lump sum award and the illustrative plaintiffs were just that—they would have illustrated typical cases for the jury's benefit in determining a lump sum award for the entire class. The illustrative plaintiffs' cases would not have been decided, and extrapolation was not part of the equation.

When the Court set the original plan aside and adopted statistical sampling as the only remaining option, it could have conducted a hearing and made necessary findings on the representativeness question—that is, what sample sizes are appropriate for each disease category—prior to trial of Phase III. However, the Court elected to defer that decision until after the damage trial to take the question of representativeness a step further. The Court determined that the impact of these cases was of sufficient importance that the Court should not limit its consideration to a "Statistics 101" analysis, but should also examine the samples to determine whether they were representative in fact. This approach requires the makeup of the randomly drawn samples to be compared to the population of each disease category.

The post-trial hearing held November 6, 1990, has persuaded the Court that the samples used were, in fact, representative. When setting the sample size for each disease category, the Court sought a confidence level of 95%, in other words $+/- 2.00$ standard deviations. The testimony adduced at the post-trial hearing indicates that the actual precision level achieved by the samples exceeds that sought by the Court. Professor Ronald G. Frankiewicz, a professor at the University of Houston who holds a Ph.D. in evaluation, measurement and statistics, conducted numerous statistical tests comparing the goodness-of-fit between the samples and their corresponding disease categories, considering the dichotomous, continuous and categorical variables. Frankiewicz's testing indicates that, with two minor exceptions,[15] the

---

15. Frankiewicz goodness-of-fit tests for the disease category "Other Cancers" indicates a 98% confidence level for the dichotomous variable of race. (See Plaintiff's

samples on the whole achieved a 99% confidence level, or in other words, a standard deviation of $+/-$ 2.56.

Defendants elected to present no evidence at the hearing either attacking Frankiewicz's methodology or comparing the sample to the entire population or class. The defendants had a data base on the 160 sample members from the trial of those cases and the data base on the entire class that included depositions in all the cases, medical examinations of approximately 1,400 class members as well as other discovery that detailed employment history, wage history, medical history, medical records and expenses, and family background. The Court can only conclude that if Frankiewicz's methodology was inappropriate or if the sample was, in fact, skewed and not representative of the class, the Court would have heard that evidence.

The Court is of the opinion that the distribution of variables between the samples and their respective subclasses is comparable. The Court finds that this procedure has proved to be a valid statistical exercise. The goodness-of-fit exceeded the acceptable limits articulated by the Court, and the Court perceives no need to try any more cases prior to extrapolation.

The Court finds no persuasive evidence why the average damage verdicts in each disease category should not be applied to the non-sample members. The averages are calculated after remittitur and take into consideration those cases where plaintiffs failed to prove the existence of an asbestos-related injury or disease resulting in a zero verdict. Individual members of a disease category who will receive an award that might be different from one they would have received had their individual case been decided by a jury have waived any objections, and the defendants cannot show that the total amount of damages would be greater under the Court's method compared to individual trials of these cases. Indeed, the millions of dollars saved in reduced transaction costs inure to defendants' benefit.

This Court, during the inception and implementation of the plan, had one additional concern—a concern similar to one expressed by Judge Higginbotham in *Vuyanich v. Republic Nat. Bank*, 505 F.Supp. 224, 394 (N.D.Tex.1980), *vacated on other grounds*, 723 F.2d 1195 (5th Cir.1984), *cert. denied*, 469 U.S. 1073 (1984). The concern is that dispute resolution under our system cannot be reduced to formula. Computers cannot replace judges who bring to their tasks experience and sensitivity to due process as well as the basic fairness that is at the core of our judicial system. Careful scrutiny has persuaded this Court

Exhibit "Frankiewicz No. 1," Table 3.) Additionally, in testing the goodness-of-fit at a 99% confidence level comparing the stratified sample with the entire population, Frankiewicz's testing indicated a lower proportion of "living" cases, according to the dichotomous variable of living, in the sample than in the general population. (*See* Plaintiff's Exhibit "Frankiewicz No. 1," Table 6.)

that, in this case, science has assumed its proper role, a role that is in aid of the court and not in replacement of it.

The siren call of numerical display has here too been resisted. It also cannot be said that this effort was not a trial. *Cimino* was a trial in the traditional sense. The 373 Orders entered and the numerous other rulings were the product of judicial opinion, not calculations. The liability verdicts and 160 damage awards were made by three juries in a traditional trial.

DUE PROCESS

Defendants, taking comfort in the language of *In re Fibreboard Corp., supra*, object to the Court's plan and assert that due process, even in the asbestos context, entitles defendants to a traditional one-on-one trial in each of the 2,298 cases. In defendants' eyes there are no common issues, irrespective of the fact that the products in each trial would be identical, the warnings would be identical, and the exposure evidence for each worksite during the time periods inquired about for each craft would be identical. Defendants further point out that damage elements vary between plaintiffs, such as the nature and extent of disease, lost wages, medical expenses, pain and suffering, and mental anguish.

In an attempt to avoid once again being sacrificed on the altar of due process, the Court has set out to address the variables that were bothersome to the Court of Appeals in *In re Fibreboard*.

It was undisputed that the product list submitted to the jury in Phase I was comprised of insulation products manufactured by the defendant indicated, that they contained asbestos, and were capable of producing dust in application, use, or removal. The warnings of each of the defendants and the time periods the products were placed in the stream of commerce were also not disputed. The jury considered each individual product and found them, once again, to be defective and unreasonably dangerous at all times marketed. These factors, therefore, would not vary from plaintiff to plaintiff. What might vary is which products a particular plaintiff was exposed to in sufficient quantities for that exposure to be a producing cause of an asbestos-related injury or disease, and when the plaintiff may have been exposed. These variables became constants as a result of the stipulation in the exposure phase—Phase II.

What remained then was the usual variables that are reflected by elements of damages in a personal injury case for a particular plaintiff. The Court addressed these variables by structuring a damages only trial in Phase III that was indistinguishable from a reverse bifurcation damage trial that defendants favor in many parts of the country. The Court then, by way of variable reduction, divided the plaintiffs into five categories by disease, from which the samples were drawn. The 160

Ch. 10 LIABILITY STANDARDS & JUDICIAL ADMINISTRATION

damage cases tried with all the variables inherent in such cases produced a result to a 99% confidence level the average of which would be comparable to the average result if all cases were tried. If the existence of variables are the driving force behind defendants' due process argument, then due process has been served.

However, a due process concern remains that is very troubling to the Court. It is apparent from the effort and time required to try these 160 cases, that unless this plan or some other procedure that permits damages to be adjudicated in the aggregate is approved, these cases cannot be tried. Defendants complain about the 1% likelihood that the result would be significantly different. However, plaintiffs are facing a 100% confidence level of being denied access to the courts. The Court will leave it to the academicians and legal scholars to debate whether our notion of due process has room for balancing these competing interests.

Judges at both trial and appellate court levels seldom have the luxury of the time required for true reflection on the consequences of what we do and how we may do it better. All too often the constraints of time militate in favor of traditional methodology even when traditional methods consistently produce a result that is quite unacceptable to litigants, the courts, and to society. The asbestos litigation mess is a classic example of this conundrum. More times than not, therefore, we find ourselves abdicating this role to others.

In commenting on the fact that the last few years have seen a revolution in thinking about mass toxic torts, Deborah Hensler, Research Director of the Institute for Civil Justice at the RAND Corporation, is one who has stepped into the breach. Professor Hensler notes:

> "When scholars and practitioners assess the appropriateness of applying various formal aggregative approaches to mass torts, they explicitly or implicitly use the 'traditional tort approach' as their standard for comparison, in effect accepting the version of legal reality that this incorporates. Judged against this standard, formal aggregative procedures frequently appear to fall short. This article argues that this version of legal reality is factitious, both with regard to process and substantive outcomes, making its use as a standard for judging formal aggregative procedures highly dubious."

Hensler, *Resolving Mass Toxic Torts: Myths and Realities*, 1989 U. Ill. L. Rev. 89, 90 (1989).

The study concludes with what is common knowledge to judges who are familiar with these cases:

1. The traditional tort approach in practice falls far short of the goals ascribed to it in both routine and mass tort cases.

chemotherapeutic agents, and countless other important pharmaceuticals.

As in medical research, private industries employ statistical techniques in the development and testing of new products. Random sampling is used in the production process for many diverse tasks, such as maintaining the dimension requirements for the plastic cards used in automatic bank teller machines or testing the specific gravity of laundry detergent. Statistical techniques are particularly valuable in the field of marketing. For example, researchers recently tested a sample of 1,277 people using questionnaires regarding 80 television commercials in order to determine the attributes of a likeable television advertisement. The insurance industry likewise makes widespread use of statistics and probability theory, particularly in the area of rate setting.

The effect of statistics reaches well beyond the market place or our medicine cabinet. In the field of education, statistical techniques are used in the administration and evaluation of various standardized tests. Studies based on random sampling may help improve curriculum for special needs pupils, such as language-minority students or illiterate adults. Statistics have likewise become very important in the political arena. Nearly every day we receive progress reports on the rise or fall of the President's popularity as determined by public opinion polls. During the previous administration, a telephone survey of a random sample of 1,000 registered voters was conducted to assess the effect of the President's support of the INF Treaty on foreign policy "hardliners." Moreover, the science of statistics frequently proves to be invaluable in such areas as evaluating the effects of changes in the law and projecting budgetary needs. At the present, the Federal Judiciary is involved in an on-going time study using a sample of all cases filed in the district courts for a two week period. The Federal Judicial Center will use the data obtained to help project the need for additional federal judges and magistrates.

[The court proceeded to survey a number of legal areas in which statistics have been employed in litigation, including employment discrimination, antitrust, torts, and civil rights.]

The reasons the courts have come to rely on statistics are the same reasons that society embraces the science. It has been proved to provide information with an acceptable degree of accuracy and economy.

Departing from the area of statistical evidence, it is incumbent upon the Court to note that various courts have permitted, or even advocated, the use of formulas or models for damage awards in class action suits, rather than employing an individual-by-individual approach. In *Pettway v. American Cast Iron Pipe Co.*, 494 F.2d 211, 258–

2. Personalized case-by-case processing is not possible and not desired by lawyers and judges.

3. Informal aggregation is many times embarked upon in such an ad hoc fashion that its implications are not carefully considered, and its consequences not subjected to careful scrutiny.

4. The expanding use of formal aggregative procedures provide for litigant control over the litigation process, more opportunity for litigant participation in the process, and a better match between victims' losses and compensation for those losses.

It is this Court's opinion that due process in the asbestos context should not be analyzed in the narrow, traditional, one-sided view of defendants, but should also encompass the impact on plaintiffs and even the obvious societal interest involved. To take defendants' argument is to embrace perfection as the benchmark; this Court submits that a confidence level of 99% will do.

THE FUTURE

The judges to whom the non-sample class member cases are assigned may now entertain motions and enter judgments consistent with this Opinion and Order. This Court will enter judgment for the class representatives, the trial sample members of the class, and its assigned cases. Plaintiffs may submit as part of this motion for judgment an affidavit concerning the termination of exposure for each individual plaintiff as reflected by that plaintiff's employment records. The affidavit may then be used by the Court to determine the time for calculating pre-judgment interest.

Judgment may be entered against Celotex only in the event the bankruptcy court lifts the stay for that purpose.

The question of whether asbestos containing insulation products are defective and unreasonably dangerous, the adequacy of warnings, the state-of-the-art, and the fiber type defenses should not be relitigated again in the Eastern District of Texas.

The question of apportionment of responsibility among all defendants should be established by one trial or by stipulation.

Damages must be determined in the aggregate. Whether it is by the mechanism of the Court's plan or by some other procedure approved or suggested by the Court of Appeals, without the ability to determine damages in the aggregate, the Court cannot try these cases.

B. CIGARETTE LITIGATION

Replace Cipollone v. Liggett Group, Inc. and note 1 on pages 880–84 with:

CIPOLLONE v. LIGGETT GROUP, INC.

Supreme Court of the United States, 1992.
___ U.S. ___, 112 S.Ct. 2608, 120 L.Ed.2d 407.

STEVENS J., announced the judgment of the Court and delivered the opinion of the Court with respect to Parts I, II, III, and IV, in which REHNQUIST, C. J., and WHITE, BLACKMUN, O'CONNOR, KENNEDY, and SOUTER, JJ., joined, and an opinion with respect to Parts V and VI, in which REHNQUIST, C. J., and WHITE, and O'CONNOR, JJ., joined. BLACKMUN, J., filed an opinion concurring in part, concurring in the judgment in part, and dissenting in part, in which KENNEDY and SOUTER JJ., joined. SCALIA, J., filed an opinion concurring in the judgment in part and dissenting in part, in which THOMAS, J., joined.

JUSTICE STEVENS delivered the opinion of the Court, except as to Parts V and VI.

"WARNING: THE SURGEON GENERAL HAS DETERMINED THAT CIGARETTE SMOKING IS DANGEROUS TO YOUR HEALTH." A federal statute enacted in 1969 requires that warning (or a variation thereof) to appear in a conspicuous place on every package of cigarettes sold in the United States. The questions presented to us by this case are whether that statute, or its 1965 predecessor which required a less alarming label, pre–empted petitioner's common law claims against respondent cigarette manufacturers.

Petitioner is the son of Rose Cipollone, who began smoking in 1942 and who died of lung cancer in 1984. He claims that respondents are responsible for Rose Cipollone's death because they breached express warranties contained in their advertising, because they failed to warn consumers about the hazards of smoking, because they fraudulently misrepresented those hazards to consumers, and because they conspired to deprive the public of medical and scientific information about smoking. The Court of Appeals held that petitioner's state law claims were pre-empted by federal statutes, 893 F.2d 541 (CA3 1990), and other courts have agreed with that analysis.[2] The highest courts of the states of Minnesota and New Jersey, however, have held that the federal statutes did not pre-empt similar common law claims.[3] Because of the

---

2. The Court of Appeals' analysis was initially set forth in *Cipollone v. Liggett Group, Inc.*, 789 F.2d 181 (CA3 1986). Other Federal Courts have adopted a similar analysis. See *Pennington v. Vistron Corp.*, 876 F.2d 414 (CA5 1989); *Roysdon v. R. J. Reynolds Tobacco Co.*, 849 F.2d 230 (CA6 1988); *Stephen v. American Brands, Inc.*, 825 F.2d 312 (CA11 1987); *Palmer v. Liggett Group, Inc.*, 825 F.2d 620 (CA1 1987).

3. *Forster v. R. J. Reynolds Tobacco Co.*, 437 N.W.2d 655 (Minn.1989); *Dewey v. R. J. Reynolds Tobacco Co.*, 121 N.J. 69, 577 A.2d 1239 (1990).

manifest importance of the issue, we granted certiorari to resolve the conflict, * * *. We now reverse in part and affirm in part.

I

On August 1, 1983, Rose Cipollone and her husband filed a complaint invoking the diversity jurisdiction of the Federal District Court. Their complaint alleged that Rose Cipollone developed Lung Cancer because she smoked cigarettes manufactured and sold by the three respondents. After her death in 1984, her husband filed an amended complaint. After trial, he also died; their son, executor of both estates, now maintains this action.

Petitioner's third amended complaint alleges several different bases of recovery, relying on theories of strict liability, negligence, express warranty, and intentional tort. These claims, all based on New Jersey Law, divided into five categories. The "design defect claims" allege that respondents' cigarettes were defective because respondents failed to use a safer alternative design for their products and because the social value of their product was outweighed by the dangers it created * * *. The "failure to warn claims" allege both that the product was "defective as a result of [respondents'] failure to provide adequate warnings of the health consequences of cigarette smoking" * * * and "that respondents were negligent in the manner [that] they tested, researched, sold, promoted, and advertised" their cigarettes * * *. The "express warranty claims" allege that respondents had expressly warranted that smoking the cigarettes which they manufactured and sold did not present any significant health consequences" * * *. The "fraudulent misrepresentation claims" allege that respondents had wilfully "through their advertising, attempted to neutralize the [federally mandated] warning" labels * * * and that they had possessed, but had "ignored and failed to act upon" medical and scientific data indicating that cigarettes were hazardous to the health of consumers" * * *. Finally, the "conspiracy to defraud claims" allege that respondents conspired to deprive the public of such medical and scientific data * * *.

As one of their defenses, respondents contended that the Federal Cigarette Labeling and Advertising Act, enacted in 1965, and its successor, the Public Health Cigarette Smoking Act of 1969, protected them from any liability based on their conduct after 1965. In a pretrial ruling, the District Court concluded that the federal statutes were intended to establish a uniform warning that would prevail throughout the country and that would protect cigarette manufacturers from being "subjected to varying requirements from state to state," *Cipollone v. Liggett Group, Inc.*, 593 F.Supp. 1146, 1148 (NJ 1984), but that the statutes did not pre-empt common law actions.

The court of appeals accepted an interlocutory appeal pursuant to 28 U.S.C. § 1292(b), and reversed. *Cipollone v. Liggett Group, Inc.*, 789

F.2d 181 (CA3 1986). The court rejected respondents' contention that the federal acts expressly pre-empted common law actions, but accepted their contention that such actions would conflict with federal law. Relying on the statement of purpose in the statutes, the court concluded that Congress' "carefully drawn balance between the purposes of warning the public of the hazards of cigarette smoking and protecting the interests of the national economy" would be upset by State Law Damages Actions based on noncompliance with warning, advertisement, and promotion obligations other than those prescribed in the [federal] Act." *Id.*, at 187. Accordingly, the court held:

> "the Act preempts those state law damages actions relating to smoking and health that challenge either the adequacy of the warning on cigarette packages or the propriety of a party's actions with respect to the advertising and promotion of cigarettes. Where the success of a state law damages claim necessarily depends on the assertion that a party bore the duty to provide a warning to consumers in addition to the warning congress has required on cigarette packages, such claims are pre-empted as conflicting with the act." *Ibid.* (footnote omitted).

The court did not, however, identify the specific claims asserted by petitioner that were pre-empted by the act.

This Court denied a petition for certiorari, 479 U.S. 1043 (1987), and the case returned to the district court for trial. Complying with the Court of Appeals mandate, the District Court held that the failure to warn, express warranty, fraudulent misrepresentation, and conspiracy to defraud claims were barred to the extent that they relied on respondents' advertising, promotional, and public relations activities after January 1, 1966 (the effective date of the 1965 act). * * * The court also ruled that while the design defect claims were not pre-empted by federal law, those claims were barred on other grounds. * * * Following extensive discovery and a four-month trial, the jury answered a series of special interrogatories and awarded $400,000 in damages to Rose Cipollone's husband. In brief, it rejected all of the fraudulent misrepresentation and conspiracy claims, but found that respondent Liggett had breached its duty to warn and its express warranties before 1966. It found, however, that Rose Cipollone had "voluntarily and unreasonably encountered a known danger by smoking cigarettes" and that 80% of the responsibility for her injuries was attributable to her. See 893 F.2D, at 554 (summarizing jury findings). For that reason, no damages were awarded to her estate. However, the jury awarded damages to compensate her husband for losses caused by respondents' breach of express warranty.

On cross-appeals from the final judgment, the Court of Appeals affirmed the District Court's pre-emption rulings but remanded for a new trial on several issues not relevant to our decision. We granted the petition for certiorari to consider the pre-emptive effect of the federal statutes.

II

Although physicians had suspected a link between smoking and illness for centuries, the first medical studies of that connection did not appear until the 1920s. See U.S. Dept. of Health and Human Services, Report of the Surgeon General, Reducing the Health Consequences of Smoking: 25 Years of Progress 5 (1989). The ensuing decades saw a wide range of epidemiologic and laboratory studies on the health hazards of smoking. Thus, by the time the Surgeon General convened an advisory committee to examine the issue in 1962, there were more than 7,000 publications examining the relationship between smoking and health. *Id.*, at 5–7.

In 1964, the advisory committee issued its report, which stated as its central conclusion: "Cigarette smoking is a health hazard of sufficient importance in the United States to warrant appropriate remedial action." U.S. Dept. of Health, Education, and Welfare, U.S. Surgeon General's Advisory Committee, Smoking and Health 33 (1964). Relying in part on that report, the Federal Trade Commission (FTC), which had long regulated unfair and deceptive advertising practices in the cigarette industry, promulgated a new trade regulation rule. That rule, which was to take effect January 1, 1965, established that it would be a violation of the Federal Trade Commission Act "to fail to disclose, clearly and prominently, in all advertising and on every pack, box, carton, or container [of cigarettes] that cigarette smoking is dangerous to health and may cause death from cancer and other diseases." 29 Fed.Reg. 8325 (1964). Several States also moved to regulate the advertising and labeling of cigarettes. See, *e.g.*, 1965 N.Y. Laws, CH.470; See also 111 Cong.Rec. 13900–13902 (1965) (Statement of Sen. Moss). Upon a congressional request, the FTC postponed enforcement of its new regulation for six months. In July 1965, Congress enacted the Federal Cigarette Labeling and Advertising Act. The 1965 act effectively adopted half of the FTC's Regulation: the Act mandated warnings on cigarette packages (§ 5(A)), but barred the requirement of such warnings in cigarette advertising (§ 5(B)).

Section 2 of the Act declares the statute's two purposes: (1) adequately informing the public that cigarette smoking may be hazardous to health, and (2) protecting the national economy from the burden imposed by diverse, nonuniform and confusing cigarette labeling and advertising regulations. In furtherance of the first purpose, § 4 of the Act made it unlawful to sell or distribute any cigarettes in the United States unless the package bore a conspicuous label stating: "CAUTION: CIGARETTE SMOKING MAY BE HAZARDOUS TO YOUR HEALTH." In furtherance of the second purpose, § 5, captioned "Pre-emption," provided in part:

"(a) No statement relating to smoking and health, other than the statement required by section 4 of this Act, shall be required on any cigarette package.

(b) No statement relating to smoking and health shall be required in the advertising of any cigarettes the packages of which are labeled in conformity with the provisions of this Act."

Although the Act took effect January 1, 1966, § 10 of the Act provided that its provisions affecting the regulation of advertising would terminate on July 1, 1969.

As that termination date approached, federal authorities prepared to issue further regulations on cigarette advertising. The FTC announced the reinstitution of its 1964 proceedings concerning a warning requirement for cigarette advertisements. [Citation.] The Federal Communications Commission (FCC) announced that it would "consider a proposed rule which would ban the broadcast of cigarette commercials by radio and television stations." [Citation.] State authorities also prepared to take actions regulating cigarette advertisements.

It was in this context that Congress enacted the Public Health Cigarette Smoking Act of 1969, which amended the 1965 Act in several ways. First, the 1969 Act strengthened the warning label, in part by requiring a statement that cigarette smoking "is dangerous" rather than that it "may be hazardous." Second, the 1969 Act banned cigarette advertising in "any medium of electronic communication subject to [FCC] jurisdiction." Third, and related, the 1969 Act modified the pre-emption provision by replacing the original § 5(b) with a provision that reads:

"(b) No requirement or prohibition based on smoking and health shall be imposed under State law with respect to the advertising or promotion of any cigarettes the packages of which are labeled in conformity with the provisions of this Act."

Although the Act also directed the FTC not to "take any action before July 1, 1971, with respect to its pending trade regulation rule proceeding relating to cigarette advertising," the narrowing of the pre-emption provision to prohibit only restrictions "imposed under State law" cleared the way for the FTC to extend the warning-label requirement to print advertisements for cigarettes. The FTC did so in 1972. * * *

III

Article VI of the Constitution provides that the laws of the United States "shall be the supreme Law of the Land; ... any Thing in the Constitution or Laws of any state to the Contrary notwithstanding." Art. VI, cl. 2. Thus, since our decision in *McCulloch v. Maryland*, 4 Wheat. 316, 427 (1819), it has been settled that state law that conflicts with federal law is "without effect." *Maryland v. Louisiana*, 451 U.S. 725, 746 (1981). Consideration of issues arising under the Supremacy

Clause start[s] with the assumption that the historic police powers of the States [are] not to be superseded by ... Federal Act unless that [is] the clear and manifest purpose of Congress." *Rice v. Santa Fe Elevator Corp.*, 331 U.S. 218, 230 (1947). Accordingly, " '[t]he purpose of Congress is the ultimate touchstone' " of pre-emption analysis. *Malone v. White Motor Corp.*, 435 U.S. 497, 504 (1978) (quoting *Retail Clerks v. Schermerhorn*, 375 U.S. 96, 103 (1963)).

Congress' intent may be "explicitly stated in the statute's language or implicitly contained in its structure and purpose." *Jones v. Rath Packing Co.*, 430 U.S. 519, 525 (1977). In the absence of an express congressional command, state law is pre-empted if that law actually conflicts with federal law, see *Pacific Gas & Elec. Co. v. Energy Resources Conservation and Development Comm'n*, 461 U.S. 190, 204 (1983), or if federal law so thoroughly occupies a legislative field " 'as to make reasonable the inference that Congress left no room for the States to supplement it.' " *Fidelity Federal Savings & Loan Assn. v. De la Cuesta*, 458 U.S. 141, 153 (1982) (quoting *Rice v. Santa Fe Elevator Corp.*, 331 U.S., at 230).

The Court of Appeals was not persuaded that the pre-emption provision in the 1969 Act encompassed state common law claims.[13] * * * It was also not persuaded that the labeling obligation imposed by both the 1965 and 1969 Acts revealed a congressional intent to exert exclusive federal control over every aspect of the relationship between cigarettes and health. *Id.*, at 186. Nevertheless, reading the statute as a whole in the light of the statement of purpose in § 2, and considering the potential regulatory effect of state common law actions on the federal interest in uniformity, the Court of Appeals concluded that Congress had impliedly pre-empted petitioner's claims challenging the adequacy of the warnings on labels or in advertising or the propriety of respondents' advertising and promotional activities. [Citation.]

In our opinion, the pre-emptive scope of the 1965 Act and the 1969 Act is governed entirely by the express language in § 5 of each Act. When Congress has considered the issue of pre-emption and has included in the enacted legislation a provision explicitly addressing that issue, and when that provision provides a "reliable indicium of congressional intent with respect to state authority," *Malone v. White Motor Corp.*, 435 U.S., at 505, "there is no need to infer congressional intent to pre-empt state laws from the substantive provisions" of the legislation. *California Federal Savings & Loan Assn. v. Guerra*, 479 U.S. 272, 282 (1987) (opinion of Marshall, J.). Such reasoning is a variant of the familiar principle of *expression unius est exclusio alterius*: Congress' enactment of a provision defining the pre-emptive reach of a statute

---

13. In its express pre-emption analysis, the court did not distinguish between the pre-emption provisions of the 1965 and 1969 Acts; it relied solely on the latter, apparently believing that the 1969 provision was at least as broad as the 1965 provision. * * *

implies that matters beyond that reach are not pre-empted. In this case, the other provisions of the 1965 and 1969 Acts offer no cause to look beyond § 5 of each Act. Therefore, we need only identify the domain expressly pre-empted by each of those sections. As the 1965 and 1969 provisions differ substantially, we consider each in turn.

IV

In the 1965 pre-emption provision regarding advertising (§ 5(b)), Congress spoke precisely and narrowly: No *statement* relating to smoking and health shall be required *in the advertising* of [properly labeled] cigarettes." Section 5(a) used the same phrase ("No *statement* relating to smoking and health") with regard to cigarette labeling. As § 5(a) made clear, that phrase referred to the sort of warning provided for in § 4, which set forth verbatim the warning Congress determined to be appropriate. Thus, on their face, these provisions merely prohibited state and federal rule-making bodies from mandating particular cautionary statements on cigarette labels (§ 5(a)) or in cigarette advertisements (§ 5(b)).

Beyond the precise words of these provisions, this reading is appropriate for several reasons. First, as discussed above, we must construe these provisions in light of the presumption against the pre-emption of state police power regulations. This presumption reinforces the appropriateness of a narrow reading of § 5. Second, the warning required in § 4 does not by its own effect foreclose additional obligations imposed under state law. That Congress requires a particular warning label does not automatically pre-empt a regulatory field. See *McDermott v. Wisconsin*, 228 U.S. 115, 131–132 (1913). Third, there is no general, inherent conflict between federal pre-emption of state warning requirements and the continued vitality of state common law damages actions. For example, in the Comprehensive Smokeless Tobacco Health Education Act of 1986, Congress expressly pre-empted State or local imposition of a "statement relating to the use of smokeless tobacco products and health" but, at the same time, preserved state law damages actions based on those products. See 15 U.S.C. § 4406. * * *

This reading comports with the 1965 Act's statement of purpose, which expressed an intent to avoid "diverse, nonuniform, and confusing labeling and advertising *regulations* with respect to any relationship between smoking and health." Read against the backdrop of regulatory activity undertaken by state legislatures and federal agencies in response to the Surgeon General's report, the term "regulation" most naturally refers to positive enactments by those bodies, not to common law damages actions.

The regulatory context of the 1965 Act also supports such a reading. As noted above, a warning requirement promulgated by the FTC and other requirements under consideration by the States were the catalyst for passage of the 1965 Act. These regulatory actions animated the passage of § 5, which reflected Congress' efforts to prevent "a multiplicity of State and local regulations pertaining to labeling of cigarette packages," * * *.

For these reasons, we conclude that § 5 of the 1965 Act only preempted state and federal rulemaking bodies from mandating particular cautionary statements and did not pre-empt state law damages actions.[17]

V

Compared to its predecessor in the 1965 Act, the plain language of the pre-emption provision in the 1969 Act is much broader. First, the later Act bars not simply "statements" but rather "requirement[s] or prohibitions . . . imposed under State law." Second, the later Act reaches beyond statements "in the advertising" to obligations "with respect to the advertising or promotion" of cigarettes.

Notwithstanding these substantial differences in language, both petitioner and respondents contend that the 1969 Act did not materially alter the pre-emptive scope of federal law. Their primary support for this contention is a sentence in a Committee Report which states that the 1969 amendment "clarified" the 1965 version of § 5(b). S. Rep. No. 91–566, p. 12 (1969). We reject the parties' reading as incompatible with the language and origins of the amendments. As we noted in another context, "[i]nferences from legislative history cannot rest on so slender a reed. Moreover, the views of a subsequent Congress form a hazardous basis for inferring the intent of an earlier one." *United States v. Price*, 361 U.S. 304, 313 (1960). The 1969 Act worked substantial changes in the law: rewriting the label warning, banning broadcast advertising, and allowing the FTC to regulate print advertising. In the context of such revisions and in light of the substantial changes in wording, we cannot accept the parties' claim that the 1969 Act did not alter the reach of § 5(b).

Petitioner next contends that § 5(b), however broadened by the 1969 Act, does not pre-empt *common law* actions. He offers two theories for limiting the reach of the amended § 5(b). First, he argues that common law damages actions do not impose "requirement[s] or prohibitions" and that Congress intended only to trump "state statutes, injunctions, or executive pronouncements." We disagree; such an analysis is at odds both with the plain words of the 1969 Act and with the general understanding of common law damages actions. The phrase "[n]o requirement or prohibition" sweeps broadly and suggests no distinction between positive enactments and common law; to the

---

17. This interpretation of the 1965 Act appears to be consistent with respondents' contemporaneous understanding of the Act. Although respondents have participated in a great deal of litigation relating to cigarette use beginning in the 1950's, it appears that this case is the first in which they have raised § 5 as a pre-emption defense.

contrary, those words easily encompass obligations that take the form of common law rules. As we noted in another context, "[state] regulation can be as effectively exerted through an award of damages as through some form of preventive relief. The obligation to pay compensation can be, indeed is designed to be, a potent method of governing conduct and controlling policy." *San Diego Building Trades Council v. Garmon*, 359 U.S. 236, 247 (1959).

Although portions of the legislative history of the 1969 Act suggest that Congress was primarily concerned with positive enactments by States and localities, see S. Rep. No. 91–566, p. 12, the language of the Act plainly reaches beyond such enactments. "We must give effect to this plain language unless there is good reason to believe Congress intended the language to have some more restrictive meaning." *Shaw v. Delta Air Lines, Inc.*, 463 U.S. 85, 97 (1983). In this case there is no "good reason to believe" that Congress meant less than what it said; indeed, in light of the narrowness of the 1965 Act, there is "good reason to believe" that Congress meant precisely what it said in amending that Act.

Moreover, common law damages actions of the sort raised by petitioner are premised on the existence of a legal duty and it is difficult to say that such actions do not impose "requirements or prohibitions." See W. Prosser, Law of Torts 4 (4th ed. 1971); Black's Law Dictionary 1489 (6th ed. 1990) (defining "tort" as "always [involving] a violation of some duty owing to plaintiff"). It is in this way that the 1969 version of § 5(b) differs from its predecessor: Whereas the common law would not normally require a vendor to use any specific *statement* on its packages or in its advertisements, it is the essence of the common law to enforce duties that are either affirmative *requirements* or negative *prohibitions*. We therefore reject petitioner's argument that the phrase "requirement or prohibition" limits the 1969 Act's pre-emptive scope to positive enactments by legislatures and agencies.

* * *

That the pre-emptive scope of § 5(b) cannot be limited to positive enactments does not mean that that section pre-empts all common law claims. For example, as respondents concede, § 5(b) does not generally pre-empt "state-law obligations to avoid marketing cigarettes with manufacturing defects or to use a demonstrably safer alternative design for cigarettes." For purposes of § 5(b), the common law is not of a piece.

Nor does the statute indicate that any familiar subdivision of common law claims is or is not pre-empted. We therefore cannot follow petitioner's passing suggestion that § 5(b) pre-empts liability for omissions but not for acts, or that § 5(b) pre-empts liability for unintentional torts but not for intentional torts. Instead we must fairly but—in light of the strong presumption against pre-emption—narrowly construe the precise language of § 5(b) and we must look to each of petitioner's common law claims to determine whether it is in fact preempted.[22] The central inquiry in each case is straightforward: we ask whether the legal duty that is the predicate of the common law damages action constitutes a "requirement or prohibition based on smoking and health ... imposed under State law with respect to ... advertising or promotion," giving that clause a fair but narrow reading. As discussed below, each phrase within that clause limits the universe of common law claims pre-empted by the statute.

We consider each category of damages actions in turn. In doing so, we express no opinion on whether these actions are viable claims as a matter of state law; we assume *arguendo* that they are.

Failure to Warn

To establish liability for a failure to warn, petitioner must show that "a warning is necessary to make a product ... reasonably safe, suitable and fit for its intended use," that respondents failed to provide such a warning, and that that failure was a proximate cause of petitioner's injury. Tr. 12738. In this case, petitioner offered two closely related theories concerning the failure to warn: first, that respondents "were negligent in the manner [that] they tested, researched, sold, promoted, and advertised" their cigarettes; and second, that respondents failed to provide "adequate warnings of the health consequences of cigarette smoking." App. 85–86.

Petitioner's claims are pre-empted to the extent that they rely on a state law "requirement or prohibition ... with respect to ... advertising or promotion." Thus, insofar as claims under either failure to warn theory require a showing that respondents' post–1969 advertising or promotions should have included additional, or more clearly stated, warnings, those claims are pre-empted. The Act does not, however, pre-empt petitioner's claims that rely solely on respondents' testing or research practices or other actions unrelated to advertising or promotion.

Breach of Express Warranty

Petitioner's claim for breach of an express warranty arises under N.J. Stat. Ann. § 12A:2– 313(1)(a) (West 1991), which provides:

22. Petitioner makes much of the fact that Congress did not expressly include common law within § 5's pre-emptive reach, as it has in other statutes. See, *e.g.*, 29 U.S.C. § 1144(c)(1); 12 U.S.C. § 1715z–17(d). Respondents make much of the fact that Congress did not include a savings clause preserving common law claims, again, as it has in other statutes. See, *e.g.*, 17 U.S.C. § 301. Under our analysis of § 5, these omissions make perfect sense: Congress was neither pre-empting nor saving common law as a whole—it was simply pre-empting particular common law claims, while saving others.

the alleged warranty is valid and enforceable) because although the breach of warranty claim is made "with respect to advertising" it does not rest on a duty imposed under state law. Accordingly, to the extent that petitioner has a viable claim for breach of express warranties made by respondents, that claim is not pre-empted by the 1969 Act.

Fraudulent Misrepresentation

Petitioner alleges two theories of fraudulent misrepresentation. First, petitioner alleges that respondents, through their advertising, neutralized the effect of federally mandated warning labels. Such a claim is predicated on a state-law prohibition against statements in advertising and promotional materials that tend to minimize the health hazards associated with smoking. Such a *prohibition*, however, is merely the converse of a state law *requirement* that warnings be included in advertising and promotional materials. Section 5(b) of the 1969 Act pre-empts both requirements and prohibitions; it therefore supersedes petitioner's first fraudulent misrepresentation theory.

* * *

Petitioner's second theory, as construed by the District Court, alleges intentional fraud and misrepresentation both by "false representation of a material fact [and by] conceal[ment of] a material fact." Tr. 12727. The predicate of this claim is a state law duty not to make false statements of material fact or to conceal such facts. Our preemption analysis requires us to determine whether such a duty is the sort of requirement or prohibition proscribed by § 5(b).

Section 5(b) pre-empts only the imposition of state law obligations "with respect to the advertising or promotion" of cigarettes. Petitioner's claims that respondents concealed material facts are therefore not pre-empted insofar as those claims rely on a state law duty to disclose such facts through channels of communication other than advertising or promotion. Thus, for example, if state law obliged respondents to disclose material facts about smoking and health to an administrative agency, § 5(b) would not pre-empt a state law claim based on a failure to fulfill that obligation.

Moreover, petitioner's fraudulent misrepresentation claims that do arise with respect to advertising and promotions (most notably claims based on allegedly false statements of material fact made in advertisements) are not pre-empted by § 5(b). Such claims are not predicated on a duty "based on smoking and health" but rather on a more general obligation—the duty not to deceive. This understanding of fraud by intentional misstatement is appropriate for several reasons. First, in the 1969 Act, Congress offered no sign that it wished to insulate cigarette manufacturers from longstanding rules governing fraud. To the contrary, both the 1965 and the 1969 Acts explicitly reserved the FTC's authority to identify and punish deceptive advertising practices—

an authority that the FTC had long exercised and continues to exercise. * * * This indicates that Congress intended the phrase "relating to smoking and health" (which was essentially unchanged by the 1969 Act) to be construed narrowly, so as not to proscribe the regulation of deceptive advertising.

Moreover, this reading of "based on smoking and health" is wholly consistent with the purposes of the 1969 Act. State law prohibitions on false statements of material fact do not create "diverse, nonuniform, and confusing" standards. Unlike state law obligations concerning the warning necessary to render a product "reasonably safe," state law proscriptions on intentional fraud rely only on a single, uniform standard: falsity. Thus, we conclude that the phrase "based on smoking and health" fairly but narrowly construed does not encompass the more general duty not to make fraudulent statements. Accordingly, petitioner's claim based on allegedly fraudulent statements made in respondents' advertisements are not pre-empted by § 5(b) of the 1969 Act.[27]

Conspiracy to Misrepresent or Conceal Material Facts

Petitioner's final claim alleges a conspiracy among respondents to misrepresent or conceal material facts concerning the health hazards of smoking. The predicate duty underlying this claim is a duty not to conspire to commit fraud. For the reasons stated in our analysis of petitioner's intentional fraud claim, this duty is not pre-empted by § 5(b) for it is not a prohibition "based on smoking and health" as that phrase is properly construed. Accordingly, we conclude that the 1969 Act does not pre-empt petitioner's conspiracy claim.

VI

To summarize our holding: The 1965 Act did not pre-empt state law damages actions; the 1969 Act pre-empts petitioner's claims based on a failure to warn and the neutralization of federally mandated warnings to the extent that those claims rely on omissions or inclusions in respondents' advertising or promotions; the 1969 Act does not pre-

---

27. Both JUSTICE BLACKMUN and JUSTICE SCALIA challenge the level of generality employed in our analysis. JUSTICE BLACKMUN contends that, as a matter of consistency, we should construe failure-to-warn claims *not* as based on smoking and health, but rather as based on the broader duty "to inform consumers of known risks." *Post*, at 2631. JUSTICE SCALIA contends that, again as a matter of consistency, we should construe fraudulent misrepresentation claims not as based on a general duty not to deceive but rather as "based on smoking and health." Admittedly, each of these positions has some conceptual attraction. However, our ambition here is not theoretical elegance, but rather a fair understanding of congressional purpose.

To analyze failure to warn claims at the highest level of generality (as JUSTICE BLACKMUN would have us do) would render the 1969 amendments almost meaningless and would pay too little respect to Congress' substantial reworking of the Act. On the other hand, to analyze fraud claims at the lowest level of generality (as JUSTICE SCALIA would have us do) would conflict both with the background presumption against preemption and with legislative history that plainly expresses an intent to preserve the "police regulations" of the States. [Citation.]

empt petitioner's claims based on express warranty, intentional fraud and misrepresentation, or conspiracy.

The judgment of the Court of Appeals is accordingly reversed in part and affirmed in part, and the case is remanded for further proceedings consistent with this opinion.

It is so ordered.

JUSTICE BLACKMUN, with whom JUSTICE KENNEDY and JUSTICE SOUTER join, concurring in part, concurring in the judgment in part, and dissenting in part.

I

* * * In my view, *neither* version of the federal legislation at issue here provides the kind of unambiguous evidence of congressional intent necessary to displace state common-law damages claims. I therefore join parts I, II, III, and IV of the Court's opinion, but dissent from parts V and VI.

A

I agree with the Court's exposition, in part III of its opinion, of the underlying principles of pre-emption law, and in particular with its recognition that the pre-emptive scope of the Federal Cigarette Labeling and Advertising Act (the 1965 Act) and the Public Health Cigarette Smoking Act of 1969 (the 1969 Act) is "governed entirely by the express language" of the statutes' pre-emption provisions. * * * Where, as here, Congress has included in legislation a specific provision addressing—and indeed, entitled—pre-emption, the Court's task is one of statutory interpretation—only to "identify the domain expressly pre-empted" by the provision. *Ante*, at 2618. * * *

B

I also agree with the Court's application of the foregoing principles in part IV of its opinion, where it concludes that none of petitioner's common-law damages claims are pre-empted by the 1965 Act. * * *

II

My agreement with the Court ceases at this point. Given the Court's proper analytical focus on the scope of the express pre-emption provisions at issue here and its acknowledgement that the 1965 Act does not pre-empt state common-law damages claims, I find the Court's conclusion that the 1969 Act pre-empts at least some common-law damages claims little short of baffling. In my view, the modified language of § 5(b), 15 U.S.C. § 1334(b) ("No requirement or prohibition based on smoking and health shall be imposed under State law with respect to the advertising or promotion of any cigarettes the packages of which are labeled in conformity with the provisions of this Act"), no more "clearly" or "manifestly" exhibits an intent to pre-empt state common-law damages actions than did the language of its predecessor in the 1965 Act. Nonetheless, the Court reaches a different conclusion, and its reasoning warrants scrutiny.

A

The Court premises its pre-emption ruling on what it terms the "substantial changes" wrought by Congress in § 5(b), * * * notably, the rewording of the provision to pre-empt any "requirement or prohibition" (as opposed merely to any "statement") "imposed under State law." As an initial matter, I do not disagree with the Court that the phrase "State law," in an appropriate case, can encompass the common law as well as positive enactments such as statutes and regulations. * * * I do disagree, however, with the Court's conclusion that "State law" as used in § 5(b) represents such an all-inclusive reference. Congress' intention in selecting that phrase cannot be understood without considering the narrow range of actions—any "requirement or prohibition"—that Congress specifically described in § 5(b) as "imposed under" state law. * * *

Although the Court flatly states that the phrase "no requirement or prohibition" "sweeps broadly" and "easily encompasses obligations that take the form of common law rules," * * * those words are in reality far from unambiguous and cannot be said clearly to evidence a congressional mandate to pre-empt state common-law damages actions. * * *

More important, the question whether common-law damages actions exert a regulatory effect on manufacturers analogous to that of positive enactments—an assumption crucial to the Court's conclusion that the phrase "requirement or prohibition" encompasses common-law actions—is significantly more complicated than the Court's brief quotation from *San Diego Building Trades Council v. Garmon*, 359 U.S. 236, 247 (1959) * * * would suggest.

The effect of tort law on a manufacturer's behavior is necessarily indirect. Although an award of damages by its very nature attaches additional consequences to the manufacturer's continued unlawful conduct, no particular course of action (e.g., the adoption of a new warning label) is required. A manufacturer found liable on, for example, a failure-to-warn claim may respond in a number of ways. It may decide to accept damages awards as a cost of doing business and not alter its behavior in any way. * * * The level of choice that a defendant retains in shaping its own behavior distinguishes the indirect regulatory effect of the common law from positive enactments such as statutes and administrative regulations. * * * Not only has the Court previously distinguished *Garmon*, but it has declined on several recent occasions to find the regulatory effects of state tort law direct or substantial enough to warrant pre-emption.

In *Goodyear Atomic Corp. v. Miller*, for example, the Court distinguished, for purposes of pre-emption analysis, "direct state regulation" of safety matters from "the incidental regulatory effects" of damages awarded pursuant to a state workers' compensation law. 486 U.S., at 185. Relying in part on its earlier decision in *Silkwood v. Kerr–McGee Corp.*, 464 U.S. 238, 256 (1984), the Court stated that "Congress may reasonably determine that incidental regulatory pressure is acceptable, whereas direct regulatory authority is not." 486 U.S., at 186. Even more recently, the Court declined in *English v. General Electric Co.*, 496 U.S., at 86, to find state common-law damages claims for emotional distress pre-empted by federal nuclear energy law. The Court concluded that, although awards to former employees for emotional distress would attach "additional consequences" to retaliatory employer conduct and could lead employers to alter the underlying conditions about which employees were complaining, *ibid.*, such an effect would be "neither direct nor substantial enough" to warrant pre-emption. *Id.*, at 85.

In light of the recognized distinction in this Court's jurisprudence between direct state regulation and the indirect regulatory effects of common-law damages actions, it cannot be said that damages claims are clearly or unambiguously "requirements" or "prohibitions" imposed under state law. The plain language of the 1969 Act's modified pre-emption provision simply cannot bear the broad interpretation the Court would impart to it.

B

Not only does the text of the revised § 5(b) fail clearly or manifestly to require pre-emption of state common-law damages actions, but there is no suggestion in the legislative history that Congress intended to expand the scope of the pre-emption provision when it amended the statute in 1969. The Court acknowledges the evidence that Congress itself perceived the changes in § 5(b) to be a mere "clarification" of the existing narrow pre-emption provision, *ante*, at 2619 (quoting S. Rep. No. 91–566, p. 12 (1969) (hereinafter S. Rep.)), but it dismisses these statements of legislative intent as the " 'views of a subsequent Congress.' " * * *, quoting *United States v. Price*, 361 U.S. 304, 313 (1960). The Court is wrong not only as a factual matter—for the statements of the Congress that amended § 5(b) are contemporaneous, not "subsequent," to enactment of the revised pre-emption provision—but as a legal matter, as well. This Court accords "great weight" to an amending Congress' interpretation of the underlying statute. See, *e.g., Red Lion Broadcasting Co. v. FCC*, 395 U.S. 367, 380–381 & n. 8 (1969).

Viewing the revisions to § 5(b) as generally nonsubstantive in nature makes sense. By replacing the word "statement" with the slightly broader term, "requirement," and adding the word "prohibition" to ensure that a State could not do through negative mandate (*e.g.*, banning all cigarette advertising) that which it already was forbidden to do through positive mandate (*e.g.*, mandating particular cautionary statements), Congress sought to "clarify" the existing precautions against confusing and nonuniform state laws and regulations. S. Rep., p. 12.

* * *

Finally, there is absolutely no suggestion in the legislative history that Congress intended to leave plaintiffs who were injured as a result of cigarette manufacturers' unlawful conduct without any alternative remedies; yet that is the regrettable effect of the Court's ruling today that many state common-law damages claims are pre-empted. The Court in the past has hesitated to find pre-emption where federal law provides no comparable remedy. See Rabin, A Sociolegal History of the Tobacco Tort Litigation, 44 Stan. L. Rev. 853, 869 (1992) (noting the "rather strong tradition of federal deference to competing state interests in compensating injury victims"). * * *

* * *

IV

By finding federal pre-emption of certain state common-law damages claims, the Court today eliminates a critical component of the States' traditional ability to protect the health and safety of their citizens. Yet such a radical readjustment of federal-state relations is warranted under this Court's precedents only if there is clear evidence that Congress intended that result. Because I believe that neither version of the Federal Cigarette Labeling and Advertising Act evidences such a clear congressional intent to pre-empt state common-law damages actions, I respectfully dissent from parts V and VI of the Court's opinion.

JUSTICE SCALIA, with whom JUSTICE THOMAS joins, concurring in the judgment in part and dissenting in part.

Today's decision announces what, on its face, is an extraordinary and unprecedented principle of federal statutory construction: that express pre-emption provisions must be construed narrowly, "in light of the presumption against the pre-emption of state police power regulations." * * * In my view, there is no merit to this newly crafted doctrine of narrow construction. Under the Supremacy Clause, U.S. Const., Art. VI, cl. 2, our job is to interpret Congress's decrees of pre-emption neither narrowly nor broadly, but in accordance with their apparent meaning. If we did that job in the present case, we would find, under the 1965 Act, pre-emption of the petitioner's failure-to-warn claims; and under the 1969 Act, we would find pre-emption of the petitioner's claims complete.

"Any affirmation of fact or promise made by the seller to the buyer which relates to the goods and becomes part of the basis of the bargain creates an express warranty that the goods shall conform to the affirmation or promise."

Petitioner's evidence of an express warranty consists largely of statements made in respondents' advertising. See 893 F.2d, at 574, 576; 683 F.Supp. 1487, 1497 (NJ 1988). Applying the Court of Appeals' ruling that Congress pre-empted "damage[s] actions ... that challenge ... the propriety of a party's actions with respect to the advertising and promotion of cigarettes," 789 F.2d, at 187, the District Court ruled that this claim "inevitably brings into question [respondents'] advertising and promotional activities, and is therefore pre-empted" after 1965. 649 F.Supp., at 675. As demonstrated above, however, the 1969 Act does not sweep so broadly: the appropriate inquiry is not whether a claim challenges the "propriety" of advertising and promotion, but whether the claim would require the imposition under state law of a requirement or prohibition based on smoking and health with respect to advertising or promotion.

A manufacturer's liability for breach of an express warranty derives from, and is measured by, the terms of that warranty. Accordingly, the "requirements" imposed by a express warranty claim are not "imposed under State law," but rather imposed *by the warrantor*. If, for example, a manufacturer expressly promised to pay a smoker's medical bills if she contracted emphysema, the duty to honor that promise could not fairly be said to be "imposed under state law," but rather is best understood as undertaken by the manufacturer itself. While the general duty not to breach warranties arises under state law, the particular "requirement ... based on smoking and health ... with respect to the advertising or promotion [of] cigarettes" in an express warranty claim arises from the manufacturer's statements in its advertisements. In short, a common law remedy for a contractual commitment voluntarily undertaken should not be regarded as a "requirement ... *imposed under State law*" within the meaning of § 5(b).[24]

That the terms of the warranty may have been set forth in advertisements rather than in separate documents is irrelevant to the pre-emption issue (though possibly not to the state law issue of whether

---

24. Justice Scalia contends that because the general duty to honor express warranties arises under state law, every express warranty obligation is a "requirement ... imposed under State law," and that, therefore, the Act pre-empts petitioner's express warranty claim. Justice Scalia might be correct if the Act pre-empted *"liability"* imposed under state law (as he suggests, post, at 8); but instead the Act expressly pre-empts only a *"requirement or prohibition"* imposed under state law. That a "contract has no legal force apart from the [state] law that acknowledges its binding character," *Norfolk & Western Railway Co. v. American Train Dispatchers Assn.*, 499 U.S. __, __ (1991), does not mean that every contractual provision is "imposed under State law." To the contrary, common understanding dictates that a contractual requirement, although only enforceable under state law, is not "imposed" by the state, but rather is "imposed" by the contracting party upon itself.

I

The Court's threshold description of the law of pre-emption is accurate enough: * * *

The Court goes beyond these traditional principles, however, to announce two new ones. First, it says that express pre-emption provisions must be given the narrowest possible construction. This is in its view the consequence of our oft-repeated assumption that, absent convincing evidence of statutory intent to pre-empt, " 'the historic police powers of the States [are] not to be superseded,' " see *ante*, at 2617. But it seems to me that assumption dissolves once there is conclusive evidence of intent to pre-empt in the express words of the statute itself, and the only remaining question is what the scope of that pre-emption is meant to be. Thereupon, I think, our responsibility is to apply to the text ordinary principles of statutory construction.

* * *

The results seem odder still when one takes into account the second new rule that the Court announces: "When Congress has considered the issue of pre-emption and has included in the enacted legislation a provision explicitly addressing that issue, ... we need only identify the domain expressly pre-empted by [that provision]." *Ante*, at 2618. Once there is an express pre-emption provision, in other words, all doctrines of implied pre-emption are eliminated. This proposition may be correct insofar as implied "field" pre-emption is concerned: The existence of an express pre-emption provision tends to contradict any inference that Congress intended to occupy a field broader than the statute's express language defines. However, with regard to implied "conflict" pre-emption—i.e., where state regulation actually conflicts with federal law, or where state regulation "stands as an obstacle to the accomplishment and execution" of Congress's purposes, *Hines, supra*, 312 U.S. at 67—the Court's second new rule works mischief. If taken seriously, it would mean, for example, that if a federal consumer protection law provided that no state agency or court shall assert jurisdiction under state law over any workplace safety issue with respect to which a federal standard is in effect, then a state agency operating under a law dealing with a subject other than workplace safety (*e.g.*, consumer protection) could impose requirements entirely contrary to federal law—forbidding, for example, the use of certain safety equipment that federal law requires. To my knowledge, we have never expressed such a rule before, and our prior cases are inconsistent with it, see, *e.g., Jones v. Rath Packing Co.*, 430 U.S. 519, 540–543 (1977). When this second novelty is combined with the first, the result is extraordinary: The statute that says *anything* about pre-emption must say *everything*; and it must do so with great exactitude, as any ambiguity concerning its scope will be read in favor of preserving state power. If this is to be the law, surely only the most sporting of congresses will dare to say anything about pre-emption.

The proper rule of construction for express pre-emption provisions is, it seems to me, the one that is customary for statutory provisions in general: Their language should be given its ordinary meaning. *FMC Corp. v. Holliday, supra*, 498 U.S. at ___, 111 S.Ct. at 407; *Shaw v. Delta Air Lines*, 463 U.S., at 97. When this suggests that the preemption provision was intended to sweep broadly, our construction must sweep broadly as well. * * * And when it bespeaks a narrow scope of pre-emption, so must our judgment. See, *e.g., Fort Halifax Packing Co., Inc. v. Coyne*, 482 U.S. 1, 7–8 (1987). Applying its niggardly rule of construction, the Court finds (not surprisingly) that none of petitioner's claims—common-law failure to warn, breach of express warranty, and intentional fraud and misrepresentation—is pre-empted under § 5(b) of the 1965 Act. And save for the failure-to-warn claims, the Court reaches the same result under § 5(b) of the 1969 Act. I think most of that is error. Applying ordinary principles of statutory construction, I believe petitioner's failure-to-warn claims are pre-empted by the 1965 Act, and all his common-law claims by the 1969 Act.

II

With much of what the plurality says in Part V of its opinion I agree—that "the language of the [1969] Act plainly reaches beyond [positive] enactments," * * * that the general tort-law duties petitioner invokes against the cigarette companies can, as a general matter, impose "requirements or prohibitions" within the meaning of § 5(b) of the 1969 Act, * * * and that the phrase "State law" as used in that provision embraces state common law, * * * I take issue with the plurality, however, on its application of these general principles to the present case. Its finding that they produce only partial pre-emption of petitioner's common-law claims rests upon three misperceptions that I shall discuss in turn, under headings indicating the erroneously permitted claims to which they apply.

A

Pre–1969 Failure–to–Warn Claims

According to the Court, § 5(b) of the 1965 Act "is best read as having superseded only positive enactments by legislatures or administrative agencies that mandate *particular* warning labels," *ante*, at 2618 (emphasis added). In essence, the Court reads § 5(b)'s critical language "No *statement* relating to smoking and health shall be required" to mean "No *particular statement* relating to smoking and health shall be required." The Court reasons that because common-law duties do not require cigarette manufacturers to include any *particular* statement in their advertising, but only *some* statement warning of health risks, those duties survive the 1965 Act. I see no basis for this element of "particularity." To require a warning about cigarette health risks is to require a "statement relating to smoking and health." If the "presumption against ... pre-emption," * * * requires us to import limiting language into the 1965 Act, I do not see why it does not require us to import similarly limiting language into the 1969 Act—so that a "requirement ... based on smoking and health ... with respect to advertising" means only a *specific* requirement, and not just general, noncigarette-specific duties imposed by tort law. The divergent treatment of the 1965 Act cannot be justified by the Act's statement of purposes, which, as the Court notes, expresses concern with "diverse, nonuniform, and confusing cigarette labeling and advertising *regulations*," 15 U.S.C. § 1331(2) (emphasis added). That statement of purposes was left untouched by Congress in 1969, and thus should be as restrictive of the scope of the later § 5(b) as the Court believes it is of the scope of the earlier one.

To the extent petitioner's claims are premised specifically on respondents' failure (during the period in which the 1965 Act was in force) to include in their *advertising* any statement relating to smoking and health, I would find those claims, no less than the similar post–1969 claims, pre-empted. In addition, for reasons I shall later explain, see *infra*, Part III, I would find pre-emption even of those claims based on respondents' failure to make health-related statements to consumers *outside* their advertising. However, since § 5(b) of the 1965 Act enjoins only those laws that *require* "statements" in cigarette advertising, those of petitioner's claims that, if accepted, would penalize statements *voluntarily* made by the cigarette companies must be deemed to survive. As these would appear to include petitioner's breach-of-express-warranty and intentional fraud and misrepresentation claims, I concur in the Court's judgment in this respect.

B

Post–1969 Breach–of–Express–Warranty Claims

In the context of this case, petitioner's breach-of-express-warranty claim necessarily embodies an assertion that respondents' advertising and promotional materials made statements to the effect that cigarette smoking is not unhealthy. Making such statements civilly actionable certainly constitutes an advertising "requirement or prohibition ... based on smoking and health." The plurality appears to accept this, but finds that liability for breach of express warranty is not "imposed under State law" within the meaning of § 5(b) of the 1969 Act. "Rather," it says, the duty "is best understood as undertaken by the manufacturer itself." * * * I cannot agree.

When liability attaches to a particular promise or representation, it attaches by law. For the making of a voluntary promise or representation, no less than for the commission of an intentional tort, it is the background law against which the act occurs, and not the act itself, that supplies the element of legal obligation. * * * Of course, New Jersey's law of express warranty attaches legal consequences to the cigarette manufacturer's voluntary conduct in making the warranty, and in that narrow sense, I suppose, the warranty obligation can be said to be "undertaken by the manufacturer." But on that logic it could also be said that the duty to warn about the dangers of cigarettes is undertaken voluntarily by manufacturers when they choose to sell in New Jersey; or, more generally, that *any* legal duty imposed on volitional behavior is not one imposed by law.

* * *

C

Post–1969 Fraud and Misrepresentation Claims

According to the plurality, at least one of petitioner's intentional fraud and misrepresentation claims survives § 5(b) of the 1969 Act because the common-law duty underlying that claim is not "based on smoking and health" within the meaning of the Act. * * * If I understand the plurality's reasoning, it proceeds from the implicit assumption that only duties deriving from laws that are specifically directed to "smoking and health," or that are uniquely crafted to address the relationship between cigarette companies and their putative victims, fall within § 5(b) of the Act, as amended. Given that New Jersey's tort-law "duty not to deceive," * * * is a general one, applicable to all commercial actors and all kinds of commerce, it follows from this assumption that § 5(b) does not pre-empt claims based on breaches of that duty.

This analysis is suspect, to begin with, because the plurality is unwilling to apply it consistently. As JUSTICE BLACKMUN cogently explains, * * * if New Jersey's common-law duty to avoid false statements of material fact—as applied to the cigarette companies' behavior—is not "based on smoking and health," the same must be said of New Jersey's common-law duty to warn about a product's dangers. *Each* duty transcends the relationship between the cigarette companies and cigarette smokers; *neither* duty was specifically crafted with an eye toward "smoking and health." None of the arguments the plurality advances to support its distinction between the two is persuasive. That Congress specifically preserved, in both the 1965 and 1969 Acts, the Federal Trade Commission's authority to police deceptive advertising practices, see § 5(c) of the 1965 Act; § 7(b) of the 1969 Act; * * * does not suggest that Congress intended comparable state authority to survive § 5(b). In fact, at least in the 1965 Act (which generally excluded federal as well as state regulation), the exemption suggested that § 5(b) was broad enough to reach laws governing fraud and misrepresentation. And it is not true that the States' laws governing fraud and misrepresentation in advertising impose identical legal standards, whereas their laws "concerning the warning necessary to render a product reasonably safe'" are quite diverse, * * *. The question whether an ad featuring a glamorous, youthful smoker with pearly-white teeth is "misrepresentative" would almost certainly be answered differently from State to State. * * *

Once one is forced to select a *consistent* methodology for evaluating whether a given legal duty is "based on smoking and health," it becomes obvious that the methodology must focus not upon the ultimate source of the duty (*e.g.*, the common law) but upon its proximate application. Use of the "ultimate source" approach (*i.e.*, a legal duty is not "based on smoking and health" unless the law from which it derives is directed only to smoking and health) would gut the statute, inviting the very "diverse, nonuniform, and confusing cigarette ... advertising regulations" Congress sought to avoid. 15 U.S.C. § 1331(2). And the problem is not simply the common law: Requirements could be imposed by state executive agencies as well, so long as they were operating under a *general* statute authorizing their supervision of "commercial advertising" or "unfair trade practices." New Jersey and many other States have such statutes already on the books. * * *

I would apply to all petitioner's claims what I have called a "proximate application" methodology for determining whether they invoke duties "based on smoking and health"—I would ask, that is, whether, whatever the source of the duty, it imposes an obligation in this case because of the effect of smoking upon health. On that basis, I would find petitioner's failure-to-warn and misrepresentation claims both pre-empted.

III

Finally, there is an additional flaw in the plurality's opinion, a systemic one that infects even its otherwise correct disposition of petitioner's post–1969 failure-to-warn claims. The opinion states that, since § 5(b) proscribes only "requirement[s] or prohibition[s] ... *'with respect to ... advertising or promotion,'*" state-law claims premised on the failure to warn consumers "through channels of communication other than advertising or promotion" are not covered. * * * This preserves not only the (somewhat fanciful) claims based on duties having no relation to the advertising and promotion (one could imagine a law requiring manufacturers to disclose the health hazards of their products to a state public-health agency), but also claims based on duties that can be complied with by taking action *either* within the advertising and promotional realm *or elsewhere.* Thus, if—as appears to be the case in New Jersey—a State's common law requires manufacturers to advise consumers of their products' dangers, but the law is indifferent as to *how* that requirement is met (*i.e.*, through "advertising or promotion" or otherwise), the plurality would apparently be unprepared to find pre-emption as long as the jury were instructed not to zero in on deficiencies in the manufacturers' advertising or promotion.

I think that is inconsistent with the law of pre-emption. Advertising and promotion are the normal means by which a manufacturer communicates required product warnings to prospective customers, and by far the most economical means. It is implausible that Congress meant to save cigarette companies from being compelled to convey such data to consumers through that means, only to allow them to be compelled to do so through means more onerous still. As a practical matter, such a "tell-the-consumers-any-way-you-wish" law compels manufacturers to relinquish the advertising and promotion immunity accorded them by the Act. The test for pre-emption in this setting should be one of practical compulsion, i.e., whether the law practically compels the manufacturers to engage in behavior that Congress has barred the States from prescribing directly. * * * Though the hypothetical law requiring disclosure to a state regulatory agency would seem to survive this test, I would have no difficulty finding that test met with respect to state laws that require the cigarette companies to meet general standards of "fair warning" regarding smoking and health.

Like JUSTICE BLACKMUN, "I can only speculate as to the difficulty lower courts will encounter in attempting to implement [today's] decision." *Ante*, at 2631 (opinion concurring in part and dissenting in part). Must express pre-emption provisions really be given their narrowest reasonable construction (as the Court says in Part III), or need they not (as the plurality does in Part V)? Are courts to ignore all doctrines of implied pre-emption whenever the statute at issue contains an express pre-emption provision, as the Court says today, or are they to continue to apply them, as we have in the past? For pre-emption purposes, does "state law" include legal duties imposed on voluntary acts (as we held last Term in Norfolk & Western R. Co.), or does it not (as the plurality says today)? These and other questions raised by today's decision will fill the law-books for years to come. A disposition that raises more questions than it answers does not serve the country well.

NOTE

1. The preemption language in the 1965 Act was:

(a) No statement relating to smoking and health, other than the statement required ... by this Act shall be required on any cigarette package.

(b) No statement relating to smoking and health shall be required in the advertising of any cigarettes the packages of which are labeled in conformity with ... this Act.

The 1969 amendments resulted in the following language:

(a) No statement relating to smoking and health, other than the statement required ... by this

Act shall be required on any cigarette package.

(b) No requirement or prohibition based on smoking and health shall be imposed under State law with respect to the advertising or promotion of any cigarettes the packages of which are labeled in conformity with the provisions of this Act.

2. What was the state of preemption of cigarette smoking cases before the Supreme Court's opinion in *Cipollone*? What tort, product liability, and warranty claims remain available for cigarette victims after the Supreme Court's decision?

3. If you were a member of Congress how would you respond to the Supreme Court's *Cipollone* decision?

REPLACE materials on pages 887–910 with:

HAINES v. LIGGETT GROUP, INC.
United States District Court, District of New Jersey, 1992.
140 F.R.D. 681.

SAROKIN, DISTRICT JUDGE.

Introduction

In light of the current controversy surrounding breast implants, one wonders when all industries will recognize their obligation to voluntarily disclose risks from the use of their products. All too often in the choice between the physical health of consumers and the financial well-being of business, concealment is chosen over disclosure, sales over safety, and money over morality. Who are these persons who knowingly and secretly decide to put the buying public at risk solely for the purpose of making profits and who believe that illness and death of consumers is an appropriate cost of their own prosperity!

As the following facts disclose, despite some rising pretenders, the tobacco industry may be the king of concealment and disinformation.

In 1954, the tobacco industry promised to disseminate the results of industry-sponsored, independent scientific research for the purpose of answering the question: "Does cigarette smoking cause illness?" Decades later, one searches in vain for a "Frank Statement to Cigarette Smokers" from the tobacco industry which purports to answer that question.

Plaintiff alleges that defendants have perpetrated a public relations fraud. Plaintiff has presented evidence from which a reasonable jury could conclude that the tobacco industry in general, and defendants in particular, were aware of the risks of smoking; were concerned about the publication of those risks by others and the consequent impact upon cigarette sales; and sought to discredit or neutralize the adverse information by proffering an independent research organization, the Council for Tobacco Research (the "CTR"), which purportedly would examine the risks of smoking and report its finding to the public. The evidence presented by plaintiff supports a finding that the industry research which might indict smoking as a cause of illness was diverted to secret research projects and that the publicized efforts were primarily directed at finding causes other than smoking for the illnesses being attributed to it.

A jury might reasonably conclude that the industry's announcement of proposed independent research into the dangers of smoking and its promise to disclose its findings was nothing but a public relations ploy—a fraud—to deflect the growing evidence against the industry, to encourage smokers to continue and non-smokers to begin, and to reassure the public that adverse information would be disclosed.

While the efforts which the CTR chose to advertise were well publicized, plaintiff learned of a secret division of the CTR, the "special projects" division. Under the auspices of the special projects program, defendants' counsel and other tobacco industry attorneys collaborated in assessing, monitoring, and directing the scope of research projects purportedly designed to identify expert witnesses and to develop evidence supporting defendants' positions in existing and anticipated litigation and Congressional hearings. Defendants insist that their "special projects" efforts are entirely distinct from and unrelated to the CTR's advertised "independent" research and thus, "special projects" documents are protected by the attorney-client privilege. However, plaintiff seeks discovery of the "special projects" documents otherwise subject to the attorney-client privilege on the ground that said documents come within the crime/fraud exception to the privilege.

Plaintiff has presented *prima facie* evidence that defendants' "special projects" program was interrelated and intermingled with the CTR's supposedly "independent" research. The facts presented support plaintiff's overall theory of fraud based on the false claims regarding the independence of CTR-sponsored research and on the likelihood that defendants mounted a public relations campaign designed to discredit the links between smoking and disease which defendants knew existed. Furthermore, there is evidence supporting the conclusion that research which might tend to prove smoking a cause of such illnesses was diverted into special projects and intentionally shielded by the attorney-client privilege so as to prevent its disclosure.

The court has conducted an *in camera* review of selected special projects documents, and, as presented in the opinion below, the documents speak for themselves in a voice filled with disdain for the consuming public and its health. Despite the industry's promise to engage independent researchers to explore the dangers of cigarette smoking and to publicize their findings, the evidence clearly suggests that the research was not independent; that potentially adverse results were shielded under the caption of "special projects;" that the attorney-client privilege was intentionally employed to guard against such unwanted disclosure; and that the promise of full disclosure was never meant to be honored, and never was. Accordingly, the court concludes that the crime/fraud exception applies and that plaintiff is entitled to discovery of the withheld special projects documents.

Procedural History

Before the court is plaintiff's appeal from Magistrate Judge Hedges' May 22, 1991 Letter–Order holding that certain documents requested by plaintiff of defendants are not subject to discovery under the crime/fraud exception to the attorney-client privilege.

Also before the court is Special Master Pisano's Report and Recommendation upholding defendants' assertion of privilege with respect to the same 1500 documents subject to the Magistrate Judge's crime/fraud ruling.

The documents in question pertain to the "Special Projects" program of the Tobacco Institute Research Council ("TIRC"), later called the Council for Tobacco Research ("CTR"). Plaintiff's counsel has previously had discovery of CTR documents in *Cipollone v. Liggett*, Civ. No. 83–2864 (HLS). As this court recognized in its Opinion denying the *Cipollone* defendants' motion for a directed verdict, 683 F.Supp. 1487, 1490–93 (D.N.J.1988), the CTR-sponsored research projects were generally unrelated to the core health issues implicated by cigarette smoking. However, during the course of that trial, plaintiff's counsel learned that the CTR had a separate "special projects" program about which defendants had not provided full discovery. The "special projects" division of the CTR did sponsor research directly relevant to the hazards of smoking.

Plaintiff's counsel also learned that the "special projects" division was specifically designed to sponsor epidemiological studies which could be of use to cigarette manufacturers in their defense of various current and future suits against them based on the hazards of cigarette smoking. Plaintiff's counsel indicated during the *Cipollone* trial that those withheld documents might be subject to discovery on the basis of the crime/fraud exception to the attorney-client and work-product privileges, but this issue was neither pressed nor resolved during the course of the *Cipollone* trial.

Now in the *Haines* case, plaintiff seeks to discover those "special projects" documents which have to this point been withheld pursuant to the attorney-client and work-product privileges. * * *

* * *

Factual Background

The factual background relevant to this motion consists of plaintiff's theory of the alleged fraud by defendants and the evidence which plaintiff has marshalled in support of that theory.

A. Plaintiff's Fraud Theory

Plaintiff's theory of the fraud in this case is that defendants knew of the hazards of cigarette smoking; concealed information which demonstrated the dangers of smoking; and affirmatively mislead the public with regard to the risks of smoking. It is this last factor—defendants' affirmative misrepresentations to the public—which constitutes the alleged fraud.

In addition to defendants' direct representations to the public regarding the risks of smoking, a crucial element of plaintiff's case is defendants "sub-fraud": the alleged abuse of the CTR as a primary vehicle for misleading the public. Defendants slavishly advertised the CTR as an entirely independent and objective scientific research body which would investigate the supposed hazards of cigarette smoking and report the results of those cigarette studies to the public. Plaintiff has provided just a few of the many advertisements by defendants as exhibits in this appeal.

* * *

Plaintiff contends that in fact, the publicized efforts of the tobacco industry to research the issues and to report the results to the public were a public relations hoax—that no meaningful research was conducted and that it was never the industry's intention to discover or publish the truth about the risks of smoking. In contrast to defendants' promotion of the CTR's "independence" and "objectivity," plaintiff alleges that defendants guided the CTR to sponsor research tending to prove that other causes existed for the illnesses being attributed to smoking, in an effort to perpetuate doubts about links between smoking and disease rather than to uncover the truth. If true, such manipulation of the CTR would be directly contrary to defendants' advertised representations regarding the industry-sponsored CTR. This "sub-fraud" with respect to the CTR is a major component of plaintiff's larger fraud theory, i.e., that defendants affirmatively mislead its consumers as to the known hazards of smoking. The court specifically concludes that plaintiff presents a viable theory of fraud, of which the role of the CTR is an integral part.[4]

* * *

---

4. Defendants' potential interest in the alleged fraud is obvious. As Rose Cipollone testified in deposition before she died, the tobacco industry advertisements which held out the CTR as an independent scientific body that had yet to link cigarette smoke to cancer afforded addicted smokers like Rose Cipollone a convenient excuse to continue smoking, despite contrary reports linking smoking to cancer. See *Cipollone*, 683 F.Supp. at 1489–91 ("This [advertising] campaign served to create doubt in the minds of the consumer as to smoking and its dangers, and played on the weaknesses of those who were either addicted and/or dependent").

Discussion

For the reasons explained below, the court finds that there is sufficient *prima facie* evidence of fraud in connection with the public assurances made by defendants to declare that the crime/fraud exception shall apply in this matter. * * *

* * *

D. The Magistrate's Order Was Clearly Erroneous

As described at length *supra*, plaintiff's theory for the application of the crime/fraud exception is grounded on the undisputed fact that the cigarette industry advertised the CTR as an "independent" research body in order to gain the public's confidence that CTR-sponsored research was not manipulated, while at the same time, defendants coordinated research between the CTR and the "special projects" program. Plaintiff contends that the existence and purpose of CTR's "special projects" is *prima facie* evidence that the tobacco industry used the CTR and the "special projects" program in order to perfect the industry's fraud on the public. Plaintiff argues that

> defendants' continued pre and post–1965 public relations reference to industry sponsored research as "independent," "totally independent," "objective," performed with "absolute objectivity" and as "completely independent of the tobacco industry" runs directly contrary to this idea that this *same* research was sponsored and promoted for the primary and/or singular purpose of defense of litigation. If that is the truth, then the "use" of *selected* information generated for "litigation" purposes in a public relations capacity as a means of undermining public awareness of the health hazards of smoking in and of itself establishes fraudulent intent.

Plt. Brief at 30–31 (emphasis in original).

In support of this theory, plaintiff relies upon the evidence adduced at the *Cipollone* trial (which this court assessed in its Opinion denying the *Cipollone* defendants' motion for a directed verdict) and upon various CTR documents which plaintiff has already received in discovery. Specifically, plaintiff contends that there is ample and overwhelmingly persuasive evidence that: (1) the cigarette manufacturers recognized and knew of the serious health risks arising from cigarette smoking; (2) despite the tobacco industry's knowledge to the contrary, defendants mounted a major public relations effort to create doubt in the public's mind as to the hazards of cigarette smoking; and (3) the CTR "special projects" program sponsored research supportive of the manufacturers' litigation strategies which was used in conjunction with the manufacturers' public relations campaign, thereby tainting the advertised independence and objectivity of the CTR. Thus, in addition to the fraudulent presentation of the CTR (the "sub-fraud"), plaintiff further argues that the cigarette manufacturers' use of the CTR "special projects" program for purposes of their litigation strategies was intimately inter-connected with the manufacturers' public relations campaign to perpetuate the alleged public fraud that cigarette smoking was not harmful.

* * *

In the court's opinion, the factual inference arising from the segregation of the "special projects" program and its avowed purpose of generating research for use in defendants' litigation is highly suggestive of the public fraud which plaintiff alleges. The fact that selective research was "siphoned off" into "special projects" protected against disclosure due the claims of privilege, strongly implies that the CTR "special projects" division was an integral part of the CTR's general practice of sponsoring and reporting selective research. Moreover, sharing the special projects, litigation oriented research with the CTR directly counters defendants' representations that CTR published research was independently selected and monitored. According to defendants themselves, the attorney involvement in the special projects program included proposing and monitoring research consistent with defendants' litigation interests. Such commingling of special projects with CTR research directly implicates the special projects program in the alleged ongoing public fraud for which this court has found *prima facie* evidence.

But in addition to the evidence and factual inferences already proffered by plaintiff, the most persuasive evidence prompting this court to apply the crime/fraud exception and to reverse the Magistrate's order as clearly erroneous comes from the disputed documents themselves. This court's own *in camera* inspection of selected documents has revealed the most explicit admissions that defendants used the special projects program to further the alleged ongoing fraud and deception surrounding the advertised function and operation of the CTR. Even more disturbing, the documents indicate that defendants specifically abused the attorney-client privilege in their efforts to effectuate their allegedly fraudulent scheme. * * *

* * *

* * * However, neither the Special Master, the Magistrate Judge, or this court has reviewed those documents in order to determine whether the scope of such an order would be too broad and would require defendants to turn over documents which are truly unrelated to plaintiff's claims and which only concern defendants' litigation strategies, etc. Therefore, this court has decided to name a new Special Master, whose task shall be to review the remaining documents in order to determine whether each document is subject to the crime/fraud exception. This Special Master shall be named at a later date.

The court shall issue the appropriate orders.

NOTE

On petition for a writ of mandamus, the Third Circuit vacated the district court's decision finding that the crime-fraud exception was available to overcome defendant's claims of privilege. The court found that the district court's review of the magistrate's initial decision was too intrusive and violated the provisions of the Federal Magistrate Act with regard to appeals of magistrate's decisions. Haines v. Liggett Group, Inc., 975 F.2d 81 (3d Cir.1992).

In the "most agonizing aspect of [the] case," the court of appeals also ruled that the first two paragraphs of Judge Sarokin's opinion in Haines created an appearance of partiality on his part. The court directed that the case be transferred to another trial judge upon remand. Id. at 98.

SECTION 2. CAUSATION

A. THE CAPACITY OF THE AGENT TO CAUSE PLAINTIFF'S DISEASE

REPLACE note 6 on page 922 with:

DELUCA v. MERRELL DOW PHARMACEUTICALS, INC.
United States Court of Appeals, Third Circuit, 1990.
911 F.2d 941.*

STAPLETON, CIRCUIT JUDGE.

This is an appeal in a diversity action brought under New Jersey law by the DeLuca family against Merrell Dow Pharmaceuticals Corporation, the manufacturer of Bendectin. The DeLucas seek damages for severe birth defects suffered by Cindy DeLuca's daughter Amy. Amy was born with limb reduction defects of the lower extremities: the lower portion of her left leg is deformed with anterior bowing of the tibia, absence of the fibula and three toes, and considerable shortening; and her right foot is missing a toe. The DeLucas allege that these birth defects were caused by Cindy DeLuca's use of Bendectin during the time she was pregnant with Amy.

Merrell Dow filed a motion for summary judgment alleging that the only causation evidence produced by the DeLucas was inadmissible because all relevant epidemiological studies have determined there is no statistically significant link between the use of Bendectin during pregnancy and the type of birth defects suffered by Amy DeLuca and these studies were the only reasonable basis for expert opinions. In

---

* References to the appellate record have been omitted.—Eds.

response, the DeLucas proffered affidavits and deposition testimony by Dr. Alan Done, an expert in pediatric pharmacology, in which Dr. Done opined that the available epidemiological data does support the conclusion that Bendectin causes limb reduction defects and that he believed, to a reasonable degree of medical certainty, Bendectin caused Amy's defects. The district court held that Dr. Done's testimony would be inadmissible at trial because it was not based on data of a type reasonably relied upon by experts in the pertinent fields in issuing opinions on these subjects, as is required by Federal Rule of Evidence 703. Since Dr. Done's testimony was the sole causation evidence the DeLucas tendered in response to Merrell Dow's motion, the district court entered summary judgment for Merrell Dow. On appeal, the DeLucas argue that the district court misapplied Federal Rule of Evidence 703 in excluding Dr. Done's testimony. We agree and we will reverse and remand for proceedings consistent with the principles articulated herein.

I. THE LEGAL AND SCIENTIFIC SETTING

This is one of the last of over 1,000 suits alleging that birth defects were caused by the drug Bendectin. Bendectin, a prescription drug prescribed for morning sickness in pregnant women, was first approved for sale by the Food and Drug Administration in 1956. Public expressions of concern about Bendectin's relationship to birth defects mounted in the 1970's. In response, Bendectin's safety was examined by the FDA, and in 1980, the FDA's Advisory Committee on Fertility and Maternal Health concluded that the relevant information "did not demonstrate an increased risk of birth defects with Bendectin use" but urged that studies be continued. The FDA continues to approve its sale for use during pregnancy.

Despite the committee report and the fact that no published study has concluded that Bendectin increases the risk of birth defects, thousands of tort cases were filed by plaintiffs alleging that Bendectin had caused their children's birth defects. While Merrell Dow prevailed in the most prominent of the trials arising out of these numerous cases, a multi-district common issues trial involving over 800 cases, it has also had large verdicts entered against it in other suits, though most of these have been reversed on appeal or overturned on a motion for judgment n.o.v. As a result of escalating insurance and litigation costs resulting from these cases, and decreased use of Bendectin flowing from the controversy surrounding its safety, Merrell Dow has ceased production of Bendectin.

In this case, the district court faced one of the difficult questions that has pervaded Bendectin litigation to this point: whether an expert may testify, in light of existing scientific knowledge, that Bendectin is a teratogen, i.e., an agent that causes birth defects. The district court held Dr. Done's testimony to be inadmissible, citing the requirement of

Federal Rule of Evidence 703, that expert opinion be based on data reasonably relied upon by experts in the relevant field. The district court reached this conclusion despite the fact that most of the data relied upon by Dr. Done was data from peer reviewed articles in medical journals that was relied upon by the authors of these articles, as well as by Merrell Dow's own expert.

In the record that served as the basis for the district court's decision, Merrell Dow did not identify particular data sets it believed Dr. Done could not reasonably rely upon. Nor did it address the specific methodology and reasoning underlying Dr. Done's conclusion that Bendectin is a teratogen. Instead, Merrell Dow relied upon the great weight of scientific opinion in its favor and upon prior cases in which testimony that Bendectin is a teratogen was held to be inadmissible or insufficient to support a verdict.[3] This was consistent with its apparent litigation strategy which was to emphasize that "in all material respects, the instant case is identical to the cases where summary judgment has been granted in Merrell Dow's favor."

Following Merrell Dow's lead, the district court did not point to specific deficiencies in the data utilized by Dr. Done and while it cited Rule 703, it made no record-supported, factual finding that Dr. Done had relied upon data experts in the field would have considered unreliable. Instead, the district court devoted most of its opinion to surveying the case law cited by Merrell Dow. In only two brief sentences of its opinion did the district court address Dr. Done's statistical analysis of the available epidemiological evidence. The first sentence states that the authors of the studies used by Dr. Done concluded that a "statistically significant" link between Bendectin and birth defects existed only for defects other than limb reduction defects or concluded that Bendectin does not cause birth defects. Dr. Done, as we shall see, readily admits that his interpretation of the data collected for these studies differs from the authors'. The second sentence appears to discard Dr. Done's analysis because he is not an epidemiologist, *id.*, despite Merrell Dow's express agreement to assume, for purposes of its motion for summary judgment, that Dr. Done was qualified to read and interpret epidemiological studies. On this basis, the district court held that the DeLucas had "not approached a showing that Dr. Done's opinion has a foundation as required by Federal Rule of Evidence 703."

* * *

3. To this end, Merrell Dow presented the following evidence in support of its motion for summary judgment: * * * (3) the affidavit of Dr. Pauline Brenholz, a board certified geneticist and cytogeneticist but not an epidemiologist, who opined that, based on the existing knowledge, "it is absolutely impossible to conclude that it is 'more probable than not' that Bendectin causes birth defects, or that a causal relationship has been shown between Bendectin and birth defects to a 'reasonable degree of medical certainty.' Indeed, the impressive and overwhelming weight of scientific authority is to the contrary." * * *

B. *The Relevant Scientific Principles and Tendered Evidence*

To competently analyze the legal issues presented by this appeal, an understanding of the relevant scientific principles, albeit necessarily a rudimentary one drawn primarily from the relevant sources cited to by the parties, is essential. Problematic issues of causation arise in Bendectin cases because the etiology of most birth defects is unknown. There is no apparent way to determine from clinical examinations of Amy DeLuca whether her limb defects were the result of her mother's exposure to Bendectin, as opposed to another possible teratogen, or whether her birth defects are simply an inexplicable natural occurrence not induced by her mother's exposure to an outside agent. Rather, the only particularistic evidence the DeLucas can show to strengthen the inference that Amy DeLuca's birth defects were caused by Bendectin is to rule in Bendectin as a possible cause by showing that Amy was exposed to it during the time her limbs were developing, i.e., during organogenesis, and to rule out other possible causes by showing that Amy was not exposed to them during the critical period of organogenesis. Merrell Dow did not contend before the district court that the DeLucas failed to present sufficient evidence in this regard.

Thus, the DeLucas must rely primarily on inferences drawn from epidemiological data to show causation in Amy's case. Epidemiology, a branch of science and medicine, uses studies to "observe the effect of exposure to a single factor upon the incidence of disease in two otherwise identical populations." Black & Lilienfeld, *Epidemiological Proof In Toxic Tort Litigation*, 52 Fordham L. Rev. 732, 755 (1984). In the Bendectin context, an epidemiological study ideally attempts to determine the incidence of birth defects among the children of two groups of women, identical in all respects except for their use of Bendectin during pregnancy. Epidemiological studies do not provide direct evidence that a particular plaintiff was injured by exposure to a substance. Such studies have the potential, however, of generating circumstantial evidence of cause and effect through a process known as hypothesis testing, a process which "amounts to an attempt to falsify the null hypothesis and by exclusion accept the alternative." K.J. Rothman, Modern Epidemiology 116 (1986) ("Rothman"). The null hypothesis is the hypothesis that there is no association between two studied variables, *id.*; in this case the key null hypothesis would be that there is no association between Bendectin exposure and an increase in limb reduction defects. The important alternative hypothesis in this case is that Bendectin use is associated with an increased incidence of limb reduction defects.

The great weight of scientific opinion, as is evidenced by the FDA committee results, sides with the view that Bendectin use does not increase the risk of having a child with birth defects. Sailing against the prevailing scientific breeze is the DeLucas' expert Dr. Alan Done, formerly a Professor of Pharmacology and Pediatrics at Wayne State

University School of Medicine, who continues to hold fast to his position that Bendectin is a teratogen. In spite of his impressive curriculum vitae, Dr. Done's opinion on this subject has been rejected as inadmissible by several courts.

Dr. Done's opinion that Bendectin is a teratogen largely rests on inferences he draws from epidemiological data, most of which he contends are the same that was utilized by the experts, including the FDA committee, to whom Merrell Dow cites to bolster its contention that Bendectin does not cause birth defects.[8] The principal difference is that Dr. Done analyzes that data using an approach, advocated by Professor Kenneth Rothman of the University of Massachusetts Medical School, that places diminished weight on so-called "significance testing." *See* K.J. Rothman, Modern Epidemiology (1986) ("Rothman"); *see also*, Rothman, *A Show of Confidence*, New Eng. J. of Medicine, Dec. 14, 1978, 1362.

Epidemiological studies, of necessity, look to the experience of sample groups as indicative of the experience of a far larger population. Epidemiologists recognize, however, that the experience of the sample groups may vary from that of the larger population by chance. Thus, a showing of increased risk for birth defects among women using Bendectin in a particular study does not automatically prove that Bendectin use creates a higher risk of having a child with birth defects because the discrepancy between the exposed and unexposed groups could be the product of chance resulting from the use of only a small sample of the relevant populations. As a result of the acknowledged risk of this

---

8. The conclusion Dr. Done draws from these studies is buttressed by inferences he draws from less probative, but nevertheless relevant, sources. These include analogies between the effect substances with a chemical structure similar to Bendectin have on human fetuses and the effect Bendectin may have, and inferences drawn from studies of the incidence of birth defects in the offspring of animals given Bendectin during pregnancy, *in vivo* studies, and the effect Bendectin has on animal fetuses outside an animal host, in vitro studies.

The animal studies Dr. Done usually relies upon to support his opinion were held in this case to be inadmissible in and of themselves, and also incapable of serving as a foundation for his testimony. The DeLucas have not challenged this ruling on appeal, however. While we, therefore, will not decide this issue, we note that an exhibit to an affidavit by Merrell Dow's medical expert indicates that it is supportive, though not a necessary prerequisite, of a conclusion that a substance is a human teratogen that it is has been shown to exhibit "teratogenicity in experimental animals." Relevant literature suggests that experts would not ignore this type of evidence if it existed, though they would give far greater weight to the human epidemiological evidence. [Citations.]

Structure activity analysis is based on the hypothesis that drugs with similar chemical structures may be expected to act in similar ways. Done alleges that drugs containing structures like Bendectin's have been associated with a higher incidence of birth defects. He infers from this that Bendectin will also be associated with an increased incidence of birth defects, though he concedes that structure activity considerations may only properly serve as a basis for concluding that greater study of Bendectin's teratogenicity is needed. The district court did not hold that Done's structural activity analysis was inadmissible. It held only that this analysis was alone insufficient to carry the DeLucas' burden on causation. The DeLucas do not contend otherwise.

so-called "sampling error," researchers typically have rejected the associations suggested by epidemiological data unless those associations survive the rigors of "significance testing." This practice has also found favor in the legal context. A number of judicial opinions, discussed below, have found Bendectin plaintiffs' causation evidence inadmissible because every published epidemiological study of the relationship of Bendectin exposure to the incidence of birth defects has concluded that there is not a "statistically significant" relationship between these two events.

Significance testing has a "P value" focus; the P value "indicates the probability, assuming the null hypothesis is true, that the observed data will depart from the absence of association to the extent that they actually do, or to a greater extent, by actual chance." Rothman, *supra*, at 116. If P is less than .05 (or 5%) a study's finding of a relationship supportive of the alternative hypothesis is considered statistically significant, if P is greater than 5% the relationship is rejected as insignificant. Accordingly, the results of a particular study are reported as simply "significant" or "not significant" or as $P<.05$ or $P>.05$.

Use of a .05 P value to determine whether to accept or reject the null hypothesis necessarily enhances one of two types of possible error. Type one error is when the null hypothesis is rejected when it is in fact true. Type two error is when the null hypothesis is in fact false but is not rejected. Rothman notes that at .05, the null hypothesis will "be rejected about 5 per cent of the time when it is true," a relatively small risk of type one error. *Id.* at 117. Unfortunately, the relationship between type one error and type two error is not simple; however, one study in the context of an employment discrimination case concluded that when the risk of type one error equalled 5%, the risk of type two error was 50%. Cohen, *Confidence in Probability: Burdens of Persuasion in a World of Imperfect Knowledge*, 60 N.Y.U.L. Rev. 329, 411 & n. 116 (1985) (citing Dawson, *Investigation of Fact—The Role of the Statistician*, 11 Forum 896, 907–08 (1976)). Type one error may be viewed here as the risk of concluding that Bendectin is a teratogen when it is not. Type two error is the risk of concluding that Bendectin is not a teratogen, when it in fact is.

Rothman contends that there is nothing magical or inherently important about .05 significance; rather this is just a common value on the tables scholars use to calculate significance. Rothman, *supra*, at 117; *see also* Cohen, *supra*, at 412 (noting that the .05 level of significance used in the social and physical sciences is a conservative and arbitrary value choice not necessarily valuable in the legal setting); Kaye, *Is Proof of Statistical Significance Relevant?*, 61 Wash. L. Rev. 1333, 1343–44 (1986). He stresses that the data in a certain study may indicate a strong relationship between two variables but still not be "statistically significant" and that the level of significance which should be required depends on the type of decision being made and the relative values placed on avoiding the two types of risk.

To convey both the extent to which two variables are associated in the data, and the extent to which this association might be the product of chance, Rothman advocates reporting both a "relative risk" (or point estimate) and "confidence intervals." In the context of an epidemiological study of Bendectin's relationship to birth defects, the relative risk is the ratio of the incidence rate of birth defects in the study group exposed to Bendectin divided by the rate in the control group not exposed to Bendectin. Black & Lilienfeld, *supra*, at 758. If a study found no difference in the rate of birth defects between the Bendectin exposed group and the control group, it yields a relative risk identical to the null hypothesis that Bendectin exposure is not associated with an increased incidence of birth defects. The relative risk would thus be reported as "1", signifying no difference between the rate of birth defects in each group.

A confidence interval is a way of graphically representing the probability that the relative risk figure or any other relationship between two studied variables is the actual relationship. The interval is a range of sets of possible values for the true parameter that is consistent with the observed data within specified limits. Rothman, *supra*, at 119; D. Barnes & J. Conley, Statistical Evidence in Litigation, § 3.15 at 107 (1986) (defining a confidence interval as a limit above or below or a range around the sample mean, beyond which the true population is unlikely to fall). A 95% confidence interval is constructed with enough width so that one can be confident that it is only 5% likely that the relative risk attained would have occurred if the true parameter, i.e., the actual unknown relationship between the two studied variables, were outside the confidence interval. If a 95% confidence interval thus contains "1", or the null hypothesis, then a researcher cannot say that the results are "statistically significant," that is, that the null hypothesis has been disproved at a .05 level of significance. Kaye, *Is Proof of Statistical Significance Relevant?, supra,* at 1348.

The result of a study should be reported, in Rothman's view, by reference to the confidence intervals at various confidence levels, e.g., 90%, 95%, 99%. The inclusion of confidence intervals of a variety of levels reflects Rothman's view that the predominating choice of a 95% confidence level is but an arbitrarily selected convention of his discipline. More importantly, however, Rothman insists that the precise locations of the boundaries of the confidence intervals, the all important focus of "significance testing," are far less important than their size and location. According to Rothman, statistical theory suggests that it is "much more likely that the [true] parameter [i.e. the true relationship between the studied variables] is located centrally within an interval than it is that the parameter is located near the limits of the interval." Rothman, *supra*, at 124. As such, the primary focus should not be on the ends of an interval but rather on the "approximate position of the interval as a whole on its scale of measurement...." *Id.*

Finally, Rothman contends that the use of significance testing is especially unhelpful when a decisionmaker is attempting to draw inferences from more than one study. Different studies may each be rejected as insignificant, yet, when the studies are looked at collectively, a majority of the data may be moderately or strongly contradictory to the null hypothesis. By failing to look at the collective data in the context of confidence intervals and the most likely estimate for the true parameter suggested by that data, researchers focusing solely on significance testing tolerate a high risk of type two error. *Id.* at 117–18.

Rothman suggests a less rigid approach in which researchers look at the confidence intervals produced by various studies. By charting the range of possibilities consistent with the data found in different studies it is possible to evaluate whether the collective data is more supportive of the proposition that the null hypothesis is false than that it is true. *Id.* at 124. At the same time, the use of confidence intervals indicates the risks inherent in generating any estimate of the true parameter from the data, and allows the decisionmaker to adjust the confidence level depending on the context in which a decision is required. *Id.* at 123–25; see also Kaye, *Is Proof of Statistical Significance Relevant?*, *supra*, at 1364.

Dr. Done attached the article and chapter by Rothman to his affidavit on behalf of the DeLucas and expressly indicated that his analysis was predicated on the methodology advocated by Rothman. Dr. Done purports to have analyzed all of the epidemiological data from the published epidemiological studies of the relationship between birth defects and Bendectin, as well the data from several unpublished studies, utilizing the author's confidence interval if calculated, a 95% confidence interval if the author indicated a preference for that figure, or 90% otherwise.

Dr. Done has graphed the relative risks and confidence intervals for each of the separate sets of data together, so that the collective trend may be visualized. He concludes from analysis of these intervals that the "bulk of the available human epidemiological data ... are indicative of Bendectin's human teratogenicity." Dr. Done contends that the effect in the data is strongest for, among other birth defects, limb reduction defects like Amy DeLuca's. Dr. Done did not, however, quantify the increased risk for limb reduction defects he believed was posed by use of Bendectin during pregnancy. Dr. Done's analysis has not been published nor has it been subjected to peer review by experts in the field.

C. The Bendectin Case Law

We recognize that the district court's decision to exclude Dr. Done's proposed testimony was heavily influenced by the decisions of other courts that have grappled with the difficult question of whether expert testimony that Bendectin causes birth defects is admissible and/or sufficient to sustain a verdict. A review of these cases is thus helpful, and should be preceded by a discussion of the most important of the prior Bendectin trials, a trial in which the admissibility and sufficiency of the plaintiffs' causation evidence was not a source of major dispute.

As federal dockets swelled in the early 1980's with Bendectin cases, the Judicial Panel on Multi–District Litigation transferred over 600 of these cases to the Southern District of Ohio for pre-trial discovery, where they were consolidated with 557 cases filed within that district. See *In re Richardson–Merrell, Inc. "Bendectin" Products Liability Litigation*, 624 F.Supp. 1212 (S.D.Ohio 1985), *aff'd in relevant part*, 857 F.2d 290 (6th Cir.1988), *cert. denied*, 109 S.Ct. 788 (1989). Over 800 of these cases were adjudicated in a common-issues trial before Chief Judge Rubin, who separated the question of whether Bendectin was a teratogen from the question of whether any particular plaintiff's birth defects were caused by Bendectin. After 21 days of testimony, during which the plaintiffs presented 10 expert witnesses, including Dr. Done, and 8 experts testified for the defense, *id.* at 1218, the jury was asked to answer this question:

> Have the plaintiffs established by a preponderance of the evidence that ingestion of Bendectin at therapeutic doses during the period of fetal organogenesis is a proximate cause, [i.e. does it in a natural and continuous sequence produce injuries that would not have otherwise occurred], of human birth defects?

Id. at 1268. The jury unanimously answered no. Judge Rubin denied a post-trial motion for j.n.o.v. by the plaintiffs because "both sides presented testimony of eminently qualified and highly credible experts who differed in regard to the safety of Bendectin." *Id.* at 1244.

Despite this verdict, Bendectin cases continued to be litigated and contrary results achieved. In *Oxendine v. Merrell Dow Pharmaceuticals Inc.*, 506 A.2d 1100 (D.C. 1986), for example, the District of Columbia Court of Appeals reinstated a verdict of $750,000 won by a plaintiff who alleged that her limb reduction defects were caused by her mother's use of Bendectin. The trial court had granted a j.n.o.v. for the defendants on the ground that the plaintiffs had not produced sufficient causation evidence.

The plaintiffs' sole causation witness in *Oxendine* was Dr. Done, who based his testimony on four types of information: (1) structure activity considerations, (2) *in vitro* animal studies, (3) *in vivo* animal studies, and (4) his interpretation of the available human epidemiological data on Bendectin's relationship to birth defects. The court of appeals was impressed by the careful and thorough nature of Dr. Done's testimony, in particular by his admissions that the first three types of evidence, while probative, could not definitively establish that Bendectin is a teratogen, and that no single epidemiological study demonstrated Bendectin's teratogenicity. *Id.* at 1108. Further, the court indicated that several of the defendant's experts conceded that Dr. Done's epidemiological methodology was sound, a concession that was bolstered by a statistical expert who testified that the more appropriate focus in analyzing epidemiological studies was on the relative risk shown in the data, rather than on statistical significance. *Id.* at 1109.

Given these factors, the reviewing court found that Dr. Done's testimony provided a sufficient basis upon which to rest plaintiff's verdict, and that the trial court had erred by fragmenting Dr. Done's testimony:

> Like the pieces of a mosaic, the individual studies showed little or nothing when viewed separately from one another, but they combined to produce a whole that was greater than the sum of its parts: a foundation for Dr. Done's opinion that Bendectin caused appellant's birth defects. The evidence also established that Dr. Done's methodology was generally accepted in the field of teratology, and his qualifications as an expert have not been challenged.

Id. at 1110.

A sharply different view of the sufficiency of Dr. Done's testimony regarding the teratogenicity of Bendectin has been taken by the Courts of Appeals for the First and District of Columbia Circuits. In *Lynch v. Merrell–National Laboratories*, 830 F.2d 1190 (1st Cir.1987), and *Richardson by Richardson v. Richardson–Merrell Inc.*, 857 F.2d 823 (D.C.Cir. 1988), *cert. denied*, 110 S.Ct. 218 (1989), those courts reviewed appeals from grants of j.n.o.v. in Bendectin limb reduction defect cases. Both held that Dr. Done's opinion that Bendectin is a teratogen is not only insufficient to support a verdict in light of the currently available scientific and medical evidence, but that it is inadmissible under Federal Rule of Evidence 703. Each court held that an opinion that Bendectin is a teratogen would be admissible under Federal Rule of Evidence 703 only if it were based on a new epidemiological study concluding that Bendectin was associated in a statistically significant way with an increase in birth defects.

In so holding, each court placed heavy emphasis on the large number of human epidemiological studies of Bendectin's relationship to birth defects in the scientific literature, and the fact that none of this peer-reviewed literature had concluded that there was a statistically significant association between Bendectin and birth defects.

> We face ... a situation in which limb reductions are a fairly unusual subspecies of defect, in which the origin of most limb

reduction is unknown, in which world-wide scientific investigations of Bendectin have produced no evidence establishing that Bendectin causes limb reduction, and in which the irrelevance of Bendectin to the incidence of limb defects has been demonstrated. The ignorance that prevails as to the etiology of most birth defects does not mean causation in a given case could not be proven; it does mean that there is a large *terra incognita* where gossip and guesswork abound, so that courts must carefully control the basis for testimony pointing to a particular cause. *A new study coming to a different conclusion and challenging the consensus would be admissible evidence. Without such a study there is nothing on which expert opinion on Bendectin as a cause may be based.*

Lynch, 830 F.2d at 1194 (emphasis added); *accord Richardson,* 857 F.2d at 832 ("the wealth of published epidemiological data ... none of which has concluded that the drug is teratogenic ... must be given their just due"); *Ealy v. Richardson–Merrell Inc.,* 897 F.2d 1159, 1163–64 (D.C.Cir.1990).

A somewhat different route arriving at the same destination was taken by the Fifth Circuit in another Bendectin limb reduction case. *Brock v. Merrell Dow Pharmaceuticals, Inc.,* 874 F.2d 307, *modified,* 884 F.2d 167 (5th Cir.1989), *cert. denied,* 110 S.Ct. 1511 (1990). The *Brock* court indicated that the conflicting evidence on the subject of Bendectin's teratogenicity, the difficulties of determining whether any given substance is a teratogen, and science's inability to trace a known birth defect back to its cause leads to the potential for inconsistent verdicts in virtually identical cases. This uncertainty creates the danger that useful medicines will be withdrawn from the market and that new medicines will not be made available, not because they are harmful, but because of manufacturers' fear of tort liability. 874 F.2d at 309 & n. 9. The court opined that "appellate courts, if they take the lead in resolving those questions upon which juries will go both ways, can reduce some of th[is] uncertainty which can tend to produce a suboptimal amount of new drug development." 874 F.2d at 310. In reversing a jury verdict for plaintiffs, the court did not hold that the plaintiffs' expert testimony that Bendectin was a teratogen was inadmissible. Instead, the court held that their evidence was insufficient to sustain a verdict absent "statistically significant epidemiological proof that Bendectin causes limb reduction defects." 884 F.2d at 167.

The court purported to base its decision on a critical analysis of the reasoning of plaintiffs' experts but it did not explain the basis for its holding that statistically significant epidemiological results were required to sustain a verdict in plaintiffs' favor. The court emphasized that it "did not wish [its decision] to stand as a bar to future Bendectin cases in the event that new and statistically significant studies emerge

* * *

We understand and sympathize with the concerns expressed in *Brock* over the costs and inequities that flow from inconsistent outcomes in Bendectin cases, the potential effect erroneous verdicts have on the availability of useful medicines, and the wastefulness of continued reconsideration of an identical scientific issue in the courts. We are also troubled, as were the courts in *Lynch* and *Richardson,* by the potential for abuse that exists whenever an expert is permitted to testify to an opinion that is based upon reasoning and data that have not been subjected to the review of professional colleagues. This concern is naturally heightened when an expert is testifying on behalf of a plaintiff as sympathetic as a child crippled by serious birth defects.

However, our concern over these issues is tempered by our recognition that we do not have the authority to create special rules to address the problems posed by continued Bendectin litigation. Principles of issue preclusion have not developed to the point where we may bind plaintiffs by the finding of previous proceedings in which they were not parties, even by a proceeding as thorough as the multidistrict common issues trial. *Lynch,* 830 F.2d at 1192–1193; *In re Bendectin Products Liability Litigation,* 732 F.Supp. at 746–48 (plaintiffs could not be bound to the results of the multi-district litigation common issues trial where (1) they had no direct financial or proprietary interest in the outcome of the trial and (2) they had no effective control over the theories or proofs advanced in that trial). Moreover, we may not manipulate our interpretation of the Federal Rules of Evidence to exclude expert testimony that on the record before us may satisfy normal standards of admissibility. Nor are we at liberty, especially in a case to be decided under our diversity jurisdiction, to impose different burdens of proof on Bendectin plaintiffs than those that would apply in analogous products liability suits. At the same time, however, we must require that Bendectin plaintiffs carry the evidentiary burdens imposed upon other plaintiffs. That is, plaintiffs must produce admissible evidence from which a jury could, applying the requisite burden of proof, reasonably find that their injuries were caused by Bendectin.

On a typical summary judgment motion in a Bendectin case, a court's task is essentially two-fold: (1) to scrutinize the admissibility of the plaintiff's expert testimony under the Federal Rules of Evidence, and (2) to measure what is admissible against the appropriate state law standard governing causation to determine whether summary judgment is appropriate. We address these issues in turn.

II. THE ADMISSIBILITY ISSUES

A. *Rule 703*

Federal Rule of Evidence 703 provides:

The facts or data in the particular case upon which an expert bases an opinion or inference may be those perceived by or made known to the expert at or before the hearing. If of a type reasonably relied upon by experts in the particular field in forming opinions or inferences upon the subject, the facts or data need not be admissible in evidence.

Rule 703 has a narrow function; it seeks to delimit the acceptable bases for expert testimony. We have read Rule 703, in conjunction with Rule 104(a), as requiring the district court to "make a factual inquiry ... as to what data experts in the field find reliable." *In re Japanese Electronics Products Antitrust Litigation*, 723 F.2d 238, 276 (3d Cir. 1983), rev'd on other grounds, 475 U.S. 574 (1986); *see also* 3 J. Weinstein & M. Berger, Weinstein's Evidence para. 703[03], at 703–16 (1988).

In performing this task, the district court must remain mindful that "the proper inquiry is not what the court deems reliable, but what experts in the relevant discipline deem it to be." *Id.* at 276; *see also Indian Coffee Corp. v. Proctor & Gamble*, 752 F.2d 891, 895 (3d Cir.), *cert. denied*, 474 U.S. 863 (1985). Further, we have noted that if an expert avers that his testimony is based on data experts in the field rely upon, then Rule 703's requirements are generally satisfied. *Id.* at 277. This reflects our recognition that Rule 703 was designed to broaden and liberalize the permissible bases for expert testimony. *Id.; see also* Fed. R. Evid. 703 advisory committee's note.

In the present case, the district court purported to apply the correct standard. However, its cursory ruling that Done's testimony was inadequate under Rule 703 does not comply with the standard set forth in *Japanese Products Litigation*, as it was not predicated upon a record-supported, factual finding that Done relied upon identified data not regarded as reliable by experts in the field. Instead, the analysis in the district court's opinion referred only to Dr. Done's qualifications and the case law we have previously discussed indicating that the testimony of Dr. Done, or similar testimony, is inadmissible under Rule 703.

The district court appeared to discard Dr. Done's reanalysis of the available epidemiological evidence in part because he is not an epidemiologist. This was improper given Merrell Dow's concession that Dr. Done was qualified to interpret epidemiological data. It was also erroneous because an objection to Dr. Done's qualifications should be analyzed under Rule of Evidence 702, not Rule 703. Given the liberal criteria that governs the expertness inquiry, *e.g., Habecker v. Copperloy Corp.*, 893 F.2d 49, 51–53 (3d Cir.1990), it is doubtful whether an expert with Dr. Done's credentials could be precluded from testifying about his interpretation of epidemiological evidence simply because he does not have a degree in epidemiology.

Putting aside the substantial question of whether the records in the prior Bendectin cases were materially different from the record here, these prior judicial opinions cannot sustain the district court's ruling because they do not address the question of whether reasonable experts would rely upon the epidemiological *data* Dr. Done bases his opinion on; rather, they primarily turn on the failure of that data to show a "statistically significant" link between Bendectin and an increased incidence of birth defects, and on the weight of scientific opinion contrary to Dr. Done's view that Bendectin is a teratogen.

While these factors may not be irrelevant to another type of challenge to Dr. Done's testimony, as we discuss hereafter, we do not view the absence of statistically significant findings or the great weight of contrary opinion as being relevant to the Rule 703 question posed here. Rule 703 is satisfied once there is a showing that an expert's testimony is based on the type of data a reasonable expert in the field would use in rendering an opinion on the subject at issue; it does not address the reliability or general acceptance of an expert's methodology. When a statistician refers to a study as "not statistically significant," he is not making a statement about the reliability of the data used, rather he is making a statement about the propriety of drawing a particular inference from that data.[12]

At oral argument, counsel for Merrell Dow conceded that Merrell Dow had not specifically challenged the data Dr. Done relied upon. Indeed, with respect to most of Dr. Done's data, Merrell Dow is hardly in a position to claim that it is not of a type reasonably relied upon by experts in the field since Merrell Dow's expert relied upon the same epidemiological data from the published literature in formulating her opinion. To the extent Merrell Dow wishes to challenge particular sets of data Dr. Done has used, it is free to do so on remand. However, it has not attempted to show that Dr. Done's reliance upon particular epidemiological data is unreasonable, and the DeLucas had no burden to address arguments not made. [Citation.]

Implicit in the district court's decision, and in the decisions in *Richardson* and *Lynch,* is the principle that Rule 703 requires an expert to accept the conclusions reached by the authors of studies if the expert wishes to utilize the data underlying those studies as a basis for testimony. However, the Federal Rules of Evidence contain no requirement that an expert's testimony be based upon reasoning subjected to peer-review and published in the professional literature. Indeed, while

---

12. He is making a statement about the degree to which the relationship found in the data may be due to chance, but his decision to use a certain significance level as a check on the permissible inference to be drawn from the data is a methodological value judgment which is separate from the question of whether the data is of the type an expert would rely upon.

Brock expressed a distrust of expert testimony based on reasoning not subjected to such scrutiny, it expressly declined to hold that this was, in itself, a sufficient reason to exclude it. 874 F.2d at 313; *Cf. Richardson*, 857 F.2d at 831 & n. 55; *Lynch*, 830 F.2d at 1195 (each expressing doubt over testimony not grounded in peer-reviewed literature but not excluding it on that ground). We thus conclude that the present record provides no basis for excluding Dr. Done's testimony under Rule 703.

B. *Rule 702*

While Merrell Dow has not challenged the reliability of specific data utilized by Dr. Done, it has challenged before us the way in which he has used his data on a number of grounds, each of which it is free to pursue on remand. As we have noted, Merrell Dow's principal emphasis in this regard has been its insistence that an expert opinion based on epidemiological data and analysis is not admissible unless the data "disprove" the null hypothesis that Bendectin is not a teratogen at a .05 level of "statistical significance". This argument presents an issue of first impression in this circuit. We conclude that it should be evaluated under Rule 702 and in accordance with the teachings of *United States v. Downing*, 753 F.2d 1224 (3d Cir.1985).

Rule 702 provides:

> If scientific, technical or other specialized knowledge will assist the trier of fact to understand the evidence or to determine a fact in issue, a witness qualified as an expert by knowledge, skill, experience, training, or education, may testify thereto in the form of an opinion or otherwise.

Rule 702 authorizes the admission of expert testimony so long as it is rendered by a qualified expert and is helpful to the trier of fact. *American Technology Resources v. United States*, 893 F.2d 651, 655 (3d Cir.1990); *Habecker*, 893 F.2d at 51; *Breidor v. Sears, Roebuck & Co.*, 722 F.2d 1134, 1138–39 (3d Cir.1983). While no Federal Rule of Evidence specifically addresses the methodological fundamentals for expert testimony, Rule 702's helpfulness requirement implicitly contains the proposition that expert testimony that is based on unreliable methodology is unhelpful and therefore excludable. *Downing*, 753 F.2d 1224.

The reliability of expert testimony founded on reasoning from epidemiological data is generally a fit subject for judicial notice; epidemiology is a well-established branch of science and medicine, and epidemiological evidence has been accepted in numerous cases. See *In re Agent Orange Product Liability Litigation*, 611 F.Supp. 1223, 1243 (acceptability of reasoning from epidemiological evidence susceptible of judicial notice) & 1255 (citing cases admitting epidemiological evidence), *aff'd*, 818 F.2d 187 (2d Cir.1987). Thus, to the extent that Dr. Done's testimony is based on traditional epidemiological methodology, Rule

702 does not require its exclusion since his qualifications were stipulated to and his testimony goes to a critical issue in the case, cause-in-fact.

To the extent that the reliability of Dr. Done's mode of analysis is not susceptible of judicial notice, i.e., deviates from that which has consistently been admitted into evidence, however, the district court on remand must conduct a hearing and analysis consistent with the counsel provided in *Downing*. In that case this court articulated a flexible test for addressing contentions that expert testimony based on arguably unreliable techniques were "unhelpful" and thus inadmissible under Rule 702:

> Rule 702 requires that a district court ruling upon the admission of (novel) scientific evidence, i.e. evidence whose scientific fundaments are not suitable candidates for judicial notice, conduct a preliminary inquiry focusing on (1) the soundness and reliability of the process or technique used in generating the evidence, (2) the possibility that admitting the evidence would overwhelm, confuse, or mislead the jury, and (3) the proffered connection between the scientific research or test result to be presented, and particular disputed factual issues in the case.

Id. at 1237. The "fit" between Dr. Done's tendered testimony and the crucial causation issues in this case is a good one and the third *Downing* factor thus cuts in favor of its admissibility. It is the other factors, reliability and jury reaction, that the district court will need to address if Merrell Dow litigates this issue on remand.

In *Downing*, we explicitly rejected reliance upon the "general acceptance" test of admissibility, most prominently articulated in *Frye v. United States*, 293 Fed. 1013 (D.C.Cir.1923). We did so, for among other reasons, because the general acceptance test was too vague and malleable to yield consistent results, and because its nose-counting emphasis often led to the exclusion of helpful evidence in contradiction to the spirit of the Federal Rules of Evidence. 753 F.2d at 1236–37. Thus, under *Downing*, Dr. Done's opinion cannot be excluded simply because the weight of scientific opinion leans against him. At the same time, however, the degree to which contrary opinion dominates the relevant literature is not wholly irrelevant to the reliability inquiry mandated by *Downing*. *Id.* at 1238.

We stress at the outset that the confidence level or "significance" of a statistical analysis is but a part of a meaningful evaluation of its reliability. *See generally*, J. Monahan & L. Walker, *Social Science in Law: Cases and Materials 33–75 (1990)*. The results of such a study may fail to correspond to reality for a number of reasons other than "sampling error." Faulty data collection resulting from design or execution flaws, for example, can create a much greater risk of error than the sampling error. Thus, a poorly conceived or conducted study that disproves the null hypothesis at a .01 level of significance may be far less reliable than a well conceived and conducted study that is significant at a .1 level. Kaye, *Is Proof of Statistical Significance Relevant?, supra* at 1362. As a result, any assessment of reliability under Section 702 should be conducted with an eye to all the risks of error posed by the proffered evidence.

By directing such an overall evaluation, however, we do not mean to reject at this point Merrell Dow's contention that a showing of a .05 level of statistical significance should be a threshold requirement for any statistical analysis concluding that Bendectin is a teratogen regardless of the presence of other indicia of reliability. That contention will need to be addressed on remand. The root issue it poses is what risk of what type of error the judicial system is willing to tolerate. This is not an easy issue to resolve and one possible resolution is a conclusion that the system should not tolerate any expert opinion rooted in statistical analysis where the results of the underlying studies are not significant at a .05 level. We believe strongly, however, that this issue should not be resolved in a case where the record contains virtually no relevant help from the parties or from qualified experts. The literature evidences that there are legal scholars and epidemiologists who have given considerable thought to this and related issues and we would hope that this expertise could be made available to the court, on remand, in some acceptable manner.

Whatever resources are made available to the district court on remand, they should be utilized with a sensitivity to the relevant policy judgments reflected in the Federal Rules of Evidence. Those rules embody a strong and undeniable preference for admitting any evidence having some potential for assisting the trier of fact and for dealing with the risk of error through the adversary process. [Citations.] Thus, Rules 401 and 402 relating to relevance, and Rule 403 relating to undue prejudice, and Rules 701–703 relating to expert testimony provide for the admission of evidence with any marginal utility absent a substantial countervailing concern.

In considering the question of reliability on remand, the district court is permitted to identify relevant scientific communities and make determinations about the degree of acceptance of Dr. Done's methodology within those communities. *Id.* at 1238. Conversely, it may consider the extent to which members of these communities decline to give any weight to inferences not supported by .05 statistical significance. The district court should keep in mind, however, that the ultimate touchstone is helpfulness to the trier of fact, and with regard to reliability helpfulness turns on whether the expert's "technique or principle [is] sufficiently reliable so that it will aid the jury in reaching accurate results." 3 Weinstein's Evidence, *supra*, para. 702[03], at 702–35. The fact that a scientific community may require a particular level of assurance for its own purposes before it will regard a null hypothesis as disproven does not necessarily mean that expert opinion with somewhat less assurance is not sufficiently reliable to be helpful in the context of civil litigation.

Even if it is found that Done's testimony meets the test of reliability, *Downing* recognizes that special dangers are posed by scientific evidence. Thus, the district court will be required to consider the "possibility that admitting the evidence could overwhelm, confuse, or mislead the jury." *Downing*, 753 F.2d at 1237. This inquiry focuses on the extent to which probative scientific evidence is capable of being properly utilized by the jury: will the jury be able to give it appropriate weight or will the evidence, because of its scientific origins, take on an importance beyond its probative value? The degree to which Dr. Done's testimony is susceptible of being understood by, rather than overwhelming, the jury, and the usefulness of cross-examination, competing expert testimony, and judicial control in this regard, factor into this calculus.

After considering the reliability of Dr. Done's testimony and the dangers it poses, the district court will have to reach the ultimate determination of whether it is "helpful" and thus admissible. That determination will require an exercise of discretion informed by the teachings of *Downing* and the record developed on remand. Once made, it will be entitled to deference. *United States v. Ferri*, 778 F.2d 985, 989–991 (3d Cir.1985) (finding no abuse of discretion where a district court's decision to admit arguably novel scientific evidence resulted from a rational application of the relevant criteria set forth in *Downing* to the record before it).

Merrell Dow is free to trigger this inquiry on remand by contending that Dr. Done's testimony is based on unreliable epidemiological methodology. But on the present record, we cannot by reference to Rule 702 affirm the district court's exclusion of that testimony. Dr. Done's qualifications were stipulated for the purposes of Merrell Dow's motion, his testimony goes to the crucial issue of causation, and his analysis purports to be based on a theory of epidemiological reasoning that has support in the published literature. Given these facts, we are unwilling in the absence of countervailing evidence or persuasive argument to conclude that his testimony would be unhelpful under Rule 702.

* * *

III. THE SUFFICIENCY OF THE EVIDENCE ISSUE

Since the district court held that the Deluca's sole evidence of causation was inadmissible, it had no difficulty in concluding that they had not met their burden under the *Celotex* trilogy to produce evidence sufficient to raise a genuine issue of material fact as to whether Amy DeLuca's birth defects were caused by Bendectin. *Celotex Corp. v.*

Catrett, 477 U.S. 317 (1986); *Anderson v. Liberty Lobby*, 477 U.S. 242 (1986); *Matsushita Electronic Industrial, Co. v. Zenith Radio Corp.*, 475 U.S. 574 (1986). If Dr. Done's testimony is ultimately held to be admissible, however, a different issue will be presented. While we express no opinion on that issue, we wish to make clear that nothing in this opinion is intended to suggest that this issue is or is not susceptible of resolution by summary judgment.

As we have earlier noted, a court presented with a motion for summary judgment must ultimately determine whether the admissible evidence tendered by the party having the burden of proof on an issue is sufficient to permit a rational factfinder to find for that party on that issue under the appropriate burden of proof. *Anderson*, 477 U.S. at 252 (in a run of the mill civil case, the judge must ask on a motion for summary judgment whether "reasonable jurors could find by a preponderance of the evidence that the plaintiff is entitled to a verdict"). In the present context, Dr. Done's testimony may be found sufficiently helpful to be admissible and sufficiently probative to support a jury finding that Bendectin *can* cause birth defects or even that Bendectin *not infrequently causes* such defects. However, assuming that New Jersey would apply the traditional "more probable than not" burden of proof standard to the causation issue in this case, this admissible testimony would not alone bar summary judgment for Merrell Dow unless it would support a jury finding that Bendectin *more likely than not caused* the birth defects in *this particular case*.

Hypothetically, Dr. Done may be able to testify, on the basis of adequate data and the application of reasonably reliable methodology, for example, that of women who took Bendectin and had children with birth defects, 25% of the cases of birth defects can be attributed to Bendectin exposure. This testimony would be admissible as it would be a basis from which a jury could rationally find that Bendectin *could have* caused Amy DeLuca's birth defects; however, it would not without more suffice to satisfy the DeLucas' burden on causation under a more likely than not standard since a fact finder could not say on the basis of this evidence alone that Amy DeLuca's birth defects were more likely than not caused by Bendectin.

If New Jersey law requires the DeLucas to show that it is more likely than not that Bendectin caused Amy DeLuca's birth defects, and they are forced to rely solely on Dr. Done's epidemiological analysis in order to avoid summary judgment, the relative risk of limb reduction defects arising from the epidemiological data Done relies upon will, at a minimum, have to exceed "2":

> A relative risk of "2" means that the disease occurs among the population subject to the event under investigation twice as frequently as the disease occurs among the population not subject to the event under investigation. Phrased another way, a relative risk of "2" means that, on the average, there is a fifty per cent likelihood that a particular case of the disease was caused by the

event under investigation and a fifty per cent likelihood that the disease was caused by chance alone. *A relative risk greater than "2" means that the disease more likely than not was caused by the event.*

Manko v. United States, 636 F.Supp. 1419, 1434 (W.D.Mo.1986), *aff'd in relevant part,* 830 F.2d 831 (8th Cir.1987).

* * *

IV. CONCLUSION

We hold that the present record cannot sustain the exclusion of Dr. Done's testimony. Therefore, we will reverse the grant of summary judgment in Merrell Dow's favor and remand for further proceedings consistent with this opinion.

NOTES

1. As the *DeLuca* opinion explains, other federal appellate courts have been less sympathetic to Bendectin plaintiffs. In a post-DeLuca decision, Daubert v. Merrell Dow Pharmaceuticals, Inc., 951 F.2d 1128, 1129–30 (9th Cir.1991), the Ninth Circuit Court of Appeals affirmed the district court's grant of summary judgment for defendant. The Court of Appeals adopted a *Frye* standard for determining the admissibility of an expert's opinion. The Supreme Court overturned the Ninth Circuit, holding that the *Frye* "general acceptance" standard was not incorporated into the Federal Rules of Evidence as a whole or into Rule 702 (concerning expert testimony) in particular. Under the Rules, "the trial judge must ensure that any and all scientific testimony or evidence admitted is not only relevant, but reliable." Rule 702 "clearly contemplates some degree of regulation of the subjects and theories about which an expert may testify." This requires a trial judge to render an initial determination of whether an expert's proffer of scientific testimony:

> "will assist the trier of fact to understand or determine a fact in issue. This entails a preliminary assessment of whether the reasoning or methodology underlying the testimony is scientifically valid and of whether that reasoning or methodology properly can be applied to the facts in issue * * *. Many factors will bear on [this] inquiry * * *.

> Ordinarily, a key question * * * will be whether it can be (and has been) tested. "Scientific methodology today is based on generating hypotheses and testing them to see if they can be falsified; indeed, this methodology is what distinguishes science from other fields of human inquiry." [Citations.]

> Another pertinent consideration is whether the theory or technique has been subjected to peer review and publication * * *.

> Additionally, in the case of a particular scientific technique, the court ordinarily should consider the known or potential rate of error, [citation], and the existence and maintenance of standards controlling the technique's operation. [Citation.]

> Finally, "general acceptance" can yet have a bearing on the inquiry. [Thus, "widespread acceptance" or "minimal support" can be important factors on admissibility. Moreover, judges should be mindful of Rules 703, concerning expert opinions based on hearsay, and 403, permitting the exclusion of relevant evidence "if its probative value is substan-

tially outweighed by the danger of unfair prejudice, confusion of the issues, or misleading the jury * * *."]

Daubert v. Merrell Dow Pharmaceuticals, Inc., ___ U.S. ___, ___ S.Ct. ___, ___ L.Ed.2d ___, 1993 WL 224478 (1993).

B. WHETHER PLAINTIFF'S DISEASE WAS CAUSED BY THE AGENT

ADD to page 936 after the first paragraph of note 6:

The matter becomes more complicated when multiple defendants and multiple toxic agents are involved. Recall the *Borel* holding that the jury could find that each of the defendants' asbestos products was a substantial factor in causing the decedent's asbestosis. But dosage is an important variable in the effect that a toxic agent has on any individual. While we may be unable to ascertain the impact of any given level of exposure, it is intuitively and logically plausible that minimal exposures may not play any (or any significant) role in the plaintiff's disease. This concern was reflected in the Fourth Circuit's decision in Lohrmann v. Pittsburgh Corning Corp., 782 F.2d 1156, 1162–64 (4th Cir. 1986). The court held that a plaintiff who had been employed as a shipyard pipefitter for 39 years could not recover against three asbestos defendants. Although the three defendants' products were present at the shipyard, there was no evidence to demonstrate that plaintiff was exposed to those products. Without proof of: (1) regular use of products, (2) proximity to them by the plaintiff, (3) over an extended period of time, plaintiff could not meet his burden of production in showing that the products were a substantial cause of his injury. The regularity, proximity, and frequency standards of *Lohrmann* has been adopted by a number of other courts.

In response to difficulties confronted by plaintiffs in meeting this burden, the "fiber drift" theory has been developed to connect the presence of asbestos products of a defendant at a worksite with a plaintiff's exposure and consequent disease. This "theory" holds that asbestos fibers present in a factory, on a ship, or at a construction worksite can migrate to other locations at the site and be breathed by persons some distance away. In Robertson v. Allied Signal, Inc., 914 F.2d 360 (3d Cir.1990), the leading case addressing the fiber drift theory, the court held that expert witness testimony on fiber migration could satisfy the "proximity" aspect of the *Lohrmann* test, but that plaintiff would still be required to prove regular use of the product and frequent presence by the plaintiff in an area to which the asbestos might have migrated. Most other courts have adopted a similar analysis. See, e.g., Thacker v. UNR Indus., Inc., 151 Ill.2d 343, 177 Ill.Dec. 379, 603 N.E.2d 449 (1992).

ADD to page 938 after note 11:

LANDRIGAN v. THE CELOTEX CORPORATION.
Supreme Court of New Jersey, 1992.
127 N.J. 404, 605 A.2d 1079.

POLLOCK, J.

Plaintiff, Angelina Landrigan, sued defendants Owens–Corning Fiberglass Corporation and Owens Illinois, Inc. for the personal injuries and death of her husband, Thomas Landrigan, claiming that exposure to defendants' asbestos had caused his death from colon cancer. She also sued The Celotex Corporation, against which all actions are stayed because it is in bankruptcy. Reference in this opinion to "defendants" is to Owens–Corning Fiberglass Corporation and Owens Illinois, Inc. To prove causation, plaintiff relied on the testimony of two witnesses, a medical doctor and an epidemiologist. The trial court rejected both experts' conclusions. It rejected the medical doctor's conclusion as a "net opinion," unsubstantiated by facts or reasons. The court ruled that the epidemiologist, not being a physician, was unqualified to render an opinion that asbestos exposure caused cancer in a specific individual. The Appellate Division affirmed. 243 N.J.Super. 449, 579 A.2d 1268 (1990). We granted certification, 127 N.J. 324, 604 A.2d 599 (1990), and now reverse and remand to the Law Division.

-I-

Decedent worked as a maintenance man and pipe insulator at the Bayonne Terminal Warehouse from 1956 until December 1981, when he was diagnosed as suffering from colon cancer. From 1956 until 1972, he allegedly worked with insulation containing asbestos supplied by defendants. In January 1982, he underwent surgery but the cancer spread, and he died in December 1982. The cause of his death was adenocarcinoma, "a malignant adenoma arising from a glandular organ," *Taber's Cyclopedic Medical Dictionary* 36 (15th ed. 1985), the most common type of colon cancer. Generally speaking, colorectal cancer is the second most common cancer in the United States, striking 140,000 persons and causing 60,000 deaths annually. *Colonoscopy Recommended, Am. Med. News*, Sept. 16, 1991, at 39. In 1984, plaintiff filed this survivorship and wrongful death action, asserting that exposure to asbestos had caused decedent's death.

* * *

At the trial in 1989, plaintiff relied on two experts, Dr. Joseph Sokolowski, Jr., a physician who is board certified in both internal medicine and pulmonary medicine, and Dr. Joseph K. Wagoner, an epidemiologist and biostatistician but not a physician. Dr. Sokolowski never treated or examined decedent. He based his conclusions on a review of decedent's history of exposure to asbestos, the absence of other risk factors in decedent's history, and on various epidemiological, animal, and *in vitro* studies. Stating that physicians regularly rely on epidemiological studies, Dr. Sokolowski testified that asbestos can cause colon cancer in humans. He also described the path asbestos fibers take from inhalation to the gastrointestinal tract.

Dr. Sokolowski testified that exposure to asbestos was the cause of decedent's colon cancer. He relied on the ability of asbestos to cause colon cancer in humans, decedent's exposure to asbestos, and the absence of other risk factors, such as a high-fat diet, excessive alcohol consumption, a family history of colon cancer, and prior bowel disease.

Dr. Sokolowski testified further that decedent would not have contracted colon cancer if he had not been exposed to asbestos.

Plaintiff also offered Dr. Wagoner to testify that asbestos exposure had caused decedent's colon cancer. After conducting a hearing pursuant to *Evidence Rule* 8, the trial court ruled that as an epidemiologist and not a physician, Dr. Wagoner was not qualified to testify that asbestos had caused decedent's cancer. The court, however, permitted the witness to testify about epidemiological methods and studies linking colon cancer to asbestos exposure. It also allowed Dr. Wagoner to state his opinion that asbestos causes colon cancer in humans. Finally, Dr. Wagoner testified that a low-fiber diet is associated with an increased risk of colon cancer, and that smoking, hemorrhoids, arthritis, and moderate alcohol consumption are not so associated.

At the close of plaintiff's case, the trial court granted defendants' motions for a directed verdict. See *Rule* 4:40–1. The court ruled that Dr. Sokolowski's testimony was a net opinion because it was supported only by epidemiological studies and the exclusion of other risk factors, explaining:

> Epidemiological evidence can only be used to show that a defendant's conduct increased a plaintiff's risk of injury to some measurable extent but it cannot be used to answer the critical question did the asbestos cause Mr. Landrigan's colon cancer. Judge Deighan so stated in the case of [*Thompson v. Merrell Dow Pharmaceuticals*, 229 N.J.Super. 230 [551 A.2d 177] (App.Div.1988)].

The court also rejected plaintiff's proffer concerning Dr. Wagoner's testimony, stating:

> Dr. Wagoner is not a medical doctor. He never prescribed a course of treatment for cancer patients. He conducted no human research. Dr. Wagoner teaches that if you can't find the cause of a disease by medical observation and you can find no other cause for it, you then go to these studies that have been conducted and pick a cause from a known risk or an increased risk factor.
>
> Again, I repeat that epidemiology cannot be used to predict an occurrence of health related events for a given specific individual. Therefore, it is this Court's decision that the colon cancer claim of Mr. Landrigan and Mrs. Landrigan is dismissed as to all defendants.

Concerning Dr. Wagoner, the Appellate Division apparently relied on the fact that he had used only epidemiological methods:

> Dr. Wagoner's qualifications as an epidemiologist and biostatistician did not endow his opinion as to proximate cause with the expertise necessary to "assist the trier of fact to understand the evidence or determine [the] fact in issue" [quoting *Evid.R.* 56(2)]. As we noted earlier, epidemiology deals with the movement of

different diseases within human populations. It does not address questions of specific causation in the individual case. While epidemiological information, taken together with other medical facts, may be useful to a physician in forming a particular diagnosis or in determining the etiology of an illness, court determinations as to such matters cannot be based on an expert opinion which rests on the application of statistical skills and studies alone. [243 N.J.Super. at 462, 579 A.2d 1268.]

Epidemiology, then, relates to two aspects of plaintiff's proof. For the physician, Dr. Sokolowski, epidemiological studies provided some of the facts on which he relied to conclude that asbestos exposure had caused decedent's colon cancer. Concerning Dr. Wagoner, the epidemiologist, the main issue was whether he was qualified as a nonphysician to render an opinion that the exposure had been the cause of decedent's cancer.

-II-

-A-

In recent years, we have sought to accommodate the requirements for the admission of expert testimony with the need for that testimony. See *Rubanick v. Witco Chem. Corp.*, 125 N.J. 421, 593 A.2d 733 (1991); *Ryan v. KDI Sylvan Pools, Inc.*, 121 N.J. 276, 579 A.2d 1241 (1990). Nowhere is that accommodation more compelling than on the issue of causation in toxic-tort litigation concerning diseases of indeterminate origin. Many such injuries remain latent for years, are associated with diverse risk factors, and occur without any apparent cause. Steve Gold, Note, *Causation in Toxic Torts: Burdens of Proof, Standards of Persuasion, and Statistical Evidence,* 96 Yale L.J. (1986). In that context, proof that a defendant's conduct caused decedent's injuries is more subtle and sophisticated than proof in cases concerned with more traditional torts.

* * *

[*Evidence Rule* 56(2)] imposes three basic requirements: (1) the intended testimony must concern a subject matter that is beyond the ken of the average juror; (2) the field testified to must be at a state of the art such that an expert's testimony could be sufficiently reliable; and (3) the witness must have sufficient expertise to offer the intended testimony. *State v. Kelly*, 97 N.J. 178, 208, 478 A.2d 364 (1984).

Our focus is on the last two requirements, that the testimony is reliable and that the witness is qualified to offer the intended testimony. In *Rubanick*, which we decided after the Appellate Division had rendered its opinion in this case, we modified the standard for the admission of expert testimony, holding that in toxic-tort litigation, a scientific theory of causation that has not yet reached general acceptance may be found to be sufficiently reliable if it is based on a sound, adequately-founded scientific methodology involving data and information of the type reasonably relied on by experts in the scientific field. The evidence of such scientific knowledge must be proffered by an expert who is sufficiently qualified by education, knowledge, training, and experience in the specific field of science. The expert must possess a demonstrated professional capability to assess the scientific significance of the underlying data and information, to apply the scientific methodology, and to explain the bases for the opinion reached. [125 N.J. at 449, 593 A.2d 733.]

Rubanick changed the emphasis for the admission of expert testimony from general acceptance in the scientific community to the methodology and reasoning supporting the testimony. * * *

* * *

Turning to the experts in this case, plaintiff's medical expert was Dr. Sokolowski. Initially, he explained that he had examined certain literature on colon cancer, including the landmark study by Dr. Irving Selikoff. See Irving Selikoff et al., *Mortality Experience of Insulation Workers in the United States and Canada*, 330 Annals N.Y. Acad. Sci. 91 (1979). The study indicated a relative risk of colon cancer from the exposure to asbestos of 1.55. The attributable risk, which would vary according to the extent and intensity of the exposure, was approximately thirty-five percent. Thus, assuming a causal relationship, the Selikoff study indicates that thirty-five percent of the cases of colon cancer in the population exposed to asbestos can be attributed to that exposure.

Dr. Sokolowski had never treated or examined decedent, but he had reviewed decedent's medical records and plaintiff's answers to interrogatories. Those materials indicated that decedent had been exposed to asbestos in his work. They also indicated the absence of other risk factors such as a family history of colon cancer, a high-fat diet, and the undue consumption of alcohol. Dr. Sokolowski acknowledged that "many studies * * * show no statistically significant increase in colon cancer in workers exposed to asbestos." Finally, he relied on the results of animal and *in vitro* studies.

The trial court rejected Dr. Sokolowski's testimony as a "net opinion" unsupported by any facts. Specifically, the court stated that "[e]pidemiological evidence can only be used to show that a defendant's conduct increased a plaintiff's risk of injury to some measurable extent but it cannot be used to answer the critical question did the asbestos cause Mr. Landrigan's colon cancer."

The Appellate Division agreed with that assessment, explaining that Dr. Sokolowski had failed to account for other factors that may have caused decedent's cancer. Although it accepted the validity of the Selikoff study, the court stated that the 1.55 relative risk was insufficient to support Dr. Sokolowski's opinion that decedent's exposure had caused the cancer. Without expressly adopting a specific standard, the court cited with approval several cases that adopted a requirement that an epidemiological study show a relative risk in excess of 2.0 to prove that causation in a specific individual was more probable than not. The significance of a relative risk greater than 2.0 representing a true causal relationship is that the ratio evidences an attributable risk of more than fifty percent, which means that more than half of the cases of the studied disease in a comparable population exposed to the substance are attributable to that exposure. This finding could support an inference that the exposure was the probable cause of the disease in a specific member of the exposed population.

Defense counsel urges that the Appellate Division opinion may be read as requiring that an expert may not rely on an epidemiological study to support a finding of individual causation unless the relative risk is greater than 2.0. See 243 N.J.Super. at 457–59, 579 A.2d 1268. At oral argument before us, they agreed that such a requirement may be unnecessary. Counsel acknowledged that under certain circumstances a study with a relative risk of less than 2.0 could support a finding of specific causation. Those circumstances would include, for example, individual clinical data, such as asbestos in or near the tumor or a documented history of extensive asbestos exposure. So viewed, a relative risk of 2.0 is not so much a password to a finding of causation as one piece of evidence, among others, for the court to consider in determining whether the expert has employed a sound methodology in reaching his or her conclusion.

If epidemiological studies are to provide the basis for an expert's opinion, they must have been "soundly and reliably generated" and be "of a type reasonably relied on by comparable experts in the particular field." * * *

* * *

In the present case, Dr. Sokolowski began by reviewing the scientific literature to establish both the ability of asbestos to cause colon cancer and the magnitude of the risk that it would cause that result. Next, he assumed that decedent was exposed to asbestos and that his exposure, in both intensity and duration, was comparable to that of the study populations described in the literature. He then assumed that other known risk factors for colon cancer did not apply to decedent. After considering decedent's exposure and the absence of those factors, Dr. Sokolowski concluded that decedent's exposure more likely than not had been the cause of his colon cancer.

Without limiting the trial court on remand, its assessment of Dr. Sokolowski's testimony should include an evaluation of the validity both of the studies on which he relied and of his assumption that the decedent's asbestos exposure was like that of the members of the study populations. The court should also verify Dr. Sokolowski's assumption concerning the absence of other risk factors. Finally, the court should ascertain if the relevant scientific community accepts the process by which Dr. Sokolowski reasoned to the conclusion that the decedent's asbestos exposure had caused his cancer. Thus, to determine the admissibility of the witness's opinion, the court, without substituting its judgment for that of the expert, should examine each step in Dr. Sokolowski's reasoning.

-B-

The trial court also rejected the testimony of plaintiff's second witness on causation, Dr. Wagoner, an epidemiologist. The court permitted Dr. Wagoner to testify generally that asbestos can cause colon cancer, but precluded him from testifying specifically that exposure to defendants' asbestos had caused decedent's cancer. In barring the witness from so testifying, the court stated that Dr. Wagoner

> cannot give an opinion as to causation, based upon the reasoning that has been argued here that the doctor is not a medical doctor. He has never treated patients. * * * He will be permitted to testify as an epidemiologist and not give any opinion as to whether or not this man's colon cancer was caused by his exposure to asbestos.

The Appellate Division agreed. 243 N.J.Super. at 462, 579 A.2d 1268.

In the interim, we decided *Rubanick,* in which we affirmed an Appellate Division ruling that a witness who was a biochemist, but not a physician, could testify that exposure to PCBs had caused colon cancer in the individual plaintiffs. Defendants' brief in the instant case, written before our opinion in *Rubanick,* acknowledges that the *Rubanick* ruling in the Appellate Division conflicts with their contention that persons other than licensed physicians, such as epidemiologists, are unqualified to offer a medical opinion about the cause of colon cancer in a specific individual. Defendants acknowledge that *Rubanick* permits an otherwise qualified witness who is not a physician to testify that a toxic substance caused colon cancer in a specific plaintiff. In light of our intervening decision in *Rubanick,* we are obliged to reverse the judgment of the Appellate Division and remand the matter to the trial court for retrial.

Our decision does not necessarily mean that on remand the trial court must reach a different result. Although the diagnosis of decedent's disease and the cause of his death are not in dispute, the parties vigorously contest the probability that decedent's colon cancer was caused by asbestos exposure. The issue posed to both Dr. Wagoner and Dr. Sokolowski was the likelihood that decedent's colon cancer was caused by asbestos exposure. Dr. Wagoner did not rely exclusively on epidemiological studies in addressing that issue. In addition to relying on such studies, he, like Dr. Sokolowski, reviewed specific evidence about decedent's medical and occupational histories. Both witnesses also excluded certain known risk factors for colon cancer, such as excessive alcohol consumption, a high-fat diet, and a positive family history. From statistical population studies to the conclusion of causation in an individual, however, is a broad leap, particularly for a witness whose training, unlike that of a physician, is oriented toward the study of groups and not of individuals. Nonetheless, proof of causation in toxic-tort cases depends largely on inferences derived from statistics about groups. Gold, *supra*, 96 *Yale L.J.* at 401. The ultimate decision whether Dr. Wagoner is qualified to render an opinion on the issue of specific causation must depend on the trial court's assessment of both his qualifications and his methodology.

Our resolution of the issue concerning the admissibility of the testimony of plaintiff's experts is consistent with *Rubanick v. Witco Chem. Corp., supra,* 125 N.J. 421, 593 A.2d 733, *Hake v. Township of Manchester,* 98 N.J. 302, 486 A.2d 836 (1985), and with opinions from other jurisdictions. In *Hake,* the plaintiffs offered the testimony of a trained first-aider to establish the lifesaving potential of cardiopulmonary resuscitation (CPR). We noted that "[w]hile the subject is ultimately medical in nature, all aspects of the subject are not within the exclusive knowledge of licensed practitioners," 98 N.J. at 314, 486 A.2d 836, and held that the plaintiffs should have been given the opportunity to demonstrate that their witness had "the minimal technical training and knowledge" required for him to express a reliable opinion, *id.* at 316, 486 A.2d 836. *See also State v. Frost,* 242 N.J.Super. 601, 616, 577 A.2d 1282 (App.Div.1990) (non-psychologist clinical director of women's resource center "eminently well qualified" to testify on battered-woman syndrome).

Courts of other jurisdictions also permit non-physician scientists to testify on matters of individual causation when their training and experience indicate sufficient expertise to support a reliable opinion. *See, e.g., In re Paoli R.R. Yard PCB Litig.,* 916 F.2d 829, 855–56 (3d Cir.1990) (toxicologist, microbiologist, and physicist, each with clinical or research experience), *cert. denied,* ___ U.S. ___, 111 S.Ct. 1584, 113 L.Ed.2d 649 (1991); *Loudermill v. Dow Chem. Co.,* 863 F.2d 566, 570 (8th Cir.1988) (toxicologist with clinical experience); *Roberts v. United States,* 316 F.2d 489, 492–93 (3d Cir.1963) (industrial hygienist/toxicologist with practical experience); *Valiulis v. Scheffels,* 191 Ill.App.3d 775, 138 Ill.Dec. 668, 547 N.E.2d 1289, 1296–97 (1989) (clinical psychologist/neuropsychologist regularly consulted by physicians); *Nicholas v. City of Alton,* 107 Ill.App.3d 404, 63 Ill.Dec. 108, 437 N.E.2d 757, 760 (1982) (toxicologist/pharmacologist with practical experience); *Karasik v. Bird*, 98 A.D.2d 359, 470 N.Y.S.2d 605, 608 (1984) (pharmacologist); *see also* Black, *supra*, 56 *Fordham L. Review* at 661 ("Causation involves fundamentally scientific questions. As one writer puts it, 'the patient seeks relief, the physician tries to provide it, and the scientist seeks understanding' [quoting Lester S. King, *Medical Thinking* 131 (1982)].").

* * *

The trial court's dismissal of the complaint flowed directly from the court's exclusion of Dr. Wagoner's testimony and its conclusion that Dr. Sokolowski's testimony was a net opinion. Without the testimony of these witnesses, plaintiff's case was devoid of proof of causation. Because the directed verdict was the inexorable result of the evidentiary rulings, our disposition of them requires that the directed verdict be set aside. *See In re Paoli R.R. Yard PCB Litig., supra*, 916 F.2d at 835.

The judgment of the Appellate Division is reversed, and the matter is remanded to the Law Division.

C. IDENTIFYING THE PARTY RESPONSIBLE FOR THE AGENT

REPLACE Sindell v. Abbott Laboratories and notes 1–4 and 11 on pages 938–951 with:

SMITH v. ELI LILLY & COMPANY
Supreme Court of Illinois, 1990.
137 Ill.2d 222, 148 Ill.Dec. 22, 560 N.E.2d 324.

JUSTICE RYAN delivered the opinion of the court.

The plaintiff in this appeal alleges that she was injured by the drug diethylstilbestrol (DES), which her mother ingested during pregnancy. She seeks relief against defendant DES manufacturers. The issue is whether, in a negligence and strict liability cause of action, Illinois should substitute for the element of causation in fact a theory of market share liability when identification of the manufacturer of the drug that injured the plaintiff is not possible. * * *

I. FACTS

The plaintiff, Sandra Smith, was born on July 13, 1953, in Chicago, Illinois. In 1978, she was admitted to the Ravenswood Hospital in Chicago, where she underwent a dilation and curettage, cervical biopsy, and an excisional biopsy of the vaginal wall. The biopsy revealed that plaintiff had a form of cancer known as clear cell adenocarcinoma of the vagina. She was then transferred to the University of Illinois Hospital, where she underwent extensive surgery. Plaintiff alleges that the DES prescribed for her mother while plaintiff was *in utero* caused the cancer.

Elizabeth Smith, plaintiff's mother, had a history of difficulty with pregnancy before she gave birth to Sandra. Therefore, in early 1953, when she learned of her pregnancy, she went to the Field Clinic in Chicago and consulted with Dr. Jack E. Davis regarding her condition. The doctor gave Mrs. Smith a prescription to be filled at the clinic pharmacy * * *. * * *

The records recovered from the Field Clinic identify numerous companies which supplied drugs to the clinic, some of which were also suppliers of DES, but these are insufficient to match the company with the drug dispensed to the plaintiff's mother. * * * Therefore, although the plaintiff knows the color, size and dosage of the drug her mother took, she is unable to identify the specific manufacturer of the product.

In 1980, plaintiff filed her initial complaint naming as defendants 138 drug companies. According to an affidavit of John Kraas, an employee of defendant Eli Lilly & Company, there were 81 companies which marketed DES in 25 milligram tablets between 1952 and 1953. This information was derived from medical and pharmaceutical industry references. Of the 81 potential manufacturers of the DES taken by plaintiff's mother, 63 were not named in the complaint. Of the 138 companies named, 70 filed appearances. Motions were filed by a number of named defendants attacking jurisdiction, asserting changes in corporate structure or ownership that would bar successor liability, or charging error of identity. Twenty companies remained in the suit after these motions were resolved.

In November 1982, plaintiff filed a second amended complaint consisting of 11 counts. Counts I through VI sound in negligence, strict liability, breach of express warranty, fraud, breach of implied warranty, and violation of the Federal Food, Drug, and Cosmetic Act. Counts VII and VIII sound in conspiracy and pray for assessment of damages on various bases of concerted action, joint and several liability and joint enterprise liability. Counts IX and X allege theories of negligence and strict liability, respectively, and invoke market share as the means for apportioning damages. The thrust of these causes of action is that the drug companies failed to properly test DES and to adequately warn of its dangers. The last count is a tort action against the Field Clinic. There are apparently no motions pending on this count.

Following completion of discovery, 14 defendants filed a joint motion for summary judgment. Some of these defendants and a number of others filed individual motions for summary judgment on the ground that the plaintiff's mother did not use their products. Twelve defendants were able to exculpate themselves on the basis that they could not have manufactured the DES that plaintiff's mother took because their product either was not of the same dosage, color or type, or was not sold to the Field Clinic. The remaining eight defendant manufacturers included Abbott Laboratories, Eli Lilly & Company, Premo Pharmaceutical Laboratories, Inc., Carroll Dunham Smith Pharmacal Company, William H. Rorer, Inc., S.E. Massengill Company, Harvey Laboratories, Inc., and Boyle & Company.

The trial court granted the joint motion for summary judgment on counts I through IX of the second amended complaint. However, the court denied the motion with respect to count X, the strict liability action, and adopted market share liability, based on the theory that the California Supreme Court articulated in *Sindell v. Abbott Laboratories* (1980), 26 Cal.3d 588, 607 P.2d 924, 163 Cal.Rptr. 132. The defendants appealed the denial of their motion for summary judgment as to count X and plaintiff cross-appealed the trial court's grant of summary judgment as to counts I through IX. [T]he appellate court likewise adopted a theory of market share liability, although different from that applied by the trial court, and extended its application to the negligence count. The appellate court affirmed the dismissals of the other counts. The defendants filed a petition for leave to appeal to this court based on the denial of their motion for summary judgment on counts IX and X, and we granted leave to appeal (107 Ill.2d R. 315). The plaintiff has not cross-appealed from the dismissal of the other counts.

II. HISTORY OF DES

The history of the development of DES and its marketing in this country has been repeatedly chronicled, especially in cases which address the issues of conspiracy and concert of action. [Citations.] Nevertheless, before getting into the market share issue, we believe that a brief account of the drug's history will be helpful.

Diethylstilbestrol is a synthetic substance which duplicates the activity of estrogen, a female sex hormone crucial to sexual development and fertility. Professor E.C. Dodds and his associates first synthesized the drug in England in 1937. The drug was not patented by Professor Dodds, but was left available for general production by pharmaceutical companies. In 1940, a number of pharmaceutical companies in the United States sought the approval of the Food and Drug Administration (FDA) to market DES in up to 5 milligram doses to treat vaginitis, engorgement of the breasts, excessive menstrual bleeding and symptoms of menopause. Standard procedure at the FDA required the filing of a new drug application (NDA), which included clinical data establishing the drug's safety, its chemical composition, methods of manufacture, the proposed uses of the drug and proposed labeling. In an effort to avoid duplication of time and effort in determining the sufficiency of the documentation presented, the FDA requested that the drug companies withdraw their NDAs and submit their data jointly in a master file. Accordingly, a working committee of four companies was formed which collected all the data, prepared the master file and submitted it to the FDA. In September 1941, the FDA approved the production and marketing of DES for the requested uses, none of which were for problems related to pregnancy.

The first supplemental NDAs seeking FDA approval for DES as a miscarriage preventative were filed in 1947. These NDAs were filed separately and relied on clinical studies published in medical journals which attested to the safety and effectiveness of DES for this purpose. The FDA subsequently approved these applications. In 1952, the FDA declared that DES was no longer a new drug within the meaning of the Federal Food, Drug, and Cosmetic Act, and was therefore considered safe for general use. This declaration meant that any manufacturer could market the drug without submitting additional data to the FDA concerning its safety and effectiveness. Between 1947 and 1952, approximately 85 companies manufactured DES. By the end of 1952 up to 191 companies were manufacturing and distributing DES.

In 1971, two medical studies suggested that there was a statistically significant association between the outbreak in young women of clear cell adenocarcinoma, a form of cancer, with the maternal ingestion of DES during pregnancy. Later that year the FDA banned the marketing of DES for use by pregnant women. It has been estimated that at the time of this ban as many as 300 companies had produced DES for sale. Many of these companies are no longer in existence, having merged with other concerns or gone into liquidation. Although DES is no longer used during pregnancy, it is still prescribed as an estrogen replacement in cases of hormone deficiency, for treatment of unusual menopausal symptoms, and for treatment of certain kinds of cancers of the breast and prostate, and is a major ingredient in the "morning after" pill, a post-coital contraceptive.

Beginning in the 1970s, hundreds of lawsuits were filed against manufacturers of DES by the daughters of women who took the drug while pregnant. These plaintiffs are commonly referred to as the "DES daughters." The seriousness of the injuries they suffer cannot be questioned and the hysterectomy required for Sandra Smith was not unusual. [Citations.] The defendants before us, however, point out that statistics regarding DES daughters have not shown a high incidence of cancer and that it is not widely accepted that the injuries suffered are the consequence of the maternal ingestion of DES (see, *e.g.*, *Sindell*, 26 Cal.3d at 620–21, 607 P.2d at 942, 163 Cal.Rptr. at 150 (Richardson, J., dissenting) (incidence of cancer is estimated at one-tenth of one percent to four-tenths of one percent)), though the plaintiff contests these assertions. Whether or not there is a correlation sufficient to establish a cause of action is an issue properly for the finder of fact. We have before us only the legal issue of the viability of the causes of action.

III. SUBSTANTIVE TORT PRINCIPLES

A fundamental principle of tort law is that the plaintiff has the burden of proving by a preponderance of the evidence that the defendant caused the complained-of harm or injury; mere conjecture or speculation is insufficient proof. [Citation.] In a negligence action this causation-in-fact requirement entails a reasonable connection between the act or omission of the defendant and the damages which the plaintiff has suffered. * * * Likewise, to recover under strict liability the plaintiff must establish some causal relationship between the defendant and the injury-producing agent. [Citation.]

In *Schmidt v. Archer Iron Works, Inc.* (1970), 44 Ill.2d 401, a defective pin used to attach a metal chute to a construction tower failed, allowing the chute to fall and strike the plaintiff. Plaintiff sued Archer and evidence established that the defective pin was similar in color to the pins manufactured by defendant, but several other manufacturers produced similar pins. We affirmed the trial court's grant of summary judgment, reasoning that:

> "The plaintiffs' evidence failed to establish sufficient connection between the admittedly defective pin and Archer. * * * [The] evidence shows no more than that Archer was one of several possible manufacturers which could have supplied the pin." (44 Ill. 2d at 405–06.)

The identification element of causation in fact serves an important function in tort law. Besides assigning blame-worthiness to culpable parties, it also limits the scope of potential liability and thereby encourages useful activity that would otherwise be deterred if there were excessive exposure to liability. Fischer, *Products Liability—An Analysis of Market Share Liability*, 34 Vand. L. Rev. 1623, 1628–29 (1981).

The plaintiff before us alleges that after extensive discovery she has been unable to identify the manufacturer of the DES her mother ingested. A number of circumstances contribute to the barrier in establishing causation in fact in DES cases. The effects caused by prenatal exposure to DES usually do not manifest themselves until at least after the child reaches puberty, and more years may pass before the cancer is linked to DES. During this long lapse, whatever records the doctor, pharmacy or manufacturer maintained have often been lost or destroyed and the memories of the persons involved have faded. Further exacerbating the problem is the fact that during the 25 years that DES was used to treat pregnancy-related problems, as many as 300 companies manufactured the drug. The manufacturers were only required by law to maintain records for five years and many manufacturers have either gone out of business or destroyed their records or have only partial records available.

Although proof of causation in fact is ordinarily an indispensable ingredient of a *prima facie* case, the plaintiff points out that competing tort interests have compelled courts to create exceptions to the causation requirement. These exceptions to the rule have allowed a plaintiff to shift to a defendant or a group of defendants the burden of proof on the causation issue. Included within the exceptions are "enterprise liability," "alternative liability" and "market share liability."

In addition to market share liability, most plaintiffs in the DES cases have argued that enterprise liability or alternative liability, as well as a concert of action and a conspiracy theory, should apply to extend liability to a group of defendants.

The criteria necessary for a cause of action based on enterprise liability have been summarized to include: "(1) The injury-causing product was manufactured by one of a small number of defendants in an industry; (2) the defendants had joint knowledge of the risks inherent in the product and possessed a joint capacity to reduce those risks; and (3) each of them failed to take steps to reduce the risk but, rather, delegated this responsibility to a trade association." (Emphasis omitted.) (*Burnside v. Abbott Laboratories* (1985), 351 Pa.Super. 264, 285, 505 A.2d 973, 984; see also *Hall v. E.I. Du Pont De Nemours & Co.* (E.D.N.Y.1972), 345 F.Supp. 353.) Alternative liability may apply when two or more defendants act tortiously toward a plaintiff who, through no fault of her own, cannot identify which one of the joined defendants caused the injury. The burden of proof shifts to each defendant to prove his innocence. (Restatement (Second) of Torts § 433B(3), at 441–42 (1965); *Summers v. Tice* (1948), 33 Cal.2d 80, 199 P.2d 1.) Concert of action applies when a tortious act is done in concert with another or pursuant to a common design, or a party gives substantial assistance to another knowing that the other's conduct constitutes a breach of duty. (Restatement (Second) of Torts §§ 876(a), (b), at 315 (1979).) A civil conspiracy involves two or more persons who combine for the purpose of accomplishing by concerted action either (1) a lawful purpose by unlawful means, or (2) an unlawful purpose by lawful means. [Citations.]

Though the market share liability theory has received some acceptance, in nearly every instance, the other theories have been soundly rejected. * * * [W]e have before us only the narrow legal issue of whether to adopt market share liability in negligence and strict liability actions filed by a DES daughter. Currently, four States have adopted some form of this theory when confronted with the issue of imposing liability on drug manufacturers for injuries caused to women whose mothers ingested DES while pregnant. However, none of these States agree on the remedy or its application.

IV. JUDICIALLY PROMULGATED MARKET SHARE THEORIES

A. California

In *Sindell v. Abbott Laboratories* (1980), 26 Cal.3d 588, 607 P.2d 924, 163 Cal.Rptr. 132, the California Supreme Court rejected the plaintiff's three bases for her cause of action and instead modified the alternative liability theory, thus fashioning its form of market share liability. In reaching this conclusion, the court reasoned that in a contemporary complex industrialized society, advances in science and technology create fungible goods which may harm consumers and which cannot be traced to any specific producer. It then went on to give three policy reasons for developing market share liability. First, as between an innocent plaintiff and a manufacturer of a defective product, the manufacturer should bear the cost of the injury. Second, it believed that the manufacturer was in a better position to bear the cost involved in an injury. Third, because the manufacturer is in the best position to recognize defects in products and to guard against them, holding the producer liable for these defects would provide an incentive to product safety.

Under the remedy as fashioned in *Sindell*, the plaintiff must first join as defendants the manufacturers of a "substantial share" of the DES which her mother may have taken, and must prove a *prima facie* case on every element except identification of the direct tortfeasor. After joining the manufacturers, the burden of proof shifts to defendants to demonstrate that they could not have manufactured the DES that caused plaintiff's injuries. If a defendant fails to meet this burden, the court fashions a market share theory to apportion damages according to the likelihood that any of defendants supplied the product by holding each defendant liable for the proportion of the judgment represented by its share of that market. The intended result of the rule is that each manufacturer's liability for an injury is approximately equivalent to the damages caused by the DES it manufactured.

The *Sindell* court realized that the rule was not flawless and, in *Brown v. Superior Court* (1988), 44 Cal.3d 1049, 751 P.2d 470, 245 Cal.Rptr. 412, the California Supreme Court resolved some of the ambiguities. *Brown* held that liability in the market share theory is not joint and several, rather it is only several. Furthermore, in cases in which all manufacturers in the market are not joined, liability will be limited to the market share represented, resulting in a less than 100% recovery for a plaintiff.

From its inception *Sindell* has not been widely accepted. In *Sindell*, Justice Richardson, joined by two other justices, dissented, arguing that the majority was abandoning a traditional tort requirement for the creation of a new, modified, industry-wide tort. Justice Richardson argued that the theory will result in imposition of liability on pure conjecture and that it rewards the plaintiff who, unlike the ordinary plaintiff, no longer has to take the chance that the responsible defendant cannot be reached or is unable to respond financially. Therefore, "it is readily apparent that 'market share' liability will fall unevenly and disproportionately upon those manufacturers who are amenable to suit in [those few jurisdictions which adopt some form of the theory]." (*Sindell*, 26 Cal.3d at 617, 607 P.2d at 940, 163 Cal.Rptr. at 148 (Richardson, J., dissenting).) The dissent stressed that the opinion has the effect of making pharmaceutical companies insurers of their industry and that because of the sweeping effect of market share liability, the policy decision to introduce and define it should rest not with the court but with the legislature.

Other than the overall concept of market share liability, which will be addressed later in this opinion, the rule as specifically developed in *Sindell* has been extensively criticized, and as of this date only one Federal district court has adopted it in the same form. (*McElhaney v. Eli Lilly & Co.* (D.S.D. 1983), 564 F.Supp. 265, 270–71 (applying what it thought would be South Dakota law).) Criticisms include that the court failed to identify the relevant market for purposes of determining a particular defendant's market share, i.e., local, countywide, statewide or national, and a manufacturer's liability will vary widely depending on which market is used. This uncertainty undermines the court's claim that market share liability approximates each defendant's responsibility for the injuries caused by its own products. (Fischer, *Products Liability—An Analysis of Market Share Liability*, 34 Vand. L. Rev. 1623, 1643–44 (1981).) The court also failed to define what constitutes a "substantial share" of the market, one which is sufficient to shift the burden of proof to the defendant. A law review article that influenced the court suggested that plaintiff join 75% to 80% of the manufacturers (Comment, *DES and a Proposed Theory of Enterprise Liability*, 46 Fordham L. Rev. 963, 995–96 (1978)), but the court rejected this as too high and held that only a substantial percentage is required (*Sindell*, 26 Cal.3d at 612, 607 P.2d at 937, 163 Cal.Rptr. at 145). Moreover, Sindell failed to specify how the market for DES can be allocated fairly when DES has been prescribed for uses other than as a miscarriage preventative. (See also Miller & Hancock, *Perspectives on Market Share Liability: Time for a Reassessment ?*, 88 W.Va. L. Rev. 81, 88–91 (1985); Note, *The DES Causation Conundrum: A Functional Analysis*, 32 N.Y.L. Sch. L. Rev. 939, 959–61 (1987).) Further attestation to the flaws in the specifically developed procedure in California is the fact that it was rejected by the three other State supreme courts which have recognized some form of market share liability, as well as by our own appellate court in the case now before us. 173 Ill.App.3d 1, 18; *Hymowitz v. Eli Lilly & Co.* (1989), 73 N.Y.2d 487, 511, 539 N.E.2d 1069, 1077–78, 541 N.Y.S.2d 941, 949–50; *Collins v. Eli Lilly Co.* (1984), 116 Wis.2d 166, 188–92, 342 N.W.2d 37, 48–49; *Martin v. Abbott Laboratories* (1984), 102 Wash. 2d 581, 600, 689 P.2d 368, 380.

B. Washington

The theory most closely paralleling the *Sindell* rule is the "market share alternate liability" theory which the Washington Supreme Court adopted in *Martin v. Abbott Laboratories* (1984), 102 Wash. 2d 581, 689 P.2d 368. As in *Sindell*, *Martin* found unavailing the enterprise and alternative liability, concert of action and civil conspiracy theories. It further believed that the California approach was insufficient because the court failed to define what constituted a "substantial" share of the market and, the *Martin* court mistakenly believed, it distorted liability by providing that the "substantial market share" bears joint responsibility for 100% of plaintiff's injuries. The Washington court nonetheless did not outrightly reject the market share theory. It reasoned that each defendant contributed to the risk of injury to the public and consequently to the risk of injury to the plaintiff. Thus, each defendant shares in some measure a degree of culpability in producing or marketing DES.

The market share alternate liability theory that the Washington court formulated allows the plaintiff to bring suit against only one defendant. The plaintiff must prove that her mother took DES; the DES caused subsequent injuries; the defendant produced or marketed the type of DES taken by plaintiff's mother; and the production and marketing of DES breached a legally recognized duty to the plaintiff. The burden then shifts to the defendant to prove by a preponderance of evidence that it did not produce or market the type of DES taken by the mother; did not produce or market DES in that geographical area; or did not produce or market DES at that time. The defendant or defendants unable to exculpate themselves become members of the plaintiff's DES market. In *George v. Parke–Davis* (1987), 107 Wash. 2d 584, 592, 733 P.2d 507, 512, the court clarified that the geographic market area ideally should be defined on a local level; however, where such evidence is unavailable, county, State, or even national figures may be admissible to determine the market share.

Defendants are presumed initially to have an equal market share and are liable on a *pro rata* basis. They may rebut this presumption by proving their actual market share and are then only liable for that percentage of the damages. The presumptive share of the defendants that are unable to establish their actual market share is adjusted upward so that 100% of the market is accounted for. If all defendants are able to establish their actual market share and the percentage of the market represented is less than 100%, plaintiff's recovery is limited to that percentage of the market which is actually represented. Our appellate court in this case and a Federal district court in Massachusetts have subsequently adopted this theory. 173 Ill.App.3d at 18; *McCormack v. Abbott Laboratories* (D.Mass.1985), 617 F.Supp. 1521, 1527 (court held the theory was consistent with statements the State supreme court made in *Payton v. Abbott Laboratories* (1982), 386 Mass. 540, 437 N.E.2d 171).

The *Martin* alternative was formulated in part on the erroneous belief that *Sindell* created joint and several liability and that it increased the share of each defendant found liable by the share attributed to nonjoined manufacturers. (*Martin*, 102 Wash. 2d at 601–02, 689 P.2d at 380–81; but see *Brown v. Superior Court*, 44 Cal.3d at 1075, 751 P.2d at 487, 245 Cal.Rptr. at 428.) Our appellate court was also under the same misconceptions. (173 Ill.App.3d at 18.) Defendants Boyle and Massengill contend that instead of refining *Sindell* so that liability will more closely equate the harm caused, this theory has the realistic potential of creating liability well in disproportion to a manufacturer's market share. First, under *Sindell* the plaintiff must at least bring a substantial number of potential defendants before the court, whereas *Martin* only requires plaintiff to sue one defendant. If that sole defendant is a small contributor to the DES market, such as Boyle and Massengill, it possibly could shoulder complete liability without proof of its being the cause in fact for the injury. Second, a smaller company which no longer has records of its actual market share will be given a presumptive share under *Martin* which is equal to that portion of the damages unattributed. Thus, the small company could be responsible for 50% or more of the damages when common sense dictates that it surely could not have distributed such a high percentage of the DES used in the market. Also, defendants assigned presumptive shares are held liable for the share of the market attributable to companies no longer in business or not otherwise amenable to suit. This makes those defendants insurers of products which others made. Therefore, this theory can be substantially unfair to any company that is unable to prove its market share, especially if that company is small.

C. Wisconsin

The Wisconsin Supreme Court addressed the DES liability issue in *Collins v. Eli Lilly Co.* (1984), 116 Wis.2d 166, 342 N.W.2d 37. The court rejected unalloyed market share liability, concluding that it "does not constitute the most desirable course to follow in DES cases because the theory, while conceptually attractive, is limited in practical applicability." (116 Wis.2d at 189, 342 N.W.2d at 48.) It found that defining the market and apportioning the market share is nearly an impossible task if it is to be done fairly and accurately and that a second mini-trial to determine market share would be a waste of judicial resources. Therefore, Wisconsin formulated its alternative, commonly referred to as the "risk contribution theory." The public policy grounds articulated in support of this theory were that:

> "Each defendant contributed to the *risk* of injury to the public and, consequently, the risk of injury to individual plaintiffs * * *. Thus each defendant shares, in some measure, a degree of culpability in

producing or marketing * * * a drug with possibly harmful side effects. Moreover, as between the injured plaintiff and the possibly responsible drug company, the drug company is in a better position to absorb the cost of the injury. * * * Finally, the cost of damages awards will act as an incentive for drug companies to test adequately the drugs they place on the market for general medical use." (Emphasis in original.) 116 Wis.2d at 191–92, 342 N.W.2d at 49.

Under the theory, the plaintiff must also allege that her mother ingested DES and this caused plaintiff's injuries; that defendant manufactured or marketed the type of DES ingested; and that the defendant's conduct constituted a breach of a legally cognizable duty to the plaintiff. The plaintiff need only sue one drug company and that company need not constitute a substantial share of the market. Once the plaintiff has proven a *prima facie* case under negligence or strict liability, the burden shifts to the defendant to prove by a preponderance of the evidence that it did not produce or market DES for the prevention of miscarriage during the relevant time period or in the relevant geographical market area. If only one company is sued and no others are impleaded, that company is liable for all the damages if it cannot exculpate itself. If more than one defendant is joined or impleaded, damages are determined according to the jury's assignment of liability under Wisconsin's comparative negligence statute. The court included a number of factors for the jury to consider in apportioning damages, such as the market share of the defendant, whether the company conducted safety tests on DES, the role the company played in seeking FDA approval of the drug, and whether the company issued warnings.

No court, other than the Wisconsin court, addressing the DES causation issue has gone so far as to impose total liability on a defendant merely for creating a risk of harm. It has been said that this theory contravenes the fundamental tort principle that a mere possibility is insufficient to satisfy causation. (See Note, *The DES Causation Conundrum: A Functional Analysis*, 32 N.Y.L. Sch. L. Rev. 939, 965–66 (1987) (imposition of liability under this approach requires a substantial reduction in the degree of proof traditionally required, and thus threatens over-deterrence and inequity).) It has been contended that Collins does not resolve its perceived errors in market share liability, but rather further exacerbates them. (Miller & Hancock, *Perspectives on Market Share Liability: Time for a Reassessment?*, 88 W.Va. L. Rev. 81, 99–101 (litigation costs will increase, there is a risk of overwhelming the jurors with evidence, and the Sindell mini-trial is transformed into a maxi-trial on a plethora of issues).) Furthermore, it is possible that liability will far exceed the probability that a defendant caused the injuries. Comment, *Torts—Products Liability—Where a Plaintiff Cannot Identify Which Drug Company Manufactured the DES Ingested, a*

Cause of Action Exists Under the Market–Share Alternate Theory of Liability, 55 Miss. L.J. 195, 210 (1985).

D. New York

The court of appeals of New York recently declined to accept Wisconsin's risk contribution theory, believing that it would only be feasible on a limited scale. (*Hymowitz v. Eli Lilly & Co.* (1989), 73 N.Y.2d 487, 539 N.E.2d 1069, 541 N.Y.S.2d 941.) The court was wary "of setting loose, for application in the hundreds of cases pending in this State, a theory which requires the fact finder's individualized and open-ended assessment of the relative liabilities of scores of defendants in every case." (*Hymowitz*, 73 N.Y.2d at 511, 539 N.E.2d at 1077–78, 541 N.Y.S.2d at 949–50.) It concluded that the injustice resulting from delays in recoveries and inconsistent results militated against adoption of the theory. New York also criticized and rejected the California and Washington versions of market share liability, noting the difficulty of determining market share. However, the *Hymowitz* court did develop its own version of market share liability.

New York's theory utilizes a national market. The court did this realizing that a national market could not provide a reasonable link between liability and the risk created by a defendant to a particular plaintiff. Instead, this theory apportions "liability so as to correspond to the over-all culpability of each defendant, measured by the amount of risk of injury each defendant created to the public-at-large." (*Hymowitz*, 73 N.Y.2d at 512, 539 N.E.2d at 1078, 541 N.Y.S.2d at 950.) A defendant can exculpate itself only through proof that it did not participate in the marketing of DES for pregnancy use. The rule also provides that liability is several only, and is not to be inflated if all the manufacturers are not before the court.

Though it is too early to determine how Hymowitz will be received, it certainly is the most radical in its departure from established tort principles and it is admittedly flawed in that it cannot equate liability to actual harm caused. (*Hymowitz*, 73 N.Y.2d at 512, 539 N.E.2d at 1078, 541 N.Y.S.2d at 950; see *Shackil v. Lederle Laboratories* (1989), 116 N.J. 155, 197, 561 A.2d 511, 532 (O'Hern, J., dissenting) (recognizing *Hymowitz* as perhaps the most controversial of the market share decisions); Note, *Hymowitz v. Eli Lilly: New York Adopts a "National Risk" Doctrine for DES*, 25 Tort & Ins. L.J. 150 (1989); but see Twerski, *Market Share—A Tale of Two Centuries*, 55 Brooklyn L. Rev. 869 (1989).) Just as the previous theories have not been embraced by subsequent courts, it is unlikely that New York's theory will receive broad acceptance.

V. COURTS WHICH HAVE REJECTED MARKET SHARE LIABILITY

Other than these cases, the concept of market share liability has not received strong support. The supreme courts of two of our sister States have outrightly rejected its application in DES daughter cases.

The Iowa Supreme Court rejected the doctrine "on a broad policy basis." (*Mulcahy v. Eli Lilly & Co.* (Iowa 1986), 386 N.W.2d 67, 75.) *Mulcahy* equated the theory with a court-constructed insurance plan which requires manufacturers to pay for injuries their product may not have caused. It recognized market share liability as a radical departure from traditional tort concepts and it rejected allowing " 'negligence in the air' " to serve as a substitute for causation in fact. (386 N.W.2d at 76, quoting F. Pollock, The Law of Torts 455 (11th ed. 1920).) The court concluded "that awarding damages to an admitted innocent party by means of a court-constructed device that places liability on manufacturers who were not proved to have caused the injury involves social engineering more appropriately within the legislative domain." *Mulcahy*, 386 N.W.2d at 76.

The Missouri Supreme Court agreed with the arguments of the drug manufacturers that market share liability was unfair, unworkable and contrary to Missouri law and violated the State's public policy. (*Zafft v. Eli Lilly & Co.* (Mo.1984), 676 S.W.2d 241, 246.) The court found that *Sindell* had not sufficiently articulated the concepts involved. Furthermore, there was too great a risk that the actual wrongdoer was not before the court and the rule exposed those who were joined to liability greater than their responsibility. *Zafft* rejected the arguments that as between an innocent plaintiff and negligent defendant, the latter should bear the cost of the injury, and that defendants can better absorb the costs. It noted that the requirement of proving causation had not been altered by the development of products liability law in Missouri. Thus, shifting the burden of proof to the defendants would significantly alter existing rights and liabilities of the litigants. It also reasoned that strong public policy arguments militated against market share liability. The court was concerned that liability of this type would "discourage desired pharmaceutical research and development while adding little incentive to production of safe products" because all companies face potential liability regardless of their safety efforts. (676 S.W.2d at 247.) The court concluded that there was insufficient public policy justification to support abandonment of so fundamental a concept of tort law as the requirement that a plaintiff prove, at a minimum, a nexus between wrongdoing and injury.

Most of the Federal courts which have addressed the issue of applying market share liability in a DES case have declined to adopt such a radical departure from the common law of the State in which each sits without a clearer direction from that State's supreme court. In *Tidler v. Eli Lilly & Co.* (D.C.Cir.1988), 851 F.2d 418, the court reasoned "that the theory that plaintiffs would have us 'construct' requires that we build on a new foundation, not on the structural underpinnings of the traditional common law of torts." (851 F.2d at 424.) Neither the highest court of Maryland nor of the District of Columbia had addressed the issue, and the *Tidler* court held that such a marked deviation from the common law was beyond the authority of a Federal court. In *Mizell v. Eli Lilly & Co.* (D.S.C.1981), 526 F.Supp. 589, the district court found that according to conflict of law principles, California substantive law, and thus the *Sindell* rule, was the appropriate choice of law. However, the court refused to apply California substantive law because it would violate the public policy of the forum. The court concluded that "[m]arket share represents a radical departure from the body of products liability law that has been developed in South Carolina" and has the potential for placing liability on defendants who bear no responsibility for the defective product. 526 F.Supp. at 596; see also *Morton v. Abbott Laboratories* (M.D.Fla.1982), 538 F.Supp. 593, 599 ("market share theory unquestionably represents a radical departure from the traditional concept of causation" and there was no indication that Florida would abandon such a fundamental principle); *Pipon v. Burroughs–Wellcome Co.* (D.N.J.1982), 532 F.Supp. 637, 639 (there is no indication that the New Jersey Supreme Court would deviate from the causation requirement), *aff'd* (3d Cir.1982), 696 F.2d 984; *Ryan v. Eli Lilly & Co.* (D.S.C.1981), 514 F.Supp. 1004, 1019.

Plaintiffs have pursued the application of market share liability with minimal success in areas other than DES cases. The plaintiff in *Shackil v. Lederle Laboratories* (1989), 116 N.J. 155, 561 A.2d 511, became severely retarded as a result of a diphtheria, pertussis and tetanus (DPT) vaccine. Unable to identify the specific manufacturer, plaintiff sued a number of manufacturers who potentially could have produced the vaccine she was given and argued for adoption of a market share liability theory. The court determined that to adopt market share liability in a DPT "case would frustrate overarching public-policy and public-health considerations by threatening the continued availability of needed drugs and impairing the prospects of the development of safer vaccines." (116 N.J. at 158, 561 A.2d at 512.) The court's decision was further influenced by the fact that Congress had already established legislation to compensate vaccine-injured plaintiffs. (National Childhood Vaccine Injury Act of 1986, 42 U.S.C. §§ 300aa—1 through 300aa—34 (Supp. V 1987).) The court also addressed the plaintiff's argument that there was a trend in New Jersey to relax the causation requirement. It noted that a trial court in *Ferrigno v. Eli Lilly & Co.* (1980), 175 N.J. 551, 420 A.2d 1305, held that alternative liability based on a percentage-share apportionment was permissible in a DES case. However, that complaint was dismissed following the appellate court opinion in *Namm v. Charles E. Frosst & Co.* (App.Div.1981), 178 N.J. Super. 19, 427 A.2d 1121, which refused to adopt alternative liability or enterprise liability in a DES action. Upon further review of New Jersey law, it found that there was no trend toward wholesale adoption of market share liability.

The Oregon Supreme Court rejected use of the theory against two DPT manufacturers in the context of a design defect. (*Senn v. Merrell–*

Dow Pharmaceuticals, Inc. (1988), 305 Or. 256, 751 P.2d 215.) The court claimed that the "adoption of any theory of alternative liability requires a profound change in fundamental tort principles," which is more properly the domain of the legislature. 305 Or. at 271, 751 P.2d at 223; [citations].

Other than in actions against drug manufacturers, the major area of cases in which plaintiffs have attempted to impose market share liability has been asbestos litigation. The success rate in these cases is considerably less than in DES cases. In *Goldman v. Johns–Manville Sales Corp.* (1987), 33 Ohio St. 3d 40, 514 N.E.2d 691, the Ohio Supreme Court rejected its application in an action against suppliers and manufacturers of products containing asbestos by the wife of a person who died allegedly due to asbestos exposure. The court reasoned that market share liability is inappropriate "in an asbestos litigation case, especially where it cannot be shown that all the products to which the injured party was exposed are completely fungible." (33 Ohio St. 3d at 50, 514 N.E.2d at 700.) Moreover, the risk the manufacturer created is not accurately reflected in its market share because many products contain different degrees of asbestos, and the largest asbestos supplier, Johns–Manville, was not amenable to suit. Instead of adopting such a divergent theory, the court concluded that the problem was more in need of a legislative solution. [Citations]; see also *Cummins v. Firestone Tire & Rubber Co.* (1985), 344 Pa.Super. 9, 495 A.2d 963 (rejecting theory in action against manufacturers of multipiece tire and rim assemblies because products are not sufficiently similar to be considered identical or fungible); *Bixler v. Avondale Mills* (Minn.App.1987), 405 N.W.2d 428 (cotton flannelette not fungible product).

VI. ANALYSIS OF MARKET SHARE IN ILLINOIS

Each of the four courts which have adopted some form of market share liability has criticized and ultimately rejected in whole or in part the theory as developed in the other jurisdictions. Our appellate court also recognized that its theory may be flawed but accepted this and believed that subsequent opinions could eventually resolve the uncertainties which develop, but which other courts apparently have been unable to resolve in the past decade. (173 Ill.App.3d at 22.) We conclude that market share liability is not a sound theory, is too great a deviation from our existing tort principles and should not be applied in cases brought by plaintiffs who were exposed to DES while *in utero.*

In addition to the criticisms already expressed by the courts which recognize market share liability, we see numerous problems with its adoption. A major flaw, in regards to DES cases, is that there is only a small amount of, or in some cases no, reliable information available to establish the defendants' percentages of the market. As mentioned earlier, no party can be blamed for this fact. It is, in part, the result of the laws in effect regarding maintenance of records and factors relating to the long lapse in time from the sale of the drug to the filing of the lawsuit. The lack of available records is evidenced in this case by the fact that after extensive discovery plaintiff was unable to identify the responsible manufacturer. Many of those defendants who have been named are no longer in business or have filed motions challenging jurisdiction and for these companies especially it is unlikely that records will be available to establish their share of any market.

The courts which have adopted market share liability have done so while ruling on pretrial motions and have not had the benefit of first having heard evidence on the availability of market share data. (See *Sindell*, 26 Cal.3d at 613, 607 P.2d at 937–38, 163 Cal.Rptr. at 145–46 ("We are not unmindful of the practical problems involved in defining the market and determining market share, but these are largely matters of proof which properly cannot be determined at the pleading stage of these proceedings").) Unlike these courts, we have the benefit of the experiences of the trial courts in California which have been instructed to apply the market share liability theory. In San Francisco, the trial court determined that the only logical or practical definition for "market" would have to be on a national scale because the parties were unable to present data on a more narrow market, which the State supreme court directed it should attempt to do. The trial judge in Los Angeles expressed exasperation with the task of attempting to formulate market shares after spending over four weeks examining the DES market. (*Stapp v. Abbott Laboratories* (Super. Ct. Los Angeles County), No. C 344407 ("The harsh blunt fact that the evidence has shown is that that information and data is just not available" and "when the Supreme Court, * * * without having any evidence says that you can determine what the [sales are] as to a particular manufacturer, it's just, just not there. That data doesn't exist").) Plaintiff here argues that the difficulty the trial judge in Los Angeles experienced could be attributed to the uncooperativeness of the defendants. The transcripts clearly refute this assertion. The judge began his analysis of the situation by thanking the parties for all their cooperation and for the highly professional manner in which the case was presented. The judge then went on to criticize those who developed the market share theory because of their obvious lack of trial experience or knowledge as to what would go into proving a case based on the theory.

Acceptance of market share liability and the concomitant burden placed on the courts and the parties will imprudently bog down the judiciary in an almost futile endeavor. This would also create a tremendous cost, both monetarily and in terms of the workload, on the court system and litigants in an attempt to establish percentages based on unreliable or insufficient data. [Citations.]

If we were to allow courts and juries to apportion damages when reliable information is not available, the clear result would be that the determinations will be arbitrary and there will be wide variances between judgments, without sufficient explanation as to these differences. The unfairness inherent in apportioning damages without adequate evidence is increased for a number of reasons. It is likely that the defendant who actually sold the product is not before the court. For example, in this case defendants have presented evidence that 63 of the potential 81 manufacturers were never before the court. Other defendants either were not served, have gone out of business, have merged with other companies and due to successor liability laws cannot be held liable for the sale of DES, or are not amenable to suit in Illinois. To impose liability when it is quite possible that the defendant is not before the court is too speculative. *Ryan v. Eli Lilly & Co.* (D.S.C.1981), 514 F.Supp. 1004, 1007, 1018.

Moreover, it is unrealistic to say that a true percentage of the market can be established by the defendants before the court. Throughout the history of the use of DES as a miscarriage preventative, hundreds of manufacturers produced the product and it is impossible to bring them before our courts. The defendants who do appear will have a difficult enough time to establish their market shares. Those who cannot meet this task but desire to reduce their potential liability will have the difficult burden of establishing the shares of manufacturers not before the court. (See *George v. Parke–Davis*, 107 Wash. 2d at 597, 733 P.2d at 514 (in order to inhibit defendants from randomly impleading insolvent corporations to reduce their share of presumptive liability, defendants are required to establish the actual market share of impleaded defendants).) The result would likely be that, even though common sense dictates that other companies are responsible, market share liability makes those companies which are unable to establish their market share liable for a wholly speculative and disproportionate amount of the damages. [Citations.] If the goal of this theory is to attribute damages in accordance with the harm caused, a truly accurate market should be limited to those manufacturers of DES which was used as a miscarriage preventative and their share of that narrower market because the drug was and is safe for the other purposes for which it was sold. (Cf. *Hymowitz*, 73 N.Y.2d at 512, 539 N.E.2d at 1078, 541 N.Y.S.2d at 950 (realizing that liability will not, over the run of cases, approximate causation).) Surely, this specific market would be nearly impossible to establish.

Market share liability also has the potential to treat plaintiffs who cannot identify the specific manufacturer responsible for the DES maternally ingested more favorably than one who can. In a typical tort case the plaintiff takes the risk that the defendant will be unable to assume financial responsibility for injuries caused. However, with the market share theory, liability is spread throughout members of the industry, reducing the risk that plaintiff will be without a solvent defendant. The theory thus punishes plaintiffs who can satisfy the identification element, while creating an incentive not to locate the particular manufacturer. [Citations.]

[The court acknowledged some similarities between the burden shifting that *res ipsa loquitur* and alternative liability accomplish and the market share liability theory advocated by plaintiff. The court rejected the analogy, however, because both of the former doctrines involve only parties "who bear some culpability for causing plaintiff's injury" and because those theories also require that all parties who could have been the cause of plaintiff's injury are joined as defendants.]

Plaintiff further attempts to support her position by contending that market share liability should be applied because she has maintained a "sufficient connection" between each of the named defendants and the form of the DES which caused her condition. This link is allegedly established because of the joint industry efforts in obtaining FDA approval to sell DES. Plaintiff points out that in 1941 a "small committee" was created to gather FDA-required data and the committee jointly submitted an application for approval to market DES for non-pregnancy-related purposes. The efforts of this committee formed the basis of subsequent FDA approval for the manufacturing of DES by other companies. The information utilized at that time was also influential in securing approval in 1947 for use of DES to prevent miscarriages. Plaintiff contends she has brought before the court "virtually all" of the companies which comprised the small committee, thus she has all the parties responsible for making DES available for use as a miscarriage preventative. Moreover, she claims to have narrowed the number of potential defendants to only a few and that liability may be imposed upon them.

We believe that plaintiff's "link" is insufficient to create what is commonly understood as the connection between a potentially responsible defendant and the injury-causing product. No court which has addressed the issue has found that the actions in 1941 constituted a joint, concerted or conspiratorial effort by defendants to market DES. (See, e.g., *Hymowitz*, 73 N.Y.2d at 506–07, 539 N.E.2d at 1074–75, 541 N.Y.S.2d at 946–47; *Collins*, 116 Wis.2d at 183–88, 342 N.W.2d at 46–48.) It was upon the request of the FDA that the small group convened to present a master file of data on behalf of the rest of the industry. Thus, it is unwarranted to make each responsible for the others' products based on some type of enterprise liability theory.

The connection between this committee and a plaintiff who suffers injuries as a result of DES' being used to prevent miscarriages is even weaker because the FDA did not approve of that use of the drug until 1947 and under different circumstances than in 1941 and upon submission of additional information. (See, *e.g.*, 173 Ill.App.3d at 28 (our appellate court recognized that the joint submission of clinical data in 1941 was distinct from 1947 application process).) Reliance on the facts comprising the 1941 filings is unwarranted unless plaintiff is able to prove that one of the companies in the "small committee" manufactured the DES maternally ingested. Moreover, plaintiff overestimates her narrowing of the likely defendants. The record discloses a much greater number of potential defendants than the eight which are before this court. To say that the true defendant has been located is speculative and improper conjecture. (See *Schmidt*, 44 Ill.2d at 405; *Tiffin v. Great Atlantic & Pacific Tea Co.* (1959), 18 Ill.2d 48, 60.) The fact that over 300 companies sold a similar product for similar purposes cannot fairly be held to have created a sufficient nexus such that each company can be responsible for the injuries caused by the others' products, even under the unique facts surrounding the approval of the manufacturing of DES.

Plaintiff next claims that certain underlying principles of products liability laws dictate that we should impose liability on the manufacturers. (See 173 Ill.App.3d at 15–16 (detailing the policy reasons for products liability).) We agree with the idea that liability based on tort law should be shouldered by the responsible manufacturer or manufacturers. However, we do not believe that we should abrogate a fundamental precept of tort law to reach this goal and ignore the effects of adopting market share liability.

Other courts have looked to these underlying principles when reaching their conclusion of whether or not to recognize market share liability. One of the bases relied upon in adopting the theory is that the drug companies are better able to insure against liability and to pass the costs on. In its opinion, the appellate court concluded that the pharmaceutical drug companies were in solid financial condition and would be able to insure against drug-related costs. 173 Ill.App.3d at 26.

Defendants have strongly contested the figures and conclusions regarding their financial status and the implications regarding other participants in the drug manufacturing industry. They further argue that the expansions in tort law are having the perverted results of eliminating production of certain useful and necessary drugs, and dramatically increasing insurance costs such that some companies either can no longer obtain insurance or cannot pass the costs on to consumers.

In support of these assertions they cite examples of drugs which no longer are being produced because of potential liability as well as areas where the Federal government has had to intercede to protect from liability and insure availability of a drug. (See generally Note, *A Question of Competence: The Judicial Role in the Regulation of Pharmaceuticals*, 103 Harv. L. Rev. 773 (1990).) The New Jersey Supreme Court recently declined on policy grounds to impose market share liability on manufacturers of DPT because of the crippling effect potential liability has had on the industry. (*Shackil v. Lederle Labora-*

tories (1989), 116 N.J. 155, 561 A.2d 511 (DPT industry was diminished to one supplier and the Federal government had established a fund to deal with liability claims).) It has also been necessary for government intervention to insure availability of the swine flu and polio vaccines.

We do not believe that in this case it is necessary to become embroiled in the "insurance crisis" or to speculate as to the relative financial security of the participants in the prescription drug industry. However, we note that market share liability will surely broaden manufacturers' liability exposure because they will need to insure against losses arising from the products of others in the industry as well as their own. (See Fischer, *Products Liability—An Analysis of Market Share Liability*, 34 Vand. L. Rev. 1623, 1654 (1981) (adoption of a market share theory will dramatically increase liability exposure and it may discourage development of new products); Comment, *Market Share Liability for Defective Products: An Ill–Advised Remedy for the Problem of Identification*, 76 Nw. U.L. Rev. 300, 321–23 (1981) (increasing liability has prompted insurers to dramatically increase premiums and they are reluctant to insure particularly risky industries; this in turn has resulted in higher prices).) This added potential for liability will likely contribute to diminishing participants in the market as well as research and availability of drugs. (See *Woodill v. Parke Davis & Co.* (1980), 79 Ill.2d 26, 37 ("This Court is acutely aware of the social desirability of encouraging the research and development of beneficial drugs"); *Zafft*, 676 S.W.2d at 247 (there are legitimate concerns that market share liability "will discourage desired pharmaceutical research and development while adding little incentive to production of safe products"); *Payton v. Abbott Laboratories* (1982), 386 Mass. 540, 574, 437 N.E.2d 171, 189–90 ("Imposition of such broad liability could have a deleterious effect on the development * * * of new drugs, especially those marketed generically").) It is tempting in this case to impose liability based on the fact that these companies profited from the sale of the type of drug which may be responsible for the plaintiff's injuries, regardless of the manufacturers' ability to cover these costs. However, this is not a strong enough reason to adopt a theory which would alter our tort law significantly while only providing a markedly flawed alternative with unclear future ramifications. [Citations.] Perhaps, as a number of other courts and commentators have suggested, this change is most appropriate for the legislature to develop, with its added ability to hold hearings and determine public policy. [Citations.]

Another underlying principle of products liability law is to enhance safer production of goods. (See Prosser, *The Assault Upon the Citadel*, 69 Yale L.J. 1099, 1119 (1960).) It is argued that adoption of market share liability in this case will provide incentive to produce safer generic drugs. However, we are not convinced that utilization of market share liability in suits against manufacturers of DES will have such an effect, though we recognize some courts and commentators believe market share liability is necessary for promotion of this safety goal. (See, *e.g., Collins,* 116 Wis.2d at 192–93, 342 N.W.2d at 49–50; *Sindell,* 26 Cal.3d at 611, 607 P.2d at 936, 163 Cal.Rptr. at 144; Robinson, *Multiple Causation in Tort Law: Reflections on the DES Cases,* 68 Va.L.Rev. 713, 741 (1982); Comment, *The DES Manufacturer Identification Problem: A Florida Public Policy Approach,* 40 U. Miami L.Rev. 857, 867–70 (1986).) First, it is not clear that the drug industry needs this even further amount of encouragement to produce safer drugs, above and beyond the incentives that products liability and negligence laws provide. (Fischer, *Products Liability—An Analysis of Market Share Liability,* 34 Vand.L.Rev. 1623, 1657 (1981) (market share liability may result in over-deterrence); Note, *A Question of Competence: The Judicial Role in the Regulation of Pharmaceuticals,* 103 Harv. L. Rev. at 780–83 (1990).) Second, it is unlikely that an overall safety incentive could result from imposition of market share liability 40 years after the undesirable behavior occurred and almost 20 years after the potential harm was discovered and the product removed from the market. (See *Zafft,* 676 S.W.2d at 247 (theory adds little incentive for production of safe products).) Third, market share liability imposes potential liability on all manufacturers in the particular industry; thus there may not be an incentive to produce safer products if liability could still be imposed as a result of the negligence of others in the industry and if the manufacturer knows that others in the industry will absorb the damages resulting from its negligence. (Miller & Hancock, *Perspectives on Market Share Liability: Time for a Reassessment?,* 88 W.Va.L.Rev. 81, 103–04 (1985).) Moreover, this theory is being accepted in a limited number of jurisdictions and is only being applied to manufacturers of DES or similar products. Thus by our adopting market share liability, the goal of warning manufacturers to produce safer products likely will not reach a wide array of producers.

* * *

The concept that liability may be imposed based merely on a breach of duty, without causation being established, has long been rejected in American tort law. * * * These principles should not be ignored merely because the defendants are members of the drug industry.

Abrogation of these concepts would also result in violating the principle that manufacturers are not insurers of their industry. In *Woodill v. Parke Davis & Co.* (1980), 79 Ill.2d 26, this court held that in a strict liability action based on a failure to warn of a danger the plaintiff must allege and prove that defendant knew or should have known of the danger and this is tested on knowledge existing at the time of production. The holding was "justified because a logical limit must be placed on the scope of a manufacturer's liability * * *. To hold a manufacturer liable for failure to warn of a danger of which it would be impossible to know based on the present state of human knowledge would make the manufacturer the virtual insurer of the product, a position rejected by this court in *Suvada*. [Citation.] Strict liability is not the equivalent of absolute liability." 79 Ill.2d at 37; see also *Coney v. J.L.G. Industries, Inc.* (1983), 97 Ill.2d 104, 111 ("imposition of strict liability was not meant to make the manufacturer an absolute insurer"); *Suvada v. White Motor Co.* (1965), 32 Ill.2d 612, 623.

The market share liability theory disregards these precedents and turns manufacturers into insurers of their own products and products made by others in the industry. (*Mulcahy v. Eli Lilly & Co.*, 386 N.W.2d at 76; Kroll, *Intra-Industry Joint Liability: The Era of Absolute Products Liability*, 687 Ins.L.J. 185, 194–97 (1980).) As illustrated in this case, the majority of plausible defendants have not been or cannot be brought before the court. Those who are present have the difficult burden of establishing their share of a market. The companies which cannot prove their share will be made to pay the unattributed portion of the damages, thus paying the damages which rightfully belong to companies which are insolvent, not amenable to suit in the jurisdiction or for some other reason are not before the court. *Sindell* justified its ruling in part on the belief that over the run of the cases a company's liability would approximate the harm it caused. (*Sindell*, 26 Cal.3d at 612, 607 P.2d at 937, 163 Cal.Rptr. at 145.) However, this is a purely illusory assumption, as recognized in *Hymowitz*, 73 N.Y.2d at 512, 539 N.E.2d at 1078, 541 N.Y.S.2d at 950. Justice Richardson, writing for the dissenters in *Sindell*, argued that market share liability makes the entire drug industry "an insurer of all injuries attributable to defective drugs of uncertain or unprovable origin, including those injuries manifesting themselves a generation later, and regardless of whether particular defendants had any part whatever in causing the claimed injury." (*Sindell*, 26 Cal.3d at 621, 607 P.2d at 942–43, 67 Cal.Rptr. at 150–51 (Richardson, J., dissenting).) We agree with his conclusion that such a solution is an unreasonable over-reaction in attempting to achieve what is perceived as a socially satisfying result.

The plaintiff contends that by not recognizing a market share liability theory we will be abdicating our responsibility in the development of Illinois common law. We have not in the past been hesitant to develop new tort concepts; however, in this instance we decline to do so because of the infirmities in the proposed theory. Furthermore, this is too great a deviation from a tort principle which we have found to serve a vital function in the law, causation in fact, especially when market share liability is a flawed concept and its application will likely be only to a narrow class of defendants.

* * *

JUSTICE CLARK, concurring in part and dissenting in part:

I agree with the majority that the appellate court should not have adopted the theory of market share liability set forth by the Washington Supreme Court in *Martin v. Abbott Laboratories* (1984), 102 Wash. 2d 581, 689 P.2d 368. However, I would adopt the theory of market share liability established by the court of appeals of New York in *Hymowitz v. Eli Lilly & Co.* (1989), 73 N.Y.2d 487, 539 N.E.2d 1069, 541 N.Y.S.2d 941, because I believe that the *Hymowitz* theory provides a fair and rational way to remedy the injustice presented by this case and avoids the shortcomings of previous theories of market share liability. I therefore dissent from the majority's outright rejection of market share liability.

This court long ago described the common law as "a system of elementary rules and of general judicial declarations of principles, which are continually expanding with the progress of society, adapting themselves to the gradual changes of trade, commerce, arts, inventions and the exigencies and usages of the country." (*Kreitz v. Behrensmeyer* (1894), 149 Ill. 496, 502; see also *Torres v. Walsh* (1983), 98 Ill.2d 338, 347; *People ex rel. Keenan v. McGuane* (1958), 13 Ill.2d 520, 535 (the common law is "a system of law whose outstanding characteristic is its adaptability and capacity for growth").) The common law, of course, does not change on its own. Instead, it is the responsibility of the legislature and the judiciary to cooperate "in examining and changing the common law to conform with the ever-changing demands of the community." (*Alvis v. Ribar* (1981), 85 Ill.2d 1, 23.) Where "the legislature has, for whatever reason, failed to act to remedy a gap in the common law that results in injustice, *it is the imperative duty of the court to repair that injustice and reform the law to be responsive to the demands of society.*" (Emphasis added.) *Alvis*, 85 Ill.2d at 23–24.

This court has frequently exercised its duty to modify the common law to remedy an injustice that has resulted from changes in society. In *Suvada v. White Motor Co.* (1965), 32 Ill.2d 612, 617, for example, this court abolished the traditional common law requirement that a manufacturer could not be held liable for injuries to a person not in privity with the manufacturer, and held that any such liability need not be based upon negligence, but instead can be based upon strict liability in tort (*Suvada*, 32 Ill.2d at 621–22). In so doing, this court rejected the idea that the abolition of negligence and privity of contract in products liability cases should be left for the legislature, stating that "'[h]aving found [the doctrines of privity in contract and negligence] to be unsound and unjust under present conditions, we consider that we have not only the power, but the duty to abolish [those doctrines].'" *Suvada*, 32 Ill.2d at 623, quoting *Molitor v. Kaneland Community Unit District No. 302* (1959), 18 Ill.2d 11, 25.

Similarly, in *Alvis*, 85 Ill.2d at 24–25, this court replaced the traditional common law doctrine of contributory negligence with the doctrine of comparative negligence. This court explained:

"Clearly, the need for stability in law must not be allowed to obscure the changing needs of society or to veil the injustice resulting from a doctrine in need of reevaluation. * * * We cannot continue to ignore the plight of plaintiffs who, because of some negligence on their part, are forced to bear the entire burden of their injuries. Neither can we condone the policy of allowing defendants to totally escape liability for injuries arising from their own negligence on the pretext that another party's negligence has contributed to such injuries." *Alvis*, 85 Ill.2d at 24-25.

The plaintiff in this case has alleged that all of the DES manufactured by the defendants was identical and shared a common defect, and that plaintiff developed cancer as a result of this defect in the DES. The defendants' sole argument on appeal is that even if the above allegations are true, the defendants cannot be held liable for negligence or strict liability because the plaintiff cannot show causation in fact. Thus, for the purposes of this appeal, the defendants have admitted that they manufactured and marketed a defective product, and that the plaintiff was injured as a result of the defective product.

Under the "elementary rules and * * * general judicial declarations of principles" (*Kreitz*, 149 Ill. at 502) which comprise our tort system, the plaintiff will not be compensated for her damages because, through no fault of her own, she cannot identify which of the wrongdoing defendants manufactured the DES that caused her injuries. The plaintiff's inability to identify the single manufacturer who caused her injuries is based upon a combination of factors, including the fungibility of DES, the length of time that it has taken for plaintiff's injuries to manifest themselves since the DES was ingested by her mother, and the DES manufacturers' inadequate record-keeping and product labeling. Unfortunately, this combination of factors prevents not only this plaintiff from recovering damages for her injuries under our current tort system, it is also likely to prevent numerous other so-called "DES daughters" from recovering damages for their injuries. That is, unless this court acts to remedy the gap in our common law which allows such injustices to occur. See *Alvis*, 85 Ill.2d at 23-24.

The principle of causation in fact, like the principles of contributory negligence, privity of contract and negligence in products liability cases, "is not an end of the legal system, but rather the means by which the legal system achieves its purposes" (*Shackil v. Lederle Laboratories* (1989), 116 N.J. 155, 200, 561 A.2d 511, 534 (O'Hern, J., dissenting)). Where such "means" prove inadequate to meet the changing needs of society, or where such "means" cause injustice, our common law tradition demands that they be modified. (See, *e.g., Alvis*, 85 Ill.2d at 24-25 (replacing contributory negligence with comparative negligence); *Suvada*, 32 Ill.2d at 623 (abolishing requirements of privity in contract and negligence in products liability actions).) Thus, as the majority notes, where necessary to avoid injustice, courts have relaxed the requirement that a plaintiff prove causation in fact by adopting doctrines such as *res ipsa loquitur* and alternative liability. (See 137 Ill.2d at 256–57.) Alternative liability, for example, as codified in the Restatement (Second) of Torts, provides:

> "Where the conduct of two or more actors is tortious, and it is proved that harm has been caused to the plaintiff by only one of them, but there is uncertainty as to which one has caused it, the burden is upon each such actor to prove that he has not caused the harm." (Restatement (Second) of Torts § 433B(3), at 441–42 (1965).)

The policy justification for relaxing the causation requirement in alternative liability situations is that it would be unjust to permit "proved wrongdoers, who among them have inflicted an injury upon the entirely innocent plaintiff, to escape liability merely because the nature of their conduct and the resulting harm has made it difficult or impossible to prove which of them has caused the harm." (Restatement (Second) of Torts § 433B, comment f, at 446.) Although the doctrines of *res ipsa loquitur* and alternative liability may not be applicable to the facts in this case (see 137 Ill.2d at 257), both doctrines illustrate the fact that traditional tort concepts such as causation in fact must occasionally be modified to meet the needs of our ever-changing society.

The highest courts of six of our sister States have directly addressed the issue that is currently before this court. Four of those courts have sought to remedy the injustice arising from gaps in their common law by replacing the element of causation in fact with some form of market share liability. [Citations.] These courts, while disagreeing as to precisely what variant of market share liability should be applied, have recognized that "the ever-evolving dictates of justice and fairness, which are the heart of our common-law system, require formation of a remedy for injuries caused by DES." (*Hymowitz*, 73 N.Y.2d at 507, 539 N.E.2d at 1075, 541 N.Y.S.2d at 947; [citations].) Only two of the six State high courts that have addressed the issue have refused to modify their common law to recognize market share liability. See *Mulcahy v. Eli Lilly & Co.* (Iowa 1986), 386 N.W.2d 67; *Zafft v. Eli Lilly & Co.* (Mo.1984), 676 S.W.2d 241.

The most recent State high court to address the issue is the court of appeals of New York. As the majority notes, that court considered each of the previous three judicially promulgated theories of market share liability, and recognized those theories' shortcomings, before developing its own theory in *Hymowitz*. (See 137 Ill.2d at 244–45; see also *Hymowitz*, 73 N.Y.2d at 509–11, 539 N.E.2d at 1076–78, 541 N.Y.S.2d at 948–50 ("we heed both the lessons learned through experience in other jurisdictions and the realities of the mass litigation of DES claims in this State").) To avoid the theoretical and practical problems of the previous theories, the court of appeals of New York adopted a theory which apportions liability based upon "the over-all culpability of each defendant, measured by the amount of risk of injury each defendant created to the public-at-large." *Hymowitz*, 73 N.Y.2d at 512, 539 N.E.2d at 1078, 541 N.Y.S.2d at 950.) The "amount of risk of injury each defendant created to the public-at-large" is equal to the defendant's share of the national market of DES sold for pregnancy use. *Hymowitz*, 73 N.Y.2d at 512, 539 N.E.2d at 1078, 541 N.Y.S.2d at 950.

Because liability under the *Hymowitz* theory "is based on the overall risk produced, and not causation in a single case," a defendant who was a part of the market of DES sold for pregnancy use cannot escape liability merely because the defendant can show that its DES could not in fact have been the DES that caused the plaintiff's injuries. (*Hymowitz*, 73 N.Y.2d at 512, 539 N.E.2d at 1078, 541 N.Y.S.2d at 950.) However, a defendant can escape liability if the defendant can show that it "was not a member of the national market of DES marketed for pregnancy [by showing, for example, that it] sold DES in a form unsuitable for use during pregnancy, or * * * that its product was not marketed for pregnancy use." *Hymowitz*, 73 N.Y.2d at 512 n.2, 539 N.E.2d at 1078 n.2, 541 N.Y.S.2d at 950 n.2.

The majority rejects the *Hymowitz* approach, concluding, in a rather cursory fashion, that "[j]ust as the previous theories have not been embraced by subsequent courts, it is unlikely that New York's theory will receive broad acceptance." (137 Ill.2d at 246.) The majority's rejection of the *Hymowitz* theory of market share liability is apparently based upon a number of specific criticisms which have been made of the market share theories previously developed by courts in this country, and upon other more general criticisms of the overall concept of market share liability. See 137 Ill.2d at 251–52.

One reason the majority rejects market share liability is the majority's fear that "market share liability will surely broaden manufacturers' liability exposure because they will need to insure against losses arising from the products of others in the industry as well as their own." According to the majority, "[t]his added potential for liability will likely contribute to diminishing participants in the market as well as research and availability of drugs." 137 Ill.2d at 261–62.

The majority apparently believes that market share liability will increase liability exposure in three ways. First, the majority notes that market share theories which variously inflate liability to account for those manufacturers that are not before the court, impose joint and several liability, or impose liability on a *pro rata* basis, may cause manufacturers to incur liability in excess of their market shares. (See 137 Ill.2d at 240–42, 267–68.) However, liability under the *Hymowitz* theory is not inflated to account for absent manufacturers, is several only, and is not imposed on a *pro rata* basis. Instead, manufacturers under the *Hymowitz* theory can only be held liable for their market share.

The majority also believes that liability imposed under market share theories, unlike liability imposed under traditional tort principles, may exceed the actual harm caused by the manufacturers. (See 137 Ill.2d at 246–47, 254.) However, as the following hypothetical illustrates, this assumption is simply not true.

Let us assume that there were only three manufacturers of DES: manufacturer X, who manufactured 50% of the DES market, and manufacturers Y and Z, who each manufactured 25% of the DES market. Because each manufacturer's DES was identical and shared a common defect, we could assume that the DES manufactured by X would cause 50% of the cancers resulting from DES, and that both Y and Z would have manufactured the DES which caused 25% of the cancers resulting from DES. If identification of the DES manufacturer could be made in all cases, X would be the sole defendant in 50% of the DES daughter cases and would be liable for 100% of the damages in those cases. Similarly, Y and Z would each be liable for 100% of the damages in 25% of the DES daughter cases. If the average amount of damages awarded in X's cases was equal to the average amount of damages awarded in Y's and Z's cases, then X would be paying 50%, and Y and Z would each be paying 25%, of the damages arising from DES.

Under market share liability, on the other hand, X, Y and Z would all be named defendants in 100% of the DES cases and each manufacturer would only be liable for its market share of the damages in each case. Thus, X would be liable for 50%, and Y and Z would each be liable for 25%, of the damages arising from DES; precisely what each would be expected to pay under traditional tort principles. See Comment, *DES and a Proposed Theory of Enterprise Liability*, 46 Fordham L. Rev. 963, 994 (1978).

The correlation between market share liability and liability under traditional tort principles may not be perfect. It is of course possible that the average amount of damages in X's cases under traditional tort principles could be less than the average amount of damages in Y's and Z's cases, in which case X would incur more liability under market share liability than under traditional tort principles. However, it is equally possible that the average amount of damages in X's cases could exceed the average amount of damages in Y's and Z's cases, in which case X would incur more liability under traditional tort principles. In either event, the correlation between the potential for liability under traditional tort principles and the potential for liability under market share theories is close enough to allay any fears that market share liability will greatly increase manufacturers' liability exposure. See

Comment, *DES and a Proposed Theory of Enterprise Liability*, 46 Fordham L. Rev. 963, 994 (1978).

A third way in which liability exposure may be increased under market share liability is that certain manufacturers may be exposed "to double liability, first to plaintiffs who can identify them as the causal party, and again to plaintiffs who cannot." (137 Ill.2d at 255, citing Comment, *Overcoming the Identification Burden in DES Litigation: The Market Share Liability Theory*, 65 Marq. L. Rev. 609, 632–33 (1982).) "Double liability" does not mean that plaintiffs will be able to recover additional damages, or bring more than one action for damages, if market share liability is adopted. Instead, "double liability" refers to the possibility that manufacturers who are liable to certain DES daughters under traditional tort principles, and who are also liable to other DES daughters under market share liability, may incur more than their market share of liability in cases arising from DES. For example, let us assume that manufacturer X from the above hypothetical, in addition to being held liable for 50% of the damages in all cases in which identification could not be made, was also identified in a number of cases as the manufacturer of the DES which was the cause in fact of the plaintiffs' injuries. Because identification could be made, the plaintiffs in those cases would seek recovery under traditional tort principles, rather than under market share liability. If those plaintiffs prevailed in their suits, X would be liable for all the damages in those cases.

Let us further assume that the DES manufactured by Y and Z could not be identified as the cause in fact of any plaintiff's injuries. Y and Z would therefore be liable for their market shares in cases in which identification could not be made, but would incur no liability in those cases involving X in which identification could be made. Under such a scenario, X's total liability in DES cases would be greater than his market share, while Y and Z would be liable for less than their market shares. X would in effect be paying for damages caused by Y and Z.

I agree with the majority that, if market share liability were adopted, manufacturers who can be causally linked to DES which caused damages in a specific case could incur a disproportionate amount of liability. However, to ameliorate any disproportionate allocation of liability that could occur from so-called "double liability," I would allow a manufacturer who has been held liable in a "cause in fact" case a right to recover contribution from other DES manufacturers. Each of the manufacturers would be liable in contribution for a percentage of the plaintiff's damages equal to the manufacturers' individual market shares. Contribution would therefore compensate the original manufacturer for any liability it incurred under traditional tort principles in excess of its market share, and would force the other manufacturers to pay the amount of damages they would have paid had identification not been made.

It is certainly true that recognizing market share liability may result in the drug manufacturers in this case incurring liability for the manufacture of defective products that, because the plaintiff cannot prove causation in fact, the manufacturers would not otherwise incur. However, I do not believe that, under the guise of limiting "liability exposure" and encouraging participation "in the market as well as research and availability of drugs" (137 Ill.2d at 261–62), wrongdoing manufacturers should be allowed to benefit from this situation. The unfortunate result of the majority's logic is that "a manufacturer must bear the same risks of liability that the majority seeks to insulate the industry from, except to the extent that the company can issue a product that would be for any reason difficult to distinguish from that of other manufacturers." *Shackil v. Lederle Laboratories* (1989), 116 N.J. 155, 202, 561 A.2d 511, 535 (O'Hern, J., dissenting).

A second reason the majority rejects market share liability is that under market share liability, "it is inevitable that some defendants wholly innocent of wrongdoing towards the particular plaintiff will shoulder part or all of the responsibility for the injury caused" (137 Ill.2d at 258; see also 137 Ill.2d at 247), and that "[t]he concept that liability may be imposed based merely on a breach of duty, without causation being established, has long been rejected in American tort law" (137 Ill.2d at 266). Although the majority's assertions are true, they simply do not address the question at issue here.

The question at issue in this case is "whether, in a negligence and strict liability cause of action, Illinois should substitute for the element of causation in fact a theory of market share liability when identification of the manufacturer of the drug that injured the plaintiff is not possible." (137 Ill.2d at 226.) The majority's claim that market share liability should not be adopted because market share liability will result in liability being imposed upon defendants who did not actually cause the plaintiff's injuries essentially amounts to an argument that market share liability should not be substituted for the element of causation in fact because, under market share liability, defendants may be held liable without a showing of causation in fact. The argument thus begs the question. The fact that causation in fact has been around a long time similarly fails to address the question.

A third reason for the majority's decision is that the majority is not convinced that adoption of market share liability will either provide incentive for production of safe drugs, or encourage drug manufacturers to adopt procedures which would enable plaintiffs to identify culpable parties. (137 Ill.2d at 264.) The majority states that "it is not clear that the drug industry needs this even *further* amount of encouragement to produce safer drugs, above and beyond the incentives that products liability and negligence laws provide." (Emphasis in original.) 137 Ill.2d at 263.

The majority may be correct that, where traditional products liability and negligence laws can be utilized to impose liability upon manufacturers of defective drugs, additional encouragement to produce safe drugs may not be needed. However, where manufacturers can escape liability because it is impossible for a plaintiff to prove causation in fact, traditional tort laws do not provide any incentive to produce safe drugs. In such situations, market share liability would not act as a *further* encouragement to produce safe drugs. Instead, market share liability would act as the *only* encouragement to produce safe drugs. Thus, market share liability insures that the incentive to produce safe products provided by traditional tort laws will remain effective in situations where identification of a particular wrongdoer is impossible.

The majority further states that "it is unlikely that an overall safety incentive could result from imposition of market share liability 40 years after the undesirable behavior occurred and almost 20 years after the potential harm was discovered and the product removed from the market." (137 Ill.2d at 263–64.) Furthermore, because market share liability "is only being applied to manufacturers of DES or similar products * * * the goal of warning manufacturers to produce safer products likely will not reach a wide array of producers." (137 Ill.2d at 264.) This aspect of the majority's reasoning is somewhat disingenuous.

When the majority considers the potential negative effects of market share liability (*i.e.*, stifling development and marketing of new drugs), the majority argues that adoption of market share liability in this case will have far-reaching, dramatic consequences on the entire pharmaceutical industry. (See, *e.g.*, 137 Ill.2d at 261–62 ("adoption of a market share theory will dramatically increase liability exposure * * * [,] dramatically increase [insurance] premiums * * * [and] will likely contribute to diminishing participants in the market as well as research and availability of drugs").) However, the majority also argues that any potential positive effects of market share liability (*i.e.*, encouraging the production of safe drugs) are unlikely to occur because this is an isolated case which will have little impact on the pharmaceutical industry as a whole. See 137 Ill.2d at 264.

If the majority believes that the potentially negative effects of adopting market share liability in this case would be felt throughout the pharmaceutical industry, then the majority should conclude that the potentially positive effects of adopting market share liability in this case would be felt throughout the pharmaceutical industry. Conversely, if the majority believes that the positive aspects of adopting market share liability would not be noticeable because they could only affect the DES market, a market which has been nonexistent for 20 years, then the majority should also conclude that the potential negative effects of market share liability would only be felt in the now nonexistent DES market (and so there would be no need for the majority to fear that adoption of market share liability would stifle the development and marketing of new drugs).

Another reason the majority is not convinced that adoption of market share liability will encourage the production of safe drugs is that "market share liability imposes potential liability on all manufacturers in the particular industry; thus there may not be an incentive to produce safer products if liability could still be imposed as a result of the negligence of others in the industry and if the manufacturer knows that others in the industry will absorb the damages resulting from its negligence." 137 Ill.2d at 264.

This argument is incorrect, as an initial matter, because market share liability would not impose liability upon all manufacturers in a particular industry. Instead, market share liability can only be imposed upon those manufacturers within a particular industry who manufacture an identical product, and only if that product shares a common defect which caused a plaintiff's injuries. Furthermore, it is incorrect to assume that market share liability would not provide an incentive to produce safe products.

If a manufacturer took steps to insure that its product was not defective, then the product manufactured by the manufacturer would not be identical to the defective products manufactured by those manufacturers subject to market share liability. For example, if any of the defendants in this case had taken precautions to insure that their DES was not defective, those defendants would have altered their DES to correct the defects before marketing it. By altering the DES to correct the defects, those defendants would have manufactured a product which was not identical to the defective DES that was manufactured by the other defendants. The defendants who took precautions and modified their DES, therefore, could not be held liable under market share liability. On the other hand, those defendants who did not take safety precautions, but instead manufactured a defective product, would be the only manufacturers subject to market share liability. It is therefore clear that market share liability does provide a strong incentive for manufacturers to produce safe products.

The majority also argues that market share liability "punishes plaintiffs who can satisfy the identification element, while creating an incentive not to locate the particular manufacturer." (137 Ill.2d at 255.) However, because liability under the *Hymowitz* market share theory is several only and is not inflated to reflect manufacturers that are not before the court, and in light of the fact that many DES manufacturers are now bankrupt, plaintiffs utilizing the market share theory of liability are certain to recover less than 100% of their damages. Plaintiffs who are able to identify the manufacturer of the DES that caused their injuries, on the other hand, will be able to recover 100% of their damages under traditional tort law. Consequently, plaintiffs would still have a strong incentive to identify specific manufacturers.

The final reason the majority refuses to adopt market share liability is the majority's belief that, as a practical matter, it will be impossible to accurately establish market shares. The majority notes that "[t]he courts which have adopted market share liability have done so while ruling on pretrial motions and have not had the benefit of first having heard evidence on the availability of market share data." (137 Ill.2d at 252.) However, I note that the majority in this case is also ruling on a pretrial motion, and therefore the majority is similarly acting "without the benefit of first having heard evidence on the availability of market share data."

The only pieces of "evidence" which the majority cites in support of its belief that market share liability is unworkable are a statement made by a San Francisco trial court judge that market share liability can only "logically or practically be applied" on a national, rather than regional, scale (*In re Complex DES Litigation* (Cal.Super.Ct. San Francisco County), No. 830—109), and a statement made by a Los Angeles trial judge which "expressed exasperation with the task of attempting to formulate market shares" (see *Stapp v. Abbott Laboratories* (Cal.Super.Ct. Los Angeles County), No. C 344407). (See 137 Ill.2d at 252–53.) Neither of these pieces of "evidence" convinces me that it would be impossible to accurately establish a manufacturer's national market share as required by the *Hymowitz* theory of market share liability. On the contrary, the San Francisco trial judge's statement actually suggests that such a national market can be established. Furthermore, according to the court of appeals of New York, a national market has in fact been established in the San Francisco case. See *Hymowitz*, 73 N.Y.2d at 509, 539 N.E.2d at 1076, 541 N.Y.S.2d at 948, citing *In re Complex DES Litigation* (Cal.Super.Ct. San Francisco County), No. 830–109.

I have no doubt that establishment of a national market would be a very difficult, costly, and time-consuming process. I also agree that a legislative response to the problems of DES daughters might provide a more efficient remedy than litigation. (See 137 Ill.2d at 253.) Until such time as the legislature acts, however, this court has a duty to continue developing the common law to keep up with the demands of our changing society. I therefore dissent.

D. APPORTIONING CAUSATION

REPLACE Martin v. Owens–Corning Fiberglas Corporation on pages 952–57 with:

DAFLER v. RAYMARK INDUSTRIES, INC.
Superior Court of New Jersey, Appellate Division, 1992.
259 N.J.Super. 17, 611 A.2d 136.

KING, P.J.A.D.

I

This appeal and cross-appeal are taken from a verdict in plaintiff's favor and a jury's apportionment of responsibility between plaintiff and defendant in an asbestos product liability case. The case presents a question of first impression in this State concerning apportionment of damages for lung cancer between an asbestos producer and a cigarette smoker. The jury found that plaintiff contributed 70% to his lung cancer by cigarette smoking and that defendant Keene Corporation (Keene) contributed 30% to plaintiff's lung cancer by its asbestos products used in shipbuilding. The damage verdict for lung cancer was molded to reflect this apportionment. We conclude that both the apportionment by the jury and the general verdict in plaintiff's favor find reasonable factual support in the record and we affirm.

II

* * * On October 10, 1986 plaintiff sued 11 defendants, all manufacturers or distributors of asbestos products. At the jury trial in May 1991 the only remaining defendant was Keene, which had stipulated to successor liability for the asbestos products of its predecessors, Ehret Magnesia Manufacturing Company and Baldwin–Hill Corporation. Plaintiff claimed that he developed asbestosis and lung cancer as a result of occupational exposure to asbestos during his six-year employment at the New York Shipyard in Camden, from 1939 to 1945.

On May 21, 1991 the jury returned liability and damage verdicts in plaintiff's favor. The jury found unanimously that "asbestos exposure was a substantial contributing cause of Mr. Dafler's lung cancer." The jury found Keene, through its predecessors, a substantial contributing cause and 95% responsible. The jury found Garlock, Inc., a defendant who had settled for $2,500 before trial, 5% responsible. The monetary awards were: for asbestosis, $60,000; for lung cancer, $140,000—an aggregate of $200,000. The $60,000 award for asbestosis was apportioned $52,500 to Mr. Dafler for his asbestosis injuries, $7,500 to Mrs. Dafler for her derivative claim. The $140,000 award for lung cancer was broken down as $122,500 to Mr. Dafler for his lung cancer, and $17,500 to Mrs. Dafler for her derivative claim.

As a result of these findings, the overall verdict of $200,000 was reduced by 5% to $190,000 because of the liability attributed to Garlock, Inc. The lung cancer verdicts alone were subjected to the 30/70% apportionment ratio between plaintiff and defendant Keene arrived at by the jury. The residual asbestosis injury award, of course, was not subject to apportionment since it was all attributable to defendant Keene. The net aggregate award to plaintiff, after these adjustments for the settlement with Garlock, Inc. and the plaintiff's own contribution to his lung cancer by smoking, was $96,900.

* * *

Both plaintiff and Keene appeal. In this appeal plaintiff * * * claims * * * there was insufficient evidence to allow the jury to apportion damages for plaintiff's lung cancer * * *.

III

These are the facts presented at trial. Plaintiff, Frank Dafler, age 70, worked as a shipfitter at the New York Shipyard in Camden from 1939 to 1945. During the World War II era New York Shipyard was one of the world's busiest ship building facilities, employing 36,000 men. During this period plaintiff worked on 12 to 13 ships. He could not recall the dates, but he remembered the names of the ships. He worked on the battleship, South Dakota; the light cruisers: Alaska, Cleveland, Guam, Hawaii and Montpelier; the carriers: Belleau Wood, Cowpens, Cabot, Princeton, Independence, and Monterey; and a tender, Vulcan.

Dafler spent all of his time at the Shipyard working on board these ships. He spent about 70% of his time working in engine rooms and boiler rooms in very close proximity to the pipefitters who used asbestos and asbestos-containing products to cover the numerous pipes housed in those areas. Dafler himself did not work with asbestos, but he said it was all around him. The pipefitters and pipe coverers worked continuously, cutting and cementing pipes. He did not recall the brand names of any of the asbestos products because these products did not relate to his job as a shipfitter, working on the steel plating of the hull and bulkheads. He saw no health warning signs anywhere. No masks were used or provided. He did recall that the pipefitters' use of asbestos made the air very dusty. There was no ventilation in the boiler or engine rooms during construction. He described the asbestos, held in 80 to 100-pound bags, as "very, very dusty" and likened it to pulverized lime. He had no further exposure to asbestos after leaving the Shipyard.

Louis Joyce, also about age 70, testified as a witness on product identification and product nexus. He worked in the Shipyard for about two and one-half years, from 1942 to 1944. He was a helper or handyman to the mechanics in the sheet metal department, putting the permanent ventilation systems in the boiler rooms or engine rooms of the ships. In his job with the fabricating mechanics, he worked right next to the shipfitters. He described the overall work as a continuous "crash-program," around-the-clock; sometimes the men worked double-shifts. He worked on board the ships about 90% of his time at the Shipyard.

Joyce remembered working on nine to ten ships. Of these, he remembered working on the battleship, South Dakota, and the carriers: Princeton, Independence, Langley, Cabot, Cowpens, Monterey, Bataan, Belleau Wood, and San Jacinto. He also worked on a number of cruisers but could not give their names. Joyce and plaintiff named seven ships in common, not including cruisers, where they both worked in the boiler and engine rooms.

Joyce and plaintiff did not know each other when they worked at the Shipyard. Up to about 500 people worked on a ship at the same time. Joyce recalled that the pipefitters and pipe coverers, who worked in the boiler and engine rooms, used Ehret asbestos pipe covering, Johns–Manville pipe covering, Baldwin Mono Block asbestos covering, and Ehret and Johns–Manville asbestos-cement bags. He said that he observed these products daily during his employment at the Shipyard. He also recalled seeing Garlock gaskets used.

Joyce saw Ehret asbestos cement in bags "from the first week he worked to the last week." He said that he saw Ehret's asbestos pipe covering 80% of the time. He saw these Ehret cement bags daily, and on each of the nine or ten ships he worked on. He said that he saw more Ehret's pipe covering and cement than Johns–Manville. He saw no health warnings anywhere; there was no ventilation system operating during the time he worked in the ships.

Joyce said that the pipefitters' use of these asbestos products created dust to the extent that "it seemed like a snowstorm." Cleaners would use air hoses and "the stuff would be flying all over the place." When the pipe coverers were dumping the bags of cement and mixing cement, "the air was dusty. It was a loose type of cement like you would pour out and then they would have to get some water to try to mix it." Joyce said their clothes "were very dusty with various dust and fibers all over our clothes and in our hair. It was itchy and some of it you couldn't get off your clothes." He recalled that when Garlock gaskets were used, some were "punched put" on the work site, sending off asbestos dust. On a scale of one to 1,000 (highest) for dustiness, Joyce estimated that Garlock gaskets were one and the pipe covering and cement were 800 or 900.

The plaintiff began experiencing shortness of breath in the 1970s. In 1984 he went to the hospital for breathing problems. The diagnosis in 1984 was asbestosis. He then decreased the time that he worked between 1984 and 1989 because of his breathing problem. In 1984 he began seeing Dr. Agia, a pulmonary specialist, twice a year for x-rays and pulmonary function tests. In 1989 the doctors found a cancerous tumor in plaintiff's lung and surgery ensued. Since his surgery plaintiff has had limited mobility and physical capacity. Plaintiff said that he smoked cigarettes for almost 45 years, since age 18. He had a pack-a-day habit until his diagnosis of asbestosis in 1984 when he quit.

The plaintiff presented two medical experts: Dr. Guidice, a pulmonary specialist, and Dr. Stone, a pathologist. Dr. Guidice explained that the cause of plaintiff's asbestosis and later bronchogenic carcinoma, or lung cancer, was his occupational exposure to asbestos at the Shipyard. His opinion, and Dr. Stone's, on causation amply created a jury question on the claimed work-connected genesis of the lung cancer, a causation which defendant's expert, Dr. DeMopolous, a pathologist, denied completely. He thought that cigarettes alone caused the plaintiff's lung cancer.

The experts also testified on the epidemiological aspects of asbestosis and cigarette smoking. Dr. Guidice explained that there is a "base line" relative risk of 11 cases of lung cancer per 100,000 persons in the general population per year. This "base line" is for people in the general population who do not smoke and are not exposed to asbestos. The relative risk of lung cancer with industrial exposure to asbestos, like plaintiff's occupational exposure, increases five-fold (5:1), or to 55 cases per 100,000 of population per year. The relative risk of exposure to asbestos *plus* cigarette smoking is not additive, *i.e.*, 10 + 5 or 15–fold, but becomes what Dr. Guidice described as "multiplicative or synergistic," or 50 times (50:1) the "base line," *i.e.*, 550 cases per 100,000 of population per year.

Dr. Guidice could not apportion the causation of plaintiff's lung cancer between his asbestosis and his long-term cigarette smoking. He said when asked about apportionment: "No, and I don't know anybody that's able to do that. That's not possible. This relationship is synergistic and multiplicative between those two cancer causing agents. It's not possible to distinguish which contribution is caused by asbestos and which is caused by cigarette smoking." He conceded that the major cause of lung cancer in the United States is cigarette smoking.

Dr. Stone essentially agreed with Dr. Guidice on the epidemiological data. He thought the relative risk for cigarette smoking alone was about 10 to 12:1 above the "base line," the relative risk for asbestosis alone was about 6 to 7:1 above the "base line." He said that "the lung cancer was caused by the synergistic interaction of his cigarette smoking and asbestos exposure." He also agreed that cigarette smoking was by far the greatest cause of all lung cancers in the United States. He did not attempt to apportion responsibility, saying that "both were significant contributory causes." Both doctors agreed that the relative risk of smoking was twice as great as the relative risk for asbestos with respect to cancer.

As noted, the defendant's expert, Dr. DeMopolous, completely discounted any role for asbestos in causing the plaintiff's lung cancer. He emphasized the role of cigarette smoking as solely causative in this case and in lung cancer in general. He appeared to think that the relative risk for cigarette smoking was somewhat higher than the estimates of plaintiff's experts, but he basically did not disagree with their epidemiological data. He recognized the theoretical synergistic effect of two causative factors but denied any role for asbestos in plaintiff's lung cancer. Dr. DeMopolous did not speak to apportionment.

The jury seemed to have apportioned the damages for plaintiff's lung cancer according to the relative risk factors for asbestos (5:1 or 30%) and cigarette smoking (10:1 or 70%), roughly one-third to two-thirds. The judge molded the jury's monetary verdict on the lung cancer aspect, $140,000, accordingly.

IV

Plaintiff's principal claim on this appeal is that the judge erred in submitting the issue of apportionment to the jury in the first place. Plaintiff contends that there was insufficient evidence in the record to provide any basis for apportionment. Judge Weinberg thought this case presented enough evidence to justify allowing the issue to go to the jury. He said:

> The case before us involves an exposure to asbestos of approximately five years. It involves cigarette smoking for almost half a century. I have never—or I have not in the past apportioned this. I did not have a case before me in the past that I felt there was sufficient facts and sufficient expert testimony that would permit the jury to do anything other that [sic] utter speculation.
>
> I think this is a case that permits the jury to consider the facts regarding exposure to asbestos and the extent and the amount and the time of cigarette smoking in conjunction with the expert evidence, if the jury accepts the same, and the jury can make a determination regarding a percentage of causation as to the lung cancer.
>
> I am not suggesting that every case where cigarette smoking happens to be involved is an appropriate case for the apportionment being made. I am making a determination that in this particular case with the facts in this case and the testimony in this case, that I believe that it is a proper item for jury consideration and I intend to submit it to them for that purpose. They will provide us a verdict as to the apportionment.

Although the issue is novel in this jurisdiction, we agree with the trial judge and affirm on this point.

Plaintiff asserts that the lung cancer was an indivisible harm with indivisible damages, that the defendant failed to meet its burden of showing that there was a reasonable basis for apportionment, and that the percentages found by the jury, 30%–70%, were against the weight of the evidence. Defendant Keene contends that the use of apportionment in this case was consistent with the evidence and the development of the law in this State.

Apportionment of damages among multiple causes is a well-recognized tort principle. The *Restatement (Second) of Torts* § 433A, at 434 (1965), regarding apportionment of harm to causes, states:

> (1) Damages for harm are to be apportioned among two or more causes where
>
> > (a) there are distinct harms, or
> >
> > (b) there is a reasonable basis for determining the contribution of each cause to a single harm.
>
> (2) Damages for any other harm cannot be apportioned among two or more causes.

Comment (a) to the *Restatement* indicates that "the rules stated apply also where one of the causes in question is the conduct of the plaintiff himself, whether it be negligent or innocent." *Restatement (Second) of Torts* § 433A, Comment (a), at 435. *Prosser and Keeton, Law of Torts* § 52, at 345 (5th ed. 1984), states the problem this way:

> Once it is determined that the defendant's conduct has been a cause of some damage suffered by the plaintiff, a further question may arise as to the portion of the total damage sustained which may properly be assigned to the defendant, as distinguished from other causes. The question is primarily not one of the fact of causation, but of the feasibility and practical convenience of splitting up the total harm into separate parts which may be attributed to each of two or more causes. Where a factual basis can be found for some rough practical apportionment, which limits a defendant's liability to that part of the harm of which that defendant's conduct has been a cause in fact, it is likely that the apportionment will be made. Where no such basis can be found, the courts generally hold the defendant for the entire loss, notwithstanding the fact that other causes have contributed to it.

The *Restatement* and *Prosser* both recognize that the concern in apportioning responsibility is more practical than theoretical: is there "a reasonable basis for determining the contribution of each cause to a single harm?" *Restatement, supra,* § 433A(1)(b) at 434. Here the single harm to the plaintiff was his lung cancer. The two causes were his six-year occupational exposure to asbestos and his 45-year cigarette smoking habit. The trial judge had to determine, as a matter of law in the first instance, whether the harm was capable of apportionment.

See *Martin v. Owens–Corning Fiberglas Corp.*, 515 Pa. 377, 528 A.2d 947, 949 (1987). The burden of proving that the harm is capable of apportionment is on the party seeking it, here defendant Keene. *Restatement, supra*, § 433B(2), at 441.

Several state and federal courts have considered the apportionment issue in similar occupational asbestos-smoking cases. The Pennsylvania Supreme Court addressed the apportionment issue in *Martin v. Owens–Corning Fiberglas Corp., supra*. The plaintiff, a former insulation worker, brought suit against various asbestos manufacturers seeking damages for asbestosis and lung impairment. Plaintiff worked with asbestos for about 39 years, and smoked for about 37 years. At trial, plaintiff's experts testified that his lung impairment was due to the combined effect of emphysema, caused by cigarette smoking, and asbestosis, from occupational asbestos exposure. They said that it was impossible to apportion the lung impairment between the two causes. 515 Pa. at 383, 528 A.2d at 950. Defendant's expert testified that the lung impairment was caused solely by plaintiff's cigarette smoking. The question presented on appeal was whether the trial judge erred in instructing the jury that it could apportion damages between the asbestos exposure and smoking. Id. at 379, 528 A.2d at 948. There were no epidemiological data or relative risk factors before the jury in *Martin*.

A plurality of the Pennsylvania Supreme Court applied § 433A of the *Restatement* and held that it was error for the trial judge to instruct the jury on apportionment since the evidence failed to establish a reasonable basis on which to apportion. Id. at 383–387, 528 A.2d at 950–951. The court commented:

> The jury, although presented with a great deal of testimony concerning appellant's history and physical condition, was provided no guidance in determining the relative contributions of asbestos exposure and cigarette smoking to appellant's disability. In fact, two experts testified that such a determination was not possible.
>
> * * *
>
> Here, as in *Offensend* [*v. Atlantic Refining Co.*, 322 Pa. 399, 185 A. 745 (1936)], the jury cannot be expected to draw conclusions which medical experts, relying on the same evidence, could not draw. The causes of disability in this case do not lend themselves to separation by lay-persons on any reasonable basis. Thus, common sense and common experience possessed by a jury do not serve as substitutes for expert guidance, and it follows that any apportionment by the jury in this case was a result of speculation and conjecture and hence, improper. "Rough approximation" is no substitute for justice. [*Id.* at 384, 528 A.2d at 950, footnotes omitted].

In his concurring opinion, Justice McDermott said that he would limit the holding of the three-judge plurality to a single proposition, that "under the facts and circumstances of this case there was not enough evidence to submit the issue of apportionment to the jury." *Id.* at 386, 528 A.2d at 951. Thus, the Pennsylvania Supreme Court did not rule out apportionment in cases where the evidence in fact supports a reasonable basis upon which to divide the harm.

In strong, separate dissents, both Chief Justice Nix, joined by Justice Zappala, and Justice Hutchinson criticized the plurality for overstepping its bounds and usurping the jury's fact-finding function. *Id.* at 385-389, 528 A.2d at 951-952. They emphasized that a jury should be allowed to make "rough approximations" where there is a reasonable basis to apportion, especially where the plaintiff's own conduct is a substantial factor in bringing about the harm. *Id.* at 385-392, 528 A.2d at 951-954. Justice Hutchinson, in his dissent, made these thoughtful comments in expressing his view that the jury should enjoy considerable latitude and employ common sense in its apportionment task:

> I am at a loss to imagine what additional testimony would satisfy the majority. Requiring the experts to speak in terms of numerical percentages introduces a false precision into the evidence. Mathematical exactitude is not found in the real world of medicine. We should not mislead lay jurors by requiring experts to falsely imply its existence. Honest, but more flexible, words such as "substantial factor," "major contribution" or "significant cause" are more suitable to the proper jury function of justly and fairly resolving uncertainties. It is unfair and unjust to place on appellee the whole burden of supporting appellant for a disability his own experts admit he himself substantially caused. [*Id.* 528 A.2d at 954; footnote omitted].

In *Borman v. Raymark Indus., Inc.*, 960 F.2d 327 (3d Cir. 1992), the Third Circuit, applying Pennsylvania law, recently declined to hold that the record was adequate to support a jury instruction on apportionment between smoking and asbestos exposure. The record contained epidemiological data on relative risks quite similar to the record before us. *Id.* at 329-331. The Circuit Court observed that appellant "Celotex argues with considerable plausibility that despite the inability of the experts to assign a percentage of contribution to each cause, the evidence provided the jury with a reasonable basis for apportioning damages between the two causes in this case." *Id.* at 334. The dissent of Justice Hutchinson in *Martin, supra*, 515 Pa. at 3, 528 A.2d at 954, to which we have alluded *supra* at 30, 611 A.2d at 143, was favorably referred to and quoted by the Circuit Court, 960 F.2d at 334, n. 12. The Circuit Court, however, noted that "we are not free to treat this issue as if it were a matter of first impression in our court." *Ibid.* Due to the holding of *Martin*, the Circuit Court felt constrained to deny an apportionment ruling favorable to the appellant. The Circuit Court, interpreting state law, said: "We predict that the Pennsylvania Supreme Court would hold this evidence insufficient to support a charge on apportionment of damages." *Ibid.*

Quite obviously, the Third Circuit thought the evidence sufficient for apportionment but was constrained under its diversity jurisdiction by applicable state law. Of course, we are not controlled by Pennsylvania law as was the Circuit Court. We are free to conclude, as the Circuit was not, "that where a factual basis exists, it is preferable in the interest of fairness to permit some rough apportionment of damages, rather than to hold the defendant entirely liable for a harm that was inflicted by separate causes. See *Prosser and Keeton, supra,* at 345." *Ibid.*

Pennsylvania's intermediate appellate court followed *Martin* in affirming a trial judge's decision not to allow the issue of apportionment to go to the jury absent some epidemiological data on relative risks of causative factors. *Taylor v. Celotex Corp.,* 393 Pa.Super. 566, 574 A.2d 1084, 1095–1098 (1990); *see also Guidry v. Johns–Manville Corp.,* 377 Pa.Super. 308, 547 A.2d 382, 386 (1988). We conclude that while Pennsylvania generally recognizes that apportionment is theoretically available where each of several causes' relative contribution can be reasonably estimated, we have no inkling yet of the threshold quantum of proof required in that jurisdiction.

Some other jurisdictions have permitted apportionment in these cases. In *Brisboy v. Fibreboard Corp.,* 429 Mich. 540, 418 N.W.2d 650 (1988), the Supreme Court of Michigan upheld a jury finding that plaintiff's smoking contributed 55% to his lung cancer while 45% was attributable to his asbestos exposure, apparently without the benefit of epidemiological testimony. *See Jenkins v. Halstead Indus.,* 17 Ark.App. 197, 706 S.W.2d 191 (1986) (92% of worker's chronic obstructive pulmonary disease apportioned to life-long cigarette smoking in workers' compensation case). *See also Gideon v. Johns–Manville Sales Corp.,* 761 F.2d 1129, 1138–1140 (5th Cir.1985) (under Texas law, determination is for the jury); *Fulgium v. Armstrong World Indus., Inc.,* 645 F.Supp. 761, 763 (W.D.La.1986) (apportionment allowed under Louisiana law); *Champagne v. Raybestos–Manhattan, Inc.,* 212 Conn. 509, 562 A.2d 1100, 1118 (1989) (plaintiff's smoking found 75% contributory to his lung cancer, citing Michigan's *Brisboy v. Fibreboard Corp., supra*); *Hao v. Owens–Illinois, Inc.,* 69 Haw. 231, 738 P.2d 416 (1987) (51% smoking; 49% asbestos exposure ratio of apportionment affirmed).

No New Jersey cases have specifically addressed the issue of apportionment of civil law damages in an asbestos-exposure cigarette smoking context. We did approve such an apportionment in a workers' compensation setting. *See Field v. Johns–Manville Sales Corp.,* 209 N.J.Super. 528, 531, 507 A.2d 1209 (App.Div.), *certif. denied,* 105 N.J.

531, 523 A.2d 172 (1986); *N.J.S.A.* 34:15–12(d) (credit to employer for loss of function from other cause). However, the concept of apportionment of damages is not alien to this jurisdiction. The theory of § 433A of the *Restatement (Second) of Torts* has been applied in varied circumstances. *See Scafidi v. Seiler,* 119 N.J. 93, 574 A.2d 398 (1990) ("increased risk" and "lost chance" concepts in medical malpractice); *Waterson v. General Motors Corp.,* 111 N.J. 238, 270, 544 A.2d 357 (1988) (automobile "crashworthiness" case); *Fosgate v. Corona,* 66 N.J. 268, 330 A.2d 355 (1974) (medical malpractice aggravating tuberculosis); *Bendar v. Rosen,* 247 N.J.Super. 219, 588 A.2d 1264 (App.Div.1991) (medical malpractice superimposed on auto accident injury). These cases involve pre-existing or concurrent injuries; apportionment was limited to instances of distinct injuries or to circumstances when a reasonable basis existed to determine the contribution of each cause. The burden with respect to proof of apportionment rested, of course, with the party seeking it. *Restatement (Second) of Torts* § 433B(2); *Scafidi, supra,* 119 N.J. at 113–114, 574 A.2d 398; *Waterson, supra,* 111 N.J. at 269, 544 A.2d 357.

In *Scafidi v. Seiler, supra,* our Supreme Court reaffirmed the principle that damages may be apportioned where causation can be attributed to more than one causative factor. In that medical malpractice action, plaintiff alleged that the defendant doctor failed to provide proper treatment for her medical condition, resulting in the premature birth and death of her infant. The court reexamined the principle set forth in *Fosgate v. Corona,* 66 N.J. 268, 330 A.2d 355 (1974), that when a preexisting injury is aggravated, the culpable defendant "should be held responsible for all damages unless he can demonstrate that the damages for which he is responsible are capable of some reasonable apportionment and what those damages are." *Id.* 119 N.J. at 110, 574 A.2d 398, *quoting Fosgate,* 66 N.J. at 272–273, 330 A.2d 355. The Court instructed that to the extent that the defendant seeks to apportion damages, he must demonstrate evidence tending to show that the premature birth and death could have been attributable solely to the preexisting condition, irrespective of the defendant's own negligence. *Id.* 119 N.J. at 113–114, 574 A.2d 398. "Based on the evidence adduced, the jury will be instructed to determine the likelihood, on a percentage basis, that the infant's birth and death would have occurred even if defendant's treatment were faultless." *Id.* at 114, 574 A.2d 398. The judge could then "mold the verdict to limit defendant's liability to the value of the lost chance for recovery attributable to defendant's negligence." *Ibid.*

The most recent pronouncement on apportionment is found in Judge Dreier's opinion in *Bendar v. Rosen,* 247 N.J.Super. 219, 588 A.2d 1264 (App.Div.1991). There plaintiff suffered injuries as a result of a car accident and was taken to a hospital where x-rays were performed. Unbeknownst to plaintiff or her doctors, she was pregnant at the time the x-rays were taken. Plaintiff, who three years earlier had undergone a sterilization procedure, elected to abort her pregnancy after her doctors determined that the x-ray may have injured the unborn child. She suffered consequent emotional distress and sued the drivers involved in the accident, the doctor who performed the prior ineffective tubal ligation, and the treating physician for the accident-related injuries, alleging that all defendants were the proximate cause of the termination of her pregnancy and her emotional distress. After a liability trial, the jury determined that both the drivers and the physician who performed the tubal ligation were proximate causes of plaintiff's abortion and awarded damages. *Id.* at 229, 588 A.2d 1264. The trial judge refused to allow the jury to apportion responsibility for damages related to the abortion, ruling that the termination of the pregnancy was a "single event" that was incapable of apportionment, and there was no testimony from which the jury could rationally apportion liability between the physician and the drivers. *Id.* at 231–232, 588 A.2d 1264.

We disagreed with both of the trial judge's conclusions and remanded for a new trial concerning the apportionment of the abortion-related damages. *Id.* at 235, 588 A.2d 1264. Regarding the "single event" analysis, Judge Dreier noted that there is usually one injury with several causes in tort actions and it is the function of a jury, pursuant to *N.J.S.A.* 2A:15-5.2b, the comparative negligence statute, to determine the percentages of fault attributable to each party. *Id.* at 232, 588 A.2d 1264. Under the rationale of *Restatement* § 433A, a single injury with multiple causes is "presumed to be joint and several unless there are either distinct harms or a reasonable basis upon which to determine the contribution of each cause of a single harm." *Ibid.* Noting that the principles applied in preexisting injury cases should also be applicable in this context, we held that there was a reasonable basis for apportionment and it should be permitted. *Id.* at 232–233, 588 A.2d 1264. In conclusion we stated:

> In short, although the injury cannot be divided, the jury heard substantial testimony concerning plaintiff's motivations for the abortion, and the effect of each occurrence upon her decision. The judge should have permitted the jury to quantify the percentage of proximate cause arising from each event, if it could do so. A basic unfairness may have been visited upon one of the parties if the jury might have determined that one event was primarily responsible for plaintiff's decision, and the other event only slightly responsible. We therefore must remand for a new trial concerning the apportionment of the sizeable abortion-related damages [$250,000] determined by the jury. [*Id.* at 234–235].

As we well know, apportionment is also consistent with the principles of the Comparative Negligence Act, *N.J.S.A.* 2A:15-5.1 to -5.3, and the Contribution Among Tortfeasors Act, *N.J.S.A.* 2A:53A-1 to -5. *See also Feldman v. Lederle Lab.*, 257 N.J.Super. 163, 608 A.2d 356 (App. Div.1992) (apportionment of damages for incremental injury approved).

We conclude that there was ample basis in the record of this trial to submit the issue of apportionment to the jury. The extant legal precedent supports rational efforts to apportion responsibility in such circumstances rather than require one party to absorb the entire burden. The jury obviously accepted the epidemiological testimony based on relative risk factors, the smoking history over 45 years, and the substantial occupational exposure over six years. The synergistically resultant disease, lung cancer, was produced by a relative risk factor of 10:1 contributed by plaintiff and 5:1 contributed by defendant. The jury probably shaded the apportionment slightly in defendant's favor, 70% instead of two-thirds, because of the strong emphasis on cigarette smoking as the greatly predominant overall cause of lung cancer in this country.

The result was rational and fair. We can ask no more. This is fairer than requiring defendant to shoulder the entire causative burden where its contribution in fact was not likely even close to 100%. Or fairer, for certain, than no recovery at all for plaintiff who, while a victim of the disease of asbestosis which probably led in part to the lung cancer, confronts a reluctant jury which might not want to saddle a defendant with a 100% verdict in the circumstances of a particular case.

We conclude that our Supreme Court's recent decision in *Landrigan v. Celotex Corp.*, 127 N.J. 404, 415–416, 605 A.2d 1079 (1992), a colon cancer asbestos claim, supports the result we reach in relying on the epidemiological data for apportionment. This discipline of epidemiology "studies the relationship between a disease and a factor suspected of causing the disease, using statistical methods...." *Id.* at 415, 608 A.2d 356. The Supreme Court recognized that "proof of causation in toxic-tort cases depends largely on inferences derived from statistics about groups," *id.* at 422, 608 A.2d 356; and conceded that plaintiffs in toxic-tort cases "may be compelled to resort to more general evidence, such as that provided by epidemiological studies." *Id.* at 415, 608 A.2d 356. *See also Caterinicchio v. Pittsburgh Corning Corp.*, 127 N.J. 428, 436, 605 A.2d 1092 (1992), a companion case to *Landrigan*.

* * *

Affirmed.

SECTION 3. STATUTES OF LIMITATION, RES JUDICATA, AND DAMAGES

ADD to page 998 right under the "Damages" heading:

SULLIVAN v. COMBUSTION ENGINEERING

Superior Court of New Jersey, Appellate Division, 1991.
248 N.J.Super. 134, 590 A.2d 681.

ANTELL, P.J.

This personal injury suit was brought by Albert E. Sullivan (plaintiff) and Patricia Sullivan, his wife, against various manufacturers and distributors of certain asbestos products to which plaintiff was exposed for a period of 33 years during the course of his employment. As a result of his exposure plaintiff developed thickening of the pleural lining of his lungs, an asbestos-related disease. The trial court dismissed his claim for present physical injury on the ground that the condition entails no loss of pulmonary function and because it is causing plaintiff no discomfort.

Dr. Donald Auerbach, plaintiff's medical expert, testified that, in 1981, plaintiff's chest x-rays first revealed the presence of asbestos-related pleural disease. He also stated that the scarring and thickening was permanent and its effect is to make the lining of the lungs "very hard.... [I]t can be just like shoe leather." Based on x-rays from 1981 to 1989 Dr. Auerbach noted that plaintiff's disease "has progressed," and "will progress." However, he indicated that symptoms such as breathing impairment, shortness of breath and coughing are only possible with extensive pleural scarring or thickening, that plaintiff's scarring is not extensive and that he is at present symptom-free. He acknowledged also that pleural thickening is the least serious of the asbestos-related diseases.

On the plaintiff's medical evidence the trial court dismissed plaintiff's claim of a present physical injury for the reason that "except for emotional damages and future damages for medical [surveillance] examinations" there could be no claim for damages arising from plaintiff's asbestos-related pleural disease.

The jury found against plaintiff on his claim for emotional distress and for punitive damages, but awarded him $2,255 for the anticipated cost of future medical surveillance. The principal point of plaintiff's appeal is that the trial court erred in dismissing his damage claim for present physical injury.

According to *Restatement (Second) of Torts* § 905, Comment b at 456 (1977), compensatory damages that may be awarded without proof of pecuniary loss include compensation for "bodily harm," which is defined as "any impairment of the physical condition of the body, including illness or physical pain." Thus, compensatory damages can

Ch. 10 STATUTES OF LIMITATION, RES JUDICATA, DAMAGES

be awarded for bodily harm, "although there is no impairment of a bodily function and, in some situations, even though the defendant's act is beneficial." *Id.*

Herber v. Johns–Manville Corp., 785 F.2d 79 (3d Cir.1986), and *Mauro v. Owens–Corning Fiberglas*, 225 N.J.Super. 196, 542 A.2d 16 (App.Div.1988), *aff'd, sub nom Mauro v. Raymark Industries*, 116 N.J. 126, 561 A.2d 257 (1989), are instructive. In *Herber*, plaintiff was exposed to asbestos products during the course of his employment and was diagnosed as having asbestos-related pleural thickening. However, he had no symptoms such as coughing, wheezing or shortness of breath. *Herber, supra*, 785 F.2d at 88. Although the jury found that plaintiff's exposure to the asbestos fibers had caused pleural thickening, and that he had suffered a physical injury to his lungs, it decided that the sum of money that would fairly, reasonably, and adequately compensate him for his "injuries" was "none." *Id.* at 81. That determination was upheld on appeal, based upon the reviewing court's conclusion that the jury's determination was one which properly lay within its authority. *Id.* at 88–89.

In *Mauro*, too, plaintiff had suffered pleural thickening as a result of long-term exposure to asbestos. The jury awarded a total of $7,500 for his "claims of bodily injury, emotional distress, pain and suffering and medical surveillance." *Mauro, supra*, 225 N.J.Super. at 211, 542 A.2d 16. In its affirming decision, the Supreme Court observed that plaintiff's x-rays showed "scarring of the lung lining," and that "although the results of his physical examination and lung function test were 'normal,' he had bilateral thickening of both chest walls and calcification of the diaphragm." *Mauro v. Raymark Industries, Inc., supra*, at 116 N.J. 129–30, 561 A.2d 257. As here, there were no "physical symptoms evidencing plaintiff's distress." *Id.* at 137, 561 A.2d 257. The Supreme Court also noted, without adverse comment, that the trial court "permitted the jury to consider Mauro's claim for damages caused by his *present medical condition*, as well as the cost of future medical surveillance." *Id.* at 131, 561 A.2d 257 (emphasis added). It specifically stated that Mauro's "exposure to asbestos has resulted in physical injury." *Id.* at 137, 561 A.2d 257. Finally, the Court observed that "our case law affords toxic-tort plaintiffs the right to receive full compensation for any provable diminution of bodily health, accommodating *all* damage claims attributable to present injury...." *Id.* at 144, 561 A.2d 257 (emphasis added).

We distinguish *Landrigan v. Celotex Corp.*, 243 N.J.Super. 449, 579 A.2d 1268 (App.Div.1990). There, suit was brought on the claim that decedent's colon cancer had been caused by the asbestos products to which decedent had been exposed during his working lifetime. During the trial, decedent's surviving spouse asserted a claim for damages based upon decedent's pleural thickening, likewise said to be asbestos related. This court affirmed the trial court's dismissal of plaintiff's claim for the "minimal pleural thickening" that was first discovered during the trial when plaintiff's expert examined an x-ray of decedent's lungs. *Id.* at 463–64, 579 A.2d 1268. The opinion pointed out that decedent "was never made aware of its existence," and expressly invited comparison of that case with *Mauro. Id.* 243 N.J.Super. at 464, 579 A.2d 1268.

We conclude that the question of whether plaintiff's pleural thickening constitutes an injury and, if so, the extent of compensation to be awarded for the physical changes brought about in the lining of plaintiff's lungs, should properly have been left to the jury's determination. We believe our view coincides with those expressed or implied by other courts which have considered comparable cases. *See Howell v. Celotex Corp.*, 904 F.2d 3, 5 (3d Cir.1990); *Herber v. Johns–Manville Corp.*, 785 F.2d 79, 88–89 (3d Cir.1986); *Giovanetti v. Johns–Manville Corp.*, 372 Pa.Super. 431, 539 A.2d 871, 876 (Pa.Super.1988); *but see In re Hawaii Federal Asbestos Cases*, 734 F.Supp. 1563, 1567–68 (D.Hawaii 1990).

In our view, *Schweitzer v. Consolidated Rail Corp. (Conrail)*, 758 F.2d 936 (3d Cir.), *cert. denied*, 474 U.S. 864, 106 S.Ct. 183, 88 L.Ed.2d 152 (1985), and *Burns v. Jaquays Min. Corp.*, 156 Ariz. 375, 752 P.2d 28 (App.1987), *appeal dismissed*, 162 Ariz. 186, 781 P.2d 1373 (1989), are distinguishable from the case now before us based on material differences in the physical facts presented to those courts. *Schweitzer* involved claims asserted by railroad workers under the Federal Employers' Liability Act, 45 *U.S.C.A.* §§ 51–60 (1986). Plaintiffs' claims of injuries seem to have consisted of nothing more than that they suffered "exposure" to asbestos fibers during the course of their employment. The opinion does not speak of any physical changes allegedly induced by the exposure, and holds only that "mere exposure to asbestos" without "manifestation of injury" would not be recognized to support a cause of action. *Schweitzer, supra,* 758 F.2d at 942.

Burns, in applying the *Schweitzer* rationale, also focused on claims primarily grounded in exposure. They differed in degree from those considered in *Schweitzer* only in that, as the court stated, all the plaintiffs "have asbestos fibers in their lungs which are causing changes in the lung tissue." *Burns, supra,* 752 P.2d at 30. While the line dividing actual pleural thickening from lung tissue which is merely undergoing the process of change is a fine one, we conclude that the *Schweitzer* and *Burns* decisions signify a determination by those courts that the pathological impact of exposure had not progressed to the point of a "manifestation of injury" which is clearly present here.

Whether plaintiff's pleural thickening constitutes an injury and, if so, the damages to be awarded, is therefore remanded to the Law Division for retrial.

Plaintiff also argues that the trial court should have submitted to the jury his claim for "possible" future consequences of his asbestos-related pleural condition. New Jersey's long-standing rule is that "prospective damages are not recoverable unless they are reasonably probable to occur." *Mauro, supra,* 116 N.J. at 133, 561 A.2d 257. "Moreover, there is no recovery allowed for the mere possible consequences of an injury inflicted by a tortfeasor." *Lesniak v. County of Bergen,* 117 N.J. 12, 20, 563 A.2d 795 (1989).[1]

Plaintiff makes the further point that the trial court should not have instructed the jury that in order for him to recover for emotional distress it must be shown that he is suffering from "serious" fear. The instruction given by the court accords with our holdings in *Mauro, supra,* 225 N.J.Super. at 208, 211, 542 A.2d 16 and *Devlin v. Johns–Manville Corp.,* 202 N.J.Super. 556, 563, 495 A.2d 495 (Law Div.1985). See also *Advisory Com'n v. Diamond Shamrock,* 243 N.J.Super. 170, 174–175, 578 A.2d 1248 (App.Div.1990), where we stated that plaintiff's anxieties were not compensable in the absence of "serious mental illness" or emotional distress which is "severe and substantial."

Plaintiff's argument that the trial court erred in precluding the testimony of his medical expert witness is lacking in merit. Plaintiff failed to inform defendants that he planned to call Dr. Tobe as a witness until the eve of trial, notwithstanding that he had the doctor's report in his hands for more than three years. The failure to furnish timely the names of expert witnesses to be called at trial or their reports may, in the sound discretion of the trial court, result in the exclusion of their testimony. *Westphal v. Guarino,* 163 N.J.Super. 139, 145, 394 A.2d 377 (App.Div.), *aff'd o.b.,* 78 N.J. 308, 394 A.2d 354 (1978); *Brown v. Mortimer,* 100 N.J.Super. 395, 401, 242 A.2d 36 (App.Div. 1968); *see also* R. 4:17–4(e); R. 4:17–7; R. 4:23–5(b). Nevertheless, although the court's ruling was faultless under the circumstances presented, in view of our determination to remand the matter for retrial as to plaintiff's present physical injury, we also direct that the retrial include plaintiff's claim for emotional distress and that in connection therewith Dr. Tobe be permitted to testify. The trial court is authorized to make whatever provision it may deem necessary to allow defendants to meet Dr. Tobe's anticipated testimony.

* * *

We reverse the trial court's dismissal of plaintiff's claim for damages resulting from the present state of his physical injury and emotional distress and remand for further proceedings consistent with this opinion. * * *

---

1. We leave for another day the question of whether plaintiff will be permitted to seek further damages in the future should symptoms develop or in the event that he experiences a more serious illness as the result of his exposure to asbestos. *See Ayers v. Jackson Tp.,* 106 N.J. 557, 584, 525 A.2d 287 (1987).

SECTION 4. INTERGENERATIONAL HARM

REPLACE Loerch v. Abbott Laboratories on pages 1003–10 with:

GROVER v. ELI LILLY & CO.
Supreme Court of Ohio, 1992.
63 Ohio St.3d 756, 591 N.E.2d 696.

WRIGHT, J.

The United States District Court for the Northern District of Ohio has certified the following question to us:

"Does Ohio recognize a cause of action on behalf of a child born prematurely, and with severe birth defects, if it can be established that such injuries were proximately caused by defects in the child's mother's reproductive system, those defects in turn being proximately caused by the child's grandmother ingesting a defective drug (DES) during her pregnancy with the child's mother?"

For purposes of this question, we are required to assume that Charles Grover can prove that his injuries were proximately caused by his mother's exposure to DES. We are not evaluating the facts of this case, but determining, as a matter of law, whether Charles Grover has a legally cognizable cause of action.

DES was prescribed to pregnant women during the 1940s, 1950s and 1960s to prevent miscarriage. The FDA banned its use by pregnant women in 1971 after medical studies discovered that female children exposed to the drug *in utero* had a high incidence of a rare type of vaginal cancer. See 36 Fed.Reg. 21,537 (1971). Candy Grover was exposed to DES as a fetus. Her son, Charles Grover, claims that his mother's DES-induced injuries were the cause of his premature birth and resulting injuries.

Because the mother and the child whose injury results from her injury are uniquely interrelated, and because it is possible that the mother may not discover the extent of her own injury until she experiences difficulties during pregnancy, the facts of this case pose a novel issue. Courts and commentators refer to the child's potential cause of action in such cases as a "preconception tort." See, *e.g.*, Note, Preconception Torts: Foreseeing the Unconceived (1977), 48 U.Colo. L.Rev. 621. The terminology stems from the fact that a child is pursuing liability against a party for a second injury that flows from an initial injury to the mother that occurred before the child was conceived.

Only a handful of courts have addressed whether a child has a cause of action for a preconception tort. One recurring issue is whether a child has a cause of action if a physician negligently performs a surgical procedure on the mother, such as an abortion or a Caesarean section, and the negligently performed procedure causes complications during childbirth several years later that injure the infant. See *Albala v. New York* (1981), 54 N.Y.2d 269, 445 N.Y.S.2d 108, 429 N.E.2d 786 (child has no cause of action for doctor's negligence during abortion performed four years prior to his conception); *Bergstreser v. Mitchell* (C.A.8, 1978), 577 F.2d 22 (construing Missouri law) (child has a cause of action against a doctor based on the doctor's negligence during a Caesarean section performed two years prior to the child's conception). In another malpractice suit, the Illinois Supreme Court recognized that a child had a cause of action against a hospital that negligently transfused her mother with Rh-positive blood eight years prior to the child's conception. *Renslow v. Mennonite Hospital* (1977), 67 Ill.2d 348, 10 Ill.Dec. 484, 367 N.E.2d 1250. As a result, the mother's body produced antibodies to the Rh-positive blood that later injured her fetus during pregnancy. See, also, *Monusko v. Postle* (1989), 175 Mich.App. 269, 437 N.W.2d 367 (allowing cause of action by child against her mother's physicians for failure to inoculate the mother with rubella vaccine prior to the child's conception).

In *McAuley v. Wills* (1983), 251 Ga. 3, 303 S.E.2d 258, the Supreme Court of Georgia evaluated a wrongful death action brought on behalf of an infant who died during childbirth due to the mother's paralysis. The suit was brought against the driver who had originally caused the mother's paralysis in an automobile accident. The court held that a person may owe a duty of care to a child conceived in the future, but also held that the injury in that case was too remote as a matter of law to support recovery. *Id.* at 6–7, 303 S.E.2d at 260–261. The driver could not reasonably foresee, as a matter of law, that his lack of care in driving a motor vehicle would result in complications during the delivery of a child who was not yet conceived at the time of the accident. *Id.*[1]

---

1. The Supreme Court of Georgia limited its holding to the facts of the case before it. The Court of Appeals for New York has taken the opposite approach and held that a plaintiff does not have a cause of action for *any* preconception tort, regardless of the facts alleged. See *Albala v. New York* (1981), 54 N.Y.2d 269, 445 N.Y.S.2d 108, 429 N.E.2d 786. It is this absolute rule that Prosser has criticized as a "blanket no-duty rule." See Prosser & Keeton, Law of Torts (5 Ed.1984) 369, Section 55.

This court declines to adopt an absolute rule at this time, but addresses an alleged cause of action that is far more tenuous than that raised in *Albala v. New York*. See, also, *Bergstreser v. Mitchell* (C.A.8, 1978), 577 F.2d 22 (for a fact pattern similar to the facts of *Albala v. New York*). At least arguably, a doctor should comprehend, at the time that he or she performs an abortion or a Caesarean section, that a negligently performed procedure could cause the woman's uterus to rupture during a subsequent pregnancy. It is more difficult to imagine that a pharmaceutical company, during the 1940s to the 1960s, could have foreseen the effect that a drug

The facts of these cases are significantly different from those of the case before us. The cause of action certified to us involves the scope of liability for the manufacture of a prescription drug that allegedly had devastating side effects on the original patient's female fetus. However, this case is not about the devastating side effects of DES on the women who were exposed to it, which have indeed been well documented in medical studies and court opinions. See authorities cited *infra* at 763–764 (Resnick, J., dissenting) and the discussion of the state of medical research at 765–766 (Resnick, J., dissenting). This case is concerned with the rippling effects of that exposure on yet another generation, when that female child reaches sexual maturity and bears a child. Because a plaintiff in Charles Grover's position cannot be injured until the original patient's child bears children, the second injury will typically have occurred more than sixteen years after the ingestion of the drug.

Several courts have addressed a fact pattern virtually identical to the facts of the case currently before this court. The New York Court of Appeals held that a child does not have a cause of action, in negligence or strict liability, against a prescription drug company based on the manufacture of DES if the child was never exposed to the drug *in utero*. *Enright v. Eli Lilly & Co.* (1991), 77 N.Y.2d 377, 568 N.Y.S.2d 550, 570 N.E.2d 198, certiorari denied (1991), 502 U.S. ___, 112 S.Ct. 197, 116 L.Ed.2d 157. The court relied in part on its earlier opinion in *Albala v. New York, supra*. In both cases, the court was concerned with the "staggering implications of any proposition which would honor claims assuming the breach of an identifiable duty for less than a perfect birth and by what standard and the difficulty in establishing a standard or definition of perfection. * * * " *Id.*, 54 N.Y.2d at 273, 445 N.Y.S.2d at 109, 429 N.E.2d at 788. See *Enright v. Eli Lilly & Co., supra*, 77 N.Y.2d at 384, 568 N.Y.S.2d at 553, 570 N.E.2d at 201. The court was troubled by the possibility that doctors would forgo certain treatments of great benefit to persons already in existence out of fear of possible effects on future children. *Albala, supra*, 54 N.Y.2d at 274, 445 N.Y.S.2d at 110, 429 N.E.2d at 788–789. In *Enright*, the court noted that "the cause of action plaintiffs ask us to recognize here could not be confined without the drawing of artificial and arbitrary boundaries. For all we know, the rippling effects of DES exposure may extend for generations. It is our duty to confine liability within manageable limits * * *. Limiting liability to those who ingested the drug or were exposed to it *in utero* serves this purpose." *Id.*, 77 N.Y.2d at 387, 568 N.Y.S.2d at 555, 570 N.E.2d at 203. See, also, *Loerch v. Eli Lilly & Co.* (Minn.1989), 445 N.W.2d 560 (the evenly divided Supreme Court of Minnesota affirmed, without opinion, a lower court's decision that a child who was not exposed to DES has no cause of action).

would have not only on a patient's unborn child, but also on that child's children.

One court has held that a plaintiff situated similarly to Charles Grover has a cause of action. The United States Court of Appeals for the Seventh District reversed a lower court's directed verdict on the issue of a pharmaceutical company's liability to a child for injuries caused by a premature birth. *McMahon v. Eli Lilly & Co.* (C.A.7, 1985), 774 F.2d 830. The court concluded that under Illinois law the company could be liable for failing to warn of the dangerous propensities of the drug, and need not have anticipated a particular side effect. *Id.* at 834–835.

We find the reasoning applied by the New York Court of Appeals persuasive on the issue currently before us. As an initial matter, we note that the pharmaceutical companies' conduct must be evaluated based on whether they knew or should have known of a particular risk through the exercise of ordinary care. The marketing of prescription drugs differs significantly from other consumer goods. Each drug is tested and approved for use by the Food and Drug Administration and is selected for use by a physician, who then prescribes the drug to the ultimate user. As a result, the drug manufacturer's primary responsibility is to provide adequate warnings to the physician. Prosser & Keeton, Law of Torts (5 Ed.1984) 688, Section 96. The manufacturer does not breach its duty to warn—in negligence, in strict liability for breach of warranty, or in strict liability in tort—until the company knew or should have known of a particular risk through the exercise of ordinary care. *Id.; Crislip v. TCH Liquidating Co.* (1990), 52 Ohio St.3d 251, 257, 556 N.E.2d 1177, 1182–1183, fn. 1.

It is on this point that Ohio law differs from Illinois law as construed in *McMahon v. Eli Lilly & Co., supra,* 774 F.2d at 834–835. The Seventh Circuit held that knowledge of the general dangerous propensities of the drug was sufficient to subject the company to liability for failure to warn. This court has stated that "[i]n a products liability case where a claimant seeks recovery for failure to warn or warn adequately, it must be proven that the manufacturer knew, or should have known, in the exercise of ordinary care, of the risk or hazard about which it failed to warn." (Footnote omitted.) *Crislip v. TCH Liquidating Co., supra,* 52 Ohio St.3d at 257, 556 N.E.2d at 1182–1183. Even if knowledge of the drug's "dangerous propensities" is sufficient to create liability to the women exposed to the drug *in utero*, this same knowledge does not automatically justify the extension of liability to those women's children. It is one thing to say that knowledge of a propensity to harm the reproductive organs is sufficient to impose liability for a variety of different injuries to the reproductive organs. It is yet another thing to say that this generalized knowledge is sufficient to impose liability for injuries to a third party that occur twenty-eight years later.[2]

2. It is on this same point of law that the dissent confuses the issue by characterizing the question as whether the pharmaceutical companies should have known

Knowledge of a risk to one class of plaintiffs does not necessarily extend an actor's liability to every potential plaintiff. While we must assume that DES was the proximate cause of Charles Grover's injuries, an actor is not liable for every harm that may result from his actions. " * * * The plaintiff sues in her own right for a wrong personal to her, and not as the vicarious beneficiary of a breach of duty to another." *Palsgraf v. Long Island RR. Co.* (1928), 248 N.Y. 339, 342, 162 N.E. 99, 100. An actor does not have a duty to a particular plaintiff unless the risk to that plaintiff is within the actor's "range of apprehension." *Id.* at 344, 162 N.E. at 100. " * * * If the actor's conduct creates such a recognizable risk of harm only to a particular class of persons, the fact that it in fact causes harm to a person of a different class, to whom the actor could not reasonably have anticipated injury, does not make the actor liable to the persons so injured." 2 Restatement of the Law 2d, Torts (1965), Section 281, Comment *c*; *Jeffers v. Olexo* (1989), 43 Ohio St.3d 140, 142–143, 539 N.E.2d 614, 616–617. The existence of a legal duty is a question for the court, unless alternate inferences are feasible based on the facts. *Palsgraf, supra*, 248 N.Y. at 345, 162 N.E. at 101.

When a pharmaceutical company prescribes drugs to a woman, the company, under ordinary circumstances, does not have a duty to her daughter's infant who will be conceived twenty-eight years later. Charles Grover's injuries are not the result of his own exposure to the drug, but are allegedly caused by his mother's injuries from her *in utero* exposure to the drug. Because of the remoteness in time and causation, we hold that Charles Grover does not have an independent cause of action, and answer the district court's question in the negative. A pharmaceutical company's liability for the distribution or manufacture of a defective prescription drug does not extend to persons who were never exposed to the drug, either directly or *in utero*.

Judgment accordingly.

Moyer, C.J., Holmes and H. Brown, JJ., concur.

Sweeney, Douglas and Resnick, JJ., dissent.

Alice Robie Resnick, J., dissenting.

I dissent from the result reached in this case, but more importantly from the superficial treatment of the issue which was certified to this court, in light of its complexity. It is critical that we consider the exact issue which the federal court certified to this court: "Does Ohio recognize a cause of action on behalf of a child born prematurely, and

that DES could cause reproductive abnormalities in a developing fetus. The issue is not whether the pharmaceutical companies knew of some dangers from the use of this drug. To the contrary, the question is whether the drug companies should have known, at the time that it was prescribed, that DES could cause a birth defect that would result in the delivery of a premature child twenty or thirty years later. Modern studies may provide us with twenty-twenty hindsight, but the only medical studies relevant to this issue are those that occurred before DES was banned in 1971.

with severe birth defects, if it can be established that such injuries were proximately caused by defects in the child's mother's reproductive system, those defects in turn being proximately caused by the child's grandmother ingesting a defective drug (DES) during her pregnancy with the child's mother?"

As the devastating effects of DES continue to mount, so too does the legal debate concerning liability for the damage caused by the drug. For a *detailed* history of DES and its catastrophic effects, as well as its treatment by medical experts, see *Hymowitz v. Eli Lilly & Co.* (1985), 73 N.Y.2d 487, 541 N.Y.S.2d 941, 539 N.E.2d 1069; *Bilcher v. Eli Lilly & Co.* (1982), 55 N.Y.2d 571, 450 N.Y.S.2d 776, 436 N.E.2d 182; *Zafft v. Eli Lilly & Co.* (Mo.1984), 676 S.W.2d 241; *Collins v. Eli Lilly & Co.* (1984), 116 Wis.2d 166, 342 N.W.2d 37. As the court in *Enright v. Eli Lilly & Co.* (1991), 77 N.Y.2d 377, 568 N.Y.S.2d 550, 570 N.E.2d 198, certiorari denied (1991), 502 U.S. ___, 112 S.Ct. 197, 116 L.Ed.2d 157, has indicated, "[t]he tragic DES tale is well documented in this Court's decisions and need not be recounted * * *. It is sufficient to note that between 1947 and 1971, the drug, a synthetic estrogenlike substance produced by approximately three hundred manufacturers, was prescribed for use and ingested by millions of pregnant women to prevent miscarriages. In 1971, the Food and Drug Administration banned the drug's use for the treatment of problems of pregnancy after studies established a link between *in utero* exposure to DES and the occurrence in teen-age women of a rare form of vaginal and cervical cancer." *Id.*, 77 N.Y.2d 377 at 382, 568 N.Y.S.2d at 552, 570 N.E.2d at 200. Plaintiffs in *Enright* had alleged that "in utero exposure to DES has since been linked to other genital tract aberrations in DES daughters, including malformations or immaturity of the uterus, cervical abnormalities, misshapen Fallopian tubes and abnormal cell and tissue growth, all of which has caused in this population a marked increase in the incidence of infertility, miscarriages, premature births and ectopic pregnancies." *Id.*

In the present case, June Rose ingested DES during her pregnancy in 1952 and 1953. June gave birth to Candace Grover on March 30, 1953. Petitioners maintain that as a result of her mother's ingestion of DES, Candace was born with an incompetent cervix. Candace gave birth, prematurely, to Charles Grover, who was born with cerebral palsy. Petitioners assert Charles' disabilities are directly and proximately attributable to his premature birth, which in turn was caused by his mother's DES-induced incompetent cervix.

The majority is persuaded by the rationale of the New York Court of Appeals' decision in *Enright, supra.* Although the basis of the holding is not entirely clear, the majority essentially holds that for public policy reasons there is no legal duty owed to a person who was not *in utero* at the time of injury.[4] As does the court in *Enright*, the majority relies upon the DES manufacturers' age-old public policy arguments that the imposition of liability would invoke "staggering implications" and "rippling effects," or would require doctors to forgo certain treatments of great benefit to persons already in existence. But as the dissent in *Enright* cogently points out, "* * * this sort of 'floodgates of litigation' [alarm] seems singularly unpersuasive in view of our Court's repeated admonitions that it is not 'a ground for denying a cause of action that there will be a proliferation of claims' and ' * * * if a cognizable wrong has been committed, that there must be a remedy, whatever the burden of the courts.' * * * Beyond that, however, when defendants' arguments are applied here to urge that although the claims of DES daughters should be allowed the claims of the granddaughters should not be, their forebodings strike a particularly ironic note: i.e., the very fact of the 'insidious nature' of DES which may make the defendants liable for injuries to a future generation is advanced as the reason why they should not be liable for injuries to that generation." *Enright, supra,* 77 N.Y.2d at 393, 568 N.Y.S.2d at 559, 570 N.E.2d at 207 (Hancock, J., dissenting).

I discern no sound basis, in law or public policy, for holding that there is no duty owed to persons in Charles Grover's position. We are dealing with a drug which was widely prescribed for many years to virtually millions of pregnant women. It was a drug which had FDA approval but, perhaps, was not adequately tested in view of a considerable body of scientific and medical literature that raised serious questions concerning the safety of DES to the developing fetus and its efficacy for treatment of pregnancy complications. Petitioners aver that, despite warnings from independent researchers dating back to the 1930s that DES caused reproductive tract abnormalities and cancer in exposed animal offspring, that drug companies, including Eli Lilly, performed no tests as to the effects of DES on the developing fetus, either in animals or humans. Petitioners also assert that by 1947 there were twenty-one studies which supported these findings; that recent medical studies have established a significant link between DES exposure and various uterine and cervical abnormalities in DES daughters; and that these studies have demonstrated that mature DES daughters have a significantly higher risk of miscarriage, infertility and premature deliveries.

In light of the foregoing there can be no question that pharmaceutical companies should have known the dangers of this drug. If in the 1930s and 1940s the manufacturers of DES knew or should have known

---

4. The reason the majority's holding is not clear is because in one breath it correctly states that "we are required to assume that Charles Grover can prove that his injuries were *proximately caused* by his mother's exposure to DES," but then ultimately concludes that "[b]ecause of the remoteness in time and *causation*, we hold that Charles Grover does not have an independent cause of action." (Emphasis added.)

of the reproductive system defects in the animal fetus exposed to DES, how then is it not foreseeable that this might mean abnormalities in the human fetus' reproductive system? In other words, it would appear that DES manufacturers knew or should have known that the human fetus exposed *in utero* might have a defect in the female reproductive system. Additionally, is it not then foreseeable that that female fetus would at some point seek to employ the defective reproductive system? The answer must be a resounding "yes." Hence, there can be no logic to the holding of the majority that "[b]ecause of the remoteness in time and causation, * * * Charles Grover does not have an independent cause of action." What could have a more direct causal connection than a premature birth by a woman who was known to have an incompetent cervix? From this it becomes readily apparent that DES grandchildren were a foreseeable group of plaintiffs. It can hardly be argued that there is no duty owed to a foreseeable plaintiff. In the landmark case of *Palsgraf v. Long Island RR. Co.* (1928), 248 N.Y. 339, 162 N.E. 99, the court held that an actor has a duty to all plaintiffs within the actor's "range of apprehension." *Id.* at 344, 162 N.E. at 100. Indeed, a federal court of appeals had recently stated: "There was sufficient evidence from which a jury could reasonably have found that in 1955 Lilly knew or should have known that DES might cause reproductive abnormalities, such as prematurity, in the female offspring of women exposed to DES during pregnancy." *McMahon v. Eli Lilly & Co.* (C.A.7, 1985), 774 F.2d 830, 835–836.

While both foreseeability and proximate cause are readily apparent in this case, it is well recognized that in strict products liability claims, unlike causes of action sounding in negligence, the concepts of duty and foreseeability are of diminished significance. See *Jorgensen v. Meade Johnson Laboratories, Inc.* (C.A.10, 1973), 483 F.2d 237; *Docken v. Ciba–Geigy* (1987), 86 Ore.App. 277, 739 P.2d 591. Even the *Enright* court recognized this concept by citing its decision in *Albala v. New York* (1981), 54 N.Y.2d 269, 445 N.Y.S.2d 108, 429 N.E.2d 786, for this proposition. Additionally, Prosser & Keeton state: "A perplexing problem that remains in this area is whether claims should be permitted where the harmful contact with the mother occurs even before the child is conceived, as from ingestion of a defective drug causing chromosomal damage to the mother's ovum, or injury to her uterus during a preconception operation. A small number of courts have allowed recovery, but New York in a *thinly reasoned* case has recently ruled that a child has no cause of action for preconception torts upon the mother. * * * These are indeed staggering problems, that will have to be dealt with *carefully* in future toxic tort contexts such as these, but they by no means require that a blanket no-duty rule be applied in preconception injury cases where such problems do not exist." (Emphasis added.) Prosser & Keeton, Law of Torts (5 Ed.1984) 369, Section 55.

Conclusion

DES continues to create difficult legal and social problems nationwide. The majority has failed to consider the uniqueness of DES. Instead, it has simply applied an arbitrary "blanket no-duty rule." Today's holding will have profound and devastating effects. To hold under these circumstances that Charles Grover's injuries were not foreseeable is to ignore an entire body of scientific information which was available or could have easily become available with a measure of care concerning the effects of DES on subsequent generations.

Having reviewed and considered the competing public policy concerns, the case law recognizing preconception torts, respected legal commentary and the available scientific studies, I would conclude that individuals such as Charles Grover properly have a cause of action for their injuries. This in no way opens the floodgates because litigation can easily be concluded with Charles Grover's generation. Moreover, the majority completely disregards the fact that the petitioners still bear the burden of proving proximate cause. I strenuously dissent.

Chapter 11

"CRISIS" AND "REFORM"

SECTION 2. THE SECOND "CRISIS":—THE 1980'S

ADD to page 1034 before "State Tort Reform":

BLANKENSHIP v. GENERAL MOTORS CORPORATION

Supreme Court of Appeals of West Virginia, 1991.
185 W.Va. 350, 406 S.E.2d 781.

NEELY, JUSTICE:

In this case the United States District Court for the District of Maryland has certified the following question to us:

> Does a complaint against the seller of a motor vehicle state a cause of action under West Virginia law if the complaint does not allege that a vehicle defect *caused* a collision, but does allege that the injuries sustained by the occupant as a result of the collision were *enhanced* by a design defect in the vehicle?

We answer the certified question in the affirmative, and like all of our sister states, we now explicitly adopt the "crashworthiness doctrine."

* * *

In the excellent briefs of General Motors and amicus, Product Liability Advisory Council, Inc., numerous issues concerning the wisdom of applying product liability law to vehicle crashworthiness problems have been raised. For example, both the defendant and amicus point out that because, under *Wright v. Hanley*, 182 W.Va. 334, 387 S.E.2d 801 (1989), a car's occupants' failure to use available seat belts cannot be introduced as contributory negligence in West Virginia, it would be unfair to allow an action for crashworthiness or "second collision." General Motors argues:

> It would be quite ironic if this court were to refuse to impose upon the passenger the duty to minimize his injuries in a collision by wearing his seat belt but, nevertheless, to impose upon the manufacturer the duty to minimize the passenger's injuries through the adoption of the crashworthiness theory of liability.

Defendant's brief, pp. 20–21. However, we did not hold in *Hanley* that failure to use an available seat belt would not be comparative contributory negligence in a crashworthiness case.

And, in a similar vein, both the defendant and amicus argue that allowing crashworthiness lawsuits invites juries to second-guess the safety standards promulgated by the National Highway Traffic Safety Administration. Thus, under the common theories of crashworthiness, defendant and amicus argue, different juries will reach different conclusions about the "reasonableness" of safety features, leaving manufacturers in the unenviable position of being unable to predict what juries will deem a "defective product [that] causes personal injury." *Morningstar, supra*. Furthermore, defendant and amicus argue, juries may find designs approved by federal regulators "defective," giving the whole regulatory effort a certain *Alice in Wonderland* quality.

In all of these regards the manufacturers and amicus have strong arguments. Nonetheless, West Virginia is a small rural state with .66 percent of the population of the United States. Although some members of this Court have reservations about the wisdom of many aspects of tort law, as a court we are utterly powerless to make the *overall* tort system for cases arising in interstate commerce more rational: Nothing that we do will have any impact whatsoever on the set of economic trade-offs that occur in the *national* economy. And, ironically, trying unilaterally to make the American tort system more rational through being uniquely responsible in West Virginia will only punish our residents severely without, in any regard, improving the system for anyone else.

* * *

[P]roduct liability is concerned with *spreading the cost of inevitable accidents*. Inherent in this cost-spreading function is the collection of what amounts to insurance premiums from all the purchasers of products, and the purchase by manufacturers of commercial insurance or the creation of self insurance funds.

The defendant before us, General Motors, is the largest producer of automobiles in the world. In light of the fact that all of our sister states have adopted a cause of action for lack of crashworthiness, General Motors is *already* collecting a product liability premium every time it sells a car anywhere in the world, including West Virginia. [Citation.] West Virginians, then, are already paying the product liability insurance premium when they buy a General Motors car, so this Court would be both foolish and irresponsible if we held that while West Virginians must pay the premiums, West Virginians can't collect the insurance after they're injured.[6]

* * *

---

6. We note that even in an oligopoly, like the automobile industry, there is an industry-wide downward sloping demand curve. Thus, any product liability insurance premium—regardless of how actuarially sound—will have some negative effect on the total volume of cars sold because, as prices rise, fewer consumers are willing to

As a fall back position in the case before us, General Motors urges that, should we adopt the doctrine of crashworthiness, we simultaneously adopt the burden of proof rule announced in *Huddell v. Levin*, 537 F.2d 726 (3rd Cir.1976). Under *Huddell* (and cases that follow Huddell's approach), the plaintiff must prove that the product defect was the cause of a particular enhanced or aggravated injury that plaintiff suffered. To meet the *Huddell* burden the plaintiff must show what injuries would have resulted from the collision in the absence of the defect, so that the plaintiff bears the heavy burden of distinguishing between first and second collision injuries. * * *

* * *

The *Huddell* standard makes a great deal of sense and, perhaps, it should be the national standard in all crashworthiness cases. But it isn't. Therefore we reject the *Huddell* standard because West Virginians are not going to pay product liability insurance premiums so that all the residents of the 10th Circuit, where *Fox v. Ford Motor Co.*, 575 F.2d 774 (10th Cir.1978) was decided, can collect the benefits. The more liberal rule announced in *Fox* (and cases that follow *Fox*) is that the plaintiff need show only a defect that was *a* factor in causing some aspect of the plaintiff's harm. Once the plaintiff has made this *prima facie* showing, the manufacturer can then limit its liability if it can show that the plaintiff's injuries are capable of apportionment between the first and second collisions. Therefore, under this more liberal standard, the burden is upon the manufacturer to make the allocation. We adopt this rule.

Because this is a certified question, we do not have a record before us of a fully litigated crashworthiness case. However, for the guidance of both the state and federal trial courts, we *hold* today that in any crashworthiness case where there is a split of authority on any issue, as for example the plaintiff's burden of proof discussed above, we adopt the rule that is most liberal to the plaintiff.

Our conclusion today to adopt the rule most favorable to the plaintiff in crashworthiness cases is based upon the same actuarial considerations that have prompted us finally to adopt the doctrine of crashworthiness—namely, that we are *already* paying for full coverage. Indeed, in some world other than the one in which we live, where this Court were called upon to make national policy, we might very well take a meat ax to some current product liability rules. Therefore, we do not claim that our adoption of rules liberal to plaintiffs comports,

buy at the new higher prices. *See, The New Palgrave: A Dictionary of Economics,* J. Eatwell, M. Milgate and P. Newman, editors, The MacMillan Press Limited (London, 1987) Vol. 3, "Oligopoly." Thus, in terms of overall national employment, product liability law is not entirely benign, but trade-offs between employment opportunities in Michigan and the compensation of accident victims here in West Virginia are entirely beyond the capacity of this Court.

necessarily, with some Platonic ideal of perfect justice. Rather, for a tiny state incapable of controlling the direction of the national law in terms of appropriate trade-offs among employment, research, development, and compensation for the injured users of products, the adoption of rules liberal to plaintiffs is simple self-defense.

However, as we recently said in *Miller v. Monongahela Power Company,* 184 W.Va. 663, 403 S.E.2d 406 (1991):

> If the federal courts wish to establish national uniformity on personal injury matters by rethinking the whole tort system and making clear, bright line rules of national application, no court would welcome such rules more hospitably than we. But until such federal rules are articulated by the Supreme Court of the United States, we shall not presume to anticipate that august body's ruling on the subject. [Footnote omitted].

Miller at 671, 403 S.E.2d at 414.[11]

Accordingly, the certified question presented to us is answered and this case is dismissed from the docket of this Court.

Certified Question Answered.

---

[11]. In any adversarial system where residents are pitted against non-residents, there will inevitably be a temptation to redistribute wealth in the direction of residents, regardless of whether the "tribunal" deciding the issue is technically a court, legislature, or administrative agency. The greatest temptation in this regard, of course, is taxation. By far the best tax is one imposed on a stranger who can't vote or otherwise retaliate. Thus, left to their own devices, the dynamics of federalism would inevitably lead the states to tax interstate commerce at a higher rate than intrastate commerce. And, for exactly this reason, the Supreme Court of the United States has said that a state can't discriminate against interstate commerce by singling out imports or exports for special taxes, and that when taxing the income or personal property of an interstate business, states must apply apportionment formulae that would yield fair taxes if applied by every other state. *See Complete Auto v. Brady,* 430 U.S. 274, 97 S.Ct. 1076, 51 L.Ed. 2d 326 (1977); *Armco Steel v. Hardesty,* 467 U.S. 638, 104 S.Ct. 2620, 81 L.Ed. 2d 540 (1984).

RESTATEMENT (SECOND) OF TORTS (1965)
SELECTED SECTIONS *

Chapter 14

LIABILITY OF PERSONS SUPPLYING CHATTELS FOR THE USE OF OTHERS

TOPIC 1. RULES APPLICABLE TO ALL SUPPLIERS

Section
388. Chattel known to be dangerous for intended use
389. Chattel unlikely to be made safe for use
390. Chattel for use by person known to be incompetent

TOPIC 2. PERSONS SUPPLYING CHATTELS TO BE USED FOR THEIR BUSINESS PURPOSES

391. Chattel known to be dangerous
392. Chattel dangerous for intended use
393. Effect of third person's duty to inspect

TOPIC 3. MANUFACTURERS OF CHATTELS

394. Chattel known to be dangerous
395. Negligent manufacture of chattel dangerous unless carefully made
396. Effect of third person's duty to inspect
397. Chattel made under secret formula
398. Chattel made under dangerous plan or design

TOPIC 4. SELLERS OF CHATTELS MANUFACTURED BY THIRD PERSONS

399. Chattel known to be dangerous
400. Selling as own product chattel made by another
401. Chattel likely to be dangerous
402. Absence of duty to inspect chattel

TOPIC 5. STRICT LIABILITY

402 A. Special liability of seller of product for physical harm to user or consumer
402 B. Misrepresentation by seller of chattels to consumer

* Copyright © 1965 by The American Law Institute. Reprinted with the permission of The American Law Institute.

Section

TOPIC 6. INDEPENDENT CONTRACTORS

403. Chattel known to be dangerous
404. Negligence in making, rebuilding, or repairing chattel

TOPIC 7. DONORS, LENDERS, AND LESSORS OF CHATTELS

405. Donors and lenders of chattels known to be dangerous
406. Manufacturer giving or lending negligently made chattel
407. Lessors of chattels known to be dangerous
408. Lease of chattel for immediate use

TOPIC 1. RULES APPLICABLE TO ALL SUPPLIERS

Scope Note: This Topic states the rules which are equally applicable to all persons who in any way or for any purpose supply chattels for the use of others or permit others to use their chattels. There are other rules which impose upon the suppliers of chattels additional duties because of the purpose for which or the manner in which the chattels are supplied or because the chattel has been made by them or put out as their product. These rules are stated hereafter. The peculiar rules which determine the liability of one who supplies a chattel or permits its use for purposes in which he himself has a business interest are stated in §§ 391–393. The peculiar rules applicable to those who manufacture the chattels which they supply are stated in §§ 394–398. The rules which determine the peculiar liability of vendors of chattels manufactured by others are stated in §§ 399–402. A special rule of strict liability applicable to sellers of articles for consumption is stated in § 402 A, and a special rule as to liability for misrepresentations made by a seller of goods to the consumer is stated in § 402 B.

The peculiar rules applicable to independent contractors and repairmen are stated in §§ 403 and 404. The peculiar rules applicable to donors, lenders, and lessors of chattels are stated in §§ 405–408.

In many instances the rules stated in the Sections in this Chapter may overlap, and the plaintiff may recover under the rules stated in two or more Sections. No attempt has been made to indicate, by way of cross-reference under any one Section, the other Sections upon which recovery may possibly be based.

§ 388. Chattel Known to Be Dangerous for Intended Use

One who supplies directly or through a third person a chattel for another to use is subject to liability to those whom the supplier should expect to use the chattel with the consent of the other or to be endangered by its probable use, for physical harm caused by the use of the chattel in the manner for which and by a person for whose use it is supplied, if the supplier

(a) knows or has reason to know that the chattel is or is likely to be dangerous for the use for which it is supplied, and

(b) has no reason to believe that those for whose use the chattel is supplied will realize its dangerous condition, and

(c) fails to exercise reasonable care to inform them of its dangerous condition or of the facts which make it likely to be dangerous.

See Reporter's Notes.

Comment:

a. The words "those whom the supplier should expect to use the chattel" and the words "a person for whose use it is supplied" include not only the person to whom the chattel is turned over by the supplier, but also all those who are members of a class whom the supplier should expect to use it or occupy it or share in its use with the consent of such person, irrespective of whether the supplier has any particular person in mind. Thus, one who lends an automobile to a friend and who fails to disclose a defect of which he himself knows and which he should recognize as making it unreasonably dangerous for use, is subject to liability not only to his friend, but also to anyone whom his friend permits to drive the car or chooses to receive in it as passenger or guest, if it is understood between them that the car may be so used. So too, one entrusting a chattel to a common carrier for transportation must expect that the chattel will be handled by the carrier's employees.

In the cases thus far decided, the rule stated in this Section has been applied only in favor of those who are injured while the chattel is being used by the person to whom it is supplied, or with his consent. In all probability the rule stated would not apply in favor of a thief of the chattel, or one injured while the thief is using it. Nor would it apply, for example, in favor of a trespasser who entered an automobile and was injured by its condition. On the other hand, no reason is apparent for limiting the rule to exclude persons who are for any reason privileged to use the chattel without the consent of the person to whom it is supplied, as in the case of a police officer who commandeers an automobile to pursue a criminal, or moves it in order to avoid danger to the public safety.

b. This Section states that one who supplies a chattel for another to use for any purpose is subject to liability for physical harm caused by his failure to exercise reasonable care to give to those whom he may expect to use the chattel any information as to the character and condition of the chattel which he possesses, and which he should recognize as necessary to enable them to realize the danger of using it. A fortiori, one so supplying a chattel is subject to liability if by word or

§ 388   RESTATEMENT (SECOND) OF TORTS

deed he leads those who are to use the chattel to believe it to be of a character or in a condition safer for use than he knows it to be or to be likely to be.

Illustration:

    1. A sells to B a shotgun, knowing that B intends to give it to his son C as a birthday present. A knows, but does not tell B, that the trigger mechanism of the gun is so defective that it is likely to be discharged by a slight jolt. B gives the gun to C. While C is using the gun it is discharged, and C is injured, by reason of the defective mechanism. A is subject to liability to C.

    c. *Persons included as "suppliers."* The rules stated in this Section and throughout this Topic apply to determine the liability of any person who for any purpose or in any manner gives possession of a chattel for another's use, or who permits another to use or occupy it while it is in his own possession or control, without disclosing his knowledge that the chattel is dangerous for the use for which it is supplied or for which it is permitted to be used. These rules, therefore, apply to sellers, lessors, donors, or lenders, irrespective of whether the chattel is made by them or by a third person. They apply to all kinds of bailors, irrespective of whether the bailment is for a reward or gratuitous, and irrespective of whether the bailment is for use, transportation, safekeeping, or repair. They also apply to one who undertakes the repair of a chattel and who delivers it back with knowledge that it is defective because of the work which he is employed to do upon it. (See § 403.)

    d. One supplying a chattel to be used or dealt with by others is subject to liability under the rule stated in this Section, not only to those for whose use the chattel is supplied but also to third persons whom the supplier should expect to be endangered by its use.

    e. *Ambit of liability.* The liability stated in this Section exists only if physical harm is caused by the use of the chattel by those for whose use the chattel is supplied, and in the manner for which it is supplied. Except possibly where there is a privilege to use the chattel, the one who supplies a chattel for another's use is not subject to liability for bodily harm caused by its use by a third person without the consent of him for whose use it is supplied. This is true although the chattel is one of a sort notoriously likely to be so used. So too, the supplier is not subject to liability for bodily harm caused by its use by a third person who uses it even with the consent of him for whom it is supplied, if the supplier has no reason to expect that such a third person may be permitted to use it.

In order that the supplier of a chattel may be subject to liability under the rule stated in this Section, not only must the person who uses the chattel be one whom the supplier should expect to use it with the consent of him to whom it is supplied, but the chattel must also be put to a use to which the supplier has reason to expect it to be put. Thus, one who lends a chattel to another to be put to a particular use for which, though defective, it is safe, is not required to give warning of the defect, although he knows of its existence and knows that it makes the chattel dangerous for other uses, unless he has reason to expect such other uses.

f. As pointed out in § 5, the phrase "subject to liability" is used to indicate that the person whose conduct is in question is liable if, but only if, there also exist the other conditions necessary to liability. The person using the chattel may disable himself from bringing an action either by his contributory negligence in voluntarily using the chattel with knowledge of its dangerous condition, or by his contributory negligence in failing to make a proper inspection which would have disclosed the defect, or in failing to use the precautions obviously necessary to the safe use of the chattel.

Comment on Clause (a):

g. The duty which the rule stated in this Section imposes upon the supplier of a chattel for another's use is to exercise reasonable care to give to those who are to use the chattel the information which the supplier possesses, and which he should realize to be necessary to make its use safe for them and those in whose vicinity it is to be used. This information enables those for whom the chattel is supplied to determine whether they shall accept and use it. Save in exceptional circumstances, as where the chattel, no matter how carefully dealt with, is incapable of any safe use, or where the person to whom it is supplied is obviously likely to misuse it, the supplier of a chattel who has given such information is entitled to assume that it will not be used for purposes for which the information given by him shows it to be unfit and, therefore, is relieved of liability for harm done by its misuse to those in the vicinity of its probable use.

A chattel may be so imperfect that it is unlikely to be safe for use for any purpose, no matter how great the care which is exercised in using it. As to the rule which determines liability in such case, see § 389.

There are many chattels which, even though perfect, are unsafe for any use or for the particular use for which they are supplied unless their properties and capabilities are known to those who use them. If such a chattel is supplied to another whom the supplier should realize to be unlikely to know its properties and capabilities, the supplier is required to exercise reasonable care to give to the other such information thereof as he himself possesses.

Illustration:

2. A is a guest in B's house. A is taken suddenly ill. B gives him a drug which B knows can only be safely used if taken in

certain doses and under certain conditions. B gives the drug to A, but forgets to instruct him as to the manner in which it is to be used. A takes it in a larger dose than is proper, or fails to take the precautions which are necessary to make it safe. In consequence A's illness is increased. B is subject to liability to A.

Comment:

h. There are many articles which are so defective as to be incapable of safe use for any of the purposes for which they are normally fit or for use in the manner in which such articles are normally capable of safe use, but which are safe for limited uses or if used with particular precautions. If the appearance of such a chattel does not disclose its defective condition, the supplier is under a duty to exercise reasonable care to disclose its condition, in so far as it is known to him, to those who are to use it, or to inform them that it is fit only for these limited uses, or if used with the particular precautions.

The supplier of a defective chattel may have had peculiar experience with such chattels, and he may, therefore, be required to realize that a disclosure of the actual condition of the chattel will not be enough to inform the user of the danger of using it except for limited purposes or with particular precautions. If such is the case, it is not enough for the supplier to inform those who are to use the chattel of its actual condition. He must exercise reasonable care to apprise them of the danger of using it otherwise than for the particular purposes for which he should know it to be fit or with the particular precautions which he should realize to be necessary to make its use safe.

i. Where lot of chattels contains a few defective ones. It is not necessary in order that a supplier of a chattel for another's use be liable under the rule stated in this Section that he should know that the particular chattel is dangerous for the use for which it is supplied. It is enough that he knows of facts which make it likely that the particular chattel may be dangerous, as where he knows that it is part of a lot, some of which he has discovered to be so imperfect as to be dangerous. If so, he is required to exercise reasonable care to acquaint those for whose use the chattel is supplied of these facts, in order that they may realize the risk they will run in using the chattel and may make an intelligent choice as to the advisability of doing so.

Illustration:

3. A sells or gives to B a can of baking powder. A knows that several, though not all, of the lot of cans of which this can is a part have exploded when opened. He does not inform B of this fact. While C, B's cook, is attempting to open the can, it explodes, causing harm to C's eyes and also the eyes of D, B's kitchen maid, who is standing nearby. A is subject to liability to C and D.

j. So too, one may put into a stock of chattels which he intends subsequently to supply for the use of others, articles which he then knows to be, or to be likely to be, dangerous for the use for which they are to be supplied. It may, however, subsequently be impossible to tell which of the chattels are of this character, and, therefore, at the time the particular article is supplied the supplier may not know that it is dangerous. He is, however, subject to liability, since he knows that it may be one of the chattels which is dangerous. This situation usually arises where the supplier is a manufacturer whose business is divided into different departments. In such a case the operative department may discover a defect in a particular chattel which the subsequent processes of manufacture may make it difficult or impossible to detect. So too, defective material may be knowingly used in the manufacture of a lot of chattels so that it is obvious that some, though not all, of these must be defective. Here again the process of manufacture may make it impossible to tell, at the time the particular chattel is supplied, which of the lot are dangerous and which safe.

Illustration:

4. The A Manufacturing Company makes a lot of ladders out of a shipment of wood of which some is knotted. It is impossible to see the knots after the ladders have been painted. One of the ladders is sold to B. While C, B's servant, is using the ladder, it breaks because of the knots in the wood of which it is made. The A Company is subject to liability to C, although at the time the ladder was sold it appeared perfectly sound and the sales department which sold the ladder had not been informed that defective material had been used in the construction of this lot of ladders.

Comment on Clause (b):

k. When warning of defects unnecessary. One who supplies a chattel to others to use for any purpose is under a duty to exercise reasonable care to inform them of its dangerous character in so far as it is known to him, or of facts which to his knowledge make it likely to be dangerous, if, but only if, he has no reason to expect that those for whose use the chattel is supplied will discover its condition and realize the danger involved. It is not necessary for the supplier to inform those for whose use the chattel is supplied of a condition which a mere casual looking over will disclose, unless the circumstances under which the chattel is supplied are such as to make it likely that even so casual an inspection will not be made. However, the condition, although readily observable, may be one which only persons of special experience would realize to be dangerous. In such case, if the supplier, having such special experience, knows that the condition involves danger and has no reason to believe that those who use it will have such special experience as will enable them to perceive the danger, he is required to inform them of the risk of which he himself knows and which he has no reason to suppose that they will realize.

Comment on Clause (c):

l. The supplier's duty is to exercise reasonable care to inform those for whose use the article is supplied of dangers which are peculiarly within his knowledge. If he has done so, he is not subject to liability, even though the information never reaches those for whose use the chattel is supplied. The factors which determine whether the supplier exercises reasonable care by giving this information to third persons through whom the chattel is supplied for the use of others, are stated in Comment *n*.

m. Inspection. The fact that a chattel is supplied for the use of others does not of itself impose upon the supplier a duty to make an inspection of the chattel, no matter how cursory, in order to discover whether it is fit for the use for which it is supplied. Such a duty may be imposed because of the purpose for which the chattel is to be used by those to whom it is supplied. (See § 392.) A manufacturer of a chattel may be under a duty to inspect the materials and parts out of which it is made and to subject the finished article to such an inspection as the danger involved in an imperfect article makes reasonable. (See § 395 and Comment *e* under that Section.) Under certain conditions, stated in §§ 403, 404, and 408, an independent contractor or lessor may be under a similar duty of inspection.

n. Warnings given to third person. Chattels are often supplied for the use of others, although the chattels or the permission to use them are not given directly to those for whose use they are supplied, as when a wholesale dealer sells to a retailer goods which are obviously to be used by the persons purchasing them from him, or when a contractor furnishes the scaffoldings or other appliances which his subcontractor and the latter's servants are to use, or when an automobile is lent for the borrower to use for the conveyance of his family and friends. In all such cases the question may arise as to whether the person supplying the chattel is exercising that reasonable care, which he owes to those who are to use it, by informing the third person through whom the chattel is supplied of its actual character.

Giving to the third person through whom the chattel is supplied all the information necessary to its safe use is not in all cases sufficient to relieve the supplier from liability. It is merely a means by which this information is to be conveyed to those who are to use the chattel. The question remains whether this method gives a reasonable assurance that the information will reach those whose safety depends upon their having it. All sorts of chattels may be supplied for the use of others, through all sorts of third persons and under an infinite variety of circumstances. This being true, it is obviously impossible to state in advance any set of rules which will automatically determine in all cases whether one supplying a chattel for the use of others through a third person has satisfied his duty to those who are to use the chattel by informing the third person of the dangerous character of the chattel, or of the precautions which must be exercised in using it in order to make its use safe. There are, however, certain factors which are important in determining this question. There is necessarily some chance that information given to the third person will not be communicated by him to those who are to use the chattel. This chance varies with the circumstances existing at the time the chattel is turned over to the third person, or permission is given to him to allow others to use it. These circumstances include the known or knowable character of the third person and may also include the purpose for which the chattel is given. Modern life would be intolerable unless one were permitted to rely to a certain extent on others' doing what they normally do, particularly if it is their duty to do so. If the chattel is one which if ignorantly used contains no great chance of causing anything more than some comparatively trivial harm, it is reasonable to permit the one who supplies the chattel through a third person to rely upon the fact that the third person is an ordinary normal man to whose discredit the supplier knows nothing, as a sufficient assurance that information given to him will be passed on to those who are to use the chattel.

If, however, the third person is known to be careless or inconsiderate or if the purpose for which the chattel is to be used is to his advantage and knowledge of the true character of the chattel is likely to prevent its being used and so to deprive him of this advantage—as when goods so defective as to be unsalable are sold by a wholesaler to a retailer—the supplier of the chattel has reason to expect, or at least suspect, that the information will fail to reach those who are to use the chattel and whose safety depends upon their knowledge of its true character. In such a case, the supplier may well be required to go further than to tell such a third person of the dangerous character of the article, or, if he fails to do so, to take the risk of being subjected to liability if the information is not brought home to those whom the supplier should expect to use the chattel. In many cases the burden of doing so is slight, as when the chattel is to be used in the presence or vicinity of the person supplying it, so that he could easily give a personal warning to those who are to use the chattel. Even though the supplier has no practicable opportunity to give this information directly and in person to those who are to use the chattel or share in its use, it is not unreasonable to require him to make good any harm which is caused by his using so unreliable a method of giving the information which is obviously necessary to make the chattel safe for those who use it and those in the vicinity of its use.

Here, as in every case which involves the determination of the precautions which must be taken to satisfy the requirements of reasonable care, the magnitude of the risk involved must be compared with the burden which would be imposed by requiring them (see § 291), and the magnitude of the risk is determined not only by the chance that some harm may result but also the serious or trivial character of the harm which is likely to result (see § 293). Since the care which must be taken always increases with the danger involved, it may be reasonable to require those who supply through others chattels which if ignorantly used involve grave risk of serious harm to those who use them and those in the vicinity of their use, to take precautions to bring the information home to the users of such chattels which it would be unreasonable to demand were the chattels of a less dangerous character.

Thus, while it may be proper to permit a supplier to assume that one through whom he supplies a chattel which is only slightly dangerous will communicate the information given him to those who are to use it unless he knows that the other is careless, it may be improper to permit him to trust the conveyance of the necessary information of the actual character of a highly dangerous article to a third person of whose character he knows nothing. It may well be that he should take the risk that this information may not be communicated, unless he exercises reasonable care to ascertain the character of the third person, or unless from previous experience with him or from the excellence of his reputation the supplier has positive reason to believe that he is careful. In addition to this, if the danger involved in the ignorant use of a particular chattel is very great, it may be that the supplier does not exercise reasonable care in entrusting the communication of the necessary information even to a person whom he has good reason to believe to be careful. Many such articles can be made to carry their own message to the understanding of those who are likely to use them by the form in which they are put out, by the container in which they are supplied, or by a label or other device, indicating with a substantial sufficiency their dangerous character. Where the danger involved in the ignorant use of their true quality is great and such means of disclosure are practicable and not unduly burdensome, it may well be that the supplier should be required to adopt them. There are many statutes which require that articles which are highly dangerous if used in ignorance of their character, such as poisons, explosives, and inflammables, shall be put out in such a form as to bear on their face notice of their dangerous character, either by the additional coloring matter, the form or color of the containers, or by labels. Such statutes are customarily construed as making one who supplies such articles not so marked liable, even though he has disclosed their actual character to the person to whom he directly gives them for the use of others, and even though the statute contains no express provisions on the subject.

o. Under the rule stated in this Section one who supplies a chattel to a third person for use is subject to the liability stated in this Section if he fails to exercise reasonable care to inform those for whose use the chattel is supplied of its dangerous condition. It follows that the supplier is equally liable if he actually conceals a defect in the chattel by painting it over or by a pretense of repair, or if by express words he represents it to be safe, knowing that it is not so.

§ 389. Chattel Unlikely to Be Made Safe for Use

One who supplies directly or through a third person a chattel for another's use, knowing or having reason to know that the chattel is unlikely to be made reasonably safe before being put to a use which the supplier should expect it to be put, is subject to liability for physical harm caused by such use to those whom the supplier should expect to use the chattel or to be endangered by its probable use, and who are ignorant of the dangerous character of the chattel or whose knowledge thereof does not make them contributorily negligent, although the supplier has informed the other for whose use the chattel is supplied of its dangerous character.

See Reporter's Notes.

Comment:

a. The rule stated in this Section, like those stated in §§ 388 and 390, determines the liability of one who supplies a chattel for another to use, irrespective of whether the chattel is to be used for the purposes of the supplier's business or for purposes which are otherwise to the supplier's advantage or, on the other hand, for purposes personal to those who are to use the chattel and of advantage only to them.

The question left open in Comment *a* under § 388, as to use of the chattel by one who is privileged to use it without the consent of the person to whom it is supplied, would appear to be equally open under this Section.

b. Chattel safe for some but not all uses. A chattel may be in such a bad condition that it is incapable of safe use for any purpose save destruction or preservation as a curiosity. On the other hand, a chattel may be reasonably safe for many uses, and dangerous for a few or even for one particular use. In the former case, the rule stated in this Section would apply even though the chattel were not supplied for any particular use. If, however, the chattel is only unsafe for one or more particular uses, the rule stated in this Section applies only if the chattel is supplied for such a use.

c. Even though a chattel when turned over to another for his own or a third person's use is in a condition dangerous for the use for which it is intended, the circumstances may be such that the supplier as a reasonable man has no reason to believe that it is unlikely that the chattel will be made safe before being used. On the other hand, the circumstances may be such that although the chattel is capable of being made safe for use, the person supplying it should realize the unlikelihood that this will be done before it is used. Among circumstances which render this unlikely are the facts that the chattel is to be used so soon after it is turned over that it is substantially certain that no change will be made in it, or that the person to whom it is supplied is financially incapable of bearing the expense of making it safe, or that he is notoriously given to taking chances with the safety of himself and others. It is, however, not enough to bring the situation within the rule stated in this Section that the supplier of the chattel should merely suspect that the chattel will be used before it is made safe. A substantial probability is necessary.

d. The rule stated in this Section determines the conditions under which the supplier of a chattel which he knows or has reason to know to be unlikely to be made safe for the use for which he supplies it is subject to liability. As defined in § 5, the phrase "subject to liability" means that the supplier will be liable if, but only if, his conduct is, in law, the cause of bodily harm sustained by another, and if the person injured by it has not so conducted himself as to disable him from recovering. Therefore, if the person using a chattel is informed of its dangerous character or learns of it from other sources, he may be barred from the recovery for any harm which he sustains by using the chattel. There may, however, be circumstances under which his use of the chattel with the knowledge of its defective character may not disable him from recovering. He may be a person whom, because of youth or other reasons, the supplier should recognize as unable to appreciate the danger involved in the use of the chattel, even though its actual condition or character is disclosed to him. Again, he may have no choice to use or refuse to use the chattel. Thus a construction company, which, during a war, builds a spur line from a railway to a training camp is liable to an enlisted man in the United States Army for injuries received while being conveyed to the camp in a wreck caused by the negligent manner in which the spur was constructed. The negligent construction of the line may be known to the construction company, the United States Government and the enlisted man. The imperative need of speedy training of troops makes it obvious to the construction company that the spur line must be used before the defective construction can be remedied, and the enlisted man, as such, cannot refuse to travel over it. So too, convicts are not free to reject any chattel which is supplied for their use or conveyance.

e. While the rule stated in this Section may, as stated in Comment *d,* occasionally apply to make the supplier of the chattel liable to those who use it with knowledge of its actual character, it is usually applicable to those who share in its use or are in the vicinity of it. Such persons, when injured, are not barred from recovery by the negligence of those who put a chattel to a use for which they know it is dangerous.

In the great majority of cases, they are ignorant of the dangerous character of the chattel. Even if they are aware of the dangerous character of the chattel, they may be entitled to be in the danger zone and, therefore, are not contributorily negligent in entering or failing to leave the area endangered, unless the danger is very great.

Illustration:

> 1. A employs B, a building contractor, to build a row of houses according to plans and specifications supplied by A. These plans require material and workmanship so cheap and inferior that any competent builder would realize that a house so built might collapse at any time. B builds the house under these plans and specifications. One of the houses collapses and harms C, a possible purchaser, inspecting the house at A's invitation, and D, a traveler upon the adjoining highway. B is subject to liability to C and D.

f. Warnings to user not always effective. Under normal conditions a chattel which is in some respects dangerous, or is dangerous when put to some uses, can still be reasonably safe if proper warning of the danger is given to the user. Thus a chain saw which is unsafe for use on hard wood may still be quite safe for use on soft wood, and is not unreasonably dangerous if that information is conveyed to the user. Again, an inflammable cleaning fluid may be very dangerous if it is used in the vicinity of an open flame, but quite safe for use if it is not; and it is not unreasonably dangerous if warning of the danger is given. The seller who has attached such a warning to his product, or taken all reasonable steps to bring it home to the ultimate user, is free to assume that it will reach him, and that he will read and heed it.

There are, however, some chattels which are so unsafe for the uses to which they are likely to be put that the seller cannot reasonably assume that the warning will be effective to protect the user. The product may be entirely unsafe for the primary use for which it is sold and intended to be used. Thus an explosive mixture of kerosene and gasoline, sold for use in kerosene lamps, can never be safe for that purpose. In such a case the warning will not relieve the seller of the responsibility, since he cannot reasonably assume that it will be heeded to the extent of foregoing the use for which the product is sold. Again, if the seller has reason to anticipate the possibility that the warning which he conveys to an intermediate dealer will not reach the ultimate user, as where it is in a separate leaflet which may not be passed on, the seller is not relieved of liability when the user does not receive the warning.

Illustration:

> 2. A manufactures and sells combs for use in permanent wave treatment in beauty shops. Heat treatment of the hair is normal and customary in such shops. A's combs are highly inflammable,

§ 389   RESTATEMENT (SECOND) OF TORTS

and dangerous in the presence of heat. A sells a quantity of the combs to B, a dealer, accompanying them with a warning that they are to be used for cold treatment only. B sells some of the combs to C, a beauty shop operator, but neglects to pass on the warning. C uses the combs in heat treatment of D's hair. They catch fire, and D is burned. A is subject to liability to D.

§ 390. Chattel for Use by Person Known to Be Incompetent

One who supplies directly or through a third person a chattel for the use of another whom the supplier knows or has reason to know to be likely because of his youth, inexperience, or otherwise, to use it in a manner involving unreasonable risk of physical harm to himself and others whom the supplier should expect to share in or be endangered by its use, is subject to liability for physical harm resulting to them.

See Reporter's Notes.

Comment:

a. The rule stated in this Section, like those stated in §§ 388 and 389, determines the liability of one who supplies a chattel for another to use, irrespective of whether the chattel is to be used for the purposes of the supplier's business or for purposes which are otherwise to the supplier's advantage or, on the other hand, for purposes personal to those who are to use the chattel and of advantage only to them.

The rule stated applies to anyone who supplies a chattel for the use of another. It applies to sellers, lessors, donors or lenders, and to all kinds of bailors, irrespective of whether the bailment is gratuitous or for a consideration.

b. The rule stated in this Section is a special application of the rule stated in § 308, and has a close analogy to the rule stated in § 307. Section 307 deals with the use of an instrumentality, whether a human being or a thing, which is known or should be known to be dangerously improper for the use to which it is put. This Section deals with the supplying of a chattel to a person incompetent to use it safely, irrespective of whether the chattel is to be used for the suppliers' purposes or for the purpose of him to whom it is supplied. In the one case as in the other, liability is based upon the rule stated in §§ 302, 302A, and 302B, and elaborated in Comment *j* under § 302, that the actor may not assume that human beings will conduct themselves properly if the facts which are known or should be known to him should make him realize that they are unlikely to do so. Thus, one who supplies a chattel for the use of another who knows its exact character and condition is not entitled to assume that the other will use it safely if the supplier knows or has reason to know that such other is likely to use it dangerously, as where the other belongs to a class which is notoriously incompetent to use the chattel safely, or lacks the training and experience necessary for such use, or the supplier knows that the other has on other occasions so acted that the supplier should realize that the chattel is likely to be dangerously used, or that the other, though otherwise capable of using the chattel safely, has a propensity or fixed purpose to misuse it. This is true even though the chattel is in perfect condition, or though defective, is capable of safe use for the purposes for which it is supplied by an ordinary person who knows of its defective condition.

Illustrations:

1. A gives a loaded gun to B, a feeble-minded girl of ten, to be carried by her to C. While B is carrying the gun she tampers with the trigger and discharges it, harming C. A is subject to liability to C.

2. A permits B, a boy of ten, who has never previously driven a motor car, to drive his motor car on an errand of B's own. B drives the car carelessly, to the injury of C. A is subject to liability to C.

3. A permits B, his chauffeur, who to his knowledge is in the habit of driving at an excessive speed, to use his car to take B's family to the seashore. While driving the car for this purpose, B drives at an excessive rate of speed and harms C. A is subject to liability to C.

4. A lends his car to his friend B for B to use to drive a party of friends to a country club dance. A knows that B has habitually become intoxicated at such dances. On the particular occasion B becomes intoxicated and while in that condition recklessly drives the car into the carefully driven car of C, and causes harm to him. A is subject to liability to C.

5. A rents an automobile to B, a young man who announces his purpose to drive it from Boston to New York on a bet that he will do so in three hours. A is subject to liability if the excessive speed at which the car is driven causes harm to travelers on the highway.

6. A sells or gives an automobile to B, his adult son, knowing that B is an epileptic, but that B nevertheless intends to drive the car. While B is driving he suffers an epileptic seizure, loses control of the car, and injures C. A is subject to liability to C.

c. The rule stated in this Section sets out the conditions under which a supplier of a chattel is subject to liability. As always this phrase denotes that a supplier is liable if, but only if, his conduct is the legal cause of the bodily harm complained of and if the person suffering the harm is not subject to any defense such as contributory negligence, which will prevent him from recovering damages therefor. One who

§ 390 RESTATEMENT (SECOND) OF TORTS

accepts and uses a chattel knowing that he is incompetent to use it safely or who associates himself in the use of a chattel by one whom he knows to be so incompetent, or one who is himself careless in the use of the chattel after receiving it, is usually in such contributory fault as to bar recovery. If, however, the person to whom the chattel is supplied is one of a class which is legally recognized as so incompetent as to prevent them from being responsible for their actions, the supplier may be liable for harm suffered by him, as when a loaded gun is entrusted to a child of tender years. So too, if the supplier knows that the condition of the person to whom the chattel is supplied is such as to make him incapable of exercising the care which it is reasonable to expect of a normal sober adult, the supplier may be liable for harm sustained by the incompetent although such person deals with it in a way which may render him liable to third persons who are also injured.

Illustration:

7. A, who makes a business of letting out boats for hire, rents his boat to B and C, who are obviously so intoxicated as to make it likely that they will mismanage the boat so as to capsize it or to collide with other boats. B and C by their drunken mismanagement collide with the boat of D, upsetting both boats. B, C, and D are drowned. A is subject to liability to the estates of B, C, and D under the death statute, although the estates of B and C may also be liable for the death of D.

d. When person using chattel knows his incompetence. The fact that the person to whom the chattel is supplied realizes his incompetence, and therefore is in such contributory fault as to bar his right to recover for any harm which he himself sustains, does not relieve the supplier from liability to third persons injured by the improper use made of the chattel by the incompetent person, unless such third persons, knowing, or having reason to know, of his incompetence, associate themselves with him in the use of the chattel or unnecessarily come within the area made dangerous by the probability that he will misuse the chattel, or knowing that the chattel is in the hands of incompetent persons, fail to take those precautions which a reasonably careful man would deem necessary under the circumstances.

Illustration:

8. A permits B, whom he knows to be an inexperienced driver, to use his car. B invites his friend C, who knows of his inexperience, to drive with him. B's inexperience leads him to drive in a way which is obviously improper. In so doing he collides with the carefully driven car of D. The collision results in harm to both B and C. While neither B nor C may recover against A, A is subject to liability to D.

TOPIC 2. PERSONS SUPPLYING CHATTELS TO BE USED FOR THEIR BUSINESS PURPOSES

§ 391. Chattel Known to Be Dangerous

One who supplies directly or through a third person a chattel for another to use for the supplier's business purposes, knowing or having reason to know that it is or is likely to be dangerous for the use for which it is supplied, is subject to liability as stated in §§ 388–390.

See Reporter's Notes.

Comment:

a. Person to whom warning must be given. As stated in § 388, Comment *n*, the liability imposed upon those who supply chattels to a third person for the use of others may often be avoided by giving to the person through whom the chattel is supplied the information necessary to enable it to be safely used, or to afford those who are to use it an opportunity to decide intelligently whether to do so or not. It is, however, not sufficient to give the information to the person through whom the chattel is supplied, if the chattel is one which is incapable of any safe use for the purposes for which it is supplied (see § 389), or if it is given to the third person for the purpose of being turned over to another whom the supplier knows to be incompetent to use it safely (see § 390), or if it is one which it is practicable to make carry its own warning and which, if ignorantly used, is very likely to involve a grave risk of death or serious bodily harm (see § 388, Comment *n*), or if the supplier has reason to believe that the information given to the third person will not be communicated to those who are to use the chattel (see § 389). This last proviso is peculiarly applicable where a chattel is supplied to a third person in order that he may turn it over for others to put it to a use so immediate that the supplier cannot expect it to be made safe before it is used.

Illustration:

1. A, a contractor, employs B, a subcontractor, to do the painting upon a building which the contractor has undertaken to build. The contract requires A to provide the necessary scaffolding. A erects a scaffolding for this purpose which he knows to be dangerously insecure. He notifies B that the scaffold is ready and requests B to send his men immediately. When B arrives on the premises with his men, A informs B of the insecure character of the scaffolding, which is not observable by any inspection which B's employees should make before going upon it, but adds, "we must get on with the work, so we will have to take a chance." B at once sends his workmen on the scaffold, which collapses, injuring C, one of B's workmen. A is subject to liability to C if there was nothing

§ 391

to indicate to him that B would tell C of the dangerous character of the scaffolding and if C was in fact ignorant of it.

§ 392. Chattel Dangerous for Intended Use

One who supplies to another, directly or through a third person, a chattel to be used for the supplier's business purposes is subject to liability to those for whose use the chattel is supplied, or to those whom he should expect to be endangered by its probable use, for physical harm caused by the use of the chattel in the manner for which and by persons for whose use the chattel is supplied

    (a) if the supplier fails to exercise reasonable care to make the chattel safe for the use for which it is supplied, or

    (b) if he fails to exercise reasonable care to discover its dangerous condition or character, and to inform those whom he should expect to use it.

See Reporter's Notes.

Comment:

a. The rules stated in §§ 388–390 determine the liability of those who for any purposes supply a chattel for the use of others. They, therefore, apply to determine the liability of a person who supplies a chattel for a use by others in which he or the others have a business interest, with knowledge that it is or is likely to be dangerous for its intended use. (See § 391.) This Section states the rule under which a peculiar liability is imposed upon one supplying chattels for another's use because of the fact that the use is one in which the supplier has a business interest. A person so supplying goods is required not only to give warning of dangers which he knows are involved in the use of the article, or which, from facts within his knowledge, he knows are likely to be so involved, but also to subject the article to such an inspection as the danger of using it in a defective condition makes it reasonable to require of him. The additional duty of inspection thrown upon the person so supplying chattels for a use in which he has a business interest, as compared with the absence of any such duty when he has no business interest in the use for which the chattel is supplied, is analogous to the duty of inspection imposed upon one who permits another to come upon his land for his business purpose.

b. The words "supplying a chattel to be used for the supplier's business purposes" apply not only where the possession or custody of the chattel is given to the other or to a third party for the use of the other, but also where others are permitted to use or share in the use of a chattel while it remains in the supplier's possession or custody. Thus, the words apply not only to a railroad company delivering a freight car on the private siding of the plaintiff's employer for the purpose of unloading the freight, or to be shifted upon the employer's private road by his own engines, but also to a railroad which permits the employees of its consignee to enter its cars for the purpose of unloading them at its own freight yards and while the train is in charge of its own train crew. So also, the vehicles and other chattels which a common carrier furnishes to its passengers for the purpose of giving them their transportation, or which are furnished by a private person who transports passengers for hire, are supplied for the purposes of the carrier's business, as are the tools and appliances which an employer furnishes to his servants to be used in performing the work which they are employed to do.

c. Ownership of chattel immaterial. In order that the rule stated in this Section shall apply, it is not necessary that the chattel be owned by the one who supplies it. It may be leased to him or borrowed by him. It is enough that he has had possession or control of it for the purpose of using it in connection with his business, and that he has supplied it for such purpose. Indeed, the rule stated in this Section would apply although the chattel had been wrongfully appropriated by the supplier to such use.

d. What uses are for supplier's business purposes. In determining whether the chattel is being supplied for the supplier's business purposes, the fact that it is being used for the purpose of completing a contract or business dealing as undertaken by the supplier is often important. Thus where a railroad company ships a car to the private siding of a manufacturing company, the persons employed as servants or otherwise by the manufacturing company to unload the car are using it in connection with the supplier's business while they are unloading it. This is true because the contract to deliver involves the unloading of the car, and also involves such movements of the car in the private yards of the manufacturing company as are necessary to place it in a position convenient for unloading.

If a railroad company accepts freight for through transportation beyond its own lines by connecting carriers, it has a business interest in the transportation of the freight beyond its own line and until the through carriage is complete. Therefore, all those who are engaged in the transportation of the freight en route to its final destination, irrespective of whether they are employees of the final carrier or of the consignee, are dealing with the car for the business purposes of the initial carrier.

On the other hand, when everything necessary to the performance of the supplier's contract or the completion of his business dealings is done, the fact that he permits his chattel to be used by those to whom he has supplied it previously for his business use, does not make such further use of the chattel a use for the supplier's business purposes.

Where a railroad accepts freight for delivery at its terminal, but on a particular occasion, as a convenience to the consignee, permits him, instead of unloading the car at its terminal, to arrange for the transportation of the car to his place of business by a connecting carrier, the transportation of the car by the connecting carrier is not a use for the railroad's business purposes.

e. Supplying tools for workmen. One who employs another to erect a structure or to do other work, and agrees for that purpose to supply the necessary tools and temporary structures, supplies them to the employees of such other for a business purpose. This is true irrespective of whether the structure or work when finished is to be used for business or residential and social purposes. On the other hand, if it is understood that the person who is to do the work is to supply his own instrumentalities, but the person for whom the work is to be done permits his own tools or appliances to be used as a favor to the person doing the work, the tools and appliances are supplied as a gratuity and not for use for the supplier's business purposes.

Illustrations:

1. A employs B, a painter, to repaint his residence. The contract provides that B be allowed to use the ladders which A has upon his premises. C, an employee of B, while using one of these ladders, is hurt by a defect which, although not readily observable, could have been discovered by the exercise of a reasonably careful inspection. A is subject to liability to C.

2. A is the principal contractor for the erection of a building. He lets out the various parts of the work to subcontractors. His contracts with them require him to provide all necessary scaffoldings. A servant of any of the subcontractors who goes upon the scaffolding is using it for the business purposes of the contractor.

3. A, a building contractor, contracts to erect a building for B and erects the necessary scaffold. The building having been completed according to the contract, B desires to have some additional work done on the exterior, and employs C by an independent contract between B and C. To do this work it is necessary to have the use of the scaffold. A says to C, "Here is the scaffold; you may as well use it." C's use of the scaffold in doing this additional work is not for a business purpose of A.

f. In order that a chattel shall be supplied for another to use for a business purpose of the supplier, it is not essential that its use is necessary for the performance of a contract between a supplier and a third person. It is enough that the chattel is to be used in furtherance of any business purpose of the supplier.

Illustration:

4. A, a contractor, for the purpose of obtaining information necessary to enable him to bid on the repair of a building, erects a scaffold so as to inspect the condition of the cornices and roofing. He permits a subcontractor, upon whose bid for the mason work the contractor's bid will depend, to use the scaffold. An employee of the subcontractor going upon the scaffold in pursuance of this arrangement for the purpose of inspecting the cornice is using the scaffold for the contractor's business purposes.

§ 393. Effect of Third Person's Duty to Inspect

One who supplies through a third person a chattel to be used for the supplier's business purposes is subject to liability under the rules stated in §§ 391 and 392 although the dangerous character or condition of the chattel is discoverable by an inspection which the third person is under a duty to the person injured to make.

See Reporter's Notes.

Comment:

a. Third person's failure to perform duty. Where a chattel is supplied to one person under circumstances which give the supplier cause to expect that such person will turn it over to others for use for a purpose in which the supplier has a business interest, the person to whom the chattel is supplied may be under a duty to inspect it before so turning it over, in order to ascertain whether it is safe for the use to which it is to be put, as where a chattel is supplied to an employer for his servants to use for a purpose in which the supplier and the employer have a mutual business interest. This duty may be owed not only to the persons to whom the chattel is thus turned over for use, but also to those in whose vicinity it should be expected to be used. The fact that the inspection, if properly made, would have disclosed the dangerous character of the chattel and would have enabled him who owed the duty to correct the defect or give such warning or instructions as were necessary to make it possible to use the chattel safely, subjects the one who fails to perform the duty to liability for bodily harm resulting to those to whom the duty is owed. It does not, however, relieve from liability the original supplier of the chattel who by his failure to inspect it has permitted it to go out of his hands in a dangerous condition.

Illustrations:

1. The A Coal Company sells coal to the B Company, a factory owner, to be delivered on the private siding of the B Company by the C Railway Company. The cars are supplied by the C Company. A reasonably careful inspection made while the cars are being

loaded by the A Company would have disclosed a defect which made the cars dangerous for unloading. D, an employee of the B Company, while unloading the cars on B's private siding is hurt because of this defect. The A Company is subject to liability to D, although the B Company is under a duty, before turning the car over to its employees for unloading, to make an inspection which would have disclosed the defect.

  2. A, the contractor for the erection of a building, lets out the painting of the exterior to B, a subcontractor. The contract between them provides that the subcontractor shall use the scaffolding erected by A. The scaffolds which have been erected for A by C, a scaffold maker, are badly erected, as an inspection made by either A or B would have disclosed. The bad condition of the scaffold is not patent to any such cursory inspection as workmen, using it, are required to make for their own protection. D, a painter employed by B, goes up the scaffold to paint the exterior of the building. The defective scaffold collapses, injuring D. A is subject to liability to D, although B is under a duty to D to inspect the scaffold as one of the appliances which he furnishes for his servants' use, and is himself concurrently liable to D.

  b. When person injured knows of defect in chattel. If the third person to whom the chattel is supplied performs his duty of inspection and discovers that the chattel is dangerous, and so informs those for whose use it is supplied, or if those who use it in any way learn of the danger of so doing, they may be barred from recovery against the supplier of the chattel by their contributory negligence in failing to take those additional precautions in using the chattel which its dangerous nature requires; or, by using a chattel which they know to be dangerous, they may thereby put themselves in such contributory fault as to disable them from maintaining an action for any injury that they suffer thereby. There are, however, situations in which this is not true, as where the person using a chattel is a passenger of a common carrier, entitled to use the chattel irrespective of the consent of the carrier, or where the person using the chattel with knowledge of its dangerous character has no choice but to use it, as when a convict uses a dangerous tool furnished to him by his employer with whom the State has contracted for the use of their convicts as laborers, or where a soldier in the Army is ordered to travel in a conveyance which he knows to be in a dangerous condition. As to the condition under which one who voluntarily subjects himself to known danger thereby puts himself in contributory fault, see § 466.

TOPIC 3. MANUFACTURERS OF CHATTELS

§ 394. Chattel Known to Be Dangerous

The manufacturer of a chattel which he knows or has reason to know to be, or to be likely to be, dangerous for

use is subject to the liability of a supplier of chattels with such knowledge.

Comment:

a. The manufacturer of a chattel is under those general liabilities which are common to all suppliers of chattels for the use of others. These liabilities are stated in §§ 388–390.

The special liabilities which attach to a manufacturer, who puts goods out on the market either by sale, lease, loan, or gift, because of the fact that the goods are manufactured by him, are stated in §§ 395–398.

§ 395. Negligent Manufacture of Chattel Dangerous Unless Carefully Made

A manufacturer who fails to exercise reasonable care in the manufacture of a chattel which, unless carefully made, he should recognize as involving an unreasonable risk of causing physical harm to those who use it for a purpose for which the manufacturer should expect it to be used and to those whom he should expect to be endangered by its probable use, is subject to liability for physical harm caused to them by its lawful use in a manner and for a purpose for which it is supplied.

See Reporter's Notes.

Comment:

a. History. The original common law rule was contrary to that stated in this Section. The case of Winterbottom v. Wright, 10 M. & W. 109, 152 Eng.Rep. 402 (1842), in which a seller who contracted with the buyer to keep a stagecoach in repair after the sale was held not to be liable to a passenger injured when he failed to do so, was for a long time misconstrued to mean that the original seller of a chattel could not be liable, in tort or in contract, to one other than his immediate buyer. To this rule various exceptions developed, the first of which involved the rule stated in §§ 388, 390, and 394, that a manufacturer who knew that the chattel was dangerous for its expected use and failed to disclose the danger became liable to a third person injured by the defect.

The most important of these exceptions, however, made the seller liable to a third person for negligence in the manufacture or sale of an article classified as "inherently" or "imminently" dangerous to human safety. By degrees this category was redefined to include articles "intended to preserve, destroy, or affect human life or health." For more than half a century, however, the category remained vague and imperfectly defined. It was held to include food, drugs, firearms, and explosives, but there was much rather pointless dispute in the decisions as to other articles, and as to whether, for example, such a product as chewing tobacco was to be classified as a food.

In 1916 the leading modern case of MacPherson v. Buick Motor Co., 217 N.Y. 382, 111 N.E. 1050, L.R.A. 1916F, 696, Ann.Cas. 1916C, 440, 13 N.C.C.A. 1029 (1916), discarded the general rule of non-liability, by holding that "inherently dangerous" articles included any article which would be dangerous to human safety if negligently made. After the passage of more than forty years, this decision is now all but universally accepted by the American courts. Although some decisions continue to speak the language of "inherent danger," it has very largely been superseded by a recognition that what is involved is merely the ordinary duty of reasonable care imposed upon the manufacturer, as to any product which he can reasonably expect to be dangerous if he is negligent in its manufacture or sale.

b. This Section states the rule thus generally adopted. The justification for it rests upon the responsibility assumed by the manufacturer toward the consuming public, which arises, not out of contract, but out of the relation resulting from the purchase of the product by the consumer; upon the foreseeability of harm if proper care is not used; upon the representation of safety implied in the act of putting the product on the market; and upon the economic benefit derived by the manufacturer from the sale and subsequent use of the chattel.

c. Not necessary that chattel be intended to affect, preserve, or destroy human life. In order that the manufacturer of a chattel shall be subject to liability under the rule stated in this Section, it is not necessary that the chattel be one the use of which is intended to affect, preserve, or destroy human life. The purpose which the article, if perfect, is intended to accomplish is immaterial. The important thing is the harm which it is likely to do if it is imperfect.

d. Not necessary that chattel be inherently dangerous. In order that the manufacturer shall be subject to liability under the rule stated in this Section, it is not necessary that the chattel be "inherently dangerous," in the sense of involving any degree of risk of harm to those who use it even if it is properly made. It is enough that the chattel, if not carefully made, will involve such a risk of harm. It is not necessary that the risk be a great one, or that it be a risk of death or serious bodily harm. A risk of harm to property, as in the case of defective animal food, is enough. All that is necessary is that the risk be an unreasonable one, as stated in § 291. The inherent danger, or the high degree of danger, is merely a factor to be considered, as in other negligence cases, as bearing upon the extent of the precautions required.

Illustration:

    1. A manufactures a mattress. Through the carelessness of one of A's employees a spring inside of the mattress is not properly tied down. A sells the mattress to B, a dealer, who resells it to C. C sleeps on the mattress, and is wounded in the back by the sharp point of the spring. The wound becomes infected, and C suffers serious illness. A is subject to liability to C.

    e. When inspections and tests necessary. As heretofore pointed out (§ 298, Comment *b*), the precaution necessary to comply with the standard of reasonable care varies with the danger involved. Consequently the character of harm likely to result from the failure to exercise care in manufacture affects the question as to what is reasonable care. It is reasonable to require those who make or assemble automobiles to subject the raw material, or parts, procured from even reputable manufacturers, to inspections and tests which it would be obviously unreasonable to require of a product which, although defective, is unlikely to cause more than some comparatively slight, though still substantial, harm to those who use it. A garment maker is not required to subject the finished garment to anything like so minute an inspection for the purpose of discovering whether a basting needle has not been left in a seam as is required of the maker of an automobile or of high speed machinery or of electrical devices, in which the slightest inaccuracy may involve danger of death.

    f. Particulars which require care. A manufacturer is required to exercise reasonable care in manufacturing any article which, if carelessly manufactured, is likely to cause harm to those who use it in the manner for which it is manufactured. The particulars in which reasonable care is usually necessary for protection of those whose safety depends upon the character of chattels are (1) the adoption of a formula or plan which, if properly followed, will produce an article safe for the use for which it is sold, (2) the selection of material and parts to be incorporated in the finished article, (3) the fabrication of the article by every member of the operative staff no matter how high or low his position, (4) the making of such inspections and tests during the course of manufacture and after the article is completed as the manufacturer should recognize as reasonably necessary to secure the production of a safe article, and (5) the packing of the article so as to be safe for those who must be expected to unpack it.

Illustrations:

    2. The A Motor Company incorporates in its car wheels manufactured by the B Wheel Company. These wheels are constructed of defective material, as an inspection made by the A Company before putting them on its car would disclose. The car is sold to C through the D Company, an independent distributor. While C is driving the car the defective wheel collapses and the car

swerves and collides with that of E, causing harm to C and E, and also to F and G, who are guests in the cars of C and E respectively. The A Motor Company is subject to liability to C, E, F, and G.

g. The exercise of reasonable care in selecting raw material and parts to be incorporated in the finished article usually requires something more than a mere inspection of the material and parts. A manufacturer should have sufficient technical knowledge to select such a type of material that its use will secure a safe finished product. So too, a manufacturer who incorporates a part made by another manufacturer into his finished product should exercise reasonable care to ascertain not only the material out of which the part is made but also the plan under which it is made. He must have sufficient technical knowledge to form a reasonably accurate judgment as to whether a part made under such a plan and of such material is or is not such as to secure a safe finished product. The part is of his own selection, and it is reasonable for the users of the product to rely not only upon a careful inspection but also sufficient technical knowledge to make a careful inspection valuable in securing an article safe for use. In all of these particulars the amount of care which the manufacturer must exercise is proportionate to the extent of the risk involved in using the article if manufactured without the exercise of these precautions. Where, as in the case of an automobile or high speed machinery or high voltage electrical devices, there is danger of serious bodily harm or death unless the article is substantially perfect, it is reasonable to require the manufacturer to exercise almost meticulous precautions in all of these particulars in order to secure substantial perfection. On the other hand, it would be ridiculous to demand equal care of the manufacturer of an article which, no matter how imperfect, is unlikely to do more than some comparatively trivial harm to those who use it.

h. Persons protected. The words "those who use the chattel" include not only the vendee but also all persons whose right or privilege to use the article is derived from him, unless the nature of the article or the conditions of the sale make it improbable that the article will be resold by the vendee or that he will permit others to use it or to share in its use. Unless the article is made to special order for the peculiar use of a particular person, the manufacturer must realize the chance that it may be sold. This becomes a substantial certainty where the article is sold to a jobber, wholesaler, or retailer. So too, many articles are obviously made for the use of several persons or are sold under conditions which make it certain that they will be used by persons other than the purchaser. Thus the manufacturer of a seven-seated automobile which is obviously intended to carry persons other than the purchaser and his chauffeur should recognize it as likely to be used by any persons whom, as members of his family, guests, or pedestrians picked up on the road, the purchaser chooses to receive in his car. A threshing machine sold to the owner of a large farm is obviously intended for the use of his employees.

The words "those who use the chattel" include, therefore, all persons whom the vendee or his subvendee or donee permits to use the article irrespective of whether they do so as his servants, as passengers for hire or otherwise, to serve his business purposes, or as licensees permitted to use a car purely for their own benefit. They also include any person to whom the vendee sells or gives the chattel, or to whom such subvendee or donee sells or gives the chattel ad infinitum, and also all persons whom such subvendee or subdonee permits to use the chattel or to share in its use. Thus they include a person to whom an improperly prepared drug is hypodermically administered by a physician who has bought it from a drugstore which has purchased it from a wholesaler or jobber.

i. Persons endangered by use. The words "those whom he should expect to be endangered by its probable use" may likewise include a large group of persons who have no connection with the ownership or use of the chattel itself. Thus the manufacturer of an automobile, intended to be driven on the public highway, should reasonably expect that, if the automobile is dangerously defective, harm will result to any person on the highway, including pedestrians and drivers of other vehicles and their passengers and guests; and he should also expect danger to those upon land immediately abutting on the highway. Likewise the manufacturer of a cable to be used in the transmission of high voltage electric current should reasonably anticipate that if its insulation is defective its use may endanger even persons miles away from the cable itself.

j. Unforeseeable use or manner of use. The liability stated in this Section is limited to persons who are endangered and the risks which are created in the course of uses of the chattel which the manufacturer should reasonably anticipate. In the absence of special reason to expect otherwise, the maker is entitled to assume that his product will be put to a normal use, for which the product is intended or appropriate; and he is not subject to liability when it is safe for all such uses, and harm results only because it is mishandled in a way which he has no reason to expect, or is used in some unusual and unforeseeable manner. Thus a shoemaker is not liable to an obstinate lady who suffers harm because she insists on wearing a size too small for her, and the manufacturer of a bottle of cleaning fluid is not liable when the purchaser splashes it into his eye.

Illustration:

3. A manufactures and sells to a dealer an automobile tire, which is in all respects safe for normal automobile driving. B, an automobile racer, buys the tire from the dealer and installs it on

§ 395 RESTATEMENT (SECOND) OF TORTS

his racing car. In the course of the race the tire blows out because of the excessive speed, and B is injured. A is not liable to B.

k. Foreseeable uses and risks. The manufacturer may, however, reasonably anticipate other uses than the one for which the chattel is primarily intended. The maker of a chair, for example, may reasonably expect that some one will stand on it; and the maker of an inflammable cocktail robe may expect that it will be worn in the kitchen in close proximity to a fire. Likewise the manufacturer may know, or may be under a duty to discover, that some possible users of the product are especially susceptible to harm from it, if it contains an ingredient to which any substantial percentage of the population are allergic or otherwise sensitive, and he fails to take reasonable precautions, by giving warning or otherwise, against harm to such persons.

l. The fact that the article is leased, given, or loaned to the user rather than sold or leased does not affect the liability of the manufacturer for his negligence in making the article.

m. Manufacturer of raw material or parts of article to be assembled by third person. It is not necessary that the manufacturer should expect his product to be used in the form in which it is delivered to his immediate buyer. A manufacturer of parts to be incorporated in the product of his buyer or others is subject to liability under the rule stated in this Section, if they are so negligently made as to render the products in which they are incorporated unreasonably dangerous for use. So too, a manufacturer of raw material made and sold to be used in the fabrication of particular articles which will be dangerous for use unless the material is carefully made, is subject to liability if he fails to exercise reasonable care in its manufacture. As to the effect to be given to the fact that the defect could have been discovered before the part or material was incorporated in the finished article, see § 396.

Illustration:

4. Under the facts stated in Illustration 2, the B Wheel Company is subject to liability to C, E, F, and G.

n. The rule stated in this Section applies where the only harm which results from the manufacturer's failure to exercise reasonable care is to the manufactured chattel itself.

Illustration:

5. A manufactures and sells to a dealer an automobile, which is purchased from the dealer by B. Because of A's failure to exercise reasonable care in manufacture the car has a defective steering gear. While B is driving the steering gear gives way, and the car goes into the ditch and is damaged. B is not injured, and there is no other damage of any kind. A is subject to liability to B for the damage to the automobile.

§ 396. Effect of Third Person's Duty to Inspect

A manufacturer of a chattel is subject to liability under the rules stated in §§ 394 and 395 although the dangerous character or condition of the chattel is discoverable by an inspection which the seller or any other person is under a duty to the person injured to make.

See Reporter's Notes.

Comment:

a. The rule stated in this Section is closely analogous to that stated in § 393, and the Comments under that Section therefore are applicable to this Section.

b. A chattel often passes through a number of hands before it reaches the person whose use of it causes bodily harm to himself or others. The buyer from the manufacturer, or any other person in the line of transmission to the ultimate user of the chattel, may have an opportunity, and be under a duty, to inspect the chattel before turning it over for use or transferring it to a third person whom he should expect so to turn it over to others. The duty of inspection may be owed only to the person to whom the chattel is transferred, but it is more usually owed to all those who should be expected to use the chattel with the consent of, or through its transfer from, the transferee and to persons likely to be in the vicinity of its probable use. The fact that the inspection, if made, would have disclosed the dangerous character of the chattel and enabled him who owed the duty to correct the defect or give a warning or instructions which would have made it possible to use it safely, subjects the one who fails to perform the duty to liability for physical harm resulting to those to whom the duty is owed. It does not, however, relieve from liability the manufacturer to whose negligence the dangerous condition is due.

Illustrations:

1. The A Motor Company sells to B a car, the steering gear of which is so negligently constructed as to make the car unsafe to drive. B makes a business of renting cars to be driven by the renter on short trips. The defect is discoverable by an inspection which B is under a duty to make (see § 408), but not by any inspection required of a person to whom cars are so rented. B rents the car to C without inspecting it. While C is carefully driving the car he collides with the car of D. The collision is due to the bad condition of the steering gear. C, D, and E, a guest in C's car, are hurt. C, D, and E can recover against either the A Motor Company or B.

2. The A Electric Company sells and ships a machine to the B Company, so packed as to be dangerous to those that unpack it. In consequence C, an employee of the B Company, is hurt while unpacking the machine. The A Company is subject to liability to C, even though his employer, the B Company, was also negligent toward him in failing to inspect the machine and container before turning it over to C for unpacking.

3. The A Manufacturing Company sells to B a threshing machine, and at B's order ships it to his farm, where B's foreman, without inspecting it, orders C and D, employed on B's farm, to operate it. The platform over the moving machinery is so badly constructed that it collapses under the weight of C and D, and they are hurt by the moving machinery. Had the foreman made a careful inspection of the machine, he could have discovered the bad condition of the platform. The A Company and B are subject to liability to C and D.

c. The situations to which the rule stated in this Section is most usually applicable are those in which a buyer of a defectively manufactured chattel, or one who derives possession of it from the buyer, turns over the chattel to his employees or others for use for his business purposes or permits others to share in its use for such purposes, or where the buyer of such a chattel leases it for immediate use (see §§ 392 and 408, which state that persons so supplying chattels are under a duty to inspect them before turning them over for use). The rule stated in this Section is also applicable where the manufacturer of raw material or of a part, such as an automobile wheel, sells it to another manufacturer who is under a duty to inspect it, before incorporating it in his product (see § 395, Comment *f*).

§ 397. Chattel Made Under Secret Formula

A manufacturer of a chattel which is compounded under a secret formula or under a formula which although disclosed should be recognized as unlikely to be understood by those whom he should expect to use it lawfully, is subject to liability for physical harm caused to them and persons whom he should expect to be endangered by its probable use by his failure to exercise reasonable care to adopt such a formula and to bring to the knowledge of those who are to use the chattel such directions as will make it reasonably safe for the use for which it is supplied.

See Reporter's Notes.

Comment:

a. The rule stated in this Section is a special application of the rule stated in § 395. The duty of care is imposed in order that the article may not be used for a purpose or in a manner for which it is unsafe.

b. When warning labels necessary. Articles which do not disclose to the ordinary intelligence their properties, either by their appearance or by the information contained on their labels, must be bought and used in reliance upon the competence and care of those who put them out to make them safe for the purposes for which they are advertised and sold, and in reliance upon the directions, in the advertisements or on the containers, given as adequate to make it safe to use the chattel in the manner directed. The maker of such article is, therefore, required not only to exercise reasonable care to adopt a formula which will make the chattel safe for its advertised use, but also to exercise reasonable care to make such directions as he appends to the chattel adequate to secure its safe use. If the chattel is one which can only be safely used for the purposes for which it is sold if adequate directions are given, a maker is required to exercise care to bring such directions home to those who may be expected to use it. If the improper use of the chattel involves grave risk of serious bodily harm or death, the maker of it does not satisfy his duty by informing the person to whom the chattel is supplied for the use of others by giving such directions to the person to whom the chattel is supplied. In such case, he is required to make the chattel carry its own directions by placing them upon the container. (See § 388, Comment *n.*)

c. When printed formula on container insufficient warning. The rule stated in this Section applies to one who puts upon the market a chattel which is advertised for sale as appropriate for particular uses, although the formula under which it is compounded is printed upon the container in which the chattel is put upon the market, if the formula is one which does not convey to the ordinary users of the chattel adequate information as to the actual qualities of the article.

d. If the chattel is of such a dangerous character as to be likely to cause death or serious bodily harm if the formula is not properly prepared, reasonable care in the selection of the formula and in giving directions for use requires the utmost skill and caution, and may require the advice of scientific specialists.

Illustrations:

1. A manufactures and puts upon the market a floor stain manufactured under a secret formula. The stain is inflammable. Of this A is ignorant, but a competent maker of such articles would have known that a stain made under such a formula would be inflammable. B purchases from a retail dealer a supply of this stain, and while C, his wife, is applying it to the floor of his kitchen, B strikes a match to light the gas. An explosion follows, causing harm to C and to D, B's infant son, who is watching his mother stain the floor. A is subject to liability to C and D, since

the explosive character of the floor stain could have been discovered if reasonable care had been exercised in selecting the formula.

2. A makes and puts upon the market a patent medicine. The dose prescribed upon the bottle contains mercury in toxic quantities. B purchases a bottle of the medicine and C, his wife, takes the dose prescribed upon the bottle and is made seriously ill. A is subject to liability to C.

3. A puts on the market a fluid for cleansing boilers made under a secret formula which he advertises as appropriate for use in all boilers. It is safe to use in any boiler except those made of cast iron; when applied to such boilers it generates explosive fumes. A does not know of this, but an analysis by a competent chemist would have discovered it. The B Company, which has contracted to overhaul C's ship, buys this fluid from A, and uses it to clean the cast iron boilers therein. The fumes generated come into contact with an open light carried by D, one of the B Company's workmen, and an explosion results by which a large part of the engine room is wrecked. C, D, and E, a watchman employed by C to guard the ship, are hurt. A is subject to liability to C, D, and E.

e. As to the liability of one who sells as his own product a chattel compounded by another under a secret or inadequately descriptive formula, see § 400.

§ 398. Chattel Made Under Dangerous Plan or Design

A manufacturer of a chattel made under a plan or design which makes it dangerous for the uses for which it is manufactured is subject to liability to others whom he should expect to use the chattel or to be endangered by its probable use for physical harm caused by his failure to exercise reasonable care in the adoption of a safe plan or design.

See Reporter's Notes.

Comment:

a. The rule stated in this Section, like that stated in § 397, is a special application of the rule stated in § 395.

b. When dangerous plan or design known to user. If the dangerous character of the plan or design is known to the user of the chattel, he may be in contributory fault if the risk involved in using it is unreasonably great or if he fails to take those special precautions which the known dangerous character of the chattel requires.

Illustration:

1. The A Stove Company makes a gas stove under a design which places the aperture through which it is lighted in dangerous proximity to the gas outlet. As a result of this B, a cook employed by C, who has bought one of these stoves from a dealer to whom A has sold it, while attempting to light the stove is hurt by an explosion of gas. The A Stove Company is subject to liability to B.

TOPIC 4. SELLERS OF CHATTELS MANUFACTURED BY THIRD PERSONS

§ 399. Chattel Known to Be Dangerous

A seller of a chattel, manufactured by a third person, who sells it knowing that it is, or is likely to be, dangerous is subject to liability as stated in §§ 388–390.

Comment:

a. A seller of a chattel supplies it for the use of others. He is, therefore, subject to liability under the conditions which are stated in §§ 388–390, as subjecting all suppliers of chattels for the use of others to liability. The special liabilities which are imposed upon a seller of a chattel manufactured by another because of the fact that he sells it as his own product, because it is bought in reliance upon his competence and care, and because of his peculiar facilities for observing the dangerous character of the chattel, are stated in §§ 400–402.

§ 400. Selling as Own Product Chattel Made by Another

One who puts out as his own product a chattel manufactured by another is subject to the same liability as though he were its manufacturer.

See Reporter's Notes.

Comment:

a. The words "one who puts out a chattel" include anyone who supplies it to others for their own use or for the use of third persons, either by sale or lease or by gift or loan.

b. The rules which determine the liability of a manufacturer of a chattel are stated in §§ 394–398.

c. One who puts out as his own product chattels made by others is under a duty to exercise care, proportionate to the danger involved in the use of the chattels if improperly made, to secure the adoption of a proper formula or plan and the use of safe materials and to inspect the chattel when made. But he does not escape liability by so doing. He is liable if, because of some negligence in its fabrication or through lack of proper inspection during the process of manufacture, the article is in a dangerously defective condition which the seller could not discover after it was delivered to him.

   d. The rule stated in this Section applies only where the actor puts out the chattel as his own product. The actor puts out a chattel as his own product in two types of cases. The first is where the actor appears to be the manufacturer of the chattel. The second is where the chattel appears to have been made particularly for the actor. In the first type of case the actor frequently causes the chattel to be used in reliance upon his care in making it; in the second, he frequently causes the chattel to be used in reliance upon a belief that he has required it to be made properly for him and that the actor's reputation is an assurance to the user of the quality of the product. On the other hand, where it is clear that the actor's only connection with the chattel is that of a distributor of it (for example, as a wholesale or retail seller), he does not put it out as his own product and the rule stated in this section is inapplicable. Thus, one puts out a chattel as his own product when he puts it out under his name or affixes to it his trade name or trademark. When such identification is referred to on the label as an indication of the quality or wholesomeness of the chattel, there is an added emphasis that the user can rely upon the reputation of the person so identified. The mere fact that the goods are marked with such additional words as "made for" the seller, or describe him as a distributor, particularly in the absence of a clear and distinctive designation of the real manufacturer or packer, is not sufficient to make inapplicable the rule stated in this Section. The casual reader of a label is likely to rely upon the featured name, trade name, or trademark, and overlook the qualification of the description of source. So too, the fact that the seller is known to carry on only a retail business does not prevent him from putting out as his own product a chattel which is marked in such a way as to indicate clearly it is put out as his product. However, where the real manufacturer or packer is clearly and accurately identified on the label or other markings on the goods, and it is also clearly stated that another who is also named has nothing to do with the goods except to distribute or sell them, the latter does not put out such goods as his own. That the goods are not the product of him who puts them out may also be indicated clearly in other ways.

Illustrations:

   1. A puts out under his own name a floor stain which is manufactured under a secret formula by B, to whom A entrusts the selection of the formula. The stain made under this formula is inflammable, as a competent maker of such articles would have known. Of this both A and B are ignorant, and neither the advertisements nor the directions contain any warning against using it near unguarded lights. C purchases from a retail dealer a supply of this stain and while D, C's wife, is applying it to the floor

of the kitchen, C strikes a match to light the gas. An explosion follows, causing harm to D and to E, a friend who is watching D stain the floor. A is subject to liability to D and E.

2. A, a wholesale distributor, sells canned corned beef labeled with A's widely known trademark and also labeled "Packed for A" and "A, distributor". The beef was negligently packed by B and is unwholesome. C buys a can of it from D, a retail grocer, and serves it to her guest, E, who is made ill. A is liable to E.

§ 401. Chattel Likely to Be Dangerous

A seller of a chattel manufactured by a third person who knows or has reason to know that the chattel is, or is likely to be, dangerous when used by a person to whom it is delivered or for whose use it is supplied, or to others whom the seller should expect to share in or be endangered by its use, is subject to liability for bodily harm caused thereby to them if he fails to exercise reasonable care to inform them of the danger or otherwise to protect them against it.

See Reporter's Notes.

Comment:

a. Reason to know. The words "reason to know", are defined in § 12(1) and are used to denote the fact that the actor has information from which a person of reasonable intelligence or of the superior intelligence of the actor would infer that the fact in question exists or that such person would govern his conduct upon the assumption that such fact exists. The words "reason to know" do not impose any duty to ascertain unknown facts, and are to be distinguished from the words "should know" as defined in § 12(2).

b. There are many situations in which a seller who does not know the chattel is dangerous none the less does know facts from which a reasonable man would conclude that the delivery of the chattel is likely to result in bodily harm. The combination of a defective chattel used by a competent person who is unaware of the defect may be a foreseeably dangerous combination; so too may be the use of a perfectly made chattel by a person incompetent to handle it properly or to appreciate the risks in using it or the limitations on its safe use. The foreseeable danger may arise out of the buyer's ignorance of facts concerning the chattel which are known to the seller. In the following comments some of the more usual types of situations are mentioned, but the comments are illustrative rather than exhaustive of possible fact patterns which would come within the rule of this Section.

c. Source of supply. Many chattels are things of danger when not properly made. To persons who deal in such chattels the known

§ 401 RESTATEMENT (SECOND) OF TORTS

reputation of the manufacturer is an important fact. A seller who buys goods of a type which he knows are dangerous when defective, and who buys them from an unknown manufacturer, or one of dubious reputation, may not know that the chattels are dangerously defective, but he does know that they may be. In such a situation, the seller knows that he does not know the condition of the chattel and he has no reasonable grounds for believing the chattel to be free from dangerous defects. A seller who sells such a chattel without a warning of its uncertain quality has reason to know that the chattel is likely to be dangerous. (Compare § 289, Comment *j.*)

Illustration:

 1. A, a retail merchant, buys a case of hair dye lotion from an unknown itinerant peddler. The lotion contains excessive chromic acid solution and is dangerous for use, although this could be discovered only by chemical analysis. A sells a bottle of the lotion to B, giving no warning of its uncertain quality. B and her sister, C, use the lotion and are harmed by it. A is subject to liability to B and to C.

 d. On the other hand, a seller who obtains his merchandise from manufacturers of established reputation or from distributors who are known for handling only high grade goods ordinarily does not have any reason to know that a chattel in a particular shipment is likely to be defective and therefore dangerous. So too, where the merchandise is of a kind which, even when defective, is not likely to cause harm, the seller does not have reason to know that the particular chattel is, or is likely to be, dangerous, regardless of the nature of his source of supply.

 e. Reckless misrepresentation. A buyer frequently relies upon the special competence which the seller has, or purports to have, in appraising the qualities of his merchandise and the function which it will perform. Even though the seller has obtained goods from a reputable source of supply, he may have no reason to believe that a particular representation made by him is true, and he may know that if it is untrue with respect to a particular article and is relied upon, it is likely to result in physical harm. A seller who knows that he does not know whether his positive statement of fact is true or false, and who knows that if it is false the safety of one who relies on it will be imperilled, utters a false representation when he assures the purchaser that the defective chattel is safe for use. This is one type of negligent act. (See § 310.)

Illustrations:

 2. A, a retail merchant, purchases a new stove blacking, without any knowledge of its qualities, from a reputable manufacturer. B, a customer of A, inquires about it, and A assures him "the warmer the stove the better it works." When used on a hot

stove the blacking explodes, injuring B. A is subject to liability to B.

    3. A, a retail merchant, buys a quantity of "first quality" rope from a manufacturer who, as A knows, has sold considerable defective rope in the past. B, a house painter, asks A for his best quality rope to hold up scaffoldings. A sells some of this "first quality" rope, which is defective, to B, saying, "This is the best rope on the market." Because of the defects the rope breaks while supporting the scaffold, and B, and C, his helper, are injured. A is subject to liability to B and to C.

    f. Even in the absence of any specific representations made by his seller concerning the article purchased, the buyer may show his reliance upon the seller's special competence, as where the buyer leaves it to the seller to select the article which will serve the buyer's described requirements. In such case the seller, by making the selection for the customer, impliedly represents that he has such special knowledge as may be necessary to make a proper choice, and the propriety of his choice will be judged in the light of his purported special knowledge. (Compare § 290, Comment *f,* and § 299 A.) The seller is also required to exercise reasonable care in making the selection.

Illustrations:

    4. A, a retail merchant who sells rope, is asked by B, a householder, to sell him a quantity of rope of sufficient strength to support two men working on a scaffold. A selects rope of perfect quality, but which is inadequate for the intended use, as any person familiar with the strength of rope would know; and while it is supporting a scaffold holding C and D, servants of B, it breaks, and they are injured. A is subject to liability to C and D.

    5. A, a retail country merchant, is told by B that he wants to purchase linseed oil as medicine for a horse. A carelessly selects boiled linseed oil, which is poisonous, instead of wholesome raw linseed oil. The poisonous oil kills B's horse. A is subject to liability to B.

    6. A, a retail druggist, is told by B that he desires something for a cough. In reaching for a bottle of cough medicine, A carelessly selects a bottle of poison instead, which B buys and uses. B is seriously injured. A is subject to liability to B.

    g. Special knowledge of seller. Retail merchants frequently have special knowledge of the characteristics and attributes of the merchandise they sell, which is not shared by the general public. For example, a butcher may know from experience that after meat is exposed to a certain temperature for x hours it may become unwholesome, and that after exposure for x plus y hours it is certain to be unwholesome. The customer may not know this fact, and he does not know the history of the temperature exposure of the meat he buys. In such case the butcher who knows that a particular piece of meat has been exposed to the given temperature for x hours knows that it may be unwholesome, as in fact it is. He does not know that the meat is unwholesome, but he has reason to know that it is, or is likely to be, and that is sufficient to create a duty at least to warn the prospective buyer of the possible danger.

So too, a grocer's experience may have taught him that certain canned foods form gas when they become unwholesome, and that such gas causes a bulge in the end of the can. When the grocer sees such a bulge in the can he has placed on the counter for the customer, that known fact is a danger signal to his trained eye. He does not know that the contents of the can are unwholesome, and they may not be, because the bulge might possibly come from other sources. But the grocer has reason to know that the food is likely to be unwholesome. What he does know requires him to look into the matter further or put the buyer on guard by warning him of the possible significance of the bulge.

The seller may have other special knowledge which warns him that a particular chattel may be dangerous, as where he has received complaints from other customers that several of the chattels received in a particular shipment were dangerously defective. In such case the seller has reason to know that the unsold chattels in that same shipment are likely to be similarly defective.

h. The seller may have reason to know from his own prior active negligence that his merchandise may not be fit for the use for which it is sold. In such case the liability for harm may be based on such active negligence.

Illustration:

    7. A, a grocer, sprinkles rat poison in such proximity to a flour bin that it is likely to be carried into the bin by the rats, which in fact occurs. Not knowing this, A sells some of the poisoned flour to B. B is made ill by eating biscuits made from the flour. A is subject to liability to B for his negligent act of placing the rat poison near the flour.

i. Evidence of seller's knowledge. The fact that the defect could have been discovered by the seller, or that a reasonable man would have discovered it, is not enough to impose liability under the rule stated in this Section. The important question is what he did know, and what would a reasonable man conclude from that knowledge. However, the fact that the defect was readily observable, or that it would usually be discovered in the course of the seller's handling of the chattel, is evidence on the issue of what the seller did know. Where it is clear that the defect was obvious to the seller who wrapped up the chattel, though not to the customer who lacked the seller's special knowledge, the triers of fact may properly find that the seller knew of the defect despite his testimony to the contrary. (Compare § 526, Comment *d.*)

j. Either a perfect or a defective chattel may be dangerous in the hands of a person who is incompetent to use it. The dealer who sells a perfect gun and ammunition to a small child is guilty of one type of negligent act. (See §§ 308 and 390.) The use of certain perfectly made chattels may be dangerous in the absence of special warnings of their normal character and properties. One who deals in such chattels is familiar with their normal attributes, and if he has reason to believe that the one who is to use the chattel is not familiar with them, the seller must exercise reasonable care to acquaint the buyer with these known facts. If the article is one the ignorant use of which threatens grave dangers of death or serious bodily harm, the retailer does not necessarily satisfy his duty by informing his purchaser of that fact. In order to escape the risk of liability, he may be required to make the article disclose its actual character to third persons, by a label or otherwise. (See § 388, Comment *n.*)

k. User's realization of risk of harm. The likelihood that a chattel will be dangerous arises primarily from the fact that the one who handles it or otherwise uses it does not know of its actual condition or, though knowing it, does not realize the risk involved in handling it or otherwise using it. Many perfectly made chattels are likely to be dangerous when used by a person who is unaware of their normal properties and dangers, and who is ignorant of the precautions necessary to be taken in order to use them safely. Many defective chattels can be used with complete safety by a person who is aware of the defect and guards against the risks created by it. There is no legal duty not to sell a chattel which involves a risk of harm. The duty relates to the delivery of the chattel to one who does not know its actual condition, or though knowing it, does not understand the risks inherent in that condition. Consequently a seller who exercises reasonable care to acquaint the buyer of a chattel with facts known to the seller which bear upon the risks inherent in using the chattel, and to explain to the buyer the significance of such facts with respect to the risks of harm they create, does not have reason to know that the chattel is likely to be dangerous when used unless the seller realizes or should realize that the buyer by reason of youth, inexperience, or otherwise is incompetent to use the chattel safely, or is likely to turn the chattel over to a third person without warning him of the risk inherent in it. So too, where the seller reasonably believes that the buyer will discover for himself the condition of the chattel and realize the danger involved and disclose it to any others who may be affected by it, the seller does not have reason to know that the chattel is likely to be dangerous when used.

Comments *g, i, j,* and *l* to § 388 are applicable to this Section.

One who voluntarily chooses to use a chattel with a complete realization, regardless of how it was acquired, of the risks to which he thus exposes himself may voluntarily assume such risks, as may one who voluntarily chooses to remain in the vicinity of a dangerous chattel with a complete realization of the risks from the chattel to one in his position. (See Chapter 17 A.)

Illustration:

8. A, a retail merchant, sells a washing machine to B, without warning her of the fact, known to him, that the safety release bar on the wringer does not operate. In using the machine, B discovers this defect. Thereafter B catches her fingers in the wringer, which does not release and crushes her hand. A is not liable to B, who has voluntarily assumed the risk of such harm.

§ 402. Absence of Duty to Inspect Chattel

A seller of a chattel manufactured by a third person, who neither knows nor has reason to know that it is, or is likely to be, dangerous, is not liable in an action for negligence for harm caused by the dangerous character or condition of the chattel because of his failure to discover the danger by an inspection or test of the chattel before selling it.

See Reporter's Notes.

Comment:

a. This Section should be read together with § 400, as to the liability of one who sells as his own product a chattel made by another, and § 402 A, as to the special strict liability of sellers of products for consumption.

b. This Section is concerned only with liability based upon negligence of the seller in failing to inspect or test the chattel sold. It is not within the scope of this Section to state when a seller warrants that a chattel sold by him is of merchantable quality or is fit for a particular purpose, or the legal consequences of a breach of such warranty.

c. For the meaning of "reason to know" see §§ 12(1) and 401, Comment *a*. The dangerous character or condition of the chattel, in the circumstances stated in this section, is not a fact which the seller "should know" as those words are defined in § 12(2).

d. There is a clear distinction between the liability of a manufacturer and that of a seller of goods made by another for harm caused by a chattel made by the former and sold by the latter. The manufacturer of a dangerously defective chattel is the creator of something which is foreseeably dangerous when it is used for the purpose for which it is manufactured. The constructing of the chattel defectively, with knowledge that it is to be sent out to be used, is an unreasonably dangerous activity. On the other hand, the seller who reasonably believes that the chattel he is selling is safe for use is not, in selling and delivering the chattel, doing anything which is foreseeably likely to cause harm. The slight risk inherent in the possibility that the chattel may be defective is not sufficient to constitute an unreasonable risk. The burden on the seller of requiring him to inspect chattels which he reasonably believes to be free from hidden danger outweighs the magnitude of the risk that a particular chattel may be dangerously defective. (See §§ 291–293.) Negligence is determined in the light of the facts known to the actor. (See § 282, Comment g.)

Illustrations:

> 1. A, a wholesale distributor, sells to B, a retail dealer, who, in turn, sells to C, a defective gas heater, obtained from a reputable manufacturer, which both A and B believe to be in perfect condition although they have not inspected it. The heater when used emits poisonous fumes, which injure C. Neither A nor B is liable to C in an action for negligence.
>
> 2. A, a retail dealer, sells to B a hot water bag purchased from a reputable manufacturer. A believes the bag to be in perfect condition, although he has not inspected it, but the bag is defective in that the stopper will not screw in securely. As a result of this defect, C, the minor son of B, is severely scalded by hot water that leaks out of the bag. A is not liable to B or to C in an action for negligence.

e. In many situations the seller who receives his goods from a reputable source of supply receives it with the firm conviction that it is free from defects; and where a chattel is of a type which is perfectly safe for use in the absence of defects, the seller who sells it with the reasonable belief that it is safe for use and represents it to be safe for use does not act negligently. Frequently, the manufacturer's literature and salesmen and his past record of sending the seller perfectly made chattels create a reasonable belief in the seller's mind that the particular chattel he is selling is made perfectly. When the seller reasonably believes that the chattel is safe, his representation in good faith to that effect is neither fraudulent, reckless, nor negligent.

Illustration:

> 3. A, a retail dealer, sells to B a defective gas heater, obtained from a reputable manufacturer, which A believes to be in perfect condition, although he has not inspected it. In making the sale, and in response to B's inquiry, A says, "This heater can be used with perfect safety." The heater when used emits poisonous fumes, injuring B. A is not liable to B in an action for negligence.

TOPIC 5. STRICT LIABILITY

§ 402 A. Special Liability of Seller of Product for Physical Harm to User or Consumer

(1) One who sells any product in a defective condition unreasonably dangerous to the user or consumer or to his property is subject to liability for physical harm thereby caused to the ultimate user or consumer, or to his property, if

    (a) the seller is engaged in the business of selling such a product, and

    (b) it is expected to and does reach the user or consumer without substantial change in the condition in which it is sold.

(2) The rule stated in Subsection (1) applies although

    (a) the seller has exercised all possible care in the preparation and sale of his product, and

    (b) the user or consumer has not bought the product from or entered into any contractual relation with the seller.

See Reporter's Notes.

Caveat:

The Institute expresses no opinion as to whether the rules stated in this Section may not apply

(1) to harm to persons other than users or consumers;

(2) to the seller of a product expected to be processed or otherwise substantially changed before it reaches the user or consumer; or

(3) to the seller of a component part of a product to be assembled.

Comment:

    a. This Section states a special rule applicable to sellers of products. The rule is one of strict liability, making the seller subject to liability to the user or consumer even though he has exercised all possible care in the preparation and sale of the product. The Section is inserted in the Chapter dealing with the negligence liability of suppliers of chattels, for convenience of reference and comparison with other Sections dealing with negligence. The rule stated here is not exclusive, and does not preclude liability based upon the alternative ground of negligence of the seller, where such negligence can be proved.

    b. History. Since the early days of the common law those engaged in the business of selling food intended for human consumption have been held to a high degree of responsibility for their products. As long ago as 1266 there were enacted special criminal statutes imposing penalties upon victualers, vintners, brewers, butchers, cooks, and other persons who supplied "corrupt" food and drink. In the earlier part of this century this ancient attitude was reflected in a series of decisions in which the courts of a number of states sought to find some method of holding the seller of food liable to the ultimate consumer even though there was no showing of negligence on the part of the seller. These decisions represented a departure from, and an exception to, the general rule that a supplier of chattels was not liable to third persons in the absence of negligence or privity of contract. In the beginning, these decisions displayed considerable ingenuity in evolving more or less fictitious theories of liability to fit the case. The various devices included an agency of the intermediate dealer or another to purchase for the consumer, or to sell for the seller; a theoretical assignment of the seller's warranty to the intermediate dealer; a third party beneficiary contract; and an implied representation that the food was fit for consumption because it was placed on the market, as well as numerous others. In later years the courts have become more or less agreed upon the theory of a "warranty" from the seller to the consumer, either "running with the goods" by analogy to a covenant running with the land, or made directly to the consumer. Other decisions have indicated that the basis is merely one of strict liability in tort, which is not dependent upon either contract or negligence.

Recent decisions, since 1950, have extended this special rule of strict liability beyond the seller of food for human consumption. The first extension was into the closely analogous cases of other products intended for intimate bodily use, where, for example, as in the case of cosmetics, the application to the body of the consumer is external rather than internal. Beginning in 1958 with a Michigan case involving cinder building blocks, a number of recent decisions have discarded any limitation to intimate association with the body, and have extended the rule of strict liability to cover the sale of any product which, if it should prove to be defective, may be expected to cause physical harm to the consumer or his property.

c. On whatever theory, the justification for the strict liability has been said to be that the seller, by marketing his product for use and consumption, has undertaken and assumed a special responsibility toward any member of the consuming public who may be injured by it; that the public has the right to and does expect, in the case of products which it needs and for which it is forced to rely upon the seller, that reputable sellers will stand behind their goods; that public policy demands that the burden of accidental injuries caused by products intended for consumption be placed upon those who market them, and be treated as a cost of production against which liability insurance can be obtained; and that the consumer of such products is entitled to the maximum of protection at the hands of someone, and the proper persons to afford it are those who market the products.

d. The rule stated in this Section is not limited to the sale of food for human consumption, or other products for intimate bodily use, although it will obviously include them. It extends to any product sold in the condition, or substantially the same condition, in which it is expected to reach the ultimate user or consumer. Thus the rule stated applies to an automobile, a tire, an airplane, a grinding wheel, a water heater, a gas stove, a power tool, a riveting machine, a chair, and an insecticide. It applies also to products which, if they are defective, may be expected to and do cause only "physical harm" in the form of damage to the user's land or chattels, as in the case of animal food or a herbicide.

e. Normally the rule stated in this Section will be applied to articles which already have undergone some processing before sale, since there is today little in the way of consumer products which will reach the consumer without such processing. The rule is not, however, so limited, and the supplier of poisonous mushrooms which are neither cooked, canned, packaged, nor otherwise treated is subject to the liability here stated.

f. Business of selling. The rule stated in this Section applies to any person engaged in the business of selling products for use or consumption. It therefore applies to any manufacturer of such a product, to any wholesale or retail dealer or distributor, and to the operator of a restaurant. It is not necessary that the seller be engaged solely in the business of selling such products. Thus the rule applies to the owner of a motion picture theatre who sells popcorn or ice cream, either for consumption on the premises or in packages to be taken home.

The rule does not, however, apply to the occasional seller of food or other such products who is not engaged in that activity as a part of his business. Thus it does not apply to the housewife who, on one occasion, sells to her neighbor a jar of jam or a pound of sugar. Nor does it apply to the owner of an automobile who, on one occasion, sells it to his neighbor, or even sells it to a dealer in used cars, and this even though he is fully aware that the dealer plans to resell it. The basis for the rule is the ancient one of the special responsibility for the safety of the public undertaken by one who enters into the business of supplying human beings with products which may endanger the safety of their persons and property, and the forced reliance upon that undertaking on the part of those who purchase such goods. This basis is lacking in the case of the ordinary individual who makes the isolated sale, and he is not liable to a third person, or even to his buyer, in the absence of his negligence. An analogy may be found in the provision of the Uniform Sales Act, § 15, which limits the implied warranty of merchantable quality to sellers who deal in such goods; and in the similar limitation of the Uniform Commercial Code, § 2–314, to a seller who is a merchant. This Section is also not intended to apply to sales of the stock of merchants out of the usual course of business, such as execution sales, bankruptcy sales, bulk sales, and the like.

g. Defective condition. The rule stated in this Section applies only where the product is, at the time it leaves the seller's hands, in a condition not contemplated by the ultimate consumer, which will be unreasonably dangerous to him. The seller is not liable when he delivers the product in a safe condition, and subsequent mishandling or other causes make it harmful by the time it is consumed. The burden of proof that the product was in a defective condition at the time that it left the hands of the particular seller is upon the injured plaintiff; and unless evidence can be produced which will support the conclusion that it was then defective, the burden is not sustained.

Safe condition at the time of delivery by the seller will, however, include proper packaging, necessary sterilization, and other precautions required to permit the product to remain safe for a normal length of time when handled in a normal manner.

h. A product is not in a defective condition when it is safe for normal handling and consumption. If the injury results from abnormal handling, as where a bottled beverage is knocked against a radiator to remove the cap, or from abnormal preparation for use, as where too much salt is added to food, or from abnormal consumption, as where a child eats too much candy and is made ill, the seller is not liable. Where, however, he has reason to anticipate that danger may result from a particular use, as where a drug is sold which is safe only in limited doses, he may be required to give adequate warning of the danger (see Comment *j*), and a product sold without such warning is in a defective condition.

The defective condition may arise not only from harmful ingredients, not characteristic of the product itself either as to presence or quantity, but also from foreign objects contained in the product, from decay or deterioration before sale, or from the way in which the product is prepared or packed. No reason is apparent for distinguishing between the product itself and the container in which it is supplied; and the two are purchased by the user or consumer as an integrated whole. Where the container is itself dangerous, the product is sold in a defective condition. Thus a carbonated beverage in a bottle which is so weak, or cracked, or jagged at the edges, or bottled under such excessive pressure that it may explode or otherwise cause harm to the person who handles it, is in a defective and dangerous condition. The container cannot logically be separated from the contents when the two are sold as a unit, and the liability stated in this Section arises not only when the consumer drinks the beverage and is poisoned by it, but also

when he is injured by the bottle while he is handling it preparatory to consumption.

i. Unreasonably dangerous. The rule stated in this Section applies only where the defective condition of the product makes it unreasonably dangerous to the user or consumer. Many products cannot possibly be made entirely safe for all consumption, and any food or drug necessarily involves some risk of harm, if only from over-consumption. Ordinary sugar is a deadly poison to diabetics, and castor oil found use under Mussolini as an instrument of torture. That is not what is meant by "unreasonably dangerous" in this Section. The article sold must be dangerous to an extent beyond that which would be contemplated by the ordinary consumer who purchases it, with the ordinary knowledge common to the community as to its characteristics. Good whiskey is not unreasonably dangerous merely because it will make some people drunk, and is especially dangerous to alcoholics; but bad whiskey, containing a dangerous amount of fusel oil, is unreasonably dangerous. Good tobacco is not unreasonably dangerous merely because the effects of smoking may be harmful; but tobacco containing something like marijuana may be unreasonably dangerous. Good butter is not unreasonably dangerous merely because, if such be the case, it deposits cholesterol in the arteries and leads to heart attacks; but bad butter, contaminated with poisonous fish oil, is unreasonably dangerous.

j. Directions or warning. In order to prevent the product from being unreasonably dangerous, the seller may be required to give directions or warning, on the container, as to its use. The seller may reasonably assume that those with common allergies, as for example to eggs or strawberries, will be aware of them, and he is not required to warn against them. Where, however, the product contains an ingredient to which a substantial number of the population are allergic, and the ingredient is one whose danger is not generally known, or if known is one which the consumer would reasonably not expect to find in the product, the seller is required to give warning against it, if he has knowledge, or by the application of reasonable, developed human skill and foresight should have knowledge, of the presence of the ingredient and the danger. Likewise in the case of poisonous drugs, or those unduly dangerous for other reasons, warning as to use may be required.

But a seller is not required to warn with respect to products, or ingredients in them, which are only dangerous, or potentially so, when consumed in excessive quantity, or over a long period of time, when the danger, or potentiality of danger, is generally known and recognized. Again the dangers of alcoholic beverages are an example, as are also those of foods containing such substances as saturated fats, which may over a period of time have a deleterious effect upon the human heart.

Where warning is given, the seller may reasonably assume that it will be read and heeded; and a product bearing such a warning, which is safe for use if it is followed, is not in defective condition, nor is it unreasonably dangerous.

k. *Unavoidably unsafe products.* There are some products which, in the present state of human knowledge, are quite incapable of being made safe for their intended and ordinary use. These are especially common in the field of drugs. An outstanding example is the vaccine for the Pasteur treatment of rabies, which not uncommonly leads to very serious and damaging consequences when it is injected. Since the disease itself invariably leads to a dreadful death, both the marketing and the use of the vaccine are fully justified, notwithstanding the unavoidable high degree of risk which they involve. Such a product, properly prepared, and accompanied by proper directions and warning, is not defective, nor is it *unreasonably* dangerous. The same is true of many other drugs, vaccines, and the like, many of which for this very reason cannot legally be sold except to physicians, or under the prescription of a physician. It is also true in particular of many new or experimental drugs as to which, because of lack of time and opportunity for sufficient medical experience, there can be no assurance of safety, or perhaps even of purity of ingredients, but such experience as there is justifies the marketing and use of the drug notwithstanding a medically recognizable risk. The seller of such products, again with the qualification that they are properly prepared and marketed, and proper warning is given, where the situation calls for it, is not to be held to strict liability for unfortunate consequences attending their use, merely because he has undertaken to supply the public with an apparently useful and desirable product, attended with a known but apparently reasonable risk.

l. *User or consumer.* In order for the rule stated in this Section to apply, it is not necessary that the ultimate user or consumer have acquired the product directly from the seller, although the rule applies equally if he does so. He may have acquired it through one or more intermediate dealers. It is not even necessary that the consumer have purchased the product at all. He may be a member of the family of the final purchaser, or his employee, or a guest at his table, or a mere donee from the purchaser. The liability stated is one in tort, and does not require any contractual relation, or privity of contract, between the plaintiff and the defendant.

"Consumers" include not only those who in fact consume the product, but also those who prepare it for consumption; and the housewife who contracts tularemia while cooking rabbits for her husband is included within the rule stated in this Section, as is also the husband who is opening a bottle of beer for his wife to drink. Consumption includes all ultimate uses for which the product is intended, and the customer in a beauty shop to whose hair a permanent wave

§ 402 A RESTATEMENT (SECOND) OF TORTS

solution is applied by the shop is a consumer. "User" includes those who are passively enjoying the benefit of the product, as in the case of passengers in automobiles or airplanes, as well as those who are utilizing it for the purpose of doing work upon it, as in the case of an employee of the ultimate buyer who is making repairs upon the automobile which he has purchased.

Illustration:

1. A manufactures and packs a can of beans, which he sells to B, a wholesaler. B sells the beans to C, a jobber, who resells it to D, a retail grocer. E buys the can of beans from D, and gives it to F. F serves the beans at lunch to G, his guest. While eating the beans, G breaks a tooth, on a pebble of the size, shape, and color of a bean, which no reasonable inspection could possibly have discovered. There is satisfactory evidence that the pebble was in the can of beans when it was opened. Although there is no negligence on the part of A, B, C, or D, each of them is subject to liability to G. On the other hand E and F, who have not sold the beans, are not liable to G in the absence of some negligence on their part.

m. *"Warranty."* The liability stated in this Section does not rest upon negligence. It is strict liability, similar in its nature to that covered by Chapters 20 and 21. The basis of liability is purely one of tort.

A number of courts, seeking a theoretical basis for the liability, have resorted to a "warranty," either running with the goods sold, by analogy to covenants running with the land, or made directly to the consumer without contract. In some instances this theory has proved to be an unfortunate one. Although warranty was in its origin a matter of tort liability, and it is generally agreed that a tort action will still lie for its breach, it has become so identified in practice with a contract of sale between the plaintiff and the defendant that the warranty theory has become something of an obstacle to the recognition of the strict liability where there is no such contract. There is nothing in this Section which would prevent any court from treating the rule stated as a matter of "warranty" to the user or consumer. But if this is done, it should be recognized and understood that the "warranty" is a very different kind of warranty from those usually found in the sale of goods, and that it is not subject to the various contract rules which have grown up to surround such sales.

The rule stated in this Section does not require any reliance on the part of the consumer upon the reputation, skill, or judgment of the seller who is to be held liable, nor any representation or undertaking on the part of that seller. The seller is strictly liable although, as is frequently the case, the consumer does not even know who he is at the time of consumption. The rule stated in this Section is not governed by the provisions of the Uniform Sales Act, or those of the Uniform

Commercial Code, as to warranties; and it is not affected by limitations on the scope and content of warranties, or by limitation to "buyer" and "seller" in those statutes. Nor is the consumer required to give notice to the seller of his injury within a reasonable time after it occurs, as is provided by the Uniform Act. The consumer's cause of action does not depend upon the validity of his contract with the person from whom he acquires the product, and it is not affected by any disclaimer or other agreement, whether it be between the seller and his immediate buyer, or attached to and accompanying the product into the consumer's hands. In short, "warranty" must be given a new and different meaning if it is used in connection with this Section. It is much simpler to regard the liability here stated as merely one of strict liability in tort.

n. Contributory negligence. Since the liability with which this Section deals is not based upon negligence of the seller, but is strict liability, the rule applied to strict liability cases (see § 524) applies. Contributory negligence of the plaintiff is not a defense when such negligence consists merely in a failure to discover the defect in the product, or to guard against the possibility of its existence. On the other hand the form of contributory negligence which consists in voluntarily and unreasonably proceeding to encounter a known danger, and commonly passes under the name of assumption of risk, is a defense under this Section as in other cases of strict liability. If the user or consumer discovers the defect and is aware of the danger, and nevertheless proceeds unreasonably to make use of the product and is injured by it, he is barred from recovery.

Comment on Caveat:

o. Injuries to non-users and non-consumers. Thus far the courts, in applying the rule stated in this Section, have not gone beyond allowing recovery to users and consumers, as those terms are defined in Comment *l*. Casual bystanders, and others who may come in contact with the product, as in the case of employees of the retailer, or a passer-by injured by an exploding bottle, or a pedestrian hit by an automobile, have been denied recovery. There may be no essential reason why such plaintiffs should not be brought within the scope of the protection afforded, other than that they do not have the same reasons for expecting such protection as the consumer who buys a marketed product; but the social pressure which has been largely responsible for the development of the rule stated has been a consumers' pressure, and there is not the same demand for the protection of casual strangers. The Institute expresses neither approval nor disapproval of expansion of the rule to permit recovery by such persons.

p. Further processing or substantial change. Thus far the decisions applying the rule stated have not gone beyond products which are sold in the condition, or in substantially the same condition, in which they are expected to reach the hands of the ultimate user or consumer. In the absence of decisions providing a clue to the rules which are likely to develop, the Institute has refrained from taking any position as to the possible liability of the seller where the product is expected to, and does, undergo further processing or other substantial change after it leaves his hands and before it reaches those of the ultimate user or consumer.

It seems reasonably clear that the mere fact that the product is to undergo processing, or other substantial change, will not in all cases relieve the seller of liability under the rule stated in this Section. If, for example, raw coffee beans are sold to a buyer who roasts and packs them for sale to the ultimate consumer, it cannot be supposed that the seller will be relieved of all liability when the raw beans are contaminated with arsenic, or some other poison. Likewise the seller of an automobile with a defective steering gear which breaks and injures the driver, can scarcely expect to be relieved of the responsibility by reason of the fact that the car is sold to a dealer who is expected to "service" it, adjust the brakes, mount and inflate the tires, and the like, before it is ready for use. On the other hand, the manufacturer of pigiron, which is capable of a wide variety of uses, is not so likely to be held to strict liability when it turns out to be unsuitable for the child's tricycle into which it is finally made by a remote buyer. The question is essentially one of whether the responsibility for discovery and prevention of the dangerous defect is shifted to the intermediate party who is to make the changes. No doubt there will be some situations, and some defects, as to which the responsibility will be shifted, and others in which it will not. The existing decisions as yet throw no light upon the questions, and the Institute therefore expresses neither approval nor disapproval of the seller's strict liability in such a case.

q. Component parts. The same problem arises in cases of the sale of a component part of a product to be assembled by another, as for example a tire to be placed on a new automobile, a brake cylinder for the same purpose, or an instrument for the panel of an airplane. Again the question arises, whether the responsibility is not shifted to the assembler. It is no doubt to be expected that where there is no change in the component part itself, but it is merely incorporated into something larger, the strict liability will be found to carry through to the ultimate user or consumer. But in the absence of a sufficient number of decisions on the matter to justify a conclusion, the Institute expresses no opinion on the matter.

§ 402 B. Misrepresentation by Seller of Chattels to Consumer

One engaged in the business of selling chattels who, by advertising, labels, or otherwise, makes to the public a misrepresentation of a material fact concerning the character or quality of a chattel sold by him is subject to liability for physical harm to a consumer of the chattel caused by justifiable reliance upon the misrepresentation, even though

(a) it is not made fraudulently or negligently, and

(b) the consumer has not bought the chattel from or entered into any contractual relation with the seller.

See Reporter's Notes.

Caveat:

The Institute expresses no opinion as to whether the rule stated in this Section may apply

(1) where the representation is not made to the public, but to an individual, or

(2) where physical harm is caused to one who is not a consumer of the chattel.

Comment:

a. The rule stated in this Section is one of strict liability for physical harm to the consumer, resulting from a misrepresentation of the character or quality of the chattel sold, even though the misrepresentation is an innocent one, and not made fraudulently or negligently. Although the Section deals with misrepresentation, it is inserted here in order to complete the rules dealing with the liability of suppliers of chattels for physical harm caused by the chattel. A parallel rule, as to strict liability for pecuniary loss resulting from such a misrepresentation, is stated in § 552 D.*

b. The rule stated in this Section differs from the rule of strict liability stated in § 402 A, which is a special rule applicable only to sellers of products for consumption and does not depend upon misrepresentation. The rule here stated applies to one engaged in the business of selling any type of chattel, and is limited to misrepresentations of their character or quality.

c. History. The early rule was that a seller of chattels incurred no liability for physical harm resulting from the use of the chattel to anyone other than his immediate buyer, unless there was privity of contract between them. (See § 395, Comment *a.*) Beginning with Langridge v. Levy, 2 M. & W. 519, 150 Eng. Rep. 863 (1837), an exception was developed in cases where the seller made fraudulent misrepresentations to the immediate buyer, concerning the character or quality of the chattel sold, and because of the fact misrepresented harm resulted to a third person who was using the chattel. The

---

* Section 552 D, in tentative form at the time § 402 B was adopted, was ultimately rejected by The American Law Institute.—Eds.

§ 402 B RESTATEMENT (SECOND) OF TORTS

remedy lay in an action for deceit, and the rule which resulted is now stated in § 557 A.

Shortly after 1930, a number of the American courts began, more or less independently, to work out a further extension of liability for physical harm to the consumer of the chattel, in cases where the seller made misrepresentations to the public concerning its character or quality, and the consumer, as a member of the public, purchased the chattel in reliance upon the misrepresentation and suffered physical harm because of the fact misrepresented. In such cases the seller was held to strict liability for the misrepresentation, even though it was not made fraudulently or negligently. The leading case is Baxter v. Ford Motor Co., 168 Wash. 456, 12 P.2d 409, 88 A.L.R. 521 (1932), adhered to on rehearing, 168 Wash. 456, 15 P.2d 1118, 88 A.L.R. 521, second appeal, 179 Wash. 123, 35 P.2d 1090 (1934), in which the manufacturer of an automobile advertised to the public that the windshield glass was "shatterproof," and the purchaser was injured when a stone struck the glass and it shattered. In the beginning various theories of liability were suggested, including strict liability in deceit, and a contract resulting from an offer made to the consumer to be bound by the representation, accepted by his purchase.

d. "Warranty." The theory finally adopted by most of the decisions, however, has been that of a non-contractual "express warranty" made to the consumer in the form of the representation to the public upon which he relies. The difficulties attending the use of the word "warranty" are the same as those involved under § 402 A, and Comment *m* under that Section is equally applicable here so far as it is pertinent. The liability stated in this Section is liability in tort, and not in contract; and if it is to be called one of "warranty," it is at least a different kind of warranty from that involved in the ordinary sale of goods from the immediate seller to the immediate buyer, and is subject to different rules.

e. Sellers included. The rule stated in this Section applies to any person engaged in the business of selling any type of chattel. It is not limited to sellers of food or products for intimate bodily use, as was until lately the rule stated in § 402 A. It is not limited to manufacturers of the chattel, and it includes wholesalers, retailers, and other distributors who sell it.

The rule stated applies, however, only to those who are engaged in the business of selling such chattels. It has no application to anyone who is not so engaged in business. It does not apply, for example, to a newspaper advertisement published by a private owner of a single automobile who offers it for sale.

f. Misrepresentation of character or quality. The rule stated applies to any misrepresentation of a material fact concerning the character or quality of the chattel sold which is made to the public by one so engaged in the business of selling such chattels. The fact misrepresented must be a material one, upon which the consumer may be expected to rely in making his purchase, and he must justifiably rely upon it. (See Comment j.) If he does so, and suffers physical harm by reason of the fact misrepresented, there is strict liability to him.

Illustration:

    1. A manufactures automobiles. He advertises in newspapers and magazines that the glass in his cars is "shatterproof." B reads this advertising, and in reliance upon it purchases from a retail dealer an automobile manufactured by A. While B is driving the car, a stone thrown up by a passing truck strikes the windshield and shatters it, injuring B. A is subject to strict liability to B.

    g. *Material fact.* The rule stated in this Section applies only to misrepresentations of material facts concerning the character or quality of the chattel in question. It does not apply to statements of opinion, and in particular it does not apply to the kind of loose general praise of wares sold which, on the part of the seller, is considered to be "sales talk," and is commonly called "puffing"—as, for example, a statement that an automobile is the best on the market for the price. As to such general language of opinion, see § 542, and Comment *d* under that Section, which is applicable here so far as it is pertinent. In addition, the fact misrepresented must be a material one, of importance to the normal purchaser, by which the ultimate buyer may justifiably be expected to be influenced in buying the chattel.

    h. *"To the public."* The rule stated in this Section is limited to misrepresentations which are made by the seller to the public at large, in order to induce purchase of the chattels sold, or are intended by the seller to, and do, reach the public. The form of the representation is not important. It may be made by public advertising in newspapers or television, by literature distributed to the public through dealers, by labels on the product sold, or leaflets accompanying it, or in any other manner, whether it be oral or written.

Illustrations:

    2. A manufactures wire rope. He issues a manual containing statements concerning its strength, which he distributes through dealers to buyers, and to members of the public who may be expected to buy. In reliance upon the statements made in the manual, B buys a quantity of the wire rope from a dealer, and makes use of it to hoist a weight of 1,000 pounds. The strength of the rope is not as great as is represented in the manual, and as a result the rope breaks and the weight falls on B and injures him. A is subject to strict liability to B.

    3. A manufactures a product for use by women at home in giving "permanent waves" to their hair. He places on the bottles

labels which state that the product may safely be used in a particular manner, and will not be injurious to the hair. B reads such a label, and in reliance upon it purchases a bottle of the product from a retail dealer. She uses it as directed, and as a result her hair is destroyed. A is subject to strict liability to B.

i. Consumers. The rule stated in this Section is limited to strict liability for physical harm to consumers of the chattel. The Caveat leaves open the question whether the rule may not also apply to one who is not a consumer, but who suffers physical harm through his justifiable reliance upon the misrepresentation.

"Consumer" is to be understood in the broad sense of one who makes use of the chattel in the manner which a purchaser may be expected to use it. Thus an employee of the ultimate purchaser to whom the chattel is turned over, and who is directed to make use of it in his work, is a consumer, and so is the wife of the purchaser of an automobile who is permitted by him to drive it.

j. Justifiable reliance. The rule here stated applies only where there is justifiable reliance upon the misrepresentation of the seller, and physical harm results because of such reliance, and because of the fact which is misrepresented. It does not apply where the misrepresentation is not known, or there is indifference to it, and it does not influence the purchase or subsequent conduct. At the same time, however, the misrepresentation need not be the sole inducement to purchase, or to use the chattel, and it is sufficient that it has been a substantial factor in that inducement. (Compare § 546 and Comments.) Since the liability here is for misrepresentation, the rules as to what will constitute justifiable reliance stated in §§ 537–545 A are applicable to this Section, so far as they are pertinent.

The reliance need not necessarily be that of the consumer who is injured. It may be that of the ultimate purchaser of the chattel, who because of such reliance passes it on to the consumer who is in fact injured, but is ignorant of the misrepresentation. Thus a husband who buys an automobile in justifiable reliance upon statements concerning its brakes, and permits his wife to drive the car, supplies the element of reliance, even though the wife in fact never learns of the statements.

Illustration:

4. The same facts as in Illustration 2, except that the harm is suffered by C, an employee of B, to whom B turns over the wire rope without informing him of the representations made by A. The same result.

TOPIC 6. INDEPENDENT CONTRACTORS

§ 403. Chattel Known to Be Dangerous

One who as an independent contractor makes, rebuilds, or repairs a chattel for another and turns it over to the other, knowing or having reason to know that his work has made it dangerous for the use for which it is turned over, is subject to the same liability as if he supplied the chattel.

See Reporter's Notes.

Caveat:

The Institute expresses no opinion that a contractor who fails to exercise reasonable care to inform his employer of a dangerous condition, which he is not employed to repair, but which he discovers in the course of making the repairs agreed upon and of which he realizes that his employer is unaware, may not be subject to the liability stated in this Section.

Comment:

a. The words "independent contractor" denote any person to whom the construction, rebuilding, or repairing of a chattel is entrusted in such a way as to give him charge and control of the details of doing the work, irrespective of whether the work is done gratuitously or is to be paid for by his employer or is in any other way of financial or other benefit to the contractor. If, however, the work is done gratuitously, the contractor is not liable because he does not have the skill necessary for the proper performance of the work, unless the work is undertaken under such circumstances that the contractor should realize that his employer is entrusting the work to him in reliance upon the contractor's expressed or implied profession of competence to do it.

b. The rule stated in this Section applies only where the contractor knows or has reason to know that the work which he has done in making, rebuilding, or repairing the chattel has made it unsafe for use. It is not, however, necessary that a contractor should know that the work which he has done in rebuilding or repairing an automobile or other chattel has made its condition worse than it was before the work was done. It is enough that the contractor knows that the rebuilding or repairs have not been sufficient to make the car or chattel as safe for use as care and competence would make it, and that it is used or permitted to be used in reliance upon his care and competence. The fact that an inadequately rebuilt or repaired automobile or other chattel is turned over by the contractor to the employer as rebuilt or repaired gives it a deceptive appearance of safety, even though its condition is in fact improved by the work which the contractor has done upon it.

§ 404. Negligence in Making, Rebuilding, or Repairing Chattel

One who as an independent contractor negligently makes, rebuilds, or repairs a chattel for another is subject to the same liability as that imposed upon negligent manufacturers of chattels.

See Reporter's Notes.

Comment:

a. When employer furnishes plan, design, or materials. The rule stated in this Section requires an independent contractor who makes, rebuilds, or repairs a chattel for an employer to do everything which he undertakes with the same competence and skill which is required of a manufacturer in doing those things which are necessary to the turning out of a safe product, under the rules stated in §§ 395–398. While the standard of care and diligence is the same in both cases, the particulars in which they are required to be exercised may, and often do, differ. One who has a car or other chattel repaired by an independent contractor usually entrusts to the contractor not only the manual labor of doing the repairs and the inspections necessary from time to time, but also the selection of the plan by which repairs are to be made and the materials which are to be used therein. In such a case, the contractor's position is substantially identical with that of a manufacturer of a chattel, and he is required to exercise care in all these particulars (see § 395, Comment *f*). On the other hand, one who employs a contractor to make a chattel for him, like one who employs a contractor to erect a structure on his premises (as to which see § 385), usually provides not only plans but also specifications, which often state the material which must be used. Indeed, chattels are often made by independent contractors from materials furnished by their employers. In such a case, the contractor is not required to sit in judgment on the plans and specifications or the materials provided by his employer. The contractor is not subject to liability if the specified design or material turns out to be insufficient to make the chattel safe for use, unless it is so obviously bad that a competent contractor would realize that there was a grave chance that his product would be dangerously unsafe. The same is true in regard to materials furnished by the employer. If, however, the employer specifies the type of material to be used, the contractor is under a duty to make an inspection of the particular material, whether procured by him or furnished by persons from whom the employer has bought it, in order to see that it conforms to the specifications.

b. In order that a contractor may be subject to liability under the rule stated in this Section it is not necessary that his negligence have changed the condition of the chattel for the worse. It is enough that the chattel because of his negligence is not in that safe condition in which a competent contractor would have put it and that it is used, or permitted to be used, in reliance upon the care and competence of the contractor. (See § 403, Comment *b*.)

TOPIC 7. DONORS, LENDERS, AND LESSORS OF CHATTELS

§ 405. Donors and Lenders of Chattels Known to Be Dangerous

One who directly or through a third person gives or lends a chattel for another to use, knowing or having reason to know that it is or is likely to be dangerous for the use for which it is given or lent, is subject to the same liability as a supplier of the chattel.

See Reporter's Notes.

Caveat:

The Institute expresses no opinion as to whether a donor or lender is subject to liability under the rule stated in § 401, if the chattel is accepted in reliance upon the donor's or lender's professed competence and care in its preparation or selection.

Comment:

a. The Comments to §§ 388–390 are applicable to this Section, so far as they are pertinent.

§ 406. Manufacturer Giving or Lending Negligently Made Chattel

A manufacturer who in the course of his business as such directly or through a third person gives or lends to another a chattel made by him, is subject to the same liability as if he had sold the chattel.

Comment:

a. The rule stated in this Section results in the same liabilities as those stated in §§ 395–398. The Comments to those Sections are applicable here, so far as they are pertinent.

§ 407. Lessors of Chattels Known to Be Dangerous

A lessor who leases a chattel for the use of others, knowing or having reason to know that it is or is likely to be dangerous for the purpose for which it is to be used, is subject to liability as a supplier of the chattel.

See Reporter's Notes.

Comment:

a. The rule stated in this Section results in the same liabilities as those stated in §§ 388–390. The Comments under those Sections are applicable here, so far as they are pertinent.

§ 408. Lease of Chattel for Immediate Use

One who leases a chattel as safe for immediate use is subject to liability to those whom he should expect to use the chattel, or to be endangered by its probable use, for physical harm caused by its use in a manner for which, and by a person for whose use, it is leased, if the lessor fails to exercise reasonable care to make it safe for such use or to disclose its actual condition to those who may be expected to use it.

See Reporter's Notes.

Comment:

a. When lessor must inspect. The fact that a chattel is leased for immediate use makes it unreasonable for the lessor to expect that the lessee will do more than give it the most cursory of inspections. The lessor must, therefore, realize that the safe use of the chattel can be secured only by precautions taken by him before turning it over to the lessee. If the chattel is made by the lessor, he is subject to liability under the same rules as are stated in §§ 395–398, as determining the liability of a manufacturer of chattels to be put upon the market. If the lessor repairs it, he is subject to liability if the repairs are not carefully made. (See § 404.) This is true although at the time that the chattel is turned over to the lessee a careful inspection would not have disclosed the dangerous condition into which the negligent construction or repair of the chattel has brought it. If the chattel is made by a third person, the lessor is required to exercise reasonable care to inspect it before turning it over to the lessee. The minuteness of the inspection required varies with the danger which will be likely to result if the chattel is defective, the source from which the lessor has obtained the chattel, and the length of time during which it has been in the lessor's possession and use. Thus, if the chattel is one which, even if defective and used in ignorance of its defective character, is unlikely to do more than some comparatively minor harm, the lessor is not required to make the minute inspections and tests which it is reasonable to require if the chattel is one which, if defective, involves a grave risk of serious bodily harm or death. So too, a lessor who has purchased a chattel from a maker who has a high reputation for the quality of his product may to a large extent rely upon the article as being well made, and is required to make only such inspections as any purchaser from such a maker should make before using it. On the other hand, if the article is bought second-hand, more intensive inspection is obviously required. In addition to the inspection required when the chattel is acquired, the lessor is required to make from time to time such inspections of the article which he keeps for hire as a reasonably careful man would make in view of the nature of the article and the use to which it is to be put.

Illustration:

    1. The A Company makes a business of letting out automobiles to be driven by the lessees for long or short trips. It buys an automobile from the X Company, whose cars have a high reputation. The A Company is required to make such an inspection as is necessary to check up any slips which may have escaped the inspection of the X Company. If the A Company buys and uses a second-hand car, it is required to subject such car to far more rigorous inspection, the intensity of which depends upon the condition in which the car is bought and the high or low reputation of the particular make for durability. The frequency and the character of the inspections which the A Company must make of its cars kept in stock for rent depend upon the nature of the use to which they are put. It may be reasonable to inspect a high grade car leased for park use at comparatively infrequent intervals. On the other hand, even such a car may require inspection after a single trip over a rough mountain road, particularly if the company has reason to suspect that the person who has driven the car is inexperienced and therefore likely to subject the car to hard usage.

    b. The rule stated in this Section is peculiarly applicable to persons who make a business of leasing chattels. In such a case, in the absence of an understanding to the contrary, it may be assumed that both lessor and lessee understand that the article is leased as fit for immediate use. On the other hand, the mere fact that on a particular occasion, a chattel is leased for immediate use does not necessarily warrant the assumption that it is understood to be leased as safe. Thus, if A's car has broken down and he asks B to lend him his car, but B refuses to do so unless A will pay him for its use, in the absence of some assurance that the car is fit for use, A would not be entitled to believe that it was leased as fit to use.

    c. While it is usually enough for the lessor of a chattel for immediate use to disclose to his lessee the actual condition of the chattel and to give such information as is necessary to enable the lessee to use it safely, the lessor does not relieve himself from liability by such disclosure if the chattel is one which cannot be used with safety even by one knowing its true condition, or if the person to whom it is leased is known to be so inexperienced or otherwise incompetent that he cannot be expected to take the precautions necessary to its safe use. As to these situations, see §§ 389 and 390.

Chapter 16

THE CAUSAL RELATION NECESSARY TO RESPONSIBILITY FOR NEGLIGENCE

TOPIC 1. CAUSAL RELATION NECESSARY TO THE EXISTENCE OF LIABILITY FOR ANOTHER'S HARM

TITLE A. GENERAL PRINCIPLES

* * *

Section
433 A. Apportionment of harm to causes
433 B. Burden of proof

* * *

TITLE C. SUPERSEDING CAUSE

440. Superseding cause defined
441. Intervening force defined
442. Considerations important in determining whether an intervening force is a superseding cause

* * *

452. Third person's failure to prevent harm

* * *

Topic 1. CAUSAL RELATION NECESSARY TO THE EXISTENCE OF LIABILITY FOR ANOTHER'S HARM

TITLE A. GENERAL PRINCIPLES

§ **433 A.** Apportionment of Harm to Causes

(1) Damages for harm are to be apportioned among two or more causes where

(a) there are distinct harms, or

(b) there is a reasonable basis for determining the contribution of each cause to a single harm.

(2) Damages for any other harm cannot be apportioned among two or more causes.

See Reporter's Notes.

Comment:

a. The rules stated in this Section apply whenever two or more causes have combined to bring about harm to the plaintiff, and each has been a substantial factor in producing the harm, as stated in §§ 431 and 433. They apply where each of the causes in question consists of the tortious conduct of a person; and it is immaterial whether all or any of such persons are joined as defendants in the particular action. The rules stated apply also where one or more of the contributing causes is an innocent one, as where the negligence of a defendant combines with the innocent conduct of another person, or with the operation of a force of nature, or with a pre-existing condition which the defendant has not caused, to bring about the harm to the plaintiff. The rules stated apply also where one of the causes in question is the conduct of the plaintiff himself, whether it be negligent or innocent.

Comment on Subsection (1):

b. Distinct harms. There are other results which, by their nature, are more capable of apportionment. If two defendants independently shoot the plaintiff at the same time, and one wounds him in the arm and the other in the leg, the ultimate result may be a badly damaged plaintiff in the hospital, but it is still possible, as a logical, reasonable, and practical matter, to regard the two wounds as separate injuries, and as distinct wrongs. The mere coincidence in time does not make the two wounds a single harm, or the conduct of the two defendants one tort. There may be difficulty in the apportionment of some elements of damages, such as the pain and suffering resulting from the two wounds, or the medical expenses, but this does not mean that one defendant must be liable for the distinct harm inflicted by the other. It is possible to make a rough estimate which will fairly apportion such subsidiary elements of damages.

c. Successive injuries. The harm inflicted may be conveniently severable in point of time. Thus if two defendants, independently operating the same plant, pollute a stream over successive periods, it is clear that each has caused a separate amount of harm, limited in time, and that neither has any responsibility for the harm caused by the other.

It should be noted that there are situations in which the earlier wrongdoer may be liable for the entire damage, while the later one will not. Thus an original tortfeasor may be liable not only for the harm which he has himself inflicted, but also for the additional damages resulting from the negligent treatment of the injury by a physician. (See § 457.) The physician, on the other hand, has played no part in causing the original injury, and will be liable only for the additional harm caused by his own negligence in treatment. There may be many other cases in which the original wrongdoer is liable for the additional harm caused by the intervening negligence of the later one, while the latter is liable only for what he has himself caused.

Illustrations:

  1. A slips on the negligently maintained platform of the B Railroad, and falls and breaks his right leg. A month later, while A is still on crutches, he is riding on the bus of C Company. The bus is negligently operated and collides with another vehicle, and A is thrown to the floor and his left leg is broken. B Company and C Company are each subject to several liability for the damages resulting from the fracture of one leg only.

  2. An automobile negligently driven by A strikes B, fractures his skull, and leaves him lying unconscious in the highway. Shortly afterward an automobile negligently driven by C runs over B and breaks his leg. A is subject to liability to B for the damages resulting from both fractures, but C is subject to liability only for the damages resulting from the broken leg.

  d. Divisible harm. There are other kinds of harm which, while not so clearly marked out as severable into distinct parts, are still capable of division upon a reasonable and rational basis, and of fair apportionment among the causes responsible. Thus where the cattle of two or more owners trespass upon the plaintiff's land and destroy his crop, the aggregate harm is a lost crop, but it may nevertheless be apportioned among the owners of the cattle, on the basis of the number owned by each, and the reasonable assumption that the respective harm done is proportionate to that number. Where such apportionment can be made without injustice to any of the parties, the court may require it to be made.

  Such apportionment is commonly made in cases of private nuisance, where the pollution of a stream, or flooding, or smoke or dust or noise, from different sources, has interfered with the plaintiff's use or enjoyment of his land. Thus where two or more factories independently pollute a stream, the interference with the plaintiff's use of the water may be treated as divisible in terms of degree, and may be apportioned among the owners of the factories, on the basis of evidence of the respective quantities of pollution discharged into the stream.

Illustrations:

  3. Five dogs owned by A and B enter C's farm and kill ten of C's sheep. There is evidence that three of the dogs are owned by A and two by B, and that all of the dogs are of the same general size and ferocity. On the basis of this evidence, A may be held liable for the death of six of the sheep, and B liable for the death of four.

  4. Through the negligence of A, B, and C, water escapes from irrigation ditches on their land, and floods a part of D's farm. There is evidence that 50 per cent of the water came from A's ditch, 30 per cent from B's and 20 per cent from C's. On the basis of this evidence, A may be held liable for 50 per cent of the

damages to C's farm, B liable for 30 per cent, and C liable for 20 per cent.

   5. Oil is negligently discharged from two factories, owned by A and B, onto the surface of a stream. As a result C, a lower riparian owner, is deprived of the use of the water for his own industrial purposes. There is evidence that 70 per cent of the oil has come from A's factory, and 30 per cent from B's. On the basis of this evidence, A may be held liable for 70 per cent of C's damages, and B liable for 30 per cent. Contrast Illustrations 14 and 15.

   e. Innocent causes. The same kind of apportionment may be made where a part of the harm can fairly be assigned to an innocent cause, as where the defendant's dam or embankment combines with an unprecedented and unforeseeable rainfall to flood the plaintiff's land, and it is clear that a part of the flood would have resulted in any event from the rainfall alone. Apportionment may also be made where a part of the harm caused would clearly have resulted from the innocent conduct of the defendant himself, and the extent of the harm has been aggravated by his tortious conduct. There may also be apportionment between harm which results from a pre-existing condition, for which the defendant is no way responsible, and the further harm which his tortious conduct has caused.

Illustrations:

   6. The same facts as in Illustration 4, except that the escape of 20 per cent of the water from C's ditch is not caused by C's negligence, but by a sudden rainfall or other innocent cause for which C is not responsible. A may be held liable for 50 per cent of the damages, and B liable for 30 per cent.

   7. Smoke from A Railroad's roundhouse interferes with B's use and enjoyment of his dwelling. There is evidence that a reasonable operation of the roundhouse, for which A Company would not be liable, would have caused one-third of the smoke and interference, and that the remaining two-thirds results from A Company's failure to take proper precautions. On the basis of this evidence, A Company may be held liable for two-thirds of the damages to B.

   8. A suffers from arthritis in his arm, as a result of which he has a 50 per cent disability in the use of the arm. He is struck by an automobile negligently driven by B, and the injury aggravates the arthritis so that he loses the use of the arm entirely. B may be held liable for 50 per cent of the disability.

   f. Contributory negligence. There are also cases where apportionment may be made between the plaintiff and the defendant when the plaintiff himself is at fault. This is true, for example, where the plaintiff has contributed to the pollution of a stream, or some other nuisance, along with one or more defendants. The damages rule as to avoidable consequences, stated in § 918, which denies recovery for the aggravation of personal injuries or other harm resulting from the plaintiff's failure to use due care to avoid it after the commission of the tort, frequently requires such apportionment, and is merely an application of the rule stated here. The apportionment is also possible in cases of the last clear chance, as where the plaintiff is struck and injured because of his own negligence, and after he is helpless the injury is aggravated, as for example by the defendant's negligent failure to remove his vehicle from the plaintiff's body.

Illustrations:

>9. Through the negligence of A, B, and C, water escapes from irrigation ditches on their land, and floods a part of C's farm. There is evidence that 50 per cent of the water came from A's ditch, 30 per cent from B's ditch, and 20 per cent from C's. On the basis of this evidence, A may be held liable for 50 per cent of the damages to C's farm, and B liable for 30 per cent.
>
>10. A negligently scratches B's arm with a nail. The wound becomes infected, and B negligently fails to consult a physician until the infection has seriously damaged the arm. A is not liable for the aggravation of the harm caused by B's negligence.
>
>11. A, who is negligently walking on the track of B Railroad, is struck by a negligently operated train, and his leg is injured. Knowing that A has been hit, the employees of B Company fail to use proper care to stop the train and extricate A, and as a result the injury to his leg is aggravated. Although B Railroad is not liable for A's original injury, it is subject to liability for the further damages resulting from the aggravation.

g. Burden of proof. As to the burden of proof, and the effect of failure to produce evidence justifying the apportionment, see § 433 B.

h. Exceptional cases. The rule stated in Clause (b) of Subsection (1) is one normally applicable to cases in which a reasonable basis can be found for the division of a single harm according to the contribution of each cause. Exceptional cases may, however, arise in which injustice to the plaintiff may result from an application of the rule. It may, for example, appear that one of two tortfeasors is so hopelessly insolvent that the plaintiff will never be able to collect from him the share of the damages allocated to him; or, in a jurisdiction in which actions for the particular tort do not survive the death of the defendant, he may have died after the infliction of the harm, but before suit has been instituted. In such cases the application of the rule stated in Clause (b) would mean that the innocent plaintiff would be forced to bear the share of the loss due to the defendant from whom he could not collect the damages, and the liability of the other tortfeasor would be reduced accordingly. Nothing in this Section, or in the Comments, is intended to say that the court may not, in a case where justice requires it, refuse to apply the rule stated in Clause (b).

Comment on Subsection (2):

i. Certain kinds of harm, by their very nature, are normally incapable of any logical, reasonable, or practical division. Death is that kind of harm, since it is impossible, except upon a purely arbitrary basis for the purpose of accomplishing the result, to say that one man has caused half of it and another the rest. The same is true of a broken leg, or any single wound, or the destruction of a house by fire, or the sinking of a barge. Such harms can be apportioned, if it all, only upon the basis of a prior reduction in value of what has been destroyed. By far the greater number of personal injuries, and of harms to tangible property, are thus normally single and indivisible. Where two or more causes combine to produce such a single result, incapable of division on any logical or reasonable basis, and each is a substantial factor in bringing about the harm, the courts have refused to make an arbitrary apportionment for its own sake, and each of the causes is charged with responsibility for the entire harm. The typical case is that of two negligently driven vehicles which collide and kill a bystander. The two drivers have not acted in concert, and the duties which they owe are separate and distinct, and may not be identical in character or scope; but the entire liability of each rests upon the obvious fact that each has caused the single result, and that no rational basis for division can be found.

Such entire liability is imposed where some of the causes are innocent, as where a fire set by the defendant is carried by a wind to burn the plaintiff's house; and it is imposed equally where two or more of the causes are culpable. It is imposed where either cause would have been sufficient in itself to bring about the result, as in the case of merging fires which burn a building. (See § 432(2).) It is imposed also where both are essential to the harm, as in the case of the vehicle collision suggested above.

It is not necessary that the misconduct of two or more tortfeasors be simultaneous. One defendant may create a situation upon which the other may act later to cause the harm. One may leave combustible material, and the other set it afire; one may leave a hole in the street, and the other drive into it. Whether there is liability in such a case may depend upon the effect of the intervening agency as a superseding cause (see Title C of this Chapter); but if the defendant is liable at all, he is liable for the entire indivisible harm which he has caused.

Illustrations:

12. Two automobiles, driven independently and negligently by A and B, collide. A's automobile is thrown against C, a

bystander, breaking C's leg. C may recover a judgment for the full amount of his damages against A or B, or both of them.

13. The motorman of the A Company's street car negligently drives it onto the tracks of the B Railroad in the path of an approaching train. B Company's crossing guard negligently lowers the crossing gates, shutting in the street car. C, a passenger, becomes frightened, and in seeking to escape negligently knocks down D, another passenger, breaking D's arm. D may recover a judgment for the full amount of his damages against A Company, or B Company, or C, or any two of them, or all of them.

14. A Company and B Company each negligently discharge oil into a stream. The oil floats on the surface and is ignited by a spark from an unknown source. The fire spreads to C's barn, and burns it down. C may recover a judgment for the full amount of his damages against A Company, or B Company, or both of them.

15. The same facts as in Illustration 14, except that C's cattle drink the water of the stream, are poisoned by the oil and die. The same result.

16. A and B, hunting deer, negligently but independently shoot in the direction of C. A's bullet wounds C in the arm, and B's bullet wounds him in the leg. C dies from the effect of both wounds. Under a wrongful death statute, C's administrator may recover the full amount of the damages for his death from A, or from B, or from both of them.

17. Two automobiles, negligently driven by A and B, collide. As a result of the collision A suffers a fractured skull. In the absence of a statute providing for apportionment, A is charged with the full amount of his own damages, and is barred by his contributory negligence from any recovery from B.

§ 433 B. Burden of Proof

(1) Except as stated in Subsections (2) and (3), the burden of proof that the tortious conduct of the defendant has caused the harm to the plaintiff is upon the plaintiff.

(2) Where the tortious conduct of two or more actors has combined to bring about harm to the plaintiff, and one or more of the actors seeks to limit his liability on the ground that the harm is capable of apportionment among them, the burden of proof as to the apportionment is upon each such actor.

(3) Where the conduct of two or more actors is tortious, and it is proved that harm has been caused to the plaintiff by only one of them, but there is uncertainty as to which

one has caused it, the burden is upon each such actor to prove that he has not caused the harm.

See Reporter's Notes.

Comment on Subsection (1):

a. Subsection (1) states the general rule as to the burden of proof on the issue of causation. As on other issues in civil cases, the plaintiff is required to produce evidence that the conduct of the defendant has been a substantial factor in bringing about the harm he has suffered, and to sustain his burden of proof by a preponderance of the evidence. This means that he must make it appear that it is more likely than not that the conduct of the defendant was a substantial factor in bringing about the harm. A mere possibility of such causation is not enough; and when the matter remains one of pure speculation and conjecture, or the probabilities are at best evenly balanced, it becomes the duty of the court to direct a verdict for the defendant.

Illustrations:

1. Through the negligence of A, B suffers a slight cut on his forehead from broken glass. Two years later a cancer develops at the point of the cut. In B's action against A, the medical evidence is that the cause of cancer is unknown; that it is possible that a cut may be a substantial factor in producing cancer, since in some comparatively rare cases cancers do develop at such a point of injury; that most cuts do not lead to cancer, and most cancers develop without any history of such injury; and that the effect of trauma in producing cancer is still a matter of medical speculation and uncertainty. On this evidence, B has not sustained his burden of proof as to A's causation of the cancer.

2. While A is driving his automobile, his three-year-old child falls out of the car, and lands on his head on the highway. Before A can stop his car and return to the child, it is run over by B's negligently driven automobile. In A's action against B for the death of the child, the evidence indicates that it is equally probable that the child was killed immediately by the fall and was dead when it was run over, or that it was still living, and was killed by B's car. On this evidence, A has not sustained his burden of proof that the death was caused by B.

b. The plaintiff is not, however, required to prove his case beyond a reasonable doubt. He is not required to eliminate entirely all possibility that the defendant's conduct was not a cause. It is enough that he introduces evidence from which reasonable men may conclude that it is more probable that the event was caused by the defendant than that it was not. The fact of causation is incapable of mathematical proof, since no man can say with absolute certainty what would have occurred if the defendant had acted otherwise. If, as a matter of ordinary experience, a particular act or omission might be expected to produce a particular result, and if that result has in fact followed, the conclusion may be justified that the causal relation exists. In drawing that conclusion, the triers of fact are permitted to draw upon ordinary human experience as to the probabilities of the case. Thus when a child is drowned in a swimming pool, no one can say with absolute certainty that a lifeguard would have saved him; but the common experience of the community permits the conclusion that the guard would more probably than not have done so, and hence that the absence of the guard has played a substantial part in bringing about the death of the child. Such questions are normally for the jury, and the court may seldom rule on them as matters of law.

Illustrations:

    3. The A Railroad Company fails to use reasonable care to light a steep and winding stairway leading from its waiting room to the train platform. B, an elderly and corpulent woman, is in the room waiting for a train. The attendant calls out the train. B hurries down the steps, and misses her footing in the dusk on the unlighted stair, falls, and is injured. On the basis of common experience that absence of light increases the likelihood of such a fall, and that people do not ordinarily fall on properly lighted stairs, it may be found that the absence of light was a substantial factor in causing the fall.

    4. The A University fails to provide a sufficient number of guards to police its campus. Juvenile hoodlums invade the campus, and shoot at pedestrians with airguns. B, a visitor on business at the University, is struck in the eye by a pellet fired from such a gun. On the basis of common experience that where there is proper policing such incidents usually do not occur, it may be found that the failure to provide enough guards has been a substantial factor in producing the injury.

    5. The town of X negligently fails to maintain a sloping sidewalk in reasonably safe condition. The defect consists of irregularities caused by lack of repair. During a storm, ice accumulates on the sidewalk. A, a pedestrian, while walking over the ice-covered slope, slips and falls. The fact that A might have slipped on the ice even if the sidewalk had been in good repair, and that the ice had not been so long on the sidewalk as to make it the duty of the town to remove it, does not prevent a finding that the negligent failure to maintain the sloping sidewalk in good repair was a substantial factor in causing the harm sustained by A.

Comment on Subsection (2):

    c. Subsection (2) states an exception to the general rule stated in Subsection (1). It arises where the tortious conduct of two or more actors combines to bring about harm to the plaintiff, and the harm which results is capable of apportionment among the causes producing it, as stated in § 433 A(1), and the Comments to that Section. A typical case is the pollution of a stream by a number of factories which discharge impurities into it. It is not essential to the application of the rule stated in Subsection (2) that all of the tortfeasors who will become liable for some part of the apportioned damages be joined as defendants in the action.

   d. The reason for the exceptional rule placing the burden of proof as to apportionment upon the defendant or defendants is the injustice of allowing a proved wrongdoer who has in fact caused harm to the plaintiff to escape liability merely because the harm which he has inflicted has combined with similar harm inflicted by other wrongdoers, and the nature of the harm itself has made it necessary that evidence be produced before it can be apportioned. In such a case the defendant may justly be required to assume the burden of producing that evidence, or if he is not able to do so, of bearing the full responsibility. As between the proved tortfeasor who has clearly caused some harm, and the entirely innocent plaintiff, any hardship due to lack of evidence as to the extent of the harm caused should fall upon the former.

Illustrations:

   6. The defendant A Company has a large steam pipe which runs through the book stacks of the public library of B City. Through the negligence of a workman employed by C Company, a contractor doing work on the library building, the steam pipe is broken and live steam escapes from it, damaging the books in the library. At the end of ten minutes A Company is notified of the break, and it then negligently delays for another thirty minutes in shutting off the steam. During that time the books are further damaged. In an action brought against A Company by B City for the harm to the books, A Company has the burden of proving the extent of the damages resulting from its delay, and if it does not do so is subject to liability for the entire damage.

   7. Through the negligence of defendants A, B, and C, water escapes from irrigation ditches on their land, and floods a part of D's farm. In D's action against A, B, and C, or any of them, each defendant has the burden of proving the extent to which his negligence contributed to the damage caused by the flood, and if he does not do so is subject to liability for the entire damage to the farm.

   8. Two automobiles negligently driven by A and B collide, and in the collision C, a passenger in A's car, suffers an injury to his right shoulder. Almost immediately afterward a car negligently driven by D drives into the wreckage, and in this second collision C's shoulder is further injured. As a result of one injury or the

other, or both, C's arm becomes paralyzed. The burden is upon D to prove that the injury inflicted by him did not cause the paralysis.

e. The cases thus far decided in which the rule stated in Subsection (2) has been applied all have involved a small number of tortfeasors, such as two or three. The possibility arises that there may be so large a number of actors, each of whom contributes a relatively small and insignificant part to the total harm, that the application of the rule may cause disproportionate hardship to defendants. Thus if a hundred factories each contribute a small, but still uncertain, amount of pollution to a stream, to hold each of them liable for the entire damage because he cannot show the amount of his contribution may perhaps be unjust. Such cases have not arisen, possibly because in such cases some evidence limiting the liability always has been in fact available.

Comment on Subsection (3):

f. Subsection (3) states a further exception to the general rule stated in Subsection (1). It arises where the conduct of two or more actors has been proved to be negligent or otherwise tortious, and it is also proved that the harm to the plaintiff has been caused by the conduct of only one of them, but there is uncertainty as to which one. In such a case the burden is upon each actor to prove that he did not cause the harm. As in the case of Subsection (2), the reason for the exception is the injustice of permitting proved wrongdoers, who among them have inflicted an injury upon the entirely innocent plaintiff, to escape liability merely because the nature of their conduct and the resulting harm has made it difficult or impossible to prove which of them has caused the harm.

g. The rule stated in Subsection (3) applies only where it is proved that each of two or more actors has acted tortiously, and that the harm has resulted from the conduct of some one of them. On these issues the plaintiff has still the burden of proof. The rule stated has no application to cases of alternative liability, where there is no proof that the conduct of more than one actor has been tortious at all. In such a case the plaintiff has the burden of proof both as to the tortious conduct and as to the causal relation.

h. The cases thus far decided in which the rule stated in Subsection (3) has been applied all have been cases in which all of the actors involved have been joined as defendants. All of these cases have involved conduct simultaneous in time, or substantially so, and all of them have involved conduct of substantially the same character, creating substantially the same risk of harm, on the part of each actor. It is possible that cases may arise in which some modification of the rule stated may be necessary because of complications arising from the fact that one of the actors involved is not or cannot be joined as a defendant, or because of the effect of lapse of time, or because of substantial differences in the character of the conduct of the actors or the risks which they have created. Since such cases have not arisen, and the situations which might arise are difficult to forecast, no attempt is made to deal with such problems in this Section. The rule stated in Subsection (3) is not intended to preclude possible modification if such situations call for it.

Illustrations:

9. A and B, independently hunting quail, both negligently shoot at the same time in the direction of C. C is struck in the face by a single shot, which could have come from either gun. In C's action against A and B, each of the defendants has the burden of proving that the shot did not come from his gun, and if he does not do so is subject to liability for the harm to C.

10. Over a period of three years A successively stores his furniture in warehouses operated by B, C, and D. At the end of that time A finds that his piano has been damaged by a large dent in one corner. The nature of the dent indicates that it was caused by careless handling on a single occasion. A has the burden of proving whether the dent was caused by the negligence of B, C, or D.

11. While A's automobile is stopped at an intersection, it is struck in the rear by B's negligently driven car. Immediately afterward C's negligently driven car strikes the rear of B's car, causing a second impact upon A's car. In one collision or the other, A sustains an injury to his neck and shoulder. In A's action against B and C, each defendant has the burden of proving that his conduct did not cause the injury.

* * *

TITLE C. SUPERSEDING CAUSE

§ 440. Superseding Cause Defined

A superseding cause is an act of a third person or other force which by its intervention prevents the actor from being liable for harm to another which his antecedent negligence is a substantial factor in bringing about.

Comment:

a. An intervening cause is defined in § 441. The rules which determine whether an intervening force is a superseding cause are stated in §§ 442–453 and Comments thereto.

b. A superseding cause relieves the actor from liability, irrespective of whether his antecedent negligence was or was not a substantial factor in bringing about the harm. Therefore, if in looking back from the harm and tracing the sequence of events by which it was produced, it is found that a superseding cause has operated, there is no need of determining whether the actor's antecedent conduct was or was not a substantial factor in bringing about the harm.

§ 441. Intervening Force Defined

(1) An intervening force is one which actively operates in producing harm to another after the actor's negligent act or omission has been committed.

(2) Whether the active operation of an intervening force prevents the actor's antecedent negligence from being a legal cause in bringing about harm to another is determined by the rules stated in §§ 442–453.

Comment on Subsection (1):

a. It is not necessary that an intervening force have been set in motion subsequent to the time when the actor's negligent conduct was committed. A force set in motion at an earlier time is an intervening force if it first operates after the actor has lost control of the situation and the actor neither knew nor should have known of its existence at the time of his negligent conduct. If the force should have been known by the actor to be existing before he has lost control of the situation, it is one of the circumstances in the light of which the negligence of the actor's subsequent conduct is to be determined.

b. "Active" and "passive" negligence. The cases in which the effect of the operation of an intervening force may be important in determining whether the negligent actor is liable for another's harm are usually, although not exclusively, cases in which the actor's negligence has created a situation harmless unless something further occurs, but capable of being made dangerous by the operation of some new force and in which the intervening force makes a potentially dangerous situation injurious. In such cases the actor's negligence is often called passive negligence, while the third person's negligence, which sets the intervening force in active operation, is called active negligence.

c. Dependent and independent intervening forces. An intervening force may be dependent or independent. A dependent, intervening force is one which operates in response to or is a reaction to the stimulus of a situation for which the actor has made himself responsible by his negligent conduct. An independent force is one the operation of which is not stimulated by a situation created by the actor's conduct. An act of a human being or animal is an independent force if the situation created by the actor has not influenced the doing of the act. Thus, if A carelessly exposes B to danger, the act of C in going to B's rescue, being C's reaction to B's peril, is a dependent intervening force. So too, if A carelessly allows his horse to run away, the act of B, who in attempting to check the speed of the horse diverts its course, is a dependent act, being done to check the harmful consequences of the defendant's negligence. On the other hand, if A so loads his truck that any slight jolt may cause a part of its heavy contents to fall and, while B is trying to pass the truck, his car skids and sideswipes the truck so slightly that, were the truck properly packed, no harm would be done by it, but because of the careless packing of the truck, it causes a heavy piece of machinery to fall on a pedestrian, the act of B is an independent intervening force.

Comment on Subsection (2):

d. The active operation of an intervening force may or may not be a superseding cause which relieves the actor from liability for another's harm occurring thereafter. Whether it has this effect is determined by the rules stated in §§ 442–453. A force due to an act of a third person which is wrongful toward the other who is harmed may be only a contributory factor in producing the harm. If so, both the actor and the third person are concurrently liable. This is true although the actor's conduct has ceased to operate actively and has merely created a condition which is made harmful by the operation of the intervening force set in motion by the third person's negligent or otherwise wrongful conduct. However, while there is concurrent liability, the two forces are not concurrent causes as that term is customarily used. To be a concurrent cause, the effects of the negligent conduct of both the actor and the third person must be in active and substantially simultaneous operation. (See § 439.)

§ 442. Considerations Important in Determining Whether an Intervening Force is a Superseding Cause

The following considerations are of importance in determining whether an intervening force is a superseding cause of harm to another:

(a) the fact that its intervention brings about harm different in kind from that which would otherwise have resulted from the actor's negligence;

(b) the fact that its operation or the consequences thereof appear after the event to be extraordinary rather than normal in view of the circumstances existing at the time of its operation;

(c) the fact that the intervening force is operating independently of any situation created by the actor's negligence, or, on the other hand, is or is not a normal result of such a situation;

(d) the fact that the operation of the intervening force is due to a third person's act or to his failure to act;

(e) the fact that the intervening force is due to an act of a third person which is wrongful toward the other and as such subjects the third person to liability to him;

(f) the degree of culpability of a wrongful act of a third person which sets the intervening force in motion.

Comment on Clause (a):

a. As to the statement in Clause (a), see § 451.

Comment on Clause (b):

b. As to the statement in Clause (b), see § 435(2) and Comments *c* and *d*.

Comment on Clause (c):

c. As to the statement in Clause (c), see §§ 443–449.

d. The words "situation created by the actor's negligence" are used to denote the fact that the actor's negligent conduct is a substantial factor in bringing about the situation and that, therefore, the actor would be liable for creating the situation if the situation were in itself a legal injury.

Comment on Clause (d):

e. As to the statement in Clause (d), see § 452.

Comment on Clause (e):

f. As to the statement in Clause (e), see §§ 447–449.

Comment on Clause (f):

g. As to the statement in Clause (f), compare § 447 with §§ 448 and 449.

* * *

§ 452. Third Person's Failure to Prevent Harm

(1) Except as stated in Subsection (2), the failure of a third person to act to prevent harm to another threatened by the actor's negligent conduct is not a superseding cause of such harm.

(2) Where, because of lapse of time or otherwise, the duty to prevent harm to another threatened by the actor's negligent conduct is found to have shifted from the actor to a third person, the failure of the third person to prevent such harm is a superseding cause.

See Reporter's Notes.

Comment:

a. The situation covered by both parts of this Section is that in which, after the original actor has been negligent and so has created an unreasonable risk of harm to another, a third person has the opportunity, by taking affirmative action, to avert the threatened harm. This implies that if such action were taken, it would prevent the negligence of the original actor from causing the harm which has in fact resulted.

Comment on Subsection (1):

b. Subsection (1) states the rule, applicable in the ordinary case, that the failure of the third person to act to prevent harm to the other threatened by the original actor's negligent conduct, is not a superseding cause of such harm, and so does not relieve the actor of liability for the harm which he has in fact caused. If the third person is under a duty to the other to take such action, his failure to do so will subject him to liability for his own negligence, which is concurrent with that of the actor, for the resulting harm which he has failed to prevent; but his failure to perform his duty does not relieve the original actor of liability for the results of his own negligence. A fortiori, where the third person is under no duty to the other to take any action, but merely has the opportunity to do so, his failure to act not only does not make him liable, but is not a superseding cause which will relieve the original actor of liability. As to the exceptional cases in which all responsibility has been shifted to the third person, see Comments on Subsection (2).

c. The rule stated in Subsection (1) applies not only where the third person makes no effort to avert the harm, but also where he makes such an effort, but the action which he takes is insufficient, or otherwise unsuccessful, in averting the harm.

Illustrations:

1. A, the owner of a house abutting on a street in B City, employs C to dig a trench across the highway to make a connection with a sewer. C does the work of replacing the sidewalk so negligently that it is left in a condition dangerous for travel. A knows of this, and B City is notified, but neither takes any steps to put the sidewalk into safe condition. Several weeks after C has completed the work, D, walking on the sidewalk at night, and without any negligence of his own, is hurt by a fall resulting from the bad condition of the sidewalk. The failure of A, and of B City, to have the sidewalk repaired makes both subject to liability to D, but is not a superseding cause relieving C of liability to D.

2. A, the truck driver of an oil company, in delivering kerosene and gasoline to B, a country storekeeper, puts gasoline into a tank used for the storage of kerosene. B demands that the gasoline be removed. A purports to do so, but carelessly fails to remove all

of the gasoline, so that the kerosene which he puts into the tank becomes unsafe for use. B sells part of the kerosene to C. D, the daughter of C, attempts to light a fire with the kerosene. Because of the presence of gasoline, an explosion ensues by which C is so severely injured that he dies. The fact that B was negligent in not seeing to it that the gasoline was effectively removed does not prevent A from being liable for the death of C.

3. The A Railroad Company negligently sets fire to the timber land of B, in a state in which, at common law or by statute, it is the duty of a landowner to use reasonable care to prevent a fire, no matter how set, from spreading to adjacent land. B, knowing that the fire has been set, either makes no effort to prevent its spread or fails to exercise reasonable care in making his efforts effectual. The fire spreads to the land of C. The failure of B to perform his duty is not a superseding cause which relieves the A Railroad Company from liability to C.

4. An automobile negligently driven by A strikes B, and leaves him on the highway, unconscious and slowly bleeding to death. C, a passing motorist, stops, looks over the situation, and decides to drive on without doing anything to aid B. B bleeds to death. Regardless of whether C is under any duty to B to render such aid, his failure to do so is not a superseding cause which will relieve A of liability for the death of B.

Comment on Subsection (2):

d. Subsection (2) covers the exceptional cases in which, because the duty, and hence the entire responsibility for the situation, has been shifted to a third person, the original actor is relieved of liability for the result which follows from the operation of his own negligence. The shifted responsibility means in effect that the duty, or obligation, of the original actor in the matter has terminated, and has been replaced by that of the third person.

e. One way in which the responsibility may be shifted is by express agreement between the actor and the third person. By contract, by gratuitous promise, or by fair implication from what is agreed, it may be understood that the third person has taken over full responsibility for the situation, and that the actor is relieved of his obligation. In many cases this is not possible, since there are duties and obligations which cannot be delegated or shifted to another; and where the personal safety of third persons is threatened, it is probably true that normally any duty to exercise reasonable care for their protection cannot be shifted. There are, however, exceptional cases, to which Subsection (2) applies. It is beyond the scope of this Restatement to attempt to state when the duty can be shifted, and when it cannot. Assuming, however, that there is no rule of law, and no reason of policy to prevent its transfer, and that there is clear understanding that it is to be shifted, the original actor can be relieved of his duty; and in such a case the failure of the one who assumes it to act to prevent the threatened harm becomes a superseding cause.

Illustrations:

5. A is one of a crew of workmen employed by a construction company to excavate a trench in the public highway. One of A's duties, at the close of a day's work, is to set out barriers and warning flares for the protection of travelers on the highway. A forgets to do so before going home at the end of the day. When halfway home he remembers, and returns to the scene, intending to make good his neglect. There he meets B, the foreman of the company, who tells him to go on home, promising that he, B, will look after the barriers and flares. A goes home. B in turn forgets, and the trench is left without guard, lights, or warning. During the night C, a traveler on the highway, drives into the trench and is injured. A is not liable to C.

6. The A Electric Company, under contract with B Village, constructs an electric transformer pole, and turns it over to the Village. The contract expressly provides that the Village assumes all responsibility for inspection, care, and maintenance of the pole, and for its condition after it is turned over. Through the negligence of A Company, two wires on the pole are set too close together, so that high winds, which are not uncommon in the vicinity, rub the wires together and wear off the insulation. B Village does nothing to inspect or maintain the pole. At the end of a year and a half, the insulation on the wires is worked through, and as a result a current of 2300 volts comes over the wire of a telephone while C is using it. C is injured. A Electric Company is not liable to C.

7. A leases a building to B for use as a motion picture theatre, to which the public will be admitted. The building is at the time in a defective and dangerous condition. The lease expressly provides that B will repair it and put it into safe condition for the admission of the public, and that the public will not be admitted until this has been done. B fails to make the necessary repairs, and opens the theatre without making it safe. C, a member of the public entering the theatre, is injured by the collapse of a defective stairway. A is not liable to C.

8. The same facts as in Illustration 7, except that the lease provides only that B will make the necessary repairs, without any provision that the public will be excluded until this is done. The full responsibility is not shifted to B, and A is not relieved of liability to C.

§ 452

f. Even in the absence of any contract or agreement, the circumstances may be such that the court will find that all duty and responsibility for the prevention of the harm has passed to the third person. It is apparently impossible to state any comprehensive rule as to when such a decision will be made. Various factors will enter into it. Among them are the degree of danger and the magnitude of the risk of harm, the character and position of the third person who is to take the responsibility, his knowledge of the danger and the likelihood that he will or will not exercise proper care, his relation to the plaintiff or to the defendant, the lapse of time, and perhaps other considerations. The most that can be stated here is that when, by reason of the interplay of such factors, the court finds that full responsibility for control of the situation and prevention of the threatened harm has passed to the third person, his failure to act is then a superseding cause, which will relieve the original actor of liability.

Illustrations:

9. The A Railroad negligently turns over to its connecting carrier B Railroad a freight car, the door of which is in defective and dangerous condition. B Railroad operates the car on its own line over a period of six months, during which time it negligently fails to inspect the car and discover the defect. At the end of that time it turns the car over to C Railroad. D, who is an employee of C Railroad, without any negligence of his own, is injured when the door falls on him. A Railroad is not liable to D.

10. A manufactures and sells an automobile with a defective hood catch, creating the danger that on a rough highway the hood will fly up and obscure the vision of the driver. The car is sold by a dealer to B. A is notified of the defect in its car and the danger, and sends out to its dealers a new safety catch for installation in all such cars, in order to remedy the defect. The dealer calls B, and offers him the new safety catch, warning him of the danger and urging him to install it. B refuses to do so. After driving the car for a year, B sells it to C, who is ignorant of the danger. While C is driving the car, the hood flies up, and C is injured. A is not liable to C.

UNIFORM COMMERCIAL CODE SELECTED SECTIONS *

Table of Jurisdictions Adopting Code.

ARTICLE 1. GENERAL PROVISIONS
PART 1. SHORT TITLE, CONSTRUCTION, APPLICATION AND SUBJECT MATTER OF THE ACT

Section
1-101. Short Title.
1-102. Purposes; Rules of Construction; Variation by Agreement.
1-103. Supplementary General Principles of Law Applicable.
1-104. Construction Against Implicit Repeal.
1-105. Territorial Application of the Act; Parties' Power to Choose Applicable Law.
1-106. Remedies to Be Liberally Administered.
1-107. Waiver or Renunciation of Claim or Right After Breach.

PART 2. GENERAL DEFINITIONS AND PRINCIPLES OF INTERPRETATION

1-201. General Definitions.
1-203. Obligation of Good Faith.
1-204. Time; Reasonable Time; "Seasonably".
1-205. Course of Dealing and Usage of Trade.

ARTICLE 2. SALES
PART 1. SHORT TITLE, GENERAL CONSTRUCTION AND SUBJECT MATTER

2-101. Short Title.
2-102. Scope; Certain Security and Other Transactions Excluded From This Article.
2-103. Definitions and Index of Definitions.
2-104. Definitions: "Merchant"; "Between Merchants"; "Financing Agency".
2-105. Definitions: Transferability; "Goods"; "Future" Goods; "Lot"; "Commercial Unit".
2-106. Definitions: "Contract"; "Agreement"; "Contract for Sale"; "Sale"; "Present Sale"; "Conforming" to Contract; "Termination"; "Cancellation".
2-107. Goods to Be Severed From Realty: Recording.

PART 2. FORM, FORMATION AND READJUSTMENT OF CONTRACT

2-201. Formal Requirements; Statute of Frauds.
2-202. Final Written Expression: Parol or Extrinsic Evidence.

* Copyright © 1987 by The American Law Institute and the National Conference of Commissioners on Uniform State Laws. Reprinted with permission of the Permanent Editorial Board for the Uniform Commercial Code.

UNIFORM COMMERCIAL CODE

Section
- 2–204. Formation in General.
- 2–206. Offer and Acceptance in Formation of Contract.
- 2–207. Additional Terms in Acceptance or Confirmation.
- 2–208. Course of Performance or Practical Construction.
- 2–209. Modification, Rescission and Waiver.

PART 3. GENERAL OBLIGATION AND CONSTRUCTION OF CONTRACT

- 2–301. General Obligations of Parties.
- 2–302. Unconscionable Contract or Clause.
- 2–303. Allocation or Division of Risks.
- 2–312. Warranty of Title and Against Infringement; Buyer's Obligation Against Infringement.
- 2–313. Express Warranties by Affirmation, Promise, Description, Sample.
- 2–314. Implied Warranty: Merchantability; Usage of Trade.
- 2–315. Implied Warranty: Fitness for Particular Purpose.
- 2–316. Exclusion or Modification of Warranties.
- 2–317. Cumulation and Conflict of Warranties Express or Implied.
- 2–318. Third Party Beneficiaries of Warranties Express or Implied.
- 2–327. Special Incidents of Sale on Approval and Sale or Return.
- 2–328. Sale by Auction.

* * *

PART 5. PERFORMANCE

- 2–503. Manner of Seller's Tender of Delivery.
- 2–507. Effect of Seller's Tender; Delivery on Condition.
- 2–508. Cure by Seller of Improper Tender or Delivery; Replacement.
- 2–510. Effect of Breach on Risk of Loss.
- 2–511. Tender of Payment by Buyer; Payment by Check.
- 2–512. Payment by Buyer Before Inspection.
- 2–513. Buyer's Right to Inspection of Goods.
- 2–515. Preserving Evidence of Goods in Dispute.

PART 6. BREACH, REPUDIATION AND EXCUSE

- 2–601. Buyer's Rights on Improper Delivery.
- 2–602. Manner and Effect of Rightful Rejection.
- 2–605. Waiver of Buyer's Objections by Failure to Particularize.
- 2–606. What Constitutes Acceptance of Goods.
- 2–607. Effect of Acceptance; Notice of Breach; Burden of Establishing Breach After Acceptance; Notice of Claim or Litigation to Person Answerable Over.
- 2–608. Revocation of Acceptance in Whole or in Part.

PART 7. REMEDIES

- 2–711. Buyer's Remedies in General; Buyer's Security Interest in Rejected Goods.
- 2–714. Buyer's Damages for Breach in Regard to Accepted Goods.
- 2–715. Buyer's Incidental and Consequential Damages.
- 2–716. Buyer's Right to Specific Performance or Replevin.
- 2–717. Deduction of Damages From the Price.
- 2–718. Liquidation or Limitation of Damages; Deposits.

Section
2–719. Contractual Modification or Limitation of Remedy.
2–720. Effect of "Cancellation" or "Rescission" on Claims for Antecedent Breach.
2–721. Remedies for Fraud.
2–725. Statute of Limitations in Contracts for Sale.

UNIFORM COMMERCIAL CODE
Table of Jurisdictions Wherein Code Has Been Adopted

Jurisdiction	Laws	Effective Date	Statutory Citation
Alabama [1]	1965, Act No. 549	1-1-1967	Code 1975, §§ 7-1-101 to 7-11-108
Alaska [1]	1962, c. 114	1-1-1963	AS §§ 45.01.101 to 45.09.507
Arizona [1]	1967, c. 3	1-1-1968	A.R.S. §§ 47-1101 to 47-11107
Arkansas [2]	1961, Act No. 185	1-1-1962	Code 1987, §§ 4-1-101 to 4-10-104
California [4]	Stats.1963, c. 819	1-1-1965	West's Ann.Cal.Com.Code, §§ 1101 to 15104
Colorado [2]	1965, c. 330	7-1-1966	C.R.S. §§ 4-1-101 to 4-11-102
Connecticut [2]	1959, No. 133	10-1-1961	C.G.S.A. §§ 42a-1-101 to 42a-10-109
Delaware [2]	1966, c. 349	7-1-1967	6 Del.C. §§ 1-101 to 11-109
Dist. of Columbia [1]	P.L. 88-243	1-1-1965	D.C.Code 1981, §§ 28:1-101 to 28:11-108
Florida [2]	1965, c. 65-254	1-1-1967	West's F.S.A. §§ 671.101 to 680.111
Georgia [1]	1962, Act 713	1-1-1964	O.C.G.A. §§ 11-1-101 to 11-11-104
Guam [1]	P.L. 13-160	1-1-1977	13 G.C.A. §§ 1101 to 10104
Hawaii [2]	1965, No. 208	1-1-1967	HRS §§ 490:1-101 to 490:11-108
Idaho [2]	1967, c. 161	1-1-1968	I.C. §§ 28-1-101 to 28-10-104
Illinois [2]	1961, p. 2101	7-2-1962	S.H.A. ch. 26, ¶¶ 1-101 to 11-108
Indiana [2]	1963, c. 317	7-1-1964	West's A.I.C. 26-1-1-101 to 26-1-10-104
Iowa [1]	1965, (61 G.A.) c. 413	7-4-1966	I.C.A. §§ 554.1101 to 554.-11109
Kansas [2]	1965, c. 564	1-1-1966	K.S.A. 84-1-101 to 84-10-102
Kentucky [2]	1958, c. 77	7-1-1960	KRS 355.1-101 to 355.11-108
Louisiana [3]	1974, No. 92	1-1-1975	LSA-R.S. 10:1-101 to 10:5-117
	1978, No. 164	6-29-1978	LSA-R.S. 10:7-101 to 10:7-701
	1978, No. 165	6-29-1978	LSA-R.S. 10:8-101 to 10:8-501
	1988, No. 528	7-1-1989	LSA-R.S. 10:9-101 to 10:9-508
Maine [2]	1963, c. 362	12-31-1964	11 M.R.S.A. §§ 1-101 to 10-108
Maryland [2]	1963, c. 538	2-1-1964	Code, Commercial Law, §§ 1-101 to 10-112
Massachusetts [2]	1957, c. 765	10-1-1958	M.G.L.A. c. 106, §§ 1-101 to 9-507
Michigan [2]	1962, P.A. 174	1-1-1964	M.C.L.A. §§ 440.1101 to 440.-11102

Jurisdiction	Laws	Effective Date	Statutory Citation
Minnesota [2]	1965, c. 811	7-1-1966	M.S.A. §§ 336.1-101 to 336.-11-108
Mississippi [1]	1966, c. 316	3-31-1968	Code 1972, §§ 75-1-101 to 75-11-108
Missouri [1]	1963, p. 503	7-1-1965	V.A.M.S. §§ 400.1-101 to 400.11-107
Montana [2]	1963, c. 264	1-2-1965	MCA 30-1-101 to 30-9-511
Nebraska [1]	1963, c. 544	9-2-1965	Neb.U.C.C. §§ 1-101 to 10-104
Nevada [2]	1965, c. 353	3-1-1967	N.R.S. 104.1101 to 104.9507
New Hampshire [2]	1959, c. 247	7-1-1961	RSA 382-A:1-101 to 382-A:9-507
New Jersey [1]	1961, c. 120	1-1-1963	N.J.S.A. 12A:1-101 to 12A:11-108
New Mexico [2]	1961, c. 96	1-1-1962	NMSA 1978, §§ 55-1-101 to 55-12-108
New York [2]	1962, c. 553	9-27-1964	McKinney's Uniform Commercial Code, §§ 1-101 to 13-105
North Carolina [1]	1965, c. 700	7-1-1967	G.S. §§ 25-1-101 to 25-11-108
North Dakota [2]	1965, c. 296	7-1-1966	NDCC 41-01-02 to 41-09-53
Ohio [2]	1961, p. 13	7-1-1962	R.C. §§ 1301.01 to 1309.50
Oklahoma [4]	1961, p. 70	1-1-1963	12A Okl.St.Ann. §§ 1-101 to 11-107
Oregon [4]	1961, c. 726	9-1-1963	ORS 71.1010 to 79.6010
Pennsylvania [1]	1953, P.L. 3	7-1-1954	13 Pa.C.S.A. §§ 1101 to 9507
Rhode Island [2]	1960, c. 147	1-2-1962	Gen.Laws 1956, §§ 6A-1-101 to 6A-9-507
South Carolina [1]	1966, c. 1065	1-1-1968	Code 1976, §§ 36-1-101 to 36-11-108
South Dakota [2]	1966, c. 150	7-1-1967	SDCL 57A-1-101 to 57A-11-108
Tennessee [2]	1963, c. 81	7-1-1964	T.C.A. §§ 47-1-101 to 47-9-607
Texas [2]	1965, c. 721	7-1-1966	V.T.C.A., Bus. & C. §§ 1.101 to 11.108
Utah [1]	1965, c. 154	1-1-1966	U.C.A.1953, 70A-1-101 to 70A-11-108
Vermont	1966, No. 29	1-1-1967	9A V.S.A. §§ 1-101 to 9-607
Virgin Islands	1965, No. 1299	7-1-1965	11A V.I.C. §§ 1-101 to 9-507

[1] Adopted 1972 Revision of Article 9.
[2] Adopted 1977 Revision of Article 8, and 1972 Revision of Article 9.
[3] Louisiana adopted only Articles 1, 3, 4, 5, 7, pre-1977 version of Article 8 and 1972 Revision of Article 9.
[4] Adopted new Article 2A-Leases, the 1977 Revision of Article 8 and the 1972 Revision of Article 9. [Note that the effective date of Article 2A enactment in California is Jan. 1, 1990.]

ARTICLE 1

GENERAL PROVISIONS

PART 1

SHORT TITLE, CONSTRUCTION, APPLICATION AND SUBJECT MATTER OF THE ACT

§ 1-101. Short Title

This Act shall be known and may be cited as Uniform Commercial Code.

* * *

§ 1-102. Purposes; Rules of Construction; Variation by Agreement

(1) This Act shall be liberally construed and applied to promote its underlying purposes and policies.

(2) Underlying purposes and policies of this Act are

(a) to simplify, clarify and modernize the law governing commercial transactions;

(b) to permit the continued expansion of commercial practices through custom, usage and agreement of the parties;

(c) to make uniform the law among the various jurisdictions.

(3) The effect of provisions of this Act may be varied by agreement, except as otherwise provided in this Act and except that the obligations of good faith, diligence, reasonableness and care prescribed by this Act may not be disclaimed by agreement but the parties may by agreement determine the standards by which the performance of such obligations is to be measured if such standards are not manifestly unreasonable.

(4) The presence in certain provisions of this Act of the words "unless otherwise agreed" or words of similar import does not imply that the effect of other provisions may not be varied by agreement under subsection (3).

(5) In this Act unless the context otherwise requires

(a) words in the singular number include the plural, and in the plural include the singular;

(b) words of the masculine gender include the feminine and the neuter, and when the sense so indicates words of the neuter gender may refer to any gender.

* * *

§ 1-103. Supplementary General Principles of Law Applicable

Unless displaced by the particular provisions of this Act, the principles of law and equity, including the law merchant and the law relative to capacity to contract, principal and agent, estoppel, fraud, misrepresentation, duress, coercion, mistake, bankruptcy, or other validating or invalidating cause shall supplement its provisions.

* * *

§ 1–104. Construction Against Implicit Repeal

This Act being a general act intended as a unified coverage of its subject matter, no part of it shall be deemed to be impliedly repealed by subsequent legislation if such construction can reasonably be avoided.

* * *

§ 1–105. Territorial Application of the Act; Parties' Power to Choose Applicable Law

(1) Except as provided hereafter in this section, when a transaction bears a reasonable relation to this state and also to another state or nation the parties may agree that the law either of this state or of such other state or nation shall govern their rights and duties. Failing such agreement this Act applies to transactions bearing an appropriate relation to this state.

* * *

Official Comment

Prior Uniform Statutory Provision: None.

Purposes:

1. Subsection (1) states affirmatively the right of the parties to a multi-state transaction or a transaction involving foreign trade to choose their own law. That right is subject to the firm rules stated in the five sections listed in subsection (2), and is limited to jurisdictions to which the transaction bears a "reasonable relation." In general, the test of "reasonable relation" is similar to that laid down by the Supreme Court in Seeman v. Philadelphia Warehouse Co., 274 U.S. 403, 47 S.Ct. 626, 71 L.Ed. 1123 (1927). Ordinarily the law chosen must be that of a jurisdiction where a significant enough portion of the making or performance of the contract is to occur or occurs. But an agreement as to choice of law may sometimes take effect as a shorthand expression of the intent of the parties as to matters governed by their agreement, even though the transaction has no significant contact with the jurisdiction chosen.

2. Where there is no agreement as to the governing law, the Act is applicable to any transaction having an "appropriate" relation to any state which enacts it. Of course, the Act applies to any transaction which takes place in its entirety in a state which has enacted the Act. But the mere fact that suit is brought in a state does not make it appropriate to apply the substantive law of that state. Cases where a relation to the enacting state is not "appropriate" include, for example, those where the parties have clearly contracted on the basis of some other law, as where the law of the place of contracting and the law of the place of contemplated performance are the same and are contrary to the law under the Code.

3. Where a transaction has significant contacts with a state which has enacted the Act and also with other jurisdictions, the question what relation is "appropriate" is left to judicial decision. In deciding that question, the court is not strictly bound by precedents established in other contexts. Thus a conflict-of-laws decision refusing to apply a purely local statute or rule of law to a particular mul-

ti-state transaction may not be valid precedent for refusal to apply the Code in an analogous situation. Application of the Code in such circumstances may be justified by its comprehensiveness, by the policy of uniformity, and by the fact that it is in large part a reformulation and restatement of the law merchant and of the understanding of a business community which transcends state and even national boundaries. Compare Global Commerce Corp. v. Clark–Babbitt Industries, Inc., 239 F.2d 716, 719 (2d Cir.1956). In particular, where a transaction is governed in large part by the Code, application of another law to some detail of performance because of an accident of geography may violate the commercial understanding of the parties.

4. The Act does not attempt to prescribe choice-of-law rules for states which do not enact it, but this section does not prevent application of the Act in a court of such a state. Common-law choice of law often rests on policies of giving effect to agreements and of uniformity of result regardless of where suit is brought. To the extent that such policies prevail, the relevant considerations are similar in such a court to those outlined above.

* * *

§ 1–106. Remedies to Be Liberally Administered

(1) The remedies provided by this Act shall be liberally administered to the end that the aggrieved party may be put in as good a position as if the other party had fully performed but neither consequential or special nor penal damages may be had except as specifically provided in this Act or by other rule of law.

(2) Any right or obligation declared by this Act is enforceable by action unless the provision declaring it specifies a different and limited effect.

Official Comment

Prior Uniform Statutory Provision: Subsection (1)—none; Subsection (2)—Section 72, Uniform Sales Act.

Changes: Reworded.

Purposes of Changes and New Matter: Subsection (1) is intended to effect three things:

1. First, to negate the unduly narrow or technical interpretation of some remedial provisions of prior legislation by providing that the remedies in this Act are to be liberally administered to the end stated in the section. Second, to make it clear that compensatory damages are limited to compensation. They do not include consequential or special damages, or penal damages; and the Act elsewhere makes it clear that damages must be minimized. Cf. Sections 1–203, 2–706(1), and 2–712(2). The third purpose of subsection (1) is to reject any doctrine that damages must be calculable with mathematical accuracy. Compensatory damages are often at best approximate: they have to be proved with whatever definiteness and accuracy the facts permit, but no more. Cf. Section 2–204(3).

2. Under subsection (2) any right or obligation described in this Act is enforceable by court action, even though no remedy may be expressly provided, unless a particular provision specifies a different and limited effect. Whether specific performance or other equitable relief is available is determined not by this section but by spe-

cific provisions and by supplementary principles. Cf. Sections 1-103, 2-716.

3. "Consequential" or "special" damages and "penal" damages are not defined in terms in the Code, but are used in the sense given them by the leading cases on the subject.

§ 1–107. Waiver or Renunciation of Claim or Right After Breach

Any claim or right arising out of an alleged breach can be discharged in whole or in part without consideration by a written waiver or renunciation signed and delivered by the aggrieved party.

Official Comment

Prior Uniform Statutory Provision: Compare Section 1, Uniform Written Obligations Act; Sections 119(3), 120(2) and 122, Uniform Negotiable Instruments Law.

Purposes:

This section makes consideration unnecessary to the effective renunciation or waiver of rights or claims arising out of an alleged breach of a commercial contract where such renunciation is in writing and signed and delivered by the aggrieved party. Its provisions, however, must be read in conjunction with the section imposing an obligation of good faith. (Section 1–203). There may, of course, also be an oral renunciation or waiver sustained by consideration but subject to Statute of Frauds provisions and to the section of Article 2 on Sales dealing with the modification of signed writings (Section 2–209). As is made express in the latter section this Act fully recognizes the effectiveness of waiver and estoppel.

* * *

PART 2

GENERAL DEFINITIONS AND PRINCIPLES OF INTERPRETATION

§ 1–201. General Definitions

Subject to additional definitions contained in the subsequent Articles of this Act which are applicable to specific Articles or Parts thereof, and unless the context otherwise requires, in this Act:

(1) "Action" in the sense of a judicial proceeding includes recoupment, counterclaim, set-off, suit in equity and any other proceedings in which rights are determined.

(2) "Aggrieved party" means a party entitled to resort to a remedy.

(3) "Agreement" means the bargain of the parties in fact as found in their language or by implication from other circumstances including course of dealing or usage of trade or course of performance as provided in this Act (Sections 1–205 and 2–208). Whether an agreement has legal consequences is determined by the provisions of this Act, if

applicable; otherwise by the law of contracts (Section 1-103). (Compare "Contract".)

* * *

(10) "Conspicuous": A term or clause is conspicuous when it is so written that a reasonable person against whom it is to operate ought to have noticed it. A printed heading in capitals (as: NON-NEGOTIABLE BILL OF LADING) is conspicuous. Language in the body of a form is "conspicuous" if it is in larger or other contrasting type or color. But in a telegram any stated term is "conspicuous". Whether a term or clause is "conspicuous" or not is for decision by the court.

(11) "Contract" means the total legal obligation which results from the parties' agreement as affected by this Act and any other applicable rules of law. (Compare "Agreement".)

* * *

(13) "Defendant" includes a person in the position of defendant in a cross-action or counterclaim.

* * *

(16) "Fault" means wrongful act, omission or breach.

* * *

(19) "Good faith" means honesty in fact in the conduct or transaction concerned.

* * *

(25) A person has "notice" of a fact when

(a) he has actual knowledge of it; or

(b) he has received a notice or notification of it; or

(c) from all the facts and circumstances known to him at the time in question he has reason to know that it exists.

A person "knows" or has "knowledge" of a fact when he has actual knowledge of it. "Discover" or "learn" or a word or phrase of similar import refers to knowledge rather than to reason to know. The time and circumstances under which a notice or notification may cease to be effective are not determined by this Act.

(26) A person "notifies" or "gives" a notice or notification to another by taking such steps as may be reasonably required to inform the other in ordinary course whether or not such other actually comes to know of it. A person "receives" a notice or notification when

(a) it comes to his attention; or

§ 1-201 *UNIFORM COMMERCIAL CODE*

(b) it is duly delivered at the place of business through which the contract was made or at any other place held out by him as the place for receipt of such communications.

(27) Notice, knowledge or a notice or notification received by an organization is effective for a particular transaction from the time when it is brought to the attention of the individual conducting that transaction, and in any event from the time when it would have been brought to his attention if the organization had exercised due diligence. An organization exercises due diligence if it maintains reasonable routines for communicating significant information to the person conducting the transaction and there is reasonable compliance with the routines. Due diligence does not require an individual acting for the organization to communicate information unless such communication is part of his regular duties or unless he has reason to know of the transaction and that the transaction would be materially affected by the information.

(28) "Organization" includes a corporation, government or governmental subdivision or agency, business trust, estate, trust, partnership or association, two or more persons having a joint or common interest, or any other legal or commercial entity.

(29) "Party", as distinct from "third party", means a person who has engaged in a transaction or made an agreement within this Act.

(30) "Person" includes an individual or an organization (See Section 1-102).

(31) "Presumption" or "presumed" means that the trier of fact must find the existence of the fact presumed unless and until evidence is introduced which would support a finding of its non-existence.

(32) "Purchase" includes taking by sale, discount, negotiation, mortgage, pledge, lien, issue or re-issue, gift or any other voluntary transaction creating an interest in property.

(33) "Purchaser" means a person who takes by purchase.

(34) "Remedy" means any remedial right to which an aggrieved party is entitled with or without resort to a tribunal.

(35) "Representative" includes an agent, an officer of a corporation or association, and a trustee, executor or administrator of an estate, or any other person empowered to act for another.

(36) "Rights" includes remedies.

* * *

Official Comment

* * *

10. "Conspicuous". New. This is intended to indicate some of the methods of making a term attention-calling. But the test is whether attention can reasonably be expected to be called to it.

* * *

19. "Good faith". See Section 76(2), Uniform Sales Act; Section 58(2), Uniform Warehouse Receipts Act; Section 53(2), Uniform Bills of Lading Act; Section 22(2), Uniform Stock Transfer Act. "Good faith", whenever it is used in the Code, means at least what is here stated. In certain Articles, by specific provision, additional requirements are made applicable. See, e.g., Secs. 2–103(1)(b), 7–404. To illustrate, in the Article on Sales, Section 2–103, good faith is expressly defined as including in the case of a merchant observance of reasonable commercial standards of fair dealing in the trade, so that throughout that Article wherever a merchant appears in the case an inquiry into his observance of such standards is necessary to determine his good faith.

* * *

25. "Notice". New. Compare N.I.L. Sec. 56. Under the definition a person has notice when he has received a notification of the fact in question. But by the last sentence the act leaves open the time and circumstances under which notice or notification may cease to be effective. Therefore such cases as Graham v. White–Phillips Co., 296 U.S. 27, 56 S.Ct. 21, 80 L.Ed. 20 (1935), are not overruled.

26. "Notifies". New. This is the word used when the essential fact is the proper dispatch of the notice, not its receipt. Compare "Send". When the essential fact is the other party's receipt of the notice, that is stated. The second sentence states when a notification is received.

27. New. This makes clear that reason to know, knowledge, or a notification, although "received" for instance by a clerk in Department A of an organization, is effective for a transaction conducted in Department B only from the time when it was or should have been communicated to the individual conducting that transaction.

28. "Organization". This is the definition of every type of entity or association, excluding an individual, acting as such. Definitions of "person" were included in Section 191, Uniform Negotiable Instruments Law; Section 76, Uniform Sales Act; Section 58, Uniform Warehouse Receipts Act; Section 53, Uniform Bills of Lading Act; Section 22, Uniform Stock Transfer Act; Section 1, Uniform Trust Receipts Act. The definition of "organization" given here includes a number of entities or associations not specifically mentioned in prior definition of "person", namely, government, governmental subdivision or agency, business trust, trust and estate.

* * *

* * *

§ 1–203. Obligation of Good Faith

Every contract or duty within this Act imposes an obligation of good faith in its performance or enforcement.

Official Comment

Prior Uniform Statutory Provision: None.

Purposes:

This section sets forth a basic principle running throughout this Act. The principle involved is that in commercial transactions good faith is required in the performance and enforcement of all agreements or duties.

***

It is to be noted that under the Sales Article definition of good faith (Section 2–103), contracts made by a merchant have incorporated in them the explicit standard not only of honesty in fact (Section 1–201), but also of observance by the merchant of reasonable commercial standards of fair dealing in the trade.

***

§ 1–204. Time; Reasonable Time; "Seasonably"

(1) Whenever this Act requires any action to be taken within a reasonable time, any time which is not manifestly unreasonable may be fixed by agreement.

(2) What is a reasonable time for taking any action depends on the nature, purpose and circumstances of such action.

(3) An action is taken "seasonably" when it is taken at or within the time agreed or if no time is agreed at or within a reasonable time.

Official Comment

Prior Uniform Statutory Provision: None.

Purposes:

1. Subsection (1) recognizes that nothing is stronger evidence of a reasonable time than the fixing of such time by a fair agreement between the parties. However, provision is made for disregarding a clause which whether by inadvertence or overreaching fixes a time so unreasonable that it amounts to eliminating all remedy under the contract. The parties are not required to fix the most reasonable time but may fix any time which is not obviously unfair as judged by the time of contracting.

2. Under the section, the agreement which fixes the time need not be part of the main agreement, but may occur separately. Notice also that under the definition of "agreement" (Section 1–201) the circumstances of the transaction, including course of dealing or usages of trade or course of performance may be material. On the question what is a reasonable time these matters will often be important.

***

§ 1–205. Course of Dealing and Usage of Trade

(1) A course of dealing is a sequence of previous conduct between the parties to a particular transaction which is fairly to be regarded as establishing a common basis of understanding for interpreting their expressions and other conduct.

(2) A usage of trade is any practice or method of dealing having such regularity of observance in a place, vocation or trade as to justify an expectation that it will be observed with respect to the transaction in question. The existence and scope of such a usage are to be proved as facts. If it is established that such a usage is embodied in a written trade code or similar writing the interpretation of the writing is for the court.

(3) A course of dealing between parties and any usage of trade in the vocation or trade in which they are engaged or of which they are or should be aware give particular meaning to and supplement or qualify terms of an agreement.

(4) The express terms of an agreement and an applicable course of dealing or usage of trade shall be construed wherever reasonable as consistent with each other; but when such construction is unreasonable express terms control both course of dealing and usage of trade and course of dealing controls usage of trade.

(5) An applicable usage of trade in the place where any part of performance is to occur shall be used in interpreting the agreement as to that part of the performance.

(6) Evidence of a relevant usage of trade offered by one party is not admissible unless and until he has given the other party such notice as the court finds sufficient to prevent unfair surprise to the latter.

Official Comment

Prior Uniform Statutory Provision: No such general provision but see Sections 9(1), 15(5), 18(2), and 71, Uniform Sales Act.

Purposes: This section makes it clear that:

1. This Act rejects both the "lay-dictionary" and the "conveyancer's" reading of a commercial agreement. Instead the meaning of the agreement of the parties is to be determined by the language used by them and by their action, read and interpreted in the light of commercial practices and other surrounding circumstances. The measure and background for interpretation are set by the commercial context, which may explain and supplement even the language of a formal or final writing.

2. Course of dealing under subsection (1) is restricted, literally, to a sequence of conduct between the parties previous to the agreement. However, the provisions of the Act on course of performance make it clear that a sequence of conduct after or under the agreement may have equivalent meaning. (Section 2-208.)

3. "Course of dealing" may enter the agreement either by explicit provisions of the agreement or by tacit recognition.

4. This Act deals with "usage of trade" as a factor in reaching the commercial meaning of the agreement which the parties have made. The language used is to be interpreted as meaning what it may fairly be expected to mean to parties involved in the particular commercial transaction in a given locality or in a given vocation or trade. By adopting in this context the term "usage of trade" this Act expresses its intent to reject those cases which see evidence of "custom" as representing an effort to displace or negate "established rules of law." A distinction is to be drawn between mandatory rules of law such as the Statute of Frauds provisions of Article 2 on Sales whose very office is to control and restrict the actions of the parties, and which cannot be abrogated by agreement, or by a usage of trade, and those rules of law (such as those in Part 3 of Article 2 on Sales) which fill in points which the parties have not considered and in fact agreed upon. The latter rules hold "unless otherwise agreed" but yield to the contrary agreement of the parties.

Part of the agreement of the parties to which such rules yield is to be sought for in the usages of trade which furnish the background and give particular meaning to the language used, and are the framework of common understanding controlling any general rules of law which hold only when there is no such understanding.

5. A usage of trade under subsection (2) must have the "regularity of observance" specified. The ancient English tests for "custom" are abandoned in this connection. Therefore, it is not required that a usage of trade be "ancient or immemorial," "universal" or the like. Under the requirement of subsection (2) full recognition is thus available for new usages and for usages currently observed by the great majority of decent dealers, even though dissidents ready to cut corners do not agree. There is room also for proper recognition of usage agreed upon by merchants in trade codes.

6. The policy of this Act controlling explicit unconscionable contracts and clauses (Sections 1–203, 2–302) applies to implicit clauses which rest on usage of trade and carries forward the policy underlying the ancient requirement that a custom or usage must be "reasonable." However, the emphasis is shifted. The very fact of commercial acceptance makes out a prima facie case that the usage is reasonable, and the burden is no longer on the usage to establish itself as being reasonable. But the anciently established policing of usage by the courts is continued to the extent necessary to cope with the situation arising if an unconscionable or dishonest practice should become standard.

7. Subsection (3), giving the prescribed effect to usages of which the parties "are or should be aware", reinforces the provision of subsection (2) requiring not universality but only the described "regularity of observance" of the practice or method. This subsection also reinforces the point of subsection (2) that such usages may be either general to trade or particular to a special branch of trade.

8. Although the terms in which this Act defines "agreement" include the elements of course of dealing and usage of trade, the fact that express reference is made in some sections to those elements is not to be construed as carrying a contrary intent or implication elsewhere. Compare Section 1–102(4).

9. In cases of a well established line of usage varying from the general rules of this Act where the precise amount of the variation has not been worked out into a single standard, the party relying on the usage is entitled, in any event, to the minimum variation demonstrated. The whole is not to be disregarded because no particular line of detail has been established. In case a dominant pattern has been fairly evidenced, the party relying on the usage is entitled under this section to go to the trier of fact on the question of whether such dominant pattern has been incorporated into the agreement.

10. Subsection (6) is intended to insure that this Act's liberal recognition of the needs of commerce in regard to usage of trade shall not be made into an instrument of abuse.

* * *

ARTICLE 2

SALES

PART 1
SHORT TITLE, GENERAL CONSTRUCTION AND SUBJECT MATTER

§ 2–101. Short Title

This Article shall be known and may be cited as Uniform Commercial Code—Sales.

Official Comment

This Article is a complete revision and modernization of the Uniform Sales Act which was promulgated by the National Conference of Commissioners on Uniform State Laws in 1906 and has been adopted in 34 states and Alaska, the District of Columbia and Hawaii.

The coverage of the present Article is much more extensive than that of the old Sales Act and extends to the various bodies of case law which have been developed both outside of and under the latter.

The arrangement of the present Article is in terms of contract for sale and the various steps of its performance. The legal consequences are stated as following directly from the contract and action taken under it without resorting to the idea of when property or title passed or was to pass as being the determining factor. The purpose is to avoid making practical issues between practical men turn upon the location of an intangible something, the passing of which no man can prove by evidence and to substitute for such abstractions proof of words and actions of a tangible character.

§ 2–102. Scope; Certain Security and Other Transactions Excluded From This Article

Unless the context otherwise requires, this Article applies to transactions in goods; it does not apply to any transaction which although in the form of an unconditional contract to sell or present sale is intended to operate only as a security transaction nor does this Article impair or repeal any statute regulating sales to consumers, farmers or other specified classes of buyers.

* * *

§ 2–103. Definitions and Index of Definitions

(1) In this Article unless the context otherwise requires

(a) "Buyer" means a person who buys or contracts to buy goods.

(b) "Good faith" in the case of a merchant means honesty in fact and the observance of reasonable commercial standards of fair dealing in the trade.

§ 2-103

(c) "Receipt" of goods means taking physical possession of them.

(d) "Seller" means a person who sells or contracts to sell goods.

* * *

§ 2–104. Definitions: "Merchant"; "Between Merchants"; "Financing Agency"

(1) "Merchant" means a person who deals in goods of the kind or otherwise by his occupation holds himself out as having knowledge or skill peculiar to the practices or goods involved in the transaction or to whom such knowledge or skill may be attributed by his employment of an agent or broker or other intermediary who by his occupation holds himself out as having such knowledge or skill.

* * *

(3) "Between merchants" means in any transaction with respect to which both parties are chargeable with the knowledge or skill of merchants.

Official Comment

Prior Uniform Statutory Provision: None. But see Sections 15(2), (5), 16(c), 45(2) and 71, Uniform Sales Act, and Sections 35 and 37, Uniform Bills of Lading Act for examples of the policy expressly provided for in this Article.

Purposes:

1. This Article assumes that transactions between professionals in a given field require special and clear rules which may not apply to a casual or inexperienced seller or buyer. It thus adopts a policy of expressly stating rules applicable "between merchants" and "as against a merchant", wherever they are needed instead of making them depend upon the circumstances of each case as in the statutes cited above. This section lays the foundation of this policy by defining those who are to be regarded as professionals or "merchants" and by stating when a transaction is deemed to be "between merchants".

2. The term "merchant" as defined here roots in the "law merchant" concept of a professional in business. The professional status under the definition may be based upon specialized knowledge as to the goods, specialized knowledge as to business practices, or specialized knowledge as to both and which kind of specialized knowledge may be sufficient to establish the merchant status is indicated by the nature of the provisions.

The special provisions as to merchants appear only in this Article and they are of three kinds. Sections 2–201(2), 2–205, 2–207 and 2–209 dealing with the statute of frauds, firm offers, confirmatory memoranda and modification rest on normal business practices which are or ought to be typical of and familiar to any person in business. For purposes of these sections almost every person in business would, therefore, be deemed to be a "merchant" under the language "who ... by his occupation holds himself out as having knowledge or skill peculiar to the practices ... involved in the transaction ..." since the practices involved in the transaction are non-specialized business practices such as answering mail. In this type of provision, banks or even universities, for example, well may be "merchants." But even these sections only apply to a merchant in his mercantile capacity; a lawyer or bank president buying fishing tackle for his own use is not a merchant.

On the other hand, in Section 2-314 on the warranty of merchantability, such warranty is implied only "if the seller is a merchant with respect to goods of that kind." Obviously this qualification restricts the implied warranty to a much smaller group than everyone who is engaged in business and requires a professional status as to particular kinds of goods. The exception in Section 2-402(2) for retention of possession by a merchant-seller falls in the same class; as does Section 2-403(2) on entrusting of possession to a merchant "who deals in goods of that kind".

A third group of sections includes 2-103(1)(b), which provides that in the case of a merchant "good faith" includes observance of reasonable commercial standards of fair dealing in the trade; 2-327(1)(c), 2-603 and 2-605, dealing with responsibilities of merchant buyers to follow seller's instructions, etc.; 2-509 on risk of loss, and 2-609 on adequate assurance of performance. This group of sections applies to persons who are merchants under either the "practices" or the "goods" aspect of the definition of merchant.

3. The "or to whom such knowledge or skill may be attributed by his employment of an agent or broker ..." clause of the definition of merchant means that even persons such as universities, for example, can come within the definition of merchant if they have regular purchasing departments or business personnel who are familiar with business practices and who are equipped to take any action required.

* * *

§ 2-105. Definitions: Transferability; "Goods"; "Future" Goods; "Lot"; "Commercial Unit"

(1) "Goods" means all things (including specially manufactured goods) which are movable at the time of identification to the contract for sale other than the money in which the price is to be paid, investment securities (Article 8) and things in action. "Goods" also includes the unborn young of animals and growing crops and other identified things attached to realty as described in the section on goods to be severed from realty (Section 2-107).

* * *

Official Comment

Prior Uniform Statutory Provision: Subsections (1), (2), (3) and (4)—Sections 5, 6 and 76, Uniform Sales Act; Subsections (5) and (6)—none.

Changes: Rewritten.

Purposes of Changes and New Matter:

1. Subsection (1) on "goods": The phraseology of the prior uniform statutory provision has been changed so that:

The definition of goods is based on the concept of movability and the term "chattels personal" is not used.

It is not intended to deal with things which are not fairly identifiable as movables before the contract is performed.

Growing crops are included within the definition of goods since they are frequently intended for sale. The concept of "industrial" growing crops has been abandoned, for under modern practices fruit, perennial hay, nursery stock and the like must be brought within the scope of this Article. The young of animals are also included expressly in this definition since they, too, are frequently intended for sale and may be contracted for before birth. The period of gestation of domestic animals is such that the provisions of the section on identification can apply as in the case of crops to be planted. The reason of this definition also leads to the inclusion of a wool crop or the like as "goods" subject to identification under this Article.

The exclusion of "money in which the price is to be paid" from the definition of goods does not mean that foreign currency which is included in the definition of money may not be the subject matter of a sales transaction. Goods is intended to cover the sale of money when money is being treated as a commodity but not to include it when money is the medium of payment.

As to contracts to sell timber, minerals, or structures to be removed from the land Section 2–107(1) (Goods to be severed from Realty: recording) controls.

The use of the word "fixtures" is avoided in view of the diversity of definitions of that term. This Article in including within its scope "things attached to realty" adds the further test that they must be capable of severance without material harm thereto. As between the parties any identified things which fall within that definition become "goods" upon the making of the contract for sale.

* * *

§ 2–106. Definitions: "Contract"; "Agreement"; "Contract for Sale"; "Sale"; "Present Sale"; "Conforming" to Contract; "Termination"; "Cancellation"

(1) In this Article unless the context otherwise requires "contract" and "agreement" are limited to those relating to the present or future sale of goods. "Contract for sale" includes both a present sale of goods and a contract to sell goods at a future time. A "sale" consists in the passing of title from the seller to the buyer for a price (Section 2–401). A "present sale" means a sale which is accomplished by the making of the contract.

(2) Goods or conduct including any part of a performance are "conforming" or conform to the contract when they are in accordance with the obligations under the contract.

(3) "Termination" occurs when either party pursuant to a power created by agreement or law puts an end to the contract otherwise than for its breach. On "termination" all obligations which are still executory on both sides are discharged but any right based on prior breach or performance survives.

(4) "Cancellation" occurs when either party puts an end to the contract for breach by the other and its effect is the same as that of "termination" except that the cancelling party also retains any remedy for breach of the whole contract or any unperformed balance.

Official Comment

Prior Uniform Statutory Provision: Subsection (1)—Section 1(1) and (2), Uniform Sales Act; Subsection (2)—none, but subsection generally continues policy of Sections 11, 44 and 69, Uniform Sales Act; Subsections (3) and (4)—none.

Changes: Completely rewritten.

Purposes of Changes and New Matter:

1. Subsection (1): "Contract for sale" is used as a general concept throughout this Article, but the rights of the parties do not vary according to whether the transaction is a present sale or a contract to sell unless the Article expressly so provides.

2. Subsection (2): It is in general intended to continue the policy of requiring exact performance by the seller of his obligations as a condition to his right to require acceptance. However, the seller is in part safeguarded against surprise as a result of sudden technicality on the buyer's part by the provisions of Section 2–508 on seller's cure of improper tender or delivery. Moreover usage of trade frequently permits commercial leeways in performance and the language of the agreement itself must be read in the light of such custom or usage and also, prior course of dealing, and in a long term contract, the course of performance.

3. Subsections (3) and (4): These subsections are intended to make clear the distinction carried forward throughout this Article between termination and cancellation.

* * *

§ 2–107. Goods to Be Severed From Realty: Recording

(1) A contract for the sale of minerals or the like (including oil and gas) or a structure or its materials to be removed from realty is a contract for the sale of goods within this Article if they are to be severed by the seller but until severance a purported present sale thereof which is not effective as a transfer of an interest in land is effective only as a contract to sell.

(2) A contract for the sale apart from the land of growing crops or other things attached to realty and capable of severance without material harm thereto but not described in subsection (1) or of timber to be cut is a contract for the sale of goods within this Article whether the subject matter is to be severed by the buyer or by the seller even though it forms part of the realty at the time of contracting, and the parties can by identification effect a present sale before severance.

* * *

PART 2

FORM, FORMATION AND READJUSTMENT OF CONTRACT

§ 2–201. Formal Requirements; Statute of Frauds

(1) Except as otherwise provided in this section a contract for the sale of goods for the price of $500 or more is not enforceable by way of action or defense unless there is some writing sufficient to indicate that a contract for sale has been made between the parties and signed by the party against whom enforcement is sought or by his authorized agent or broker. A writing is not insufficient because it omits or incorrectly states a term agreed upon but the contract is not enforceable under this paragraph beyond the quantity of goods shown in such writing.

(2) Between merchants if within a reasonable time a writing in confirmation of the contract and sufficient against the sender is received and the party receiving it has reason to know its contents, it satisfies the requirements of subsection (1) against such party unless written notice of objection to its contents is given within 10 days after it is received.

(3) A contract which does not satisfy the requirements of subsection (1) but which is valid in other respects is enforceable

  (a) if the goods are to be specially manufactured for the buyer and are not suitable for sale to others in the ordinary course of the seller's business and the seller, before notice of repudiation is received and under circumstances which reasonably indicate that the goods are for the buyer, has made either a substantial beginning of their manufacture or commitments for their procurement; or

  (b) if the party against whom enforcement is sought admits in his pleading, testimony or otherwise in court that a contract for sale was made, but the contract is not enforceable under this provision beyond the quantity of goods admitted; or

  (c) with respect to goods for which payment has been made and accepted or which have been received and accepted (Sec. 2–606).

Official Comment

Prior Uniform Statutory Provision: Section 4, Uniform Sales Act (which was based on Section 17 of the Statute of 29 Charles II).

Changes: Completely rephrased; restricted to sale of goods. See also Sections 1–206, 8–319 and 9–203.

Purposes of Changes: The changed phraseology of this section is intended to make it clear that:

1. The required writing need not contain all the material terms of the contract and such material terms as are stated need not be precisely stated. All that is required is that the writing afford a basis for believing that the offered oral evidence rests on a real transaction. It may be written in lead pencil on a scratch pad. It need not indicate which party is the buyer and which the seller. The only term which must appear is the quantity term which need not be accurately stated but recovery is limited to the amount stated. The price, time and place of payment or delivery, the gen-

eral quality of the goods, or any particular warranties may all be omitted.

Special emphasis must be placed on the permissibility of omitting the price term in view of the insistence of some courts on the express inclusion of this term even where the parties have contracted on the basis of a published price list. In many valid contracts for sale the parties do not mention the price in express terms, the buyer being bound to pay and the seller to accept a reasonable price which the trier of the fact may well be trusted to determine. Again, frequently the price is not mentioned since the parties have based their agreement on a price list or catalogue known to both of them and this list serves as an efficient safeguard against perjury. Finally, "market" prices and valuations that are current in the vicinity constitute a similar check. Thus if the price is not stated in the memorandum it can normally be supplied without danger of fraud. Of course if the "price" consists of goods rather than money the quantity of goods must be stated.

Only three definite and invariable requirements as to the memorandum are made by this subsection. First, it must evidence a contract for the sale of goods; second, it must be "signed", a word which includes any authentication which identifies the party to be charged; and third, it must specify a quantity.

2. "Partial performance" as a substitute for the required memorandum can validate the contract only for the goods which have been accepted or for which payment has been made and accepted.

Receipt and acceptance either of goods or of the price constitutes an unambiguous overt admission by both parties that a contract actually exists. If the court can make a just apportionment, therefore, the agreed price of any goods actually delivered can be recovered without a writing or, if the price has been paid, the seller can be forced to deliver an apportionable part of the goods. The overt actions of the parties make admissible evidence of the other terms of the contract necessary to a just apportionment. This is true even though the actions of the parties are not in themselves inconsistent with a different transaction such as a consignment for resale or a mere loan of money.

Part performance by the buyer requires the delivery of something by him that is accepted by the seller as such performance. Thus, part payment may be made by money or check, accepted by the seller. If the agreed price consists of goods or services, then they must also have been delivered and accepted.

3. Between merchants, failure to answer a written confirmation of a contract within ten days of receipt is tantamount to a writing under subsection (2) and is sufficient against both parties under subsection (1). The only effect, however, is to take away from the party who fails to answer the defense of the Statute of Frauds; the burden of persuading the trier of fact that a contract was in fact made orally prior to the written confirmation is unaffected. Compare the effect of a failure to reply under Section 2–207.

4. Failure to satisfy the requirements of this section does not render the contract void for all purposes, but merely prevents it from being judicially enforced in favor of a party to the contract. For example, a buyer who takes possession of goods as provided in an oral contract which the seller has not meanwhile repudiated, is not a trespasser. Nor would the Statute of Frauds provisions of this section be a defense to a third person who wrongfully induces a party to refuse to perform an oral contract, even

though the injured party cannot maintain an action for damages against the party so refusing to perform.

5. The requirement of "signing" is discussed in the comment to Section 1–201.

6. It is not necessary that the writing be delivered to anybody. It need not be signed or authenticated by both parties but it is, of course, not sufficient against one who has not signed it. Prior to a dispute no one can determine which party's signing of the memorandum may be necessary but from the time of contracting each party should be aware that to him it is signing by the other which is important.

7. If the making of a contract is admitted in court, either in a written pleading, by stipulation or by oral statement before the court, no additional writing is necessary for protection against fraud. Under this section it is no longer possible to admit the contract in court and still treat the Statute as a defense. However, the contract is not thus conclusively established. The admission so made by a party is itself evidential against him of the truth of the facts so admitted and of nothing more; as against the other party, it is not evidential at all.

* * *

§ 2–202. Final Written Expression: Parol or Extrinsic Evidence

Terms with respect to which the confirmatory memoranda of the parties agree or which are otherwise set forth in a writing intended by the parties as a final expression of their agreement with respect to such terms as are included therein may not be contradicted by evidence of any prior agreement or of a contemporaneous oral agreement but may be explained or supplemented

(a) by course of dealing or usage of trade (Section 1–205) or by course of performance (Section 2–208); and

(b) by evidence of consistent additional terms unless the court finds the writing to have been intended also as a complete and exclusive statement of the terms of the agreement.

Official Comment

Prior Uniform Statutory Provision: None.

Purposes:

1. This section definitely rejects:

(a) Any assumption that because a writing has been worked out which is final on some matters, it is to be taken as including all the matters agreed upon;

(b) The premise that the language used has the meaning attributable to such language by rules of construction existing in the law rather than the meaning which arises out of the commercial context in which it was used; and

(c) The requirement that a condition precedent to the admissibility of the type of evidence specified in paragraph (a) is an original determination by the court that the language used is ambiguous.

2. Paragraph (a) makes admissible evidence of course of dealing, usage of trade and course of performance to explain or supplement the terms of any writing stating the

agreement of the parties in order that the true understanding of the parties as to the agreement may be reached. Such writings are to be read on the assumption that the course of prior dealings between the parties and the usages of trade were taken for granted when the document was phrased. Unless carefully negated they have become an element of the meaning of the words used. Similarly, the course of actual performance by the parties is considered the best indication of what they intended the writing to mean.

3. Under paragraph (b) consistent additional terms, not reduced to writing, may be proved unless the court finds that the writing was intended by both parties as a complete and exclusive statement of all the terms. If the additional terms are such that, if agreed upon, they would certainly have been included in the document in the view of the court, then evidence of their alleged making must be kept from the trier of fact.

* * *

* * *

§ 2–204. Formation in General

(1) A contract for sale of goods may be made in any manner sufficient to show agreement, including conduct by both parties which recognizes the existence of such a contract.

(2) An agreement sufficient to constitute a contract for sale may be found even though the moment of its making is undetermined.

(3) Even though one or more terms are left open a contract for sale does not fail for indefiniteness if the parties have intended to make a contract and there is a reasonably certain basis for giving an appropriate remedy.

* * *

§ 2–206. Offer and Acceptance in Formation of Contract

(1) Unless otherwise unambiguously indicated by the language or circumstances

   (a) an offer to make a contract shall be construed as inviting acceptance in any manner and by any medium reasonable in the circumstances;

   (b) an order or other offer to buy goods for prompt or current shipment shall be construed as inviting acceptance either by a prompt promise to ship or by the prompt or current shipment of conforming or non-conforming goods, but such a shipment of non-conforming goods does not constitute an acceptance if the seller seasonably notifies the buyer that the shipment is offered only as an accommodation to the buyer.

(2) Where the beginning of a requested performance is a reasonable mode of acceptance an offeror who is not notified of acceptance

within a reasonable time may treat the offer as having lapsed before acceptance.

* * *

§ 2–207. Additional Terms in Acceptance or Confirmation

(1) A definite and seasonable expression of acceptance or a written confirmation which is sent within a reasonable time operates as an acceptance even though it states terms additional to or different from those offered or agreed upon, unless acceptance is expressly made conditional on assent to the additional or different terms.

(2) The additional terms are to be construed as proposals for addition to the contract. Between merchants such terms become part of the contract unless:

   (a) the offer expressly limits acceptance to the terms of the offer;

   (b) they materially alter it; or

   (c) notification of objection to them has already been given or is given within a reasonable time after notice of them is received.

(3) Conduct by both parties which recognizes the existence of a contract is sufficient to establish a contract for sale although the writings of the parties do not otherwise establish a contract. In such case the terms of the particular contract consist of those terms on which the writings of the parties agree, together with any supplementary terms incorporated under any other provisions of this Act.

* * *

§ 2–208. Course of Performance or Practical Construction

(1) Where the contract for sale involves repeated occasions for performance by either party with knowledge of the nature of the performance and opportunity for objection to it by the other, any course of performance accepted or acquiesced in without objection shall be relevant to determine the meaning of the agreement.

(2) The express terms of the agreement and any such course of performance, as well as any course of dealing and usage of trade, shall be construed whenever reasonable as consistent with each other; but when such construction is unreasonable, express terms shall control course of performance and course of performance shall control both course of dealing and usage of trade (Section 1–205).

(3) Subject to the provisions of the next section on modification and waiver, such course of performance shall be relevant to show a waiver or modification of any term inconsistent with such course of performance.

Official Comment

Prior Uniform Statutory Provision: No such general provision but concept of this section recognized by terms such as "course of dealing", "the circumstances of the case," "the conduct of the parties," etc., in Uniform Sales Act.

Purposes:

1. The parties themselves know best what they have meant by their words of agreement and their action under that agreement is the best indication of what that meaning was. This section thus rounds out the set of factors which determines the meaning of the "agreement" and therefore also of the "unless otherwise agreed" qualification to various provisions of this Article.

2. Under this section a course of performance is always relevant to determine the meaning of the agreement. Express mention of course of performance elsewhere in this Article carries no contrary implication when there is a failure to refer to it in other sections.

3. Where it is difficult to determine whether a particular act merely sheds light on the meaning of the agreement or represents a waiver of a term of the agreement, the preference is in favor of "waiver" whenever such construction, plus the application of the provisions on the reinstatement of rights waived (see Section 2–209), is needed to preserve the flexible character of commercial contracts and to prevent surprise or other hardship.

4. A single occasion of conduct does not fall within the language of this section but other sections such as the ones on silence after acceptance and failure to specify particular defects can affect the parties' rights on a single occasion (see Sections 2–605 and 2–607).

* * *

§ 2–209. Modification, Rescission and Waiver

(1) An agreement modifying a contract within this Article needs no consideration to be binding.

(2) A signed agreement which excludes modification or rescission except by a signed writing cannot be otherwise modified or rescinded, but except as between merchants such a requirement on a form supplied by the merchant must be separately signed by the other party.

(3) The requirements of the statute of frauds section of this Article (Section 2–201) must be satisfied if the contract as modified is within its provisions.

(4) Although an attempt at modification or rescission does not satisfy the requirements of subsection (2) or (3) it can operate as a waiver.

(5) A party who has made a waiver affecting an executory portion of the contract may retract the waiver by reasonable notification received by the other party that strict performance will be required of any term waived, unless the retraction would be unjust in view of a material change of position in reliance on the waiver.

Official Comment

Prior Uniform Statutory Provision: Subsection (1)—Compare Section 1, Uniform Written Obligations Act; Subsections (2) to (5)—none.

Purposes of Changes and New Matter:

1. This section seeks to protect and make effective all necessary and desirable modifications of sales contracts without regard to the technicalities which at present hamper such adjustments.

2. Subsection (1) provides that an agreement modifying a sales contract needs no consideration to be binding.

However, modifications made thereunder must meet the test of good faith imposed by this Act. The effective use of bad faith to escape performance on the original contract terms is barred, and the extortion of a "modification" without legitimate commercial reason is ineffective as a violation of the duty of good faith. Nor can a mere technical consideration support a modification made in bad faith.

The test of "good faith" between merchants or as against merchants includes "observance of reasonable commercial standards of fair dealing in the trade" (Section 2–103), and may in some situations require an objectively demonstrable reason for seeking a modification. But such matters as a market shift which makes performance come to involve a loss may provide such a reason even though there is no such unforeseen difficulty as would make out a legal excuse from performance under Sections 2–615 and 2–616.

3. Subsections (2) and (3) are intended to protect against false allegations of oral modifications. "Modification or rescission" includes abandonment or other change by mutual consent, contrary to the decision in Green v. Doniger, 300 N.Y. 238, 90 N.E.2d 56 (1949); it does not include unilateral "termination" or "cancellation" as defined in Section 2–106.

The Statute of Frauds provisions of this Article are expressly applied to modifications by subsection (3). Under those provisions the "delivery and acceptance" test is limited to the goods which have been accepted, that is, to the past. "Modification" for the future cannot therefore be conjured up by oral testimony if the price involved is $500.00 or more since such modification must be shown at least by an authenticated memo. And since a memo is limited in its effect to the quantity of goods set forth in it there is safeguard against oral evidence.

Subsection (2) permits the parties in effect to make their own Statute of Frauds as regards any future modification of the contract by giving effect to a clause in a signed agreement which expressly requires any modification to be by signed writing. But note that if a consumer is to be held to such a clause on a form supplied by a merchant it must be separately signed.

4. Subsection (4) is intended, despite the provisions of subsections (2) and (3), to prevent contractual provisions excluding modification except by a signed writing from limiting in other respects the legal effect of the parties' actual later conduct. The effect of such conduct as a waiver is further regulated in subsection (5).

* * *

PART 3

GENERAL OBLIGATION AND CONSTRUCTION OF CONTRACT

§ 2–301. General Obligations of Parties

The obligation of the seller is to transfer and deliver and that of the buyer is to accept and pay in accordance with the contract.

Official Comment

Prior Uniform Statutory Provision: Sections 11 and 41, Uniform Sales Act.

Changes: Rewritten.

Purposes of Changes: This section uses the term "obligation" in contrast to the term "duty" in order to provide for the "condition" aspects of delivery and payment insofar as they are not modified by other sections of this Article such as those on cure of tender. It thus replaces not only the general provisions of the Uniform Sales Act on the parties' duties, but also the general provisions of that Act on the effect of conditions. In order to determine what is "in accordance with the contract" under this Article usage of trade, course of dealing and performance, and the general background of circumstances must be given due consideration in conjunction with the lay meaning of the words used to define the scope of the conditions and duties.

* * *

§ 2–302. Unconscionable Contract or Clause

(1) If the court as a matter of law finds the contract or any clause of the contract to have been unconscionable at the time it was made the court may refuse to enforce the contract, or it may enforce the remainder of the contract without the unconscionable clause, or it may so limit the application of any unconscionable clause as to avoid any unconscionable result.

(2) When it is claimed or appears to the court that the contract or any clause thereof may be unconscionable the parties shall be afforded a reasonable opportunity to present evidence as to its commercial setting, purpose and effect to aid the court in making the determination.

Official Comment

Prior Uniform Statutory Provision: None.

Purposes:

1. This section is intended to make it possible for the courts to police explicitly against the contracts or clauses which they find to be unconscionable. In the past such policing has been accomplished by adverse construction of language, by manipulation of the rules of offer and acceptance or by determinations that the clause is contrary to public policy or to the dominant purpose of the contract. This section is intended to allow the court to pass directly on the unconscionability of the contract or particular clause therein and to make a conclusion of law as to its unconscionability. The basic test is whether, in the light of the general commercial background and the commercial needs of the particular trade or case, the clauses involved are so one-sided as to be unconscionable under the circumstances existing at the time of the making of the contract. Subsection (2) makes it clear that it is proper for the court to hear evidence upon these

questions. The principle is one of the prevention of oppression and unfair surprise (Cf. Campbell Soup Co. v. Wentz, 172 F.2d 80, 3d Cir.1948) and not of disturbance of allocation of risks because of superior bargaining power. The underlying basis of this section is illustrated by the results in cases such as the following:

Kansas City Wholesale Grocery Co. v. Weber Packing Corporation, 93 Utah 414, 73 P.2d 1272 (1937), where a clause limiting time for complaints was held inapplicable to latent defects in a shipment of catsup which could be discovered only by microscopic analysis; Hardy v. General Motors Acceptance Corporation, 38 Ga.App. 463, 144 S.E. 327 (1928), holding that a disclaimer of warranty clause applied only to express warranties, thus letting in a fair implied warranty; Andrews Bros. v. Singer & Co. (1934 CA) 1 K.B. 17, holding that where a car with substantial mileage was delivered instead of a "new" car, a disclaimer of warranties, including those "implied," left unaffected an "express obligation" on the description, even though the Sale of Goods Act called such an implied warranty; New Prague Flouring Mill Co. v. G.A. Spears, 194 Iowa 417, 189 N.W. 815 (1922), holding that a clause permitting the seller, upon the buyer's failure to supply shipping instructions, to cancel, ship, or allow delivery date to be indefinitely postponed 30 days at a time by the inaction, does not indefinitely postpone the date of measuring damages for the buyer's breach, to the seller's advantage; and Kansas Flour Mills Co. v. Dirks, 100 Kan. 376, 164 P. 273 (1917), where under a similar clause in a rising market the court permitted the buyer to measure his damages for non-delivery at the end of only one 30 day postponement; Green v. Arcos, Ltd. (1931 CA) 47 T.L.R. 336, where a blanket clause prohibiting rejection of shipments by the buyer was restricted to apply to shipments where discrepancies represented merely mercantile variations; Meyer v. Packard Cleveland Motor Co., 106 Ohio St. 328, 140 N.E. 118 (1922), in which the court held that a "waiver" of all agreements not specified did not preclude implied warranty of fitness of a rebuilt dump truck for ordinary use as a dump truck; Austin Co. v. J.H. Tillman Co., 104 Or. 541, 209 P. 131 (1922), where a clause limiting the buyer's remedy to return was held to be applicable only if the seller had delivered a machine needed for a construction job which reasonably met the contract description; Bekkevold v. Potts, 173 Minn. 87, 216 N.W. 790, 59 A.L.R. 1164 (1927), refusing to allow warranty of fitness for purpose imposed by law to be negated by clause excluding all warranties "made" by the seller; Robert A. Munroe & Co. v. Meyer (1930) 2 K.B. 312, holding that the warranty of description overrides a clause reading "with all faults and defects" where adulterated meat not up to the contract description was delivered.

2. Under this section the court, in its discretion, may refuse to enforce the contract as a whole if it is permeated by the unconscionability, or it may strike any single clause or group of clauses which are so tainted or which are contrary to the essential purpose of the agreement, or it may simply limit unconscionable clauses so as to avoid unconscionable results.

3. The present section is addressed to the court, and the decision is to be made by it. The commercial evidence referred to in subsection (2) is for the court's consideration, not the jury's. Only the agreement which results from the court's action on these matters is to be submitted to the general triers of the facts.

* * *

§ 2–303. Allocation or Division of Risks

Where this Article allocates a risk or a burden as between the parties "unless otherwise agreed", the agreement may not only shift the allocation but may also divide the risk or burden.

Official Comment

Prior Uniform Statutory Provision: None.

Purposes:

1. This section is intended to make it clear that the parties may modify or allocate "unless otherwise agreed" risks or burdens imposed by this Article as they desire, always subject, of course, to the provisions on unconscionability.

Compare Section 1–102(4).

2. The risk or burden may be divided by the express terms of the agreement or by the attending circumstances, since under the definition of "agreement" in this Act the circumstances surrounding the transaction as well as the express language used by the parties enter into the meaning and substance of the agreement.

* * *

* * *

§ 2–312. Warranty of Title and Against Infringement; Buyer's Obligation Against Infringement

(1) Subject to subsection (2) there is in a contract for sale a warranty by the seller that

   (a) the title conveyed shall be good, and its transfer rightful; and

   (b) the goods shall be delivered free from any security interest or other lien or encumbrance of which the buyer at the time of contracting has no knowledge.

(2) A warranty under subsection (1) will be excluded or modified only by specific language or by circumstances which give the buyer reason to know that the person selling does not claim title in himself or that he is purporting to sell only such right or title as he or a third person may have.

(3) Unless otherwise agreed a seller who is a merchant regularly dealing in goods of the kind warrants that the goods shall be delivered free of the rightful claim of any third person by way of infringement or the like but a buyer who furnishes specifications to the seller must hold the seller harmless against any such claim which arises out of compliance with the specifications.

* * *

§ 2–313. Express Warranties by Affirmation, Promise, Description, Sample

(1) Express warranties by the seller are created as follows:

§ 2-313

(a) Any affirmation of fact or promise made by the seller to the buyer which relates to the goods and becomes part of the basis of the bargain creates an express warranty that the goods shall conform to the affirmation or promise.

(b) Any description of the goods which is made part of the basis of the bargain creates an express warranty that the goods shall conform to the description.

(c) Any sample or model which is made part of the basis of the bargain creates an express warranty that the whole of the goods shall conform to the sample or model.

(2) It is not necessary to the creation of an express warranty that the seller use formal words such as "warrant" or "guarantee" or that he have a specific intention to make a warranty, but an affirmation merely of the value of the goods or a statement purporting to be merely the seller's opinion or commendation of the goods does not create a warranty.

Official Comment

Prior Uniform Statutory Provision: Sections 12, 14 and 16, Uniform Sales Act.

Changes: Rewritten.

Purposes of Changes: To consolidate and systematize basic principles with the result that:

1. "Express" warranties rest on "dickered" aspects of the individual bargain, and go so clearly to the essence of that bargain that words of disclaimer in a form are repugnant to the basic dickered terms. "Implied" warranties rest so clearly on a common factual situation or set of conditions that no particular language or action is necessary to evidence them and they will arise in such a situation unless unmistakably negated.

This section reverts to the older case law insofar as the warranties of description and sample are designated "express" rather than "implied".

2. Although this section is limited in its scope and direct purpose to warranties made by the seller to the buyer as part of a contract for sale, the warranty sections of this Article are not designed in any way to disturb those lines of case law growth which have recognized that warranties need not be confined either to sales contracts or to the direct parties to such a contract. They may arise in other appropriate circumstances such as in the case of bailments for hire, whether such bailment is itself the main contract or is merely a supplying of containers under a contract for the sale of their contents. The provisions of Section 2-318 on third party beneficiaries expressly recognize this case law development within one particular area. Beyond that, the matter is left to the case law with the intention that the policies of this Act may offer useful guidance in dealing with further cases as they arise.

3. The present section deals with affirmations of fact by the seller, descriptions of the goods or exhibitions of samples, exactly as any other part of a negotiation which ends in a contract is dealt with. No specific intention to make a warranty is necessary if any of these factors is made part of the basis of the bargain. In actual practice affirmations of fact made by the seller about the goods during a

bargain are regarded as part of the description of those goods; hence no particular reliance on such statements need be shown in order to weave them into the fabric of the agreement. Rather, any fact which is to take such affirmations, once made, out of the agreement requires clear affirmative proof. The issue normally is one of fact.

4. In view of the principle that the whole purpose of the law of warranty is to determine what it is that the seller has in essence agreed to sell, the policy is adopted of those cases which refuse except in unusual circumstances to recognize a material deletion of the seller's obligation. Thus, a contract is normally a contract for a sale of something describable and described. A clause generally disclaiming "all warranties, express or implied" cannot reduce the seller's obligation with respect to such description and therefore cannot be given literal effect under Section 2–316.

This is not intended to mean that the parties, if they consciously desire, cannot make their own bargain as they wish. But in determining what they have agreed upon good faith is a factor and consideration should be given to the fact that the probability is small that a real price is intended to be exchanged for a pseudo-obligation.

5. Paragraph (1)(b) makes specific some of the principles set forth above when a description of the goods is given by the seller.

A description need not be by words. Technical specifications, blueprints and the like can afford more exact description than mere language and if made part of the basis of the bargain goods must conform with them. Past deliveries may set the description of quality, either expressly or impliedly by course of dealing. Of course, all descriptions by merchants must be read against the applicable trade usages with the general rules as to merchantability resolving any doubts.

6. The basic situation as to statements affecting the true essence of the bargain is no different when a sample or model is involved in the transaction. This section includes both a "sample" actually drawn from the bulk of goods which is the subject matter of the sale, and a "model" which is offered for inspection when the subject matter is not at hand and which has not been drawn from the bulk of the goods.

Although the underlying principles are unchanged, the facts are often ambiguous when something is shown as illustrative, rather than as a straight sample. In general, the presumption is that any sample or model just as any affirmation of fact is intended to become a basis of the bargain. But there is no escape from the question of fact. When the seller exhibits a sample purporting to be drawn from an existing bulk, good faith of course requires that the sample be fairly drawn. But in mercantile experience the mere exhibition of a "sample" does not of itself show whether it is merely intended to "suggest" or to "be" the character of the subject-matter of the contract. The question is whether the seller has so acted with reference to the sample as to make him responsible that the whole shall have at least the values shown by it. The circumstances aid in answering this question. If the sample has been drawn from an existing bulk, it must be regarded as describing values of the goods contracted for unless it is accompanied by an unmistakable denial of such responsibility. If, on the other hand, a model of merchandise not on hand is offered, the mercantile presumption that it has become a literal description of the subject matter is not so strong, and particularly so if modification on the buyer's initiative impairs any feature of the model.

7. The precise time when words of description or affirmation are made or samples are shown is not material. The sole question is whether the language or samples or models are fairly to be regarded as part of the contract. If language is used after the closing of the deal (as when the buyer when taking delivery asks and receives an additional assurance), the warranty becomes a modification, and need not be supported by consideration if it is otherwise reasonable and in order (Section 2-209).

8. Concerning affirmations of value or a seller's opinion or commendation under subsection (2), the basic question remains the same: What statements of the seller have in the circumstances and in objective judgment become part of the basis of the bargain? As indicated above, all of the statements of the seller do so unless good reason is shown to the contrary. The provisions of subsection (2) are included, however, since common experience discloses that some statements or predictions cannot fairly be viewed as entering into the bargain. Even as to false statements of value, however, the possibility is left open that a remedy may be provided by the law relating to fraud or misrepresentation.

* * *

§ 2-314. Implied Warranty: Merchantability; Usage of Trade

(1) Unless excluded or modified (Section 2-316), a warranty that the goods shall be merchantable is implied in a contract for their sale if the seller is a merchant with respect to goods of that kind. Under this section the serving for value of food or drink to be consumed either on the premises or elsewhere is a sale.

(2) Goods to be merchantable must be at least such as

(a) pass without objection in the trade under the contract description; and

(b) in the case of fungible goods, are of fair average quality within the description; and

(c) are fit for the ordinary purposes for which such goods are used; and

(d) run, within the variations permitted by the agreement, of even kind, quality and quantity within each unit and among all units involved; and

(e) are adequately contained, packaged, and labeled as the agreement may require; and

(f) conform to the promises or affirmations of fact made on the container or label if any.

(3) Unless excluded or modified (Section 2-316) other implied warranties may arise from course of dealing or usage of trade.

Official Comment

Prior Uniform Statutory Provision: Section 15(2), Uniform Sales Act.

Changes: Completely rewritten.

Purposes of Changes: This section, drawn in view of the steadily developing case law on the subject, is intended to make it clear that:

1. The seller's obligation applies to present sales as well as to contracts to sell subject to the effects of any examination of specific goods. (Subsection (2) of Section 2–316). Also, the warranty of merchantability applies to sales for use as well as to sales for resale.

2. The question when the warranty is imposed turns basically on the meaning of the terms of the agreement as recognized in the trade. Goods delivered under an agreement made by a merchant in a given line of trade must be of a quality comparable to that generally acceptable in that line of trade under the description or other designation of the goods used in the agreement. The responsibility imposed rests on any merchant-seller, and the absence of the words "grower or manufacturer or not" which appeared in Section 15(2) of the Uniform Sales Act does not restrict the applicability of this section.

3. A specific designation of goods by the buyer does not exclude the seller's obligation that they be fit for the general purposes appropriate to such goods. A contract for the sale of second-hand goods, however, involves only such obligation as is appropriate to such goods for that is their contract description. A person making an isolated sale of goods is not a "merchant" within the meaning of the full scope of this section and, thus, no warranty of merchantability would apply. His knowledge of any defects not apparent on inspection would, however, without need for express agreement and in keeping with the underlying reason of the present section and the provisions on good faith, impose an obligation that known material but hidden defects be fully disclosed.

4. Although a seller may not be a "merchant" as to the goods in question, if he states generally that they are "guaranteed" the provisions of this section may furnish a guide to the content of the resulting express warranty. This has particular significance in the case of second-hand sales, and has further significance in limiting the effect of fine-print disclaimer clauses where their effect would be inconsistent with large-print assertions of "guarantee".

5. The second sentence of subsection (1) covers the warranty with respect to food and drink. Serving food or drink for value is a sale, whether to be consumed on the premises or elsewhere. Cases to the contrary are rejected. The principal warranty is that stated in subsections (1) and (2)(c) of this section.

6. Subsection (2) does not purport to exhaust the meaning of "merchantable" nor to negate any of its attributes not specifically mentioned in the text of the statute, but arising by usage of trade or through case law. The language used is "must be at least such as ...," and the intention is to leave open other possible attributes of merchantability.

7. Paragraphs (a) and (b) of subsection (2) are to be read together. Both refer, as indicated above, to the standards of that line of the trade which fits the transaction and the seller's business. "Fair average" is a term directly appropriate to agricultural bulk products and means goods centering around the middle belt of quality, not the least or the worst that can be understood in the particular

trade by the designation, but such as can pass "without objection." Of course a fair percentage of the least is permissible but the goods are not "fair average" if they are all of the least or worst quality possible under the description. In cases of doubt as to what quality is intended, the price at which a merchant closes a contract is an excellent index of the nature and scope of his obligation under the present section.

8. Fitness for the ordinary purposes for which goods of the type are used is a fundamental concept of the present section and is covered in paragraph (c). As stated above, merchantability is also a part of the obligation owing to the purchaser for use. Correspondingly, protection, under this aspect of the warranty, of the person buying for resale to the ultimate consumer is equally necessary, and merchantable goods must therefore be "honestly" resalable in the normal course of business because they are what they purport to be.

9. Paragraph (d) on evenness of kind, quality and quantity follows case law. But precautionary language has been added as a reminder of the frequent usages of trade which permit substantial variations both with and without an allowance or an obligation to replace the varying units.

10. Paragraph (e) applies only where the nature of the goods and of the transaction require a certain type of container, package or label. Paragraph (f) applies, on the other hand, wherever there is a label or container on which representations are made, even though the original contract, either by express terms or usage of trade, may not have required either the labelling or the representation. This follows from the general obligation of good faith which requires that a buyer should not be placed in the position of reselling or using goods delivered under false representations appearing on the package or container. No problem of extra consideration arises in this connection since, under this Article, an obligation is imposed by the original contract not to deliver mislabeled articles, and the obligation is imposed where mercantile good faith so requires and without reference to the doctrine of consideration.

11. Exclusion or modification of the warranty of merchantability, or of any part of it, is dealt with in the section to which the text of the present section makes explicit precautionary references. That section must be read with particular reference to its subsection (4) on limitation of remedies. The warranty of merchantability, wherever it is normal, is so commonly taken for granted that its exclusion from the contract is a matter threatening surprise and therefore requiring special precaution.

12. Subsection (3) is to make explicit that usage of trade and course of dealing can create warranties and that they are implied rather than express warranties and thus subject to exclusion or modification under Section 2–316. A typical instance would be the obligation to provide pedigree papers to evidence conformity of the animal to the contract in the case of a pedigreed dog or blooded bull.

13. In an action based on breach of warranty, it is of course necessary to show not only the existence of the warranty but the fact that the warranty was broken and that the breach of the warranty was the proximate cause of the loss sustained. In such an action an affirmative showing by the seller that the loss resulted from some action or event following his own delivery of the goods can operate as a defense. Equally, evidence indicating that the seller exercised care in the manufacture, processing or selec-

tion of the goods is relevant to the issue of whether the warranty was in fact broken. Action by the buyer following an examination of the goods which ought to have indicated the defect complained of can be shown as matter bearing on whether the breach itself was the cause of the injury.

* * *

§ 2–315. Implied Warranty: Fitness for Particular Purpose

Where the seller at the time of contracting has reason to know any particular purpose for which the goods are required and that the buyer is relying on the seller's skill or judgment to select or furnish suitable goods, there is unless excluded or modified under the next section an implied warranty that the goods shall be fit for such purpose.

Official Comment

Prior Uniform Statutory Provision: Section 15(1), (4), (5), Uniform Sales Act.

Changes: Rewritten.

Purposes of Changes:

1. Whether or not this warranty arises in any individual case is basically a question of fact to be determined by the circumstances of the contracting. Under this section the buyer need not bring home to the seller actual knowledge of the particular purpose for which the goods are intended or of his reliance on the seller's skill and judgment, if the circumstances are such that the seller has reason to realize the purpose intended or that the reliance exists. The buyer, of course, must actually be relying on the seller.

2. A "particular purpose" differs from the ordinary purpose for which the goods are used in that it envisages a specific use by the buyer which is peculiar to the nature of his business whereas the ordinary purposes for which goods are used are those envisaged in the concept of merchantability and go to uses which are customarily made of the goods in question. For example, shoes are generally used for the purpose of walking upon ordinary ground, but a seller may know that a particular pair was selected to be used for climbing mountains.

A contract may of course include both a warranty of merchantability and one of fitness for a particular purpose.

The provisions of this Article on the cumulation and conflict of express and implied warranties must be considered on the question of inconsistency between or among warranties. In such a case any question of fact as to which warranty was intended by the parties to apply must be resolved in favor of the warranty of fitness for particular purpose as against all other warranties except where the buyer has taken upon himself the responsibility of furnishing the technical specifications.

3. In connection with the warranty of fitness for a particular purpose the provisions of this Article on the allocation or division of risks are particularly applicable in any transaction in which the purpose for which the goods are to be used combines requirements both as to the quality of the goods themselves and compliance with certain laws or regulations. How the risks are divided is a question of fact to be determined, where not expressly contained in the agreement, from the circumstances of contracting, usage of trade, course of per-

formance and the like, matters which may constitute the "otherwise agreement" of the parties by which they may divide the risk or burden.

4. The absence from this section of the language used in the Uniform Sales Act in referring to the seller, "whether he be the grower or manufacturer or not," is not intended to impose any requirement that the seller be a grower or manufacturer. Although normally the warranty will arise only where the seller is a merchant with the appropriate "skill or judgment," it can arise as to non-merchants where this is justified by the particular circumstances.

5. The elimination of the "patent or other trade name" exception constitutes the major extension of the warranty of fitness which has been made by the cases and continued in this Article. Under the present section the existence of a patent or other trade name and the designation of the article by that name, or indeed in any other definite manner, is only one of the facts to be considered on the question of whether the buyer actually relied on the seller, but it is not of itself decisive of the issue. If the buyer himself is insisting on a particular brand he is not relying on the seller's skill and judgment and so no warranty results. But the mere fact that the article purchased has a particular patent or trade name is not sufficient to indicate nonreliance if the article has been recommended by the seller as adequate for the buyer's purposes.

6. The specific reference forward in the present section to the following section on exclusion or modification of warranties is to call attention to the possibility of eliminating the warranty in any given case. However it must be noted that under the following section the warranty of fitness for a particular purpose must be excluded or modified by a conspicuous writing.

* * *

§ 2–316. Exclusion or Modification of Warranties

(1) Words or conduct relevant to the creation of an express warranty and words or conduct tending to negate or limit warranty shall be construed wherever reasonable as consistent with each other; but subject to the provisions of this Article on parol or extrinsic evidence (Section 2–202) negation or limitation is inoperative to the extent that such construction is unreasonable.

(2) Subject to subsection (3), to exclude or modify the implied warranty of merchantability or any part of it the language must mention merchantability and in case of a writing must be conspicuous, and to exclude or modify any implied warranty of fitness the exclusion must be by a writing and conspicuous. Language to exclude all implied warranties of fitness is sufficient if it states, for example, that "There are no warranties which extend beyond the description on the face hereof."

(3) Notwithstanding subsection (2)

(a) unless the circumstances indicate otherwise, all implied warranties are excluded by expressions like "as is," "with all faults" or other language which in common understanding calls the buyer's attention to the exclusion of warranties and makes plain that there is no implied warranty; and

(b) when the buyer before entering into the contract has examined the goods or the sample or model as fully as he desired or has refused to examine the goods there is no implied warranty with regard to defects which an examination ought in the circumstances to have revealed to him; and

(c) an implied warranty can also be excluded or modified by course of dealing or course of performance or usage of trade.

(4) Remedies for breach of warranty can be limited in accordance with the provisions of this Article on liquidation or limitation of damages and on contractual modification of remedy (Sections 2–718 and 2–719).

Official Comment

Prior Uniform Statutory Provision: None. See sections 15 and 71, Uniform Sales Act.

Purposes:

1. This section is designed principally to deal with those frequent clauses in sales contracts which seek to exclude "all warranties, express or implied." It seeks to protect a buyer from unexpected and unbargained language of disclaimer by denying effect to such language when inconsistent with language of express warranty and permitting the exclusion of implied warranties only by conspicuous language or other circumstances which protect the buyer from surprise.

2. The seller is protected under this Article against false allegations of oral warranties by its provisions on parol and extrinsic evidence and against unauthorized representations by the customary "lack of authority" clauses. This Article treats the limitation or avoidance of consequential damages as a matter of limiting remedies for breach, separate from the matter of creation of liability under a warranty. If no warranty exists, there is of course no problem of limiting remedies for breach of warranty. Under subsection (4) the question of limitation of remedy is governed by the sections referred to rather than by this section.

3. Disclaimer of the implied warranty of merchantability is permitted under subsection (2), but with the safeguard that such disclaimers must mention merchantability and in case of a writing must be conspicuous.

4. Unlike the implied warranty of merchantability, implied warranties of fitness for a particular purpose may be excluded by general language, but only if it is in writing and conspicuous.

5. Subsection (2) presupposes that the implied warranty in question exists unless excluded or modified. Whether or not language of disclaimer satisfies the requirements of this section, such language may be relevant under other sections to the question whether the warranty was ever in fact created. Thus, unless the provisions of this Article on parol and extrinsic evidence prevent, oral language of disclaimer may raise issues of fact as to whether reliance by the buyer occurred and whether the seller had "reason to know" under the section on implied warranty of fitness for a particular purpose.

§ 2-316

6. The exceptions to the general rule set forth in paragraphs (a), (b) and (c) of subsection (3) are common factual situations in which the circumstances surrounding the transaction are in themselves sufficient to call the buyer's attention to the fact that no implied warranties are made or that a certain implied warranty is being excluded.

7. Paragraph (a) of subsection (3) deals with general terms such as "as is," "as they stand," "with all faults," and the like. Such terms in ordinary commercial usage are understood to mean that the buyer takes the entire risk as to the quality of the goods involved. The terms covered by paragraph (a) are in fact merely a particularization of paragraph (c) which provides for exclusion or modification of implied warranties by usage of trade.

8. Under paragraph (b) of subsection (3) warranties may be excluded or modified by the circumstances where the buyer examines the goods or a sample or model of them before entering into the contract. "Examination" as used in this paragraph is not synonymous with inspection before acceptance or at any other time after the contract has been made. It goes rather to the nature of the responsibility assumed by the seller at the time of the making of the contract. Of course if the buyer discovers the defect and uses the goods anyway, or if he unreasonably fails to examine the goods before he uses them, resulting injuries may be found to result from his own action rather than proximately from a breach of warranty. See Sections 2—314 and 2—715 and comments thereto.

In order to bring the transaction within the scope of "refused to examine" in paragraph (b), it is not sufficient that the goods are available for inspection. There must in addition be a demand by the seller that the buyer examine the goods fully. The seller by the demand puts the buyer on notice that he is assuming the risk of defects which the examination ought to reveal. The language "refused to examine" in this paragraph is intended to make clear the necessity for such demand.

Application of the doctrine of "caveat emptor" in all cases where the buyer examines the goods regardless of statements made by the seller is, however, rejected by this Article. Thus, if the offer of examination is accompanied by words as to their merchantability or specific attributes and the buyer indicates clearly that he is relying on those words rather than on his examination, they give rise to an "express" warranty. In such cases the question is one of fact as to whether a warranty of merchantability has been expressly incorporated in the agreement. Disclaimer of such an express warranty is governed by subsection (1) of the present section.

The particular buyer's skill and the normal method of examining goods in the circumstances determine what defects are excluded by the examination. A failure to notice defects which are obvious cannot excuse the buyer. However, an examination under circumstances which do not permit chemical or other testing of the goods would not exclude defects which could be ascertained only by such testing. Nor can latent defects be excluded by a simple examination. A professional buyer examining a product in his field will be held to have assumed the risk as to all defects which a professional in the field ought to observe, while a nonprofessional buyer will be held to have assumed the risk only for such defects as a layman might be expected to observe.

9. The situation in which the buyer gives precise and complete specifications to the seller is not explicitly

covered in this section, but this is a frequent circumstance by which the implied warranties may be excluded. The warranty of fitness for a particular purpose would not normally arise since in such a situation there is usually no reliance on the seller by the buyer. The warranty of merchantability in such a transaction, however, must be considered in connection with the next section on the cumulation and conflict of warranties. Under paragraph (c) of that section in case of such an inconsistency the implied warranty of merchantability is displaced by the express warranty that the goods will comply with the specifications. Thus, where the buyer gives detailed specifications as to the goods, neither of the implied warranties as to quality will normally apply to the transaction unless consistent with the specifications.

* * *

§ 2–317. Cumulation and Conflict of Warranties Express or Implied

Warranties whether express or implied shall be construed as consistent with each other and as cumulative, but if such construction is unreasonable the intention of the parties shall determine which warranty is dominant. In ascertaining that intention the following rules apply:

(a) Exact or technical specifications displace an inconsistent sample or model or general language of description.

(b) A sample from an existing bulk displaces inconsistent general language of description.

(c) Express warranties displace inconsistent implied warranties other than an implied warranty of fitness for a particular purpose.

Official Comment

Prior Uniform Statutory Provision: On cumulation of warranties see Sections 14, 15, and 16, Uniform Sales Act.

Changes: Completely rewritten into one section.

Purposes of Changes:

1. The present section rests on the basic policy of this Article that no warranty is created except by some conduct (either affirmative action or failure to disclose) on the part of the seller. Therefore, all warranties are made cumulative unless this construction of the contract is impossible or unreasonable.

This Article thus follows the general policy of the Uniform Sales Act except that in case of the sale of an article by its patent or trade name the elimination of the warranty of fitness depends solely on whether the buyer has relied on the seller's skill and judgment; the use of the patent or trade name is but one factor in making this determination.

2. The rules of this section are designed to aid in determining the intention of the parties as to which of inconsistent warranties which have arisen from the circumstances of their transaction shall prevail. These rules of intention are to be applied only where factors making for an equitable

estoppel of the seller do not exist and where he has in perfect good faith made warranties which later turn out to be inconsistent. To the extent that the seller has led the buyer to believe that all of the warranties can be performed, he is estopped from setting up any essential inconsistency as a defense.

3. The rules in subsections (a), (b) and (c) are designed to ascertain the intention of the parties by reference to the factor which probably claimed the attention of the parties in the first instance. These rules are not absolute but may be changed by evidence showing that the conditions which existed at the time of contracting make the construction called for by the section inconsistent or unreasonable.

* * *

§ 2–318. Third Party Beneficiaries of Warranties Express or Implied

Note: *If this Act is introduced in the Congress of the United States this section should be omitted. (States to select one alternative.)*

Alternative A

A seller's warranty whether express or implied extends to any natural person who is in the family or household of his buyer or who is a guest in his home if it is reasonable to expect that such person may use, consume or be affected by the goods and who is injured in person by breach of the warranty. A seller may not exclude or limit the operation of this section.

Alternative B

A seller's warranty whether express or implied extends to any natural person who may reasonably be expected to use, consume or be affected by the goods and who is injured in person by breach of the warranty. A seller may not exclude or limit the operation of this section.

Alternative C

A seller's warranty whether express or implied extends to any person who may reasonably be expected to use, consume or be affected by the goods and who is injured by breach of the warranty. A seller may not exclude or limit the operation of this section with respect to injury to the person of an individual to whom the warranty extends. As amended 1966.

Official Comment

Purposes:

1. The last sentence of this section does not mean that a seller is precluded from excluding or disclaiming a warranty which might otherwise arise in connection with the sale provided such exclusion or modification is permitted by Section 2–316. Nor does

that sentence preclude the seller from limiting the remedies of his own buyer and of any beneficiaries, in any manner provided in Sections 2–718 or 2–719. To the extent that the contract of sale contains provisions under which warranties are excluded or modified, or remedies for breach are limited, such provisions are equally operative against beneficiaries of warranties under this section. What this last sentence forbids is exclusion of liability by the seller to the persons to whom the warranties which he has made to his buyer would extend under this section.

2. The purpose of this section is to give certain beneficiaries the benefit of the same warranty which the buyer received in the contract of sale, thereby freeing any such beneficiaries from any technical rules as to "privity." It seeks to accomplish this purpose without any derogation of any right or remedy resting on negligence. It rests primarily upon the merchant-seller's warranty under this Article that the goods sold are merchantable and fit for the ordinary purposes for which such goods are used rather than the warranty of fitness for a particular purpose. Implicit in the section is that any beneficiary of a warranty may bring a direct action for breach of warranty against the seller whose warranty extends to him [As amended in 1966].

3. The first alternative expressly includes as beneficiaries within its provisions the family, household and guests of the purchaser. Beyond this, the section in this form is neutral and is not intended to enlarge or restrict the developing case law on whether the seller's warranties, given to his buyer who resells, extend to other persons in the distributive chain. The second alternative is designed for states where the case law has already developed further and for those that desire to expand the class of beneficiaries. The third alternative goes further, following the trend of modern decisions as indicated by Restatement of Torts 2d § 402 A (Tentative Draft No. 10, 1965) in extending the rule beyond injuries to the person [As amended in 1966].

* * *

* * *

§ 2–327. Special Incidents of Sale on Approval and Sale or Return

(1) Under a sale on approval unless otherwise agreed

(a) although the goods are identified to the contract the risk of loss and the title do not pass to the buyer until acceptance; and

(b) use of the goods consistent with the purpose of trial is not acceptance but failure seasonably to notify the seller of election to return the goods is acceptance, and if the goods conform to the contract acceptance of any part is acceptance of the whole; and

(c) after due notification of election to return, the return is at the seller's risk and expense but a merchant buyer must follow any reasonable instructions.

(2) Under a sale or return unless otherwise agreed

(a) the option to return extends to the whole or any commercial unit of the goods while in substantially their original condition, but must be exercised seasonably; and

(b) the return is at the buyer's risk and expense.

* * *

§ 2–328. Sale by Auction

(1) In a sale by auction if goods are put up in lots each lot is the subject of a separate sale.

(2) A sale by auction is complete when the auctioneer so announces by the fall of the hammer or in other customary manner. Where a bid is made while the hammer is falling in acceptance of a prior bid the auctioneer may in his discretion reopen the bidding or declare the goods sold under the bid on which the hammer was falling.

(3) Such a sale is with reserve unless the goods are in explicit terms put up without reserve. In an auction with reserve the auctioneer may withdraw the goods at any time until he announces completion of the sale. In an auction without reserve, after the auctioneer calls for bids on an article or lot, that article or lot cannot be withdrawn unless no bid is made within a reasonable time. In either case a bidder may retract his bid until the auctioneer's announcement of completion of the sale, but a bidder's retraction does not revive any previous bid.

(4) If the auctioneer knowingly receives a bid on the seller's behalf or the seller makes or procures such a bid, and notice has not been given that liberty for such bidding is reserved, the buyer may at his option avoid the sale or take the goods at the price of the last good faith bid prior to the completion of the sale. This subsection shall not apply to any bid at a forced sale.

* * *

PART 5
PERFORMANCE

* * *

§ 2–503. Manner of Seller's Tender of Delivery

(1) Tender of delivery requires that the seller put and hold conforming goods at the buyer's disposition and give the buyer any notification reasonably necessary to enable him to take delivery. The manner, time and place for tender are determined by the agreement and this Article, and in particular

(a) tender must be at a reasonable hour, and if it is of goods they must be kept available for the period reasonably necessary to enable the buyer to take possession; but

(b) unless otherwise agreed the buyer must furnish facilities reasonably suited to the receipt of the goods.

(2) Where the case is within the next section respecting shipment tender requires that the seller comply with its provisions.

(3) Where the seller is required to deliver at a particular destination tender requires that he comply with subsection (1) and also in any appropriate case tender documents as described in subsections (4) and (5) of this section.

(4) Where goods are in the possession of a bailee and are to be delivered without being moved

(a) tender requires that the seller either tender a negotiable document of title covering such goods or procure acknowledgment by the bailee of the buyer's right to possession of the goods; but

(b) tender to the buyer of a non-negotiable document of title or of a written direction to the bailee to deliver is sufficient tender unless the buyer seasonably objects, and receipt by the bailee of notification of the buyer's rights fixes those rights as against the bailee and all third persons; but risk of loss of the goods and of any failure by the bailee to honor the non-negotiable document of title or to obey the direction remains on the seller until the buyer has had a reasonable time to present the document or direction, and a refusal by the bailee to honor the document or to obey the direction defeats the tender.

(5) Where the contract requires the seller to deliver documents

(a) he must tender all such documents in correct form, except as provided in this Article with respect to bills of lading in a set (subsection (2) of Section 2–323); and

(b) tender through customary banking channels is sufficient and dishonor of a draft accompanying the documents constitutes non-acceptance or rejection.

* * *

§ 2–507. Effect of Seller's Tender; Delivery on Condition

(1) Tender of delivery is a condition to the buyer's duty to accept the goods and, unless otherwise agreed, to his duty to pay for them. Tender entitles the seller to acceptance of the goods and to payment according to the contract.

(2) Where payment is due and demanded on the delivery to the buyer of goods or documents of title, his right as against the seller to retain or dispose of them is conditional upon his making the payment due.

* * *

§ 2-508. Cure by Seller of Improper Tender or Delivery; Replacement

(1) Where any tender or delivery by the seller is rejected because non-conforming and the time for performance has not yet expired, the seller may seasonably notify the buyer of his intention to cure and may then within the contract time make a conforming delivery.

(2) Where the buyer rejects a non-conforming tender which the seller had reasonable grounds to believe would be acceptable with or without money allowance the seller may if he seasonably notifies the buyer have a further reasonable time to substitute a conforming tender.

Official Comment

Prior Uniform Statutory Provision: None.

Purposes:

1. Subsection (1) permits a seller who has made a non-conforming tender in any case to make a conforming delivery within the contract time upon seasonable notification to the buyer. It applies even where the seller has taken back the non-conforming goods and refunded the purchase price. He may still make a good tender within the contract period. The closer, however, it is to the contract date, the greater is the necessity for extreme promptness on the seller's part in notifying of his intention to cure, if such notification is to be "seasonable" under this subsection.

The rule of this subsection, moreover, is qualified by its underlying reasons. Thus if, after contracting for June delivery, a buyer later makes known to the seller his need for shipment early in the month and the seller ships accordingly, the "contract time" has been cut down by the supervening modification and the time for cure of tender must be referred to this modified time term.

2. Subsection (2) seeks to avoid injustice to the seller by reason of a surprise rejection by the buyer. However, the seller is not protected unless he had "reasonable grounds to believe" that the tender would be acceptable. Such reasonable grounds can lie in prior course of dealing, course of performance or usage of trade as well as in the particular circumstances surrounding the making of the contract. The seller is charged with commercial knowledge of any factors in a particular sales situation which require him to comply strictly with his obligations under the contract as, for example, strict conformity of documents in an overseas shipment or the sale of precision parts or chemicals for use in manufacture. Further, if the buyer gives notice either implicitly, as by a prior course of dealing involving rigorous inspections, or expressly, as by the deliberate inclusion of a "no replacement" clause in the contract, the seller is to be held to rigid compliance. If the clause appears in a "form" contract evidence that it is out of line with trade usage or the prior course of dealing and was not called to the seller's attention may be sufficient to show that the seller had reasonable grounds to believe that the tender would be acceptable.

3. The words "a further reasonable time to substitute a conforming tender" are intended as words of limitation to protect the buyer. What is a "reasonable time" depends upon the attending circumstances. Compare Section 2-511 on the comparable case

of a seller's surprise demand for legal tender.

4. Existing trade usages permitting variations without rejection but with price allowance enter into the agreement itself as contractual limitations of remedy and are not covered by this section.

* * *

§ 2–510. Effect of Breach on Risk of Loss

(1) Where a tender or delivery of goods so fails to conform to the contract as to give a right of rejection the risk of their loss remains on the seller until cure or acceptance.

(2) Where the buyer rightfully revokes acceptance he may to the extent of any deficiency in his effective insurance coverage treat the risk of loss as having rested on the seller from the beginning.

(3) Where the buyer as to conforming goods already identified to the contract for sale repudiates or is otherwise in breach before risk of their loss has passed to him, the seller may to the extent of any deficiency in his effective insurance coverage treat the risk of loss as resting on the buyer for a commercially reasonable time.

* * *

§ 2–511. Tender of Payment by Buyer; Payment by Check

(1) Unless otherwise agreed tender of payment is a condition to the seller's duty to tender and complete any delivery.

(2) Tender of payment is sufficient when made by any means or in any manner current in the ordinary course of business unless the seller demands payment in legal tender and gives any extension of time reasonably necessary to procure it.

(3) Subject to the provisions of this Act on the effect of an instrument on an obligation (Section 3–802), payment by check is conditional and is defeated as between the parties by dishonor of the check on due presentment.

* * *

§ 2–512. Payment by Buyer Before Inspection

(1) Where the contract requires payment before inspection non-conformity of the goods does not excuse the buyer from so making payment unless

(a) the non-conformity appears without inspection; or

(b) despite tender of the required documents the circumstances would justify injunction against honor under the provisions of this Act (Section 5–114).

(2) Payment pursuant to subsection (1) does not constitute an acceptance of goods or impair the buyer's right to inspect or any of his remedies.

* * *

§ 2–513. Buyer's Right to Inspection of Goods

(1) Unless otherwise agreed and subject to subsection (3), where goods are tendered or delivered or identified to the contract for sale, the buyer has a right before payment or acceptance to inspect them at any reasonable place and time and in any reasonable manner. When the seller is required or authorized to send the goods to the buyer, the inspection may be after their arrival.

(2) Expenses of inspection must be borne by the buyer but may be recovered from the seller if the goods do not conform and are rejected.

(3) Unless otherwise agreed and subject to the provisions of this Article on C.I.F. contracts (subsection (3) of Section 2–321), the buyer is not entitled to inspect the goods before payment of the price when the contract provides

    (a) for delivery "C.O.D." or on other like terms; or

    (b) for payment against documents of title, except where such payment is due only after the goods are to become available for inspection.

(4) A place or method of inspection fixed by the parties is presumed to be exclusive but unless otherwise expressly agreed it does not postpone identification or shift the place for delivery or for passing the risk of loss. If compliance becomes impossible, inspection shall be as provided in this section unless the place or method fixed was clearly intended as an indispensable condition failure of which avoids the contract.

Official Comment

Prior Uniform Statutory Provision: Section 47(2), (3), Uniform Sales Act.

Changes: Rewritten, Subsections (2) and (3) being new.

Purposes of Changes and New Matter: To correspond in substance with the prior uniform statutory provision and to incorporate in addition some of the results of the better case law so that:

1. The buyer is entitled to inspect goods as provided in subsection (1) unless it has been otherwise agreed by the parties. The phrase "unless otherwise agreed" is intended principally to cover such situations as those outlined in subsections (3) and (4) and those in which the agreement of the parties negates inspection before tender of delivery. However, no agreement by the parties can displace the entire right of inspection except where the contract is simply for the sale of "this thing." Even in a sale of boxed goods "as is" inspection is a right of the buyer, since if the boxes prove to contain some other merchandise altogether the price can be recovered back; nor do the limitations of

the provision on effect of acceptance apply in such a case.

2. The buyer's right of inspection is available to him upon tender, delivery or appropriation of the goods with notice to him. Since inspection is available to him on tender, where payment is due against delivery he may, unless otherwise agreed, make his inspection before payment of the price. It is also available to him after receipt of the goods and so may be postponed after receipt for a reasonable time. Failure to inspect before payment does not impair the right to inspect after receipt of the goods unless the case falls within subsection (4) on agreed and exclusive inspection provisions. The right to inspect goods which have been appropriated with notice to the buyer holds whether or not the sale was by sample.

3. The buyer may exercise his right of inspection at any reasonable time or place and in any reasonable manner. It is not necessary that he select the most appropriate time, place or manner to inspect or that his selection be the customary one in the trade or locality. Any reasonable time, place or manner is available to him and the reasonableness will be determined by trade usages, past practices between the parties and the other circumstances of the case.

The last sentence of subsection (1) makes it clear that the place of arrival of shipped goods is a reasonable place for their inspection.

4. Expenses of an inspection made to satisfy the buyer of the seller's performance must be assumed by the buyer in the first instance. Since the rule provides merely for an allocation of expense there is no policy to prevent the parties from providing otherwise in the agreement. Where the buyer would normally bear the expenses of the inspection but the goods are rightly rejected because of what the inspection reveals, demonstrable and reasonable costs of the inspection are part of his incidental damage caused by the seller's breach.

5. In the case of payment against documents, subsection (3) requires payment before inspection, since shipping documents against which payment is to be made will commonly arrive and be tendered while the goods are still in transit. This Article recognizes no exception in any peculiar case in which the goods happen to arrive before the documents. However, where by the agreement payment is to await the arrival of the goods, inspection before payment becomes proper since the goods are then "available for inspection."

Where by the agreement the documents are to be held until arrival the buyer is entitled to inspect before payment since the goods are then "available for inspection". Proof of usage is not necessary to establish this right, but if inspection before payment is disputed the contrary must be established by usage or by an explicit contract term to that effect.

For the same reason, that the goods are available for inspection, a term calling for payment against storage documents or a delivery order does not normally bar the buyer's right to inspection before payment under subsection (3)(b). This result is reinforced by the buyer's right under subsection (1) to inspect goods which have been appropriated with notice to him.

6. Under subsection (4) an agreed place or method of inspection is generally held to be intended as exclusive. However, where compliance with such an agreed inspection term becomes impossible, the question is basically one of intention. If the parties clearly intend that the method

of inspection named is to be a necessary condition without which the entire deal is to fail, the contract is at an end if that method becomes impossible. On the other hand, if the parties merely seek to indicate a convenient and reliable method but do not intend to give up the deal in the event of its failure, any reasonable method of inspection may be substituted under this Article.

Since the purpose of an agreed place of inspection is only to make sure at that point whether or not the goods will be thrown back, the "exclusive" feature of the named place is satisfied under this Article if the buyer's failure to inspect there is held to be an acceptance with the knowledge of such defects as inspection would have revealed within the section on waiver of buyer's objections by failure to particularize. Revocation of the acceptance is limited to the situations stated in the section pertaining to that subject. The reasonable time within which to give notice of defects within the section on notice of breach begins to run from the point of the "acceptance."

7. Clauses on time of inspection are commonly clauses which limit the time in which the buyer must inspect and give notice of defects. Such clauses are therefore governed by the section of this Article which requires that such a time limitation must be reasonable.

8. Inspection under this Article is not to be regarded as a "condition precedent to the passing of title" so that risk until inspection remains on the seller. Under subsection (4) such an approach cannot be sustained. Issues between the buyer and seller are settled in this Article almost wholly by special provisions and not by the technical determination of the locus of the title. Thus "inspection as a condition to the passing of title" becomes a concept almost without meaning. However, in peculiar circumstances inspection may still have some of the consequences hitherto sought and obtained under that concept.

9. "Inspection" under this section has to do with the buyer's checkup on whether the seller's performance is in accordance with a contract previously made and is not to be confused with the "examination" of the goods or of a sample or model of them at the time of contracting which may affect the warranties involved in the contract.

* * *

* * *

§ 2–515. Preserving Evidence of Goods in Dispute

In furtherance of the adjustment of any claim or dispute

(a) either party on reasonable notification to the other and for the purpose of ascertaining the facts and preserving evidence has the right to inspect, test and sample the goods including such of them as may be in the possession or control of the other; and

(b) the parties may agree to a third party inspection or survey to determine the conformity or condition of the goods and may agree that the findings shall be binding upon them in any subsequent litigation or adjustment.

Official Comment

Prior Uniform Statutory Provision: None.

Purposes:

1. To meet certain serious problems which arise when there is a dispute as to the quality of the goods and thereby perhaps to aid the parties in reaching a settlement, and to further the use of devices which will promote certainty as to the condition of the goods, or at least aid in preserving evidence of their condition.

2. Under paragraph (a), to afford either party an opportunity for preserving evidence, whether or not agreement has been reached, and thereby to reduce uncertainty in any litigation and, in turn perhaps, to promote agreement.

Paragraph (a) does not conflict with the provisions on the seller's right to resell rejected goods or the buyer's similar right. Apparent conflict between these provisions which will be suggested in certain circumstances is to be resolved by requiring prompt action by the parties. Nor does paragraph (a) impair the effect of a term for payment before inspection. Short of such defects as amount to fraud or substantial failure of consideration, non-conformity is neither an excuse nor a defense to an action for non-acceptance of documents. Normally, therefore, until the buyer has made payment, inspected and rejected the goods, there is no occasion or use for the rights under paragraph (a).

3. Under paragraph (b), to provide for third party inspection upon the agreement of the parties, thereby opening the door to amicable adjustments based upon the findings of such third parties.

The use of the phrase "conformity or condition" makes it clear that the parties' agreement may range from a complete settlement of all aspects of the dispute by a third party to the use of a third party merely to determine and record the condition of the goods so that they can be resold or used to reduce the stake in controversy. "Conformity", at one end of the scale of possible issues, includes the whole question of interpretation of the agreement and its legal effect, the state of the goods in regard to quality and condition, whether any defects are due to factors which operate at the risk of the buyer, and the degree of non-conformity where that may be material. "Condition", at the other end of the scale, includes nothing but the degree of damage or deterioration which the goods show. Paragraph (b) is intended to reach any point in the gamut which the parties may agree upon.

The principle of the section on reservation of rights reinforces this paragraph in simplifying such adjustments as the parties wish to make in partial settlement while reserving their rights as to any further points. Paragraph (b) also suggests the use of arbitration, where desired, of any points left open, but nothing in this section is intended to repeal or amend any statute governing arbitration. Where any question arises as to the extent of the parties' agreement under the paragraph, the presumption should be that it was meant to extend only to the relation between the contract description and the goods as delivered, since that is what a craftsman in the trade would normally be expected to report upon. Finally, a written and authenticated report of inspection or tests by a third party, whether or not sampling has been practicable, is entitled to be admitted as evidence under this Act, for it is a third party document.

* * *

PART 6

BREACH, REPUDIATION AND EXCUSE

§ 2–601. Buyer's Rights on Improper Delivery

Subject to the provisions of this Article on breach in installment contracts (Section 2–612) and unless otherwise agreed under the sections on contractual limitations of remedy (Sections 2–718 and 2–719), if the goods or the tender of delivery fail in any respect to conform to the contract, the buyer may

(a) reject the whole; or

(b) accept the whole; or

(c) accept any commercial unit or units and reject the rest.

Official Comment

Prior Uniform Statutory Provision: No one general equivalent provision but numerous provisions, dealing with situations of non-conformity where buyer may accept or reject, including Sections 11, 44 and 69(1), Uniform Sales Act.

Changes: Partial acceptance in good faith is recognized and the buyer's remedies on the contract for breach of warranty and the like, where the buyer has returned the goods after transfer of title, are no longer barred.

Purposes of Changes: To make it clear that:

1. A buyer accepting a nonconforming tender is not penalized by the loss of any remedy otherwise open to him. This policy extends to cover and regulate the acceptance of a part of any lot improperly tendered in any case where the price can reasonably be apportioned. Partial acceptance is permitted whether the part of the goods accepted conforms or not. The only limitation on partial acceptance is that good faith and commercial reasonableness must be used to avoid undue impairment of the value of the remaining portion of the goods. This is the reason for the insistence on the "commercial unit" in paragraph (c). In this respect, the test is not only what unit has been the basis of contract, but whether the partial acceptance produces so materially adverse an effect on the remainder as to constitute bad faith.

2. Acceptance made with the knowledge of the other party is final. An original refusal to accept may be withdrawn by a later acceptance if the seller has indicated that he is holding the tender open. However, if the buyer attempts to accept, either in whole or in part, after his original rejection has caused the seller to arrange for other disposition of the goods, the buyer must answer for any ensuing damage since the next section provides that any exercise of ownership after rejection is wrongful as against the seller. Further, he is liable even though the seller may choose to treat his action as acceptance rather than conversion, since the damage flows from the misleading notice. Such arrangements for resale or other disposition of the goods by the seller must be viewed as within the normal contemplation of a buyer who has given notice of rejection. However, the buyer's attempts in good faith to dispose of defective goods where the seller has failed to give instructions within a

reasonable time are not to be regarded as an acceptance.

* * *

§ 2–602. Manner and Effect of Rightful Rejection

(1) Rejection of goods must be within a reasonable time after their delivery or tender. It is ineffective unless the buyer seasonably notifies the seller.

(2) Subject to the provisions of the two following sections on rejected goods (Sections 2–603 and 2–604),

   (a) after rejection any exercise of ownership by the buyer with respect to any commercial unit is wrongful as against the seller; and

   (b) if the buyer has before rejection taken physical possession of goods in which he does not have a security interest under the provisions of this Article (subsection (3) of Section 2–711), he is under a duty after rejection to hold them with reasonable care at the seller's disposition for a time sufficient to permit the seller to remove them; but

   (c) the buyer has no further obligations with regard to goods rightfully rejected.

(3) The seller's rights with respect to goods wrongfully rejected are governed by the provisions of this Article on Seller's remedies in general (Section 2–703).

Official Comment

Prior Uniform Statutory Provision: Section 50, Uniform Sales Act.

Changes: Rewritten.

Purposes of Changes: To make it clear that:

1. A tender or delivery of goods made pursuant to a contract of sale, even though wholly non-conforming, requires affirmative action by the buyer to avoid acceptance. Under subsection (1), therefore, the buyer is given a reasonable time to notify the seller of his rejection, but without such seasonable notification his rejection is ineffective. The sections of this Article dealing with inspection of goods must be read in connection with the buyer's reasonable time for action under this subsection. Contract provisions limiting the time for rejection fall within the rule of the section on "Time" and are effective if the time set gives the buyer a reasonable time for discovery of defects. What constitutes a due "notifying" of rejection by the buyer to the seller is defined in Section 1–201.

2. Subsection (2) lays down the normal duties of the buyer upon rejection, which flow from the relationship of the parties. Beyond his duty to hold the goods with reasonable care for the buyer's [seller's] disposition, this section continues the policy of prior uniform legislation in generally relieving the buyer from any duties with respect to them, except when the circumstances impose the limited obli-

gation of salvage upon him under the next section.

3. The present section applies only to rightful rejection by the buyer. If the seller has made a tender which in all respects conforms to the contract, the buyer has a positive duty to accept and his failure to do so constitutes a "wrongful rejection" which gives the seller immediate remedies for breach. Subsection (3) is included here to emphasize the sharp distinction between the rejection of an improper tender and the non-acceptance which is a breach by the buyer.

4. The provisions of this section are to be appropriately limited or modified when a negotiation is in process.

* * *

* * *

§ 2–605. Waiver of Buyer's Objections by Failure to Particularize

(1) The buyer's failure to state in connection with rejection a particular defect which is ascertainable by reasonable inspection precludes him from relying on the unstated defect to justify rejection or to establish breach

(a) where the seller could have cured it if stated seasonably; or

(b) between merchants when the seller has after rejection made a request in writing for a full and final written statement of all defects on which the buyer proposes to rely.

(2) Payment against documents made without reservation of rights precludes recovery of the payment for defects apparent on the face of the documents.

* * *

§ 2–606. What Constitutes Acceptance of Goods

(1) Acceptance of goods occurs when the buyer

(a) after a reasonable opportunity to inspect the goods signifies to the seller that the goods are conforming or that he will take or retain them in spite of their nonconformity; or

(b) fails to make an effective rejection (subsection (1) of Section 2–602), but such acceptance does not occur until the buyer has had a reasonable opportunity to inspect them; or

(c) does any act inconsistent with the seller's ownership; but if such act is wrongful as against the seller it is an acceptance only if ratified by him.

(2) Acceptance of a part of any commercial unit is acceptance of that entire unit.

Official Comment

Prior Uniform Statutory Provision: Section 48, Uniform Sales Act.

Changes: Rewritten, the qualification in paragraph (c) and subsection (2) being new; otherwise the general policy of the prior legislation is continued.

Purposes of Changes and New Matter: To make it clear that:

1. Under this Article "acceptance" as applied to goods means that the buyer, pursuant to the contract, takes particular goods which have been appropriated to the contract as his own, whether or not he is obligated to do so, and whether he does so by words, action, or silence when it is time to speak. If the goods conform to the contract, acceptance amounts only to the performance by the buyer of one part of his legal obligations.

2. Under this Article acceptance of goods is always acceptance of identified goods which have been appropriated to the contract or are appropriated by the contract. There is no provision for "acceptance of title" apart from acceptance in general, since acceptance of title is not material under this Article to the detailed rights and duties of the parties. (See Section 2–401). The refinements of the older law between acceptance of goods and of title become unnecessary in view of the provisions of the sections on effect and revocation of acceptance, on effects of identification and on risk of loss, and those sections which free the seller's and buyer's remedies from the complications and confusions caused by the question of whether title has or has not passed to the buyer before breach.

3. Under paragraph (a), payment made after tender is always one circumstance tending to signify acceptance of the goods but in itself it can never be more than one circumstance and is not conclusive. Also, a conditional communication of acceptance always remains subject to its expressed conditions.

4. Under paragraph (c), any action taken by the buyer, which is inconsistent with his claim that he has rejected the goods, constitutes an acceptance. However, the provisions of paragraph (c) are subject to the sections dealing with rejection by the buyer which permit the buyer to take certain actions with respect to the goods pursuant to his options and duties imposed by those sections, without effecting an acceptance of the goods. The second clause of paragraph (c) modifies some of the prior case law and makes it clear that "acceptance" in law based on the wrongful act of the acceptor is acceptance only as against the wrongdoer and then only at the option of the party wronged.

In the same manner in which a buyer can bind himself, despite his insistence that he is rejecting or has rejected the goods, by an act inconsistent with the seller's ownership under paragraph (c), he can obligate himself by a communication of acceptance despite a prior rejection under paragraph (a). However, the sections on buyer's rights on improper delivery and on the effect of rightful rejection, make it clear that after he once rejects a tender, paragraph (a) does not operate in favor of the buyer unless the seller has re-tendered the goods or has taken affirmative action indicating that he is holding the tender open. See also Comment 2 to Section 2–601.

5. Subsection (2) supplements the policy of the section on buyer's rights on improper delivery, recognizing the validity of a partial acceptance but insisting that the buyer exercise

this right only as to whole commercial units.

* * *

§ 2–607. Effect of Acceptance; Notice of Breach; Burden of Establishing Breach After Acceptance; Notice of Claim or Litigation to Person Answerable Over

(1) The buyer must pay at the contract rate for any goods accepted.

(2) Acceptance of goods by the buyer precludes rejection of the goods accepted and if made with knowledge of a non-conformity cannot be revoked because of it unless the acceptance was on the reasonable assumption that the non-conformity would be seasonably cured but acceptance does not of itself impair any other remedy provided by this Article for non-conformity.

(3) Where a tender has been accepted

(a) the buyer must within a reasonable time after he discovers or should have discovered any breach notify the seller of breach or be barred from any remedy; and

(b) if the claim is one for infringement or the like (subsection (3) of Section 2–312) and the buyer is sued as a result of such a breach he must so notify the seller within a reasonable time after he receives notice of the litigation or be barred from any remedy over for liability established by the litigation.

(4) The burden is on the buyer to establish any breach with respect to the goods accepted.

(5) Where the buyer is sued for breach of a warranty or other obligation for which his seller is answerable over

(a) he may give his seller written notice of the litigation. If the notice states that the seller may come in and defend and that if the seller does not do so he will be bound in any action against him by his buyer by any determination of fact common to the two litigations, then unless the seller after seasonable receipt of the notice does come in and defend he is so bound.

(b) if the claim is one for infringement or the like (subsection (3) of Section 2–312) the original seller may demand in writing that his buyer turn over to him control of the litigation including settlement or else be barred from any remedy over and if he also agrees to bear all expense and to satisfy any adverse judgment, then unless the buyer after seasonable receipt of the demand does turn over control the buyer is so barred.

(6) The provisions of subsections (3), (4) and (5) apply to any obligation of a buyer to hold the seller harmless against infringement or the like (subsection (3) of Section 2–312).

Official Comment

Prior Uniform Statutory Provision: Subsection (1)—Section 41, Uniform Sales Act; Subsections (2) and (3)—Sections 49 and 69, Uniform Sales Act.

Changes: Rewritten.

Purposes of Changes: To continue the prior basic policies with respect to acceptance of goods while making a number of minor though material changes in the interest of simplicity and commercial convenience so that:

1. Under subsection (1), once the buyer accepts a tender the seller acquires a right to its price on the contract terms. In cases of partial acceptance, the price of any part accepted is, if possible, to be reasonably apportioned, using the type of apportionment familiar to the courts in quantum valebat cases, to be determined in terms of "the contract rate," which is the rate determined from the bargain in fact (the agreement) after the rules and policies of this Article have been brought to bear.

2. Under subsection (2) acceptance of goods precludes their subsequent rejection. Any return of the goods thereafter must be by way of revocation of acceptance under the next section. Revocation is unavailable for a non-conformity known to the buyer at the time of acceptance, except where the buyer has accepted on the reasonable assumption that the non-conformity would be seasonably cured.

3. All other remedies of the buyer remain unimpaired under subsection (2). This is intended to include the buyer's full rights with respect to future installments despite his acceptance of any earlier non-conforming installment.

4. The time of notification is to be determined by applying commercial standards to a merchant buyer. "A reasonable time" for notification from a retail consumer is to be judged by different standards so that in his case it will be extended, for the rule of requiring notification is designed to defeat commercial bad faith, not to deprive a good faith consumer of his remedy.

The content of the notification need merely be sufficient to let the seller know that the transaction is still troublesome and must be watched. There is no reason to require that the notification which saves the buyer's rights under this section must include a clear statement of all the objections that will be relied on by the buyer, as under the section covering statements of defects upon rejection (Section 2–605). Nor is there reason for requiring the notification to be a claim for damages or of any threatened litigation or other resort to a remedy. The notification which saves the buyer's rights under this Article need only be such as informs the seller that the transaction is claimed to involve a breach, and thus opens the way for normal settlement through negotiation.

5. Under this Article various beneficiaries are given rights for injuries sustained by them because of the seller's breach of warranty. Such a beneficiary does not fall within the reason of the present section in regard to discovery of defects and the giving of notice within a reasonable time after acceptance, since he has nothing to do with acceptance. However, the reason of this section does extend to

requiring the beneficiary to notify the seller that an injury has occurred. What is said above, with regard to the extended time for reasonable notification from the lay consumer after the injury is also applicable here; but even a beneficiary can be properly held to the use of good faith in notifying, once he has had time to become aware of the legal situation.

6. Subsection (4) unambiguously places the burden of proof to establish breach on the buyer after acceptance. However, this rule becomes one purely of procedure when the tender accepted was non-conforming and the buyer has given the seller notice of breach under subsection (3). For subsection (2) makes it clear that acceptance leaves unimpaired the buyer's right to be made whole, and that right can be exercised by the buyer not only by way of cross-claim for damages, but also by way of recoupment in diminution or extinction of the price.

7. Subsections (3)(b) and (5)(b) give a warrantor against infringement an opportunity to defend or compromise third-party claims or be relieved of his liability. Subsection (5)(a) codifies for all warranties the practice of voucher to defend. Compare Section 3–803. Subsection (6) makes these provisions applicable to the buyer's liability for infringement under Section 2–312.

8. All of the provisions of the present section are subject to any explicit reservation of rights.

* * *

§ 2–608. Revocation of Acceptance in Whole or in Part

(1) The buyer may revoke his acceptance of a lot or commercial unit whose non-conformity substantially impairs its value to him if he has accepted it

  (a) on the reasonable assumption that its non-conformity would be cured and it has not been seasonably cured; or

  (b) without discovery of such non-conformity if his acceptance was reasonably induced either by the difficulty of discovery before acceptance or by the seller's assurances.

(2) Revocation of acceptance must occur within a reasonable time after the buyer discovers or should have discovered the ground for it and before any substantial change in condition of the goods which is not caused by their own defects. It is not effective until the buyer notifies the seller of it.

(3) A buyer who so revokes has the same rights and duties with regard to the goods involved as if he had rejected them.

Official Comment

Prior Uniform Statutory Provision: Section 69(1)(d), (3), (4) and (5), Uniform Sales Act.

Changes: Rewritten.

Purposes of Changes: To make it clear that:

1. Although the prior basic policy is continued, the buyer is no longer required to elect between revocation of acceptance and recovery of damages for breach. Both are now available to him. The non-alternative character of the two remedies is stressed by the terms used in the pres-

ent section. The section no longer speaks of "rescission," a term capable of ambiguous application either to transfer of title to the goods or to the contract of sale and susceptible also of confusion with cancellation for cause of an executed or executory portion of the contract. The remedy under this section is instead referred to simply as "revocation of acceptance" of goods tendered under a contract for sale and involves no suggestion of "election" of any sort.

2. Revocation of acceptance is possible only where the non-conformity substantially impairs the value of the goods to the buyer. For this purpose the test is not what the seller had reason to know at the time of contracting; the question is whether the non-conformity is such as will in fact cause a substantial impairment of value to the buyer though the seller had no advance knowledge as to the buyer's particular circumstances.

3. "Assurances" by the seller under paragraph (b) of subsection (1) can rest as well in the circumstances or in the contract as in explicit language used at the time of delivery. The reason for recognizing such assurances is that they induce the buyer to delay discovery. These are the only assurances involved in paragraph (b). Explicit assurances may be made either in good faith or bad faith. In either case any remedy accorded by this Article is available to the buyer under the section on remedies for fraud.

4. Subsection (2) requires notification of revocation of acceptance within a reasonable time after discovery of the grounds for such revocation. Since this remedy will be generally resorted to only after attempts at adjustment have failed, the reasonable time period should extend in most cases beyond the time in which notification of breach must be given, beyond the time for discovery of non-conformity after acceptance and beyond the time for rejection after tender. The parties may by their agreement limit the time for notification under this section, but the same sanctions and considerations apply to such agreements as are discussed in the comment on manner and effect of rightful rejection.

5. The content of the notice under subsection (2) is to be determined in this case as in others by considerations of good faith, prevention of surprise, and reasonable adjustment. More will generally be necessary than the mere notification of breach required under the preceding section. On the other hand the requirements of the section on waiver of buyer's objections do not apply here. The fact that quick notification of trouble is desirable affords good ground for being slow to bind a buyer by his first statement. Following the general policy of this Article, the requirements of the content of notification are less stringent in the case of a non-merchant buyer.

6. Under subsection (2) the prior policy is continued of seeking substantial justice in regard to the condition of goods restored to the seller. Thus the buyer may not revoke his acceptance if the goods have materially deteriorated except by reason of their own defects. Worthless goods, however, need not be offered back and minor defects in the articles reoffered are to be disregarded.

7. The policy of the section allowing partial acceptance is carried over into the present section and the buyer may revoke his acceptance, in appropriate cases, as to the entire lot or any commercial unit thereof.

* * *

PART 7

REMEDIES

* * *

§ **2–711.** Buyer's Remedies in General; Buyer's Security Interest in Rejected Goods

(1) Where the seller fails to make delivery or repudiates or the buyer rightfully rejects or justifiably revokes acceptance then with respect to any goods involved, and with respect to the whole if the breach goes to the whole contract (Section 2–612), the buyer may cancel and whether or not he has done so may in addition to recovering so much of the price as has been paid

- (a) "cover" and have damages under the next section as to all the goods affected whether or not they have been identified to the contract; or

- (b) recover damages for non-delivery as provided in this Article (Section 2–713).

(2) Where the seller fails to deliver or repudiates the buyer may also

- (a) if the goods have been identified recover them as provided in this Article (Section 2–502); or

- (b) in a proper case obtain specific performance or replevy the goods as provided in this Article (Section 2–716).

(3) On rightful rejection or justifiable revocation of acceptance a buyer has a security interest in goods in his possession or control for any payments made on their price and any expenses reasonably incurred in their inspection, receipt, transportation, care and custody and may hold such goods and resell them in like manner as an aggrieved seller (Section 2–706).

Official Comment

Prior Uniform Statutory Provision: No comparable index section; Subsection (3)—Section 69(5), Uniform Sales Act.

Changes: The prior uniform statutory provision is generally continued and expanded in Subsection (3).

Purposes of Changes and New Matter:

1. To index in this section the buyer's remedies, subsection (1) covering those remedies permitting the recovery of money damages, and subsection (2) covering those which permit reaching the goods themselves. The remedies listed here are those available to a buyer who has not accepted the goods or who has justifiably revoked his acceptance. The remedies available to a buyer with regard to goods finally accepted appear in the section dealing with breach in regard to accepted goods. The buyer's right to proceed as to all goods when the

breach is as to only some of the goods is determined by the section on breach in installment contracts and by the section on partial acceptance.

Despite the seller's breach, proper retender of delivery under the section on cure of improper tender or replacement can effectively preclude the buyer's remedies under this section, except for any delay involved.

2. To make it clear in subsection (3) that the buyer may hold and resell rejected goods if he has paid a part of the price or incurred expenses of the type specified. "Paid" as used here includes acceptance of a draft or other time negotiable instrument or the signing of a negotiable note. His freedom of resale is coextensive with that of a seller under this Article except that the buyer may not keep any profit resulting from the resale and is limited to retaining only the amount of the price paid and the costs involved in the inspection and handling of the goods. The buyer's security interest in the goods is intended to be limited to the items listed in subsection (3), and the buyer is not permitted to retain such funds as he might believe adequate for his damages. The buyer's right to cover, or to have damages for non-delivery, is not impaired by his exercise of his right of resale.

3. It should also be noted that this Act requires its remedies to be liberally administered and provides that any right or obligation which it declares is enforceable by action unless a different effect is specifically prescribed (Section 1–106).

* * *

* * *

§ 2–714. Buyer's Damages for Breach in Regard to Accepted Goods

(1) Where the buyer has accepted goods and given notification (subsection (3) of Section 2–607) he may recover as damages for any non-conformity of tender the loss resulting in the ordinary course of events from the seller's breach as determined in any manner which is reasonable.

(2) The measure of damages for breach of warranty is the difference at the time and place of acceptance between the value of the goods accepted and the value they would have had if they had been as warranted, unless special circumstances show proximate damages of a different amount.

(3) In a proper case any incidental and consequential damages under the next section may also be recovered.

Official Comment

Prior Uniform Statutory Provision: Section 69(6) and (7), Uniform Sales Act.

Changes: Rewritten.

Purposes of Changes:

1. This section deals with the remedies available to the buyer after the goods have been accepted and the time for revocation of acceptance has gone by. In general this section adopts the rule of the prior uniform statutory provision for measuring

damages where there has been a breach of warranty as to goods accepted, but goes further to lay down an explicit provision as to the time and place for determining the loss.

The section on deduction of damages from price provides an additional remedy for a buyer who still owes part of the purchase price, and frequently the two remedies will be available concurrently. The buyer's failure to notify of his claim under the section on effects of acceptance, however, operates to bar his remedies under either that section or the present section.

2. The "non-conformity" referred to in subsection (1) includes not only breaches of warranties but also any failure of the seller to perform according to his obligations under the contract. In the case of such non-conformity, the buyer is permitted to recover for his loss "in any manner which is reasonable."

3. Subsection (2) describes the usual, standard and reasonable method of ascertaining damages in the case of breach of warranty but it is not intended as an exclusive measure. It departs from the measure of damages for non-delivery in utilizing the place of acceptance rather than the place of tender. In some cases the two may coincide, as where the buyer signifies his acceptance upon the tender. If, however, the non-conformity is such as would justify revocation of acceptance, the time and place of acceptance under this section is determined as of the buyer's decision not to revoke.

4. The incidental and consequential damages referred to in subsection (3), which will usually accompany an action brought under this section, are discussed in detail in the comment on the next section.

* * *

§ 2–715. Buyer's Incidental and Consequential Damages

(1) Incidental damages resulting from the seller's breach include expenses reasonably incurred in inspection, receipt, transportation and care and custody of goods rightfully rejected, any commercially reasonable charges, expenses or commissions in connection with effecting cover and any other reasonable expense incident to the delay or other breach.

(2) Consequential damages resulting from the seller's breach include

(a) any loss resulting from general or particular requirements and needs of which the seller at the time of contracting had reason to know and which could not reasonably be prevented by cover or otherwise; and

(b) injury to person or property proximately resulting from any breach of warranty.

Official Comment

Prior Uniform Statutory Provisions: Subsection (2)(b)—Sections 69(7) and 70, Uniform Sales Act.
Changes: Rewritten.

Purposes of Changes and New Matter:

1. Subsection (1) is intended to provide reimbursement for the buyer

who incurs reasonable expenses in connection with the handling of rightfully rejected goods or goods whose acceptance may be justifiably revoked, or in connection with effecting cover where the breach of the contract lies in non-conformity or non-delivery of the goods. The incidental damages listed are not intended to be exhaustive but are merely illustrative of the typical kinds of incidental damage.

2. Subsection (2) operates to allow the buyer, in an appropriate case, any consequential damages which are the result of the seller's breach. The "tacit agreement" test for the recovery of consequential damages is rejected. Although the older rule at common law which made the seller liable for all consequential damages of which he had "reason to know" in advance is followed, the liberality of that rule is modified by refusing to permit recovery unless the buyer could not reasonably have prevented the loss by cover or otherwise. Subparagraph (2) carries forward the provisions of the prior uniform statutory provision as to consequential damages resulting from breach of warranty, but modifies the rule by requiring first that the buyer attempt to minimize his damages in good faith, either by cover or otherwise.

3. In the absence of excuse under the section on merchant's excuse by failure of presupposed conditions, the seller is liable for consequential damages in all cases where he had reason to know of the buyer's general or particular requirements at the time of contracting. It is not necessary that there be a conscious acceptance of an insurer's liability on the seller's part, nor is his obligation for consequential damages limited to cases in which he fails to use due effort in good faith.

Particular needs of the buyer must generally be made known to the seller while general needs must rarely be made known to charge the seller with knowledge.

Any seller who does not wish to take the risk of consequential damages has available the section on contractual limitation of remedy.

4. The burden of proving the extent of loss incurred by way of consequential damage is on the buyer, but the section on liberal administration of remedies rejects any doctrine of certainty which requires almost mathematical precision in the proof of loss. Loss may be determined in any manner which is reasonable under the circumstances.

5. Subsection (2)(b) states the usual rule as to breach of warranty, allowing recovery for injuries "proximately" resulting from the breach. Where the injury involved follows the use of goods without discovery of the defect causing the damage, the question of "proximate" cause turns on whether it was reasonable for the buyer to use the goods without such inspection as would have revealed the defects. If it was not reasonable for him to do so, or if he did in fact discover the defect prior to his use, the injury would not proximately result from the breach of warranty.

6. In the case of sale of wares to one in the business of reselling them, resale is one of the requirements of which the seller has reason to know within the meaning of subsection (2)(a).

* * *

§ 2–716. Buyer's Right to Specific Performance or Replevin

(1) Specific performance may be decreed where the goods are unique or in other proper circumstances.

(2) The decree for specific performance may include such terms and conditions as to payment of the price, damages, or other relief as the court may deem just.

(3) The buyer has a right of replevin for goods identified to the contract if after reasonable effort he is unable to effect cover for such goods or the circumstances reasonably indicate that such effort will be unavailing or if the goods have been shipped under reservation and satisfaction of the security interest in them has been made or tendered.

Official Comment
Prior Uniform Statutory Provision: Section 68, Uniform Sales Act.
Changes: Rephrased.
Purposes of Changes: To make it clear that:

1. The present section continues in general prior policy as to specific performance and injunction against breach. However, without intending to impair in any way the exercise of the court's sound discretion in the matter, this Article seeks to further a more liberal attitude than some courts have shown in connection with the specific performance of contracts of sale.

2. In view of this Article's emphasis on the commercial feasibility of replacement, a new concept of what are "unique" goods is introduced under this section. Specific performance is no longer limited to goods which are already specific or ascertained at the time of contracting. The test of uniqueness under this section must be made in terms of the total situation which characterizes the contract. Output and requirements contracts involving a particular or peculiarly available source or market present today the typical commercial specific performance situation, as contrasted with contracts for the sale of heirlooms or priceless works of art which were usually involved in the older cases. However, uniqueness is not the sole basis of the remedy under this section for the relief may also be granted "in other proper circumstances" and inability to cover is strong evidence of "other proper circumstances".

3. The legal remedy of replevin is given the buyer in cases in which cover is reasonably unavailable and goods have been identified to the contract. This is in addition to the buyer's right to recover identified goods on the seller's insolvency (Section 2–502).

4. This section is intended to give the buyer rights to the goods comparable to the seller's rights to the price.

5. If a negotiable document of title is outstanding, the buyer's right of replevin relates of course to the document not directly to the goods. See Article 7, especially Section 7–602.

* * *

§ 2–717. Deduction of Damages From the Price

The buyer on notifying the seller of his intention to do so may deduct all or any part of the damages resulting from any breach of the contract from any part of the price still due under the same contract.

Official Comment

Prior Uniform Statutory Provision: See Section 69(1)(a), Uniform Sales Act.

Purposes:

1. This section permits the buyer to deduct from the price damages resulting from any breach by the seller and does not limit the relief to cases of breach of warranty as did the prior uniform statutory provision. To bring this provision into application the breach involved must be of the same contract under which the price in question is claimed to have been earned.

2. The buyer, however, must give notice of his intention to withhold all or part of the price if he wishes to avoid a default within the meaning of the section on insecurity and right to assurances. In conformity with the general policies of this Article, no formality of notice is required and any language which reasonably indicates the buyer's reason for holding up his payment is sufficient.

* * *

§ 2–718. Liquidation or Limitation of Damages; Deposits

(1) Damages for breach by either party may be liquidated in the agreement but only at an amount which is reasonable in the light of the anticipated or actual harm caused by the breach, the difficulties of proof of loss, and the inconvenience or nonfeasibility of otherwise obtaining an adequate remedy. A term fixing unreasonably large liquidated damages is void as a penalty.

(2) Where the seller justifiably withholds delivery of goods because of the buyer's breach, the buyer is entitled to restitution of any amount by which the sum of his payments exceeds

(a) the amount to which the seller is entitled by virtue of terms liquidating the seller's damages in accordance with subsection (1), or

(b) in the absence of such terms, twenty per cent of the value of the total performance for which the buyer is obligated under the contract or $500, whichever is smaller.

(3) The buyer's right to restitution under subsection (2) is subject to offset to the extent that the seller establishes

(a) a right to recover damages under the provisions of this Article other than subsection (1), and

(b) the amount or value of any benefits received by the buyer directly or indirectly by reason of the contract.

(4) Where a seller has received payment in goods their reasonable value or the proceeds of their resale shall be treated as payments for the purposes of subsection (2); but if the seller has notice of the buyer's breach before reselling goods received in part performance, his resale is

subject to the conditions laid down in this Article on resale by an aggrieved seller (Section 2-706).

Official Comment

Prior Uniform Statutory Provision: None.

Purposes:

1. Under subsection (1) liquidated damage clauses are allowed where the amount involved is reasonable in the light of the circumstances of the case. The subsection sets forth explicitly the elements to be considered in determining the reasonableness of a liquidated damage clause. A term fixing unreasonably large liquidated damages is expressly made void as a penalty. An unreasonably small amount would be subject to similar criticism and might be stricken under the section on unconscionable contracts or clauses.

2. Subsection (2) refuses to recognize a forfeiture unless the amount of the payment so forfeited represents a reasonable liquidation of damages as determined under subsection (1). A special exception is made in the case of small amounts (20% of the price or $500, whichever is smaller) deposited as security. No distinction is made between cases in which the payment is to be applied on the price and those in which it is intended as security for performance. Subsection (2) is applicable to any deposit or down or part payment. In the case of a deposit or turn in of goods resold before the breach, the amount actually received on the resale is to be viewed as the deposit rather than the amount allowed the buyer for the trade in. However, if the seller knows of the breach prior to the resale of the goods turned in, he must make reasonable efforts to realize their true value, and this is assured by requiring him to comply with the conditions laid down in the section on resale by an aggrieved seller.

* * *

§ 2-719. Contractual Modification or Limitation of Remedy

(1) Subject to the provisions of subsections (2) and (3) of this section and of the preceding section on liquidation and limitation of damages,

(a) the agreement may provide for remedies in addition to or in substitution for those provided in this Article and may limit or alter the measure of damages recoverable under this Article, as by limiting the buyer's remedies to return of the goods and repayment of the price or to repair and replacement of nonconforming goods or parts; and

(b) resort to a remedy as provided is optional unless the remedy is expressly agreed to be exclusive, in which case it is the sole remedy.

(2) Where circumstances cause an exclusive or limited remedy to fail of its essential purpose, remedy may be had as provided in this Act.

(3) Consequential damages may be limited or excluded unless the limitation or exclusion is unconscionable. Limitation of consequential damages for injury to the person in the case of consumer goods is prima

facie unconscionable but limitation of damages where the loss is commercial is not.

Official Comment

Prior Uniform Statutory Provision: None.

Purposes:

1. Under this section parties are left free to shape their remedies to their particular requirements and reasonable agreements limiting or modifying remedies are to be given effect.

However, it is of the very essence of a sales contract that at least minimum adequate remedies be available. If the parties intend to conclude a contract for sale within this Article they must accept the legal consequence that there be at least a fair quantum of remedy for breach of the obligations or duties outlined in the contract. Thus any clause purporting to modify or limit the remedial provisions of this Article in an unconscionable manner is subject to deletion and in that event the remedies made available by this Article are applicable as if the stricken clause had never existed. Similarly, under subsection (2), where an apparently fair and reasonable clause because of circumstances fails in its purpose or operates to deprive either party of the substantial value of the bargain, it must give way to the general remedy provisions of this Article.

2. Subsection (1)(b) creates a presumption that clauses prescribing remedies are cumulative rather than exclusive. If the parties intend the term to describe the sole remedy under the contract, this must be clearly expressed.

3. Subsection (3) recognizes the validity of clauses limiting or excluding consequential damages but makes it clear that they may not operate in an unconscionable manner. Actually such terms are merely an allocation of unknown or undeterminable risks. The seller in all cases is free to disclaim warranties in the manner provided in Section 2–316.

* * *

§ 2–720. Effect of "Cancellation" or "Rescission" on Claims for Antecedent Breach

Unless the contrary intention clearly appears, expressions of "cancellation" or "rescission" of the contract or the like shall not be construed as a renunciation or discharge of any claim in damages for an antecedent breach.

Official Comment

Prior Uniform Statutory Provision: None.

Purpose: This section is designed to safeguard a person holding a right of action from any unintentional loss of rights by the ill-advised use of such terms as "cancellation", "rescission", or the like. Once a party's rights have accrued they are not to be lightly impaired by concessions made in business decency and without intention to forego them. Therefore, unless the cancellation of a contract expressly declares that it is "without reservation of rights", or the like, it cannot be considered to be a renunciation under this section.

* * *

§ 2-721. Remedies for Fraud

Remedies for material misrepresentation or fraud include all remedies available under this Article for non-fraudulent breach. Neither rescission or a claim for rescission of the contract for sale nor rejection or return of the goods shall bar or be deemed inconsistent with a claim for damages or other remedy.

Official Comment

Prior Uniform Statutory Provision: None.

Purposes: To correct the situation by which remedies for fraud have been more circumscribed than the more modern and mercantile remedies for breach of warranty. Thus the remedies for fraud are extended by this section to coincide in scope with those for non-fraudulent breach. This section thus makes it clear that neither rescission of the contract for fraud nor rejection of the goods bars other remedies unless the circumstances of the case make the remedies incompatible.

* * *

* * *

§ 2-725. Statute of Limitations in Contracts for Sale

(1) An action for breach of any contract for sale must be commenced within four years after the cause of action has accrued. By the original agreement the parties may reduce the period of limitation to not less than one year but may not extend it.

(2) A cause of action accrues when the breach occurs, regardless of the aggrieved party's lack of knowledge of the breach. A breach of warranty occurs when tender of delivery is made, except that where a warranty explicitly extends to future performance of the goods and discovery of the breach must await the time of such performance the cause of action accrues when the breach is or should have been discovered.

(3) Where an action commenced within the time limited by subsection (1) is so terminated as to leave available a remedy by another action for the same breach such other action may be commenced after the expiration of the time limited and within six months after the termination of the first action unless the termination resulted from voluntary discontinuance or from dismissal for failure or neglect to prosecute.

(4) This section does not alter the law on tolling of the statute of limitations nor does it apply to causes of action which have accrued before this Act becomes effective.

Official Comment

Prior Uniform Statutory Provision: None.

Purposes: To introduce a uniform statute of limitations for sales contracts, thus eliminating the jurisdictional variations and providing needed relief for concerns doing business on a nationwide scale whose contracts have heretofore been governed by several different periods of limitation depending upon the state in which the transaction occurred. This Article takes sales contracts out of the general laws limiting the time for commencing contractual actions and selects a four year period as the most appropriate to modern business practice. This is within the normal commercial record keeping period.

Subsection (1) permits the parties to reduce the period of limitation. The minimum period is set at one year. The parties may not, however, extend the statutory period.

Subsection (2), providing that the cause of action accrues when the breach occurs, states an exception where the warranty extends to future performance.

Subsection (3) states the saving provision included in many state statutes and permits an additional short period for bringing new actions, where suits begun within the four year period have been terminated so as to leave a remedy still available for the same breach.

Subsection (4) makes it clear that this Article does not purport to alter or modify in any respect the law on tolling of the statute of limitations as it now prevails in the various jurisdictions.

* * *

SELECTED STATE PRODUCTS LIABILITY STATUTES

Arizona Revised Statutes Annotated
(1978 and (§ 12-701) 1989)

§ 12-551. Product liability. A product liability action as defined in § 12-681 shall be commenced and prosecuted within the period prescribed in § 12-542, except that no product liability action may be commenced and prosecuted if the cause of action accrues more than twelve years after the product was first sold for use or consumption, unless the cause of action is based upon the negligence of the manufacturer or seller or a breach of an express warranty provided by the manufacturer or seller.

§ 12-681. Definitions. In this article, unless the context otherwise requires:

1. "Manufacturer" means a person or entity who designs, assembles, fabricates, produces, constructs or otherwise prepares a product or component part of a product prior to its sale to a user or consumer, including a seller owned in whole or significant part by the manufacturer or a seller, owning the manufacturer in whole or significant part.

2. "Product" means the individual product or any component part of such product which is the subject of a product liability action.

3. "Product liability action" means any action brought against a manufacturer or seller of a product for damages for bodily injury, death or property damage caused by or resulting from the manufacture, construction, design, formula, installation, preparation, assembly, testing, packaging, labeling, sale, use or consumption of any product, the failure to warn or protect against a danger or hazard in the use or misuse of the product or the failure to provide proper instructions for the use or consumption of any product.

4. "Reasonably foreseeable alteration, modification, use or consumption" means an alteration, modification, use or consumption of the product which would be expected of an ordinary and prudent purchaser, user or consumer and which an ordinary and prudent manufacturer should have anticipated.

5. "Seller" means a person or entity, including a wholesaler, distributor, retailer or lessor, engaged in the business of leasing any product or selling any product for resale, use or consumption.

6. "State of the art" means the technical, mechanical and scientific knowledge of manufacturing, designing, testing or labeling the same or similar products which was in existence and reasonably feasible for use at the time of manufacture.

§ 12–682. **Limitation.** The previously existing common law of products liability is modified only to the extent specifically stated in this article and § 12–551.

§ 12–683. **Affirmative defenses.** In any product liability action, a defendant shall not be liable if the defendant proves that any of the following apply:

1. The defect in the product is alleged to result from inadequate design or fabrication, and if the plans or designs for the product or the methods and techniques of manufacturing, inspecting, testing and labeling the product conformed with the state of the art at the time the product was first sold by the defendant.

2. The proximate cause of the incident giving rise to the action was an alteration or modification of the product which was not reasonably foreseeable, made by a person other than the defendant and subsequent to the time the product was first sold by the defendant.

3. The proximate cause of the incident giving rise to the action was a use or consumption of the product which was for a purpose, in a manner or in an activity other than that which was reasonably foreseeable or was contrary to any express and adequate instructions or warnings appearing on or attached to the product or on its original container or wrapping, if the injured person knew or with the exercise of reasonable and diligent care should have known of such instructions or warnings.

§ 12–684. **Indemnification—Tender of defense—Execution.** A. In any product liability action where the manufacturer refuses to accept a tender of defense from the seller, the manufacturer shall indemnify the seller for any judgment rendered against the seller and shall also reimburse the seller for reasonable attorneys' fees and costs incurred by the seller in defending such action, unless either paragraph 1 or 2 applies:

1. The seller had knowledge of the defect in the product.

2. The seller altered, modified or installed the product, and such alteration, modification or installation was a substantial cause of the incident giving rise to the action, was not authorized or requested by the manufacturer and was not performed in compliance with the directions or specifications of the manufacturer.

B. If a judgment is rendered in favor of the plaintiff and a seller is granted indemnity against a manufacturer, the plaintiff shall first attempt to satisfy the judgment by levying execution upon the manufacturer in this state or in the state where the manufacturer's principal place of business is located and by making demand upon any liability insurance carrier of the manufacturer whose identity is known to plaintiff before attempting to collect the judgment from the seller or the seller's liability insurance carrier. The return of a writ of execution partially or wholly unsatisfied or the failure of the manufacturer's insurance carrier to pay the judgment upon demand shall be deemed full compliance with the plaintiff's obligation to attempt to collect from the manufacturer.

C. In any product liability action the manufacturer of the product shall be indemnified by the seller of the product for any judgment rendered against the manufacturer and shall also reimburse the manufacturer for reasonable attorneys' fees and costs incurred in defending such action, if the seller provided the plans or specifications for the manufacturer or preparation of the product and such plans or specifications were a substantial cause of the product's alleged defect and if the product was manufactured in compliance with and according to the plans or specifications of the seller. If a judgment is rendered in favor of the plaintiff and a manufacturer is granted indemnity against a seller, the plaintiff shall first attempt to satisfy the judgment by levying execution upon the seller in this state or in the state where the seller's principal place of business is located and by making demand upon any liability insurance carrier of the seller whose identity is known to plaintiff before attempting to collect the judgment from the manufacturer or manufacturer's liability insurance carrier. The return of a writ of execution partially or wholly unsatisfied or the failure of the seller's insurance carrier to pay the judgment upon demand shall be deemed full compliance with the plaintiff's obligation to attempt to collect from the seller. The provisions of this subsection shall not apply if the manufacturer had knowledge or with the exercise of reasonable and diligent care should have had knowledge of the defect in the product.

§ 12–685. Contents of complaint—Amount of recovery. In any product liability action no dollar amount or figure shall be included in the complaint. The complaint shall pray for such damages as are reasonable in the premises. The complaint shall include a statement reciting that the jurisdictional amount established for filing the action is satisfied.

§ 12–686. Inadmissible evidence—State of the art—Modification. In any product liability action, the following shall not be admissible as direct evidence of a defect:

1. Evidence of advancements or changes in the state of the art subsequent to the time the product was first sold by the defendant.

2. Evidence of any change made in the design or methods of manufacturing or testing the product or any similar product subsequent to the time the product was first sold by the defendant.

§ 12–701. Drugs—Exemplary or punitive damages—Definition.

A. The manufacturer or seller of a drug is not liable for exemplary or punitive damages if the drug alleged to cause the harm either:

1. was manufactured and labeled in relevant and material respects in accordance with the terms of an approval or license issued by the federal food and drug administration under the food, drug and cosmetic act (21 United States Code Section 301, et seq.) or the Public Health Service Act (42 United States Code Section 201, et seq.) or

2. is generally recognized as safe and effective pursuant to conditions established by the federal food and drug administration and applicable regulations, including packaging and labeling regulations.

B. Subsection A does not apply if the plaintiff proves, by clear and convincing evidence, that the defendant, either before or after making the drug available for public use, knowingly, in violation of applicable federal food and drug administration regulations, withheld from or misrepresented to the administration information known to be material and relevant to the harm which the plaintiff allegedly suffered.

C. In this section, "drug" means the same as provided in Section 201(g)(1) of the federal food, drug and cosmetic act (21 United States Code Section 321(g)(1).

CALIFORNIA HEALTH & SAFETY CODE
(1986, concerning AIDS vaccine)

§ 199.49. (a)(1) Except as provided in paragraph (2), a manufacturer of an FDA-approved AIDS vaccine that is sold, delivered, administered, or dispensed in California shall be liable for all damages proximately or legally caused by that AIDS vaccine.

(2) A manufacturer of an FDA-approved AIDS vaccine that is sold, delivered, administered, or dispensed in California, shall not be liable in strict products liability for any damages proximately or legally caused by any design or warning defect of the AIDS vaccine, or for breach of implied warranty, if, upon motion and after the hearing provided in subdivision (b), the trial judge determines that the subject AIDS vaccine is unavoidably dangerous. For purposes of this section, an AIDS vaccine is unavoidably dangerous if the trial judge determines that all three of the following criteria are met:

(A) At the time of distribution, the vaccine was intended to confer an exceptionally important benefit on society that made its availability highly desirable.

(B) At the time of distribution, the then-existing risk posed by the vaccine was both substantial and unavoidable.

(i) In determining whether the risk posed by the vaccine was substantial, the court shall consider whether the risk posed permanent or long-term disability as opposed to temporary or insignificant inconvenience.

(ii) In determining whether the risk posed was unavoidable, the court shall consider whether the vaccine was designed to minimize, to the extent scientifically knowable at the time it was distributed, the risk inherent in the vaccine, and also, the availability, at the time of distribution, of an alternative AIDS vaccine or product that would have as effectively accomplished the full intended purpose of the subject vaccine.

(C) At the time of distribution, the interest in availability of the subject AIDS vaccine outweighed the interest in promoting enhanced accountability through either strict products liability design and warning defect, or implied warranty, review.

(3) For purposes of this section, it shall be conclusively presumed that any FDA-approved AIDS vaccine that is sold, delivered, administered, or dispensed in California is intended to confer an exceptionally important benefit on society that makes its availability highly desirable.

(b) In any civil action governed by the provisions of this section, the defendant manufacturer shall, upon motion be entitled to a determination of whether the subject AIDS vaccine is unavoidably dangerous within the meaning of subdivision (a). The manufacturer shall have the burden of proving by a preponderance of the evidence all the criteria established in paragraph (2) of subdivision (a) except as to those matters for which a presumption exists.

(c) In enacting this section, it is the intent of the Legislature to codify, in part, certain portions of the court ruling in *Kearl v. Lederle Laboratories,* 172 Cal.App.3d 812.

This section is intended with respect to design and warning defect only, to deny recovery under strict liability, whether based upon the theories of strict liability, implied warranty, or any other theory of liability without fault. For purposes of this section, breach of express warranty shall not be affected by a finding of "unavoidably dangerous."

This section is not intended to, nor shall it be construed to, repeal, modify, or otherwise preclude any recovery based on negligence or fault, or any theory of liability except this section is intended, with respect to design and warning defect only, to deny recovery under strict liability, whether based upon theories of strict liability, implied warranty, or any other theory of liability without fault.

For purposes of this section, "unavoidably dangerous" means unavoidably unsafe. It is the intent of the Legislature that the terms "unavoidably dangerous" and "unavoidably unsafe" may be used interchangeably.

This section does not apply to any other vaccine, drug, or similar product, other than an FDA-approved AIDS vaccine that is sold, distributed, administered, or dispensed in California, and does not apply to any manufacturer of any vaccine, drug, or similar product, other than a manufacturer of an FDA-approved AIDS vaccine that is sold, distributed, administered, or dispensed in California.

(1983, concerning firearms and ammunition liability)

§ 1714.4. (a) In a product liability action, no firearm or ammunition shall be deemed defective in design on the basis that the benefits of the product do not outweigh the risk of injury posed by its potential to cause serious injury, damage, or death when discharged.

(b) For purposes of this section:

(1) The potential of a firearm or ammunition to cause serious injury, damage, or death when discharged does not make the product defective in design.

(2) Injuries or damages resulting from the discharge of a firearm or ammunition are not proximately caused by its potential to cause serious injury, damage, or death, but are proximately caused by the actual discharge of the product.

(c) This section shall not affect a products liability cause of action based upon the improper selection of design alternatives.

(d) This section is declaratory of existing law.

(1987, concerning certain inherent dangers)

§ 1714.45. (a) In a products liability action, a manufacturer or seller shall not be liable if:

(1) The product is inherently unsafe and the product is known to be unsafe by the ordinary consumer who consumes the product with the ordinary knowledge common to the community; and

(2) The product is a common consumer product intended for personal consumption, such as sugar, castor oil, alcohol, tobacco, and butter, as identified in comment *i* to Section 402A of the *Restatement (Second) of Torts*.

(b) For purposes of this section, the term "product liability action" means any action for injury or death caused by a product, except that the term does not include an action based on a manufacturing defect or breach of an express warranty.

(c) This section is intended to be declarative of and does not alter or amend existing California law, including *Cronin v. J.B.E. Olson Corp.*, (1972) 8 Cal.3d 121, and shall apply to all product liability actions pending on, or commenced after, January 1, 1988.

(1970–79, concerning warranties)

§ 1792. Unless disclaimed in the manner prescribed by this chapter, every sale of consumer goods that are sold at retail in this state shall be accompanied by the manufacturer's and the retail seller's implied warranty that the goods are merchantable. The retail seller shall have a right of indemnity against the manufacturer in the amount of any liability under this section.

§ 1792.1. Every sale of consumer goods that are sold at retail in this state by a manufacturer who has reason to know at the time of the retail sale that the goods are required for a particular purpose and that the buyer is relying on the manufacturer's skill or judgment to select or furnish suitable goods shall be accompanied by such manufacturer's implied warranty of fitness.

§ 1792.2. (a) Every sale of consumer goods that are sold at retail in this state by a retailer or distributor who has reason to know at the time of the retail sale that the goods are required for a particular purpose, and that the buyer is relying on the retailer's or distributor's skill or judgment to select or furnish suitable goods shall be accompanied by such retailer's or distributor's implied warranty that the goods are fit for that purpose.

(b) Every sale of an assistive device sold at retail in this state shall be accompanied by the retail seller's implied warranty that the device is specifically fit for the particular needs of the buyer.

§ **1792.3.** No implied warranty of merchantability and, where applicable, no implied warranty of fitness shall be waived, except in the case of a sale of consumer goods on an "as is" or "with all faults" basis where the provisions of this chapter affecting "as is" or "with all faults" sales are strictly complied with.

§ **1792.4.** (a) No sale of goods, governed by the provisions of this chapter, on an "as is" or "with all faults" basis, shall be effective to disclaim the implied warranty of merchantability or, where applicable, the implied warranty of fitness, unless a conspicuous writing is attached to the goods which clearly informs the buyer, prior to the sale, in simple and concise language of each of the following:

(1) The goods are being sold on an "as is" or "with all faults" basis.

(2) The entire risk as to the quality and performance of the goods is with the buyer.

(3) Should the goods prove defective following their purchase, the buyer and not the manufacturer, distributor, or retailer assumes the entire cost of all necessary servicing or repair.

(b) In the event of sale of consumer goods by means of a mail order catalog, the catalog offering such goods shall contain the required writing as to each item so offered in lieu of the requirement of notification prior to the sale.

§ **1792.5.** Every sale of goods that are governed by the provisions of this chapter, on an "as is" or "with all faults" basis, shall constitute a waiver by the buyer of the implied warranty of merchantability and, where applicable, of the implied warranty of fitness.

Connecticut General Statutes
(1982–90)

§ 52–572h. Negligence actions—Doctrines applicable. (a) For purposes of this section: (1) "economic damages" means compensation determined by the trier of fact for pecuniary losses including, but not limited to, the cost of reasonable and necessary medical care, rehabilitative services, custodial care and loss of earnings or earning capacity excluding any noneconomic damages; (2) "noneconomic damages" means compensation determined by the trier of fact for all nonpecuniary losses including, but not limited to, physical pain and suffering and mental or emotional pain and suffering; (3) "recoverable economic damages" means the economic damages reduced by any applicable findings including, but not limited to, set-offs, credits, comparative negligence, additur and remittitur, and any reduction provided by section 52–225a, as amended by section 4 of this Act; (4) "recoverable noneconomic damages" means the noneconomic damages reduced by any applicable findings including but not limited to set-offs, credits, comparative negligence, additur and remittitur.

(b) In causes of action based on negligence, contributory negligence shall not bar recovery in an action by any person or his legal representative to recover damages resulting from personal injury, wrongful death or damage to property if the negligence was not greater than the combined negligence of the person or persons against whom recovery is sought including settled or released persons under subsection (n) of this section. The economic or noneconomic damages allowed shall be diminished in the proportion of the percentage of negligence attributable to the person recovering which percentage shall be determined pursuant to subsection (f) of this section.

(c) In a negligence action to recover damages resulting from personal injury, wrongful death or damage to property occurring on or after October 1, 1987, if the damages are determined to be proximately caused by the negligence of more than one party, each party against whom recovery is allowed shall be liable to the claimant only for his proportionate share of the recoverable economic damages and the recoverable noneconomic damages except as provided in subsection (g) of this section.

(d) The proportionate share of damages for which each party is liable is calculated by multiplying the recoverable economic damages and the recoverable noneconomic damages by a fraction in which the numerator is the party's percentage of negligence, which percentage shall be determined pursuant to subsection (f) of this section, and the denominator is the total of the percentages of negligence, which percentages shall be determined pursuant to subsection (f) of this section, to be attributable to all parties whose negligent actions were a proximate cause of the injury, death or damage to property including settled or released parties under subsection (n) of this section. Any percentage of negligence attributable to the claimant shall not be included in the denominator of the fraction.

(e) In any action to which this section is applicable, the instructions to the jury given by the court shall include an explanation of the effect on awards and liabilities of the percentage of negligence found by the jury to be attributable to each party.

(f) The jury or, if there is no jury, the court shall specify: (1) The amount of economic damages; (2) the amount of noneconomic damages; (3) any findings of fact necessary for the court to specify recoverable economic damages and recoverable noneconomic damages; (4) the percentage of negligence that proximately caused the injury, death or damage to property in relation to one hundred per cent, that is attributable to each party whose negligent actions were a proximate cause of the injury, death or damage to property including settled or released persons under subsection (n) of this section; and (5) the percentage of such negligence attributable to the claimant.

* * *

(l) The legal doctrines of last clear chance and assumption of risk in actions to which this section is applicable are abolished.

(m) The family car doctrine shall not be applied to impute contributory or comparative negligence pursuant to this section to the owner of any motor vehicle or motor boat.

(n) A release, settlement or similar agreement entered into by a claimant and a person discharges that person from all liability for contribution, but it does not discharge any other persons liable upon the same claim unless it so provides. However, the total award of damages is reduced by the amount of the released person's percentage of negligence determined in accordance with subsection (f) of this section.

* * *

§ 52-5721. Strict tort liability, contributory negligence and comparative negligence not bar to recovery. In causes of action based on strict tort liability, contributory negligence or comparative negligence shall not be a bar to recovery. The provisions of this section shall apply to all actions pending on or brought after June 7, 1977, claiming strict tort liability notwithstanding the date on which the cause of action accrued. Nothing in this section shall be construed as barring the defense of misuse of the product or the defense of knowingly using the product in a defective condition in an action based on strict tort liability.

§ 52–572m. Product liability actions—Definitions. As used in this section and sections 52–240a, 52–572n to 52–572r, inclusive, and 52–577a, as amended by sections 243 to 245, inclusive, and 247 of this act:

(a) "Product seller" means any person or entity, including a manufacturer, wholesaler, distributor or retailer who is engaged in the business of selling such products whether the sale is for resale or for use or consumption. The term "product seller" also includes lessors or bailors of products who are engaged in the business of leasing or bailment of products.

(b) "Product liability claim" includes all claims or actions brought for personal injury, death or property damage caused by the manufacture, construction, design, formula, preparation, assembly, installation, testing, warnings, instructions, marketing, packaging or labeling of any product. "Product liability claim" shall include, but is not limited to, all actions based on the following theories: strict liability in tort; negligence; breach of or failure to discharge a duty to warn or instruct, whether negligent or innocent; misrepresentation or nondisclosure, whether negligent or innocent.

(c) "Claimant" means a person asserting a product liability claim for damages incurred by the claimant or one for whom the claimant is acting in a representative capacity.

(d) "Harm" includes damage to property, including the product itself, and personal injuries including wrongful death. As between commercial parties, "harm" does not include commercial loss.

(e) "Manufacturer" includes product sellers who design, assemble, fabricate, construct, process, package or otherwise prepare a product or component part of a product prior to its sale to a user or consumer. It includes a product seller or entity not otherwise a manufacturer that holds itself out as a manufacturer.

§ 52–572n. Product liability claims. (a) A product liability claim as provided in sections 52–240a, 52–240b, 52–572m to 52–572r, inclusive, and 52–577a may be asserted and shall be in lieu of all other claims against product sellers, including actions of negligence, strict liability and warranty, for harm caused by a product.

(b) A claim may be asserted successfully under said sections notwithstanding the claimant did not buy the product from or enter into any contractual relationship with the product seller.

(c) As between commercial parties, commercial loss caused by a product is not harm and may not be recovered by a commercial claimant in a product liability claim. An action for commercial loss caused by a product may be brought only under, and shall be governed by, title 42a, the Uniform Commercial Code.

§ 52–572o. Comparative responsibility—Award of damages—Action for contribution. (a) In any claim under sections 52–240a, 52–240b, 52–572m to 52–572r, inclusive, or 52–577a, the comparative responsibility of, or attributed to, the claimant, shall not bar recovery but shall diminish the award of compensatory damages proportionately, according to the measure of responsibility attributed to the claimant.

(b) In any claim involving comparative responsibility, the court may instruct the jury to give answers to special interrogatories, or if there is no jury, the court may make its own findings, indicating (1) the amount of damages each claimant would receive if comparative responsibility were disregarded, and (2) the percentage of responsibility allocated to each party, including the claimant, as compared with the combined responsibility of all parties to the action. For this purpose, the court may decide that it is appropriate to treat two or more persons as a single party.

(c) In determining the percentage of responsibility, the trier of fact shall consider, on a comparative basis, both the nature and quality of the conduct of the party.

(d) The court shall determine the award for each claimant according to these findings and shall enter judgment against parties liable on the basis of the common law joint and several liability of joint tortfeasors. The judgment shall also specify the proportionate amount of damages allocated against each party liable, according to the percentage of responsibility established for such party.

(e) If a judgment has been rendered, any action for contribution must be brought within one year after the judgment becomes final. If no judgment has been rendered, the person bringing the action for contribution either must have (1) discharged by payment the common liability within the period of the statute of limitations applicable to the right of action of the claimant against him and commenced the action for contribution within one year after payment, or (2) agreed while action was pending to discharge the common liability and, within one year after the agreement, have paid the liability and brought an action for contribution.

§ 52–572p. Limitation of liability of product seller. (a) A product seller shall not be liable for harm that would not have occurred but for the fact that his product was altered or modified by a third party unless: (1) The alteration or modification was in accordance with the instructions or specifications of the product seller; (2) the alteration or modification was made with the consent of the product seller; or (3) the alteration or modification was the result of conduct that reasonably should have been anticipated by the product seller.

(b) For the purposes of this section, alteration or modification includes changes in the design, formula, function or use of the product from that originally designed, tested or intended by the product seller.

§ **52–572q. Liability of product seller—Adequate warnings or instructions.** (a) A product seller may be subject to liability for harm caused to a claimant who proves by a fair preponderance of the evidence that the product was defective in that adequate warnings or instructions were not provided.

(b) In determining whether instructions or warnings were required and, if required, whether they were adequate the trier of fact may consider: (1) The likelihood that the product would cause the harm suffered by the claimant; (2) the ability of the product seller to anticipate at the time of manufacture that the expected product user would be aware of the product risk, and the nature of the potential harm; and (3) the technological feasibility and cost of warnings and instructions.

(c) In claims based on this section, the claimant shall prove by a fair preponderance of the evidence that if adequate warnings or instructions had been provided, the claimant would not have suffered the harm.

(d) A product seller may not be considered to have provided adequate warnings or instructions unless they were devised to communicate with the person best able to take or recommend precautions against the potential harm.

§ **52–572r. Product liability claims against third parties.** (a) Notwithstanding any provision of the general statutes to the contrary, in any product liability claim against a third party this section shall govern the rights of the employee, or in the event of death, his dependents or representative, the employer or insurance carrier and the third party.

(b) The plaintiff, upon verdict or settlement against a third party resulting from a product liability claim shall receive the amount of the verdict or settlement reduced by his attorney's fees and costs, and further reduced by an amount equal to the amount paid as compensation, including medical expenses, under the provisions of chapter 568 and an amount equal to the present worth of any probable future payments to which he has become entitled by award on account of such injury.

(c) Neither an employer nor, in the event the employer is insured against liability under chapter 568, the insurer of such employer, shall have any lien upon any judgment received in any product liability claim, or any right of subrogation if the claim against the third party is a product liability claim.

(d) In any product liability claim for personal injury or death arising out of and in the course of employment subject to the provisions of sections 52–240a, 52–240b, 52–572m to 52–572r, inclusive, and 52–577a, brought against any third party, such third party may not maintain any action for indemnity against any person immune from liability.

(e) The provisions of this section shall not apply to product liability claims in which the claimant's employer is the state of Connecticut, any political subdivision thereof, or any district or authority created by law providing governmental functions.

(f) If any subsection of this section is adjudicated to be unconstitutional, the entire section shall be void.

(1979)

§ 52-240a. Award of attorney's fees in product liability action. If the court determines that the claim or defense is frivolous, the court may award reasonable attorney's fees to the prevailing party in a products liability action.

§ 52-240b. Punitive damages in product liability actions. Punitive damages may be awarded if the claimant proves that the harm suffered was the result of the product seller's reckless disregard for the safety of product users, consumers or others who were injured by the product. If the trier of fact determines that punitive damages should be awarded, the court shall determine that amount of damages not to exceed an amount equal to twice the damages awarded to the plaintiff.

(Laws 1991, H.B. 5624, concerning AIDS vaccine)

§ 4. **[Definitions.]** As used in sections 4 to 7, inclusive, of this act: (1) "AIDS vaccine" means a vaccine which has been developed by a manufacturer, is being tested and administered at a research institution for purposes of determining whether it provides immunity to acquired immune deficiency syndrome or is of therapeutic benefit to persons or fetuses infected with the acquired immune deficiency syndrome virus, and for which an investigational new drug application is on file with the federal Food and Drug Administration and is in effect.

(2) "Manufacturer" means any person who is domiciled or has his principal place of business in this state and has developed an AIDS vaccine.

(3) "Research institution" means a hospital which is accredited by the Joint Commission on the Accreditation of Healthcare Organizations, or a recognized medical school which operates, or is affiliated with, or is operated by an accredited hospital.

(4) "Research subject" means a person who is administered an AIDS vaccine, or a fetus of a person administered an AIDS vaccine, or a child born to a person administered an AIDS vaccine.

(5) "Researcher" means a person employed by or affiliated with a manufacturer or a research institution, who participates in the develop-

ment or testing or administration of an AIDS vaccine, or who is involved in the diagnosis and treatment of a research subject.

§ 5. A manufacturer, research institution or researcher shall, prior to the administration of an AIDS vaccine to a person, provide a written explanation of the immunity provisions of section 6 of this act to such person and obtain such person's informed consent. A parent or legal guardian of a child may give informed consent for such child. A copy of the informed consent shall be maintained with such person's medical records.

§ 6. A manufacturer, research institution or researcher shall not be liable to a research subject for civil damages for personal injury resulting from the administration of any AIDS vaccine to such research subject, unless such injury was caused by the gross negligence or reckless, wilful or wanton misconduct of such manufacturer, research institution or researcher or such manufacturer, research institution or researcher has failed to comply with the provisions of section 5 of this act. The immunity provided by this section shall not apply to a manufacturer, research institution or researcher who intentionally provided false information in connection with an investigational new drug application.

§ 7. No person shall be denied the opportunity to be a research subject because of the inability to pay for medical treatment.

DISTRICT OF COLUMBIA CODE ANNOTATED

ILLEGAL FIREARM SALE AND DISTRIBUTION STRICT LIABILITY ACT OF 1992

§ 6–2381. **Definitions.** For the purposes of this act, the term:

(1) "Dealer" means:

(A) Any person engaged in the business of selling firearms at wholesale or retail;

(B) Any person engaged in the business of repairing firearms or of making or fitting special barrels, stocks, or trigger mechanisms to firearms; or

(C) Any person who is a pawnbroker who takes or receives by way of pledge or pawn, any firearm as security for the payment or repayment of money.

(2) "Engaged in the business" means:

(A) A person who devotes time, attention, and labor to dealing in firearms as a regular course of trade or business with the principal objective of livelihood and profit through the repetitive purchase and resale of firearms. The term "engaged in business" shall not include a person who makes occasional sales, exchanges, or purchases of firearms for the enhancement of a personal collection or for a hobby, or who sells all or part of this personal collection of firearms; or

(B) A person who devotes time, attention, and labor to importing firearms as a regular course of trade or business with the principal objective of livelihood and profit through the sale or distribution of the firearms imported.

(3) "Firearm" shall have the same meaning as in paragraph 9 of section 101 of the Firearms Control Regulations Act of 1975, effective September 24, 1976 (D.C.Law 1–85; D.C.Code § 6–2302(9)).

(4) "Illegal sale" means:

(A) Failure to establish proof of the purchaser's residence in a jurisdiction where the purchase of the weapon is legal or ignoring proof of the purchaser's residence in the District of Columbia;

(B) Failure to comply with District of Columbia registration and waiting requirements prior to delivery of the firearm to the purchaser when proof of District of Columbia residence is provided;

(C) Failure to maintain full, complete, and accurate records of firearm sales as required by local, state, and federal law; or

(D) Knowingly and willfully maintaining false records with the intent to misrepresent the name and address of persons purchasing firearms, or the type of firearm sold to those persons.

(5) "Importer" means any person engaged in the business of importing or bringing firearms or ammunition into the United States for purposes of sale or distribution.

(6) "Law enforcement agency" means a federal, state, or local law enforcement agency, state militia, or an agency of the United States government.

(7) "Law enforcement officer" means any employee or agent of a law enforcement agency who is authorized to use a firearm in the course of employment.

(8) "Manufacturer" means any person in business to manufacture or assemble a firearm or ammunition for sale or distribution.

(9) "Pawnbroker" means any person whose business or occupation includes the taking or receiving, by way of pledge or pawn, of any firearm as security for the payment or repayment of money.

§ 6–2382. Liability. (a) Any manufacturer, importer, or dealer of a firearm who can be shown by a preponderance of the evidence to have knowingly and willfully engaged in the illegal sale of a firearm shall be held strictly liable in tort, without regard to fault and without regard to either: (1) an intent to interfere with a legally protected interest, or (2) a breach of duty to exercise reasonable care, for all direct and consequential damages that arise from bodily injury or death if the bodily injury or death proximately results from the discharge of the firearm in the District of Columbia, regardless of whether or not the person operating the firearm is the original, illegal purchaser.

(b) Any individual who can be shown by a preponderance of the evidence to have knowingly and willfully engaged in the illegal sale, loan, lease, or rental of a firearm for money or anything of value shall be held strictly liable in tort, without regard to fault and without regard to either: (1) an intent to interfere with a legally protected interest, or (2) a breach of duty to exercise reasonable care, for all direct and consequential damages that arise from bodily injury or death if the bodily injury or death proximately results from the discharge of the firearm in the District of Columbia regardless of whether or not the person operating the firearm is the original, illegal purchaser.

(c) Nothing in this act shall relieve from liability any person who commits a crime, is negligent, or who might otherwise be liable for acts committed with the firearm.

§ 6–2383. Exemptions. (a) No firearm originally distributed to a law enforcement agency or a law enforcement officer shall provide the basis for liability under this act.

(b) No action may be brought pursuant to this act by a person who can be shown by a preponderance of the evidence to have committed a self-inflicted injury or by a person injured by a firearm while committing a crime, attempting to commit a crime, engaged in criminal activity, or engaged in a delinquent act.

(c) No action may be brought pursuant to this act by a person who can be shown by a preponderance of the evidence to be engaged in the sale or distribution of illegal narcotics.

(d) No action may be brought pursuant to this act by a person who either: (1) assumed the risk of the injury that occurred, or (2) negligently contributed to the injury that occurred.

§ 6–2384. Firearms Bounty Fund. (a) There is established a fund to be known as the Firearms Bounty Fund ("Fund") to be administered by the Metropolitan Police Department. The Fund shall be operated as a proprietary fund and shall consist of monies appropriated to the Fund, federal grants to the Fund, or private monies donated to the Fund.

(b) Disbursements from the Fund shall be used exclusively for the payment of cash rewards to persons who provide District of Columbia law enforcement agencies with tips that lead to the adjudication or conviction of:

(1) A person or entity engaged in the illegal sale, rental, lease, or loan of a firearm in exchange for money or other thing of value; or

(2) A person who has committed a crime with a firearm.

(c) The amount of each cash reward shall be determined at the discretion of the Chief of the Metropolitan Police Department and the cash reward may range up to $100,000 per tip.

(d) The Chief of the Metropolitan Police Department shall report annually to the Mayor and Council all income and expenditures of the Fund.

(e) The Mayor, by a proposed notice to the Council, may terminate the Fund if the Mayor determines that the Fund is no longer necessary to pay cash rewards.

(f) If monies exist in the Fund at the time of its termination, the monies shall be deposited in the General Fund of the District of Columbia.

(g) The proposed notice to terminate the fund shall be submitted to the Council for a 45–day period of review, excluding Saturdays, Sundays, legal holidays, and days of Council recess. If the Council does not approve or disapprove by resolution within the 45–day review period, the proposed notice to terminate the Fund shall be deemed approved.

ASSAULT WEAPON MANUFACTURING STRICT LIABILITY ACT OF 1990

§ 6–2391. Definitions. For the purposes of this act, the term:

(1) "Assault weapon" includes:

(A) The following weapons:

(i) Norinco, Mitchell, and Poly Technologies Avtomat Kalashnikovs (all models);

(ii) Action Arms Israeli Military Industries UZI and Galil;

(iii) Beretta AR–70 (SC–70);

(iv) Colt AR–15 and CAR–15;

(v) Fabrique Nationale FN/FAL, FN/LAR, and FNC;

(vi) MAC 10 and MAC 11;

(vii) Steyr AUG;

(viii) INTRATEC TEC–9; and

(ix) Street Sweeper and Striker 12.

(2) "Handgun" means a firearm with a barrel less than 12 inches in length at the time of manufacture.

(3) "Dealer" and "importer" shall have the same meaning as in section 902 of the Gun Control Act of 1968, approved June 19, 1968 (82 Stat. 226; 18 U.S.C. 921).

(4) "Machine gun" shall have the same meaning as in section 101 of the Firearms Control Regulations Act of 1975, effective September 24, 1976 (D.C.Law 1–85; D.C.Code, sec. 6–2302(10)).

(5) "Manufacturer" means any person in business to manufacture or assemble a firearm or ammunition for sale or distribution.

(6) "Law enforcement agency" means a federal, state, or local law enforcement agency, state militia, or an agency of the United States government.

(7) "Law enforcement officer" means any officer or agent of an agency defined in paragraph (6) of this section who is authorized to use a handgun or machine gun in the course of his or her work.

§ 6–2392. Liability. Any manufacturer, importer, or dealer of an assault weapon shall be held strictly liable in tort, without regard to fault or proof of defect, for all direct and consequential damages that arise from bodily injury or death if the bodily injury or death proximately results from the discharge of the assault weapon in the District of Columbia.

§ 6–2393. Exemptions. (a) No assault weapon originally distributed to a law enforcement agency or a law enforcement officer shall provide the basis for liability under this act.

(b) No action may be brought pursuant to this act by a person injured by an assault weapon while committing a crime.

(c) This section shall not operate to limit in scope any cause of action, other than that provided by this act, available to a person injured by an assault weapon.

(d) Any defense that is available in a strict liability action shall be available as a defense under this act.

(e) Recovery shall not be allowed under this act for a self-inflicted injury that results from a reckless, wanton, or willful discharge of an assault weapon.

Idaho Code
(1980 and (§ 6–1410) 1986)

6–1401. Scope. The previous existing applicable law of this state on product liability is modified only to the extent set forth in this act.

6–1402. Definitions. (1) "Product seller" means any person or entity that is engaged in the business of selling products, whether the sale is for resale, or for use or consumption. The term includes a manufacturer, wholesaler, distributor, or retailer of the relevant product. The term also includes a party who is in the business of leasing or bailing such products. The term "product seller" does not include:

(a) A provider of professional services who utilizes or sells products within the legally authorized scope of its professional practice. A nonprofessional provider of services is not included unless the sale or use of a product is the principal part of the transaction, and the essence of the relationship between the seller and purchaser is not the furnishing of judgment, skill, or services;

(b) A commercial seller of used products who resells a product after use by a consumer or other product user, provided the used product is in essentially the same condition as when it was acquired for resale; and

(c) A finance lessor who is not otherwise a product seller. A "finance lessor" is one who acts in a financial capacity, who is not a manufacturer, wholesaler, distributor, or retailer, and who leases a product without having a reasonable opportunity to inspect and discover defects in the product, under a lease arrangement in which the selection, possession, maintenance, and operation of the product are controlled by a person other than the lessor.

(2) "Manufacturer" includes a product seller who designs, produces, makes, fabricates, constructs, or remanufactures the relevant product or component part of a product before its sale to a user or consumer. It includes a product seller or entity not otherwise a manufacturer that holds itself out as a manufacturer. A product seller acting primarily as a wholesaler, distributor, or retailer of a product may be a "manufacturer" but only to the extent that it designs, produces, makes, fabricates, constructs, or remanufactures the product before its sale.

(3) "Product" means any object possessing intrinsic value, capable of delivery either as an assembled whole or as a component part or parts, and produced for introduction into trade or commerce. Human tissue and organs, including human blood and its components, are excluded from this term. The "relevant product" under this chapter is that product, or its component part or parts, which gave rise to the product liability claim.

(4) "Claimant" means a person or entity asserting a product liability claim, including a wrongful death action, and, if the claim is asserted through or on behalf of an estate, the term includes claimant's decedent. "Claimant" includes any person or entity that suffers harm.

(5) "Reasonably anticipated conduct" means the conduct which would be expected of an ordinary reasonably prudent person who is likely to use the product in the same or similar circumstances.

6–1403. Length of time product sellers are subject to liability.
(1) Useful safe life.

(a) Except as provided in subsection (1)(b) hereof, a product seller shall not be subject to liability to a claimant for harm under this chapter if the product seller proves by a preponderance of the evidence that the harm was caused after the product's "useful safe life" had expired.

"Useful safe life" begins at the time of delivery of the product and extends for the time during which the product would normally be likely to perform or be stored in a safe manner. For the purposes of this chapter, "time of delivery" means the time of delivery of a product to its first purchaser or lessee who was not engaged in the business of either selling such products or using them as component parts of another product to be sold.

(b) A product seller may be subject to liability for harm caused by a product used beyond its useful safe life to the extent that the product seller has expressly warranted the product for a longer period.

(2) Statute of repose.

(a) Generally. In claims that involve harm caused more than ten (10) years after time of delivery, a presumption arises that the harm was caused after the useful safe life had expired. This presumption may only be rebutted by clear and convincing evidence.

(b) Limitations on statute of repose.

1. If a product seller expressly warrants that its product can be utilized safely for a period longer than ten (10) years, the period of repose, after which the presumption created in subsection (2)(a) hereof arises, shall be extended according to that warranty or promise.

2. The ten (10) year period of repose established in subsection (2)(a) hereof does not apply if the product seller intentionally misrepresents facts about its product, or fraudulently conceals information about it, and that conduct was a substantial cause of the claimant's harm.

3. Nothing contained in subsection (2) of this section shall affect the right of any person found liable under this chapter to seek and obtain contribution or indemnity from any other person who is responsible for harm under this chapter.

4. The ten (10) year period of repose established in subsection (2)(a) hereof shall not apply if the harm was caused by prolonged exposure to a defective product, or if the injury-causing aspect of the product that existed at the time of delivery was not discoverable by an ordinary reasonably prudent person until more than ten (10) years after the time of delivery, or if the harm, caused within ten (10) years after the time of delivery, did not manifest itself until after that time.

(3) Statute of limitation. No claim under this chapter may be brought more than two (2) years from the time the cause of action accrued as defined in section 5-219, Idaho Code.

6-1404. Comparative responsibility. Comparative responsibility shall not bar recovery in an action by any person or his legal representative to recover damages for product liability resulting in death or injury to person or property, if such responsibility was not as great as the responsibility of the person against whom recovery is sought, but any damages allowed shall be diminished in the proportion to the amount of responsibility attributable to the person recovering.

6-1405. Conduct affecting comparative responsibility. (1) Failure to discover a defective condition.

(a) Claimant's failure to inspect. A claimant is not required to have inspected the product for a defective condition. Failure to have done so does not render the claimant responsible for the harm caused or reduce the claimant's damages.

(b) Claimant's failure to observe an obvious defective condition. When the product seller proves by a preponderance of the evidence that the claimant, while using the product, was injured by a defective condition that would have been obvious to an ordinary reasonably prudent person, the claimant's damages shall be subject to reduction.

(c) A nonclaimant's failure to inspect for defects or to observe an obvious defective condition. A nonclaimant's failure to inspect for a defective condition or to observe a defective condition that would have been obvious to an ordinary reasonably prudent person, shall not reduce claimant's damages.

(2) Use of a product with a known defective condition.

(a) By a claimant. When the product seller proves, by a preponderance of the evidence, that the claimant knew about the product's defective condition, and voluntarily used the product or voluntarily assumed the risk of harm from the product, the claimant's damages shall be subject to reduction to the extent that the claimant did not act as an ordinary reasonably prudent person under the circumstances.

(b) By a nonclaimant product user. If the product seller proves by a preponderance of the evidence that a product user, other than the claimant, knew about a product's defective condition, but voluntarily and unreasonably used or stored the product and thereby proximately caused claimant's harm, the claimant's damages shall be subject to apportionment.

(3) Misuse of a product.

(a) "Misuse" occurs when the product user does not act in a manner that would be expected of an ordinary reasonably prudent person who is likely to use the product in the same or similar circumstances.

(b) When the product seller proves, by a preponderance of the evidence, that product misuse by a claimant, or by a party other than the claimant or the product seller has proximately caused the claimant's harm, the claimant's damages shall be subject to reduction or apportionment to the extent that the misuse was a proximate cause of the harm.

(4) Alteration or modification of a product.

(a) "Alteration or modification" occurs when a person or entity other than the product seller changes the design, construction, or formula of the product, or changes or removes warnings or instructions that accompanied or were displayed on the product. "Alteration or modification" of a product includes the failure to observe routine care and maintenance, but does not include ordinary wear and tear.

(b) When the product seller proves, by a preponderance of the evidence, that an alteration or modification of the product by the claimant, or by a party other than the claimant or the product seller has proximately caused the claimant's harm, the claimant's damages shall be subject to reduction or apportionment to the extent that the alteration or modification was a proximate cause of the harm.

This subsection shall not be applicable if:

1. The alteration or modification was in accord with the product seller's instructions or specifications;

2. The alteration or modification was made with the express or implied consent of the product seller; or

3. The alteration or modification was reasonably anticipated conduct, and the product was defective because of the product seller's failure to provide adequate warnings or instructions with respect to the alteration or modification.

6–1406. Relevance of industry custom, safety or performance standards, and technological feasibility. (1) Evidence of changes in (a) a product's design, (b) warnings or instructions concerning the product, (c) technological feasibility, (d) "state of the art," or (e) the custom of the product seller's industry or business, occurring after the product was manufactured and delivered to its first purchaser or lessee who was not engaged in the business of either selling such products or using them as component parts of another product to be sold, is not admissible for the purpose of proving that the product was defective in design or that a warning or instruction should have accompanied the product at the time of manufacture. The provisions of this section shall not relieve the product seller of any duty to warn of known defects discovered after the product was designed and manufactured.

(2) If the court finds outside the presence of a jury that the probative value of such evidence substantially outweighs its prejudicial effect and that there is no other proof available, this evidence may be admitted for other relevant purposes, including but not limited to proving ownership or control, or impeachment.

(3) For purposes of this section, "custom" refers to the practices followed by an ordinary product seller in the product seller's industry or business.

(4) For purposes of this section, "technological feasibility" means the technological, mechanical and scientific knowledge relating to product safety that was reasonably feasible for use, in light of economic practicality, at the time of manufacture.

6–1407. Individual rights and responsibilities of product sellers other than manufacturers. (1) In the absence of express warranties to the contrary, product sellers other than manufacturers shall not be subject to liability in circumstances where they do not have a reasonable opportunity to inspect the product in a manner which would or should, in the exercise of reasonable care, reveal the existence of the defective condition which is in issue; or where the product seller acquires the product in a sealed package or container and sells the product in the same sealed package or container. The liability limitation of this subsection shall not apply if:

(a) The product seller had knowledge or reason to know of the defect in the product;

(b) The product seller altered, modified, or installed the product, and such alteration, modification or installation was a substantial proximate cause of the incident giving rise to the action, was not authorized or requested by the manufacturer and was not performed in compliance with the directions or specifications of the manufacturer;

(c) The product seller provided the plans or specifications for the manufacturer or preparation of the product and such plans or specifications were a substantial cause of the product's alleged defect;

(d) The product seller is a wholly-owned subsidiary of the manufacturer, the manufacturer is a wholly-owned subsidiary of the product seller;

(e) The product seller sold the product after the expiration date placed on the product or its package by the manufacturer.

(2) In an action where the liability limitation of subsection (1) applies, any manufacturer who refuses to accept a tender of defense from the product seller, shall indemnify the product seller for reasonable attorney's fees and costs incurred by the product seller in defending such action.

(3) In any product liability action, the manufacturer of the product shall be indemnified by the product seller of the product for any judgment rendered against the manufacturer and shall also be reimbursed for reasonable attorney's fees and costs incurred in defending such action:

(a) If the product seller provided the plans or specifications for the manufacture or preparation of the product;

(b) If such plans or specifications were a substantial cause of the product's alleged defect; and

(c) If the product was manufactured in compliance with and according to the plans or specifications of the seller.

The provisions of this subsection shall not apply if the manufacturer had knowledge or with the exercise of reasonable and diligent care should have had knowledge of the defect in the product.

(4) A product seller, other than a manufacturer, is also subject to the liability of manufacturer if:

(a) The manufacturer is not subject to service of process under the laws of the claimant's domicile; or

(b) The manufacturer has been judicially declared insolvent in that the manufacturer is unable to pay its debts as they become due in the ordinary course of business; or

(c) The court outside the presence of a jury determines that it is highly probable that the claimant would be unable to enforce a judgment against the product manufacturer.

6–1408. Contents of complaint—Amount of recovery. In any product liability action no dollar amount or figure shall be included in the complaint. The complaint shall pray for such damages as are reasonable in the premises. The complaint shall include a statement reciting that the jurisdictional amount established for filing the action is satisfied.

6–1409. Short title. This act shall be known and may be cited as the "Idaho Product Liability Reform Act."

6–1410. Products liability—Defectiveness of firearms or ammunition. (1) In a products liability action, no firearm or ammunition shall be deemed defective in design on the basis that the benefits of the product do not outweigh the risk of injury posed by its potential to cause serious injury, damage, or death when discharged.

(2) For purposes of this section:

(a) The potential of a firearm or ammunition to cause serious injury, damage, or death when discharged does not make the product defective in design;

(b) Injuries or damages resulting from the discharge of a firearm or ammunition are not proximately caused by its potential to cause serious injury, damage, or death, but are proximately caused by the actual discharge of the product;

(3) The provisions of this section shall not affect a products liability cause of action based upon the improper selection of design alternatives.

Illinois Revised Statutes
(1991)
CHAPTER 110

§ 2–621. Product liability actions. (a) In any product liability action based in whole or in part on the doctrine of strict liability in tort commenced or maintained against a defendant or defendants other than the manufacturer, that party shall upon answering or otherwise pleading file an affidavit certifying the correct identity of the manufacturer of the product allegedly causing injury, death or damage. The commencement of a product liability action based in whole or in part on the doctrine of strict liability in tort against said defendant or said defendants shall toll the applicable statute of limitation and statute of repose relative to said defendant or defendants for purposes of asserting a strict liability in tort cause of action.

(b) Once the plaintiff has filed a complaint against the manufacturer or manufacturers, and the manufacturer or manufacturers have or are required to have answered or otherwise pleaded, the court shall order the dismissal of a strict liability in tort claim against the certifying defendant or defendants, provided the certifying defendant or defendants are not within the categories set forth in subsection (c) of this Section. Due diligence shall be exercised by the certifying defendant or defendants in providing the plaintiff with the correct identity of the manufacturer or manufacturers, and due diligence shall be exercised by the plaintiff in filing a law suit and obtaining jurisdiction over the manufacturer or manufacturers.

The plaintiff may at any time subsequent to the dismissal move to vacate the order of dismissal and reinstate the certifying defendant or defendants, provided plaintiff can show one or more of the following:

(1) That the applicable period of statute of limitation or statute of repose bars the assertion of a strict liability in tort cause of action against the manufacturer or manufacturers of the product allegedly causing the injury, death or damage; or

(2) That the identity of the manufacturer given to the plaintiff by the certifying defendant or defendants was incorrect. Once the correct identity of the manufacturer has been given by the certifying defendant or defendants the court shall again dismiss the certifying defendant or defendants; or

(3) That the manufacturer no longer exists, cannot be subject to the jurisdiction of the courts of this state, or, despite due diligence, the manufacturer is not amenable to service of process; or

(4) That the manufacturer is unable to satisfy any judgment as determined by the court; or

§ 2–621   *SELECTED STATE PRODUCTS LIABILITY STATUTES*

(5) That the court determines that the manufacturer would be unable to satisfy a reasonable settlement or other agreement with plaintiff.

(c) A court shall not enter a dismissal order relative to any certifying defendant or defendants other than the manufacturer even though full compliance with subsection (a) of this Section has been made where the plaintiff can show one or more of the following:

(1) That the defendant has exercised some significant control over the design or manufacture of the product, or has provided instructions or warnings to the manufacturer relative to the alleged defect in the product which caused the injury, death or damage; or

(2) That the defendant had actual knowledge of the defect in the product which caused the injury, death or damage; or

(3) That the defendant created the defect in the product which caused the injury, death or damage.

(d) Nothing contained in this Section shall be construed to grant a cause of action in strict liability in tort or any other legal theory, or to affect the right of any person to seek and obtain indemnity or contribution.

(e) This section applies to all causes of action accruing on or after September 24, 1979.

§ 13–213. (a) As used in this Section, the term:

(1) "alteration, modification or change" or "altered, modified, or changed" means an alteration, modification or change that was made in the original makeup characteristics, function or design of a product or in the original recommendations, instructions and warnings given with respect to a product including the failure properly to maintain and care for a product.

(2) "product" means any tangible object or goods distributed in commerce, including any service provided in connection with the product. Where the term "product unit" is used, it refers to a single item or unit of a product.

(3) "product liability action" means any action based on the doctrine of strict liability in tort brought against the seller of a product on account of personal injury, (including illness, disease, disability and death) or property, economic or other damage allegedly caused by or resulting from the manufacture, construction, preparation, assembly, installation, testing, makeup, characteristics, functions, design, formula, plan, recommendation, specification, prescription, advertising, sale, marketing, packaging, labeling, repair, maintenance or disposal of, or warning or instruction regarding any product. This definition excludes actions brought by State or federal regulatory agencies pursuant to statute.

(4) "seller" means one who, in the course of a business conducted for the purpose, sells, distributes, leases, assembles, installs, produces, manufactures, fabricates, prepares, constructs, packages, labels, markets, repairs, maintains, or otherwise is involved in placing a product in the stream of commerce.

(b) Subject to the provisions of subsections (c) and (d) no product liability action based on the doctrine of strict liability in tort shall be commenced except within the applicable limitations period and, in any event, within 12 years from the date of first sale, lease or delivery of possession by a seller or 10 years from the date of first sale, lease or delivery of possession to its initial user, consumer, or other non-seller, whichever period expires earlier, of any product unit that is claimed to have injured or damaged the plaintiff, unless the defendant expressly has warranted or promised the product for a longer period and the action is brought within that period.

(c) No product liability action based on the doctrine of strict liability in tort to recover for injury or damage claimed to have resulted from an alteration, modification or change of the product unit subsequent to the date of first sale, lease or delivery of possession of the product unit to its initial user, consumer or other non-seller shall be limited or barred by subsection (b) hereof if:

(1) the action is brought against a seller making, authorizing, or furnishing materials for the accomplishment of such alteration, modification or change (or against a seller furnishing specifications or instructions for the accomplishment of such alteration, modification or change when the injury is claimed to have resulted from failure to provide adequate specifications or instructions), and

(2) the action commenced within the applicable limitation period and, in any event, within 10 years from the date such alteration, modification or change was made, unless defendant expressly has warranted or promised the product for a longer period and the action is brought within that period, and

(3) when the injury or damage is claimed to have resulted from an alteration, modification or change of a product unit, there is proof that such alteration, modification or change had the effect of introducing into the use of the product unit, by reason of defective materials or workmanship, a hazard not existing prior to such alteration, modification or change.

(d) Notwithstanding the provisions of subsection (b) and paragraph (2) of subsection (c) if the injury complained of occurs within any of the periods provided by subsection (b) and paragraph (2) of subsection (c), the plaintiff may bring an action within 2 years after the date on which the claimant knew, or through the use of reasonable diligence should have known, of the existence of the personal injury, death or property damage, but in no event shall such action be brought more than 8 years after the date on which such personal injury, death or property damage occurred. In any such case, if the person entitled to bring the action was, at the time the personal injury, death or property damage occurred, under the age of 18 years, or under a legal disability, then the period of limitations does not begin to run until the person attains the age of 18 years, or the disability is removed.

(e) Replacement of a component part of a product unit with a substitute part having the same formula or design as the original part shall not be deemed a sale, lease or delivery of possession or an alteration, modification or change for the purpose of permitting commencement of a product liability action based on the doctrine of strict liability in tort to recovery for injury or damage claimed to have resulted from the formula or design of such product unit or of the substitute part when such action would otherwise be barred according to the provisions of subsection (b) of this Section.

(f) Nothing in this Section shall be construed to create a cause of action or to affect the right of any person to seek and obtain indemnity or contribution.

(g) The provisions of this Section 13–213 of this Act apply to any cause of action accruing on or after January 1, 1979, involving any product which was in or entered the stream of commerce prior to, on, or after January 1, 1979.

KANSAS STATUTES ANNOTATED
(1981-90)

60-3301. Short title. The act shall be known and may be cited as the "Kansas product liability act."

60-3302. Definitions. (a) "Product seller" means any person or entity that is engaged in the business of selling products, whether the sale is for resale, or for use or consumption. The term includes a manufacturer, wholesaler, distributor or retailer of the relevant product.

(b) "Manufacturer" includes a product seller who designs, produces, makes, fabricates, constructs, or remanufactures the relevant product or component part of a product before its sale to a user or consumer. It includes a product seller or entity not otherwise a manufacturer that holds itself out as a manufacturer, or that is owned in whole or in part by the manufacturer.

(c) "Product liability claim" includes any claim or action brought for harm caused by the manufacture, production, making, construction, fabrication, design, formula, preparation, assembly, installation, testing, warnings, instructions, marketing, packaging, storage or labeling of the relevant product. It includes, but is not limited to, any action based on strict liability in tort, negligence, breach of express or implied warranty, breach of, or failure to discharge a duty to warn or instruct, whether negligent or innocent, misrepresentation, concealment or nondisclosure, whether negligent or innocent, or under any other substantive legal theory.

(d) "Harm" includes: 1. Damage to property; 2. personal physical injuries, illness and death; 3. mental anguish or emotional harm attendant to such personal physical injuries, illness or death. The term "harm" does not include direct or consequential economic loss.

60-3303. Useful safe life, ten-year period of repose, evidence. (a)(1) Except as provided in paragraph 2 of subsection (a) of this section, a product seller shall not be subject to liability in a product liability claim if the product seller proves by a preponderance of the evidence that the harm was caused after the product's "useful safe life" had expired. "Useful safe life" begins at the time of delivery of the product and extends for the time during which the product would normally be likely to perform or be stored in a safe manner. For the purposes of this section, "time of delivery" means the time of delivery of a product to its first purchaser or lessee who was not engaged in the business of either selling such products or using them as component parts of another product to be sold.

Examples of evidence that is especially probative in determining whether a product's useful safe life had expired include:

(A) The amount of wear and tear to which the product had been subject;

(B) the effect of deterioration from natural causes, and from climate and other conditions under which the product was used or stored;

(C) the normal practices of the user, similar users and the product seller with respect to the circumstances, frequency and purposes of the product's use, and with respect to repairs, renewals and replacements;

(D) any representations, instructions or warnings made by the product seller concerning proper maintenance, storage and use of the product or the expected useful safe life of the product; and

(E) any modification or alteration of the product by a user or third party.

(2) A product seller may be subject to liability for harm caused by a product used beyond its useful safe life to the extent that the product seller has expressly warranted the product for a longer period.

(b)(1) In claims that involve harm caused more than 10 years after time of delivery, a presumption arises that the harm was caused after the useful safe life had expired. This presumption may only be rebutted by clear and convincing evidence.

(2)(A) If a product seller expressly warrants that its product can be utilized safely for a period longer than 10 years, the period of repose, after which the presumption created in paragraph 1. of this subsection arises, shall be extended according to that warranty or promise.

(B) The ten-year period of repose established in paragraph 1. of this subsection does not apply if the product seller intentionally misrepresents facts about its product, or fraudulently conceals information about it, and that conduct was a substantial cause of the claimant's harm.

(C) Nothing contained in this subsection shall affect the right of any person liable under a product liability claim to seek and obtain indemnity from any other person who is responsible for the harm which gave rise to the product liability claim.

(D) The ten-year period of repose established in paragraph 1. of this subsection shall not apply if the harm was caused by prolonged exposure to a defective product, or if the injury-causing aspect of the product that existed at the time of delivery was not discoverable by a reasonably prudent person until more than 10 years after the time of delivery, or if the harm caused within 10 years after the time of delivery did not manifest itself until after that time.

(c) Except as provided in subsections (d) and (e), nothing contained in subsections (a) and (b) above shall modify the application of K.S.A. 60–513, and amendments thereto.

(d)(1) In a product liability claim against the product seller, the ten-year limitation, as defined in K.S.A. 60–513, and amendments thereto, shall not apply to the time to discover a disease which is latent caused by exposure to a harmful material, in which event the action shall be deemed to have accrued when the disease and such disease's cause have been made known to the person or at the point the person should have been aware of the disease and such disease's cause.

(2) The term "harmful material" means any chemical substances commonly known as asbestos, dioxins, or polychlorinated byphenyls, whether alone or as part of any product, or any substance which is determined to present an unreasonable risk of injury to health or the environment by the United States Environmental Protection Agency pursuant to the Federal Toxic Substances Control Act, 15 U.S.C. § 2601 et seq., or the state of Kansas, and because of such risk is regulated by the state or the Environmental Protection Agency.

(e) Upon the effective date of this act through July 1, 1991, the provisions of this subsection shall revive such causes of action for latent diseases caused by exposure to a harmful material for: (1) Any person whose cause of action had accrued, as defined in subsection (d) on or after March 3, 1987; or (2) any person who had an action pending in any court on March 3, 1989, and because of the judicial interpretation of the ten-year limitation contained in subsection (b) of K.S.A. 60–512, and amendments thereto, as applied to latent disease caused by exposure to a harmful material the: (a) action was dismissed; (b) dismissal of the action was affirmed; or (c) action was subject to dismissal. The intent of this subsection is to revive causes of action for latent diseases caused by exposure to a harmful material which were barred by interpretation of K.S.A. 60–513, and amendments thereto, in effect prior to this enactment.

60–3304. Legislative regulatory standards or administrative regulatory safety standards or mandatory government contract specifications—Defenses. (a) When the injury-causing aspect of the product was, at the time of manufacture, in compliance with legislative regulatory standards or administrative regulatory safety standards relating to design or performance, the product shall be deemed not defective by reason of design or performance, or, if the standard addressed warnings or instructions, the product shall be deemed not defective by reason of warnings or instructions, unless the claimant proves by a preponderance of the evidence that a reasonably prudent product seller could and would have taken additional precautions.

(b) When the injury-causing aspect of the product was not, at the time of manufacture, in compliance with legislative regulatory standards or administrative regulatory safety standards relating to design, performance, warnings or instructions, the product shall be deemed defective unless the product seller proves by a preponderance of the evidence that its failure to comply was a reasonably prudent course of conduct under the circumstances.

(c) When the injury-causing aspect of the product was, at the time of manufacture, in compliance with a mandatory government contract specification relating to design, this shall be an absolute defense and the product shall be deemed not defective for that reason, or, if the specification related to warnings or instructions, then the product shall be deemed not defective for that reason.

(d) When the injury-causing aspect of the product was not, at the time of manufacture, in compliance with a mandatory government contract specification relating to design, the product shall be deemed defective for that reason, or if the specification related to warnings or instructions, the product shall be deemed defective for that reason.

60-3305. Manufacturer's or seller's duty to warn or protect against danger, when. In any product liability claim any duty on the part of the manufacturer or seller of the product to warn or protect against a danger or hazard which could or did arise in the use or misuse of such product, and any duty to have properly instructed in the use of such product shall not extend: (a) To warnings, protecting against or instructing with regard to those safeguards, precautions and actions which a reasonable user or consumer of the product, with the training, experience, education and any special knowledge the user or consumer did, should or was required to possess, could and should have taken for such user or consumer or others, under all the facts and circumstances;

(b) to situations where the safeguards, precautions and actions would or should have been taken by a reasonable user or consumer of the product similarly situated exercising reasonable care, caution and procedure; or

(c) to warnings, protecting against or instructing with regard to dangers, hazards or risks which are patent, open or obvious and which should have been realized by a reasonable user or consumer of the product.

60-3306. Seller not subject to liability. A product seller shall not be subject to liability in a product liability claim arising from an alleged defect in a product, if the product seller establishes that: (a) Such seller had no knowledge of the defect;

(b) such seller in the performance of any duties the seller performed, or was required to perform, could not have discovered the defect while exercising reasonable care;

(c) the seller was not a manufacturer of the defective product or product component;

(d) the manufacturer of the defective product or product component is subject to service of process either under the laws of the state of

Kansas or the domicile of the person making the product liability claim; and

(e) any judgment against the manufacturer obtained by the person making the product liability claim would be reasonably certain of being satisfied.

60-3307. Inadmissible evidence. (a) In a product liability claim, the following evidence shall not be admissible for any purpose:

(1) Evidence of any advancements or changes in technical or other knowledge or techniques, in design theory or philosophy, in manufacturing or testing knowledge, techniques or processes in labeling, warning of risks or hazards, instructions for the use of such product, if such advancements or changes have been made, learned or placed into common use subsequent to the time the product in issue was designed, formulated, tested, manufactured or sold by the manufacturer; and

(2) evidence of any changes made in the designing, planning, formulating, testing, preparing, manufacturing, packaging, warnings, labeling or instructing for use of, or with regard to, the product in issue, or any similar product, which changes were made subsequent to the time the product in issue was designed, formulated, tested, manufactured or sold by the manufacturer.

(b) This section does not require the exclusion of evidence of a subsequent measure if offered to impeach a witness for the manufacturer or seller of a product who has expressly denied the feasibility of such a measure.

Louisiana Revised Statutes Annotated
(1988)

§ 2800.51. Short title. This Chapter shall be known and may be cited as the "Louisiana Products Liability Act."

§ 2800.52. Scope of this chapter. This Chapter establishes the exclusive theories of liability for manufacturers for damage caused by their products. A claimant may not recover from a manufacturer for damage caused by a product on the basis of any theory of liability that is not set forth in this Chapter. Conduct or circumstances that result in liability under this Chapter are "fault" within the meaning of Civil Code Article 2315. This Chapter does not apply to the rights of an employee or his personal representatives, dependents or relations against a manufacturer who is the employee's employer or against any principal or any officer, director, stockholder, partner or employee of such manufacturer or principal as limited by R.S. 23:1032, or to the rights of a claimant against the following, unless they assume the status of a manufacturer as defined in R.S. 9:2800.53(1):

(1) Providers of professional services, even if the service results in a product.

(2) Providers of nonprofessional services where the essence of the service is the furnishing of judgment or skill, even if the service results in a product.

(3) Producers of natural fruits and other raw products in their natural state that are derived from animals, fowl, aquatic life or invertebrates, including but not limited to milk, eggs, honey and wool.

(4) Farmers and other producers of agricultural plants in their natural state.

(5) Ranchers and other producers of animals, fowl, aquatic life or invertebrates in their natural state.

(6) Harvesters and other producers of fish, crawfish, oysters, crabs, mollusks or other aquatic animals in their natural state.

§ 2800.53. Definitions. The following terms have the following meanings for the purpose of this Chapter:

(1) "Manufacturer" means a person or entity who is in the business of manufacturing a product for placement into trade or commerce. "Manufacturing a product" means producing, making, fabricating, constructing, designing, remanufacturing, reconditioning or refurbishing a product. "Manufacturer" also means:

(a) A person or entity who labels a product as his own or who otherwise holds himself out to be the manufacturer of the product.

(b) A seller of a product who exercises control over or influences a characteristic of the design, construction or quality of the product that causes damage.

(c) A manufacturer of a product who incorporates into the product a component or part manufactured by another manufacturer.

(d) A seller of a product of an alien manufacturer if the seller is in the business of importing or distributing the product for resale and the seller is the alter ego of the alien manufacturer. The court shall take into consideration the following in determining whether the seller is the alien manufacturer's alter ego: whether the seller is affiliated with the alien manufacturer by way of common ownership or control; whether the seller assumes or administers product warranty obligations of the alien manufacturer; whether the seller prepares or modifies the product for distribution; or any other relevant evidence. A "product of an alien manufacturer" is a product that is manufactured outside the United States by a manufacturer who is a citizen of another country or who is organized under the laws of another country.

(2) "Seller" means a person or entity who is not a manufacturer and who is in the business of conveying title to or possession of a product to another person or entity in exchange for anything of value.

(3) "Product" means a corporeal movable that is manufactured for placement into trade or commerce, including a product that forms a component part of or that is subsequently incorporated into another product or an immovable. "Product" does not mean human blood, blood components, human organs, human tissue or approved animal tissue to the extent such are governed by R.S. 9:2797.

(4) "Claimant" means a person or entity who asserts a claim under this Chapter against the manufacturer of a product or his insurer for damage caused by the product.

(5) "Damage" means all damage caused by a product, including survival and wrongful death damages, for which Civil Code Articles 2315, 2315.1 and 2315.2 allow recovery. "Damage" includes damage to the product itself and economic loss arising from a deficiency in or loss of use of the product only to the extent that Section 3 of Chapter 6 of Title VII of Book III of the Civil Code, entitled "Of the Vices of the Thing Sold," does not allow recovery for such damage or economic loss. Attorneys' fees are not recoverable under this Chapter.

(6) "Express warranty" means a representation, statement of alleged fact or promise about a product or its nature, material or workmanship that represents, affirms or promises that the product or its nature, material or workmanship possesses specified characteristics or qualities or will meet a specified level of performance. "Express warranty" does not mean a general opinion about or general praise of a product. A sample or model of a product is an express warranty.

(7) "Reasonably anticipated use" means a use or handling of a product that the product's manufacturer should reasonably expect of an ordinary person in the same or similar circumstances.

(8) "Reasonably anticipated alteration or modification" means a change in a product that the product's manufacturer should reasonably expect to be made by an ordinary person in the same or similar circumstances, and also means a change arising from ordinary wear and tear. "Reasonably anticipated alteration or modification" does not mean the following:

(a) Alteration, modification or removal of an otherwise adequate warning provided about a product.

(b) The failure of a person or entity, other than the manufacturer of a product, reasonably to provide to the product user or handler an adequate warning that the manufacturer provided about the product, when the manufacturer has satisfied his obligation to use reasonable care to provide the adequate warning by providing it to such person or entity rather than to the product user or handler.

(c) Changes to or in a product or its operation because the product does not receive reasonable care and maintenance.

(9) "Adequate warning" means a warning or instruction that would lead an ordinary reasonable user or handler of a product to contemplate the danger in using or handling the product and either to decline to use or handle the product or, if possible, to use or handle the product in such a manner as to avoid the damage for which the claim is made.

§ 2800.54. Manufacturer responsibility and burden of proof.
A. The manufacturer of a product shall be liable to a claimant for damage proximately caused by a characteristic of the product that renders the product unreasonably dangerous when such damage arose from a reasonably anticipated use of the product by the claimant or another person or entity.

B. A product is unreasonably dangerous if and only if:

(1) The product is unreasonably dangerous in construction or composition as provided in R.S. 9:2800.55;

(2) The product is unreasonably dangerous in design as provided in R.S. 9:2800.56;

(3) The product is unreasonably dangerous because an adequate warning about the product has not been provided as provided in R.S. 9:2800.57; or

(4) The product is unreasonably dangerous because it does not conform to an express warranty of the manufacturer about the product as provided in R.S. 9:2800.58.

C. The characteristic of the product that renders it unreasonably dangerous under R.S. 9:2800.55 must exist at the time the product left the control of its manufacturer. The characteristic of the product that renders it unreasonably dangerous under R.S. 9:2800.56 or 9:2800.57 must exist at the time the product left the control of its manufacturer or result from a reasonably anticipated alteration or modification of the product.

D. The claimant has the burden of proving the elements of Subsections A, B and C of this Section.

§ 2800.55. Unreasonably dangerous in construction or composition. A product is unreasonably dangerous in construction or composition if, at the time the product left its manufacturer's control, the product deviated in a material way from the manufacturer's specifications or performance standards for the product or from otherwise identical products manufactured by the same manufacturer.

§ 2800.56. Unreasonably dangerous in design. A product is unreasonably dangerous in design if, at the time the product left its manufacturer's control:

(1) There existed an alternative design for the product that was capable of preventing the claimant's damage; and

(2) The likelihood that the product's design would cause the claimant's damage and the gravity of that damage outweighed the burden on the manufacturer of adopting such alternative design and the adverse effect, if any, of such alternative design on the utility of the product. An adequate warning about a product shall be considered in evaluating the likelihood of damage when the manufacturer has used reasonable care to provide the adequate warning to users and handlers of the product.

§ 2800.57. Unreasonably dangerous because of inadequate warning. A. A product is unreasonably dangerous because an adequate warning about the product has not been provided if, at the time the product left its manufacturer's control, the product possessed a characteristic that may cause damage and the manufacturer failed to use reasonable care to provide an adequate warning of such characteristic and its danger to users and handlers of the product.

B. A manufacturer is not required to provide an adequate warning about his product when:

(1) The product is not dangerous to an extent beyond that which would be contemplated by the ordinary user or handler of the product, with the ordinary knowledge common to the community as to the product's characteristics; or

(2) The user or handler of the product already knows or reasonably should be expected to know of the characteristic of the product that may cause damage and the danger of such characteristic.

C. A manufacturer of a product who, after the product has left his control, acquires knowledge of a characteristic of the product that may cause damage and the danger of such characteristic, or who would have acquired such knowledge had he acted as a reasonably prudent manufacturer, is liable for damage caused by his subsequent failure to use reasonable care to provide an adequate warning of such characteristic and its danger to users and handlers of the product.

§ 2800.58. Unreasonably dangerous because of nonconformity to express warranty. A product is unreasonably dangerous when it does not conform to an express warranty made at any time by the manufacturer about the product if the express warranty has induced the claimant or another person or entity to use the product and the claimant's damage was proximately caused because the express warranty was untrue.

§ 2800.59. Manufacturer knowledge, design feasibility and burden of proof. A. Notwithstanding R.S. 9:2800.56, a manufacturer of a product shall not be liable for damage proximately caused by a characteristic of the product's design if the manufacturer proves that, at the time the product left his control:

(1) He did not know and, in light of then-existing reasonably available scientific and technological knowledge, could not have known of the design characteristic that caused the damage or the danger of such characteristic; or

(2) He did not know and, in light of then-existing reasonably available scientific and technological knowledge, could not have known of the alternative design identified by the claimant under R.S. 9:2800.-56(1); or

(3) The alternative design identified by the claimant under R.S. 9:2800.56(1) was not feasible, in light of then-existing reasonably available scientific and technological knowledge or then-existing economic practicality.

B. Notwithstanding R.S. 9:2800.57(A) or (B), a manufacturer of a product shall not be liable for damage proximately caused by a characteristic of the product if the manufacturer proves that, at the time the product left his control, he did not know and, in light of then-existing reasonably available scientific and technological knowledge, could not have known of the characteristic that caused the damage or the danger of such characteristic.

SELECTED STATE PRODUCTS LIABILITY STATUTES

GENERAL LAWS OF MISSISSIPPI
(1993)

Summary of Mississippi H.B. 1270
(As Passed by the House)

The purpose of H.B. 1270 is to clearly state the rules which apply to Mississippi products liability actions and to cases seeking punitive damages. The bill as amended:

- Codifies the common-sense rule that a manufacturer should not be liable unless a product contains a defect and the defect caused the claimant's harm.

- Provides that liability should not be imposed for harm caused by products that are inherently risky (e.g., guns and knives) if the risk is recognized by the ordinary consumer and cannot be eliminated without substantially reducing the product's usefulness.

- Recognizes that a company should not be required to warn of dangers that were not known or knowable when the product was manufactured.

- Does not allow recovery of damages if the danger posed by a product is open or obvious or if the injured person knew of the danger and voluntarily chose to expose himself to the danger.

- Provides that liability should not be imposed in a design-defect case unless there was a feasible alternative design that would have prevented the alleged harm.

- Requires a manufacturer who is found liable to indemnify the product seller for litigation costs, reasonable expenses, attorneys' fees and any damages awarded against a seller who had no control over the manufacture or design of the product.

- Requires punitive damages awards to be supported by clear and convincing evidence that the defendant acted with actual malice, actual fraud or with willful, wanton, or reckless disregard for the safety of others.

- Requires the question of liability for compensatory damages to be decided by the jury before the punitive damages issue is addressed.

- Prohibits punitive damages in the absence of a compensatory damage award.

- Provides several factors for the jury to consider when determining the amount of punitive damages and requires the amount to be rationally related to the harm caused.

- Protects innocent retailers and wholesalers from liability for punitive damages if the seller had no control over the manufacture or design of the product.

AN ACT TO CODIFY CERTAIN RULES AND ESTABLISH NEW RULES APPLICABLE TO PRODUCT LIABILITY ACTIONS; ETC.

BE IT ENACTED BY THE LEGISLATURE OF THE STATE OF MISSISSIPPI:

SECTION 1. In any action for damages caused by a product except for commercial damage to the product itself:

(a) The manufacturer or seller of the product shall not be liable if the claimant does not prove by the preponderance of the evidence that at the time the product left the control of the manufacturer or seller:

(i) 1. The product was defective because it deviated in a material way from the manufacturer's specifications or from otherwise identical units manufactured to the same manufacturing specifications, or

2. The product was defective because it failed to contain adequate warnings or instructions, or

3. The product was designed in a defective manner, or

4. The product breached an express warranty or failed to conform to other express factual representations upon which the claimant justifiably relied in electing to use the product; and

(ii) The defective condition rendered the product unreasonably dangerous to the user or consumer; and

(iii) The defective and unreasonably dangerous condition of the product proximately caused the damages for which recovery is sought.

(b) A product is not defective in design or formulation if the harm for which the claimant seeks to recover compensatory damages was caused by an inherent characteristic of the product which is a generic aspect of the product that cannot be eliminated without substantially compromising the product's usefulness or desirability and which is recognized by the ordinary person with the ordinary knowledge common to the community.

(c)(i) In any action alleging that a product is defective because it failed to contain adequate warnings or instructions pursuant to paragraph (a)(i)2 of this section, the manufacturer or seller shall not be liable if the claimant does not prove by the preponderance of the evidence that at the time the product left the control of the manufacturer or seller, the manufacturer or seller knew or in light of reasonably available knowledge should have known about the danger that caused the damage for which recovery is sought and that the ordinary user or consumer would not realize its dangerous condition.

(ii) An adequate product warning or instruction is one that a reasonably prudent person in the same or similar circumstances would have provided with respect to the danger and that communicates sufficient information on the dangers and safe use of the product, taking into account the characteristics of, and the ordinary knowledge common to an ordinary consumer who purchases the product; or in the case of a prescription drug, medical device or other product that is intended to be used only under the supervision of a physician or other licensed professional person, taking into account the characteristics of, and the ordinary knowledge common to, a physician or other licensed professional who prescribes the drug, device or other product.

(d) In any action alleging that a product is defective pursuant to paragraph (a) of this section, the manufacturer or seller shall not be liable if the claimant (i) had knowledge of a condition of the product that was inconsistent with his safety; (ii) appreciated the danger in the condition; and (iii) deliberately and voluntarily chose to expose himself to the danger in such a manner to register assent on the continuance of the dangerous condition.

(e) In any action alleging that a product is defective pursuant to paragraph (a)(i)2 of this section, the manufacturer or seller shall not be liable if the danger posed by the product is known or is open and obvious to the user or consumer of the product, or should have been known or open and obvious to the user or consumer of the product, taking into account the characteristics of, and the ordinary knowledge common to, the persons who ordinarily use or consume the product.

(f) In any action alleging that a product is defective because of its design pursuant to paragraph (a)(i)3 of this section, the manufacturer or product seller shall not be liable if the claimant does not prove by the preponderance of the evidence that at the time the product left the control of the manufacturer or seller:

(i) The manufacturer or seller knew, or in light of reasonably available knowledge or in the exercise of reasonable care should have known, about the danger that caused the damage for which recovery is sought; and

(ii) The product failed to function as expected and there existed a feasible design alternative that would have to a reasonable probability prevented the harm. A feasible design alternative is a design that would have to a reasonable probability prevented the harm without impairing the utility, usefulness, practicality or desirability of the product to users or consumers.

(g)(i) The manufacturer of a product who is found liable for a defective product pursuant to Section 1(a) shall indemnify a product seller for the costs of litigation, any reasonable expenses, reasonable attorney's fees and any damages awarded by the trier of fact unless the seller exercised substantial control over that aspect of the design, testing, manufacture, packaging or labeling of the product that caused the harm for which recovery of damages is sought; the seller altered or modified the product, and the alteration or modification was a substantial factor in causing the harm for which recovery of damages is sought; the seller had actual knowledge of the defective condition of the product at the time he supplied same; or the seller made an express factual representation about the aspect of the product which caused the harm for which recovery of damages is sought.

(ii) Subparagraph (i) shall not apply unless the seller has given prompt notice of the suit to the manufacturer within thirty (30) days of the filing of the complaint against the seller.

(h) Nothing in this section shall be construed to eliminate any common law defense to an action for damages caused by a product.

SECTION 2. (1) In any action in which punitive damages are sought:

(a) Punitive damages may not be awarded if the claimant does not prove by clear and convincing evidence that the defendant against whom punitive damages are sought acted with actual malice, gross negligence which evidences a willful, wanton or reckless disregard for the safety of others, or committed actual fraud.

(b) In any action in which the claimant seeks an award of punitive damages, the trier of fact shall first determine whether compensatory damages are to be awarded and in what amount, before addressing any issues related to punitive damages.

(c) If, but only if, an award of compensatory damages has been made against a party, the court shall promptly commence an evidentiary hearing before the same trier of fact to determine whether punitive damages may be considered.

(d) The court shall determine whether the issue of punitive damages may be submitted to the trier of fact; and, if so, the trier of fact shall determine whether to award punitive damages and in what amount.

(e) In all cases involving an award of punitive damages, the fact finder, in determining the amount of punitive damages, shall consider, to the extent relevant, the following: the defendant's financial condition and net worth; the nature and reprehensibility of the defendant's wrongdoing, for example, the impact of the defendant's conduct on the plaintiff, or the relationship of the defendant to the plaintiff; the defendant's awareness of the amount of harm being caused and the defendant's motivation in causing such harm; the duration of the defendant's misconduct and whether the defendant attempted to conceal such misconduct; and any other circumstances shown by the evidence that bear on determining a proper amount of punitive damages. The trier of fact shall be instructed that the primary purpose of punitive damages is to punish the wrongdoer and deter similar misconduct in the future by the defendant and others while the purpose of compensatory damages is to make the plaintiff whole.

(f)(i) Before entering judgment for an award of punitive damages the trial court shall ascertain that the award is reasonable in its amount and rationally related to the purpose to punish what occurred giving rise to the award and to deter its repetition by the defendant and others.

(ii) In determining whether the award is excessive, the court shall take into consideration the following factors:

1. Whether there is a reasonable relationship between the punitive damage award and the harm likely to result from the defendant's conduct as well as the harm that actually occurred;

2. The degree of reprehensibility of the defendant's conduct, the duration of that conduct, the defendant's awareness, any concealment, and the existence and frequency of similar past conduct;

3. The financial condition and net worth of the defendant; and

4. In mitigation, the imposition of criminal sanctions on the defendant for its conduct and the existence of other civil awards against the defendant for the same conduct.

(g) The seller of a product other than the manufacturer shall not be liable for punitive damages unless the seller exercised substantial control over that aspect of the design, testing, manufacture, packaging or labeling of the product that caused the harm for which recovery of damages is sought; the seller altered or modified the product, and the alteration or modification was a substantial factor in causing the harm for which recovery of damages is sought; the seller had actual knowledge of the defective condition of the product at the time he supplied same; or the seller made an express factual representation about the aspect of the product which caused the harm for which recovery of damages is sought.

(2) The provisions of Section 2 of this act shall not apply to:

(a) Contracts;

(b) Libel and slander; or

(c) Causes of action for persons and property arising out of asbestos.

[Sections 3, 4, and 5, pertaining to compensatory damages and date of effectiveness, omitted.]

Missouri Revised Statutes
(1987)

§ 537.760. As used in sections 33 to 36 of this act, the term "products liability claim" means a claim or portion of a claim in which the plaintiff seeks relief in the form of damages on a theory that the defendant is strictly liable for such damages because:

(1) The defendant, wherever situated in the chain of commerce, transferred a product in the course of his business; and

(2) The product was used in a manner reasonably anticipated; and

(3) Either or both of the following:

(a) The product was then in a defective condition unreasonably dangerous when put to a reasonably anticipated use, and the plaintiff was damaged as a direct result of such defective condition as existed when the product was sold; or

(b) The product was then unreasonably dangerous when put to a reasonably anticipated use without knowledge of its characteristics, and the plaintiff was damaged as a direct result of the product being sold without an adequate warning.

§ 537.762. 1. A defendant whose liability is based solely on his status as a seller in the stream of commerce may be dismissed from a products liability claim as provided in this section.

2. This section shall apply to any products liability claim in which another defendant, including the manufacturer, is properly before the court and from whom total recovery may be had for plaintiff's claim.

3. A defendant may move for dismissal under this section within the time for filing an answer or other responsive pleading unless permitted by the court at a later time for good cause shown. The motion shall be accompanied by an affidavit which shall be made under oath and shall state that the defendant is aware of no facts or circumstances upon which a verdict might be reached against him, other than his status as a seller in the stream of commerce.

4. The parties shall have sixty days in which to conduct discovery on the issues raised in the motion and affidavit. The court for good cause shown, may extend the time for discovery, and may enter a protective order pursuant to the rules of civil procedure regarding the scope of discovery on other issues.

5. Any party may move for a hearing on a motion to dismiss under this section. If the requirements of subsections 2 and 3 of this section are met, and no party comes forward at such a hearing with evidence of facts which would render the defendant seeking dismissal under this section liable on some basis other than his status as a seller

in the stream of commerce, the court shall dismiss without prejudice the claim as to that defendant.

6. No order of dismissal under this section shall operate to divest a court of venue or jurisdiction otherwise proper at the time the action was commenced. A defendant dismissed pursuant to this section shall be considered to remain a party to such action only for such purposes.

7. An order of dismissal under this section shall be interlocutory until final disposition of plaintiff's claim by settlement or judgment and may be set aside for good cause shown at anytime prior to such disposition.

§ 537.764. 1. As used in this section, "state of the art" means that the dangerous nature of the product was not known and could not reasonably be discovered at the time the product was placed into the stream of commerce.

2. The state of the art shall be a complete defense and relevant evidence only in an action based upon strict liability for failure to warn of the dangerous condition of a product. This defense shall be pleaded as an affirmative defense and the party asserting it shall have the burden of proof.

3. Nothing in this section shall be construed as limiting the rights of an injured party to maintain an action for negligence whenever such a cause of action would otherwise exist.

4. This section shall not be construed to permit or prohibit evidence of feasibility in products liability claims.

§ 537.765. 1. Contributory fault, as a complete bar to plaintiff's recovery in a products liability claim, is abolished. The doctrine of pure comparative fault shall apply to products liability claims as provided in this section.

2. Defendant may plead and prove the fault of the plaintiff as an affirmative defense. Any fault chargeable to the plaintiff shall diminish proportionately the amount awarded as compensatory damages but shall not bar recovery.

3. For purposes of this section, "fault" is limited to:

(1) The failure to use the product as reasonably anticipated by the manufacturer;

(2) Use of the product for a purpose not intended by the manufacturer;

(3) Use of the product with knowledge of a danger involved in such use with reasonable appreciation of the consequences and the voluntary and unreasonable exposure to said danger;

(4) Unreasonable failure to appreciate the danger involved in use of the product or the consequences thereof and the unreasonable exposure to said danger;

(5) The failure to undertake the precautions a reasonably careful user of the product would take to protect himself against dangers which he would reasonably appreciate under the same or similar circumstances; or

(6) The failure to mitigate damages.

SELECTED STATE PRODUCTS LIABILITY STATUTES

NEW JERSEY REVISED STATUTES
(1987)

2A:58c-1. a. * * *

2A.58c-1. b. As used in this Act:

(1) "Claimant" means any person who brings a product liability action, and if such an action is brought through or on behalf of an estate, the term includes the person's decedent, or if an action is brought through or on behalf of a minor, the term includes the person's parent or guardian.

(2) "Harm" means (a) physical damage to property, other than to the product itself; (b) personal physical illness, injury or death; (c) pain and suffering, mental anguish or emotional harm; and (d) any loss of consortium or services or other loss deriving from any type of harm described in subparagraphs (a) through (c) of this paragraph.

(3) "Product liability action" means any claim or action brought by a claimant for harm caused by a product, irrespective of the theory underlying the claim, except actions for harm caused by breach of an express warranty.

(4) "Environmental tort action" means a civil action seeking damages for harm where the cause of the harm is exposure to toxic chemicals or substances, but does not mean actions involving drugs or products intended for personal consumption or use.

2A:58c-2.1. Liability of manufacturer or seller—Proof by preponderance of evidence product not reasonably fit, suitable or safe for its intended purpose. A manufacturer or seller of a product shall be liable in a product liability action only if the claimant proves by a preponderance of the evidence that the product causing the harm was not reasonably fit, suitable or safe for its intended purpose because it: a. deviated from the design specifications, formulae, or performance standards of the manufacturer or from otherwise identical units manufactured to the same manufacturing specifications or formulae, or b. failed to contain adequate warnings or instructions, or c. was designed in a defective manner.

2A:58c-3. Defenses. a. In any product liability action against a manufacturer or seller for harm allegedly caused by a product that was designed in a defective manner, the manufacturer or seller shall not be liable if:

(1) At the time the product left the control of the manufacturer, there was not a practical and technically feasible alternative design that would have prevented the harm without substantially impairing the reasonably anticipated or intended function of the product; or

(2) The characteristics of the product are known to the ordinary consumer or user, and the harm was caused by an unsafe aspect of the product that is an inherent characteristic of the product and that would be recognized by the ordinary person who uses or consumes the product with the ordinary knowledge common to the class of persons for whom the product is intended, except that this paragraph shall not apply to industrial machinery or other equipment used in the workplace and it is not intended to apply to dangers posed by products such as machinery or equipment that can feasibly be eliminated without impairing the usefulness of the product; or

(3) The harm was caused by an unavoidably unsafe aspect of the product and the product was accompanied by an adequate warning or instruction as defined in section 4 of this act.

b. The provisions of paragraph (1) of subsection a. of this section shall not apply if the court, on the basis of clear and convincing evidence, makes all of the following determinations:

(1) The product is egregiously unsafe or ultra-hazardous;

(2) The ordinary user or consumer of the product cannot reasonably be expected to have knowledge of the product's risks, or the product poses a risk of serious injury to persons other than the user or consumer; and

(3) The product has little or no usefulness.

c. No provision of subsection a. of this section is intended to establish any rule, or alter any existing rule, with respect to the burden of proof.

2A:58c–4. Adequate product warning or instruction—Rebuttable presumption of adequacy after approval. In any product liability action the manufacturer or seller shall not be liable for harm caused by a failure to warn if the product contains an adequate warning or instruction or, in the case of dangers a manufacturer or seller discovers or reasonably should discover after the product leaves its control, if the manufacturer or seller provides an adequate warning or instruction. An adequate product warning or instruction is one that a reasonably prudent person in the same or similar circumstances would have provided with respect to the danger and that communicates adequate information on the dangers and safe use of the product, taking into account the characteristics of, and the ordinary knowledge common to, the persons by whom the product is intended to be used, or in the case of prescription drugs, taking into account the characteristics of, and the ordinary knowledge common to, the prescribing physician. If the warning or instruction given in connection with a drug or device or food or food additive has been approved or prescribed by the federal Food and Drug Administration under the "Federal Food, Drug, and Cosmetic Act," 52 Stat. 1040, 21 U.S.C. § 301 *et seq.* or the "Public

Health Service Act," 58 Stat. 682, 42 U.S.C. § 201 *et seq.*, a rebuttable presumption shall arise that the warning or instruction is adequate. For purposes of this section, the terms "drug", "device", "food", and "food additive" have the meanings defined in the "Federal Food, Drug, and Cosmetic Act."

2A:58c–5. Punitive damages. a. Punitive damages may be awarded to the claimant only if the claimant proves, by a preponderance of the evidence, that the harm suffered was the result of the product manufacturer's or seller's acts or omissions, and such acts or omissions were actuated by actual malice or accompanied by a wanton and willful disregard of the safety of product users, consumers, or others who foreseeably might be harmed by the product. For the purposes of this section "actual malice" means an intentional wrongdoing in the sense of an evil-minded act, and "wanton and willful disregard" means a deliberate act or omission with knowledge of a high degree of probability of harm to another and reckless indifference to the consequences of such action or omission. Punitive damages shall not be awarded in the absence of an award of compensatory damages.

b. The trier of fact shall first determine whether compensatory damages are to be awarded. Evidence relevant only to punitive damages shall not be admissible in that proceeding. After such determination has been made, the trier of fact shall, in a separate proceeding, determine whether punitive damages are to be awarded. In determining whether punitive damages are to be awarded, the trier of fact shall consider all relevant evidence, including, but not limited to, the following:

(1) The likelihood at the relevant time that serious harm would arise from the tortfeasor's conduct;

(2) The tortfeasor's awareness of reckless disregard of the likelihood that the serious harm at issue would arise from the tortfeasor's conduct;

(3) The conduct of the tortfeasor upon learning that its initial conduct would likely cause harm; and

(4) The duration of the conduct or any concealment of it by the tortfeasor.

c. Punitive damages shall not be awarded if a drug or device or food or food additive which caused the claimant's harm was subject to premarket approval or licensure by the federal Food and Drug Administration under the "Federal Food, Drug, and Cosmetic Act," 52 Stat. 1040, 21 U.S.C. § 301 *et seq.* or the "Public Health Service Act," 58 Stat. 682, 42 U.S.C. § 201 *et seq.* and was approved or licensed; or is generally recognized as safe and effective pursuant to conditions established by the federal Food and Drug Administration and applicable regulations, including packaging and labeling regulations. However,

SELECTED STATE PRODUCTS LIABILITY STATUTES

where the product manufacturer knowingly withheld or misrepresented information required to be submitted under the agency's regulations, which information was material and relevant to the harm in question, punitive damages may be awarded. For purposes of this subsection, the terms "drug", "device", "food", and "food additive" have the meanings defined in the "Federal Food, Drug, and Cosmetic Act."

d. If the trier of fact determines that punitive damages should be awarded, the trier of fact shall then determine the amount of those damages. In making that determination, the trier of fact shall consider all relevant evidence, including, but not limited to, the following:

(1) All relevant evidence relating to the factors set forth in subsection b. of this section;

(2) The profitability of the misconduct to the tortfeasor;

(3) When the misconduct was terminated; and

(4) The financial condition of the tortfeasor.

2A:58c-6. Environmental tort action—Inapplicability of Act. The provisions of this act shall not apply to any environmental tort action.

2A:58c-7. Burden of proof in product liability action—Establishment or alteration of existing rule. Except as otherwise expressly provided in this act, no provision of this act is intended to establish any rule, or alter any existing rule, with respect to the burden of proof in a product liability action.

SELECTED STATE PRODUCTS LIABILITY STATUTES

OHIO REVISED CODE ANNOTATED
(1987)

§ 2307.71. [Definitions.] As used in sections 2307.71 to 2307.80 of the Revised Code:

(A) "claimant" means either of the following:

(1) a person who asserts a product liability claim or on whose behalf such a claim is asserted;

(2) if a product liability claim is asserted on behalf of the surviving spouse, children, parents, or other next of kin of a decedent or on behalf of the estate of a decedent, whether as a claim in a wrongful death action under chapter 2125 of the Revised Code or as a survivorship claim, whichever of the following is appropriate:

(a) the decedent, if the reference is to the person who allegedly sustained harm or economic loss for which, or in connection with which, compensatory damages or punitive or exemplary damages are sought to be recovered;

(b) the personal representative of the decedent or the estate of the decedent, if the reference is to the person who is asserting or has asserted the product liability claim.

(B) "Economic loss" means direct, incidental, or consequential pecuniary loss, including, but not limited to, damage to the product in question, and nonphysical damage to property other than the product. Harm is not "economic loss."

(C) "Environment" means navigable waters, surface water, ground water, drinking water supplies, land surface, subsurface strata, and air.

(D) "Ethical drug" means a prescription drug that is prescribed or dispensed by a physician or any other person who is legally authorized to prescribe or dispense a prescription drug.

(E) "Ethical medical device" means a medical device that is prescribed, dispensed, or implanted by a physician or any other person who is legally authorized to prescribe, dispense, or implant a medical device and that is regulated under the "Federal Food, Drug, and Cosmetic Act," 52 STAT. 1040, 21 U.S.C. 301–392, as amended.

(F) "Foreseeable risk" means a risk of harm that satisfies both of the following:

(1) it is associated with an intended or reasonably foreseeable use, modification, or alteration of a product in question;

(2) it is a risk that the manufacturer in question should recognize while exercising both of the following:

(a) the attention, perception, memory, knowledge, and intelligence that a reasonable manufacturer should possess;

(b) any superior attention, perception, memory, knowledge, or intelligence that the manufacturer in question possesses.

(G) "Harm" means death, physical injury to person, serious emotional distress, or physical damage to property other than the product in question. Economic loss is not "harm."

(H) "Hazardous or toxic substances" include, but are not limited to, hazardous waste as defined in section 3734.01 of the Revised Code, hazardous waste as specified in the rules of the director of environmental protection pursuant to division (A) of section 3734.12 of the Revised Code, hazardous substances as defined in section 3716.01 of the Revised Code, and hazardous substances, pollutants, and contaminants as defined in or by regulations adopted pursuant to the "Comprehensive Environmental Response, Compensation, and Liability Act of 1980." 94 STAT. 2767, 42 U.S.C. 9601, as amended.

(I) "Manufacturer" means a person engaged in a business to design, formulate, produce, create, make, construct, assemble, or rebuild a product or a component of a product.

(J) "Person" has the same meaning as in division (C) of section 1.59 of the Revised Code and also includes governmental entities.

(K) "Physician" means a person who is licensed to practice medicine and surgery or osteopathic medicine and surgery by the state medical board.

(L)(1) "Product" means, subject to division (L)(2) of this section, any object, substance, mixture, or raw material that constitutes tangible personal property and that satisfies all of the following:

(a) it is capable of delivery itself, or as an assembled whole in a mixed or combined state, or as a component or ingredient;

(b) it is produced, manufactured, or supplied for introduction into trade or commerce;

(c) it is intended for sale or lease to persons for commercial or personal use.

(2) "product" does not include human tissue, blood, or organs.

(M) "Product liability claim" means a claim that is asserted in a civil action and that seeks to recover compensatory damages from a manufacturer or supplier for death, physical injury to person, emotional distress, or physical damage to property other than the product in question, that allegedly arose from any of the following:

(1) the design, formulation, production, construction, creation, assembly, rebuilding, testing, or marketing of that product;

(2) any warning or instruction, or lack of warning or instruction, associated with that product;

(3) any failure of that product to conform to any relevant representation or warranty.

(N) "Representation" means an express representation of a material fact concerning the character, quality, or safety of a product.

(O)(1) "Supplier" means, subject to division (O)(2) of this section, either of the following:

(a) a person that, in the course of a business conducted for the purpose, sells, distributes, leases, prepares, blends, packages, labels, or otherwise participates in the placing of a product in the stream of commerce;

(b) a person that, in the course of a business conducted for the purpose, installs, repairs, or maintains any aspect of a product that allegedly causes harm.

(2) "Supplier" does not include any of the following:

(a) a manufacturer;

(b) a seller of real property;

(c) a provider of professional services who, incidental to a professional transaction the essence of which is the furnishing of judgment, skill, or services, sells or uses a product;

(d) any person who acts only in a financial capacity with respect to the sale of a product, or who leases a product under a lease arrangement in which the selection, possession, maintenance, and operation of the product are controlled by a person other than the lessor.

(P) "Unavoidably unsafe" means that, in the state of technical, scientific, and medical knowledge at the time a product in question left the control of its manufacturer, an aspect of that product was incapable of being made safe.

§ 2307.72. (A) Any recovery of compensatory damages based on a product liability claim is subject to sections 2307.71 to 2307.79 of the Revised Code.

(B) Any recovery of punitive or exemplary damages in connection with a product liability claim is subject to sections 2307.71 to 2307.80 of the Revised Code.

(C) Any recovery of compensatory damages for economic loss based on a claim that is asserted in a civil action, other than a product liability claim, is not subject to sections 2307.71 to 2307.79 of the Revised Code, but may occur under the common law of this state or other applicable sections of the Revised Code.

(D)(1) Sections 2307.71 to 2307.80 of the Revised Code do not supersede, modify, or otherwise affect any statute, regulation, or rule of this state or of the United States, or the common law of this state or of the United States, that relates to liability in compensatory damages or punitive or exemplary damages for injury, death, or loss to person or property, or to relief in the form of the abatement of a nuisance, civil penalties, cleanup costs, cost recovery, an injunction or temporary restraining order, or restitution, that arises, in whole or in part, from contamination or pollution of the environment or a threat of contamination or pollution of the environment, including contamination or pollution or a threat of contamination or pollution from hazardous or toxic substances.

(2) Consistent with the rules of civil procedure, in the same civil action against the same defendant or different defendants, a claimant may assert both of the following:

(a) a product liability claim, including a claim for the recovery of punitive or exemplary damages in connection with a product liability claim;

(b) a claim for the recovery of compensatory damages or punitive or exemplary damages for injury, death, or loss to person or property, or for relief in the form of the abatement of a nuisance, civil penalties, cleanup costs, cost recovery, an injunction or temporary restraining order, or restitution, that arises, in whole or in part, from contamination or pollution of the environment or a threat of contamination or pollution of the environment, including contamination or pollution or a threat of contamination or pollution from hazardous or toxic substances.

§ **2307.73.** (A) A manufacturer is subject to liability for compensatory damages based on a product liability claim only if the claimant establishes, by a preponderance of the evidence, both of the following:

(1) subject to division B of this section, the product in question was defective in manufacture or construction as described in section 2307.74 of the Revised Code, was defective in design or formulation as described in section 2307.75 of the Revised Code, was defective due to inadequate warning or instruction as described in section 2307.76 of the Revised Code, or was defective because it did not conform to a representation made by its manufacturer as described in section 2307.77 of the Revised Code;

(2) a defective aspect of the product in question as described in division (A)(1) of this section was a proximate cause of harm for which the claimant seeks to recover compensatory damages.

(B) If a claimant is unable because a product in question was destroyed to establish by direct evidence that the product in question was defective or if a claimant otherwise is unable to establish by direct evidence that a product in question was defective, then, consistent with the rules of evidence, it shall be sufficient for the claimant to present circumstantial or other competent evidence that establishes, by a pre-

SELECTED STATE PRODUCTS LIABILITY STATUTES

ponderance of the evidence, that the product in question was defective in any one of the four respects specified in division (A)(1) of this section.

§ 2307.74. A product is defective in manufacture or construction if, when it left the control of its manufacturer, it deviated in a material way from the design specifications, formula, or performance standards of the manufacturer, or from otherwise identical units manufactured to the same design specifications, formula, or performance standards. A product may be defective in manufacture or construction as described in this section even though its manufacturer exercised all possible care in its manufacture or construction.

§ 2307.75. (A) Subject to divisions (D), (E), and (F) of this section, a product is defective in design or formulation if either of the following applies:

(1) when it left the control of its manufacturer, the foreseeable risks associated with its design or formulation as determined pursuant to division (B) of this section exceeded the benefits associated with that design or formulation as determined pursuant to division (C) of this section;

(2) it is more dangerous than an ordinary consumer would expect when used in an intended or reasonably foreseeable manner.

(B) The foreseeable risks associated with the design or formulation of a product shall be determined by considering factors including, but not limited to, the following:

(1) the nature and magnitude of the risks of harm associated with that design or formulation in light of the intended and reasonably foreseeable uses, modifications, or alterations of the product;

(2) the likely awareness of product users, whether based on warnings, general knowledge, or otherwise, of those risks of harm;

(3) the likelihood that that design or formulation would cause harm in light of the intended and reasonably foreseeable uses, modifications, or alterations of the product;

(4) the extent to which that design or formulation conformed to any applicable public or private product standard that was in effect when the product left the control of its manufacturer.

(C) The benefits associated with the design or formulation of a product shall be determined by considering factors including, but not limited to, the following:

(1) the intended or actual utility of the product, including any performance or safety advantages associated with that design or formulation;

(2) the technical and economic feasibility, when the product left the control of its manufacturer, of using an alternative design or formulation;

(3) the nature and magnitude of any foreseeable risks associated with such an alternative design or formulation.

(D) An ethical drug or ethical medical device is not defective in design or formulation because some aspect of it is unavoidably unsafe, if the manufacturer of the ethical drug or ethical medical device provides adequate warning and instruction under section 2307.76 of the revised code concerning that unavoidably unsafe aspect.

(E) A product is not defective in design or formulation if the harm for which the claimant seeks to recover compensatory damages was caused by an inherent characteristic of the product which is a generic aspect of the product that cannot be eliminated without substantially compromising the product's usefulness or desirability and which is recognized by the ordinary person with the ordinary knowledge common to the community.

(F) A product is not defective in design or formulation if, at the time the product left the control of its manufacturer, a practical and technically feasible alternative design or formulation was not available that would have prevented the harm for which the claimant seeks to recover compensatory damages without substantially impairing the usefulness or intended purpose of the product, unless the manufacturer acted unreasonably in introducing the product into trade or commerce.

§ 2307.76. (A) Subject to divisions (B) and (C) of this section, a product is defective due to inadequate warning or instruction if either of the following applies:

(1) it is defective due to inadequate warning or instruction at the time of marketing if, when it left the control of its manufacturer, both of the following applied:

(a) the manufacturer knew or, in the exercise of reasonable care, should have known about a risk that is associated with the product and that allegedly caused harm for which the claimant seeks to recover compensatory damages;

(b) the manufacturer failed to provide the warning or instruction that a manufacturer exercising reasonable care would have provided concerning that risk, in light of the likelihood that the product would cause harm of the type for which the claimant seeks to recover compensatory damages and in light of the likely seriousness of that harm.

(2) It is defective due to inadequate post-marketing warning or instruction if, at a relevant time after it left the control of its manufacturer, both of the following applied:

(a) the manufacturer knew or, in the exercise of reasonable care, should have known about a risk that is associated with the product and that allegedly caused harm for which the claimant seeks to recover compensatory damages;

(b) the manufacturer failed to provide the post-marketing warning or instruction that a manufacturer exercising reasonable care would have provided concerning that risk, in light of the likelihood that the product would cause harm of the type for which the claimant seeks to recover compensatory damages and in light of the likely seriousness of that harm.

(B) A product is not defective due to lack of warning or instruction or inadequate warning or instruction as a result of the failure of its manufacturer to warn or instruct about an open and obvious risk or a risk that is a matter of common knowledge.

(C) An ethical drug is not defective due to inadequate warning or instruction if its manufacturer provides otherwise adequate warning and instruction to the physician or other legally authorized person who prescribes or dispenses that ethical drug for a claimant in question and if the federal Food and Drug Administration has not provided that warning or instruction relative to that ethical drug is to be given directly to the ultimate user of it.

§ 2307.77. A product is defective if it did not conform, when it left the control of its manufacturer, to a representation made by that manufacturer. A product may be defective because it did not conform to a representation even though its manufacturer did not act fraudulently, recklessly, or negligently in making the representation.

§ 2307.78. (A) Subject to division (B) of this section, a supplier is subject to liability for compensatory damages based on a product liability claim only if the claimant establishes, by a preponderance of the evidence, that either of the following applies:

(1) the supplier in question was negligent and that negligence was a proximate cause of harm for which the claimant seeks to recover compensatory damages;

(2) the product in question did not conform, when it left the control of the supplier in question, to a representation made by that supplier, and that representation and the failure to conform to it were a proximate cause of harm for which the claimant seeks to recover compensatory damages. A supplier is subject to liability for such a representation and the failure to conform to it even though the supplier did not act fraudulently, recklessly, or negligently in making the representation.

(B) A supplier of a product is subject to liability for compensatory damages based on a product liability claim under sections 2307.71 to 2307.77 of the Revised Code, as if it were the manufacturer of that product, if the manufacturer of that product is or would be subject to liability for compensatory damages based on a product liability claim under sections 2307.71 to 2307.77 of the Revised Code and any of the following applies:

(1) the manufacturer of that product is not subject to judicial process in this state;

(2) the claimant will be unable to enforce a judgment against the manufacturer of that product due to actual or asserted insolvency of the manufacturer;

(3) the supplier in question owns or, when it supplied that product, was owned, in whole or in part, by the manufacturer of that product;

(4) the supplier in question is owned or, when it supplied that product, was owned, in whole or in part, by the manufacturer of that product;

(5) the supplier in question created or furnished a manufacturer with the design or formulation that was used to produce, create, make, construct, assemble, or rebuild that product or a component of that product;

(6) the supplier in question altered, modified, or failed to maintain that product after it came into the possession of, and before it left the possession of, the supplier in question, and the alteration, modification, or failure to maintain that product rendered it defective;

(7) the supplier in question marketed that product under its own label or trade name;

(8) the supplier in question failed to respond timely and reasonably to a written request by or on behalf of the claimant to disclose to the claimant the name and address of the manufacturer of that product.

§ 2307.7. (A) If a claimant is entitled to recover compensatory damages for harm from a manufacturer in accordance with section 2307.73 of the Revised Code or from a supplier in accordance with division (B) of section 2307.78 of the Revised Code, the claimant may recover from the manufacturer or supplier in question, in that action, compensatory damages for any economic loss that proximately resulted from the defective aspect of the product in question.

(B) If a claimant is entitled to recover compensatory damages for harm from a supplier in accordance with division (A) of section 2307.78 of the Revised Code, the claimant may recover from the supplier in question, in that action, compensatory damages for any economic loss that proximately resulted from the negligence of that supplier or from the representation made by that supplier and the failure of the product in question to conform to that representation.

§ 2307.80. (A) Subject to division (C) of this section, punitive or exemplary damages shall not be awarded against a manufacturer or supplier in question in connection with a product liability claim unless the claimant establishes, by clear and convincing evidence, that harm for which he is entitled to recover compensatory damages in accordance with section 2307.73 or 2307.78 of the Revised Code was the result of misconduct of the manufacturer or supplier in question that manifested a flagrant disregard of the safety of persons who might be harmed by the product in question. The fact by itself that a product is defective

SELECTED STATE PRODUCTS LIABILITY STATUTES

does not establish a flagrant disregard of the safety of persons who might be harmed by that product.

(B) Whether the trier of fact is a jury or the court, if the trier of fact determines that a manufacturer or supplier in question is liable for punitive or exemplary damages in connection with a product liability claim, the amount of those damages shall be determined by the court. In determining the amount of punitive or exemplary damages, the court shall consider factors including, but not limited to, the following:

(1) the likelihood that serious harm would arise from the misconduct of the manufacturer or supplier in question;

(2) the degree of the awareness of the manufacturer or supplier in question of that likelihood;

(3) the profitability of the misconduct to the manufacturer or supplier in question;

(4) the duration of the misconduct and any concealment of it by the manufacturer or supplier in question;

(5) the attitude and conduct of the manufacturer or supplier in question upon the discovery of the misconduct and whether the misconduct has terminated;

(6) the financial condition of the manufacturer or supplier in question;

(7) the total effect of other punishment imposed or likely to be imposed upon the manufacturer or supplier in question as a result of the misconduct, including awards of punitive or exemplary damages to persons similarly situated to the claimant and the severity of criminal penalties to which the manufacturer or supplier in question has been or is likely to be subjected.

(C) If a claimant alleges in a product liability claim that a drug caused harm to him, the manufacturer of the drug shall not be liable for punitive or exemplary damages in connection with that product liability claim if the drug that allegedly caused the harm was manufactured and labeled in relevant and material respects in accordance with the terms of an approval or license issued by the Federal Food and Drug Administration under the "Federal Food, Drug, and Cosmetic Act," 52 STAT. 1040, 21 U.S.C. 301–392, as amended, or the "Public Health Service Act," 58 STAT. 682, 42 U.S.C. 201–300CC–15, as amended, unless it is established, by a preponderance of the evidence, that the manufacturer fraudulently and in violation of applicable regulations of the Food and Drug Administration withheld from the Food and Drug Administration information known to be material and relevant to the harm that the claimant allegedly suffered or misrepresented to the Food and Drug Administration information of that type. For purposes of this division, "drug" has the meaning given to that term in section 1201(g)(1) of the "Federal Food, Drug, and Cosmetic Act," 52 STAT. 1040, 21 U.S.C. 301–392, as amended.

SELECTED STATE PRODUCTS LIABILITY STATUTES

OREGON REVISED STATUTES
(1977, (§ 30.907) 1989, and (§§ 30.920–25) 1979)

30.900. "Product liability civil action" defined. As used in ORS 30.900 to 30.920 "product liability civil action" means a civil action brought against a manufacturer, distributor, seller or lessor of a product for damages for personal injury, death or property damage arising out of:

(1) Any design, inspection, testing, manufacturing or other defect in a product;

(2) Any failure to warn regarding a product; or

(3) Any failure to properly instruct in the use of a product.

30.905. Time limitation for commencement of action. (1) Notwithstanding ORS 12.115 or 12.140 and except as provided in subsection (2) of this section and ORS 30.907, a product liability civil action shall be commenced not later than eight years after the date on which the product was first purchased for use or consumption.

(2) Except as provided in ORS 30.907, a product liability civil action shall be commenced not later than two years after the date on which the death, injury or damage complained of occurs.

Note: Section 5, chapter 4, Oregon Laws 1987, is repealed on July 1, 1995. See section 7, chapter 4, Oregon Laws 1987, as amended by section 1, chapter 642, Oregon Laws 1989. The text is set forth for the user's convenience.

Sec. 5. Notwithstanding ORS 30.905, a product liability civil action against the manufacturer of an intrauterine contraceptive device must be commenced not later than two years after the date on which the plaintiff first discovered or, in the exercise of reasonable care, should have discovered the specific disease, injury or permanent disability for which the plaintiff is suing and the tortious act or acts of the manufacturer which caused the disease, injury or permanent disability.

30.907 Action for damages from asbestos related disease; limitations. A product liability civil action for damages resulting from asbestos related disease shall be commenced not later than two years after the date on which the plaintiff first discovered, or in the exercise of reasonable care should have discovered, the disease and the cause thereof.

30.910. Product disputably presumed not unreasonably dangerous. It is a disputable presumption in a products liability civil action that a product as manufactured and sold or leased is not unreasonably dangerous for its intended use.

§ 30.915. Defenses. It shall be a defense to a product liability civil action that an alteration or modification of a product occurred under the following circumstances:

(1) The alteration or modification was made without the consent of or was made not in accordance with the instructions or specifications of the manufacturer, distributor, seller or lessor;

(2) The alteration or modification was a substantial contributing factor to the personal injury, death or property damage; and

(3) If the alteration or modification was reasonably foreseeable, the manufacturer, distributor, seller or lessor gave adequate warning.

30.920. When seller or lessor of product liable—Effect of liability rule. (1) One who sells or leases any product in a defective condition unreasonably dangerous to the user or consumer or to his property is subject to liability for physical harm or damage to property caused by that condition, if:

(a) The seller or lessor is engaged in the business of selling or leasing such a product; and

(b) The product is expected to and does reach the user or consumer without substantial change in the condition in which it is sold or leased.

(2) The rule stated in subsection (1) of this section shall apply, even though:

(a) The seller or lessor has exercised all possible care in the preparation and sale or lease of the product; and

(b) The user, consumer or injured party has not purchased or leased the product from or entered into any contractual relations with the seller or lessor.

(3) It is the intent of the Legislative Assembly that the rule stated in subsections (1) and (2) of this section shall be construed in accordance with the *Restatement (Second) of Torts* § 402A, Comments *a* to *m* (1965). All references in these comments to sale, sell, selling or seller shall be construed to include lease, leases, leasing or lessor.

(4) Nothing in this section shall be construed to limit the rights and liabilities of sellers and lessors under principles of common law negligence or under ORS chapter 72.

30.925. Punitive damages—Evidence of defendant's ability to pay. (1) In a product liability civil action, punitive damages shall not be recoverable unless it is proven by clear and convincing evidence that the party against whom punitive damages is sought has shown wanton disregard for the health, safety and welfare of others.

(2) During the course of trial, evidence of the defendant's ability to pay shall not be admitted unless and until the party entitled to recover establishes a prima facie right to recover under subsection (1) of this section.

(3) Punitive damages, if any, shall be determined and awarded based upon the following criteria:

(a) The likelihood at the time that serious harm would arise from the defendant's misconduct;

(b) The degree of the defendant's awareness of that likelihood;

(c) The profitability of the defendant's misconduct;

(d) The duration of the misconduct and any concealment of it;

(e) The attitude and conduct of the defendant upon discovery of the misconduct;

(f) The financial condition of the defendant; and

(g) The total deterrent effect of other punishment imposed upon the defendant as a result of the misconduct, including, but not limited to, punitive damage awards to persons in situations similar to the claimant's and the severity of criminal penalties to which the defendant has been or may be subjected.

(Laws 1989, Ch. 642, concerning IUDs)

2. The statutes of repose in ORS 12.115, 30.905(1) or any other statute of repose contained in Oregon Revised Statutes shall not apply to a product liability civil action against a manufacturer of an intrauterine device, resulting in IUD-related injuries.

4. This Act applies to any product liability civil action against the manufacturer of an intrauterine device resulting from IUD-related injuries which is tried, arbitrated or settled after the effective date of this Act, even if such an action has already been dismissed, so long as the dismissal is based on a previous version of the applicable statute of limitations or repose. This Act shall also apply to any product liability civil action against a manufacturer of an intrauterine device currently pending in the trial court or on appeal, in which the defendant manufacturer has raised the statute of limitations or repose as a defense. Any such action in which final judgment has been entered in favor of the manufacturer based solely on a previous version of the statute of limitations or repose may be refiled within one year of the effective date of this Act.

5. If a product liability civil action that was allowed to be commenced or refiled under authority of section 8 or 9, chapter 4, Oregon Laws 1987 was not refiled or commenced in timely fashion under the provisions of either of those sections because of the pending bankruptcy of the defendant, such action may be refiled or commenced within one year after the effective date of this Act.

6. This Act shall not apply to product liability actions against manufacturers that had, at the time the intrauterine device was sold, received approval of an application filed under 21 U.S.C. section 355 with the Food and Drug Administration for the sale of the intrauterine device which caused the injury unless the plaintiff proves, by clear and convincing evidence, that the defendant drug manufacturer, acting in wanton disregard for the health, safety and welfare of others, fraudulently withheld from or misrepresented to the United States Food and Drug Administration, information that was both:

(1) Required to be submitted by Food and Drug Administration regulations; and

(2) Material and relevant to the harm suffered by the plaintiff.

7. [Chapter 642 is scheduled for repeal on July 1, 1995.]

South Carolina Code Annotated
(1974)

§ 15–73–10. Liability of seller for defective product. (1) One who sells any product in a defective condition unreasonably dangerous to the user or consumer or to his property is subject to liability for physical harm caused to the ultimate user or consumer, or to his property, if

a. The seller is engaged in the business of selling such a product, and

b. It is expected to and does reach the user or consumer without substantial change in the condition in which it is sold.

2. The rule stated in subsection (1) shall apply although

a. The seller has exercised all possible care in the preparation and sale of his product, and

b. The user or consumer has not brought the product from or entered into any contractual relation with the seller.

§ 15–73–20. Situation in which recovery shall be barred. If the user or consumer discovers the defect and is aware of the danger, and nevertheless proceeds unreasonably to make use of the product and is injured by it, he is barred from recovery.

§ 15–73–30. Intent of chapter. Comments to § 402A of the Restatement of Torts, 2d, are incorporated herein by reference thereto as the legislative intent of this chapter.

SELECTED STATE PRODUCTS LIABILITY STATUTES

TEXAS GENERAL LAWS

(S.B. 4, 1993)

AN ACT

relating to products liability.

BE IT ENACTED BY THE LEGISLATURE OF THE STATE OF TEXAS:

SECTION 1. Title 4, Civil Practice and Remedies Code, is amended by adding Chapter 82 to read as follows:

CHAPTER 82. PRODUCTS LIABILITY

Sec. 82.001. DEFINITIONS. In this chapter:

(1) "Claimant" means a party seeking relief, including a plaintiff, counterclaimant, or cross-claimant.

(2) "Products liability action" means any action against a manufacturer or seller for recovery of damages arising out of personal injury, death, or property damage allegedly caused by a defective product whether the action is based in strict tort liability, strict products liability, negligence, misrepresentation, breach of express or implied warranty, or any other theory or combination of theories.

(3) "Seller" means a person who is engaged in the business of distributing or otherwise placing, for any commercial purpose, in the stream of commerce for use or consumption a product or any component part thereof.

(4) "Manufacturer" means a person who is a designer, formulator, constructor, rebuilder, fabricator, producer, compounder, processor, or assembler of any product or any component part thereof and who places the product or any component part thereof in the stream of commerce.

Sec. 82.002. MANUFACTURER'S DUTY TO INDEMNIFY. (a) A manufacturer shall indemnify and hold harmless a seller against loss arising out of a products liability action, except for any loss caused by the seller's negligence, intentional misconduct, or other act or omission, such as negligently modifying or altering the product, for which the seller is independently liable.

(b) For purposes of this section, "loss" includes court costs and other reasonable expenses, reasonable attorney fees, and any reasonable damages.

(c) Damages awarded by the trier of fact shall, on final judgment, be deemed reasonable for purposes of this section.

(d) For purposes of this section, a wholesale distributor or retail seller who completely or partially assembles a product in accordance with the manufacturer's instructions shall be considered a seller.

(e) The duty to indemnify under this section:

(1) applies without regard to the manner in which the action is concluded; and

(2) is in addition to any duty to indemnify established by law, contract, or otherwise.

(f) A seller eligible for indemnification under this section shall give reasonable notice to the manufacturer of a product claimed in a petition or complaint to be defective, unless the manufacturer has been served as a party or otherwise has actual notice of the action.

(g) A seller is entitled to recover from the manufacturer court costs and other reasonable expenses, reasonable attorney fees, and any reasonable damages incurred by the seller to enforce the seller's right to indemnification under this section.

[Sec. 82.003 omitted by legislature.]

Sec. 82.004. INHERENTLY UNSAFE PRODUCTS. (a) In a products liability action, a manufacturer or seller shall not be liable if:

(1) the product is inherently unsafe and the product is known to be unsafe by the ordinary consumer who consumes the product with the ordinary knowledge common to the community; and

(2) the product is a common consumer product intended for personal consumption, such as sugar, castor oil, alcohol, tobacco, and butter, as identified in Comment i to Section 402A of the Restatement (Second) of Torts.

(b) For purposes of this section, the term "products liability action" does not include an action based on manufacturing defect or breach of an express warranty.

Sec. 82.005. DESIGN DEFECTS. (a) In a products liability action in which a claimant alleges a design defect, the burden is on the claimant to prove by a preponderance of the evidence that:

(1) there was a safer alternative design; and

(2) the defect was a producing cause of the personal injury, property damage, or death for which the claimant seeks recovery.

(b) In this section, "safer alternative design" means a product design other than the one actually used that in reasonable probability:

(1) would have prevented or significantly reduced the risk of the claimant's personal injury, property damage, or death without substantially impairing the product's utility; and

(2) was economically and technologically feasible at the time the product left the control of the manufacturer or seller by the application of existing or reasonably achievable scientific knowledge.

(c) This section does not supersede or modify any statute, regulation, or other law of this state or of the United States that relates to liability for, or to relief in the form of, abatement of nuisance, civil penalties, cleanup costs, cost recovery, an injunction, or restitution that arises from contamination or pollution of the environment.

(d) This section does not apply to:

(1) a cause of action based on a toxic or environmental tort as defined by Sections 33.013(c)(2) and (3); or

(2) a drug or device, as those terms are defined in the federal Food, Drug, and Cosmetic Act (21 U.S.C. Section 321).

(e) This section is not declarative, by implication or otherwise, of the common law with respect to any product and shall not be construed to restrict the courts of this state in developing the common law with respect to any product which is not subject to this section.

Sec. 82.006. FIREARMS AND AMMUNITION. (a) In a products liability action brought against a manufacturer or seller of a firearm or ammunition that alleges a design defect in the firearm or ammunition, the burden is on the claimant to prove, in addition to any other elements that the claimant must prove, that:

(1) the actual design of the firearm or ammunition was defective, causing the firearm or ammunition not to function in a manner reasonably expected by an ordinary consumer of firearms or ammunition; and

(2) the defective design was a producing cause of the personal injury, property damage, or death.

(b) The claimant may not prove the existence of the defective design by a comparison or weighing of the benefits of the firearm or ammunition against the risk of personal injury, property damage, or death posed by its potential to cause such injury, damage, or death when discharged.

SECTION 2. Subchapter A, Chapter 16, Civil Practice and Remedies Code, is amended by adding Section 16.012 to read as follows:

Sec. 16.012. PRODUCTS LIABILITY: MANUFACTURING EQUIPMENT. (a) In this section:

(1) "Claimant," "products liability action," "seller," and "manufacturer" have the meanings assigned by Section 82.001.

(2) "Manufacturing equipment" means equipment and machinery used in the manufacturing, processing, or fabrication of tangible personal property but does not include agricultural equipment or machinery.

(b) Except as provided by Subsection (c), a claimant must commence a products liability action against a manufacturer or seller of manufacturing equipment before the end of 15 years after the date of the sale of the equipment by the defendant.

(c) If a manufacturer or seller expressly represents that the manufacturing equipment has a useful safe life of longer than 15 years, a claimant must commence a products liability action against that manufacturer or seller of the equipment before the end of the number of years represented after the date of the sale of the equipment by that seller.

(d) This section does not reduce a limitations period that applies to a products liability action involving manufacturing equipment that accrues before the end of the limitations period under this section.

(e) This section does not extend the limitations period within which a products liability action involving manufacturing equipment may be commenced under any other law.

(f) This section applies only to the sale and not to the lease of manufacturing equipment.

SECTION 3. (a) Sections 82.002 through 82.004, Civil Practice and Remedies Code, as added by this Act, apply only to a cause of action commenced on or after the effective date of this Act. A cause of action commenced before the effective date of this Act is governed by the law in effect at the time the action accrued, and that law is continued in effect for that purpose.

(b) Sections 16.012, 82.005, and 82.006, Civil Practice and Remedies Code, as added by this Act, apply only to a cause of action that accrues on or after the effective date of this Act. A cause of action that accrued before the effective date of this Act is governed by the law in effect at the time the action accrued, and that law is continued in effect for that purpose.

(c) Section 82.001, Civil Practice and Remedies Code, as added by this Act, takes effect on the effective date of this Act.

SECTION 4. This Act takes effect September 1, 1993.

SECTION 5. The importance of this legislation and the crowded condition of the calendars in both houses create an emergency and an imperative public necessity that the constitutional rule requiring bills to be read on three several days in each house be suspended, and this rule is hereby suspended.

SELECTED STATE PRODUCTS LIABILITY STATUTES

Washington Revised Code Annotated
(1981-91)

7.72.010. Definitions. For the purposes of this chapter, unless the context clearly indicates to the contrary:

(1) Product seller. "Product seller" means any person or entity that is engaged in the business of selling products, whether the sale is for resale, or for use or consumption. The term includes a manufacturer, wholesaler, distributor, or retailer of the relevant product. The term also includes a party who is in the business of leasing or bailing such products. The term "product seller" does not include:

(a) A seller of real property, unless that person is engaged in the mass production and sale of standardized dwellings or is otherwise a product seller;

(b) A provider of professional services who utilizes or sells products within the legally authorized scope of the professional practice of the provider;

(c) A commercial seller of used products who resells a product after use by a consumer or other product user: Provided, That when it is resold, the used product is in essentially the same condition as when it was acquired for resale;

(d) A finance lessor who is not otherwise a product seller. A "finance lessor" is one who acts in a financial capacity, who is not a manufacturer, wholesaler, distributor, or retailer, and who leases a product without having a reasonable opportunity to inspect and discover defects in the product, under a lease arrangement in which the selection, possession, maintenance, and operation of the product are controlled by a person other than the lessor; and

(e) A licensed pharmacist who dispenses a prescription product in the form manufactured by a commercial manufacturer pursuant to a prescription issued by a licensed prescribing practitioner if the claim against the pharmacist is based upon strict liability in tort or the implied warranty provisions under the uniform commercial code, Title 62A RCW, and if the pharmacist complies with recordkeeping requirements pursuant to chapters 18.64, 69.41, and 69.50 RCW, and related administrative rules as provided in RCW 7.72.040. Nothing in this subsection (1)(e) affects a pharmacist's liability under RCW 7.72.040(1).

(2) Manufacturer. "Manufacturer" includes a product seller who designs, produces, makes, fabricates, constructs, or remanufactures the relevant product or component part of a product before its sale to a user or consumer. The term also includes a product seller or entity not otherwise a manufacturer that holds itself out as a manufacturer.

A product seller acting primarily as a wholesaler, distributor, or retailer of a product may be a "manufacturer" but only to the extent that it designs, produces, makes, fabricates, constructs, or remanufactures the product for its sale. A product seller who performs minor assembly of a product in accordance with the instructions of the manufacturer shall not be deemed a manufacturer. A product seller that did not participate in the design of a product and that constructed the product in accordance with the design specifications of the claimant or another product seller shall not be deemed a manufacturer for the purposes of RCW 7.72.030(1)(a).

(3) Product. "Product" means any object possessing intrinsic value, capable of delivery either as an assembled whole or as a component part or parts, and produced for introduction into trade or commerce. Human tissue and organs, including human blood and its components, are excluded from this term.

The "relevant product" under this chapter is that product or its component part or parts, which gave rise to the product liability claim.

(4) Product liability claim. "Product liability claim" includes any claim or action brought for harm caused by the manufacture, production, making, construction, fabrication, design, formula, preparation, assembly, installation, testing, warnings, instructions, marketing, packaging, storage or labeling of the relevant product. It includes, but is not limited to, any claim or action previously based on: Strict liability in tort; negligence; breach of express or implied warranty; breach of, or failure to, discharge a duty to warn or instruct, whether negligent or innocent; misrepresentation, concealment, or nondisclosure, whether negligent or innocent; or other claim or action previously based on any other substantive legal theory except fraud, intentionally caused harm or a claim or action under the consumer protection act, chapter 19.86 RCW.

(5) Claimant. "Claimant" means a person or entity asserting a product liability claim, including a wrongful death action, and, if the claim is asserted through or on behalf of an estate, the term includes claimant's decedent. "Claimant" includes any person or entity that suffers harm. A claim may be asserted under this chapter even though the claimant did not buy the product from, or enter into any contractual relationship with, the product seller.

(6) Harm. "Harm" includes any damages recognized by the courts of this state: Provided, That the term "harm" does not include direct or consequential economic loss under Title 62A RCW [Uniform Commercial Code].

7.72.020. Scope. (1) The previous existing applicable law of this state on product liability is modified only to the extent set forth in this chapter.

(2) Nothing in [this] chapter shall prevent the recovery of direct or consequential economic loss under Title 62A RCW [Uniform Commercial Code].

7.72.030. Liability of manufacturers. (1) A product manufacturer is subject to liability to a claimant if the claimant's harm was proximately caused by the negligence of the manufacturer in that the product was not reasonably safe as designed or not reasonably safe because adequate warnings or instructions were not provided.

(a) A product is not reasonably safe as designed, if, at the time of manufacture, the likelihood that the product would cause the claimant's harm or similar harms, and the seriousness of those harms, outweighed the burden on the manufacturer to design a product that would have prevented those harms and the adverse effect that an alternative design that was practical and feasible would have on the usefulness of the product: Provided, That a firearm or ammunition shall not be deemed defective in design on the basis that the benefits of the product do not outweigh the risk of injury posed by its potential to cause serious injury, damage, or death when discharged.

(b) A product that is not reasonably safe because adequate warnings or instructions were not provided with the product, if, at the time of manufacture, the likelihood that the product would cause the claimant's harm or similar harms, and the seriousness of those harms, rendered the warnings or instructions of the manufacturer inadequate and the manufacturer could have provided the warnings or instructions which the claimant alleges would have been adequate.

(c) A product is not reasonably safe because adequate warnings or instructions were not provided after the product was manufactured where a manufacturer learned or where a reasonably prudent manufacturer should have learned about a danger connected with the product after it was manufactured. In such a case, the manufacturer is under a duty to act with regard to issuing warnings or instructions concerning the danger in the manner that a reasonably prudent manufacturer would act in the same or similar circumstances. This duty is satisfied if the manufacturer exercises reasonable care to inform product users.

(2) A product manufacturer is subject to strict liability to a claimant if the claimant's harm was proximately caused by the fact that the product was not reasonably safe in construction or not reasonably safe because it did not conform to the manufacturer's express warranty or to the implied warranties under Title 62A RCW [Uniform Commercial Code].

(a) A product is not reasonably safe in construction if, when the product left the control of the manufacturer, the product deviated in some material way from the design specifications or performance standards of the manufacturer, or deviated in some material way from otherwise identical units of the same product line.

(b) A product does not conform to the express warranty of the manufacturer if it is made part of the basis of the bargain and relates to a material fact or facts concerning the product and the express warranty proved to be untrue.

(c) Whether or not a product conforms to an implied warranty created under Title 62A RCW [Uniform Commercial Code] shall be determined under that title.

(3) In determining whether a product was not reasonably safe under this section, the trier of fact shall consider whether the product was unsafe to an extent beyond that which would be contemplated by the ordinary consumer.

7.72.040. Liability of product sellers other than manufacturers. (1) Except as provided in subsection (2) of this section, a product seller other than a manufacturer is liable to the claimant only if the claimant's harm was proximately caused by:

(a) The negligence of such product seller; or

(b) Breach of an express warranty made by such product seller; or

(c) The intentional misrepresentation of facts about the product by such product seller or the intentional concealment of information about the product by such product seller.

(2) A product seller, other than a manufacturer, shall have the liability of a manufacturer to the claimant if:

(a) No solvent manufacturer who would be liable to the claimant is subject to service of process under the laws of the claimant's domicile or the state of Washington; or

(b) The court determines that it is highly probable that the claimant would be unable to enforce a judgment against any manufacturer; or

(c) The product seller is a controlled subsidiary of a manufacturer, or the manufacturer is a controlled subsidiary of the product seller; or

(d) The product seller provided the plans or specifications for the manufacture or preparation of the product and such plans or specifications were a proximate cause of the defect in the product; or

(e) The product was marketed under a trade name or brand name of the product seller.

(3) Subsection (2) of this section does not apply to a pharmacist who dispenses a prescription product in the form manufactured by a commercial manufacturer pursuant to a prescription issued by a licensed practitioner if the pharmacist complies with recordkeeping requirements pursuant to chapters 18.64, 69.41, and 69.50 RCW, and related administrative rules.

7.72.050. Relevance of industry custom, technological feasibility, and nongovernmental, legislative or administrative regulatory standards. (1) Evidence of custom in the product seller's industry, technological feasibility or that the product was or was not, in compliance with nongovernmental standards or with legislative regulatory standards or administrative regulatory standards, whether relating to design, construction or performance of the product or to warnings or instructions as to its use may be considered by the trier of fact.

(2) When the injury-causing aspect of the product was, at the time of manufacture, in compliance with a specific mandatory government contract specification relating to design or warnings, this compliance shall be an absolute defense. When the injury-causing aspect of the product was not, at the time of manufacture, in compliance with a specific mandatory government specification relating to design or warnings, the product shall be deemed not reasonably safe under RCW 7.72.030(1).

7.72.060. Length of time product sellers are subject to liability. (1) *Useful safe life.* (a) Except as provided in subsection (1)(b) hereof, a product seller shall not be subject to liability to a claimant for harm under this chapter if the product seller proves by a preponderance of the evidence that the harm was caused after the product's "useful safe life" had expired.

"Useful safe life" begins at the time of delivery of the product and extends for the time during which the product would normally be likely to perform or be stored in a safe manner. For the purposes of this chapter, "time of delivery" means the time of delivery of a product to its first purchaser or lessee who was not engaged in the business of either selling such products or using them as component parts of another product to be sold. In the case of a product which has been remanufactured by a manufacturer, "time of delivery" means the time of delivery of the remanufactured product to its first purchaser or lessee who was not engaged in the business of either selling such products or using them as component parts of another product to be sold.

(b) A product seller may be subject to liability for harm caused by a product used beyond its useful safe life, if:

(i) The product seller has warranted that the product may be utilized safely for such longer period; or

(ii) The product seller intentionally misrepresents facts about its product, or intentionally conceals information about it, and that conduct was a proximate cause of the claimant's harm; or

(iii) The harm was caused by exposure to a defective product, which exposure first occurred within the useful safe life of the product, even though the harm did not manifest itself until after the useful safe life had expired.

(2) *Presumption regarding useful safe life.* If the harm was caused more than twelve years after the time of delivery, a presumption arises

that the harm was caused after the useful safe life had expired. This presumption may only be rebutted by a preponderance of the evidence.

(3) *Statute of limitation.* Subject to the applicable provisions of chapter 4.16 RCW pertaining to the tolling and extension of any statute of limitation, no claim under this chapter may be brought more than three years from the time the claimant discovered or in the exercise of due diligence should have discovered the harm and its cause.

CONSUMER PRODUCT SAFETY ACT AS AMENDED *

Act of October 27, 1972, Public Law 92–573,
86 Stat. 1207–33; 15 U.S.C.A. §§ 2051–82.

SELECTED SECTIONS

Section
2051. Congressional findings and declaration of purpose.
2052. Definitions.
2053. Consumer Product Safety Commission.
    (a) Establishment; Chairman.
    (b) Term; vacancies.
    (c) Restrictions on Commissioners' outside activities.
    (d) Quorum; seal; Vice Chairman.
    (e) Offices.
    (f) Functions of Chairman.
    (g) Executive Director; officers and employees.
    (h) Civil action against the United States.
2054. Product safety information and research.
    (a) Injury Information Clearinghouse; duties.
    (b) Research, investigation and testing of consumer products.
    (c) Grants and contracts for conduct of functions.
    (d) Availability to public of information.
2055. Public disclosure of information.
    (a) Disclosure requirements for manufacturers or private labelers; procedures applicable.
    (b) Additional disclosure requirements for manufacturers or private labelers; procedures applicable.
    (c) Communications with manufacturers.
    (d) Definition; coverage.
2056. Consumer product safety standards.
    (a) Types of requirements.
    (b) Reliance of Commission upon voluntary standards.
    (c) Contribution of Commission to development cost.
2057. Banned hazardous products.
2058. Procedure for consumer product safety rules.
    (a) Commencement of proceeding; publication of prescribed notice of proposed rulemaking; transmittal of notice.
    (b) Voluntary standard; publication as proposed rule; notice of reliance of Commission on standard.
    (c) Publication of proposed rule; preliminary regulatory analysis; contents; transmittal of notice.
    (d) Promulgation of rule; time.

---

* By Consumer Product Safety Amendments of 1981, Pub.L. 97–35, 95 Stat. 724, Emergency Interim Consumer Product Safety Standard Act of 1978, Pub.L. 95–319, 92 Stat. 386, and Consumer Product Safety Commission Improvements Act of 1976, Pub.L. 94–284, 90 Stat. 503.

CONSUMER PRODUCT SAFETY ACT

Section
2058. Procedure for consumer product safety rules.—Continued
    (e) Expression of risk of injury; consideration of available product data; needs of elderly and handicapped.
    (f) Findings; final regulatory analysis; judicial review of rule.
    (g) Effective date of rule or standard; stockpiling of product.
    (h) Amendment or revocation of rule.

* * *

2060. Judicial review of consumer product safety rules.
    (a) Petition by persons adversely affected, consumers, or consumer organizations.
    (b) Additional data, views, or arguments.
    (c) Jurisdiction; costs and attorneys' fees; substantial evidence to support administrative findings.
    (d) Supreme Court review.
    (e) Availability of other remedies.
    (f) Computation of reasonable fee for attorney.
2061. Imminent hazards.
    (a) Filing of action.
    (b) Relief; product condemnation and seizure.
    (c) Consumer product safety rule.
    (d) Jurisdiction and venue; process; subpena.
    (e) Employment of attorneys by Commission.

* * *

2063. Product certification and labeling.
2064. Substantial product hazards.
    (a) Definition.
    (b) Noncompliance with applicable consumer product safety rules; product defects; notice to Commission by manufacturer, distributor, or retailer.
    (c) Public notice of defect or failure to comply; mail notice.
    (d) Repair; replacement; refunds; action plan.
    (e) Reimbursement.
    (f) Hearing.
    (g) Preliminary injunction.
2065. Inspection and recordkeeping.
2066. Imported products.
    (a) Refusal of admission.
    (b) Samples.
    (c) Modification.
    (d) Supervision of modifications.
    (e) Product destruction.
    (f) Payment of expenses occasioned by refusal of admission.
    (g) Importation conditioned upon manufacturer's compliance.
2067. Exemption of exports.
    (a) Risk of injury to consumers within United States.
    (b) Statement of exportation: filing period, information; notification of foreign country; petition for minimum filing period: good cause.
2068. Prohibited acts.
2069. Civil penalties.
    (a) Amount of penalty.
    (b) Relevant factors in assessment of penalty.
    (c) Compromise of penalty; deductions from penalty.
    (d) "Knowingly" defined.
2070. Criminal penalties.

CONSUMER PRODUCT SAFETY ACT

Section
2071. Injunctive enforcement and seizure.
2072. Suits for damages.
    (a) Persons injured; costs; amount in controversy.
    (b) Denial and imposition of costs.
    (c) Remedies available.
2073. Private enforcement.
2074. Private remedies.
    (a) Liability at common law or under State statute not relieved by compliance.
    (b) Evidence of Commission's inaction inadmissible in actions relating to consumer products.
    (c) Public information.
2075. State standards.
    (a) State compliance to Federal standards.
    (b) Consumer product safety requirements which impose performance standards more stringent than Federal standards.
    (c) Exemptions.
2076. Additional functions of Consumer Product Safety Commission.
    (a) Authority to conduct hearings or other inquiries.
    (b) Commission powers; orders.
    (c) Noncompliance with subpena or Commission order; contempt.
    (d) Disclosure of information.
    (e) Performance and technical data.
    (f) Purchase of consumer products by Commission.
    (g) Contract authority.
    (h) Research, development, and testing facilities.
    (i) Recordkeeping; audit.
    (j) Report to President and Congress.
    (k) Budget estimates and requests; legislative recommendations; testimony; comments on legislation.
2077. Chronic Hazard Advisory Panels.
    (a) Appointment; purposes.
    (b) Composition; membership.
    (c) Chairman and Vice Chairman; election; term.
    (d) Majority vote.
    (e) Administrative support services.
    (f) Compensation.
    (g) Requests for and disclosures of information.
    (h) Information from other Federal departments and agencies.
2078. Cooperation with States and other Federal agencies.
2079. Transfers of functions.
    (a) Hazardous substances and poisons.
    (b) Flammable fabrics.
    (c) Household refrigerators.
    (d) Regulation by Commission of consumer products in accordance with other provisions of law.
    (e) Transfer of personnel, property, records, etc; continued application of orders, rules, etc.
    (f) Definition of "function."
2080. Limitation on Jurisdiction of Consumer Product Safety Commission.
    (a) Authority to regulate.
    (b) Certain notices of proposed rulemaking; duties of Chronic Hazard Advisory Panel.
    (c) Panel report; incorporation into advance notice and final rule.
2081. Authorization of appropriations.

Section
2082. Interim cellulose insulation safety standard.
  (a) Applicability of specification of General Services Administration; authority and effect of interim standard; modifications; criteria; labeling requirements.
  (b) Scope of judicial review.
  (c) Enforcement; violations; promulgation of final standard; procedures applicable to promulgation; revision of interim standard; procedures applicable to revision.
  (d) Reporting requirements of other Federal departments, agencies, etc. of violations.
  (e) Reporting requirements of Commission to Congressional committees; contents, time of submission, etc.
  (f) Compliance with certification requirements; implementation; waiver; rules and regulations.
  (g) Authorization of appropriations.
2083. Congressional veto of consumer product safety rules.
  (a) Transmission to Congress.
  (b) Disapproval by concurrent resolution.
  (c) Presumptions from Congressional action or inaction.
  (d) Continuous session of Congress.

§ 2051. Congressional findings and declaration of purpose

(a) The Congress finds that—

(1) an unacceptable number of consumer products which present unreasonable risks of injury are distributed in commerce;

(2) complexities of consumer products and the diverse nature and abilities of consumers using them frequently result in an inability of users to anticipate risks and to safeguard themselves adequately;

(3) the public should be protected against unreasonable risks of injury associated with consumer products;

(4) control by State and local governments of unreasonable risks of injury associated with consumer products is inadequate and may be burdensome to manufacturers;

(5) existing Federal authority to protect consumers from exposure to consumer products presenting unreasonable risks of injury is inadequate; and

(6) regulation of consumer products the distribution or use of which affects interstate or foreign commerce is necessary to carry out this chapter.

(b) The purposes of this chapter are—

(1) to protect the public against unreasonable risks of injury associated with consumer products;

(2) to assist consumers in evaluating the comparative safety of consumer products;

(3) to develop uniform safety standards for consumer products and to minimize conflicting State and local regulations; and

(4) to promote research and investigation into the causes and prevention of product-related deaths, illnesses, and injuries.

Pub.L. 92–573, § 2, Oct. 27, 1972, 86 Stat. 1207.

§ 2052. Definitions

(a) For purposes of this chapter:

(1) The term "consumer product" means any article, or component part thereof, produced or distributed (i) for sale to a consumer for use in or around a permanent or temporary household or residence, a school, in recreation, or otherwise, or (ii) for the personal use, consumption or enjoyment of a consumer in or around a permanent or temporary household or residence, a school, in recreation, or otherwise; but such term does not include—

(A) any article which is not customarily produced or distributed for sale to, or use or consumption by, or enjoyment of, a consumer,

(B) tobacco and tobacco products,

(C) motor vehicles or motor vehicle equipment (as defined by sections 102(3) and (4) of the National Traffic and Motor Vehicle Safety Act of 1966),

(D) pesticides (as defined by the Federal Insecticide, Fungicide, and Rodenticide Act),

(E) any article which, if sold by the manufacturer, producer, or importer, would be subject to the tax imposed by section 4181 of the Internal Revenue Code of 1954 (determined without regard to any exemptions from such tax provided by section 4182 or 4221, or any other provision of such Code), or any component of any such article,

(F) aircraft, aircraft engines, propellers, or appliances (as defined in section 101 of the Federal Aviation Act of 1958),

(G) boats which could be subjected to safety regulation under the Federal Boat Safety Act of 1971; vessels, and appurtenances to vessels (other than such boats), which could be subjected to safety regulation under title 52 of the Revised Statutes or other marine safety statutes administered by the department in which the Coast Guard is operating; and equipment (including associated equipment, as defined in section 3(8) of the Federal Boat Safety Act of 1971) to the extent that a risk of injury associated with the use of such equipment on boats or vessels could be eliminated or reduced by actions taken under any statute referred to in this subparagraph,

(H) drugs, devices, or cosmetics (as such terms are defined in sections 201(g), (h), and (i) of the Federal Food, Drug, and Cosmetic Act), or

(I) food. The term "food", as used in this subparagraph means all "food", as defined in section 201(f) of the Federal Food, Drug, and Cosmetic Act, including poultry and poultry products (as defined in sections 4(e) and (f) of the Poultry Products Inspection Act), meat, meat food products (as defined in section 1(j) of the Federal Meat Inspection Act), and eggs and egg products (as defined in section 4 of the Egg Products Inspection Act).

Such term includes any mechanical device which carries or conveys passengers along, around, or over a fixed or restricted route or course or within a defined area for the purpose of giving its passengers amusement, which is customarily controlled or directed by an individual who is employed for that purpose and who is not a consumer with respect to such device, and which is not permanently fixed to a site. Such term does not include such a device which is permanently fixed to a site. Except for the regulation under this chapter or the Federal Hazardous Substances Act of fireworks devices or any substance intended for use as a component of any such device, the Commission shall have no authority under the functions transferred pursuant to section 2079 of this title to regulate any product or article described in subparagraph (E) of this paragraph or described, without regard to quantity, in section 845(a)(5) of Title 18. See sections 2079(d) and 2080 of this title, for other limitations on Commission's authority to regulate certain consumer products.

(2) The term "consumer product safety rule" means a consumer products safety standard described in section 2056(a) of this title, or a rule under this chapter declaring a consumer product a banned hazardous product.

(3) The term "risk of injury" means a risk of death, personal injury, or serious or frequent illness.

(4) The term "manufacturer" means any person who manufactures or imports a consumer product.

(5) The term "distributor" means a person to whom a consumer product is delivered or sold for purposes of distribution in commerce, except that such term does not include a manufacturer or retailer of such product.

(6) The term "retailer" means a person to whom a consumer product is delivered or sold for purposes of sale or distribution by such person to a consumer.

(7)(A) The term "private labeler" means an owner of a brand or trademark on the label of a consumer product which bears a private label.

(B) A consumer product bears a private label if (i) the product (or its container) is labeled with the brand or trademark of a person other than a manufacturer of the product, (ii) the person with whose brand or trademark the product (or container) is labeled has authorized or caused the product to be so labeled, and (iii) the brand or trademark of a manufacturer of such product does not appear on such label.

(8) The term "manufactured" means to manufacture, produce, or assemble.

(9) The term "Commission" means the Consumer Product Safety Commission, established by section 2053 of this title.

(10) The term "State" means a State, the District of Columbia, the Commonwealth of Puerto Rico, the Virgin Islands, Guam, Wake Island, Midway Island, Kingman Reef, Johnston Island, the Canal Zone, American Samoa, or the Trust Territory of the Pacific Islands.

(11) The terms "to distribute in commerce" and "distribution in commerce" mean to sell in commerce, to introduce or deliver for introduction into commerce, or to hold for sale or distribution after introduction into commerce.

(12) The term "commerce" means trade, traffic, commerce, or transportation—

(A) between a place in a State and any place outside thereof, or

(B) which affects trade, traffic, commerce, or transportation described in subparagraph (A).

(13) The terms "import" and "importation" include reimporting a consumer product manufactured or processed, in whole or in part, in the United States.

(14) The term "United States", when used in the geographic sense, means all of the States (as defined in paragraph (10)).

(b) A common carrier, contract carrier, or freight forwarder shall not, for purposes of this chapter, be deemed to be a manufacturer, distributor, or retailer of a consumer product solely by reason of receiving or transporting a consumer product in the ordinary course of its business as such a carrier or forwarder.

As amended Pub.L. 94–284, § 3(b), (d), May 11, 1976, 90 Stat. 503; Pub.L. 97–35, Title XII, § 1213, Aug. 13, 1981, 95 Stat. 724.

§ 2053. Consumer Product Safety Commission

(a) Establishment; Chairman

(a) An independent regulatory commission is hereby established, to be known as the Consumer Product Safety Commission, consisting of five Commissioners who shall be appointed by the President, by and with the advice and consent of the Senate. The Chairman shall be appointed by the President, by and with the advice and consent of the Senate, from among the members of the Commission. An individual may be appointed as a member of the Commission and as Chairman at the same time. Any member of the Commission may be removed by the President for neglect of duty or malfeasance in office but for no other cause.

(b) Term; vacancies

(b)(1) Except as provided in paragraph (2), (A) the Commissioners first appointed under this section shall be appointed for terms ending three, four, five, six, and seven years, respectively, after October 27, 1972, the term of each to be designated by the President at the time of nomination; and (B) each of their successors shall be appointed for a term of seven years from the date of the expiration of the term for which his predecessor was appointed.

(2) Any Commissioner appointed to fill a vacancy occurring prior to the expiration of the term for which his predecessor was appointed shall be appointed only for the remainder of such term. A Commissioner may continue to serve after the expiration of his term until his successor has taken office, except that he may not so continue to serve more than one year after the date on which his term would otherwise expire under this subsection.

(c) Restrictions on Commissioners' outside activities

(c) Not more than three of the Commissioners shall be affiliated with the same political party. No individual (1) in the employ of, or holding any official relation to, any person engaged in selling or manufacturing consumer products, or (2) owning stock or bonds of substantial value in a person so engaged, or (3) who is in any other manner pecuniarily interested in such a person, or in a substantial supplier of such a person, shall hold the office of Commissioner. A Commissioner may not engage in any other business, vocation, or employment.

(d) Quorum; seal; Vice Chairman

(d) No vacancy in the Commission shall impair the right of the remaining Commissioners to exercise all the powers of the Commission, but three members of the Commission shall constitute a quorum for the transaction of business. The Commission shall have an official seal of which judicial notice shall be taken. The Commission shall annually elect a Vice Chairman to act in the absence or disability of the Chairman or in case of a vacancy in the office of the Chairman.

(e) Offices

(e) The Commission shall maintain a principal office and such field offices as it deems necessary and may meet and exercise any of its powers at any other place.

(f) Functions of Chairman

(f)(1) The Chairman of the Commission shall be the principal executive officer of the Commission, and he shall exercise all of the executive and administrative functions of the Commission, including functions of the Commission with respect to (A) the appointment and supervision of personnel employed under the Commission (other than personnel employed regularly and full time in the immediate offices of commissioners other than the Chairman), (B) the distribution of business among personnel appointed and supervised by the Chairman and among administrative units of the Commission, and (C) the use and expenditure of funds.

(2) In carrying out any of his functions under the provisions of this subsection the Chairman shall be governed by general policies of the Commission and by such regulatory decisions, findings, and determinations as the Commission may by law be authorized to make.

(3) Requests or estimates for regular, supplemental, or deficiency appropriations on behalf of the Commission may not be submitted by the Chairman without the prior approval of the Commission.

(g) Executive Director; officers and employees

(g)(1) The Chairman, subject to the approval of the Commission, shall appoint an Executive Director, a General Counsel, a Director of Engineering Sciences, a Director of Epidemiology, and a Director of Information. No individual so appointed may receive pay in excess of the annual rate of basic pay in effect for grade GS–18 of the General Schedule.

(2) The Chairman, subject to subsection (f)(2), of this section, may employ such other officers and employees (including attorneys) as are necessary in the execution of the Commission's functions. No regular officer or employee of the Commission who was at any time during the 12 months preceding the termination of his employment with the Commission compensated at a rate in excess of the annual rate of basic pay in effect for grade GS–14 of the General Schedule, shall accept employment or compensation from any manufacturer subject to this chapter, for a period of 12 months after terminating employment with the Commission.

(3) In addition to the number of positions authorized by section 5108(a) of Title 5, the Chairman, subject to the approval of the Commission, and subject to the standards and procedures prescribed by chapter 51 of Title 5, may place a total of twelve positions in grades GS–16, GS–17, and GS–18.

(4) The appointment of any officer (other than a Commissioner) or employee of the Commission shall not be subject, directly or indirectly, to review or approval by any officer or entity within the Executive Office of the President.

(h) Civil action against the United States

(h) Subsections (a) and (h) of section 2680 of Title 28 do not prohibit the bringing of a civil action on a claim against the United States which—

(1) is based upon—

(A) misrepresentation or deceit on the part of the Commission or any employee thereof, or

(B) any exercise or performance, or failure to exercise or perform, a discretionary function on the part of the Commission or any employee thereof, which exercise, performance, or failure was grossly negligent; and

(2) is not made with respect to any agency action (as defined in section 551(13) of Title 5).

In the case of a civil action on a claim based upon the exercise or performance of, or failure to exercise or perform, a discretionary function, no judgment may be entered against the United States unless the court in which such action was brought determines (based upon consideration of all the relevant circumstances, including the statutory responsibility of the Commission and the public interest in encouraging rather than inhibiting the exercise of discretion) that such exercise, performance, or failure to exercise or perform was unreasonable.

As amended Pub.L. 94–284, §§ 4, 5(a), May 11, 1976, 90 Stat. 504; Pub.L. 95–631, § 2, Nov. 10, 1978, 92 Stat. 3742.

§ 2054. Product safety information and research

(a) Injury Information Clearinghouse; duties

(a) The Commission shall—

(1) maintain an Injury Information Clearinghouse to collect, investigate, analyze, and disseminate injury data, and information, relating to the causes and prevention of death, injury, and illness associated with consumer products;

(2) conduct such continuing studies and investigations of deaths, injuries, diseases, other health impairments, and economic losses resulting from accidents involving consumer products as it deems necessary;

(3) following publication of an advance notice of proposed rulemaking or a notice of proposed rulemaking for a product safety rule under any rulemaking authority administered by the Commission, assist public and private organizations or groups of manufacturers, administratively and technically, in the development of safety standards addressing the risk of injury identified in such notice; and

(4) to the extent practicable and appropriate (taking into account the resources and priorities of the Commission), assist public and private organizations or groups of manufacturers, administratively and technically, in the development of product safety standards and test methods.

(b) Research, investigation and testing of consumer products

(b) The Commission may—

(1) conduct research, studies, and investigations on the safety of consumer products and on improving the safety of such products;

(2) test consumer products and develop product safety test methods and testing devices; and

(3) offer training in product safety investigation and test methods.

(c) Grants and contracts for conduct of functions

(c) In carrying out its functions under this section, the Commission may make grants or enter into contracts for the conduct of such functions with any person (including a governmental entity).

(d) Availability to public of information

(d) Whenever the Federal contribution for any information, research, or development activity authorized by this chapter is more than minimal, the Commission shall include in any contract, grant, or other arrangement for such activity, provisions effective to insure that the rights to all information, uses, processes, patents, and other developments resulting from that activity will be made available to the public without charge on a nonexclusive basis. Nothing in this subsection shall be construed to deprive any person of any right which he may have had, prior to entering into any arrangement referred to in this subsection, to any patent, patent application, or invention.

As amended Pub.L. 97–35, Title XII, § 1209(a), (b), Aug. 13, 1981, 95 Stat. 720.

§ 2055. Public disclosure of information

(a) Disclosure requirements for manufacturers or private labelers; procedures applicable

(a)(1) Nothing contained in this Act shall be construed to require the release of any information described by subsection (b) of section 552 of Title 5 or which is otherwise protected by law from disclosure to the public.

(2) All information reported to or otherwise obtained by the Commission or its representative under this Act which information contains or relates to a trade secret or other matter referred to in section 1905 of Title 18 or subject to section 552(b)(4) of Title 5 shall be considered confidential and shall not be disclosed.

(3) The Commission shall, prior to the disclosure of any information which will permit the public to ascertain readily the identity of a manufacturer or private labeler of a consumer product, offer such manufacturer or private labeler an opportunity to mark such information as confidential and therefore barred from disclosure under paragraph (2).

(4) All information that a manufacturer or private labeler has marked to be confidential and barred from disclosure under paragraph (2), either at the time of submission or pursuant to paragraph (3), shall not be disclosed, except in accordance with the procedures established in paragraphs (5) and (6).

(5) If the Commission determines that a document marked as confidential by a manufacturer or private labeler to be barred from disclosure under paragraph (2) may be disclosed because it is not confidential information as provided in paragraph (2), the Commission

shall notify such person in writing that the Commission intends to disclose such document at a date not less than 10 days after the date of receipt of notification.

(6) Any person receiving such notification may, if he believes such disclosure is barred by paragraph (2), before the date set for release of the document, bring an action in the district court of the United States in the district in which the complainant resides, or has his principal place of business, or in which the documents are located, or in the United States District Court for the District of Columbia to restrain disclosure of the document. Any person receiving such notification may file with the appropriate district court or court of appeals of the United States, as appropriate, an application for a stay of disclosure. The documents shall not be disclosed until the court has ruled on the application for a stay.

(7) Nothing in this Act shall authorize the withholding of information by the Commission or any officer or employee under its control from the duly authorized committees or subcommittees of the Congress, and the provisions of paragraphs (2) through (6) shall not apply to such disclosures, except that the Commission shall immediately notify the manufacturer or private labeler of any such request for information designated as confidential by the manufacturer or private labeler.

(8) The provisions of paragraphs (2) through (6) shall not prohibit the disclosure of information to other officers or employees concerned with carrying out this Act or when relevant in any administrative proceeding under this Act, or in judicial proceedings to which the Commission is a party. Any disclosure of relevant information in Commission administrative proceedings, or in judicial proceedings to which the Commission is a party, shall be governed by the rules of the Commission (including in camera review rules for confidential material) for such proceedings or by court rules or orders, except that the rules of the Commission shall not be amended in a manner inconsistent with the purposes of this section.

(b) Additional disclosure requirements for manufacturers or private labelers; procedures applicable

(b)(1) Except as provided by paragraph (4) of this subsection, not less than 30 days prior to its public disclosure of any information obtained under this Act, or to be disclosed to the public in connection therewith (unless the Commission finds that the public health and safety requires a lesser period of notice and publishes such a finding in the Federal Register), the Commission shall, to the extent practicable, notify and provide a summary of the information to each manufacturer or private labeler of any consumer product to which such information pertains, if the manner in which such consumer product is to be designated or described in such information will permit the public to ascertain readily the identity of such manufacturer or private labeler, and shall provide such manufacturer or private labeler with a reasonable opportunity to submit comments to the Commission in regard to such information. The Commission shall take reasonable steps to assure, prior to its public disclosure thereof, that information from which the identity of such manufacturer or private labeler may be readily ascertained is accurate, and that such disclosure is fair in the circumstances and reasonably related to effectuating the purposes of this Act. In disclosing any information under this subsection, the Commission may, and upon the request of the manufacturer or private labeler shall, include with the disclosure any comments or other information or a summary thereof submitted by such manufacturer or private labeler to the extent permitted by and subject to the requirements of this section.

(2) If the Commission determines that a document claimed to be inaccurate by a manufacturer or private labeler under paragraph (1) should be disclosed because the Commission believes it has complied with paragraph (1), the Commission shall notify the manufacturer or private labeler that the Commission intends to disclose such document at a date not less than 10 days after the date of the receipt of notification. The Commission may provide a lesser period of notice of intent to disclose if the Commission finds that the public health and safety requires a lesser period of notice and publishes such finding in the Federal Register.

(3) Prior to the date set for release of the document, the manufacturer or private labeler receiving the notice described in paragraph (2) may bring an action in the district court of the United States in the district in which the complainant resides, or has his principal place of business, or in which the documents are located or in the United States District Court for the District of Columbia to enjoin disclosure of the document. The district court may enjoin such disclosure if the Commission has failed to take the reasonable steps prescribed in paragraph (1).

(4) Paragraphs (1) through (3) of this subsection shall not apply to the public disclosure of (A) information about any consumer product with respect to which product the Commission has filed an action under section 2061 of this title (relating to imminently hazardous products), or which the Commission has reasonable cause to believe is in violation of section 2068 of this title (relating to prohibited acts); or (B) information in the course of or concerning a rulemaking proceeding (which shall commence upon the publication of an advance notice of proposed rulemaking or a notice of proposed rulemaking), an adjudicatory proceeding (which shall commence upon the issuance of a complaint) or other administrative or judicial proceeding under this Act.

§ 2055　　　CONSUMER PRODUCT SAFETY ACT

(5) In addition to the requirements of paragraph (1), the Commission shall not disclose to the public information submitted pursuant to section 2064(b) of this title respecting a consumer product unless—

(A) the Commission has issued a complaint under section 2064(c) or (d) of this title alleging that such product presents a substantial product hazard;

(B) in lieu of proceeding against such product under section 2064(c) or (d) of this title, the Commission has accepted in writing a remedial settlement agreement dealing with such product; or

(C) the person who submitted the information under section 2064(b) of this title agrees to its public disclosure.

The provisions of this paragraph shall not apply to the public disclosure of information with respect to a consumer product which is the subject of an action brought under section 2061 of this title, or which the Commission has reasonable cause to believe is in violation of section 2068(a) of this title, or information in the course of or concerning a judicial proceeding.

(6) Where the Commission initiates the public disclosure of information that reflects on the safety of a consumer product or class of consumer products, whether or not such information would enable the public to ascertain readily the identity of a manufacturer or private labeler, the Commission shall establish procedures designed to ensure that such information is accurate and not misleading.

(7) If the Commission finds that, in the administration of this Act, it has made public disclosure of inaccurate or misleading information which reflects adversely upon the safety of any consumer product or class of consumer products, or the practices of any manufacturer, private labeler, distributor, or retailer of consumer products, it shall, in a manner equivalent to that in which such disclosure was made, take reasonable steps to publish a retraction of such inaccurate or misleading information.

(8) If, after the commencement of a rulemaking or the initiation of an adjudicatory proceeding, the Commission decides to terminate the proceeding before taking final action, the Commission shall, in a manner equivalent to that in which such commencement or initiation was publicized, take reasonable steps to make known the decision to terminate.

(c) **Communications with manufacturers**

(c) The Commission shall communicate to each manufacturer of a consumer product, insofar as may be practicable, information as to any significant risk of injury associated with such product.

(d) Definition; coverage

(d)(1) For purposes of this section, the term "Act" means the Consumer Product Safety Act, the Flammable Fabrics Act, the Poison Prevention Packaging Act, and the Federal Hazardous Substances Act.

(2) The provisions of this section shall apply whenever information is to be disclosed by the Commission, any member of the Commission, or any employee, agent, or representative of the Commission in an official capacity. Commission shall include in any contract, grant, or other arrangement for such activity, provisions effective to insure that the rights to all information, uses, processes, patents, and other developments resulting from that activity will be made available to the public without charge on a nonexclusive basis. Nothing in this subsection shall be construed to deprive any person of any right which he may have had, prior to entering into any arrangement referred to in this subsection, to any patent, patent application, or invention.

As amended Pub.L. 97–35, Title XII, § 1209(a), (b), Aug. 13, 1981, 95 Stat. 720, Pub.L. 97–414, § 9(j)(1), Jan. 4, 1983, 96 Stat. 2064.

§ 2056. Consumer product safety standards

(a) Types of requirements

(a) The Commission may promulgate consumer product safety standards in accordance with the provisions of section 2058 of this title. A consumer product safety standard shall consist of one or more of any of the following types of requirements:

> (1) Requirements expressed in terms of performance requirements.
>
> (2) Requirements that a consumer product be marked with or accompanied by clear and adequate warnings or instructions, or requirements respecting the form of warnings or instructions.

Any requirement of such a standard shall be reasonably necessary to prevent or reduce an unreasonable risk of injury associated with such product.

(b) Reliance of Commission upon voluntary standards

(b) The Commission shall rely upon voluntary consumer product safety standards rather than promulgate a consumer product safety standard prescribing requirements described in subsection (a) of this section whenever compliance with such voluntary standards would eliminate or adequately reduce the risk of injury addressed and it is likely that there will be substantial compliance with such voluntary standards.

(c) Contribution of Commission to development cost

(c) If any person participates with the Commission in the development of a consumer product safety standard, the Commission may agree to contribute to the person's cost with respect to such participation, in any case in which the Commission determines that such contribution is likely to result in a more satisfactory standard than would be developed without such contribution, and that the person is financially responsible. Regulations of the Commission shall set forth the items of cost in which it may participate, and shall exclude any contribution to the acquisition of land or buildings. Payments under agreements entered into under this subsection may be made without regard to section 3324(a) and (b) of Title 31.

As amended Pub.L. 94–284, §§ 6–8(a), May 11, 1976, 90 Stat. 505, 506; Pub.L. 95–631, §§ 3, 4(a)-(c), 5, Nov. 10, 1978, 92 Stat. 3742–3744; Pub.L. 97–35, Title XII, § 1202, Aug. 13, 1981, 95 Stat. 703, 97–258, § 4(b), Sept. 13, 1982, 96 Stat. 1067.

§ 2057. Banned hazardous products

Whenever the Commission finds that—

(1) a consumer product is being, or will be, distributed in commerce and such consumer product presents an unreasonable risk of injury; and

(2) no feasible consumer product safety standard under this chapter would adequately protect the public from the unreasonable risk of injury associated with such product,

the Commission may, in accordance with section 2058 of this title, promulgate a rule declaring such product a banned hazardous product.

As amended Pub.L. 97–35, Title XII, § 1203(c), Aug. 13, 1981, 95 Stat. 713.

§ 2058. Procedure for consumer product safety rules

(a) Commencement of proceeding; publication of prescribed notice of proposed rulemaking; transmittal of notice

(a) A proceeding for the development of a consumer product safety rule shall be commenced by the publication in the Federal Register of an advance notice of proposed rulemaking which shall—

(1) identify the product and the nature of the risk of injury associated with the product;

(2) include a summary of each of the regulatory alternatives under consideration by the Commission (including voluntary consumer product safety standards);

(3) include information with respect to any existing standard known to the Commission which may be relevant to the proceedings, together with a summary of the reasons why the Commission believes preliminarily that such standard does not eliminate or adequately reduce the risk of injury identified in paragraph (1);

(4) invite interested persons to submit to the Commission, within such period as the Commission shall specify in the notice (which period shall not be less than 30 days or more than 60 days after the date of publication of the notice), comments with respect to the risk of injury identified by the Commission, the regulatory alternatives being considered, and other possible alternatives for addressing the risk;

(5) invite any person (other than the Commission) to submit to the Commission, within such period as the Commission shall specify in the notice (which period shall not be less than 30 days after the date of publication of the notice), an existing standard or a portion of a standard as a proposed consumer product safety standard; and

(6) invite any person (other than the Commission) to submit to the Commission, within such period as the Commission shall specify in the notice (which period shall not be less than 30 days after the date of publication of the notice), a statement of intention to modify or develop a voluntary consumer product safety standard to address the risk of injury identified in paragraph (1) together with a description of a plan to modify or develop the standard.

The Commission shall transmit such notice within 10 calendar days to the Committee on Commerce, Science, and Transportation of the Senate and the Committee on Energy and Commerce of the House of Representatives.

(b) Voluntary standard; publication as proposed rule; notice of reliance of Commission on standard

(b)(1) If the Commission determines that any standard submitted to it in response to an invitation in a notice published under subsection (a)(5) of this section if promulgated (in whole, in part, or in combination with any other standard submitted to the Commission or any part of such a standard) as a consumer product safety standard, would eliminate or adequately reduce the risk of injury identified in the notice under subsection (a)(1), of this section, the Commission may publish such standard, in whole, in part, or in such combination and with nonmaterial modifications, as a proposed consumer product safety rule.

(2) If the Commission determines that—

(A) compliance with any standard submitted to it in response to an invitation in a notice published under subsection (a)(6) of this section is likely to result in the elimination or adequate reduction of the risk of injury identified in the notice, and

(B) it is likely that there will be substantial compliance with such standard,

the Commission shall terminate any proceeding to promulgate a consumer product safety rule respecting such risk of injury and shall publish in the Federal Register a notice which includes the determination of the Commission and which notifies the public that the Commission will rely on the voluntary standard to eliminate or reduce the risk of injury.

(c) Publication of proposed rule; preliminary regulatory analysis; contents; transmittal of notice

(c) No consumer product safety rule may be proposed by the Commission unless, not less than 60 days after publication of the notice required in subsection (a) of this section, the Commission publishes in the Federal Register the text of the proposed rule, including any alternatives, which the Commission proposes to promulgate, together with a preliminary regulatory analysis containing—

(1) a preliminary description of the potential benefits and potential costs of the proposed rule, including any benefits or costs that cannot be quantified in monetary terms, and an identification of those likely to receive the benefits and bear the costs;

(2) a discussion of the reasons any standard or portion of a standard submitted to the Commission under subsection (a)(5) of this section was not published by the Commission as the proposed rule or part of the proposed rule;

(3) a discussion of the reasons for the Commission's preliminary determination that efforts proposed under subsection (a)(6) of this section and assisted by the Commission as required by section 2054(a)(3) of this title would not, within a reasonable period of time, be likely to result in the development of a voluntary consumer product safety standard that would eliminate or adequately reduce the risk of injury addressed by the proposed rule; and

(4) a description of any reasonable alternatives to the proposed rule, together with a summary description of their potential costs and benefits, and a brief explanation of why such alternatives should not be published as a proposed rule.

The Commission shall transmit such notice within 10 calendar days to the Committee on Commerce, Science, and Transportation of the Senate and the Committee on Energy and Commerce of the House of Representatives.

(d) Promulgation of rule; time

(d)(1) Within 60 days after the publication under subsection (c) of this section of a proposed consumer product safety rule respecting a risk of injury associated with a consumer product, the Commission shall—

(A) promulgate a consumer product safety rule respecting the risk of injury associated with such product, if it makes the findings required under subsection (f) of this section, or

(B) withdraw the applicable notice of proposed rulemaking if it determines that such rule is not (i) reasonably necessary to eliminate or reduce an unreasonable risk of injury associated with the product, or (ii) in the public interest;

except that the Commission may extend such 60-day period for good cause shown (if it publishes its reasons therefor in the Federal Register).

(2) Consumer product safety rules shall be promulgated in accordance with section 553 of Title 5 except that the Commission shall give interested persons an opportunity for the oral presentation of data, views, or arguments, in addition to an opportunity to make written submissions. A transcript shall be kept of any oral presentation.

(e) Expression of risk of injury; consideration of available product data; needs of elderly and handicapped

(e) A consumer product safety rule shall express in the rule itself the risk of injury which the standard is designed to eliminate or reduce. In promulgating such a rule the Commission shall consider relevant available product data including the results of research, development, testing, and investigation activities conducted generally and pursuant to this chapter. In the promulgation of such a rule the Commission shall also consider and take into account the special needs of elderly and handicapped persons to determine the extent to which such persons may be adversely affected by such rule.

(f) Findings; final regulatory analysis; judicial review of rule

(f)(1) Prior to promulgating a consumer product safety rule, the Commission shall consider, and shall make appropriate findings for inclusion in such rule with respect to—

(A) the degree and nature of the risk of injury the rule is designed to eliminate or reduce;

(B) the approximate number of consumer products, or types or classes thereof, subject to such rule;

§ 2058   CONSUMER PRODUCT SAFETY ACT

(C) the need of the public for the consumer products subject to such rule, and the probable effect of such rule upon the utility, cost, or availability of such products to meet such need; and

(D) any means of achieving the objective of the order while minimizing adverse effects on competition or disruption or dislocation of manufacturing and other commercial practices consistent with the public health and safety.

(2) The Commission shall not promulgate a consumer product safety rule unless it has prepared, on the basis of the findings of the Commission under paragraph (1) and on other information before the Commission, a final regulatory analysis of the rule containing the following information:

(A) A description of the potential benefits and potential costs of the rule, including costs and benefits that cannot be quantified in monetary terms, and the identification of those likely to receive the benefits and bear the costs.

(B) A description of any alternatives to the final rule which were considered by the Commission, together with a summary description of their potential benefits and costs and a brief explanation of the reasons why these alternatives were not chosen.

(C) A summary of any significant issues raised by the comments submitted during the public comment period in response to the preliminary regulatory analysis, and a summary of the assessment by the Commission of such issues.

The Commission shall publish its final regulatory analysis with the rule.

(3) The Commission shall not promulgate a consumer product safety rule unless it finds (and includes such finding in the rule)—

(A) that the rule (including its effective date) is reasonably necessary to eliminate or reduce an unreasonable risk of injury associated with such product;

(B) that the promulgation of the rule is in the public interest;

(C) in the case of a rule declaring the product a banned hazardous product, that no feasible consumer product safety standard under this chapter would adequately protect the public from the unreasonable risk of injury associated with such product;

(D) in the case of a rule which relates to a risk of injury with respect to which persons who would be subject to such rule have adopted and implemented a voluntary consumer product safety standard, that—

(i) compliance with such voluntary consumer product safety standard is not likely to result in the elimination or adequate reduction of such risk of injury; or

(ii) it is unlikely that there will be substantial compliance with such voluntary consumer product safety standard;

(E) that the benefits expected from the rule bear a reasonable relationship to its costs; and

(F) that the rule imposes the least burdensome requirement which prevents or adequately reduces the risk of injury for which the rule is being promulgated.

(4)(A) Any preliminary or final regulatory analysis prepared under subsection (c) or (f)(2) of this section shall not be subject to independent judicial review, except that when an action for judicial review of a rule is instituted, the contents of any such regulatory analysis shall constitute part of the whole rulemaking record of agency action in connection with such review.

(B) The provisions of subparagraph (A) shall not be construed to alter the substantive or procedural standards otherwise applicable to judicial review of any action by the Commission.

(g) Effective date of rule or standard; stockpiling of product

(g)(1) Each consumer product safety rule shall specify the date such rule is to take effect not exceeding 180 days from the date promulgated, unless the Commission finds, for good cause shown, that a later effective date is in the public interest and publishes its reasons for such finding. The effective date of a consumer product safety standard under this chapter shall be set at a date at least 30 days after the date of promulgation unless the Commission for good cause shown determines that an earlier effective date is in the public interest. In no case may the effective date be set at a date which is earlier than the date of promulgation. A consumer product safety standard shall be applicable only to consumer products manufactured after the effective date.

(2) The Commission may by rule prohibit a manufacturer of a consumer product from stockpiling any product to which a consumer product safety rule applies, so as to prevent such manufacturer from circumventing the purpose of such consumer product safety rule. For purposes of this paragraph, the term "stockpiling" means manufacturing or importing a product between the date of promulgation of such consumer product safety rule and its effective date at a rate which is significantly greater (as determined under the rule under this paragraph) than the rate at which such product was produced or imported during a base period (prescribed in the rule under this paragraph) ending before the date of promulgation of the consumer product safety rule.

(h) Amendment or revocation of rule

(h) The Commission may by rule amend or revoke any consumer product safety rule. Such amendment or revocation shall specify the date on which it is to take effect which shall not exceed 180 days from the date the amendment or revocation is published unless the Commission finds for good cause shown that a later effective date is in the public interest and publishes its reasons for such finding. Where an amendment involves a material change in a consumer product safety rule, sections 2056 and 2057 of this title, and subsections (a) through (g) of this section shall apply. In order to revoke a consumer product safety rule, the Commission shall publish a proposal to revoke such rule in the Federal Register, and allow oral and written presentations in accordance with subsection (d)(2) of this section. It may revoke such rule only if it determines that the rule is not reasonably necessary to eliminate or reduce an unreasonable risk of injury associated with the product. Section 2060 of this title shall apply to any amendment of a consumer product safety rule which involves a material change and to any revocation of a consumer product safety rule, in the same manner and to the same extent as such section applies to the Commission's action in promulgating such a rule.

As amended Pub.L. 94–284, § 9, May 11, 1976, 90 Stat. 506; Pub.L. 95–631, § 4(d), Nov. 10, 1978, 92 Stat. 3744; Pub.L. 97–35, Title XII, § 1203(a), Aug. 13, 1981, 95 Stat. 704.

* * *

§ 2060. Judicial review of consumer product safety rules

(a) Petition by persons adversely affected, consumers, or consumer organizations

(a) Not later than 60 days after a consumer product safety rule is promulgated by the Commission, any person adversely affected by such rule, or any consumer or consumer organization, may file a petition with the United States court of appeals for the District of Columbia or for the circuit in which such person, consumer, or organization resides or has his principal place of business for judicial review of such rule. Copies of the petition shall be forthwith transmitted by the clerk of the court to the Commission or other officer designated by it for that purpose and to the Attorney General. The record of the proceedings on which the Commission based its rule shall be filed in the court as provided for in section 2112 of Title 28. For purposes of this section, the term "record" means such consumer product safety rule; any notice or proposal published pursuant to section 2056, 2057, or 2058 of this title; the transcript required by section 2058(d)(2) of this title of any oral presentation; any written submission of interested parties; and any other information which the Commission considers relevant to such rule.

(b) Additional data, views, or arguments

(b) If the petitioner applies to the court for leave to adduce additional data, views, or arguments and shows to the satisfaction of the court that such additional data, views, or arguments are material and that there were reasonable grounds for the petitioner's failure to adduce such data, views, or arguments in the proceeding before the Commission, the court may order the Commission to provide additional opportunity for the oral presentation of data, views, or arguments and for written submissions. The Commission may modify its findings, or make new findings by reason of the additional data, views, or arguments so taken and shall file such modified or new findings, and its recommendation, if any, for the modification or setting aside of its original rule, with the return of such additional data, views, or arguments.

(c) Jurisdiction; costs and attorneys' fees; substantial evidence to support administrative findings

(c) Upon the filing of the petition under subsection (a) of this section the court shall have jurisdiction to review the consumer product safety rule in accordance with chapter 7 of Title 5, and to grant appropriate relief, including interim relief, as provided in such chapter. A court may in the interest of justice include in such relief an award of the costs of suit, including reasonable attorneys' fees (determined in accordance with subsection (f) of this section) and reasonable expert witnesses' fees. Attorneys' fees may be awarded against the United States (or any agency or official of the United States) without regard to section 2412 of Title 28 or any other provision of law. The consumer product safety rule shall not be affirmed unless the Commission's findings under sections 2058(f)(1) and 2058(f)(3) of this title are supported by substantial evidence on the record taken as a whole.

(d) Supreme Court review

(d) The judgment of the court affirming or setting aside, in whole or in part, any consumer product safety rule shall be final, subject to review by the Supreme Court of the United States upon certiorari or certification, as provided in section 1254 of Title 28.

(e) Availability of other remedies

(e) The remedies provided for in this section shall be in addition to and not in lieu of any other remedies provided by law.

(f) Computation of reasonable fee for attorney

(f) For purposes of this section and sections 2072(a) and 2073 of this title, a reasonable attorney's fee is a fee (1) which is based upon (A) the actual time expended by an attorney in providing advice and other legal services in connection with representing a person in an action brought under this section, and (B) such reasonable expenses as may be incurred by the attorney in the provision of such services, and (2) which is computed at the rate prevailing for the provision of similar services with respect to actions brought in the court which is awarding such fee.

As amended Pub.L. 94–284, §§ 10(b), 11(a), May 11, 1976, 90 Stat. 507; Pub.L. 97–35, Title XII, § 1211(h)(1)–(3)(A), Aug. 13, 1981, 95 Stat. 723; Pub.L. 97–414, § 9(j)(2), Jan. 4, 1983, 96 Stat. 2064.

§ 2061. Imminent hazards

(a) Filing of action

(a) The Commission may file in a United States district court an action (1) against an imminently hazardous consumer product for seizure of such product under subsection (b)(2) of this section, or (2) against any person who is a manufacturer, distributor, or retailer of such product, or (3) against both. Such an action may be filed notwithstanding the existence of a consumer product safety rule applicable to such product, or the pendency of any administrative or judicial proceedings under any other provision of this chapter. As used in this section, and hereinafter in this chapter, the term "imminently hazardous consumer product" means a consumer product which presents imminent and unreasonable risk of death, serious illness, or severe personal injury.

(b) Relief; product condemnation and seizure

(b)(1) The district court in which such action is filed shall have jurisdiction to declare such product an imminently hazardous consumer product, and (in the case of an action under subsection (a)(2) of this section) to grant (as ancillary to such declaration or in lieu thereof) such temporary or permanent relief as may be necessary to protect the public from such risk. Such relief may include a mandatory order requiring the notification of such risk to purchasers of such product known to the defendant, public notice, the recall, the repair or the replacement of, or refund for, such product.

(2) In the case of an action under subsection (a)(1) of this section, the consumer product may be proceeded against by process of libel for the seizure and condemnation of such product in any United States district court within the jurisdiction of which such consumer product is found. Proceedings and cases instituted under the authority of the preceding sentence shall conform as nearly as possible to proceedings in rem in admiralty.

(c) **Consumer product safety rule**

(c) Where appropriate, concurrently with the filing of such action or as soon thereafter as may be practicable, the Commission shall initiate a proceeding to promulgate a consumer product safety rule applicable to the consumer product with respect to which such action is filed.

(d) **Jurisdiction and venue; process; subpena**

(d)(1) An action under subsection (a)(2) of this section may be brought in the United States district court for the District of Columbia or in any judicial district in which any of the defendants is found, is an inhabitant or transacts business; and process in such an action may be served on a defendant in any other district in which such defendant resides or may be found. Subpenas requiring attendance of witnesses in such an action may run into any other district. In determining the judicial district in which an action may be brought under this section in instances in which such action may be brought in more than one judicial district, the Commission shall take into account the convenience of the parties.

(2) Whenever proceedings under this section involving substantially similar consumer products are pending in courts in two or more judicial districts, they shall be consolidated for trial by order of any such court upon application reasonably made by any party in interest, upon notice to all other parties in interest.

(e) **Employment of attorneys by Commission**

(e) Notwithstanding any other provision of law, in any action under this section, the Commission may direct attorneys employed by it to appear and represent it.

As amended Pub.L. 97–35, Title XII, § 1205(a)(2), Aug. 13, 1981, 95 Stat. 716.

* * *

§ 2063. Product certification and labeling

(a)(1) Every manufacturer of a product which is subject to a consumer product safety standard under this chapter and which is distributed in commerce (and the private labeler of such product if it bears a private label) shall issue a certificate which shall certify that such product conforms to all applicable consumer product safety standards, and shall specify any standard which is applicable. Such certificate shall accompany the product or shall otherwise be furnished to any distributor or retailer to whom the product is delivered. Any certificate under this subsection shall be based on a test of each product or upon a reasonable testing program; shall state the name of the manufacturer or private labeler issuing the certificate; and shall include the date and place of manufacture.

(2) In the case of a consumer product for which there is more than one manufacturer or more than one private labeler, the Commission may by rule designate one or more of such manufacturers or one or more of such private labelers (as the case may be) as the persons who shall issue the certificate required by paragraph (1) of this subsection, and may exempt all other manufacturers of such product or all other private labelers of the product (as the case may be) from the requirement under paragraph (1) to issue a certificate with respect to such product.

(b) The Commission may by rule prescribe reasonable testing programs for consumer products which are subject to consumer product safety standards under this chapter and for which a certificate is required under subsection (a) of this section. Any test or testing program on the basis of which a certificate is issued under subsection (a) of this section may, at the option of the person required to certify the product, be conducted by an independent third party qualified to perform such tests or testing programs.

(c) The Commission may by rule require the use and prescribe the form and content of labels which contain the following information (or that portion of it specified in the rule)—

(1) The date and place of manufacture of any consumer product.

(2) A suitable identification of the manufacturer of the consumer product, unless the product bears a private label in which case it shall identify the private labeler and shall also contain a code mark which will permit the seller of such product to identify the manufacturer thereof to the purchaser upon his request.

(3) In the case of a consumer product subject to a consumer product safety rule, a certification that the product meets all applicable consumer product safety standards and a specification of the standards which are applicable.

Such labels, where practicable, may be required by the Commission to be permanently marked on or affixed to any such consumer product. The Commission may, in appropriate cases, permit information required under paragraphs (1) and (2) of this subsection to be coded.

Pub.L. 92-573, § 14, Oct. 27, 1972, 86 Stat. 1220.

§ 2064. Substantial product hazards

(a) Definition

(a) For purposes of this section, the term "substantial product hazard" means—

(1) a failure to comply with an applicable consumer product safety rule which creates a substantial risk of injury to the public, or

(2) a product defect which (because of the pattern of defect, the number of defective products distributed in commerce, the severity of the risk, or otherwise) creates a substantial risk of injury to the public.

(b) Noncompliance with applicable consumer product safety rules; product defects; notice to Commission by manufacturer, distributor, or retailer

(b) Every manufacturer of a consumer product distributed in commerce, and every distributor and retailer of such product, who obtains information which reasonably supports the conclusion that such product—

(1) fails to comply with an applicable consumer product safety rule; or

(2) contains a defect which could create a substantial product hazard described in subsection (a)(2) of this section,

shall immediately inform the Commission of such failure to comply or of such defect, unless such manufacturer, distributor, or retailer has actual knowledge that the Commission has been adequately informed of such defect or failure to comply.

(c) Public notice of defect or failure to comply; mail notice

(c) If the Commission determines (after affording interested persons, including consumers and consumer organizations, an opportunity for a hearing in accordance with subsection (f) of this section) that a product distributed in commerce presents a substantial product hazard and that notification is required in order to adequately protect the public from such substantial product hazard, the Commission may order the manufacturer or any distributor or retailer of the product to take any one or more of the following actions:

(1) To give public notice of the defect or failure to comply.

(2) To mail notice to each person who is a manufacturer, distributor, or retailer of such product.

(3) To mail notice to every person to whom the person required to give notice knows such product was delivered or sold.

Any such order shall specify the form and content of any notice required to be given under such order.

(d) Repair; replacement; refunds; action plan

(d) If the Commission determines (after affording interested parties, including consumers and consumer organizations, an opportunity for a hearing in accordance with subsection (f) of this section) that a product distributed in commerce presents a substantial product hazard and that action under this subsection is in the public interest, it may order the manufacturer or any distributor or retailer of such product to take whichever of the following actions the person to whom the order is directed elects:

(1) To bring such product into conformity with the requirements of the applicable consumer product safety rule or to repair the defect in such product.

(2) To replace such product with a like or equivalent product which complies with the applicable consumer product safety rule or which does not contain the defect.

(3) To refund the purchase price of such product (less a reasonable allowance for use, if such product has been in the possession of a consumer for one year or more (A) at the time of public notice under subsection (c) of this section, or (B) at the time the consumer receives actual notice of the defect or noncompliance, whichever first occurs).

An order under this subsection may also require the person to whom it applies to submit a plan, satisfactory to the Commission, for taking action under whichever of the preceding paragraphs of this subsection under which such person has elected to act. The Commission shall specify in the order the persons to whom refunds must be made if the person to whom the order is directed elects to take the action described in paragraph (3). If an order under this subsection is directed to more than one person, the Commission shall specify which person has the election under this subsection. An order under this subsection may prohibit the person to whom it applies from manufacturing for sale, offering for sale, distributing in commerce, or importing into the customs territory of the United States (as defined in general headnote 2 to the Tariff Schedules of the United States), or from doing any combination of such actions, the product with respect to which the order was issued.

(e) Reimbursement

(e)(1) No charge shall be made to any person (other than a manufacturer, distributor, or retailer) who avails himself of any remedy provided under an order issued under subsection (d) of this section, and the person subject to the order shall reimburse each person (other than a manufacturer, distributor, or retailer) who is entitled to such a remedy for any reasonable and foreseeable expenses incurred by such person in availing himself of such remedy.

(2) An order issued under subsection (c) or (d) of this section with respect to a product may require any person who is a manufacturer, distributor, or retailer of the product to reimburse any other person who is a manufacturer, distributor, or retailer of such product for such other person's expenses in connection with carrying out the order, if the Commission determines such reimbursement to be in the public interest.

(f) Hearing

(f) An order under subsection (c) or (d) of this section may be issued only after an opportunity for a hearing in accordance with section 554 of Title 5, except that, if the Commission determines that any person who wishes to participate in such hearing is a part of a class of participants who share an identity of interest, the Commission may limit such person's participation in such hearing to participation through a single representative designated by such class (or by the Commission if such class fails to designate such a representative).

Pub.L. 92–573, § 15, Oct. 27, 1972, 86 Stat. 1221.

(g) Preliminary injunction

(g)(1) If the Commission has initiated a proceeding under this section for the issuance of an order under subsection (d) of this section with respect to a product which the Commission has reason to believe presents a substantial product hazard, the Commission (without regard to section 2076(b)(7) of this title) or the Attorney General may, in accordance with section 2061(g)(1) of this title, apply to a district court of the United States for the issuance of a preliminary injunction to restrain the distribution in commerce of such product pending the completion of such proceeding. If such a preliminary injunction has been issued, the Commission (or the Attorney General if the preliminary injunction was issued upon an application of the Attorney General) may apply to the issuing court for extensions of such preliminary injunction.

(2) Any preliminary injunction, and any extension of a preliminary injunction, issued under this subsection with respect to a product shall be in effect for such period as the issuing court prescribes not to exceed a period which extends beyond the thirtieth day from the date of the issuance of the preliminary injunction (or, in the case of a preliminary injunction which has been extended, the date of its extension) or the date of the completion or termination of the proceeding under this section respecting such product, whichever date occurs first.

(3) The amount in controversy requirement of section 1331 of Title 28, does not apply with respect to the jurisdiction of a district court of the United States to issue or exend [1] a preliminary injunction under this subsection.

As amended Pub.L. 94–284, § 12(a), May 11, 1976, 90 Stat. 508.

§ 2065. Inspection and recordkeeping

(a) For purposes of implementing this chapter, or rules or orders prescribed under this chapter, officers or employees duly designated by the Commission, upon presenting appropriate credentials and a written notice from the Commission to the owner, operator, or agent in charge, are authorized—

(1) to enter, at reasonable times, (A) any factory, warehouse, or establishment in which consumer products are manufactured or held, in connection with distribution in commerce, or (B) any conveyance being used to transport consumer products in connection with distribution in commerce; and

(2) to inspect, at reasonable times and in a reasonable manner such conveyance or those areas of such factory, warehouse, or establishment where such products are manufactured, held, or transported and which may relate to the safety of such products. Each such inspection shall be commenced and completed with reasonable promptness.

(b) Every person who is a manufacturer, private labeler, or distributor of a consumer product shall establish and maintain such records, make such reports, and provide such information as the Commission may, by rule, reasonably require for the purposes of implementing this chapter, or to determine compliance with rules or orders prescribed under this chapter. Upon request of an officer or employee duly designated by the Commission, every such manufacturer, private labeler, or distributor shall permit the inspection of appropriate books,

---

1. So in original. Probably should read "extend".

records, and papers relevant to determining whether such manufacturer, private labeler, or distributor has acted or is acting in compliance with this chapter and rules under this chapter.

Pub.L. 92–573, § 16, Oct. 27, 1972, 86 Stat. 1222.

§ 2066. Imported products

(a) Refusal of admission

(a) Any consumer product offered for importation into the customs territory of the United States (as defined in general headnote 2 to the Tariff Schedules of the United States) shall be refused admission into such customs territory if such product—

(1) fails to comply with an applicable consumer product safety rule;

(2) is not accompanied by a certificate required by section 2063 of this title, or is not labeled in accordance with regulations under section 2063(c) of this title;

(3) is or has been determined to be an imminently hazardous consumer product in a proceeding brought under section 2061 of this title;

(4) has a product defect which constitutes a substantial product hazard (within the meaning of section 2064(a)(2) of this title); or

(5) is a product which was manufactured by a person who the Commission has informed the Secretary of the Treasury is in violation of subsection (g) of this section.

(b) Samples

(b) The Secretary of the Treasury shall obtain without charge and deliver to the Commission, upon the latter's request, a reasonable number of samples of consumer products being offered for import. Except for those owners or consignees who are or have been afforded an opportunity for a hearing in a proceeding under section 2061 of this title with respect to an imminently hazardous product, the owner or consignee of the product shall be afforded an opportunity by the Commission for a hearing in accordance with section 554 of Title 5 with respect to the importation of such products into the customs territory of the United States. If it appears from examination of such samples or otherwise that a product must be refused admission under the terms of subsection (a) of this section, such product shall be refused admission, unless subsection (c) of this section applies and is complied with.

(c) Modification

(c) If it appears to the Commission that any consumer product which may be refused admission pursuant to subsection (a) of this section can be so modified that it need not (under the terms of paragraphs (1) through (4) of subsection (a) of this section) be refused admission, the Commission may defer final determination as to the admission of such product and, in accordance with such regulations as the Commission and the Secretary of the Treasury shall jointly agree to, permit such product to be delivered from customs custody under bond for the purpose of permitting the owner or consignee an opportunity to so modify such product.

(d) Supervision of modifications

(d) All actions taken by an owner or consignee to modify such product under subsection (c) of this section shall be subject to the supervision of an officer or employee of the Commission and of the Department of the Treasury. If it appears to the Commission that the product cannot be so modified or that the owner or consignee is not proceeding satisfactorily to modify such product, it shall be refused admission into the customs territory of the United States, and the Commission may direct the Secretary to demand redelivery of the product into customs custody, and to seize the product in accordance with section 2071(b) of this title if it is not so redelivered.

(e) Product destruction

(e) Products refused admission into the customs territory of the United States under this section must be exported, except that upon application, the Secretary of the Treasury may permit the destruction of the product in lieu of exportation. If the owner or consignee does not export the product within a reasonable time, the Department of the Treasury may destroy the product.

(f) Payment of expenses occasioned by refusal of admission

(f) All expenses (including travel, per diem or subsistence, and salaries of officers or employees of the United States) in connection with the destruction provided for in this section (the amount of such expenses to be determined in accordance with regulations of the Secretary of the Treasury) and all expenses in connection with the storage, cartage, or labor with respect to any consumer product refused admission under this section, shall be paid by the owner or consignee and, in default of such payment, shall constitute a lien against any future importations made by such owner or consignee.

(g) Importation conditioned upon manufacturer's compliance

(g) The Commission may, by rule, condition the importation of a consumer product on the manufacturer's compliance with the inspection and recordkeeping requirements of this chapter and the Commission's rules with respect to such requirements.

Pub.L. 92–573, § 17, Oct. 27, 1972, 86 Stat. 1223.

§ 2067. Exemption of exports

(a) Risk of injury to consumers within United States

(a) This chapter shall not apply to any consumer product if (1) it can be shown that such product is manufactured, sold, or held for sale for export from the United States (or that such product was imported for export), unless (A) such consumer product is in fact distributed in commerce for use in the United States, or (B) the Commission determines that exportation of such product presents an unreasonable risk of injury to consumers within the United States, and (2) such consumer product when distributed in commerce, or any container in which it is enclosed when so distributed, bears a stamp or label stating that such consumer product is intended for export; except that this chapter shall apply to any consumer product manufactured for sale, offered for sale, or sold for shipment to any installation of the United States located outside of the United States.

(b) Statement of exportation: filing period, information; notification of foreign country; petition for minimum filing period: good cause

(b) Not less than thirty days before any person exports to a foreign country any product—

>   (1) which is not in conformity with an applicable consumer product safety standard in effect under this chapter, or

>   (2) which is declared to be a banned hazardous substance by a rule promulgated under section 2058 of this title,

such person shall file a statement with the Commission notifying the Commission of such exportation, and the Commission, upon receipt of such statement, shall promptly notify the government of such country of such exportation and the basis for such safety standard or rule. Any statement filed with the Commission under the preceding sentence shall specify the anticipated date of shipment of such product, the country and port of destination of such product, and the quantity of such product that will be exported, and shall contain such other information as the Commission may by regulation require. Upon petition filed with the Commission by any person required to file a statement under this subsection respecting an exportation, the Commission may, for good cause shown, exempt such person from the requirement of this subsection that such a statement be filed no less than thirty days before the date of the exportation, except that in no case shall the Commission permit such a statement to be filed later than the tenth day before such date.

As amended Pub.L. 95–631, § 6(a), Nov. 10, 1978, 92 Stat. 3745.

§ 2068. Prohibited acts

(a) It shall be unlawful for any person to—

(1) manufacture for sale, offer for sale, distribute in commerce, or import into the United States any consumer product which is not in conformity with an applicable consumer product safety standard under this chapter;

(2) manufacture for sale, offer for sale, distribute in commerce, or import into the United States any consumer product which has been declared a banned hazardous product by a rule under this chapter;

(3) fail or refuse to permit access to or copying of records, or fail or refuse to establish or maintain records, or fail or refuse to make reports or provide information, or fail or refuse to permit entry or inspection, as required under this chapter or rule thereunder;

(4) fail to furnish information required by section 2064(b) of this title;

(5) fail to comply with an order issued under section 2064(c) or (d) of this title (relating to notification, to repair, replacement, and refund, and to prohibited acts);

(6) fail to furnish a certificate required by section 2063 of this title or issue a false certificate if such person in the exercise of due care has reason to know that such certificate is false or misleading in any material respect; or to fail to comply with any rule under section 2063(c) of this title (relating to labeling);

(7) fail to comply with any rule under section 2058(g)(2) of this title (relating to stockpiling); or

(8) fail to comply with any rule under section 2076(e) of this title (relating to provision of performance and technical data); and

(9) fail to comply with any rule or requirement under section 2082 of this title (relating to labeling and testing of cellulose insulation).

(10) fail to file a statement with the Commission pursuant to section 2067(b) of this title.

(b) Paragraphs (1) and (2) of subsection (a) of this section shall not apply to any person (1) who holds a certificate issued in accordance with section 2063(a) of this title to the effect that such consumer product conforms to all applicable consumer product safety rules, unless such person knows that such consumer product does not conform, or (2) who relies in good faith on the representation of the manufacturer or a distributor of such product that the product is not subject to an applicable product safety rule.

As amended Pub.L. 97–414, § 9(j)(4), Jan. 4, 1983, 96 Stat. 2064.

§ 2069. Civil penalties

(a) Amount of penalty

(a)(1) Any person who knowingly violates section 2068 of this title shall be subject to a civil penalty not to exceed $2,000 for each such violation. Subject to paragraph (2), a violation of section 2068(a)(1), (2), (4), (5), (6), (7), (8), (9), or (10) of this title shall constitute a separate offense with respect to each consumer product involved, except that the maximum civil penalty shall not exceed $500,000 for any related series of violations. A violation of section 2068(a)(3) of this title shall constitute a separate violation with respect to each failure or refusal to allow or perform an act required thereby; and, if such violation is a continuing one, each day of such violation shall constitute a separate offense, except that the maximum civil penalty shall not exceed $500,000 for any related series of violations.

(2) The second sentence of paragraph (1) of this subsection shall not apply to violations of paragraph (1) or (2) of section 2068(a) of this title—

(A) if the person who violated such paragraphs is not the manufacturer or private labeler or a distributor of the products involved, and

(B) if such person did not have either (i) actual knowledge that his distribution or sale of the product violated such paragraphs or (ii) notice from the Commission that such distribution or sale would be a violation of such paragraphs.

(b) Relevant factors in assessment of penalty

(b) In determining the amount of any penalty to be sought upon commencing an action seeking to assess a penalty for a violation of section 2068(a) of this title, the Commission shall consider the nature of the product defect, the severity of the risk of injury, the occurrence or absence of injury, the number of defective products distributed, and the appropriateness of such penalty in relation to the size of the business of the person charged.

(c) Compromise of penalty; deductions from penalty

(c) Any civil penalty under this section may be compromised by the Commission. In determining the amount of such penalty or whether it should be remitted or mitigated and in what amount, the Commission shall consider the appropriateness of such penalty to the size of the business of the person charged, the nature of the product defect, the severity of the risk of injury, the occurrence or absence of injury, and the number of defective products distributed. The amount of such penalty when finally determined, or the amount agreed on compromise, may be deducted from any sums owing by the United States to the person charged.

(d) "Knowingly" defined

(d) As used in the first sentence of subsection (a)(1) of this section, the term "knowingly" means (1) the having of actual knowledge, or (2) the presumed having of knowledge deemed to be possessed by a reasonable man who acts in the circumstances, including knowledge obtainable upon the exercise of due care to ascertain the truth of representations.

As amended Pub.L. 94–284, § 13(b), May 11, 1976, 90 Stat. 509; Pub.L. 95–631, § 6(c), Nov. 10, 1978, 92 Stat. 3745; Pub.L. 97–35, Title XII, § 1211(c), Aug. 13, 1981, 95 Stat. 721.

§ 2070. Criminal penalties

(a) Any person who knowingly and willfully violates section 2068 of this title after having received notice of noncompliance from the Commission shall be fined not more than $50,000 or be imprisoned not more than one year, or both.

(b) Any individual director, officer, or agent of a corporation who knowingly and willfully authorizes, orders, or performs any of the acts or practices constituting in whole or in part a violation of section 2068 of this title, and who has knowledge of notice of noncompliance received by the corporation from the Commission, shall be subject to penalties under this section without regard to any penalties to which that corporation may be subject under subsection (a) of this section.

Pub.L. 92–573, § 21, Oct. 27, 1972, 86 Stat. 1225.

§ 2071. Injunctive enforcement and seizure

(a) The United States district courts shall have jurisdiction to take the following action:

(1) Restrain any violation of section 2068 of this title.

(2) Restrain any person from manufacturing for sale, offering for sale, distributing in commerce, or importing into the United States a product in violation of an order in effect under section 2064(d) of this title.

(3) Restrain any person from distributing in commerce a product which does not comply with a consumer product safety rule.

Such actions may be brought by the Commission (without regard to section 2076(b)(7)(A) of this title) or by the Attorney General in any United States district court for a district wherein any act, omission, or transaction constituting the violation occurred, or in such court for the district wherein the defendant is found or transacts business. In any action under this section process may be served on a defendant in any other district in which the defendant resides or may be found.

(b) Any consumer product—

(1) which fails to conform with an applicable consumer product safety rule, or

(2) the manufacture for sale, offering for sale, distribution in commerce, or the importation into the United States of which has been prohibited by an order in effect under section 2064(d) of this title,

when introduced into or while in commerce or while held for sale after shipment in commerce shall be liable to be proceeded against on libel of information and condemned in any district court of the United States within the jurisdiction of which such consumer product is found. Proceedings in cases instituted under the authority of this subsection shall conform as nearly as possible to proceedings in rem in admiralty. Whenever such proceedings involving substantially similar consumer products are pending in courts of two or more judicial districts they shall be consolidated for trial by order of any such court upon application reasonably made by any party in interest upon notice to all other parties in interest.

As amended Pub.L. 94–284, §§ 11(b), 12(c), May 11, 1976, 90 Stat. 507, 508.

§ 2072. Suits for damages

(a) Persons injured; costs; amount in controversy

(a) Any person who shall sustain injury by reason of any knowing (including willful) violation of a consumer product safety rule, or any other rule or order issued by the Commission may sue any person who knowingly (including willfully) violated any such rule or order in any district court of the United States in the district in which the defendant resides or is found or has an agent, shall recover damages sustained,

§ 2072   CONSUMER PRODUCT SAFETY ACT

and may, if the court determines it to be in the interest of justice, recover the costs of suit, including reasonable attorneys' fees (determined in accordance with section 2060(f) of this title) and reasonable expert witnesses' fees: Provided, That the matter in controversy exceeds the sum or value of $10,000, exclusive of interest and costs, unless such action is brought against the United States, any agency thereof, or any officer or employee thereof in his official capacity.

(b) Denial and imposition of costs

(b) Except when express provision is made in a statute of the United States, in any case in which the plaintiff is finally adjudged to be entitled to recover less than the sum or value of $10,000, computed without regard to any setoff or counterclaim to which the defendant may be adjudged to be entitled, and exclusive of interests and costs, the district court may deny costs to the plaintiff and, in addition, may impose costs on the plaintiff.

(c) Remedies available

(c) The remedies provided for in this section shall be in addition to and not in lieu of any other remedies provided by common law or under Federal or State law.

As amended Pub.L. 94–284, § 10(c), May 11, 1976, 90 Stat. 507; Pub.L. 96–486, § 3, Dec. 1, 1980, 94 Stat. 2369; Pub.L. 97–35, Title XII, § 1211(h)(3)(B), Aug. 13, 1981, 95 Stat. 723.

§ 2073. Private enforcement

Any interested person (including any individual or nonprofit, business, or other entity) may bring an action in any United States district court for the district in which the defendant is found or transacts business to enforce a consumer product safety rule or an order under section 2064 of this title, and to obtain appropriate injunctive relief. Not less than thirty days prior to the commencement of such action, such interested person shall give notice by registered mail to the Commission, to the Attorney General, and to the person against whom such action is directed. Such notice shall state the nature of the alleged violation of any such standard or order, the relief to be requested, and the court in which the action will be brought. No separate suit shall be brought under this section if at the time the suit is brought the same alleged violation is the subject of a pending civil or criminal action by the United States under this chapter. In any action under this section the court may in the interest of justice award the costs of suit, including reasonable attorneys' fees (determined in accordance with section 2060(f) of this title) and reasonable expert witnesses' fees.

As amended Pub.L. 94–284, § 10(d), May 11, 1976, 90 Stat. 507; Pub.L. 97–35, Title XII, § 1211(a), (h)(3)(C), Aug. 13, 1981, 95 Stat. 721, 723.

§ 2074. Private remedies

(a) Liability at common law or under State statute not relieved by compliance

(a) Compliance with consumer product safety rules or other rules or orders under this chapter shall not relieve any person from liability at common law or under State statutory law to any other person.

(b) Evidence of Commission's inaction inadmissible in actions relating to consumer products

(b) The failure of the Commission to take any action or commence a proceeding with respect to the safety of a consumer product shall not be admissible in evidence in litigation at common law or under State statutory law relating to such consumer product.

(c) Public information

(c) Subject to sections 2055(a)(2) and 2055(b) of this title but notwithstanding section 2055(a)(1) of this title, (1) any accident or investigation report made under this chapter by an officer or employee of the Commission shall be made available to the public in a manner which will not identify any injured person or any person treating him, without the consent of the person so identified, and (2) all reports on research projects, demonstration projects, and other related activities shall be public information.

Pub.L. 92–573, § 25, Oct. 27, 1972, 86 Stat. 1227.

§ 2075. State standards

(a) State compliance to Federal standards

(a) Whenever a consumer product safety standard under this chapter is in effect and applies to a risk of injury associated with a consumer product, no State or political subdivision of a State shall have any authority either to establish or to continue in effect any provision of a safety standard or regulation which prescribes any requirements as to the performance, composition, contents, design, finish, construction, packaging, or labeling of such product which are designed to deal with the same risk of injury associated with such consumer product, unless such requirements are identical to the requirements of the Federal standard.

(b) Consumer product safety requirements which impose performance standards more stringent than Federal standards

(b) Subsection (a) of this section does not prevent the Federal Government or the government of any State or political subdivision of a State from establishing or continuing in effect a safety requirement applicable to a consumer product for its own use which requirement is designed to protect against a risk of injury associated with the product and which is not identical to the consumer product safety standard applicable to the product under this chapter if the Federal, State, or political subdivision requirement provides a higher degree of protection from such risk of injury than the standard applicable under this chapter.

(c) Exemptions

(c) Upon application of a State or political subdivision of a State, the Commission may by rule, after notice and opportunity for oral presentation of views, exempt from the provisions of subsection (a) of this section (under such conditions as it may impose in the rule) any proposed safety standard or regulation which is described in such application and which is designed to protect against a risk of injury associated with a consumer product subject to a consumer product safety standard under this chapter if the State or political subdivision standard or regulation—

(1) provides a significantly higher degree of protection from such risk of injury than the consumer product safety standard under this chapter, and

(2) does not unduly burden interstate commerce.

In determining the burden, if any, of a State or political subdivision standard or regulation on interstate commerce, the Commission shall consider and make appropriate (as determined by the Commission in its discretion) findings on the technological and economic feasibility of complying with such standard or regulation, the cost of complying with such standard or regulation, the geographic distribution of the consumer product to which the standard or regulation would apply, the probability of other States or political subdivisions applying for an exemption under this subsection for a similar standard or regulation, and the need for a national, uniform standard under this chapter for such consumer product.

As amended Pub.L. 94–284, § 17(d), May 11, 1976, 90 Stat. 514.

§ 2076. Additional functions of Consumer Product Safety Commission

(a) Authority to conduct hearings or other inquiries

(a) The Commission may, by one or more of its members or by such agents or agency as it may designate, conduct any hearing or other inquiry necessary or appropriate to its functions anywhere in the United States. A Commissioner who participates in such a hearing or other inquiry shall not be disqualified solely by reason of such participation from subsequently participating in a decision of the Commission in the same matter. The Commission shall publish notice of any proposed hearing in the Federal Register and shall afford a reasonable opportunity for interested persons to present relevant testimony and data.

(b) Commission powers; orders

(b) The commission shall also have the power—

(1) to require, by special or general orders, any person to submit in writing such reports and answers to questions as the Commission may prescribe to carry out a specific regulatory or enforcement function of the Commission; and such submission shall be made within such reasonable period and under oath or otherwise as the Commission may determine;

(2) to administer oaths;

(3) to require by subpena the attendance and testimony of witnesses and the production of all documentary evidence relating to the execution of its duties;

(4) in any proceeding or investigation to order testimony to be taken by deposition before any person who is designated by the Commission and has the power to administer oaths and, in such instances, to compel testimony and the production of evidence in the same manner as authorized under paragraph (3) of this subsection;

(5) to pay witnesses the same fees and mileage as are paid in like circumstances in the courts of the United States;

(6) to accept gifts and voluntary and uncompensated services, notwithstanding the provisions of section 1342 of Title 31;

(7) to—

(A) initiate, prosecute, defend, or appeal (other than to the Supreme Court of the United States), through its own legal representative and in the name of the Commission, any civil action if the Commission makes a written request to the Attorney General for representation in such civil action and the Attorney General does not within the 45-day period beginning on the date such request was made notify the Commission in writing that the Attorney General will represent the Commission in such civil action, and

(B) initiate, prosecute, or appeal, through its own legal representative, with the concurrence of the Attorney General or through the Attorney General, any criminal action,

for the purpose of enforcing the laws subject to its jurisdiction;

(8) to lease buildings or parts of buildings in the District of Columbia, without regard to the Act of March 3, 1877 (section 34 of Title 40), for the use of the Commission; and

(9) to delegate any of its functions or powers, other than the power to issue subpenas under paragraph (3), to any officer or employee of the Commission.

An order issued under paragraph (1) shall contain a complete statement of the reason the Commission requires the report or answers specified in the order to carry out a specific regulatory or enforcement function of the Commission. Such an order shall be designed to place the least burden on the person subject to the order as is practicable taking into account the purpose for which the order was issued.

(c) Noncompliance with subpena or Commission order; contempt

(c) Any United States district court within the jurisdiction of which any inquiry is carried on, may, upon petition by the Commission (subject to subsection (b)(7) of this section) or by the Attorney General, in case of refusal to obey a subpena or order of the Commission issued under subsection (b) of this section, issue an order requiring compliance therewith; and any failure to obey the order of the court may be punished by the court as a contempt thereof.

(d) Disclosure of information

(d) No person shall be subject to civil liability to any person (other than the Commission or the United States) for disclosing information at the request of the Commission.

(e) Performance and technical data

(e) The Commission may by rule require any manufacturer of consumer products to provide to the Commission such performance and technical data related to performance and safety as may be required to carry out the purposes of this chapter, and to give such notification of such performance and technical data at the time of original purchase to prospective purchasers and to the first purchaser of such product for purposes other than resale, as it determines necessary to carry out the purposes of this chapter.

(f) Purchase of consumer products by Commission

(f) For purposes of carrying out this chapter, the Commission may purchase any consumer product and it may require any manufacturer, distributor, or retailer of a consumer product to sell the product to the Commission at manufacturer's, distributor's, or retailer's cost.

(g) Contract authority

(g) The Commission is authorized to enter into contracts with governmental entities, private organizations, or individuals for the conduct of activities authorized by this chapter.

(h) Research, development, and testing facilities

(h) The Commission may plan, construct, and operate a facility or facilities suitable for research, development, and testing of consumer products in order to carry out this chapter.

(i) Recordkeeping; audit

(i)(1) Each recipient of assistance under this chapter pursuant to grants or contracts entered into under other than competitive bidding procedures shall keep such records as the Commission by rule shall prescribe, including records which fully disclose the amount and disposition by such recipient of the proceeds of such assistance, the total cost of the project undertaken in connection with which such assistance is given or used, and the amount of that portion of the cost of the project or undertaking supplied by other sources, and such other records as will facilitate an effective audit.

(2) The Commission and the Comptroller General of the United States, or their duly authorized representatives, shall have access for the purpose of audit and examination to any books, documents, papers, and records of the recipients that are pertinent to the grants or contracts entered into under this chapter under other than competitive bidding procedures.

(j) Report to President and Congress

(j) The Commission shall prepare and submit to the President and the Congress at the beginning of each regular session of Congress a comprehensive report on the administration of this chapter for the preceding fiscal year. Such report shall include—

(1) a thorough appraisal, including statistical analyses, estimates, and long-term projections, of the incidence of injury and effects to the population resulting from consumer products, with a breakdown, insofar as practicable, among the various sources of such injury;

(2) a list of consumer product safety rules prescribed or in effect during such year;

(3) an evaluation of the degree of observance of consumer product safety rules, including a list of enforcement actions, court decisions, and compromises of alleged violations, by location and company name;

(4) a summary of outstanding problems confronting the administration of this chapter in order of priority;

(5) an analysis and evaluation of public and private consumer product safety research activities;

(6) a list, with a brief statement of the issues, of completed or pending judicial actions under this chapter;

(7) the extent to which technical information was disseminated to the scientific and commercial communities and consumer information was made available to the public;

(8) the extent of cooperation between Commission officials and representatives of industry and other interested parties in the implementation of this chapter, including a log or summary of meetings held between Commission officials and representatives of industry and other interested parties;

(9) an appraisal of significant actions of State and local governments relating to the responsibilities of the Commission;

(10) with respect to voluntary consumer product safety standards for which the Commission has participated in the development through monitoring or offering of assistance and with respect to voluntary consumer product safety standards relating to risks of injury that are the subject of regulatory action by the Commission, a description of—

   (A) the number of such standards adopted;

   (B) the nature and number of the products which are the subject of such standards;

(C) the effectiveness of such standards in reducing potential harm from consumer products;

(D) the degree to which staff members of the Commission participate in the development of such standards;

(E) the amount of resources of the Commission devoted to encouraging development of such standards; and

(F) such other information as the Commission determines appropriate or necessary to inform the Congress on the current status of the voluntary consumer product safety standard program; and

(11) such recommendations for additional legislation as the Commission deems necessary to carry out the purposes of this chapter.

(k) Budget estimates and requests; legislative recommendations; testimony; comments on legislation

(k)(1) Whenever the Commission submits any budget estimate or request to the President or the Office of Management and Budget, it shall concurrently transmit a copy of that estimate or request to the Congress.

(2) Whenever the Commission submits any legislative recommendations, or testimony, or comments on legislation to the President or the Office of Management and Budget, it shall concurrently transmit a copy thereof to the Congress. No officer or agency of the United States shall have any authority to require the Commission to submit its legislative recommendations, or testimony, or comments on legislation, to any officer or agency of the United States for approval, comments, or review, prior to the submission of such recommendations, testimony, or comments to the Congress.

Pub.L. 94–273, § 31, Apr. 21, 1976, 90 Stat. 380; Pub.L. 94–284, §§ 8(b), 11(c), (d), 14, May 11, 1976, 90 Stat. 506–509; Pub.L. 95–631, § 11, Nov. 10, 1978, 92 Stat. 3748; Pub.L. 97–35, Title XII, §§ 1207(b), 1208, 1209(c), 1211(d), Aug. 13, 1981, 95 Stat. 718, 720, 721, Pub.L. 97–258, § 4(b), Sept. 13, 1982, 96 Stat. 1067.

§ 2077. Chronic Hazard Advisory Panels

(a) Appointment; purposes

(a) The Commission shall appoint Chronic Hazard Advisory Panels (hereinafter referred to as the Panel or Panels) to advise the Commission in accordance with the provisions of section 2080(b) of this title respecting the chronic hazards of cancer, birth defects, and gene mutations associated with consumer products.

(b) Composition; membership

(b) Each Panel shall consist of 7 members appointed by the Commission from a list of nominees who shall be nominated by the President of the National Academy of Sciences from scientists—

(1) who are not officers or employees of the United States, and who do not receive compensation from or have any substantial financial interest in any manufacturer, distributor, or retailer of a consumer product; and

(2) who have demonstrated the ability to critically assess chronic hazards and risks to human health presented by the exposure of humans to toxic substances or as demonstrated by the exposure of animals to such substances.

The President of the National Academy of Sciences shall nominate for each Panel a number of individuals equal to three times the number of members to be appointed to the Panel.

(c) Chairman and Vice Chairman; election; term

(c) The Chairman and Vice Chairman of the Panel shall be elected from among the members and shall serve for the duration of the Panel.

(d) Majority vote

(d) Decisions of the Panel shall be made by a majority of the Panel.

(e) Administrative support services

(e) The Commission shall provide each Panel with such administrative support services as it may require to carry out its duties under section 2080 of this title.

(f) Compensation

(f) A member of a Panel appointed under subsection (a) of this section shall be paid at a rate not to exceed the daily equivalent of the annual rate of basic pay in effect for grade GS–18 of the General Schedule for each day (including traveltime) during which the member is engaged in the actual performance of the duties of the Panel.

(g) Requests for and disclosures of information

(g) Each Panel shall request information and disclose information to the public, as provided in subsection (h) of this section, only through the Commission.

(h) Information from other Federal departments and agencies

(h)(1) Notwithstanding any statutory restriction on the authority of agencies and departments of the Federal Government to share information, such agencies and departments shall provide the Panel with such information and data as each Panel, through the Commission, may request to carry out its duties under section 2080 of this title. Each Panel may request information, through the Commission, from States, industry and other private sources as it may require to carry out its responsibilities.

(2) Section 2055 of this title shall apply to the disclosure of information by the Panel but shall not apply to the disclosure of information to the Panel.

Pub.L. 92-573, § 28, as added Pub.L. 97-35, Title XII, § 1206(a), Aug. 13, 1981, 95 Stat. 716.

§ 2078. Cooperation with States and other Federal agencies

(a) The Commission shall establish a program to promote Federal-State cooperation for the purposes of carrying out this chapter. In implementing such program the Commission may—

(1) accept from any State or local authorities engaged in activities relating to health, safety, or consumer protection assistance in such functions as injury data collection, investigation, and educational programs, as well as other assistance in the administration and enforcement of this chapter which such States or localities may be able and willing to provide and, if so agreed, may pay in advance or otherwise for the reasonable cost of such assistance, and

(2) commission any qualified officer or employee of any State or local agency as an officer of the Commission for the purpose of conducting examinations, investigations, and inspections.

(b) In determining whether such proposed State and local programs are appropriate in implementing the purposes of this chapter, the Commission shall give favorable consideration to programs which establish separate State and local agencies to consolidate functions relating to product safety and other consumer protection activities.

(c) The Commission may obtain from any Federal department or agency such statistics, data, program reports, and other materials as it may deem necessary to carry out its functions under this chapter. Each such department or agency may cooperate with the Commission

§ 2078   CONSUMER PRODUCT SAFETY ACT

and, to the extent permitted by law, furnish such materials to it. The Commission and the heads of other departments and agencies engaged in administering programs related to product safety shall, to the maximum extent practicable, cooperate and consult in order to insure fully coordinated efforts.

(d) The Commission shall, to the maximum extent practicable, utilize the resources and facilities of the National Bureau of Standards, on a reimbursable basis, to perform research and analyses related to risks of injury associated with consumer products (including fire and flammability risks), to develop test methods, to conduct studies and investigations, and to provide technical advice and assistance in connection with the functions of the Commission.

Pub.L. 92–573, § 29, Oct. 27, 1972, 86 Stat. 1230.

(e) The Commission may provide to another Federal agency or a State or local agency or authority engaged in activities relating to health, safety, or consumer protection, copies of any accident or investigation report made under this chapter by any officer, employee, or agent of the Commission only if (1) information which under section 2055(a)(2) of this title is to be considered confidential is not included in any copy of such report which is provided under this subsection; and (2) each Federal agency and State and local agency and authority which is to receive under this subsection a copy of such report provides assurances satisfactory to the Commission that the identity of any injured person and any person who treated an injured person will not, without the consent of the person identified, be included in—

    (A) any copy of any such report, or

    (B) any information contained in any such report,

which the agency or authority makes available to any member of the public. No Federal agency or State or local agency or authority may disclose to the public any information contained in a report received by the agency or authority under this subsection unless with respect to such information the Commission has complied with the applicable requirements of section 2055(b) of this title.

As amended Pub.L. 94–284, § 15, May 11, 1976, 90 Stat. 510.

§ 2079. Transfers of functions

(a) Hazardous substances and poisons

(a) The functions of the Secretary of Health, Education, and Welfare under the Federal Hazardous Substances Act and the Poison Prevention Packaging Act of 1970 are transferred to the Commission. The functions of the Secretary of Health, Education, and Welfare under the Federal Food, Drug, and Cosmetic Act (15 U.S.C. 301 et seq.[1]), to the extent such functions relate to the administration and enforcement of the Poison Prevention Packaging Act of 1970, are transferred to the Commission.

(b) Flammable fabrics

(b) The functions of the Secretary of Health, Education, and Welfare, the Secretary of Commerce, and the Federal Trade Commission under the Flammable Fabrics Act are transferred to the Commission. The functions of the Federal Trade Commission under the Federal Trade Commission Act, to the extent such functions relate to the administration and enforcement of the Flammable Fabrics Act, are transferred to the Commission.

(c) Household refrigerators

(c) The functions of the Secretary of Commerce and the Federal Trade Commission under the Act of August 2, 1956, are transferred to the Commission.

(d) Regulation by Commission of consumer products in accordance with other provisions of law

(d) A risk of injury which is associated with a consumer product and which could be eliminated or reduced to a sufficient extent by action under the Federal Hazardous Substances Act, the Poison Prevention Packaging Act of 1970, or the Flammable Fabrics Act may be regulated under this chapter only if the Commission by rule finds that it is in the public interest to regulate such risk of injury under this chapter. Such a rule shall identify the risk of injury proposed to be regulated under this chapter and shall be promulgated in accordance with section 553 of Title 5; except that the period to be provided by the Commission pursuant to subsection (c) of such section for the submission of data, views, and arguments respecting the rule shall not exceed thirty days from the date of publication pursuant to subsection (b) of such section of a notice respecting the rule.

(e) Transfer of personnel, property, records, etc.; continued application of orders, rules, etc.

(e)(1)(A) All personnel, property, records, obligations, and commitments, which are used primarily with respect to any function transferred under the provisions of subsections (a), (b) and (c) of this section

---

1. So in original. Probably should be "21 U.S.C. 301 et seq.".

shall be transferred to the Commission, except those associated with fire and flammability research in the National Bureau of Standards. The transfer of personnel pursuant to this paragraph shall be without reduction in classification or compensation for one year after such transfer, except that the Chairman of the Commission shall have full authority to assign personnel during such one-year period in order to efficiently carry out functions transferred to the Commission under this section.

(B) Any commissioned officer of the Public Health Service who upon the day before the effective date of this section, is serving as such officer primarily in the performance of functions transferred by this chapter to the Commission, may, if such officer so elects, acquire competitive status and be transferred to a competitive position in the Commission subject to subparagraph (A) of this paragraph, under the terms prescribed in paragraphs (3) through (8)(A) of section 15(b) of the Clean Air Amendments of 1970.

(2) All orders, determinations, rules, regulations, permits, contracts, certificates, licenses, and privileges (A) which have been issued, made, granted, or allowed to become effective in the exercise of functions which are transferred under this section by any department or agency, any functions of which are transferred by this section, and (B) which are in effect at the time this section takes effect, shall continue in effect according to their terms until modified, terminated, superseded, set aside, or repealed by the Commission, by any court of competent jurisdiction, or by operation of law.

(3) The provisions of this section shall not affect any proceedings pending at the time this section takes effect before any department or agency, functions of which are transferred by this section; except that such proceedings, to the extent that they relate to functions so transferred, shall be continued before the Commission. Orders shall be issued in such proceedings, appeals shall be taken therefrom, and payments shall be made pursuant to such orders, as if this section had not been enacted; and orders issued in any such proceedings shall continue in effect until modified, terminated, superseded, or repealed by the Commission, by a court of competent jurisdiction, or by operation of law.

(4) The provisions of this section shall not affect suits commenced prior to the date this section takes effect and in all such suits proceedings shall be had, appeals taken, and judgments rendered, in the same manner and effect as if this section had not been enacted; except that if before the date on which this section takes effect, any department or agency (or officer thereof in his official capacity) is a party to a suit involving functions transferred to the Commission, then such suit shall be continued by the Commission. No cause of action, and no suit, action, or other proceeding, by or against any department or agency (or

officer thereof in his official capacity) functions of which are transferred by this section, shall abate by reason of the enactment of this section. Causes of actions, suits, actions, or other proceedings may be asserted by or against the United States or the Commission as may be appropriate and, in any litigation pending when this section takes effect, the court may at any time, on its own motion or that of any party, enter an order which will give effect of the provisions of this paragraph.

(f) Definition of "function"

(f) For purposes of this section, (1) the term "function" includes power and duty, and (2) the transfer of a function, under any provision of law, of an agency or the head of a department shall also be a transfer of all functions under such law which are exercised by any office or officer of such agency or department.

As amended Pub.L. 94-284, §§ 3(f), 16, May 11, 1976, 90 Stat. 504, 510.

§ 2080. Limitations on Jurisdiction of Consumer Product Safety Commission

(a) Authority to regulate

(a) The Commission shall have no authority under this chapter to regulate any risk of injury associated with a consumer product if such risk could be eliminated or reduced to a sufficient extent by actions taken under the Occupational Safety and Health Act of 1970; the Atomic Energy Act of 1954; or the Clean Air Act. The Commission shall have no authority under this chapter to regulate any risk of injury associated with electronic product radiation emitted from an electronic product (as such terms are defined by sections 355(1) and (2) of the Public Health Service Act) if such risk of injury may be subjected to regulation under subpart 3 of part F of title III of the Public Health Service Act.

(b) Certain notices of proposed rulemaking; duties of Chronic Hazard Advisory Panel

(1) The Commission may not issue—

(A) an advance notice of proposed rulemaking for a consumer product safety rule,

(B) a notice of proposed rulemaking for a rule under section 2076(e) of this title, or

(C) an advance notice of proposed rulemaking for regulations under section 1261(q)(1) of this title, relating to a risk of cancer, birth defects, or gene mutations from a consumer product unless a Chronic Hazard Advisory Panel, established under section 2077 of this title, has, in accordance with paragraph (2), submitted a report to the Commission with respect to whether a substance contained in such product is a carcinogen, mutagen, or teratogen.

(2)(A) Before the Commission issues an advance notice of proposed rulemaking for—

(i) a consumer product safety rule,

(ii) a rule under section 2076(e) of this title, or

(iii) a regulation under section 1261(q)(1) of this title,

relating to a risk of cancer, birth defects, or gene mutations from a consumer product, the Commission shall request the Panel to review the scientific data and other relevant information relating to such risk to determine if any substance in the product is a carcinogen, mutagen, or a teratogen and to report its determination to the Commission.

(B) When the Commission appoints a Panel, the Panel shall convene within 30 days after the date the final appointment is made to the Panel. The Panel shall report its determination to the Commission not later than 120 days after the date the Panel is convened or, if the Panel requests additional time, within a time period specified by the Commission. If the determination reported to the Commission states that a substance in a product is a carcinogen, mutagen, or a teratogen, the Panel shall include in its report an estimate, if such an estimate is feasible, of the probable harm to human health that will result from exposure to the substance.

(C) A Panel appointed under section 2077 of this title shall terminate when it has submitted its report unless the Commission extends the existence of the Panel.

(D) The Federal Advisory Committee Act shall not apply with respect to any Panel established under this section.

(c) Panel report; incorporation into advance notice and final rule

(c) Each Panel's report shall contain a complete statement of the basis for the Panel's determination. The Commission shall consider the report of the Panel and incorporate such report into the advance notice of proposed rulemaking and final rule.

Pub.L. 97–35, Title XII, § 1206(b), Aug. 13, 1981, 95 Stat. 717, Pub.L. 97–414, § 9(j)(5), Jan. 4, 1983, 96 Stat. 2064.

§ 2081. Authorization of appropriations

(a) There are authorized to be appropriated for the purposes of carrying out the provisions of this chapter (other than the provisions of section 2076(h) of this title which authorize the planning and construction of research, development, and testing facilities) and for the purpose of carrying out the functions, powers, and duties transferred to the Commission under section 2079 of this title, not to exceed—

(1) $51,000,000 for the fiscal year ending June 30, 1976;

(2) $14,000,000 for the period beginning July 1, 1976, and ending September 30, 1976;

(3) $60,000,000 for the fiscal year ending September 30, 1977;

(4) $68,000,000 for the fiscal year ending September 30, 1978; and [1]

(5) $55,000,000 for the fiscal year ending September 30, 1979;

(6) $60,000,000 for the fiscal year ending September 30, 1980;

(7) $65,000,000 for the fiscal year ending September 30, 1981;

(8) $33,000,000 for the fiscal year ending September 30, 1982; and

(9) $35,000,000 for the fiscal year ending September 30, 1983.

For payment of accumulated and accrued leave under section 5551 of Title 5 severance pay under section 5595 under such title, and any other expense related to a reduction in force in the Commission, there are authorized to be appropriated such sums as may be necessary.

(b)(1) There are authorized to be appropriated such sums as may be necessary for the planning and construction of research, development and testing facilities described in section 2076(h) of this title; except that no appropriation shall be made for any such planning or construction involving an expenditure in excess of $100,000 if such planning or construction has not been approved by resolutions adopted in substantially the same form by the Committee on Energy and Commerce of the House of Representatives, and by the Committee on Commerce, Science, and Transportation of the Senate. For the purpose of securing consideration of such approval the Commission shall transmit to Congress a prospectus of the proposed facility including (but not limited to)—

(A) a brief description of the facility to be planned or constructed;

(B) the location of the facility, and an estimate of the maximum cost of the facility;

(C) a statement of those agencies, private and public, which will use such facility, together with the contribution to be made by each such agency toward the cost of such facility; and

(D) a statement of justification of the need for such facility.

---

1. So in original. The word "and" probably should not appear.

§ 2081   CONSUMER PRODUCT SAFETY ACT

(2) The estimated maximum cost of any facility approved under this subsection as set forth in the prospectus may be increased by the amount equal to the percentage increase, if any, as determined by the Commission, in construction costs, from the date of the transmittal of such prospectus to Congress, but in no event shall the increase authorized by this paragraph exceed 10 per centum of such estimated maximum cost.

(c) No funds appropriated under subsection (a) of this section may be used to pay any claim described in section 2053(h) of this title whether pursuant to a judgment of a court or under any award, compromise, or settlement of such claim made under section 2672 of Title 28, or under any other provision of law.

As amended Pub.L. 94–284, §§ 2, 5(b), May 11, 1976, 90 Stat. 503, 505; S.Res. 4, Feb. 4, 1977; Pub.L. 95–631, § 1, Nov. 10, 1978, 92 Stat. 3742; H.Res. 459, Mar. 25, 1980; Pub.L. 97–35, Title XII, § 1214, Aug. 13, 1981, 95 Stat. 724.

§ 2082. Interim cellulose insulation safety standard

(a) Applicability of specification of General Services Administration; authority and effect of interim standard; modifications; criteria; labeling requirements

(a)(1) Subject to the provisions of paragraph (2), on and after the last day of the 60-day period beginning on the effective date of this section, the requirements for flame resistance and corrosiveness set forth in the General Services Administration's specification for cellulose insulation, HH–I–515C (as such specification was in effect on February 1, 1978), shall be deemed to be an interim consumer product safety standard which shall have all the authority and effect of any other consumer product safety standard promulgated by the Commission under this chapter. During the 45-day period beginning on the effective date of this section, the Commission may make, and shall publish in the Federal Register, such technical, nonsubstantive changes in such requirements as it deems appropriate to make such requirements suitable for promulgation as a consumer product safety standard. At the end of the 60-day period specified in the first sentence of this paragraph, the Commission shall publish in the Federal Register such interim consumer product safety standard, as altered by the Commission under this paragraph.

(2) The interim consumer product safety standard established in paragraph (1) shall provide that any cellulose insulation which is produced or distributed for sale or use as a consumer product shall have a flame spread rating of 0 to 25, as such rating is set forth in the General Services Administration's specification for cellulose insulation, HH–I–515C.

(3) During the period for which the interim consumer product safety standard established in subsection (a) of this section is in effect, in addition to complying with any labeling requirement established by the Commission under this chapter, each manufacturer or private labeler of cellulose insulation shall include the following statement on any container of such cellulose insulation: "ATTENTION: This material meets the applicable minimum Federal flammability standard. This standard is based upon laboratory tests only, which do not represent actual conditions which may occur in the home". Such statement shall be located in a conspicuous place on such container and shall appear in conspicuous and legible type in contrast by typography, layout, and color with other printed matter on such container.

(b) Scope of judicial review

(b) Judicial review of the interim consumer product safety standard established in subsection (a) of this section, as such standard is in effect on and after the last day of the 60–day period specified in such subsection, shall be limited solely to the issue of whether any changes made by the Commission under paragraph (1) are technical, nonsubstantive changes. For purposes of such review, any change made by the Commission under paragraph (1) which requires that any test to determine the flame spread rating of cellulose insulation shall include a correction for variations in test results caused by equipment used in the test shall be considered a technical, nonsubstantive change.

(c) Enforcement; violations; promulgation of final standard; procedures applicable to promulgation; revision of interim standard; procedures applicable to revision

(c)(1)(A) Any interim consumer product safety standard established pursuant to this section shall be enforced in the same manner as any other consumer product safety standard until such time as there is in effect a final consumer product safety standard promulgated by the Commission, as provided in subparagraph (B), or until such time as it is revoked by the Commission under section 2058(e) of this title. A violation of the interim consumer product safety standard shall be deemed to be a violation of a consumer product safety standard promulgated by the Commission under section 2058 of this title.

(B) If the Commission determines that the interim consumer product safety standard does not adequately protect the public from the unreasonable risk of injury associated with flammable or corrosive cellulose insulation, it shall promulgate a final consumer product safety standard to protect against such risk. Such final standard shall be promulgated pursuant to section 553 of Title 5, except that the Commission shall give interested persons an opportunity for the oral presentation of data, views, or arguments, in addition to an opportunity to make written submissions. A transcript shall be kept of any oral presentation. The provisions of section 2058(b), (c), and (d) of this title shall apply to any proceeding to promulgate such final standard. In any judicial review of such final standard under section 2060 of this title, the court shall not require any demonstration that each particular finding made by the Commission under section 2058(c) of this title is supported by substantial evidence. The court shall affirm the action of the Commission unless the court determines that such action is not supported by substantial evidence on the record taken as a whole.

(2)(A) Until there is in effect such a final consumer product safety standard, the Commission shall incorporate into the interim consumer product safety standard, in accordance with the provisions of this paragraph, each revision superseding the requirements for flame resistance and corrosiveness referred to in subsection (a) of this section and promulgated by the General Services Administration.

(B) At least 45 days before any revision superseding such requirements is to become effective, the Administrator of the General Services Administration shall notify the Commission of such revision. In the case of any such revision which becomes effective during the period beginning on February 1, 1978, and ending on the effective date of this section, such notice from the Administrator of the General Services Administration shall be deemed to have been made on the effective date of this section.

(C)(i) No later than 45 days after receiving any notice under subparagraph (B), the Commission shall publish the revision, including such changes in the revision as it considers appropriate to make the revision suitable for promulgation as an amendment to the interim consumer product safety standard, in the Federal Register as a proposed amendment to the interim consumer product safety standard.

(ii) The Commission may extend the 45-day period specified in clause (i) for an additional period of not more than 150 days if the Commission determines that such extension is necessary to study the technical and scientific basis for the revision involved, or to study the safety and economic consequences of such revision.

(D)(i) Additional extensions of the 45-day period specified in subparagraph (C)(i) may be taken by the Commission if—

(I) the Commission makes the determination required in subparagraph (C)(ii) with respect to each such extension; and

(II) in the case of further extensions proposed by the Commission after an initial extension under this clause, such further extensions have not been disapproved under clause (iv).

(ii) Any extension made by the Commission under this subparagraph shall be for a period of not more than 45 days.

(iii) Prior notice of each extension made by the Commission under this subparagraph, together with a statement of the reasons for such extension and an estimate of the length of time required by the Commission to complete its action upon the revision involved, shall be published in the Federal Register and shall be submitted to the Committee on Commerce, Science, and Transportation of the Senate and the Committee on Interstate and Foreign Commerce of the House of Representatives.

(iv) In any case in which the Commission takes an initial 45-day extension under clause (i), the Commission may not take any further extensions under clause (i) if each committee referred to in clause (iii) disapproves by committee resolution any such further extensions before the end of the 15-day period following notice of such initial extension made by the Commission in accordance with clause (iii).

(E) The Commission shall give interested persons an opportunity to comment upon any proposed amendment to the interim consumer product safety standard during the 30-day period following any publication by the Commission under subparagraph (C).

(F) No later than 90 days after the end of the period specified in subparagraph (E), the Commission shall promulgate the amendment to the interim consumer product safety standard unless the Commission determines, after consultation with the Secretary of Energy, that—

(i) such amendment is not necessary for the protection of consumers from the unreasonable risk of injury associated with flammable or corrosive cellulose insulation; or

(ii) implementation of such amendment will create an undue burden upon persons who are subject to the interim consumer product safety standard.

(G) The provisions of section 2060 of this title shall not apply to any judicial review of any amendment to the interim product safety standard promulgated under this paragraph.

(d) Reporting requirements of other Federal departments, agencies, etc. of violations

(d) Any Federal department, agency, or instrumentality, or any Federal independent regulatory agency, which obtains information which reasonably indicates that cellulose insulation is being manufactured or distributed in violation of this chapter shall immediately inform the Commission of such information.

(e) Reporting requirements of Commission to Congressional committees; contents, time of submission, etc.

(e)(1) The Commission, no later than 45 days after the effective date of this section, shall submit a report to the Committee on Commerce, Science, and Transportation of the Senate and to the Committee on Interstate and Foreign Commerce of the House of Representatives which shall contain a detailed statement of the manner in which the Commission intends to carry out the enforcement of this section.

(2)(A) The Commission, no later than 6 months after the date upon which the report required in paragraph (1) is due (and no later than the end of each 6-month period thereafter), shall submit a report to each committee referred to in paragraph (1) which shall describe the enforcement activities of the Commission with respect to this section during the most recent 6-month period.

(B) The first report which the Commission submits under subparagraph (A) shall include the results of tests of cellulose insulation manufactured by at least 25 manufacturers which the Commission shall conduct to determine whether such cellulose insulation complies with the interim consumer product safety standard. The second such report shall include the results of such tests with respect to 50 manufacturers who were not included in testing conducted by the Commission for inclusion in the first report.

(f) Compliance with certification requirements; implementation; waiver; rules and regulations

(f)(1) The Commission shall have the authority to require that any person required to comply with the certification requirements of section 2063 of this title with respect to the manufacture of cellulose insulation shall provide for the performance of any test or testing program required for such certification through the use of an independent third party qualified to perform such test or testing program. The Commission may impose such requirement whether or not the Commission has established a testing program for cellulose insulation under section 2063(b) of this title.

(2) The Commission, upon petition by a manufacturer, may waive the requirements of paragraph (1) with respect to such manufacturer if the Commission determines that the use of an independent third party is not necessary in order for such manufacturer to comply with the certification requirements of section 2063 of this title.

(3) The Commission may prescribe such rules as it considers necessary to carry out the provisions of this subsection.

(g) Authorization of appropriations

(g) There are authorized to be appropriated, for each of the fiscal years 1978, 1979, 1980, and 1981, such sums as may be necessary to carry out the provisions of this section.

Pub.L. 92–573, § 35, as added Pub.L. 95–319, § 3(a), July 11, 1978, 92 Stat. 386.

§ 2083. Congressional veto of consumer product safety rules

(a) Transmission to Congress

(a) The Commission shall transmit to the Secretary of the Senate and the Clerk of the House of Representatives a copy of any consumer product safety rule promulgated by the Commission under section 2058 of this title.

(b) Disapproval by concurrent resolution

(b) Any rule specified in subsection (a) of this section shall not take effect if—

(1) within the 90 calendar days of continuous session of the Congress which occur after the date of the promulgation of such rule, both Houses of the Congress adopt a concurrent resolution, the matter after the resolving clause of which is as follows (with the blank spaces appropriately filled): "That the Congress disapproves the consumer product safety rule which was promulgated by the Consumer Product Safety Commission with respect to _____ and which was transmitted to the Congress on _____ and disapproves the rule for the following reasons: _____."; or

(2) within the 60 calendar days of continuous session of the Congress which occur after the date of the promulgation of such rule, one House of the Congress adopts such concurrent resolution and transmits such resolution to the other House and such resolution is not disapproved by such other House within the 30 calendar days of continuous session of the Congress which occur after the date of such transmittal.

(c) Presumptions from Congressional action or inaction

(c) Congressional inaction on, or rejection of, a concurrent resolution of disapproval under this section shall not be construed as an expression of approval of the rule involved, and shall not be construed to create any presumption of validity with respect to such rule.

(d) Continuous session of Congress

(d) For purposes of this section—

(1) continuity of session is broken only by an adjournment of the Congress sine die; and

(2) the days on which either House is not in session because of an adjournment of more than 3 days to a day certain are excluded in the computation of the periods of continuous session of the Congress specified in subsection (b) of this section.

Pub.L. 92–573, § 36, as added Pub.L. 97–35, Title XII, § 1207(a), Aug. 13, 1981, 95 Stat. 718.

MAGNUSON–MOSS WARRANTY ACT

Act of January 4, 1975, Public Law 93–637, 88 Stat. 2183–93; 15 U.S.C.A. §§ 2301–12

Enacted as Title I of "Magnuson–Moss Warranty— Federal Trade Commission Improvement Act"

Sec.
2301. Definitions.
2302. Rules governing contents of warranties.
    (a) Full and conspicuous disclosure of terms and conditions; additional requirements for contents.
    (b) Availability of terms to consumer; manner and form for presentation and display of information; duration; extension of period for written warranty or service contract.
    (c) Prohibition on conditions for written or implied warranty; waiver by Commission.
    (d) Incorporation by reference of detailed substantive warranty provisions.
    (e) Applicability to consumer products costing more than $5.00.
2303. Designation of written warranties.
    (a) Full (statement of duration) or limited warranty.
    (b) Applicability of requirements, standards, etc., to representations or statements of customer satisfaction.
    (c) Exemptions by Commission.
    (d) Applicability to consumer products costing more than $10.00 and not designated as full warranties.
2304. Federal minimum standards for warranties.
    (a) Remedies under written warranty; duration of implied warranty; exclusion or limitation on consequential damages for breach of written or implied warranty; election of refund or replacement.
    (b) Duties and conditions imposed on consumer by warrantor.
    (c) Waiver of standards.
    (d) Remedy without charge.
    (e) Incorporation of standards to products designated with full warranty for purposes of judicial actions.
2305. Full and limited warranting of a consumer product.
2306. Service contracts; rules for full, clear and conspicuous disclosure of terms and conditions; addition to or in lieu of written warranty.
2307. Designation of representatives by warrantor to perform duties under written or implied warranty.
2308. Implied warranties.
    (a) Restrictions on disclaimers or modifications.
    (b) Limitation on duration.
    (c) Effective of disclaimers, modifications, or limitations.
2309. Procedures applicable to promulgation of rules by Commission; rulemaking proceeding for warranty and warranty practices involved in sale of used motor vehicles.

Sec.
2310. Remedies in consumer disputes.
    (a) Informal dispute settlement procedures; establishment; rules setting forth minimum requirements; effect of compliance by warrantor; review of informal procedures or implementation by Commission; application to existing informal procedures.
    (b) Prohibited acts.
    (c) Injunction proceedings by Attorney General or Commission for deceptive warranty, noncompliance with requirements, or violating prohibitions; procedures; definitions.
    (d) Civil action by consumer for damages, etc.; jurisdiction; recovery of costs and expenses; cognizable claims.
    (e) Class actions; conditions; procedures applicable.
    (f) Warrantors subject to enforcement of remedies.
2311. Applicability of provisions to other Federal or State laws and requirements.
2312. Effective dates; time for promulgation of rules by Commission.

Code of Federal Regulations

Rules, Regulations, Statements and Interpretations under the Magnuson–Moss Warranty Act, see 16 CFR 701.1 et seq.

§ 2301. Definitions

For the purposes of this chapter:

(1) The term "consumer product" means any tangible personal property which is distributed in commerce and which is normally used for personal, family, or household purposes (including any such property intended to be attached to or installed in any real property without regard to whether it is so attached or installed).

(2) The term "Commission" means the Federal Trade Commission.

(3) The term "consumer" means a buyer (other than for purposes of resale) of any consumer product, any person to whom such product is transferred during the duration of an implied or written warranty (or service contract) applicable to the product, and any other person who is entitled by the terms of such warranty (or service contract) or under applicable State law to enforce against the warrantor (or service contractor) the obligations of the (warranty or service contract).

(4) The term "supplier" means any person engaged in the business of making a consumer product directly or indirectly available to consumers.

(5) The term "warrantor" means any supplier or other person who gives or offers to give a written warranty or who is or may be obligated under an implied warranty.

(6) The term "written warranty" means—

    (A) any written affirmation of fact or written promise made in connection with the sale of a consumer product by a supplier to a buyer which relates to the nature of the material or workmanship and affirms or promises that such material or workmanship is defect free or will meet a specified level of performance over a specified period of time, or

(B) any undertaking in writing in connection with the sale by a supplier of a consumer product to refund, repair, replace, or take other remedial action with respect to such product in the event that such product fails to meet the specifications set forth in the undertaking.

which written affirmation, promise, or undertaking becomes part of the basis of the bargain between a supplier and a buyer for purposes other than resale of such product.

(7) The term "implied warranty" means an implied warranty arising under State law (as modified by sections 2308 and 2304(a) of this title) in connection with the sale by a supplier of a consumer product.

(8) The term "service contract" means a contract in writing to perform, over a fixed period of time or for a specified duration, services relating to the maintenance or repair (or both) of a consumer product.

(9) The term "reasonable and necessary maintenance" consists of those operations (A) which the consumer reasonably can be expected to perform or have performed and (B) which are necessary to keep any consumer product performing its intended function and operating at a reasonable level of performance.

(10) The term "remedy" means whichever of the following actions the warrantor elects:

(A) repair,

(B) replacement, or

(C) refund;

except that the warrantor may not elect refund unless (i) the warrantor is unable to provide replacement and repair is not commercially practicable or cannot be timely made, or (ii) the consumer is willing to accept such refund.

(11) The term "replacement" means furnishing a new consumer product which is identical or reasonably equivalent to the warranted consumer product.

(12) The term "refund" means refunding the actual purchase price (less reasonable depreciation based on actual use where permitted by rules of the Commission).

(13) The term "distributed in commerce" means sold in commerce, introduced or delivered for introduction into commerce, or held for sale or distribution after introduction into commerce.

(14) The term "commerce" means trade, traffic, commerce, or transportation—

(A) between a place in a State and any place outside thereof, or

(B) which affects trade, traffic, commerce, or transportation described in subparagraph (A).

(15) The term "State" means a State, the District of Columbia, the Commonwealth of Puerto Rico, the Virgin Islands, Guam, the Canal Zone, or American Samoa. The term "State law" includes a law of the United States applicable only to the District of Columbia or only to a territory or possession of the United States; and the term "Federal law" excludes any State law.

Pub.L. 93–637, Title I, § 101, Jan. 4, 1975, 88 Stat. 2183.

§ 2302. Rules governing contents of warranties

(a) Full and conspicuous disclosure of terms and conditions; additional requirements for contents

(a) In order to improve the adequacy of information available to consumers, prevent deception, and improve competition in the marketing of consumer products any warrantor warranting a consumer product to a consumer by means of a written warranty shall, to the extent required by rules of the Commission, fully and conspicuously disclose in simple and readily understood language the terms and conditions of such warranty. Such rules may require inclusion in the written warranty of any of the following items among others:

(1) The clear identification of the names and addresses of the warrantors.

(2) The identity of the party or parties to whom the warranty is extended.

(3) The products or parts covered.

(4) A statement of what the warrantor will do in the event of a defect, malfunction, or failure to conform with such written warranty—at whose expense—and for what period of time.

(5) A statement of what the consumer must do and expenses he must bear.

(6) Exceptions and exclusions from the terms of the warranty.

(7) The step-by-step procedure which the consumer should take in order to obtain performance of any obligation under the warran-

ty, including the identification of any person or class of persons authorized to perform the obligation set forth in the warranty.

(8) Information respecting the availability of any informal dispute settlement procedure offered by the warrantor and a recital, where the warranty so provides, that the purchaser may be required to resort to such procedure before pursuing any legal remedies in the courts.

(9) A brief, general description of the legal remedies available to the consumer.

(10) The time at which the warrantor will perform any obligations under the warranty.

(11) The period of time within which, after notice of a defect, malfunction, or failure to conform with the warranty, the warrantor will perform any obligations under the warranty.

(12) The characteristics or properties of the products, or parts thereof, that are not covered by the warranty.

(13) The elements of the warranty in words or phrases which would not mislead a reasonable, average consumer as to the nature or scope of the warranty.

(b) Availability of terms to consumer; manner and form for presentation and display of information; duration; extension of period for written warranty or service contract

(b)(1)(A) The Commission shall prescribe rules requiring that the terms of any written warranty on a consumer product be made available to the consumer (or prospective consumer) prior to the sale of the product to him.

(B) The Commission may prescribe rules for determining the manner and form in which information with respect to any written warranty of a consumer product shall be clearly and conspicuously presented or displayed so as not to mislead the reasonable, average consumer, when such information is contained in advertising, labeling, point-of-sale material, or other representations in writing.

(2) Nothing in this chapter (other than paragraph (3) of this subsection) shall be deemed to authorize the Commission to prescribe the duration of written warranties given or to require that a consumer product or any of its components be warranted.

(3) The Commission may prescribe rules for extending the period of time a written warranty or service contract is in effect to correspond with any period of time in excess of a reasonable period (not less than 10 days) during which the consumer is deprived of the use of such consumer product by reason of failure of the product to conform with the written warranty or by reason of the failure of the warrantor (or

(c) Prohibition on conditions for written or implied warranty; waiver by Commission

(c) No warrantor of a consumer product may condition his written or implied warranty of such product on the consumer's using, in connection with such product, any article or service (other than article or service provided without charge under the terms of the warranty) which is identified by brand, trade, or corporate name; except that the prohibition of this subsection may be waived by the Commission if—

(1) the warrantor satisfies the Commission that the warranted product will function properly only if the article or service so identified is used in connection with the warranted product, and

(2) the Commission finds that such a waiver is in the public interest.

The Commission shall identify in the Federal Register, and permit public comment on, all applications for waiver of the prohibition of this subsection, and shall publish in the Federal Register its disposition of any such application, including the reasons therefor.

(d) Incorporation by reference of detailed substantive warranty provisions

(d) The Commission may by rule devise detailed substantive warranty provisions which warrantors may incorporate by reference in their warranties.

(e) Applicability to consumer products costing more than $5.00

(e) The provisions of this section apply only to warranties which pertain to consumer products actually costing the consumer more than $5.

Pub.L. 93–637, Title I, § 102, Jan. 4, 1975, 88 Stat. 2185.

§ 2303. Designation of written warranties

(a) Full (statement of duration) or limited warranty

(a) Any warrantor warranting a consumer product by means of a written warranty shall clearly and conspicuously designate such warranty in the following manner, unless exempted from doing so by the Commission pursuant to subsection (c) of this section:

(1) If the written warranty meets the Federal minimum standards for warranty set forth in section 2304 of this title, then it

shall be conspicuously designated a "full (statement of duration) warranty".

(2) If the written warranty does not meet the Federal minimum standards for warranty set forth in section 2304 of this title, then it shall be conspicuously designated a "limited warranty".

(b) Applicability of requirements, standards, etc., to representations or statements of customer satisfaction

(b) This section and sections 2302 and 2304 of this title shall not apply to statements or representations which are similar to expressions of general policy concerning customer satisfaction and which are not subject to any specific limitations.

(c) Exemptions by Commission

(c) In addition to exercising the authority pertaining to disclosure granted in section 2302 of this title, the Commission may by rule determine when a written warranty does not have to be designated either "full (statement of duration)" or "limited" in accordance with this section.

(d) Applicability to consumer products costing more than $10.00 and not designated as full warranties

(d) The provisions of subsections (a) and (c) of this section apply only to warranties which pertain to consumer products actually costing the consumer more than $10 and which are not designated "full (statement of duration) warranties".

Pub.L. 93-637, Title I, § 103, Jan. 4, 1975, 88 Stat. 2187.

§ 2304. Federal minimum standards for warranties

(a) Remedies under written warranty; duration of implied warranty; exclusion or limitation on consequential damages for breach of written or implied warranty; election of refund or replacement

(a) In order for a warrantor warranting a consumer product by means of a written warranty to meet the Federal minimum standards for warranty—

(1) such warrantor must as a minimum remedy such consumer product within a reasonable time and without charge, in the case of a defect, malfunction, or failure to conform with such written warranty;

(2) notwithstanding section 2308(b) of this title, such warrantor may not impose any limitation on the duration of any implied warranty on the product;

(3) such warrantor may not exclude or limit consequential damages for breach of any written or implied warranty on such product, unless such exclusion or limitation conspicuously appears on the face of the warranty; and

(4) if the product (or a component part thereof) contains a defect or malfunction after a reasonable number of attempts by the warrantor to remedy defects or malfunctions in such product, such warrantor must permit the consumer to elect either a refund for, or replacement without charge of, such product or part (as the case may be). The Commission may by rule specify for purposes of this paragraph, what constitutes a reasonable number of attempts to remedy particular kinds of defects or malfunctions under different circumstances. If the warrantor replaces a component part of a consumer product, such replacement shall include installing the part in the product without charge.

(b) Duties and conditions imposed on consumer by warrantor

(b)(1) In fulfilling the duties under subsection (a) of this section respecting a written warranty, the warrantor shall not impose any duty other than notification upon any consumer as a condition of securing remedy of any consumer product which malfunctions, is defective, or does not conform to the written warranty, unless the warrantor has demonstrated in a rulemaking proceeding, or can demonstrate in an administrative or judicial enforcement proceeding (including private enforcement), or in an informal dispute settlement proceeding, that such a duty is reasonable.

(2) Notwithstanding paragraph (1), a warrantor may require, as a condition to replacement of, or refund for, any consumer product under subsection (a) of this section, that such consumer product shall be made available to the warrantor free and clear of liens and other encumbrances, except as otherwise provided by rule or order of the Commission in cases in which such a requirement would not be practicable.

(3) The Commission may, by rule define in detail the duties set forth in subsection (a) of this section and the applicability of such duties to warrantors of different categories of consumer products with "full (statement of duration)" warranties.

(4) The duties under subsection (a) of this section extend from the warrantor to each person who is a consumer with respect to the consumer product.

(c) Waiver of standards

(c) The performance of the duties under subsection (a) of this section shall not be required of the warrantor if he can show that the defect, malfunction, or failure of any warranted consumer product to conform with a written warranty, was caused by damage (not resulting from defect or malfunction) while in the possession of the consumer, or unreasonable use (including failure to provide reasonable and necessary maintenance).

(d) Remedy without charge

(d) For purposes of this section and of section 2302(c) of this title, the term "without charge" means that the warrantor may not assess the consumer for any costs the warrantor or his representatives incur in connection with the required remedy of a warranted consumer product. An obligation under subsection (a)(1)(A) of this section to remedy without charge does not necessarily require the warrantor to compensate the consumer for incidental expenses; however, if any incidental expenses are incurred because the remedy is not made within a reasonable time or because the warrantor imposed an unreasonable duty upon the consumer as a condition of securing remedy, then the consumer shall be entitled to recover reasonable incidental expenses which are so incurred in any action against the warrantor.

(e) Incorporation of standards to products designated with full warranty for purposes of judicial actions

(e) If a supplier designates a warranty applicable to a consumer product as a "full (statement of duration)" warranty, then the warranty on such product shall, for purposes of any action under section 2310(d) of this title or under any State law, be deemed to incorporate at least the minimum requirements of this section and rules prescribed under this section.

Pub.L. 93–637, Title I, § 104, Jan. 4, 1975, 88 Stat. 2187.

§ 2305. Full and limited warranting of a consumer product

Nothing in this chapter shall prohibit the selling of a consumer product which has both full and limited warranties if such warranties are clearly and conspicuously differentiated.

Pub.L. 93–637, Title I, § 105, Jan. 4, 1975, 88 Stat. 2188.

§ 2306. Service contracts; rules for full, clear and conspicuous disclosure of terms and conditions; addition to or in lieu of written warranty

(a) The Commission may prescribe by rule the manner and form in which the terms and conditions of service contracts shall be fully, clearly, and conspicuously disclosed.

(b) Nothing in this chapter shall be construed to prevent a supplier or warrantor from entering into a service contract with the consumer in addition to or in lieu of a written warranty if such contract fully, clearly, and conspicuously discloses its terms and conditions in simple and readily understood language.

Pub.L. 93–637, Title I, § 106, Jan. 4, 1975, 88 Stat. 2188.

§ 2307. Designation of representatives by warrantor to perform duties under written or implied warranty

Nothing in this chapter shall be construed to prevent any warrantor from designating representatives to perform duties under the written or implied warranty: *Provided,* That such warrantor shall make reasonable arrangements for compensation of such designated representatives, but no such designation shall relieve the warrantor of his direct responsibilities to the consumer or make the representative a cowarrantor.

Pub.L. 93–637, Title I, § 107, Jan. 4, 1975, 88 Stat. 2189.

§ 2308. Implied warranties

(a) Restrictions on disclaimers or modifications

(a) No supplier may disclaim or modify (except as provided in subsection (b) of this section) any implied warranty to a consumer with respect to such consumer product if (1) such supplier makes any written warranty to the consumer with respect to such consumer product, or (2) at the time of sale, or within 90 days thereafter, such supplier enters into a service contract with the consumer which applies to such consumer product.

(b) Limitation on duration

(b) For purposes of this chapter (other than section 2304(a)(2) of this title), implied warranties may be limited in duration to the duration of a written warranty of reasonable duration, if such limitation is conscionable and is set forth in clear and unmistakable language and prominently displayed on the face of the warranty.

(c) Effectiveness of disclaimers, modifications, or limitations

(c) A disclaimer, modification, or limitation made in violation of this section shall be ineffective for purposes of this chapter and State law.

Pub.L. 93–637, Title I, § 108, Jan. 4, 1975, 88 Stat. 2189.

§ 2309. Procedures applicable to promulgation of rules by Commission; rulemaking proceeding for warranty and warranty practices involved in sale of used motor vehicles

(a) Any rule prescribed under this chapter shall be prescribed in accordance with section 553 of Title 5; except that the Commission shall give interested persons an opportunity for oral presentations of data, views, and arguments, in addition to written submissions. A transcript shall be kept of any oral presentation. Any such rule shall be subject to judicial review under section 57a(e) of this title in the same manner as rules prescribed under section 57a(a)(1)(B) of this title, except that section 57a(e)(3)(B) of this title shall not apply.

(b) The Commission shall initiate within one year after January 4, 1975, a rulemaking proceeding dealing with warranties and warranty practices in connection with the sale of used motor vehicles; and, to the extent necessary to supplement the protections offered the consumer by this chapter, shall prescribe rules dealing with such warranties and practices. In prescribing rules under this subsection, the Commission may exercise any authority it may have under this chapter, or other law, and in addition it may require disclosure that a used motor vehicle is sold without any warranty and specify the form and content of such disclosure.

Pub.L. 93–637, Title I, § 109, Jan. 4, 1975, 88 Stat. 2189.

§ 2310. Remedies in consumer disputes

(a) Informal dispute settlement procedures; establishment; rules setting forth minimum requirements; effect of compliance by warrantor; review of informal procedures or implementation by Commission; application to existing informal procedures

(a)(1) Congress hereby declares it to be its policy to encourage warrantors to establish procedures whereby consumer disputes are fairly and expeditiously settled through informal dispute settlement mechanisms.

(2) The Commission shall prescribe rules setting forth minimum requirements for any informal dispute settlement procedure which is incorporated into the terms of a written warranty to which any provi-

§ 2310   MAGNUSON–MOSS WARRANTY ACT

sion of this chapter applies. Such rules shall provide for participation in such procedure by independent or governmental entities.

(3) One or more warrantors may establish an informal dispute settlement procedure which meets the requirements of the Commission's rules under paragraph (2). If—

(A) a warrantor establishes such a procedure,

(B) such procedure, and its implementation, meets the requirements of such rules, and

(C) he incorporates in a written warranty a requirement that the consumer resort to such procedure before pursuing any legal remedy under this section respecting such warranty,

then (i) the consumer may not commence a civil action (other than a class action) under subsection (d) of this section unless he initially resorts to such procedure; and (ii) a class of consumers may not proceed in a class action under subsection (d) of this section except to the extent the court determines necessary to establish the representative capacity of the named plaintiffs, unless the named plaintiffs (upon notifying the defendant that they are named plaintiffs in a class action with respect to a warranty obligation) initially resort to such procedure. In the case of such a class action which is brought in a district court of the United States, the representative capacity of the named plaintiffs shall be established in the application of rule 23 of the Federal Rules of Civil Procedure. In any civil action arising out of a warranty obligation and relating to a matter considered in such a procedure, any decision in such procedure shall be admissible in evidence.

(4) The Commission on its own initiative may, or upon written complaint filed by any interested person shall, review the bona fide operation of any dispute settlement procedure resort to which is stated in a written warranty to be a prerequisite to pursuing a legal remedy under this section. If the Commission finds that such procedure or its implementation fails to comply with the requirements of the rules under paragraph (2), the Commission may take appropriate remedial action under any authority it may have under this chapter or any other provision of law.

(5) Until rules under paragraph (2) take effect, this subsection shall not affect the validity of any informal dispute settlement procedure respecting consumer warranties, but in any action under subsection (d) of this section, the court may invalidate any such procedure if it finds that such procedure is unfair.

(b) Prohibited acts

(b) It shall be a violation of section 45(a)(1) of this title for any person to fail to comply with any requirement imposed on such person by this chapter (or a rule thereunder) or to violate any prohibition contained in this chapter (or a rule thereunder).

(c) Injunction proceedings by Attorney General or Commission for deceptive warranty, noncompliance with requirements, or violating prohibitions; procedures; definitions

(c)(1) The district courts of the United States shall have jurisdiction of any action brought by the Attorney General (in his capacity as such), or by the Commission by any of its attorneys designated by it for such purpose, to restrain (A) any warrantor from making a deceptive warranty with respect to a consumer product, or (B) any person from failing to comply with any requirement imposed on such person by or pursuant to this chapter or from violating any prohibition contained in this chapter. Upon proper showing that, weighing the equities and considering the Commission's or Attorney General's likelihood of ultimate success, such action would be in the public interest and after notice to the defendant, a temporary restraining order or preliminary injunction may be granted without bond. In the case of an action brought by the Commission, if a complaint under section 45 of Title 15 is not filed within such period (not exceeding 10 days) as may be specified by the court after the issuance of the temporary restraining order or preliminary injunction, the order or injunction shall be dissolved by the court and be of no further force and effect. Any suit shall be brought in the district in which such person resides or transacts business. Whenever it appears to the court that the ends of justice require that other persons should be parties in the action, the court may cause them to be summoned whether or not they reside in the district in which the court is held, and to that end process may be served in any district.

(2) For the purposes of this subsection, the term "deceptive warranty" means (A) a written warranty which (i) contains an affirmation, promise, deception, or representation which is either false or fraudulent, or which, in light of all the circumstances, would mislead a reasonable individual exercising due care; or (ii) fails to contain information which is necessary in light of all of the circumstances, to make the warranty not misleading to a reasonable individual exercising due care; or (B) a written warranty created by the use of such terms as "guaranty" or "warranty", if the terms and conditions of such warranty so limit its scope and application as to deceive a reasonable individual.

(d) Civil action by consumer for damages, etc.; jurisdiction; recovery of costs and expenses; cognizable claims

(d)(1) Subject to subsections (a)(3) and (e) of this section, a consumer who is damaged by the failure of a supplier, warrantor, or service contractor to comply with any obligation under this chapter, or under a written warranty, implied warranty, or service contract, may bring suit for damages and other legal and equitable relief—

    (A) in any court of competent jurisdiction in any State or the District of Columbia; or

    (B) in an appropriate district court of the United States, subject to paragraph (3) of this subsection.

(2) If a consumer finally prevails in any action brought under paragraph (1) of this subsection, he may be allowed by the court to recover as part of the judgment a sum equal to the aggregate amount of cost and expenses (including attorneys' fees based on actual time expended) determined by the court to have been reasonably incurred by the plaintiff for or in connection with the commencement and prosecution of such action, unless the court in its discretion shall determine that such an award of attorneys' fees would be inappropriate.

(3) No claim shall be cognizable in a suit brought under paragraph (1)(B) of this subsection—

    (A) if the amount in controversy of any individual claim is less than the sum or value of $25;

    (B) if the amount in controversy is less than the sum or value of $50,000 (exclusive of interests and costs) computed on the basis of all claims to be determined in this suit; or

    (C) if the action is brought as a class action, and the number of named plaintiffs is less than one hundred.

(e) Class actions; conditions; procedures applicable

(e) No action (other than a class action or an action respecting a warranty to which subsection (a)(3) of this section applies) may be brought under subsection (d) of this section for failure to comply with any obligation under any written or implied warranty or service contract, and a class of consumers may not proceed in a class action under such subsection with respect to such a failure except to the extent the court determines necessary to establish the representative capacity of the named plaintiffs, unless the person obligated under the warranty or service contract is afforded a reasonable opportunity to cure such failure to comply. In the case of such a class action (other than a class action respecting a warranty to which subsection (a)(3) of this section applies) brought under subsection (d) of this section for breach of any written or implied warranty or service contract, such reasonable opportunity will be afforded by the named plaintiffs and they shall at that time notify the defendant that they are acting on behalf of the class. In the case of such a class action which is brought in a district court of the United States, the representative capacity of the named plaintiffs shall be established in the application of rule 23 of the Federal Rules of Civil Procedure.

(f) Warrantors subject to enforcement of remedies

(f) For purposes of this section, only the warrantor actually making a written affirmation of fact, promise, or undertaking shall be deemed to have created a written warranty, and any rights arising thereunder may be enforced under this section only against such warrantor and no other person.

Pub.L. 93–637, Title I, § 110, Jan. 4, 1975, 88 Stat. 2189.

§ 2311. Applicability of provisions to other Federal or State laws and requirements

(a)(1) Nothing contained in this chapter shall be construed to repeal, invalidate, or supersede the Federal Trade Commission Act or any statute defined therein as an Antitrust Act.

(2) Nothing in this chapter shall be construed to repeal, invalidate, or supersede the Federal Seed Act and nothing in this chapter shall apply to seed for planting.

(b)(1) Nothing in this chapter shall invalidate or restrict any right or remedy of any consumer under State law or any other Federal law.

(2) Nothing in this chapter (other than sections 2304(a)(2) and (4) and 2308 of this title) shall (A) affect the liability of, or impose liability on, any person for personal injury, or (B) supersede any provision of State law regarding consequential damages for injury to the person or other injury.

(c)(1) Except as provided in subsection (b) of this section and in paragraph (2) of this subsection, a State requirement—

(A) which relates to labeling or disclosure with respect to written warranties or performance thereunder;

(B) which is within the scope of an applicable requirement of sections 2302, 2303, and 2304 of this title (and rules implementing such sections), and

(C) which is not identical to a requirement of section 2302, 2303, or 2304 of this title (or a rule thereunder),

shall not be applicable to written warranties complying with such sections (or rules thereunder).

(2) If, upon application of an appropriate State agency, the Commission determines (pursuant to rules issued in accordance with section 2309 of this title) that any requirement of such State covering any transaction to which this chapter applies (A) affords protection to consumers greater than the requirements of this chapter and (B) does

not unduly burden interstate commerce, then such State requirement shall be applicable (notwithstanding the provisions of paragraph (1) of this subsection) to the extent specified in such determination for so long as the State administers and enforces effectively any such greater requirement.

(d) This chapter (other than section 2302(c) of this title) shall be inapplicable to any written warranty the making or content of which is otherwise governed by Federal law. If only a portion of a written warranty is so governed by Federal law, the remaining portion shall be subject to this chapter.

Pub.L. 93–637, Title I, § 111, Jan. 4, 1975, 88 Stat. 2192.

§ 2312. Effective dates; time for promulgation of rules by Commission

(a) Except as provided in subsection (b) of this section, this chapter shall take effect 6 months after January 4, 1975, but shall not apply to consumer products manufactured prior to such date.

(b) Section 2302(a) of this title shall take effect 6 months after the final publication of rules respecting such section; except that the Commission, for good cause shown, may postpone the applicability of such sections until one year after such final publication in order to permit any designated classes of suppliers to bring their written warranties into compliance with rules promulgated pursuant to this chapter.

(c) The Commission shall promulgate rules for initial implementation of this chapter as soon as possible after January 4, 1975, but in no event later than one year after such date.

Pub.L. 93–637, Title I, § 112, Jan. 4, 1975, 88 Stat. 2192.

MODEL UNIFORM PRODUCT LIABILITY ACT

Outline: Uniform Product Liability Act

Introduction.
Preamble.
Sec.
100. Short Title.
101. Findings.
102. Definitions.
   (A) Product Seller.
   (B) Manufacturer.
   (C) Product.
   (D) Product Liability Claim.
   (E) Claimant.
   (F) Harm.
   (G) Reasonably Anticipated Conduct.
   (H) Preponderance of the Evidence.
   (I) Clear and Convincing Evidence.
   (J) Reckless Disregard.
   (K) Express Warranty.
103. Scope of This Act.
104. Basic Standards of Responsibility for Manufacturers.
   (A) Unsafe in Construction.
   (B) Unsafe in Design.
   (C) Warnings or Instructions.
   (D) Express Warranty.
105. Basic Standards of Responsibility for Product Sellers Other Than Manufacturers.
106. Unavoidably Dangerous Aspects of Products.
107. Relevance of Industry Custom, Safety or Performance Standards, and Practical Technological Feasibility.
108. Relevance of Legislative or Administrative Regulatory Standards and Mandatory Government Contract Specifications.
109. Notice of Possible Claim Required.
110. Length of Time Product Sellers Are Subject to Liability.
   (A) Useful Safe Life.
   (B) Statute of Repose.

Sec.
   (C) Statute of Limitation.
111. Comparative Responsibility and Apportionment of Damages.
   (A) Comparative Responsibility.
   (B) Apportionment of Damages.
112. Conduct Affecting Comparative Responsibility.
   (A) Failure to Discover a Defective Condition.
   (B) Use of a Product With a Known Defective Condition.
   (C) Misuse of a Product.
   (D) Alteration or Modification of a Product.
113. Multiple Defendants: Contribution and Implied Indemnity.
114. Relationship Between Product Liability and Worker Compensation.
115. Sanctions Against the Bringing of Frivolous Claims and Defenses.
116. Arbitration.
   (A) Applicability.
   (B) Rules Governing.
   (C) Arbitrators.
   (D) Arbitrators' Powers.
   (E) Commencement.
   (F) Evidence.
   (G) Transcript of Proceeding.
   (H) Arbitration Decision and Judgment.
   (I) Trial Following Arbitration.
117. Expert Testimony.
   (A) Appointment of Experts.
   (B) Compensation.
   (C) Disclosure of Appointment.
   (D) Parties' Selection of Own Experts.
   (E) Pre-trial Evaluation of Experts.
118. Non-pecuniary Damages.
119. The Collateral Source Rule.
120. Punitive Damages.

Sec.
121. Severance Clause.
122. Effective Date.

Introduction

The Department of Commerce publishes herein its "Model Uniform Product Liability Act." It is offered for voluntary use by the states.

This Model Law will help to assure that persons injured by unreasonably unsafe products receive reasonable compensation for their injuries. It should also help to stabilize product liability insurance rates.

The Model Law, if enacted by the states, would introduce uniformity and stability into the law of product liability. This, in turn, would help stabilize product liability insurance rates. Uniformity and stability in this area are needed because product liability insurance rates are set on a countrywide basis. Thus, product liability law differs from medical malpractice, automobile, and other standard lines of liability.

The current system of having individual state courts develop product liability law on a case-by-case basis is not consistent with commercial necessity. Product sellers and insurers need uniformity in product liability law so they will know the rules by which they are to be judged. At the same time, product users are entitled to the assurance that their rights will be protected and will not be restricted by "reform" legislation formulated in a crisis atmosphere. Thus, the Model Law meets the needs of product users, sellers, and insurers.

Background of the Act

The Department of Commerce chaired an 18–month interagency study on the topic of product liability and published its final report [1] on November 1, 1977.

The genesis of the "Uniform Product Liability Act" can be traced directly to the Task Force study. The Task Force found that uncertainties in the tort-litigation system were a principal cause of the product liability problem. The "Task Force Report" noted that a few courts had come

> very close to holding that the tort-litigation system should provide a recovery for persons who merely proved that they were injured by a product [and that] while these cases appear to be relatively few in number, insurers have regarded them as quite important in their pricing practices.[2]

The "Task Force Report" called for improvement in insurer ratemaking practices but indicated that even if this were done, "the specter of these cases could still serve as an arguable justification for increasing premiums." [3] Decisions supporting this view continue to appear.

On the basis of the "Task Force Report," representatives

---

1. The "Final Report (cited as the "Task Force Report") of the Federal Interagency Task Force on Product Liability" (cited as the "Task Force").

2. "Task Force Report" at p. I–27.

3. *Id.*

from the Office of Management and Budget and the Domestic Policy Staff of the White House asked Commerce to prepare an options paper regarding what action, if any, the Federal Government should take to address the product liability problem. That paper was published in the **Federal Register** on April 6, 1978. 43 FR 14612 (1978).[4]

One of Commerce's recommendations was that a uniform product liability law be prepared. The overwhelming majority of public comment received in response to the "Options Paper" supported this recommendation.[5]

On July 20, 1978, the Administration announced its program to address the product liability problem. Included in that program as the principal long-range measure was the drafting of a model uniform product liability law.

On January 12, 1979, Commerce's "Draft Uniform Product Liability Law" was published in the **Federal Register** for public comment.[6] The written commentary received by Commerce regarding the Draft Law totals approximately 1500 pages, representing 240 separate communications.[7] The Department also made a special effort to bring the Draft Law to the attention of consumers. Working with its Director of Consumer Affairs and the Office of the Special Assistant to the President for Consumer Affairs, Commerce conducted consumer forums in Washington, D.C., Detroit, Los Angeles, and Atlanta.

In addition to meeting with consumer groups, the drafters of this Act met with representatives of product seller and insurer groups which expressed an interest in the proposal. The Draft Law was also reviewed at hearings before the Subcommittee on Oversight and Minority Enterprises of the House Committee on Small Business, and before the Subcommittee on Consumer Protection and Finance of the House Committee on Interstate and Foreign Commerce.

The final version of the "Uniform Product Liability Act" has benefited substantially from its review by, and input from, the various groups affected by the product liability problem.

Other Sources of the Act

Apart from the public comment, this Act is based on the work products of the Interagency Task Force on Product Liability, including its "Final Report," its "Legal Study," its "Industry Study," and its "Insurance Study."[8] Also, a thorough review

---

4. Public comment on the "Options Paper" was later published in the **Federal Register** on September 11, 1978. 43 FR 40438 (1978).
5. 43 FR 40443.
6. 44 FR 2996.
7. On file, Law Library, U.S. Department of Commerce.

8. The Task Force's reports are available from the National Technical Information Service, Springfield, Virginia 22161 (Attention: Sales Desk). Reference should be made to the appropriate accession number, and a check made payable to NTIS in the proper amount should be enclosed:

was conducted of all major case law and law review literature that had been published since the time of the Task Force's "Legal Study."

As will be apparent from the Act's section-by-section analysis, attention was given to:

(1) The findings of the extensive "Product Liability Closed Claims Survey" conducted by the Insurance Services Office in 1976–77;

(2) All product liability legislation enacted at the state level, plus major proposals introduced in state legislatures in the past two years;

(3) Congressional hearings on product liability and the Report of the House Subcommittee on Capital, Investment and Business Opportunities of the Committee on Small Business. *See* H.R.Report No. 95–997, 95th Cong., 2d Sess. (1978) (Honorable John J. LaFalce, Chairman); and

(4) Privately drafted model product liability legislation.

A bibliography of some of the major resources considered by the Department is set forth in Appendix A.

Criteria for the Act

The criteria [9] utilized in evaluating the provisions of the Model Law were:

Final Report—PB 273–220, $20.00 (1 vol.) (1977).

Selected Papers—PB 278–625, $17.50 (1 vol.) (1978).

Legal Study—PB 263–601, $31.25 (7 vol.) (1977) (The Research Group, Inc.).

Legal Study:

Executive Summary—PB 265–450, $6.00 (first of 7 vol.) (1977).

(1) *To ensure that persons injured by unreasonably unsafe products receive reasonable compensation for their injuries.*

Many proposed alternatives in product liability law are primarily justified by the fact that they contain "cost-saving devices" for product liability insurers or their insureds. However, these projected "cost savings" must be balanced against the responsibility of a product seller to provide reasonable compensation to persons harmed by unreasonably unsafe products. The cost of an accident should be shifted from a claimant to a product seller when there is a logical and articulated rationale for deeming it (as compared with the injured individual or society at large) "responsible" for the claimant's injuries.

(2) *To ensure the availability of affordable product liability insurance with adequate coverage to product sellers that engage in reasonably safe manufacturing practices.*

Product liability law should attempt to create a situation in which affordable product liability insurance is available to manufacturers that follow reasonably safe manufacturing practices. The

Industry Study—PB 265–542, $21.25 (2 vol.) (1977) (Gordon Associates, Inc.).

Insurance Study—PB 263–600, $9.00 (1 vol.) (1977) (McKinsey, Inc.).

9. A more extensive discussion of these criteria appears in the "Task Force Report" at VII–29. The criteria are also set forth in Subsection 103(C) of the Act and are discussed in the corresponding section-by-section analysis.

law should not, however, be modified in order to provide such insurance to manufacturers who are unwilling or unable to follow reasonably safe manufacturing practices.

(3) *To place the incentive for loss prevention on the party or parties who are best able to accomplish that goal.*

Part of the product liability problem has been caused by unsafe manufacturing practices. Obviously, it is in the interest of all groups affected by the product liability problem to reduce the number of accidents caused by products. The Task Force study showed that product liability law can help bring about this goal. The threat of tort liability and product liability judgments has prompted manufacturers to make a greater effort to produce safe products. Nevertheless, existing state product liability law does not always place the incentive for loss prevention on the party or parties who can best achieve that goal.

The decision of where to place the incentive for loss prevention was not an easy one, and at least two factors helped determine the drafters' decision. One was based on pure economics—which party can prevent the loss at lowest cost? Economic analysis of preliminary drafts of this Act were helpful in this consideration.

A second factor focused on the question of who is in the best practical position to prevent a product-related harm. This consideration may be at counterpoint with pure economic analysis. Sometimes a product seller may be in a better practical position to implement a loss prevention technique although a product user could theoretically do so at a lesser cost.

(4) *To expedite the reparations process from the time of injury to the time the claim is paid.*

Delays in the reparations process do not serve any social interest. Seriously injured claimants can ill afford to endure long delays between the time of their injury and the time they are paid. Therefore, the Act has placed emphasis on arbitration and other means that will help expedite the reparations process.

(5) *To minimize the sum of accident costs, prevention costs, and transaction costs.*

The goal of minimizing accident, prevention, and transaction costs, while worthwhile, is not easy to fulfill within the tort-litigation system. For example, one can minimize "transaction costs" by abolishing trial by jury. However, this would be at the expense of other societal values which are particularly important in product liability cases, such as the need for the individualized judgment of cases and the experience of ordinary persons in making those judgments. Nevertheless, this consideration was significant enough to weigh in formulating the Act.

(6) *To use language that is comparatively clear and concise.*

Many product liability proposals that appear sound when stated in a broad and general manner break down when one focuses on the practicality of their implementation. In drafting the Act, practicality, together with conciseness and clarity of language, were important goals. The Act was drafted as a guideline for courts, not as a detailed legal contract between product seller and user.

Other considerations were utilized in the process of formulating each of the provisions. They are highlighted in the section-by-section analysis that accompanies the Act. Again, permeating the discussion of each provision is the concern that it is fair to all groups having an interest in the product liability problem.

It is important to understand the basic philosophy that underlies the Act. Product liability law is a branch of the law of torts. Its function is to shift the cost of an accident from a claimant to a defendant when the latter is deemed "responsible" for the claimant's injuries. This "responsibility" should be defined in terms that everyone can understand. Product liability law should indicate why a particular individual product seller was sufficiently blameworthy that it should bear the cost of that injury.

Tort law is not a compensation system similar to Social Security or Worker Compensation. A product seller should not, through the medium of tort law, be asked to pay merely because its product caused an injury. If a social judgment is made that product sellers are to bear the costs of all injuries caused by their products, it would be far more efficient to make purchasers of products third-party beneficiaries of product sellers' insurance policies as is the case with other compensation systems. Such systems also utilize cost-saving devices such as limiting recovery for lost earnings, eliminating recovery for pain and suffering, and abolishing the collateral source rule. In contrast, product liability law, with its full tort law recovery, reflects the social judgment that liability should be imposed only when it is fair to hold the individual product seller responsible for an injury.

This proposal is offered in the hope that it will stabilize product liability law and benefit product sellers and users alike.

C.L. Haslam,

General Counsel, Department of Commerce.

Victor E. Schwartz,

Chairman, Task Force on Product Liability and Accident Compensation.

Uniform Product Liability Act Code

Preamble

This Act sets forth uniform standards for state product liability tort law. It does not cover all issues that may be litigated in product liability cases; rather, it focuses on those where the need for uniform rules is the greatest. The principal purposes of the Act are to provide a fair balance of the interests of both product users and sellers and to eliminate existing confusion and uncertainty about their respective legal rights and obligations. The fulfillment of these goals should help, first, to assure that persons injured by unreasonably unsafe products will be adequately compensated for their injuries and, second, to make product liability insurance more widely available and affordable, with greater stability in rates and premiums.

* * *

Analysis

Preamble

The importance this Act places on increasing the degree of certainty in the product liability litigation process is tempered by the recognition that, even with nationwide adoption of a uniform code, its application may vary from state to state on some issues. One of the Act's goals, the development of a fair balance of interests, has been achieved by applying the general criteria set forth in Subsection 103(C) of the Act and by revising the first draft of the Act (*see* 44 FR 2996 (1979)) in light of the public comment it generated. A second goal is to promote a greater degree of certainty than exists under the present system. This can be achieved if the Act is adopted by the states in which a substantial majority of product liability claims are brought.

* * *

Code

§ 100. Short Title

This Act shall be known and may be cited as the "Uniform Product Liability Act."

* * *

Analysis

§ 100. Short Title

This is the customary "short title" provision. It may be placed wherever state legislative practice dictates. If a state legislature introduces parts of the "Uniform Product Liability Act" as separate measures, the short title should be adjusted accordingly.

* * *

Code

§ 101. Findings

(A) Sharply rising product liability insurance premiums have created serious problems in commerce resulting in:

(1) Increased prices of consumer and industrial products;

(2) Disincentives for innovation and for the development of high-risk but potentially beneficial products;

(3) An increase in the number of product sellers attempting to do business without product liability insurance coverage, thus jeopardizing both their continued existence and the availability of compensation to injured persons; and

(4) Legislative initiatives enacted in a crisis atmosphere that may, as a result, unreasonably curtail the rights of product liability claimants.

(B) One cause of these problems is that product liability law is fraught with uncertainty and sometimes reflects an imbalanced consideration of the interests it affects. The rules vary from jurisdiction to jurisdiction and are subject to rapid and substantial change. These facts militate against predictability of litigation outcome.

(C) Insurers have cited this uncertainty and imbalance as justifications for setting rates and premiums that, in fact, may not reflect actual product risk or liability losses.

(D) Product liability insurance rates are set on the basis of countrywide, rather than individual state, experience. Insurers utilize countrywide experience because a product manufactured in one state can readily cause injury in any one of the other states, the District of Columbia, or the Commonwealth of Puerto Rico. One ramification of this practice is that there is little an individual state can do to solve the problems caused by product liability.

(E) Uncertainty in product liability law and litigation outcome has added to litigation costs and may put an additional strain on the judicial system.

(F) Recently enacted state product liability legislation has widened existing disparities in the law.

* * *

Analysis

§ 101. Findings

Chapters VI and VII of the "Final Report of the Interagency Task Force on Product Liability" (hereinafter cited as "Task Force Report") provide support for most of the findings made here. Additional support comes from the Report of the Subcommittee on Capital, Investment, and Business Opportunities, "Product Liability Insurance," H.R.Rep. No. 95-997, 95th Cong., 2d Sess. (1978) (Honorable John J. LaFalce, Chairman) (hereinafter cited as "LaFalce Subcommittee Report"). Among other things, the "LaFalce Subcommittee Report" called for clarification and simplification of "present tort law relating to product liability by formulating Federal standards to be adopted by the States...." *Id.* at 76.

Individual state studies on product liability conducted in Missouri (Report of the Senate Select Committee on Product Liability, 1977), Illinois (Judiciary I Subcommittee on Product Liability: Report and Recommendations—Part 1, undated), Georgia (Report of the Senate Products Liability Study Committee, 1978), Maine (Governor's Task Force, 1978), Michigan (Department of Commerce Task Force on Product Liability Insurance, 1978), and Wisconsin (Product Liability: An Overview, Wisconsin Legislative Council Staff, 1978) provide additional support for individual findings.

The Maine and Georgia reports emphasize that individual state tort reforms can do little to affect the product liability problem. This conclusion was reaffirmed in Governor Grasso's message vetoing a product liability tort bill passed by the Connecticut legislature in 1978, and Governor Brown's message vetoing a product liability tort bill passed by the California legislature in 1979. Both messages stressed that uncoordinated, individual state tort action will not stabilize product liability insurance rates.

More specific references to the findings of this Section appear in the following citations keyed to the various findings in each Subsection:

101(A)(1) "Task Force Report" at V-19, VI-27-28.

(2) "Task Force Report" at VI-28-32.

(3) "Task Force Report" at VI-2-26.

(4) "Options Paper on Product Liability and Accident Compensation Issues," 43 FR 14612-14 (1978); "Georgia Report", Appendix B; Johnson, "Products Liability 'Reform': A Hazard to Consumers," 56 "N.C.L.Rev." 677 (1978); Phillips, "A Synopsis of the Developing Law of Products Liability," 28 "Drake L.Rev." 317, 388 (1979); Comment, "State Legislative Restrictions on Product Liability Actions," 29 "Mercer L.Rev." 619 (1978). *See also* "Federal–State Product Liability Legislation for Client and Counsel," Federal–State Reports, Inc. (1977-79).

101(B) "Task Force Report" at I-26-28, VII-15-17; "LaFalce Subcommittee Report" at 72; "Michigan Department of Commerce Task Force on Product Liability Insurance Report" at 6 (1978).

(C) Task Force "Insurance Study" at IV-88 (citing uncertainty); "Task Force Report" at V-48-49 (relationship of premium to risk).

(D) "Task Force Report" at I-28; "Maine Report" at 23.

(E) "Task Force Report" at VII-214-16; *see also* Insurance Services Office, "Product Liability Closed Claims Survey" (hereinafter cited as "ISO Closed Claims Survey") at 118-30 (1977).

(F) *See* "Federal–State Product Liability Legislation for Client and Counsel," Federal–State Reports, Inc. (1977-79); "Product Liability Trends," at 97-98, 104-05, 157-58 (The Research Group, Inc., 1978); "Business Insurance," July 23, 1979 at 31; *see also* "Wisconsin Report" at 29-37 (describing 25 separate bills on product liability introduced in one legislative session).

Code

§ 102. Definitions

(A) *Product Seller.* "Product seller" means any person or entity that is engaged in the business of selling products, whether the sale is for resale, or for use or consumption. The term includes a manufacturer, wholesaler, distributor, or retailer of the relevant product. The term also includes a party who is in the business of leasing or bailing such products.

The term "product seller" does not include:

(1) A seller of real property, unless that person is engaged in the mass production and sale of standardized dwellings or is otherwise a product seller;

(2) A provider of professional services who utilizes or sells products within the legally authorized scope of its professional practice. A nonprofessional provider of services is not included unless the sale or use of a product is the principal part of the transaction, and the essence of the relationship between the seller and purchaser is not the furnishing of judgment, skill, or services;

(3) A commercial seller of used products who resells a product after use by a consumer or other product user, provided the used product is in essentially the same condition as when it was acquired for resale; and

(4) A finance lessor who is not otherwise a product seller. A "finance lessor" is one who acts in a financial capacity, who is not a manufacturer, wholesaler, distributor, or retailer, and who leases a product without having a reasonable opportunity to inspect and discover defects in the product, under a lease arrangement in which the selection, possession, maintenance, and operation of the product are controlled by a person other than the lessor.

(B) *Manufacturer.* "Manufacturer" includes a product seller who designs, produces, makes, fabricates, constructs, or remanufactures the relevant product or component part of a product before its sale to a user or consumer. It includes a product seller or entity not otherwise a manufacturer that holds itself out as a manufacturer.

A product seller acting primarily as a wholesaler, distributor, or retailer of a product may be a "manufacturer" but only to the extent that it designs, produces, makes, fabricates, constructs, or remanufactures the product before its sale.

(C) *Product.* "Product" means any object possessing intrinsic value, capable of delivery either as an assembled whole or as a component part or parts, and produced for introduction into trade or commerce. Human tissue and organs, including human blood and its components, are excluded from this term.

The "relevant product" under this Act is that product, or its component part or parts, which gave rise to the product liability claim.

(D) *Product Liability Claim.* "Product liability claim" includes any claim or action brought for harm caused by the manufacture, production, making, construction, fabrication, design, formula, preparation, assembly, installation, testing, warnings, instructions, marketing, packaging, storage, or labeling of the relevant product. It includes, but is not limited to, any action previously based on: strict liability in tort; negligence; breach of express or implied warranty; breach of, or failure to, discharge a duty to warn or instruct, whether negligent or innocent; misrepresentation, concealment, or nondisclosure, whether negligent or innocent; or under any other substantive legal theory.

(E) *Claimant.* "Claimant" means a person or entity asserting a product liability claim, including a wrongful death action, and, if the claim is asserted through or on behalf of an estate, the term includes claimant's decedent. "Claimant" includes any person or entity that suffers harm.

(F) *Harm.* "Harm" includes: (1) damage to property; (2) personal physical injuries, illness and death; (3) mental anguish or emotional harm attendant to such personal physical injuries, illness or death; and (4) mental anguish or emotional harm caused by the claimant's being placed in direct personal physical danger and manifested by a substantial objective symptom. The term "harm" does not include direct or consequential economic loss.

(G) *Reasonably Anticipated Conduct.* "Reasonably anticipated conduct" means the conduct which would be expected of an ordinary reasonably prudent person who is likely to use the product in the same or similar circumstances.

(H) *Preponderance of the Evidence.* "A preponderance of the evidence" is that measure or degree of proof which, by the weight, credit, and value of the aggregate evidence on either side, establishes that it is more probable than not that a fact occurred or did not occur.

(I) *Clear and Convincing Evidence.* "Clear and convincing evidence" is that measure or degree of proof that will produce in the mind of the trier of fact a firm belief or conviction as to the allegations sought to be established. This level of proof is greater than mere "preponderance of the evidence," but less than proof beyond a reasonable doubt.

(J) *Reckless Disregard.* "Reckless disregard" means a conscious indifference to the safety of persons or entities that might be harmed by a product.

(K) *Express Warranty.* "Express warranty" means any positive statement, affirmation of fact, promise, description, sample, or model relating to the product.

Analysis

§ 102. Definitions

(A) *Product Seller.* "Product seller" includes any party in the regular commercial distribution chain. It does not include the occasional private seller. This is in accord with the "Restatement (Second) of Torts" Section 402A, Comment f (1965). The term also includes lessors (except finance lessors) and bailors of products, in accord with the majority of decisions that have addressed the issue. *See* Annot., 52 "A.L.R.3d" 121 (1973); "Francioni v. Gibsonia Truck Corp.," 472 Pa. 362, 372 A.2d 736 (1977) (finance lessor); Fraser, "Application of Strict Tort Liability to the Leasing Industry," 34 "Bus.Law." 605 (1979).

The Act excludes the seller of real property from its coverage, except for a builder-vendor engaged in the mass production and sale of standardized dwellings, including modular homes. *See* "Schipper v. Levitt & Sons," 44 N.J. 70, 207 A.2d 314 (1965); "Berman v. Watergate West, Inc.," 391 A.2d 1351 (D.C.1978) (extending

§ 102 MODEL UNIFORM PRODUCT LIABILITY ACT

"Schipper" to cooperative apartments); "Fuqua Homes, Inc. v. Evanston Bldg. & Loan Co.," 52 Ohio App.2d 399, 370 N.E.2d 780 (1977) (modular homes). *But see* "Wright v. Creative Corp.," 30 Colo.App. 575, 498 P.2d 1179 (1972) (rejecting "Schipper"). The potential liability of sellers of real property not engaged in such large-scale operations is left to each state's laws governing real property transactions. However, all sellers of building materials, furnishings, appliances, and other products made part of improvements to real property are not exempted from the coverage of the Act. *See* Maldonado, "Builder Beware: Strict Tort Liability for Mass Produced Housing, 7 Real Estate L.J." 283 (1979).

The Act also excludes from its coverage the provider of professional services when a product is utilized or sold as part of the rendition of such services. *Compare* "Barbee v. Rogers," 425 S.W.2d 342 (Tex.1968), *with* "Newmark v. Gimbel's, Inc.," 54 N.J. 585, 258 A.2d 697 (1969) (differentiating "sales-service hybrid transaction" of a beautician from "professional ministration" of a physician or dentist). The majority of current decisions look to the factual circumstances of each case and generally exclude persons exercising professional judgment within their legally authorized scope of practice. Thus, in the absence of any product preparation or modification, of any representation by service providers that the products are their own, or of warranty, the courts have generally not applied product liability doctrines where the provider is called upon to exercise such professional judgment. However, appropriate remedies may be available to injured parties under other theories of law, including malpractice. *See* "Batiste v. American Home Prods. Corp.," 32 N.C.App. 1, 231 S.E.2d 269 (1977).

Consequently, it is the intent of the drafters of this Act that professionals, such as pharmacists, physicians, optometrists, and opticians, should *not* be considered product sellers in those circumstances where they are selling a product while acting within their legally authorized scope of professional practice. *See* "Bichler v. Willing," 5 App.Div.2d 331, 397 N.Y.S.2d 57 (1977); "Batiste v. American Home Prods. Corp.," *supra*. In addition, pharmacists or other professionals, employed by and working within the scope of their employment for a hospital or other health-related facility, would *not* be considered product sellers within this context since they would be rendering a part of the overall services of such facilities.

On the other hand, a pharmacist or other professional who is engaged in a commercial, non-professional sales transaction, such as the sale of perfume or photographic film, *would* be considered a product seller. Thus, the Act states that a party shall be considered a product seller when the sale of a product is the principal part of the transaction and when the essence of the relationship between the buyer and seller is *not* the furnishing of a professional skill or service. *See* Annot., 2 "A.L.R.3d" 1425 (1970).

With respect to non-professional services, when the sale of a product is the principal part of the transaction, and the essence of the relationship is not the furnishing of judgment, skill, or services, the non-manufacturer product seller is responsible under Section 105 of this Act. Therefore, when a non-professional service, such as application, installation, or dealer preparation, is an incidental part of the overall transaction of sale of a product, the provisions of Section 105 govern the entire transaction. *See* "Newmark v. Gimbel's, Inc.," 54 N.J. 585, 258 A.2d 697 (1969); "Winters v. Sears, Roebuck & Co.," 89 "A.L.R.3d" 196, 554 S.W.2d 656 (Mo.1977). However, when the non-professional service is the predominant element of the transaction, or when the service and sale elements are clearly distinguishable or contracted for separately, the Act does not apply to such non-professional service. Instead, it is governed by other applicable law of the state. *See* "Nickel v. Hyster Co.," 97 Misc.2d 770, 412 N.Y.S.2d 273 (1978). *See also* Brook, "Sales–Service Hybrid Transactions: A Policy Approach," 28 Sw.L.J. 575 (1975); and Greenfield, "Consumer Protection in Service Transactions— Implied Warranties and Strict Liability in Tort," 1974 "Utah L.Rev." 661.

It is also the intent of the drafters that this Act include manufacturers and other product sellers of new or remanufactured products, but not ordinary commercial sellers of used products. In this context, the commercial seller of used products is one who resells a product after it has been used by a consumer or other product user and is in essentially the same condition as when it was acquired for resale. Thus, the commercial seller of used products may be differentiated from sellers of fully rebuilt or remanufactured products that are included within the definition of "manufacturer" under Subsection (B). The slight majority of decisions indicate that product liability law does apply to sellers of used products; however, such sellers are not held to the same standards as are sellers of new products, due to the different nature and condition of the used product at the time of sale. Therefore, the issue of the potential liability of sellers of used products is left for resolution not under this Act, but rather under the other law of the state. *See* "Tillman v. Vance Equip. Co.," 596 P.2d 1299, 286 Or. 747 (1979); "Mickle v. Blackmon," 252 S.C. 202, 166 S.E.2d 173 (1969) (manufacturer); "Peterson v. Lou Bachrodt Chevrolet Co.," 61 Ill.2d 17, 329 N.E.2d 785 (1975) ("as is" sale by dealer).

(B) *Manufacturer.* The term encompasses those product sellers who initiate and carry out the process of production. It also includes manufacturers of component parts, "private labelers" who hold themselves out to the public as manufacturers, and those product sellers who rebuild or remanufacture products for resale in "like new" condition. It does not include independent product designers whose services are contracted for by product sellers, if such designers are not otherwise engaged in the business of selling products. See Subsection (A) (definition of "product seller"). Unless they actually engage in some element of manufacture, traditional wholesalers, distributors, and retailers are excluded from the definition. However, if they do participate in the actual manufacturing process, they are deemed manufacturers, but only to the extent that they engage in such activity. They do not become manufacturers of the product as a whole.

This definition is drawn in part from Arizona's product liability law. See "Ariz.Rev.Stat.Ann." Section 12–681(1) (Supp.1978). Its greatest import within this Act is in regard to the responsibility of a manufacturer for defective products, as contrasted with that of other product sellers. See Section 105, "The Basic Standards of Responsibility for Product Sellers Other Than Manufacturers."

(C) *Product.* "Product" means property which, as a component part or an assembled whole, is movable, and possesses intrinsic value. Therefore, included are all goods, wares, merchandise, and their components, as well as articles and commodities capable of delivery for introduction into trade or commerce.

The definition follows existing case law by including movable dwellings, such as mobile homes, campers and similar vehicles. See "Morrow v. New Moon Homes, Inc.," 548 P.2d 279 (Alaska 1976) (mobile home). Also included are water, natural gas, and electrical energy provided by public utilities or other product sellers. See "Moody v. City of Galveston," 524 S.W.2d 583 (Tex.Civ.App.1975) (water); "Harris v. Northwest Natural Gas Co.," 284 Or. 571, 588 P.2d 18 (1978) (warnings regarding gas); "Ransome v. Wisconsin Elec. Power Co.," 87 Wis.2d 605, 275 N.W.2d 641 (1979) (electricity). However, human biologicals, such as blood and other bodily tissues or organs, are expressly excluded from the definition. In addition, representations of value, such as money or choses in action, are excluded, although the physical document and the ink or any other material used in printing the document do fall within the definition. See 72 *C.J.S.* "Product" (1951), and Sections 85–92 (Supp. 1975); 63 "Am.Jur.2d" "Products Liability" Section 5 (1972).

In a specific case, the particular product with which this Act is concerned is the "relevant product" which actually gave rise to the product liability claim. The "relevant product" may be the product as a whole or the particular component part or parts which gave rise to the product liability claim.

(D) *Product Liability Claim.* An important purpose of this Act is to consolidate product liability actions that have, at times, been separated under theories of negligence, warranty, and strict liability. This approach was suggested by the Task Force's "Legal Study" as well as by the "LaFalce Subcommittee Report." While an argument may be made that negligence theory is qualitatively different from strict liability and, therefore, should be preserved, product liability theory and practice have merged into a single entity and can only be stabilized if there is one, and not a multiplicity of, causes of action.

"Product liability claim" embraces express as well as implied warranty actions.

(E) *Claimant.* Living persons and those claiming through or on behalf of an estate in wrongful death or survival actions are both included within the meaning of the word "claimant."

Although the "Restatement (Second) of Torts" leaves open the question of whether persons other than product users should be included within the compass of product liability claims, subsequent case law has been almost uniform in ruling that such persons should be included. *See* "Giberson v. Ford Motor Co.," 504 S.W.2d 8 (Mo.1974) (collecting cases). *See also* Annot., 33 "A.L.R.3d" 415 (1970). The definition follows this line of decisions. *See* "Guarino v. Mine Safety Appliance Co.," 25 N.Y.2d 460, 255 N.E.2d 173, 306 N.Y.S.2d 942 (1969) (rescuer).

(F) *Harm.* Section 402A of the "Restatement" includes physical harm to persons and property. This Act provides that harm may manifest itself as damage to property, disability, including personal physical injuries and illness, death, and mental anguish or emotional harm attendant to such disability or death. It also includes mental anguish or emotional harm in circumstances in which the claimant is actually placed in personal danger, and the mental anguish or emotional harm is accompanied by substantial objective symptomatology. *See* "Wallace v. Coca-Cola Bottling Plants, Inc.," 269 A.2d 117 (Me.1970).

The term also includes damage to the product itself. There is strong case law support for leaving direct economic loss cases to the field of commercial law. "Hawkins Constr. Co. v. Matthews Co., Inc." 190 Neb. 546, 209 N.W.2d 643 (1973); "Dennis v. Willys-Overland Motors, Inc.," 111 F.Supp. 875 (W.D.Mo.1958); "Price v. Gatlin," 241 Or. 315, 405 P.2d 502 (1965). Courts that have allowed recovery in tort where the purchased property is "destroyed," but not where there is "mere loss of the bargain," have had difficulty applying this distinction where the product is wholly ineffective. *See* "Anthony v. Kelsey-Hayes Co.," 25 Cal.App.3d 442, 102 Cal. Rptr. 113 (1972); "States Steamship Co. v. Stone Manganese Marine Ltd.," 371 F.Supp. 500, 504–505 (D.N.J.1973) (collecting cases). For this reason and the fact that loss of the bargain damages are in essence a part of commercial law, claims for direct economic harm have been left to the "Uniform Commercial Code" ("U.C.C.").

The Act also does not include damages for consequential economic losses. Almost all courts have been in accord with "Seely v. White Motor Co.," 63 Cal.2d 9, 403

P.2d 145, 45 Cal.Rptr. 17 (1965), on this issue and have left claimants with whatever rights they have under the "U.C.C." Pursuant to Section 103, the Act follows the weight of authority in this regard, and does not preempt such recovery under the "U.C.C." *See* "Brown v. Western Farmers Ass'n.," 268 Or. 470, 521 P.2d 537 (1974); "Eli Lilly & Co. v. Casey," 472 S.W.2d 598 (Tex.Civ.App. 1971); "Paul O'Leary Lumber Corp. v. Mill Equip., Inc.," 448 F.2d 536 (5th Cir.1971).

The insurance costs of extending consequential economic losses beyond parties to a contract would be enormous. It is much less expensive and more efficient for the product purchaser to obtain insurance against consequential economic losses caused by business stoppage. Also, most courts believe that a commercial purchaser should be charged with the risk that the purchased product will not match its economic expectations unless the manufacturer agrees that it will. *See* Note, "Economic Loss in Products Liability Jurisprudence," 66 "Colum.L.Rev." 917 (1966).

(G) *Reasonably Anticipated Conduct.* The definition is based in part on Arizona product liability law. *See* "Ariz.Rev.Stat.Ann." Section 12–681(4) (Supp.1978). "Anticipated" conduct includes occurrences which are expected, ordinary, usual, and familiar. The definition focuses on the class of persons which the product seller knows is likely to use the product. *See* "Thibault v. Sears, Roebuck & Co.", 395 A.2d 843 (N.H.1978).

The concept of "reasonably anticipated conduct" should be contrasted with "foreseeable conduct." Almost any kind of misconduct with regard to products can be "foreseeable"—especially if the trier of fact is permitted to use hindsight, *e.g.,* that a soda bottle will be used for a hammer, that someone will attempt to drive a land vehicle on water, that perfume will be poured on a candle in order to scent it. *See* "Moran v. Faberge, Inc.," 273 Md. 538, 332 A.2d 11 (1975). This same conduct may not be reasonably anticipated by a potential product litigant, or by the trier of fact.

The Act's reliance on the concept of "reasonably anticipated conduct" places incentives for loss prevention on both product sellers and product users. It also helps to ensure that the price of products is not affected by the liability insurance costs that would spring from providing coverage for abnormal product use.

(H) *Preponderance of the Evidence.* Unless otherwise stated, the standard of evidence under this Act is the standard utilized in most civil litigation—a preponderance of the evidence. This standard requires a showing that it is more probable than not that a fact occurred or did not occur. *See* 30 "Am.Jur.2d" "Evidence" Section 1164 (1967).

(I) *Clear and Convincing Evidence.* Proof that is "clear and convincing" not only carries with it the power to persuade the mind as to its probable truth or correctness of fact, but also has an additional element of clinching such truth. The term is best understood in context. It requires more proof than does the preponderance of the evidence standard (the ordinary standard under this Act), but does not require proof beyond a reasonable doubt. *See, e.g.,* "Aiello v. Knoll Golf Club," 64 N.J.Super. 156, 165 A.2d 531 (1960); "Cross v. Ledford," 161 Ohio St. 469, 120 N.E.2d 118 (1954); "Brown v. Warner," 78 S.D. 647, 107 N.W.2d 1 (1961).

(J) *Reckless Disregard.* As Prosser has indicated, "reckless disregard" occurs where the actor

has intentionally done an act of an unreasonable character in disregard of a risk known to him or [one that was] so obvious that he must be taken to have been aware of it, and so great as to make it highly probable that harm would follow.

W. Prosser, "Torts" 185 (4th ed. 1971).

The term denotes aggravated conduct which represents a major departure from ordinary negligence.

(K) *Express Warranty.* This definition is based on its counterpart in the "Uniform Commercial Code" and includes any positive statement, affirmation of fact, promise, description, sample, or model relating to the product. *See* "U.C.C." Section 2–313; 63 "Am.Jur.2d" "Products Liability" Section 93 (1972). The product seller may give an express warranty orally or in writing, or through any other actions intended as a communication. *See* "Alan Wood Steel Co. v. Capital Equip. Enterprises, Inc.," 39 Ill.App.3d 48, 349 N.E.2d 627 (1976); "Larutan Corp. v. Magnolia Homes Mfg. Co.," 190 Neb. 425, 209 N.W.2d 177 (1973). It should be noted that an action based on a violation of an express warranty must include the element of reliance, and the breach must relate to a misrepresentation of material facts. *See* Subsection 104(D).

* * *

Code

§ 103. Scope of This Act

(A) This Act is in lieu of and preempts all existing law governing matters within its coverage, including the "Uniform Commercial Code" and similar laws; however, nothing in this Act shall prevent the recovery, under the "Uniform Commercial Code" or similar laws, of direct or consequential economic losses.

(B) A claim may be asserted under this Act even though the claimant did not buy the product from, or enter into any contractual relationship with, the product seller.

(C) Whenever this Act does not provide a rule of decision, reference may be made to other sources of law, provided that such reference conforms to the intent and spirit of this Act as set forth in the following criteria used as guidelines for its development:

(1) To ensure that persons injured by unreasonably unsafe

products receive reasonable compensation for their injuries;

(2) To ensure the availability of affordable product liability insurance with adequate coverage to product sellers that engage in reasonably safe manufacturing practices;

(3) To place the incentive for loss prevention on the party or parties who are best able to accomplish that goal;

(4) To expedite the reparations process from the time of injury to the time the claim is paid;

(5) To minimize the sum of accident costs, prevention costs, and transaction costs; and

(6) To use language that is comparatively clear and concise.

* * *

Analysis

§ **103. Scope of This Act**

(A) The Act consolidates all product liability recovery theories into one. The approach taken is in accord with the Task Force's "Legal Study." While some have argued that for trial tactics purposes, it is useful to retain the negligence and breach of warranty causes of action as distinct from strict tort liability, a claimant's attorney can retain the essence of this utility by showing the basic wrongfulness of the product seller's conduct under Sections 104 or 105.

The Act explicitly preempts the "Uniform Commercial Code" ("U.C.C.") and similar laws in instances where such laws have governed matters within the Act's coverage. The purpose of this provision is to prevent conflicting product liability rules and remedies. See, e.g., "Swartz v. General Motors Corp.," 378 N.E.2d 61 (Mass.1978). Although the Act eliminates breach of warranty as a separate cause of action in product liability cases, express warranties continue to play an important role in the Act. See, e.g., Subsections 102(K), 104(D), 105(B), 106(B)(4), 107(E)(4), 110(A)(2), 110(B)(2)(a).

Because the Act does not provide remedies for purely economic losses, Subsection (A) ensures that the Act does not prevent recovery under commercial law for loss of the use of a product. Thus, product liability actions for personal injury, illness, death, or damage to property (other than the product itself) are governed by this Act. On the other hand, recovery under the "U.C.C." or similar law for economic losses is not precluded by this Act.

(B) The Act is in accord with the "Restatement (Second) of Torts" in that it is unnecessary for the claimant to be in contractual privity with the product seller in order to recover for harm. See "Restatement (Second) of Torts" Section 402A, Comment 1.

(C) The Act and its accompanying commentary do not purport to be an exhaustive compilation of the entire subject of product liability law. Rather, they focus on subject matter areas that the "Task Force Report" suggested have created the most problems and are of major importance.

The interstices of the Act will be filled by statutory or common law additions of the individual states. Some of these interstitial issues will be pointed out in the section-by-section analysis. Others will be discovered in the course of litigation under the Act.

It is the intent of Subsection (C) that these additions of statutory or common law should enhance, rather than conflict with, the basic purposes of this Act. Those courts or legislatures that make such additions should keep in mind the "Criteria for the Act" set forth in this Subsection. A full explanation of the criteria is set forth in the Introduction to the Act. In regard to these criteria, it is essential to note that this Act does not intend to set up a compensation system similar to Worker Compensation. Rather, the purpose of the Act is to impose liability "only where it is fair to deem the product seller responsible for an injury." "Introduction," p. 14, *supra*.

* * *

Code

§ 104. Basic Standards of Responsibility for Manufacturers

A product manufacturer is subject to liability to a claimant who proves by a preponderance of the evidence that the claimant's harm was proximately caused because the product was defective.

A product may be proven to be defective if, and only if:

(1) It was unreasonably unsafe in construction (Subsection A);

(2) It was unreasonably unsafe in design (Subsection B);

(3) It was unreasonably unsafe because adequate warnings or instructions were not provided (Subsection C); or

(4) It was unreasonably unsafe because it did not conform to the product seller's express warranty (Subsection D).

Before submitting the case to the trier of fact, the court shall determine that the claimant has introduced sufficient evidence to allow a reasonable person to find, by a preponderance of the evidence, that one or more of the above conditions existed and was a proximate cause of the claimant's harm.

(A) *The Product Was Unreasonably Unsafe in Construction.* In order to determine that the product was unreasonably unsafe in construction, the trier of fact must find that, when the product left the control of the manufacturer, the product deviated in some material way from the manufacturer's design specifications or performance standards, or from otherwise identical units of the same product line.

(B) *The Product Was Unreasonably Unsafe in Design.*

(1) In order to determine that the product was unreasonably unsafe in design, the trier of fact must find that, at the time of manufacture, the likelihood that

the product would cause the claimant's harm or similar harms, and the seriousness of those harms outweighed the burden on the manufacturer to design a product that would have prevented those harms, and the adverse effect that alternative design would have on the usefulness of the product.

(2) Examples of evidence that is especially probative in making this evaluation include:

(a) Any warnings and instructions provided with the product;

(b) The technological and practical feasibility of a product designed and manufactured so as to have prevented claimant's harm while substantially serving the likely user's expected needs;

(c) The effect of any proposed alternative design on the usefulness of the product;

(d) The comparative costs of producing, distributing, selling, using, and maintaining the product as designed and as alternatively designed; and

(e) The new or additional harms that might have resulted if the product had been so alternatively designed.

(C) *The Product Was Unreasonably Unsafe Because Adequate Warnings or Instructions Were Not Provided.*

(1) In order to determine that the product was unreasonably unsafe because adequate warnings or instructions were not provided about a danger connected with the product or its proper use, the trier of fact must find that, at the time of manufacture, the likelihood that the product would cause the claimant's harm or similar harms and the seriousness of those harms rendered the manufacturer's instructions inadequate and that the manufacturer should and could have provided the instructions or warnings which claimant alleges would have been adequate.

(2) Examples of evidence that is especially probative in making this evaluation include:

(a) The manufacturer's ability, at the time of manufacture, to be aware of the product's danger and the nature of the potential harm;

(b) The manufacturer's ability to anticipate that the likely product user would be aware of the product's danger and the nature of the potential harm;

(c) The technological and practical feasibility of providing adequate warnings and instructions;

(d) The clarity and conspicuousness of the warnings or instructions that were provided; and

(e) The adequacy of the warnings or instructions that were provided.

(3) In any claim under this Subsection, the claimant must prove by a preponderance of the evidence that if adequate warnings or instructions had been provided, they would have been effective because a reasonably prudent product user would have either declined to use the product or would have used the product in a man-

ner so as to have avoided the harm.

(4) A manufacturer shall not be liable for its failure to warn or instruct about dangers that are obvious; for "product misuse" as defined in Subsection 112(C)(1); or for alterations or modifications of the product which do not constitute "reasonably anticipated conduct" under Subsection 102(G).

(5) A manufacturer is under an obligation to provide adequate warnings or instructions to the actual product user unless the manufacturer provided such warnings to a person who may be reasonably expected to assure that action is taken to avoid the harm, or that the risk of the harm is explained to the actual product user.

For products that may be legally used only by or under the supervision of a class of experts, warnings or instructions may be provided to the using or supervisory expert.

For products that are tangible goods sold or handled only in bulk or other workplace products, warnings or instructions may be provided to the employer of the employee-claimant if there is no practical and feasible means of transmitting them to the employee-claimant.

(6) *Post–Manufacture Duty to Warn.* In addition to the claim provided in Subsection (C)(1), a claim may arise under this Subsection where a reasonably prudent manufacturer should have learned about a danger connected with the product after it was manufactured. In such a case, the manufacturer is under an obligation to act with regard to the danger as a reasonably prudent manufacturer in the same or similar circumstances. This obligation is satisfied if the manufacturer makes reasonable efforts to inform product users or a person who may be reasonably expected to assure that action is taken to avoid the harm, or that the risk of harm is explained to the actual product user.

(D) *The Product Was Unreasonably Unsafe Because It Did Not Conform to an Express Warranty.* In order to determine that the product was unreasonably unsafe because it did not conform to an express warranty, the trier of fact must find that the claimant, or one acting on the claimant's behalf, relied on an express warranty made by the manufacturer or its agent about a material fact or facts concerning the product and this express warranty proved to be untrue.

A "material fact" is any specific characteristic or quality of the product. It does not include a general opinion about, or praise of, the product.

The product seller may be subject to liability under Subsection (D) although it did not engage in negligent or fraudulent conduct in making the express warranty.

* * *

Analysis

§ 104. Basic Standards of Responsibility for Manufacturers

No single product liability issue has generated more controversy than the question of defining the basic standards of responsibility to which product manufacturers are to be held. *See, e.g.,* Epstein, "Products Liability: The Search for the Middle Ground," 56 "N.C.L.Rev." 643 (1978); *see also* Vetri, "Products Liability: Developing a Framework for Analysis," 54 "Or.L.Rev." 293, 310 (1975); Henderson, "Judicial Review of Manufacturers' Conscious Design Choice: The Limits of Adjudication," 73 "Colum.L.Rev." 1531 (1973); Keeton, "Product Liability and the Meaning of Defect," 5 "St. Mary's L.J." 30 (1973); Wade, "On the Nature of Strict Tort Liability for Products," 44 "Miss. L.J." 825 (1973); Walkowiak, "Product Liability Litigation and the Concept of Defective Goods: 'Reasonableness' Revisited," 44 "J. Air Law & Commerce" 705 (1978).

Much of the controversy appears to have sprung from the fact that the authors of Section 402A of the "Restatement (Second) of Torts" were focusing on problems relating to product mismanufacture or defective construction, and not on problems relating to defective design or the duty to warn. *See* "Restatement (Second) of Torts" Section 402A, Appendix (1965) (most cases cited deal with defects in construction cases); Wade, *supra,* 44 "Miss.L.J." at 830–32. In the 15 years following the publication of the "Restatement," courts have struggled to define standards of responsibility with respect to design and the duty to warn. *See, e.g.,* "Barker v. Lull Eng'r. Co.," 20 Cal. 3d 413, 573 P.2d 443, 143 Cal.Rptr. 225 (1978); "Cepeda v. Cumberland Eng'r. Co.," 76 N.J. 152, 386 A.2d 816 (1978); "Phillips v. Kimwood Mach. Co.," 269 Or. 485, 525 P.2d 1033 (1974).

In the course of this struggle, courts appear to have drifted away from rationales for imposing liability and toward verbal formulae that attempt to distinguish between negligence and strict liability.

The drafters of this Act have focused on the basic rationale of product liability and made decisions that should make it easier for courts to decide these cases. It was determined that "strict liability" is justified in two product liability areas—defects in construction and breach of express warranty.

The "Task Force Report" concluded that strict liability for defective construction can be absorbed within the existing liability insurance system. There is a degree of predictability with regard to these defective products that is not found with respect to products that are defective in design or to failure to warn. Strict liability for defective construction has also been predicated on Section 402A of the "Restatement" and implied warranty claims under commercial law. These sources support the position that consumers have the right to expect that products are free from construction defects.

Strict liability cases involving breach of an express warranty can also be justified. If a manufacturer makes a specific representation about its product, it is fair to hold the manufacturer to that promise. Moreover, the consumer has the right to expect that a product will live up to the manufacturer's representations.

While some courts have indicated that strict liability should also be applied in design and duty-to-warn cases, it is difficult to find an adequate rationale to support that result. A few courts have sought to justify the result under a theory of "risk distribution" wherein the product seller distributes the costs of all product-related risks through liability insurance; however, this rationale breaks down in practice. The application of uncertain strict liability principles in the areas of design and duty to warn places a whole product line at risk; therefore, a firmer liability foundation is needed. In terms of creating incentives for loss prevention, the approach of applying strict liability principles to design and duty-to-warn cases represents an "overkill;" a fault system will provide the needed incentive.

If the costs of product-related injuries are always to be distributed through the price of the product, the mechanism to bring about this result should be an appropriate compensation system with limited damages, not the tort-litigation system. The former is the approach taken in Worker Compensation and automobile no-fault reparations systems. While courts that have applied strict liability in design and duty-to-warn cases have often stated that they are not imposing "absolute" insurer liability, they have not been able to articulate why they draw a line short of that particular point. The reason for this is that the risk distribution rationale provides no stopping point short of absolute liability. Thus, a number of courts have plunged into a foggy area that is neither true strict liability nor negligence. The result has been the creation of a wide variety of legal "formulae," unpredictability for consumers, and instability in the insurance market.

In light of these facts, this Act places both design and duty-to-warn cases on a fault basis.

The Act utilizes the word "defective" as a generic term covering all four types of unreasonably unsafe products. A product cannot be proven defective unless the claimant shows that it is unreasonably unsafe under one or more Subsections under Section 104.[10]

This approach should not lead to problems of characterization. The claimant's pleading should indicate the theory on which it is based within the framework of Subsections (A), (B), (C), or (D). Of course, a product may be unreasonably unsafe in more than one way.

The manufacturer of a component part or parts is subject to liability under this Section for harms caused because that component part was defective. The

---

10. Liability can be imposed on non-manufacturer product sellers under Section 105 when they have been negligent.

manufacturer of a whole product is subject to liability under this Section for harms caused because the product, or any of its components, was defective.

The following commentary discusses each Subsection in turn.

(A) *The Product Was Unreasonably Unsafe in Construction.* The history of imposing strict liability for products which are unreasonably unsafe in construction goes back as far as 1913 when sellers of foods were first held liable for their failure to produce a product reasonably fit for its intended use. *See* "Mazetti v. Armour & Co.," 75 Wash. 622, 135 P. 633 (1913); Prosser, "The Assault Upon the Citadel (Strict Liability to the Consumer)," 69 "Yale L.J." 1099 (1960).

Subsection (A) imposes pure strict liability on the manufacturer in accordance with Section 402A of the "Restatement (Second) of Torts." *Cf.* "Pabon v. Hackensack Auto Sales, Inc.," 63 N.J.Super. 476, 164 A.2d 773, 783 (1960) (implied warranty for defective ball bearing). The approach is also in accord with the overwhelming trend in case law in the United States. *See* Phillips, "A Synopsis of the Developing Law of Products Liability," 28 "Drake L.Rev." 317, 344–45 (1979).

In the course of its study, the Task Force found that most product sellers can absorb the financial impact of strict liability for products which are defective in construction. *See* "Task Force Report" at VII–17.

The approach taken here is subject to theoretical criticism because

> [A] standard which judges a manufacturer by his own rather than industry standards could penalize the manufacturer who goes out of his way to build into his product a high safety level not mandated or followed by the industry.

Twerski & Weinstein, "A Critique of the Uniform Product Liability Law—A Rush to Judgment," 28 "Drake L.Rev." 221, 225 (1979).

Nevertheless, this criticism overlooks the fact that the manufacturer's self-imposition of a higher standard will function as a shield against claims alleging liability in the more costly area of defective design. By adopting a higher standard, a manufacturer may occasionally be subject to liability under Subsection (A), while another manufacturer may not be, but the first manufacturer does not place its whole product line at risk of being found unreasonably unsafe in design.

Not every minor variation from a standard will result in liability; rather, the variation must be a material one causing the claimant's harm.

In point of fact, there is no practical way to define defective construction except by the manufacturer's own standards. It is an optimal area for strict liability "because societal expectations are fairly well established with regard to such defects, and a ready gauge of acceptability exists by reference to like products that are non-defective." Phillips, "The Standard for Determining Defectiveness in Products Liability," 46 "U.Cin. L.Rev." 101, 104–05 (1977). Moreover, the imposition of strict liability with regard to defective construction is fair to the product user. Under a negligence system, the claimant would have the very difficult burden of showing that a manufacturer knew or should have known about a latent defect in one of thousands of mass-produced products.

(B) *The Product Was Unreasonably Unsafe in Design.* No court, in spite of some loose language that has been used, has imposed true strict or absolute liability on manufacturers for products which are unreasonably unsafe in design. See Henderson, "Manufacturers' Liability for Defective Design: A Proposed Statutory Reform," 56 "N.C.L.Rev." 625, 634–35 (1978). This is true because courts have appreciated the liability potential inherent in such cases—it is almost always possible to design a product more safely. Nevertheless, some courts in their instructions to the trier of fact have left juries "at sea." The jury is told to decide design cases by "considering" a number of factors; it is not given a guideline or formula for making the evaluation.

The approach taken here provides such a guideline. The trier of fact is instructed to impose liability if it finds that the product was unreasonably unsafe in design. The trier of fact is also given a formula to assist it in making this determination. The approach has its roots in the law of negligence [11] and has been put into modern and appropriate product liability terminology by some courts in their attempt to resolve the defective design dilemma. See "Hagans v. Oliver Mach. Co.," 576 F.2d 97, 99–100 (5th Cir.1978); "Dreisonstok v. Volkswagenwerk, A.G.," 489 F.2d 1066, 1071 (4th Cir.1974); "Jeng v. Witters," 452 F.Supp. 1349, 1356 (M.D.Pa.1978).

Section 104 requires the court to make an initial determination as to whether the claimant has introduced enough evidence for the case to be considered by the jury. This requirement is especially important with respect to conscious design cases under Subsection (B). The dangers of the trier of fact introducing hindsight into the risk-utility analysis make it imperative for the court to apply its screening function carefully. See "Owens v. Allis–Chalmers Corp.," 83 Mich.App. 74, 268 N.W.2d 291 (1978); Henderson, *supra,* 73 "Colum.L.Rev." at 1531. *Cf.* Wade, *supra,* 44 "Miss.L.J." at 837–38 (suggesting that such formulae can *only* be applied by the court).

The formula set forth in Subsection (B) requires the trier of fact to balance two pairs of factors existing at the time of manufacture: (1) the likelihood that the product would cause the claim-

11. *See* "United States v. Carroll Towing Co.," 159 F.2d 169, 173 (2d Cir.1947) (the "Learned Hand formula").

ant's harm or similar harms, and the seriousness of those harms; against (2) the manufacturer's burden of designing a product that would have prevented those harms, and the adverse effect that alternative design would have on the usefulness of the product. *See* "Kerns v. Engelke," 390 N.E.2d 859, 865 (1979).

If the case is sent to the jury, the balancing formula should be placed in a jury instruction indicating that the claimant has the burden of showing, in light of the formula, that the product was unreasonably unsafe in design.

The Subsection also sets forth examples of important evidence that may be considered with respect to applying the formula.

First, warnings and instructions are important because, in an appropriate case, a product may be found not to be defective in design if the product seller has given an adequate warning about the product risk. *See, e.g.,* "Wagner v. Larson," 257 Iowa 1202, 136 N.W.2d 312 (1965); "Penn v. Inferno Mfg. Corp.," 199 So.2d 210 (La. App.) *aff'd*, 251 La. 27, 202 So.2d 649 (1967). There are limits to this possibility, however, since a product seller will not be shielded from liability for an unreasonably unsafe product simply by indicating that the product "may be hazardous." Only a warning or instruction which, at the time of manufacture, substantially reduces the likelihood that the product would cause harm in the manner in which the claimant's harm was caused will affect the question of whether the product was defective in design.

Second, evidence relating to the technological and practical feasibility of designing and manufacturing a product which would have substantially served the expected user's needs, and would have also prevented the claimant's harm, addresses the side of the formula dealing with the manufacturer's burden. If an alternatively designed product which would have prevented the harm while preserving its usefulness could have been produced with a slight increase in cost, it is likely that the product is unreasonably unsafe. On the other hand, the manufacturer need not incorporate safety features that render a product incapable of performing some or all of the very functions that create its public demand. *See* "Hagans v. Oliver Mach., Inc.," 576 F.2d 97 (5th Cir.1978); "Dreisonstok v. Volkswagenwerk, A.G.," 489 F.2d 1066 (4th Cir. 1974).

Third, it is important to consider evidence relating to the effect of the alternative design on the usefulness of the product. As learned scholars have observed, "it is virtually impossible to [evaluate a design defect case] without balancing risk and utility factors." *See* Twerski & Weinstein, *supra*, 28 "Drake L.Rev." at 229. *See also* "Phillips v. Kimwood Mach. Co.," 269 Or. 485, 525 P.2d 1033, 1038 (1974). It is important to note that this evidence is not directed to the general usefulness of the product in society, *i.e.,* the overall social worth of pharmaceuticals, lawnmowers, or other products.

Fourth, it is essential to consider evidence relating to the comparative costs of producing, distributing, selling, using, and maintaining the product as designed and as alternatively designed. This places the court and the trier of fact in the "real world" of design options.

Finally, if new or additional harms might have resulted if the product had been alternatively designed, the trier of fact should consider this factor in making its evaluation. Since this evidence will probably be introduced by the defendant manufacturer, it may be placed before the court and jury *after* the claimant's case has been presented.

In sum, Subsection (B) places the burden of proof on the claimant to show that in light of a balance of practical, objective factors, the product seller should bear the full cost of the injury and have the responsibility for attempting to distribute that cost through the price of its product. In light of the fact that the judgment is the equivalent of holding that the whole product line is defective, it is important that traditional tort law principles be followed and that the claimant retain the burden of proof. See Kalven, "Torts: The Quest for Appropriate Standards," 53 "Cal.L.Rev." 189 (1965). *But see* "Barker v. Lull Engineering, Inc.," 20 Cal.3d 413, 573 P.2d 443, 143 Cal.Rptr. 225 (1978).

Neither the formula nor the detailed list of the more important evidentiary items includes what has been called the "consumer expectation test." The reasons for not including it are rooted in both economics and practicality. As Professor Wade, Reporter for "The Restatement (Second) of Torts," has stated:

> In many situations, particularly involving design matters, the consumer would not know what to expect, because he would have no idea how safe the product could be made.

Wade, *supra*, "Miss.L.J.," at 829.

The consumer expectation test takes subjectivity to its most extreme end. Each trier of fact is likely to have a different understanding of abstract consumer expectations. Moreover, most consumers are not familiar with the details of the manufacturing process and cannot abstractly evaluate conscious design alternatives. This has been recently recognized by the Supreme Court of Texas. "Turner v. General Motors Corp.," ___ S.W.2d ___, No. B-7747 (Tex. June 13, 1979); *see also* Green, "Strict Liability Under Sections 402A and 402B: A Decade of Litigation," 54 "Tex.L.Rev." 1185 (1976).

(C) *The Product Was Unreasonably Unsafe Because Adequate Warnings or Instructions Were Not Provided.* A manufacturer may be held liable under Subsection (C) regardless of whether the product was found to be unreasonably unsafe in construction or design. Even where the lack of scientific knowledge or cost factors preclude the use of an alternative design, the manufacturer may still be required to provide a warning about the product's hazard or to provide adequate instructions about the product's use. *See* "Jacobson v. Colorado Fuel & Iron Corp.," 409 F.2d 1263, 1271 (9th Cir.1969).

It is important to note that Subsection (C) covers two arguably separate problems. First, was there a duty to warn or instruct about a particular matter? Second, assuming that a warning or instruction was given, was it adequate? While these two problems are theoretically separate, the underlying factors that must be taken into consideration in evaluating a manufacturer's duty with respect to them overlap; therefore, the two issues have been combined in Subsection (C). As will be indicated below, there may be a different evidentiary emphasis in the two types of cases.

The basic standard of responsibility for Subsection (C) is predicated on a fault basis. A "strict liability" base in this area creates unacceptable uncertainty within the tort-litigation system. This has recently been recognized by the Supreme Court of Michigan. "Smith v. E.R. Squibb & Sons," 405 Mich. 79, 273 N.W.2d 476 (1979).

Under Subsection (C), the trier of fact is to place itself in the manufacturer's position at the time the product was manufactured. In order to impose liability on the manufacturer, the claimant must prove that the probability that the product would cause the claimant's harm and similar harms and the seriousness of those harms rendered the manufacturer's instructions inadequate, and that the manufacturer should and could have provided the warnings or instructions which claimant alleges would have been adequate. Obviously, where harms were likely to occur and unlikely to be recognized by the product user, the necessity of adequate warnings and instructions is correspondingly acute. On the other hand, the duty to provide adequate warnings and instructions cannot go beyond the technological and other information that was reasonably available at the time of manufacture. This concept is in accord with the overwhelming majority of court decisions. *See* "Robbins v. Farmers Union Grain Terminal Ass'n," 552 F.2d 788 (8th Cir.1977) (collecting cases).

Unlike the basic formula for design cases, the utility of the product is not a consideration in deciding whether a warning is necessary. The focus is on the likelihood that the product would cause the claimant's harm, and the seriousness of that harm, the adequacy of the warnings that were provided, and the practical need for providing the warnings or instructions which claimant alleges would have been adequate.

Subsection (C)(2) lists examples of some of the more probative evidence that can assist the court and the jury in applying this formula.

Factor (a) focuses on the manufacturer's ability, at the time of manufacture, to be aware of the product's danger and the nature of the potential harm. This factor should not operate through hindsight.

Factor (b) involves evidence relating to the manufacturer's ability to anticipate that the likely product user would be aware of the product risk and the nature of the potential harm. The more serious the anticipated harm, the greater the duty to warn. *See* "Braniff Airways, Inc. v. Curtiss-Wright Corp.," 411 F.2d 451 (2d Cir.1969), *on rehearing,* 424 F.2d 427 (2d Cir.1970); "Davis v. Wyeth Laboratories, Inc.," 399 F.2d 121 (9th Cir.1968).

Factor (c), the technological and practical feasibility of providing effective warnings and instructions, may not be significant in many cases because warnings are often relatively inexpensive to provide. However, in some situations, it may not be feasible as a practical technological matter to provide a warning or the type of warning that the claimant suggests should have been provided.

Factor (d), the clarity and conspicuousness of the warnings or instructions, is material in cases where claimant alleges that the warnings given were not adequate. As Professor Phillips has noted:

> To be adequate, warnings must be reasonably conspicuous, strong and clear. They must describe the danger and, where pertinent, the means of avoiding it.

Phillips, *supra,* 28 "Drake L.Rev." at 351.

Also highly relevant to this issue is Factor (e), evidence relating to the adequacy of the warnings or instructions that were provided. Again, as Professor Phillips has noted:

> The effectiveness of a warning may be diluted by other supplier representations of safety that lull the user into a false sense of security. While little or no warning may have to be given to the expert user, a clear and strong warning is required for dangerous products which the supplier can reasonably expect to be used by inexperienced persons. *Id.* at 351-52.

Subsection (C)(3) sets forth a basic causation link for the Subsection. The claimant must show that if adequate warnings or instructions had been provided, the harm would have been avoided either because a reasonably prudent product user would have declined to use the product (a situation which may be most pertinent with respect to a pharmaceutical with a known risk), or because the product would have been used in a manner so as to have avoided the harm. *See* "Technical Chem. Co. v. Jacobs," 480 S.W.2d 602 (Tex. 1972); *cf.* "Potthoff v. Alms," ___ Colo.App. ___, 583 P.2d 309 (Colo. Ct.App.1978). While it has been suggested that no causation requirement should be required with respect to unavoidable pharmaceutical risks (*see* Twerski & Weinstein, *supra,* 28 "Drake L.Rev." at 236–37), the Act addresses itself to tort law, not the general public regulation of products. It is a basic requirement of tort law for the claimant to show that if the defendant had acted in a manner in which the claimant alleges was appropriate, then he or she would not have suffered harm. See W. Prosser, "Torts" at 236 (4th ed. 1971).

Subsection (C)(4) recognizes that a manufacturer should be able to assume that the ordinary product user is familiar with obvious hazards—that knives cut, that alcohol burns, that it is dangerous to drive automobiles at high speeds. Thus, the Act states that the manufacturer does not have to warn about dangers that are obvious. See "Kimble v. Waste Systems International, Inc.," ___ Wash.App. ___, 595 P.2d 569 (1979). While it has been suggested that this approach may encourage the manufacture of "obviously dangerous" products, this is unlikely to occur under this Act, since the manufacturer of an unreasonably unsafe product may be subject to liability under Subsection (B).

Requiring a manufacturer to warn about matters that are obvious would tend to reduce the effectiveness of warnings. As experts in the field have observed, "Warnings, in order to be effective, must be selective." Twerski, Weinstein, Donaher, & Piehler, "The Use and Abuse of Warnings in Products Liability—Design Defect Litigation Comes of Age," 61 "Cornell L.Rev." 495, 514 (1976). It is recognized that, in some jurisdictions, there is an open-ended duty to warn about obvious dangers when they are highly likely to cause very serious injuries. See Marschall, "An Obvious Wrong Does Not Make a Right: Manufacturers' Liability for Patently Dangerous Products," 48 "N.Y.U.L.Rev." 1065 (1973) (collecting cases). Again, the Act approaches this problem by potentially subjecting a manufacturer of a patently dangerous product to liability for an unreasonably unsafe design.

Similarly, the product manufacturer is not under an obligation to warn about misuses or alterations of products that would not be expected by an ordinary reasonably prudent person who is likely to use the product in the same or similar circumstances. See also Section 112(C).

Subsection (C)(5) indicates that in the normal course of events, a manufacturer should place its warning or instruction in a place or in a form where it can be communicated to the actual product user. On the other hand, there are some situations in which this is impossible or impracticable. See "Bryant v. Hercules, Inc.," 325 F.Supp. 241 (W.D.Ky.1970). Therefore, the Subsection indicates that a warning or instruction may be given to a person who may be reasonably expected to assure that action is taken to avoid the harm, or that the risk of the harm is explained to the actual product user. By way of example, the Act sets forth situations where such a process is appropriate. Thus, communication to a using or supervising expert is explicitly stated to be adequate when the product—such as a prescription drug or a radioactive material—is one which may be legally used only by, or under, the supervision of such an expert. *See* "Carmichael v. Reitz," 17 Cal.App.3d 958, 95 Cal.Rptr. 381 (Dist.Ct.App. 1971); "Terhune v. A.H. Robbins Co.," 90 Wash.2d 9, 577 P.2d 975 (1978).

The manufacturer of tangible goods sold or handled only in bulk or of other workplace products may communicate warnings or instructions to the employer of the claimant when that is the only practical and feasible avenue for making a warning. *See* "Reed v. Pennwalt Corp.," 22 Wash.App. 718, 591 P.2d 478 (1979).

Other situations not specifically pointed out in the Act may arise where it is permissible for the manufacturer to convey warnings to persons other than a product user, *e.g.,* warnings to the parent of a young child with respect to a food product. *Cf.* "Spruill v. Boyle–Midway Inc.," 308 F.2d 79 (4th Cir.1962).

Post–Manufacture Duty to Warn. Subsection (C)(6) recognizes a manufacturer's duty to warn after its product has been produced. The Subsection places an obligation on a manufacturer to act with reasonable prudence to learn about serious risks connected with products after they are manufactured. When it learns of such a risk, it is to act as a reasonably prudent manufacturer in the same or similar situation. This obligation is satisfied if the manufacturer makes reasonable efforts to inform product users or appropriate persons about the risk. The Subsection is in accord with basic negligence case law. *See* "Comstock v. General Motors Corp." 358 Mich. 163, 99 N.W.2d 627 (1959); "Schenebeck v. Sterling Drug, Inc.," 423 F.2d 919 (8th Cir.1970). The Subsection recognizes that in some situations, a general warning through an advertising medium may be all a manufacturer can provide. The standard is reasonableness, not absolute or strict liability.

(D) *The Product Was Unreasonably Unsafe Because It Did Not Conform to an Express Warranty.* When there has been an express warranty concerning the product, strict liability can readily be justified. The product seller has used specific words to induce the purchase of the product, and the Act indicates that it must be accountable for its representations. The term "express warranty" is separately defined in the Act in Subsection 102(K).

Since the case of "Baxter v. Ford Motor Co.," 179 Wash. 123, 35 P.2d 1090 (1934), courts have been virtually unanimous in imposing strict liability on product sellers when their statements about their products prove to be untrue. *See* W. Prosser, "Torts" at 652 (4th ed. 1971) ("decisions to the contrary have been amazingly few").

Thus, where a product seller advertised that its pharmaceutical was "free and safe from all dangers of addiction" and claimant, because of a rare and totally unforeseeable susceptibility, became physically dependent on the drug, strict liability was imposed. "Crocker v. Winthrop Lab., Div. of Sterling Drug, Inc.," 514 S.W.2d 429 (Tex.1974); "Spiegel v. Saks 34th Street," 43 Misc.2d 1065, 252 N.Y.S.2d 852 (App.Term 1964), *aff'd,* 272 N.Y.S.2d 972 (App.Div. 1966) (perfume advertised as "non-allergenic").

While many courts use the term "express warranty" to describe the cause of action set forth in Subsection (D), "warranty" is a term of commercial law which is appropriate in the ordinary sale of goods from an immediate buyer to an immediate seller. Here, the focus is solely on tort claims for personal injury and damage to property. In order to convey the tort basis of this cause of action, Section 402B of the "Restatement (Second) of Torts" (1965), utilized the term "misrepresentation" in place of the term "express warranty." Nevertheless, this parlance has not been generally accepted by courts, although they do appreciate the distinction between the tort action and commercial law. *See* "Drayton v. Jiffee Chem. Corp.," 591 F.2d 352, 359 (6th Cir. 1978) ("sounds distinctly in tort"). In deference to this common usage, the term "express warranty," as defined in Subsection 102(K), has been utilized.

Subsection (D) applies only to representations or warranties made by the manufacturer or by a person for whom it is legally responsible. In general, the representation must have been made to the claimant, who must have relied on the warranty, and the harm must have resulted because of that reliance and because of the fact which was misrepresented. However, Subsection (D) does permit reliance by "one acting on behalf" of the claimant. Thus, if a wife purchases an automobile in reliance on a statement concerning its brakes and permits her husband to drive the car, this supplies the element of reliance although the husband, in fact, never learned of the statement. Otherwise, the Section is limited to consumers of products. *See* "Restatement (Second) of Torts" Section 402B, Comment j (1965).

The statement made by the product seller must be about a material fact or facts concerning the product. This does not include mere "puffing" or sales talk. Thus, the manufacturer of a grinding disk that broke was not deemed liable for a breach of an express warranty after stating that the product was "stronger, sharper, and longer lived than ever before available anywhere." "Jakubowski v. Minnesota Mining & Mfg.," 80 N.J.Super. 184, 193 A.2d 275 (1963), *rev'd on other grounds,* 42 N.J. 177, 199 A.2d 826 (1964); *cf.* "Berkebile v. Brantly Helicopter Corp.," 462 Pa. 83, 337 A.2d 893 (1975) (helicopter "easy to operate"). In contrast, a manufacturer was deemed strictly liable when it advertised that a golf training device could be operated and the "ball will not hit player." A player of limited golfing ability was indeed hit by the ball, and the defendant was held liable. "Hauter v. Zogarts," 14 Cal.3d 104, 120 Cal.Rptr. 681, 534 P.2d 377 (1975).

Code

§ 105. Basic Standards of Responsibility for Product Sellers Other Than Manufacturers

(A) A product seller, other than a manufacturer, is subject to liability to a claimant who proves by a preponderance of the evidence that claimant's harm was proximately caused by such product seller's failure to use reasonable care with respect to the product.

Before submitting the case to the trier of fact, the court shall determine that the claimant has introduced sufficient evidence to allow a reasonable person to find by a preponderance of the evidence that such product seller has failed to exercise reasonable care and that this failure was a proximate cause of the claimant's harm.

In determining whether a product seller, other than a manufacturer, is subject to liability under Subsection (A), the trier of fact shall consider the effect of such product seller's own conduct with respect to the design, construction, inspection, or condition of the product, and any failure of such product seller to transmit adequate warnings or instructions about the dangers and proper use of the product.

Unless Subsection (B) or (C) is applicable, product sellers shall not be subject to liability in circumstances in which they did not have a reasonable opportunity to inspect the product in a manner which would or should, in the exercise of reasonable care, reveal the existence of the defective condition.

(B) A product seller, other than a manufacturer, who makes an express warranty about a material fact or facts concerning a product is subject to the standards of liability set forth in Subsection 104(D).

(C) A product seller, other than a manufacturer, is also subject to the liability of manufacturer under Section 104 if:

(1) The manufacturer is not subject to service of process under the laws of the claimant's domicile; or

(2) The manufacturer has been judicially declared insolvent in that the manufacturer is unable to pay its debts as they become due in the ordinary course of business; or

(3) The court determines that it is highly probable that the claimant would be unable to enforce a judgment against the product manufacturer.

(D) Except as provided in Subsections (A), (B), and (C), a product seller, other than a manufacturer, shall not otherwise be subject to liability under this Act.

Analysis

§ 105. Basic Standards of Responsibility for Product Sellers Other Than Manufacturers

Section 105 is derived in part from Tennessee law. "Tenn.Code

Ann." Section 23–3706 (Supp. 1978). The Section addresses the problem of excessive product liability costs for parties other than manufacturers in the distribution chain in a way that does not compromise incentives for loss prevention. It also leaves the claimant with a viable defendant whenever a defective product has caused harm.

The "ISO Closed Claims Survey" shows that manufacturers account for 87 percent of the total amount of product liability payments, while distributors, wholesalers, and retailers account for 4.6 percent. "ISO Closed Claims Survey," Report 3, at 35 (1977). Case law suggests that these non-manufacturer product sellers can usually shift their costs to the manufacturer through an indemnity suit. See, e.g., "Hales v. Monroe," 544 F.2d 331, 332 (8th Cir. 1976); "Anderson v. Somberg," 158 N.J.Super. 384, 386 A.2d 413, 419–20 (1978); "Litton Systems, Inc. v. Shaw's Sales & Serv., Ltd.," 119 Ariz. 10, 579 P.2d 48, 50 (1978).

Despite their relatively small role vis-a-vis manufacturers as product liability defendants, wholesalers, retailers, and distributors are frequently brought into a product liability suit. See, e.g., "Tucson Indus., Inc. v. Schwartz," 108 Ariz. 464, 501 P.2d 936 (1972); "Vergott v. Deseret Pharmaceutical Co.," 463 F.2d 12 (5th Cir. 1972); "Duckworth v. Ford Motor Co.," 320 F.2d 130 (3d Cir.1963). In light of ISO data showing that for every dollar of claims paid, at least 35 cents is spent in defense costs,[12] the net result is that wholesalers, retailers, and distributors are subject to substantial product liability costs in terms of both premiums and defense costs. These costs are added to the price of products and waste legal resources. See "Pender v. Skillcraft Indus., Inc.," 358 So.2d 45 (Fla. Dist.Ct.App.1978).

Under Section 105, product sellers other than manufacturers must exercise reasonable care in their handling of products. This obligation includes inspecting for hazards which a reasonably prudent product seller would have reason to discover. The focus of judicial inquiry will be on the opportunity the non-manufacturer product seller had to discover the hazard and on whether circumstances would permit a reasonable product seller to take corrective action. See "Edwards v. E.I. DuPont de Nemours & Co.," 183 F.2d 165, 167 (5th Cir.1950).

On the other hand, product sellers other than manufacturers are not liable for harms caused by products which are defective in construction or design, if those products were defective when they were received and the product seller had no reasonable opportunity to discover the defective condition. In addition, such product sellers are generally not liable for harms caused by breaches of the duty to warn or an express warranty unless the product seller's own conduct gave rise to the claim.

---

12. See "ISO Closed Claims Survey," Report 14, at 118.

Subsection (A) provides that non-manufacturer product sellers are not subject to liability when they had no reasonable opportunity for product inspection which, in the exercise of reasonable care, would or should have revealed the existence of the defective condition. For example, if a retailer receives a defective product in a sealed container and there is no way for the retailer to be aware of the condition, the retailer will not be held liable. In general, Section 105 does not impose liability on non-manufacturer product sellers where there are defects in construction or defects in design that a reasonably prudent product seller would have had no opportunity to discover. The manufacturer can avoid many of these defects; the distributor or retailer cannot. However, a non-manufacturer product seller can waive the benefits of Subsection (A) through an express warranty that it makes or transmits to the product user. *Cf.* "Ky.Rev.Stat.Ann." Section 411.-340 (Supp.1978). The term "manufacturer" is defined in Subsection 102(B).

Under Subsection (A), non-manufacturer product sellers are required to exercise reasonable care in their handling and storage of products and to pass along warnings from the manufacturer. Non-manufacturer product sellers are also responsible for defects introduced into the product by virtue of their own negligent conduct (*e.g.,* faulty product preparation or storage). Failure to fulfill their responsibilities will subject non-manufacturer product sellers to liability for their contribution to the harm which results.

Under Subsection (B), the non-manufacturer product seller is subject to the same liability as a manufacturer if the non-manufacturer product seller makes an express warranty. In these situations, such product seller has induced the purchase of the product by these specific words, and courts have been virtually unanimous in holding them responsible if the words prove to be untrue. *See* W. Prosser, "Torts" at 652 (4th ed. 1971).

Subsection (C) addresses the justifiable concern of Justice Traynor in "Vandermark v. Ford Motor Co.," 61 Cal.2d 256, 391 P.2d 168, 171, 37 Cal.Rptr. 896, 899 (1964), that:

> In some cases the retailer may be the only member of that enterprise reasonably available to the injured plaintiff. In other cases the retailer himself may play a substantial part in ensuring that the product is safe or may be in a position to exert pressure on the manufacturer to that end.

A majority of courts have followed the "Vandermark" case and have extended strict liability to retailers. *See, e.g.* "McKisson v. Sales Affiliates, Inc.," 416 S.W.2d 787 (Tex.1967); "Housman v. C.A. Dawson & Co.," 106 Ill.App.2d 225, 245 N.E.2d 886 (1969). *See also* "U.C.C." Section 2–314.

Section 105 responds to Justice Traynor's concern in cases in which it is necessary to do so. If the manufacturer is not subject to service of process or has been judicially declared insolvent, or if a court determines that it would be highly likely that the claimant would be unable to enforce a judgment against the product manufacturer, the retailer, wholesaler, or distributor has the same strict liability obligations as a manufacturer. Thus, the limited liability shield set forth in Subsection (D) only operates when the product manufacturer is reasonably available for suit by the injured claimant.

Some economists may criticize the exception to the general rule set forth in Section 105. Another approach is that of a recently enacted Nebraska statute which flatly exempts non-manufacturer product sellers from liability unless they have been negligent. *See* "Neb.Rev.Stat." Section 25–21, 181 (Supp.1978). *See also* "Shainberg v. Barlow," 258 So.2d 242, 244 (Miss.1972) (same result under case law). However, the Nebraska approach can leave a person injured by a *defective* product (as defined in Section 104) without compensation. The Act makes clear that in these situations, the party who actually sold or commercially leased the defective product should bear the loss.

Procedurally, if the claimant commences an action against the retailer, wholesaler, or distributor, and the action is based upon a theory other than the retailer's, wholesaler's, or distributor's own negligence—such as Subsection 104(A)—the defendant would make a motion for dismissal. At that time, the claimant must show that the manufacturer is unavailable under the provisions of Subsection (C). The court would then consider and make a determination regarding the three conditions listed in Subsection (C) concerning the manufacturer. If the claimant commences an action against the retailer, wholesaler, or distributor, and one of the claimant's theories is the negligent conduct of the defendant, the defendant may move to dismiss on the other theory, but the negligence theory will be litigated. If the action is dismissed against the retailer, wholesaler, or distributor under Section 105, the claimant retains the option to proceed against the manufacturer.

Subsection (D) makes clear that the Section sets forth the entire scope of liability of non-manufacturer product sellers.

However, it should be noted that retailers, wholesalers, distributors, or others can become manufacturers for the purposes of this Act to the extent that they design, produce, make, fabricate, construct, or remanufacture a product or component part of a product prior to sale. Such parties can also become manufacturers for the purposes of this Act if they hold themselves out as a manufacturer. *See* Section 102(B) ("manufacturer") and accompanying analysis.

In order for Section 105 to operate fairly toward claimants as well as non-manufacturer product sellers, it is suggested that:

(1) The non-manufacturer product seller be treated as a par-

ty for the purposes of discovery under the applicable procedural code. If this step is not taken, the Act may place an undue burden on the claimant in his or her attempt to prove the case; and

(2) The statute of limitation vis-a-vis the non-manufacturer product seller be deemed to have tolled in case the claimant is unable to enforce his or her product liability judgment against the manufacturer.

* * *

Code

§ 106. Unavoidably Dangerous Aspects of Products

(A) An unavoidably dangerous aspect of a product is that aspect incapable, in light of the state of scientific and technological knowledge at the time of manufacture, of being made safe without seriously impairing the product's usefulness.

(B) A product seller shall not be subject to liability for harm caused by an unavoidably dangerous aspect of a product unless:

(1) The product seller knew or had reason to know of the aspect and with that knowledge acted unreasonably in selling the product at all;

(2) The aspect was a defect in construction under Subsection 104(A);

(3) The product seller knew or had reason to know of the aspect and failed to meet a duty to instruct or warn under Subsection 104(C), or to transmit warnings or instructions under Subsection 105(A); or

(4) The product seller expressly warranted that the product was free of the unavoidably dangerous aspect under Subsection 104(D) or 105(B).

* * *

Analysis

§ 106. Unavoidably Dangerous Aspects of Products

Section 106 provides that, in general, a product seller will not be subject to liability for a product which is defective in design when a harm stems from an aspect of the product that is incapable of being made safe in light of the state of scientific and technical knowledge at the time of manufacture. The term "incapable" is meaningless unless it is placed in context. Therefore, Subsection (A) indicates that it applies when the danger cannot be avoided without seriously impairing the product's usefulness.

The approach taken in Section (A) recognizes that there may be circumstances in which a seriously injured person is left without compensation for an injury caused by an unavoidably dangerous aspect of a product; however, for reasons of policy that consumers can appreciate, Section 106 proposes that a product seller not be held responsible for harms that are simply unavoidable. *See* Johnson, "Products Liability 'Reform': A Hazard to Consumers," 56 "N.C.L.Rev." 676, 690 (1978).

If the costs of unavoidable harms are to be shifted from the individual, they should be borne by society at large. The policy predicate underlying Section 106 is that it should help encourage research and development without unleashing unreasonably unsafe products on the public. It also makes clear to policymakers that the tort-litigation system is not the means for addressing injuries caused by all product hazards.

Section 106 is based on the "Restatement (Second) of Torts" Section 402A, Comment k (1965). *See also* "N.H.Rev.Stat.Ann." Section 507–D:4 (Supp.1978).

With the exception of one Illinois decision, "Cunningham v. MacNeal Memorial Hosp.," 47 Ill.2d 443, 266 N.E.2d 897 (1970), *subsequently overruled by* "Ill. Ann.Stat." ch. 91, Sections 181–84 (Supp.1979), this approach has been followed by the common law courts throughout the United States. *See, e.g.,* "Moore v. Underwood Memorial Hosp.," 147 N.J.Super. 252, 371 A.2d 105 (1977) (serum hepatitis contracted from blood supplied); "Dalke v. Upjohn Co.," 555 F.2d 245 (9th Cir.1977) (tooth discoloration from tetracycline); "Chambers v. G.D. Searle & Co.," 441 F.Supp. 377 (D.Md.1975) (stroke allegedly from birth control pills); "Coffer v. Standard Brands, Inc.," 30 N.C.App. 134, 226 S.E.2d 534 (1976) (shell in nuts); "Hines v. St. Joseph's Hospital," 86 N.M. 763, 527 P.2d 1075 (1974) (blood transfusion).

Subsection (A) indicates that the time from which to judge the state of scientific and technological knowledge is the time of manufacture. *See* "Cochran v. Brooke," 243 Or. 89, 409 P.2d 904 (1966).

Subsection (B) indicates that the product seller shall not be subject to liability for harms caused by unavoidably dangerous aspects of products unless the claimant proves that one of four circumstances occurred.

The first circumstance involves the unusual situation in which the product seller knew or had reason to know of the unavoidably dangerous aspect and, with that knowledge, acted unreasonably in selling the product at all. An example is a product seller who markets a toy that is highly dangerous to children. This example can be contrasted with a pharmaceutical approved by the Food and Drug Administration, when both the government and the manufacturer know of the dangers connected with that product. In that situation, it is clear that this exception should not apply because it would not be unreasonable to sell the product.

The second circumstance deals with defects in construction. It is arguable that, even with the finest quality control, a product that is defective in construction can slip by inspection. Nevertheless, a judgment has been made by a majority of courts to impose strict liability on manufacturers for defects in construction. That judgment is preserved in this Act.

The third circumstance deals with the situation in which the product seller has failed to provide an adequate warning about an unavoidably dangerous aspect of a product. Section 106 is in accord with Subsections 104(C) and 105(A) and is predicated on a fault base—it is only to apply with respect to dangers which were known or could be discovered through the exercise of reasonable care. *See* "Dalke v. Upjohn," *supra;* "Chambers v. G.D. Searle & Co.," *supra;* "Toole v. Richardson–Merrell, Inc.," 251 Cal.App.2d 689, 60 Cal.Rptr. 398 (1967). As these cases reflect, the factual question underlying the legal issue of whether warnings or instructions were adequate is whether a product seller has met its duty to promulgate warnings and instructions commensurate with its actual knowledge gained from research and adverse reaction reports, and its constructive knowledge as measured by scientific literature and other available means of communication. *See* "Dalke v. Upjohn Co.," *supra,* 555 F.2d, at 248; "McEwen v. Ortho Pharmaceutical Corp.," 270 Or. 375, 528 P.2d 522, 528–29 (1974). *Contra,* "Bruce v. Martin–Marietta Corp.," 544 F.2d 442 (10th Cir.1976).

The Section's cross-reference to Subsections 104(C) and 105(A) makes clear that the product seller must meet its obligation to warn, instruct, or transmit warnings or instructions based on new information about an unavoidably dangerous aspect of a product that is discovered *after* the product has been manufactured. *See* "Love v. Wolf," 226 Cal.App.2d 378, 38 Cal. Rptr. 183 (1964); "Sterling Drug, Inc. v. Yarrow," 408 F.2d 1978 (8th Cir.1969). Only those harmed after the duty to warn arose would be entitled to a claim.

Finally, Section 106 makes clear that a product seller can be liable for an unavoidably dangerous aspect of a product if the product seller expressly warranted that the product was free from such aspect. *See* Subsections 104(D) and 105(B).

* * *

Code

§ 107. Relevance of Industry Custom, Safety or Performance Standards, and Practical Technological Feasibility

(A) Evidence of changes in (1) a product's design, (2) warnings or instructions concerning the product, (3) technological feasibility, (4) "state of the art", or (5) the custom of the product seller's industry or business, occurring after the product was manufactured, is not admissible for the purpose of proving that the product was defective in design under Subsection 104(B) or that a warning or instruction should have accompanied the product at the time of manufacture under Subsection 104(C).

If the court finds that the probative value of such evidence substantially outweighs its prejudicial effect and that there is no other proof available, this evidence may be admitted for other relevant purposes if confined to those purposes in a specific court instruction. Examples of "other relevant purposes" include proving ownership or control, or impeachment.

(B) For the purposes of Section 107, "custom" refers to the practices followed by an ordinary product seller in the product seller's industry or business.

(C) Evidence of custom in the product seller's industry or business or of the product seller's compliance or non-compliance with a non-governmental safety or performance standard, existing at the time of manufacture, may be considered by the trier of fact in determining whether a product was defective in design under Subsection 104(B), or whether there was a failure to warn or instruct under Subsection 104(C) or to transmit warnings or instructions under Subsection 105(A).

(D) For the purposes of Section 107, "practical technological feasibility" means the technological, mechanical, and scientific knowledge relating to product safety that was reasonably feasible for use, in light of economic practicality, at the time of manufacture.

(E) If the product seller proves, by a preponderance of the evidence, that it was not within practical technological feasibility for it to make the product safer with respect to design and warnings or instructions at the time of manufacture so as to have prevented claimant's harm, the product seller shall not be subject to liability for harm caused by the product unless the trier of fact determines that:

(1) The product seller knew or had reason to know of the danger and, with that knowledge, acted unreasonably in selling the product at all;

(2) The product was defective in construction under Subsection 104(A);

(3) The product seller failed to meet the post-manufacture duty to warn or instruct under Subsection 104(C)(6); or

(4) The product seller was subject to liability for express warranty under Subsection 104(D) or 105(B).

Analysis

§ 107. Relevance of Industry Custom, Safety or Performance Standards, and Practical Technological Feasibility

Subsection (A) adopts a fundamental principle of evidence law for the purposes of product liability cases. It excludes the showing of post-manufacture changes in the design of or warnings about a product, technological feasibility, "state of the art," or industry custom when evidence of those changes is offered to show that the product was defective at the time of manufacture. See Fed.R.Evid. 407 and Advisory Committee Commentary. The term "state of the art," as used in the listing of evidentiary items in Subsection 107(A), is a general, commonly used phrase whose meaning may include industry custom or the most scientifically advanced developments in the field. As will be indicated in the discussion of Subsections (B) through (E), the Act has generally eschewed the phrase because of its ambiguity. Nevertheless, it has been utilized in Subsection (A) in order to assure that all post-manufacture change is excluded from evidence.

The reasons underlying the rule on which Subsection 107(A) is based are twofold: first, subsequent changes are deemed irrelevant (all they show is that "as one gets older, one may get wiser"); and second, admission of such evidence may discourage the making of improvements or repairs. While the latter rationale has been challenged (*see* "Ault v. International Harvester Co.," 13 Cal.3d 113, 528 P.2d 1148, 117 Cal. Rptr. 812 (1975); Schwartz, "The Exclusionary Rule on Evidence of Repair—A Rule in Need of Repair," 7 "The Forum" 1 (1971)), the relevance of such evidence on the issue of defectiveness is of very limited value. On the other hand, the prejudicial effect of showing the subsequent change or repair—particularly one undertaken by the product seller itself—is quite substantial. *See* "LaMonica v. Outboard Marine Corp.," 48 Ohio App.2d 43, 355 N.E.2d 533 (1976); "Haysom v. Coleman Lantern Co.," 89 Wash.2d 474, 573 P.2d 785 (1978).

Subsection (A) permits the introduction of evidence which would otherwise be excluded under the Subsection, if that evidence is highly probative and necessary to prove a relevant matter other than the fact that the product was defective at the time of manufacture. Thus, evidence of such changes may be admissible to show that the product seller knew of the defect at a certain point in time after manufacture. In appropriate circumstances, this evidence may suggest that the product seller had a duty to take reasonable steps to warn product users about a newly discovered hazard. It may also be admissible when the product seller claims the product hazard was impossible to avoid. In cases of this kind, the court should make a finding that the probative value of the evidence substantially outweighs its prejudicial nature and that there is no other equally probative proof available. Allowing the introduction of evidence in these cases should *not* become a vehicle for avoiding the basic purpose of the rule.

Subsections (B), (C), (D), and (E) address one of the major issues that has divided product sellers and consumer groups concerned about product liability. Product sellers have vigorously argued that when their products comply with the "state of the art," it is unfair to deem them defective. Further, they contend that industry custom is likely to incorporate all cost-justified product safety features. They have received some support for this contention from members of the academic community, at least in regard to purchasers, as contrasted with nonpurchaser product users, of the product. *See* R. Posner, "Economic Analysis of Law" 71 (1972).

Consumer groups respond that it is inappropriate to allow product sellers to fix indirectly their own standard of liability. See Johnson, "Products Liability 'Reform': A Hazard to Consumers," 56 "N.C.L.Rev." 677, 680–81 (1978).

When the issue is carefully analyzed, there is less dispute between product sellers and consumer groups than appears on the surface. Part of the sound and fury is a debate over the ambiguous term "state of the art." The approach taken in Subsections (B), (C), (D), and (E) of not using the term "state of the art" eliminates that ambiguity and focuses on what is fair to each party.

Subsection (B) defines "custom" as the "practices followed by the ordinary product seller in the defendant product seller's industry or business." See W. Prosser, "Torts" at 166 (4th ed. 1971).

Subsection (C) indicates that compliance with industry custom is merely evidence that the trier of fact may consider in determining whether a product was defective under Subsections 104(B) and (C). There is strong support in the case law for this approach. See, e.g., "Bruce v. Martin–Marietta Corp.," 544 F.2d 442 (10th Cir. 1976); "Baker v. Chrysler Corp.," 55 Cal.App.3d 710, 127 Cal.Rptr. 745 (1976); "Maxted v. Pacific Car & Foundry Co.," 527 P.2d 832 (Wyo.1974); "Roach v. Kononen," 269 Or. 457, 525 P.2d 125 (1974); "Olson v. Arctic Enterprises, Inc." 349 F.Supp. 761 (D.N.D.1972).

Subsection (C) also permits introduction of evidence of non-compliance with custom—evidence likely to be introduced by a product liability claimant. While it might be argued that non-compliance with custom should indicate that the product was defective, situations may arise where a product seller followed an alternative procedure that was no less safe (perhaps even safer) than the custom in the industry. For that reason, non-compliance with custom does not create a situation where the trier of fact should consider the product defective *per se*.

Subsection (C) treats compliance or non-compliance with non-governmental product standards in the same manner as custom. Compliance or non-compliance with such standards is admissible in evidence when relevant to the issue before the court. Privately developed standards—for both design and performance—vary widely in their nature and quality. While almost all privately developed standards are labeled "minimum" (suggesting a standard below that which a product seller could reasonably achieve), some standards reach the best level that can be obtained as a practical technological matter. See "Task Force Report" at IV–13–17. On the other hand, some are clearly below the level of safety appropriate as a defense in a product liability case. See "Report of the National Commission on Product Safety" at 48 (1978) ("chronically inadequate both in scope and permissible level of risk").

Compliance with standards that are rigorous and objective (in that they were developed through careful, thorough product testing and a formal product safety evaluation, and up-to-date in light of the technological and scientific knowledge reasonably available at the time the product was manufactured) suggests that a product was not defective. Failure to comply with such standards, especially performance standards, suggests that it was defective. Nevertheless, because of the variance in the nature and quality of privately developed safety standards, the Act has eschewed *per se* rules in this area. See "Poches v. J.J. Newberry Co.," 549 F.2d 1166 (8th Cir.1977).

Subsection (D), defining "practical technological feasibility," should be contrasted with Subsection (B)'s definition of "custom." The Subsection (D) definition contemplates a level of safety that was feasible, as a practical matter, at the time of manufacture. "Feasibility" includes economic considerations such as the ability of a product seller to price a product so that it is competitive, but excludes financial considerations peculiar to a particular product seller, such as its cash flow at the relevant time.

The definition's emphasis on *feasibility* addresses consumer concerns with "state-of-the-art" or "custom" defenses that could allow an industry or business to be shielded from liability when it has "negligently" lagged behind in both developing and utilizing safety technology.

Subsection (E) indicates that when a product seller proves by a preponderance of the evidence that it was not within practical technological feasibility to make the product safer, the product seller shall not be subject to liability. This is in accord with the great majority of case law. See, e.g., "Olson v. Arctic Enterprises, Inc.," *supra;* "Wilson v. Piper Aircraft Corp.," 282 Or. 61, 577 P.2d 1322, 1326 (1978) ("... plaintiff's *prima facie* case of a defect must show more than the technical possibility of a safe design"); "Bruce v. Martin–Marietta Corp.," *supra;* "Maxted v. Pacific Car & Foundry Co.," *supra;* "Roach v. Kononen," *supra. Cf.* "Ky.Rev.Stat.Ann." Section 411.310(2) (Supp.1978) (includes custom). *But cf.* "Colo.Rev. Stat." Section 13–21–403 (Supp. 1978) ("state of the art" presumption only).

Significantly, only a few intermediate appellate court decisions, primarily from one state, impose liability if the product was in accord with the technological, mechanical, and scientific knowledge reasonably feasible for use at the time of manufacture. See, e.g., "Gelsumino v. E.W. Bliss Co.," 10 Ill.App.3d 604, 295 N.E.2d 110 (1973), and its progeny. *But see* "McClellan v. Chicago Transit Authority," 34 Ill.App.3d 151, 340 N.E.2d 61 (1975). *Compare* "Olson v. A.W. Chesterton Co.," 256 N.W.2d 530 (N.D.1977).

In order to meet appropriate consumer group concerns, Subsection (E) provides four exceptions to the defense. First, the defense

§ 107   MODEL UNIFORM PRODUCT LIABILITY ACT

will not apply if the product seller knew or had reason to know of the danger and, with that knowledge, acted unreasonably in selling the product at all. *See also* Subsection 106(B)(1) and analysis. This exception would only apply in very unusual situations. For example, a child's toy might comply with what was technologically feasible but, because of its danger, it would be unreasonable behavior to market the product for young children. Similarly, it would be unreasonable to manufacture a home heating unit with a radium core unless technology had reached a point at which the inhabitants of the home (and others) would be protected from radiation.

Second, although the product was in accord with the "practical technological feasibility," it may be defective in construction. It is a basic principle of this Act to apply strict liability against the manufacturer in that case. *See* Subsection 104(A) and analysis.

Third, although the product complied with the "practical technological feasibility" at the time of manufacture, the product seller may have failed to meet its post-manufacture duty to warn or instruct under Subsection 104(C)(6).

Finally, although its product was in accord with "practical technological feasibility," a product seller cannot escape strict liability for express warranty under Subsection 104(D) or 105(B).

* * *

Code

§ 108. Relevance of Legislative or Administrative Regulatory Standards and Mandatory Government Contract Specifications

(A) When the injury-causing aspect of the product was, at the time of manufacture, in compliance with legislative regulatory standards or administrative regulatory safety standards relating to design or performance, the product shall be deemed not defective under Subsection 104(B), or, if the standard addressed warnings or instructions, under Subsection 104(C) or 105(A), unless the claimant proves by a preponderance of the evidence that a reasonably prudent product seller could and would have taken additional precautions.

(B) When the injury-causing aspect of the product was not, at the time of manufacture, in compliance with legislative regulatory standards or administrative regulatory safety standards relating to design or performance, the product shall be deemed defective under Subsection 104(B), or, if the standard addressed warnings or instructions, under Subsection 104(C) or 105(A), unless the product seller proves by a preponderance of the evidence that its failure to comply was a reasonably prudent course of conduct under the circumstances.

(C) When the injury-causing aspect of the product was, at the time of manufacture, in compliance with a mandatory government contract specification relating to design, this shall be an absolute defense and the product shall be deemed not defective under Subsection 104(B), or, if the specification related to warnings or instructions, under Subsection 104(C) or 105(A).

(D) When the injury-causing aspect of the product was not, at the time of manufacture, in compliance with a mandatory government contract specification relating to design, the product shall be deemed defective under Subsection 104(B), or, if the specification related to warnings or instructions, under Subsection 104(C) or 105(A).

Analysis

§ 108. Relevance of Legislative or Administrative Regulatory Standards and Mandatory Government Contract Specifications

Product sellers have contended that it is unfair to deem a product defective when the challenged aspect of that product conformed to an applicable administrative or legislative regulatory standard. They note that considerable time and thought are spent in the development of such standards and that the standards are frequently subject to intense public scrutiny prior to the time of their official adoption. Product sellers point to legislative and administrative standards as a resource to provide some predictability within the scope of product liability law. They contend that it is unfair to allow lay jurors to reevaluate a standard that has presumably been drafted by government experts. Furthermore, some product liability loss prevention experts suggest that a defense based on compliance with standards will create incentives for manufacturers to comply with such standards. *See* Task Force "Selected Papers" at 266 (Remarks of Professor Alvin S. Weinstein).

On the other hand, some consumer groups maintain that government standards are often the result of compromise decisions—decisions that are sometimes unduly influenced by industry. These consumer groups point out that some government regulatory bodies may have insufficient personnel or expertise to make independent judgments. The general approach of courts, as well as that embodied in the "Consumer Product Safety Act," 15 "U.S.C." Section 2074(A) (1976) and the "National Traffic and Motor Vehicle Safety Act," 15 "U.S.C." Section 1391(2) (1976), is that government standards are only minimum standards, and that compliance should not be deemed an absolute defense in product liability actions. *See* "Roberts v. May," ___ Colo.App. ___, 583 P.2d 305, 308 (1978). In spite of this, some states have enacted statutes that grant this effect to such compliance. *See* "N.D.Cent.Code" Section 28–01.1–05(3) (Supp.1979); "Utah Code Ann." Section 78–15–6 (1977); "Colo.Rev.Stat." Section 13–21–403 (Supp.1978).

Nevertheless, case law also suggests that government safety standards are often deemed sound and appropriate for application to tort law claims. *See* "Jones v. Hittle Serv., Inc.," 219 Kan. 627, 549 P.2d 1383 (1976) (universally accepted standards for odorizing LP gas outweigh expert opinion); "McDaniel v. McNeil Laboratories, Inc.," 196 Neb. 190, 241 N.W.2d 822 (1976) (determination of the FDA prevails in absence of proof that the manufacturer furnished incomplete, misleading, or fraudulent information); "Simien v. S.S. Kresge Co.," 566 F.2d 551 (5th Cir.1978) (compliance with flammability standard); "Bruce v. Martin–Marietta Corp.," 544 F.2d 442, 446 (10th Cir.1976) (claimants did "not present any more stringent standards which might have been applicable at the time of manufacture").

The approach taken in Subsection (A) is based on these cases and on the "Restatement (Second) of Torts" Section 288C (1965). When the specific injury-causing aspect of the product conformed to or was in compliance with the legislative or administrative regulatory standard, the product is deemed not defective under Subsection 104(B) when design is relevant, or under Subsection 104(C) or 105(A) when the duty to warn or instruct is relevant, unless the claimant proves by a preponderance of the evidence that a reasonably prudent product seller could and would have taken additional precautions.

This approach has enabled claimants to prevail when legislative or administrative standards did not meet an appropriate level of safety. For example, in "Raymond v. Riegel Textile Corp.," 484 F.2d 1025 (1st Cir.1973), the claimant was able to show that a standard promulgated under the "Flammable Fabrics Act" was outdated. *See also* "Burch v. Amsterdam Corp.," 366 A.2d 1079 (D.C. 1976) (when manufacturer knows of greater dangers not included in a statutorily mandated warning, it should bring those precautions to the attention of product users). On the other hand, it recognizes that government safety standards *may* provide an adequate basis for evaluating safety in tort law.

Subsection (B) makes it clear that when the injury-causing aspect of the product did not conform or was not in compliance with a legislative or administrative regulatory standard, the product shall be deemed defective under Subsection 104(B), when design is relevant, or Subsection 104(C), when duty to warn is relevant, unless the product seller shows by a preponderance of the evidence that its failure to comply amounted to reasonably prudent conduct under the circumstances. *See* "Restatement (Second) of Torts" Section 286 (1965). A product seller may be able to prevail under Subsection (B) by showing that compliance would have created greater dangers than non-compliance would have. *Cf.* "Davison v. Williams," 251 Ind. 448, 242 N.E.2d 101 (1968) (violation of safety regulation may be justified in circumstances).

Subsection (C) addresses a highly specialized problem with respect to a product that had been manufactured strictly in accordance with mandatory specifications set forth in a government contract. When compliance with such a standard leads to an injury, the government, not the product seller, is the appropriate defendant. As the court in "Hunt v. Blasius," 55 Ill.App.3d 14, 370 N.E.2d 617, 621–22 (1977), indicated, "public policy dictates that bidders who comply strictly with governmental specifications should be shielded from liability in any respect in which the product complies." When enacting this provision, a legislature should ensure that its own state government bears financial responsibility (either through tort law or through a compensation system) for the harm it has caused by directing that the product conform to contract specifications.

Subsection (D) provides a counterweight to Subsection (C). If the bidder fails to comply with a mandatory government contract specification, and this failure to comply caused the claimant's injury, the product seller will be deemed liable under Subsection 104(B) if the specification related to design, or under Subsection 104(C) or 105(A) of the specification related to instruction or warnings. If the manufacturer's compliance exceeded the government regulation and the product failed, liability should not be imposed under this Section—in that case, the technical "failure to comply" would not be the proximate cause of the injury that befell claimant.

* * *

Code

§ 109. Notice of Possible Claim Required

(A) An attorney who anticipates filing a claim shall notify all product sellers against whom the claim is likely to be made. The notice of claim shall:

(1) Identify the product as specifically as possible;

(2) State the time, place, circumstances, and events giving rise to the claim;

(3) Give an estimate of compensation or other relief to be sought.

(B) The attorney shall give notice of claim within six (6) months of the date of entering into an attorney-client relationship with the claimant in regard to the claim. For the purposes of Section 109, such a relationship arises when the attorney, or any member or associate of the attorney's firm, agrees to serve the claimant's interests in regard to the anticipated claim.

(C) If the claimant's attorney requests the information at the time the notice of claim is given, the product seller receiving the notice of claim shall promptly furnish the claimant's attorney with the names and addresses of each person whom the product seller knows to be in the chain of manufacture and distribution of the product, and who is likely to be subject to liability under Sections 104 or 105. Any product seller who fails to furnish such information may be subject to liability as provided in Subsection (E).

(D) A claimant who delays entering into an attorney-client relationship so as to delay unreasonably the notice of claim required by Subsection (A) may be subject to liability as provided in Subsection (E).

(E) Any party to the product liability claim or any attorney representing such a party who suffers a monetary loss associated with the litigation of the claim caused by the failure of a claimant or a claimant's attorney, or of a product seller or its attorney, to comply with the requirements of this Section may recover pecuniary damages, costs, and reasonable attorneys' fees from that party. Failure to comply with the requirements of Section 109 does not affect the validity of any claim or defense under this Act.

Analysis

§ 109. Notice of Possible Claim Required

The purpose of Section 109 is to inform product sellers at an early date that the products they produce may be defective. Under present law, a claimant can delay informing a product seller of a claim until the statute of limitation has nearly expired. In most jurisdictions, this period is two or three years. Although 77.8 percent of all bodily injury claims are reported within six months, the 22.2 percent that are not reported during this period are of concern because they represent about 68 percent of the claim payments. "ISO Closed Claims Survey" at 100 (1977).

A reasonable notice of claim requirement in product liability law promotes the interests of consumers and product users because it is a low-cost means of helping to assure product safety. Presumably, if informed about defective conditions at an early stage, a product seller is likely to take action to correct such conditions and thus prevent future injuries. This is why notice-of-claim provisions have been utilized in other contexts. See, e.g., "U.C.C." Section 2–607 (warranty breaches); 18 E. McQuillan, "Municipal Corporations" Section 53.154 (3d ed. 1977) (suits against municipalities for injuries); 3 A. Larson, "Workmen's Compensation Law" Section 78.00 et seq. (1976) (notice of injury to employer). See also Comment, "Notice Requirement in Warranty Actions Involving Personal Injury," 51 "Calif.L.Rev." 586 (1963); Phillips, "Notice of Breach in Sales and Strict Tort Liability Law: Should There Be a Difference?," 47 "Ind.L.J." 457, 468–69 (1972) (observing that requiring notice of claim may encourage defendants to make reasonable settlements).

This Section is adapted from the recently enacted "Minn.Stat. Ann." Section 604.04 (Supp.1978). It differs from analogous notice-of-claim provisions in that it does not provide that a claim or defense will be barred by the failure of the injured party to meet its conditions. As the court noted in "Greenman v. Yuba Power Prods., Inc.," 59 Cal.2d 57, 377 P.2d 897, 27 Cal.Rptr. 697, 700 (1963), such a provision may become a booby trap for the unwary. The injured consumer is seldom 'steeped in the business practice which justifies the rule.' [James, "Products Liability" (pt. 2), 34 "Tex. L.Rev." 192, 197 (1955)] and at least until he has had legal advice it will not occur to him to give notice....

Instead, Section 109 places a duty on the attorney to give the notice of claim. It imposes on the attorney the costs of investigation and other litigation expenses which stem from the failure to give notice.

Section 109 also places a burden on the product seller who is notified of an anticipated claim to provide the claimant's attorney with the names and addresses of others whom the product seller knows to be in the chain of manufacture and distribution of the product, and who are likely to be subject to liability under Sections 104 or 105. The product seller is not obligated, however, to supply long lists of every supplier of a component part of its product or every possible wholesale and retail purchaser of it. Product sellers may also be held liable under this Section for litigation costs that stem from the failure to provide the required names.

Subsection 109(E) is limited to losses associated directly with the litigation of the claim in issue and does not apply to possible losses suffered by persons other than a party to the product liability claim or any attorney representing such a party.

Claims arising under Section 109 can be consolidated with the principal product liability claim brought under this Act.

* * *

Code

§ 110. Length of Time Product Sellers are Subject to Liability

(A) *Useful Safe Life.*

(1) Except as provided in Subsection (A)(2), a product seller shall not be subject to liability to a claimant for harm under this Act if the product seller proves by a preponderance of the evidence that the harm was caused after the product's "useful safe life" had expired.

"Useful safe life" begins at the time of delivery of the product and extends for the time during which the product would normally be likely to perform or be stored in a safe manner. For the purposes of Section 110, "time of delivery" means the time of delivery of a product to its first purchaser or lessee who was not engaged in the business of either selling such products or using them as component parts of another product to be sold.

Examples of evidence that is especially probative in determining whether a product's useful safe life had expired include:

(a) The amount of wear and tear to which the product had been subject;

(b) The effect of deterioration from natural causes, and from climate and other conditions under which the product was used or stored;

(c) The normal practices of the user, similar users, and the product seller with respect to the circumstances, frequency, and purposes of the product's use, and with respect to repairs, renewals, and replacements;

(d) Any representations, instructions, or warnings made by the product seller concerning proper maintenance, storage, and use of the product or the expected useful safe life of the product; and

(e) Any modification or alteration of the product by a user or third party.

(2) A product seller may be subject to liability for harm caused by a product used beyond its useful safe life to the extent that the product seller has expressly warranted the product for a longer period.

(B) *Statute of Repose.*

(1) *Generally.* In claims that involve harm caused more than ten (10) years after time of delivery, a presumption arises that the harm was caused after the useful safe life had expired. This presumption may only be rebutted by clear and convincing evidence.

(2) *Limitations on Statute of Repose.*

(a) If a product seller expressly warrants that its product can be utilized safely for a period longer than ten (10) years, the period of repose, after which the presumption created in Subsection (B)(1) arises, shall be extended according to that warranty or promise.

(b) The ten- (10-) year period of repose established in Subsection (B)(1) does not apply if the product seller intentionally misrepresents facts about its product, or fraudulently conceals information about it, and that conduct was a substantial cause of the claimant's harm.

(c) Nothing contained in Subsection (B) shall affect the right of any person found liable under this Act to seek and obtain contribution or indemnity from any other person who is responsible for harm under this Act.

(d) The ten- (10-) year period of repose established in Subsection (B)(1) shall not apply if the harm was caused by prolonged exposure to a defective product, or if the injury-causing aspect of the product that existed at the time of delivery was not discoverable by an ordinary reasonably prudent person until more than ten (10) years after the time of delivery, or if the harm, caused within ten (10) years after the time of delivery, did not manifest itself until after that time.

(C) *Statute of Limitation.* No claim under this Act may be brought more than two (2) years from the time the claimant discovered, or in the exercise of due diligence should have discovered, the harm and the cause thereof.

* * *

Analysis

§ 110. Length of Time Product Sellers are Subject to Liability

Perhaps more significant than any other single factor alleged to be the cause of the nationwide product liability insurance problem are the rules governing the responsibility of product sellers for older products. Most product liability policies include claims based not only on products manufactured or sold during the given policy year, but also on products manufactured or sold in the past. In the case of sellers of durable goods, this creates an "open-ended" liability situation.

The Supreme Court of Oregon summarized the general common law rule for products with the statement: "[P]rolonged use of a manufactured article is but one factor, albeit an important one, in the determination of whether a defect in the product made it unsafe...." "Tucker v. Unit Crane & Shovel Corp.," 256 Or. 318, 473 P.2d 862 (1970) (boom crane manufactured in 1956, collapsed in 1965). See also "Gates v. Ford Motor Company," 494 F.2d 458 (10th Cir.1974) (24-year-old tractor); "Kaczmarek v. Mesta Machinery Co.," 463 F.2d 675 (3d Cir. 1972) (30-year-old pickling machine); "Mondshour v. General Motors Corp.," 298 F.Supp. 111 (D.Md.1969) (bus designed 17 years prior to accident).

Partly in response to this open-ended liability potential, a number of states have enacted statutes of repose that begin at the time a product is first sold and distributed. See, e.g., "1979 Ala. Acts" No. 79–468 Section 3(b) ("10 years after the manufactured product is first put to use"); "Ariz. Rev.Stat.Ann." Section 12–551 (Supp.1978) ("12 years after the product was first sold for use or consumption ..."); "Fla.Stat. Ann." Section 95.031(2) (Supp. 1979) ("12 years after the date of delivery of the completed product"); "Ill.Ann.Stat." ch. 83, Section 22.2(b) (Supp.1979) (12 years from date of first sale or 10 years from sale to actual user-claimant—strict liability); "Ind.Code Ann." Section 33–1–1.5–5 (Supp. 1978) ("10 years after the delivery ... to the initial user"); "Neb. Rev.Stat." Section 25–224 (Supp. 1978) (10 years after first sale); "Utah Code Ann." Section 78–15–3(1) (1977) (6 years after date of initial purchase; 10 years after date of manufacture).

The advantages of these statutes are that they: (1) establish an actuarially certain date after which no liability can be assessed; and (2) eliminate tenuous claims involving older products for which evidence of defective conditions may be difficult to produce. See "Order of Railroad Telegraphers v. Railway Express Agency," 321 U.S. 342, 348–49 (1944).

On the other hand, a fundamental problem with these statutes is that they *may* deprive a person injured by a product of the right to bring a claim based on a defective product before the injury has actually occurred. See Johnson, "Products Liability 'Reform': A Hazard to Consumers," 56

"N.C.L.Rev." 677, 689–90 (1978); "Victorson v. Bock Laundry Mach. Co.," 37 N.Y.2d 395, 335 N.E.2d 275, 373 N.Y.S.2d 39 (1975).

The limited available data show that insurers' apprehension about older products may be exaggerated. See "ISO Closed Claims Survey" at 105–08 (indicating that over 97 percent of product-related accidents occur within six years of the time the product was purchased and, in the capital goods area, 83.5 percent of all bodily injury accidents occur within ten years of manufacture). Nevertheless, as the "Task Force Report" indicated, the underwriters' concern about *potential* losses associated with older products may be an important factor in the recent increase in liability insurance premiums for manufacturers of durable goods. See "Task Force Report" at VII–21.

Section 110 attempts to provide insurers and product sellers with some security against stale claims, while preserving the claimant's right to obtain damages for injuries caused by defective products. It accomplishes this result through provisions on useful safe life, a statute of repose, and a statute of limitation.

(A) *Useful Safe Life.* The common law in most states is that "[t]he age of an allegedly defective product must be considered in light of its expected useful life and the stress to which it has been subjected." "Kuisis v. Baldwin–Lima–Hamilton Corp.," 457 Pa. 321, 319 A.2d 914, 923 (1974) (brake-locking mechanism on a crane failed after more than 20 years of use). The "Kuisis" court noted further that "in certain situations the prolonged use factor may loom so large as to obscure all others in a case." *Id.*

The basic problem has been the vagueness of the concept. Thus, while the "Task Force Report" noted that "if a useful life limitation were identified in statutory form, it might be expected that it would be given more serious attention by both judge and jury" ("Task Force Report" at VII–27), it also observed that "the concept would still lack specificity." *Id.* Subsection (A) is designed to define the concept with as much specificity as possible.

The Subsection was derived from "Minn.Stat.Ann." Section 604.03 (Supp.1978). It serves to remind the court and the trier of fact that a product seller may be held liable only for harms caused during the useful *safe* life of the product. It does not attempt to apply fixed useful safe life standards for all products. Such an approach is not possible as a practical matter. See Phillips, "An Analysis of Proposed Reform of Products Liability Statutes of Limitations," 56 "N.C.L.Rev." 663, 673 (1978). Rather, it identifies factors that will assist the court and the trier of fact in determining how long a product can reasonably be expected to perform or be stored in a safe manner.

Section 110 uses the term "useful safe life" (not "useful life," a term which has already acquired a meaning in the law of taxation), because the period in which the product can have some "utility" may be well beyond the period in which the product is "safe." For example, a driver may continue to "use" tires that lack sufficient treads for safety.

A product seller may raise the "useful safe life" of a product as an affirmative defense in a product liability claim. The period of time begins at the time of delivery of the product and extends through the time during which the product would normally be likely to perform in a safe manner.

"Time of delivery" is defined as the time of delivery of a product to its first purchaser or lessee not engaged in the business of either selling such products or using them as component parts of another product to be sold. "Time of delivery" is an important concept in the Act because it marks the last time a product seller has physical control of the product and the first time that the product is in the hands of someone other than a product seller. The useful safe life and repose periods of Section 110 begin to run from this point in time.

The Section then sets forth a series of factors that will be of assistance to the court and jury in determining whether the period of time has expired. The product seller need not introduce evidence with respect to each of the listed factors. Rather, each of the litigants in a product liability claim may introduce evidence on those factors listed which, they believe, will support their respective contentions. In some cases, evidence on one or a few of the factors may be regarded as dispositive of the "useful safe life" issue and, when this occurs, the lack of evidence on one of the other factors normally will not affect the outcome of the case. The product seller has the burden of proof upon the issue.

Factors (a) through (c) under Subsection (A) are basically self-explanatory. Factor (d) refers to the useful safe life stated *by the product seller*. A product seller can place some reliance on this provision when it has indicated that a product should not be used beyond a certain period of time. However, Subsection (A) does not give the product seller absolute power to limit a product's useful safe life. While this was suggested in "Velez v. Craine & Clark Lumber Corp.," 33 N.Y.2d 117, 305 N.E.2d 750, 350 N.Y.S.2d 617 (1973), almost all courts would insist on retaining judicial power to determine whether the product seller's limitation was a reasonable one. *Cf.* "Henningsen v. Bloomfield Motors, Inc.," 32 N.J. 358, 161 A.2d 69 (1960). Further, even the "Velez" court indicated that a product seller's limitation on useful life could not bind the rights of a non-purchaser claimant. Nevertheless, where the product seller imposes a reasonable limitation, made in good faith to protect the user, the trier of fact should give very serious consideration to this fact in determining whether the product was used beyond its useful safe life.

Factor (e), dealing with modifications of the product by users or third parties, relates to conduct that might shorten or lengthen the useful life of the product. While the Act treats product modifications in Section 112, they are also factors in determining whether a product has been used beyond its useful safe life.

(B) *Statute of Repose.*

(1) *Generally.* Statutes of repose differ from statutes of limitation in that they set a fixed limit after the time of the product's manufacture, sale, or delivery beyond which the product seller will not be held liable. The rationale of such statutes is threefold. First, the fact that a product has been used safely for a substantial period of time is some indication that it was not defective at the time of delivery. Second, if a product seller is not aware of a claim, the passing of time may make it extremely difficult to construct a good defense because of the obstacle of securing evidence. Although the burden of proof on the issue of defectiveness remains on the claimant under the Act, a jury, as a practical matter, may demand an explanation from a product seller when the claimant has suffered a severe injury. The third rationale is that persons ought to be allowed, as a matter of policy, to plan their affairs with a reasonable degree of certainty. This goes to the heart of the product liability insurance rate-setting problem. Even though past data show that 83.5 percent of bodily injury claims arise within a ten-year period,[13] there is no safeguard in the existing law that the past will portend the future. There is always the possibility that the number of claims for older products will increase. *See* "ISO Closed Claims Survey" at 107.

On the other hand, consumers are justifiably concerned about overly broad absolute cut-offs of their right to sue. This provision recognizes consumer concerns in three basic ways:

(1) The term of the statute is ten years—beyond the term enacted or proposed in a number of states;

(2) The statute begins to run at the time of delivery, not the time of manufacture; and

(3) The statute does not contain an absolute cut-off, but rather a presumption that the product has been used beyond its useful safe life. Colorado law utilizes this approach. "Colo.Rev.Stat." Section 13–21–403(3) (Supp.1978). Most other state product liability statutes do not.

Consumer concerns are also addressed by three of the four additional restrictions contained in Subsection (B)(2).

(2) *Limitations on Statute of Repose.* This Subsection contains four key limitations on its scope of operation.

First, Subsection (B) does not apply when a product seller has expressly warranted or promised that a product can be used safely for a period longer than ten years.

---

13. Figure for capital goods.

See Subsection 102(K) (definition of "express warranty").

Second, the statute of repose provisions do not apply when a product seller intentionally misrepresented facts about its product and this misrepresentation was a substantial cause of claimant's harm.

Third, Subsection (B) does not affect contribution and indemnity claims. Thus, an intermediate product seller will not have to absorb a liability loss that was the true responsibility of the original manufacturer. *See* Defense Research Institute, "Products Liability Position Paper" at 22 (monograph 1976); *see also* Phillips, *supra,* 56 "N.C.L.Rev." at 670–71 (1978).

Fourth, there is an exception for products that cause perceptible harm only through prolonged exposure (*see, e.g.,* "Michie v. Great Lakes Steel Div., National Steel Corp.," 495 F.2d 213 (6th Cir. 1974)), or that cause harms that take many years to manifest themselves. *See* "Sindell v. Abbott Laboratories," 85 Cal.App.3d 1, 149 Cal.Rptr. 138 (1978). An exception is also made for the unusual situation in which a product contains, at the time of delivery, a hidden defect that is not discoverable by a reasonably prudent product user and does not manifest itself until after a ten-year period has expired. *See* "Mickel v. Blackmon," 252 S.C. 202, 166 S.E.2d 173 (1969) (plastic used on gearshift lost its resiliency when exposed to sunlight).

If the ten-year presumption does not apply, a product seller can still prove that the product has been utilized beyond its useful safe life under Subsection (A).

(C) *Statute of Limitation.* Tort statutes of limitation traditionally begin at the time a person is injured. This Subsection follows that approach. Nevertheless, in accord with justified consumer concerns, Subsection (C) extends the limitation period beyond the time of harm in situations where the claimant would have no reason to know about the harm or the causal connection to a defective product (*e.g.,* the case of long-term pharmaceutical harms). This reflects a general trend in both statutory and case law. *See* Birnbaum, "'First Breath's' Last Gasp: The Discovery Rule in Products Liability Cases," 13 "Forum" 279 (1977); and Annot., 91 "A.L.R.3d" 991 (1979). The two-year period represents the length of the traditional state statute of limitation based on claims for negligence. In light of the Act's adoption of the discovery rule, this is the maximum period that seemed to be appropriate.

The underlying philosophy of this Section is congruent with Sections 105 and 106, which shield product sellers from liability for risks that they would have no reason to discover at the time of manufacture.

* * *

Code

§ 111. Comparative Responsibility and Apportionment of Damages

(A) *Comparative Responsibility.* All claims under this Act

shall be governed by the principles of comparative responsibility. In any claim under this Act, the comparative responsibility of, or attributed to, the claimant shall not bar recovery but shall diminish the award of compensatory damages proportionately, according to the measure of responsibility attributed to the claimant.

(B) *Apportionment of Damages.*

(1) In all claims involving comparative responsibility, the court, unless otherwise agreed by all parties, shall instruct the jury to answer special interrogatories or, if there is no jury, the court shall make findings, indicating:

(a) The amount of damages each claimant would be entitled to recover if the comparative responsibility of each party were disregarded; and

(b) The percentage of the total responsibility of all parties to each claim that is to be allocated to each claimant; defendant; third-party defendant; person or entity who misused, modified, or altered a product under Subsection 112(C) or (D), [or who voluntarily and unreasonably used or stored a product with a known defective condition under Subsection 112(B)]; and person released from liability under Subsection 113(E). Under this Subsection, the court may determine that two or more persons are to be treated as a single party.

(2) When the claimant's employer's or co-employee's fault is considered, damages shall be reduced in accordance with Subsection 114(A), if applicable, or by the percentage of responsibility apportioned to such employer or co-employee, if that amount is greater. When a person released from liability under Subsection 113(E) would otherwise be liable under this Act, damages shall be reduced by the percentage of responsibility apportioned to such person.

(3) In determining the percentages of responsibility, the trier of fact shall consider, on a comparative basis, both the nature of the conduct of each person or entity responsible and the extent of the proximate causal relation between the conduct and the damages claimed.

(4) The court shall determine the award of damages to each claimant in accordance with the findings and enter judgment against each party liable. For purposes of contribution under Section 113, the court shall also determine and state in the judgment each party's equitable share of the obligation to each claimant in accordance with the respective percentages of responsibility.

(5) Damages are to be apportioned severally, and not jointly, when a party is responsible for a distinct harm, or when there is some other reasonable basis for apportioning that party's responsibility for the harm. Otherwise, judgment shall be entered against each party liable on the basis of the rules of joint and several liability.

(6) When one or more parties made a substantial contribution to an indivisible harm, or for other

reasons under the common law of the state is a joint tortfeasor, upon motion made not later than one (1) year after judgment is entered, the court shall determine whether all or part of a joint tortfeasor's share of the obligation is uncollectible from that joint tortfeasor.

If the court's finding is in the affirmative, the court shall reallocate any uncollectible amount among a claimant found to be responsible and other parties who are joint tortfeasors with the party whose share is uncollectible. The reallocation shall be made according to the respective percentages of responsibility of each party.

* * *

Analysis

§ 111. Comparative Responsibility and Apportionment of Damages

(A) *Comparative Responsibility.* Subsection (A) attempts to resolve existing legal uncertainty about the relevance of a claimant's conduct and the comparative responsibility of others who contributed to the claimant's harm. It applies principles of comparative responsibility to situations where more than one person has some responsibility for the product-related incident. *Cf.* "Uniform Comparative Fault Act" ("UCFA") Section 1. The consumer-oriented fairness of pure comparative responsibility is adopted, as compared with the "non-discriminating rough justice of the modified type...." "Prefatory Note," "UCFA".

Although there is no assurance that the use of comparative responsibility principles will lower the cost of product liability claims, the inherent fairness of such principles has led to their inclusion in the "UCFA" by the National Conference of Commissioners of Uniform State Laws. Section 111 borrows extensively from the "UCFA" and its accompanying commentary.

Some courts and commentators have voiced concern about the semantic and theoretical difficulties of mixing the "apples" of negligence with the "oranges" of strict liability. *See, e.g.,* "Kirkland v. General Motors Corp.," 521 P.2d 1353 (Okla.1974); Robinson, "Square Pegs (Products Liability) in Round Holes (Comparative Negligence)," 52 "Cal.St.B.J." 16 (1977). Nevertheless, these concerns appear to be more theoretical than real.

The utility of comparative responsibility for product liability cases has been appreciated both by state legislatures [14] and courts.[15] It has also been recom-

14. *E.g.,* "Ark.Stat.Ann." Section 27–1763–1765 (Supp.1977); "Me.Rev.Stat." tit. 14 Section 156 (Supp.1978); "Mich.Comp. Laws Ann." Section 600.2949 (Supp.1978), "Mich.Stat.Ann." Section 27A.2949; Conn. (1979 Conn.Pub.Acts 79–483, Section 4).

15. *E.g.,* "Thibault v. Sears, Roebuck & Co.," 395 A.2d 843 (N.H.1978); "Daly v. General Motors Corp.," 20 Cal.3d 725, 575 P.2d 1162, 144 Cal.Rptr. 380 (1978); "Busch v. Busch Constr., Inc.," 262 N.W.2d 377 (Minn.1977); "Butaud v. Suburban Marine & Sport. Goods, Inc.," 555 P.2d 42 (Alaska 1976).

§ 111   MODEL UNIFORM PRODUCT LIABILITY ACT

mended by a congressional subcommittee. "LaFalce Subcommittee Report," *supra* at 76.

Section 111 places a strong incentive for loss prevention on the party who is best able to accomplish that goal. It also avoids burdening the careful product user with liability insurance costs assessed to persons who misuse or are otherwise at fault in their handling of products. While some economic analyses indicate that a comparative responsibility system creates a risk of economic inefficiency because of an overinvestment in safety, the drafters of the Act have made a value judgment that such an "overinvestment" is worth making.

(B) *Apportionment of Damages.* In order to apply comparative responsibility principles under this Act, it is necessary for the trier of fact to supply certain information in special interrogatories. Subsection (B)(1)(a), which is based on "UCFA" Subsection 2(A)(1), indicates that the trier of fact should set forth the amount of damages a claimant would receive if each party's comparative responsibility were disregarded. This helps assure that the trier of fact does not inflate or deflate the amount of damages claimant would receive if the claimant were free from responsibility.

Subsection (B)(1)(b), which is based on "UCFA" Subsection 2(a)(2), requires the trier of fact to indicate the percentage of responsibility allocated to each claimant; defendant; third-party defendant; and person or entity who has misused, altered, or modified products under Subsections 112(C) or (D). It also includes persons or entities who voluntarily and unreasonably used or stored a product with a known defective condition under Subsection 112(B)(2). As is noted in the analysis to that Subsection, this is an optional provision.

Although it is difficult to apportion the responsibility of an absent employer or co-employee who is immune from tort liability due to Worker Compensation laws, such an approach is necessary to ensure fairness to product sellers. It is also fair to employees because they have given up their right to sue in tort for harms caused by their employers' or co-employees' fault in exchange for their Worker Compensation benefits.

Subsection 111(B)(2) indicates that in cases of product misuse or alteration where an employer's or co-employee's fault is considered, damages should be reduced by the amount of Worker Compensation benefits the worker received or will receive in accordance with Subsection 114(A), or by the percentage of responsibility apportioned to such employer or co-employee, whichever is greater.

Thus, for example, in a case in which a manufacturer is found to have been 40 percent responsible, the injured employee's employer was 60 percent responsible, and Worker Compensation benefits constituted 15 percent of the damages, then the claimant's damages would be reduced by 60 percent, not 85 percent. On the other hand, if the manufacturer had been 80 percent responsible,

574

the employer was 20 percent responsible, and Worker Compensation benefits constituted 30 percent of the damages, then the claimant's damages would be reduced by 30 percent, which was the amount of the Worker Compensation benefits and was greater than the employer's percentage (20 percent) of responsibility.

When a released party's fault is considered, the process is simpler. Damages are reduced according to the percentage of fault which the trier of fact attributes to that person or entity.

Subsection (B)(1)(b) also indicates that persons who have been released under Subsection 113(E) shall be included in the apportionment of responsibility. This approach is in accord with the "UCFA" and the majority of cases that have addressed this issue. Again, while it is difficult to apportion an absent person's fault, the approach helps to ensure that all releases are executed in good faith. See "Frey v. Snelgrove," __ Minn. __, 269 N.W.2d 918 (1978); "Bartels v. City of Williston," 276 N.W.2d 113 (N.D.1979); "Pierringer v. Hoger," 21 Wis.2d 182, 124 N.W.2d 106 (1963).

Subsection (B)(3), which is based on "UCFA" Subsection 2(b), provides a general guideline to assist the trier of fact in comparing responsibility among the parties. The "UCFA" comments (Section 2) indicate that in appropriate cases, the trier of fact may also consider:

(1) Whether the conduct was mere inadvertence or engaged in with an awareness of the danger involved;

(2) The magnitude of the risk created by the conduct, including the number of persons endangered and the potential seriousness of the injury;

(3) The significance of what the actor was seeking to attain by his conduct;

(4) The actor's superior or inferior capacities; and

(5) The particular circumstances, such as the existence of an emergency requiring a hasty decision.

"UCFA Comment" Section 2 ("percentages of fault").

"The extent of the proximate causal relation between the conduct and the damages claimed" refers to proximate cause as opposed to cause-in-fact. While, at times, the distinction may be a difficult one to draw, this Act is premised on apportioning responsibility only—pure causation in terms of cause-in-fact is irrelevant to that concept. See Malone, "Ruminations on Cause-in-Fact," 9 "Stan.L.Rev." 60 (1956). Proximate cause, on the other hand, is an important concept in this Section. In order for the product user's conduct to bring about a reduction or apportionment of damages, it must be a proximate cause of the harm.

The importance of the distinction between cause-in-fact and proximate cause as applied to this Section may be illustrated by the so-called "second collision case" in which the claimant sues the manufacturer for enhanced injuries due to an alleged defect in the automobile, although the initial impact of the accident was caused by the claimant's or another person's negligent driving. When the enhanced injuries caused by the "second collision" within the automobile can be reasonably separated from those injuries caused by the initial collision, damages should be approximately divided. Nevertheless, the negligent driving should not be compared with the manufacturer's conduct because it is not the proximate cause of the enhanced injuries, even though it is clearly a cause-in-fact. *See* "Austin v. Ford Motor Co.," 86 Wis.2d 628, 273 N.W.2d 233, 239 (1979).

On the other hand, there may be "second collision cases" in which the enhanced injuries and the initial impact injuries cannot be reasonably separated. Such a case might arise when an allegedly defective automobile was hit at high speed. *See* "Fietzer v. Ford Motor Co.," 590 F.2d 215 (7th Cir. 1978). In such a case, the driver's conduct is considered a proximate cause of the harm for purposes of comparative responsibility.

Subsection (B)(3), which is based on "UCFA" Subsection 2(c), helps to assure that the mathematics of comparative responsibility will be correctly determined. The court must determine the award for each claimant according to the findings made under this Subsection.

Subsections (B)(4) and (5) indicate that the common law rules of joint and several liability continue to apply under this Act. In this connection, it is important for the court to determine whether the defendant *is* a joint tortfeasor, *i.e.*, if its tortious conduct was a substantial cause of an indivisible injury, or it is otherwise deemed to have that status (*e.g.*, persons acting in concert, express or implied; persons vicariously liable for the torts of another). *See* W. Prosser, "Torts" at 297–99 (4th ed. 1971). A defendant who caused only a divisible part of the claimant's harm is only severally liable for that portion. *See* "UCFA Comment" Section 4, and "Restatement (Second) of Torts" Section 433A (1965).

As with "UCFA" Subsection 2(c), the judgment for each claimant will also show the share of each party's total obligation to the claimant. This should save litigation costs and avoid the need for a special motion or a separate action on the issue.

Subsection (B)(5) follows "UCFA" Subsection 2(d) in providing for the reallocation of damages among the parties responsible when one of the parties' share is uncollectible. The reallocation procedure applies to claimants who are contributorily at fault and joint tortfeasors who have made a substantial contribution to claimant's harm.

* * *

Code

§ 112. Conduct Affecting Comparative Responsibility

(A) *Failure to Discover a Defective Condition.*

(1) *Claimant's Failure to Inspect.* A claimant is not required to have inspected the product for a defective condition. Failure to have done so does not render the claimant responsible for the harm caused or reduce the claimant's damages.

(2) *Claimant's Failure to Observe an Apparent Defective Condition.* When the product seller proves by a preponderance of the evidence that the claimant, while using the product, was injured by a defective condition that would have been apparent, without inspection, to an ordinary reasonably prudent person, the claimant's damages shall be subject to reduction. The procedural principles governing reduction of damages are set forth in Section 111.

(3) *A Non–Claimant's Failure to Inspect for Defects or to Observe an Apparent Defective Condition.* A non-claimant's failure to inspect for a defective condition or to observe an apparent defective condition that would have been obvious, without inspection, to an ordinary reasonably prudent person, shall not reduce claimant's damages.

(B) *Use of a Product With a Known Defective Condition.*

(1) *By a Claimant.* When the product seller proves, by a preponderance of the evidence, that the claimant knew about the product's defective condition, and voluntarily used the product or voluntarily assumed the risk of harm from the product, the claimant's damages shall be subject to reduction to the extent that the claimant did not act as an ordinary reasonably prudent person under the circumstances. Under this Subsection, the trier of fact may determine that the claimant should bear sole responsibility for harm caused by a defective product. The procedural principles governing reduction of damages are set forth in Section 111.

* **Optional Section**

[(2) *By a Non-claimant Product User.* If the product seller proves by a preponderance of the evidence that a product user, other than the claimant, knew about a product's defective condition, but voluntarily and unreasonably used or stored the product and thereby caused claimant's harm, the claimant's damages shall be subject to apportionment. The procedural principles governing apportionment of damages are set forth in Section 111.]

(C) *Misuse of a Product.*

(1) "Misuse" occurs when the product user does not act in a manner that would be expected of an ordinary reasonably prudent person who is likely to use the product in the same or similar circumstances.

(2) When the product seller proves, by a preponderance of the evidence, that product misuse by a claimant, or by a party other than the claimant or the product seller, has caused the claimant's harm, the claimant's damages shall be subject to reduction or apportionment to the extent that the misuse was a cause of the harm. Under this Subsection, the trier of fact may determine that the harm arose solely because of product

misuse. The procedural principles governing reduction or apportionment of damages are set forth in Section 111.

(3) Under this Subsection, subject to state and federal law regarding immunity in tort, the trier of fact may determine that a party or parties who misused the product and thereby caused claimant's harm should bear partial or sole responsibility for harm caused by the product and are subject to liability to the claimant.

(D) *Alteration or Modification of a Product.*

(1) "Alteration or modification" occurs when a person or entity other than the product seller changes the design, construction, or formula of the product, or changes or removes warnings or instructions that accompanied or were displayed on the product. "Alteration or modification" of a product includes the failure to observe routine care and maintenance, but does not include ordinary wear and tear.

(2) When the product seller proves, by a preponderance of the evidence, that an alteration or modification of the product by the claimant, or by a party other than the claimant or the product seller, has caused the claimant's harm, the claimant's damages shall be subject to reduction or apportionment to the extent that the alteration or modification was a cause of the harm. Under this Subsection, the trier of fact may determine that the harm arose solely because of the product alteration or modification.

This Subsection shall not be applicable if:

(a) The alteration or modification was in accord with the product seller's instructions or specifications;

(b) The alteration or modification was made with the express or implied consent of the product seller; or

(c) The alteration or modification was reasonably anticipated conduct under Subsection 102(G), and the product was defective under Subsection 104(C) because of the product seller's failure to provide adequate warnings or instructions with respect to the alteration or modification.

The procedural principles governing reduction or apportionment of damages are set forth in Section 111.

(3) Under this Subsection, subject to state and federal law regarding immunity in tort, the trier of fact may determine that a party or parties who altered or modified the product and thereby caused claimant's harm should bear partial or sole responsibility for harm caused by the product and are subject to liability to the claimant.

* * *

Analysis

§ 112. Conduct Affecting Comparative Responsibility

(A) *Failure to Discover a Defective Condition.*

(1) *Claimant's Failure to Inspect.* Under common law, the product user had an obligation to inspect for defects; failure to do so could bar a claim. *See* "Palmer v. Massey–Ferguson, Inc.," 3 Wash. App. 508, 476 P.2d 713 (1970). However, under modern tort law, the product user is entitled to assume that the product is reasonably safe for its ordinary use. *See* "Restatement (Second) of Torts" Section 402A (1965); "Cepeda v. Cumberland Eng'r. Co.," 76 N.J. 152, 386 A.2d 816 (1978). Subsection (A) follows these cases and does not require the product user or consumer to inspect a product for a defect. *See* "Kassouf v. Lee Bros.," 209 Cal.App.2d 568, 26 Cal. Rptr. 276 (1962) (plaintiff, without inspection, ate a chocolate bar containing worms and maggots).

(2) *Claimant's Failure to Observe an Apparent Defective Condition.* Cases can arise where a defect would be apparent, without inspection, to an ordinary reasonably prudent person. Subsection (A)(2) incorporates the Task Force's views in this area, permitting the trier of fact to consider this conduct and reduce claimant's damages. Under Comment n to the "Restatement (Second) of Torts" Section 402A, an individual who failed to discover an apparent defective condition would, theoretically, still be allowed a full claim. On the other hand, if that person knew about the defect and proceeded anyway, the claim would be totally barred. This approach has led to considerable litigation and expense over the issue of whether a claimant knew or did not know about a particular defect. *See* "Task Force Report" at VII–51–53; *see also* "Karabatsos v. Spivey Co.," 49 Ill.App.3d 317, 364 N.E.2d 319 (1977); "Teagle v. Fischer & Porter Co.," 89 Wash.2d 149, 570 P.2d 438 (1977); "Poches v. J.J. Newberry Co.," 549 F.2d 1166 (8th Cir.1977). The Act eliminates this distinction and focuses on the true responsibility of the product user.

Thus, if a claimant with good eyesight ate a candy bar that had bright green worms crawling over it, Subsection (A)(2) permits the trier of fact to find that the claimant should bear some responsibility for any ill effects suffered. This example involves a defective condition that can be discovered without inspection. *Cf.* "Auburn Mach. Works Co. v. Jones," 366 So.2d 1167 (Fla.1979).

Subsection (A)(2) will not promote misconduct by product sellers. If they were aware of the defect in the goods at the time of sale, the punitive damages section of the Act (Section 120) would provide a strong incentive not to sell such a product.

(3) *A Non-claimant's Failure to Inspect for Defects or to Observe an Apparent Defective Condition.* When a product seller has sold a defective product and an intervening product user negligently fails to discover the defect or to take precautions against the possible harm, case law is uniform that the product user's conduct does not relieve the product seller of liability.

§ 112 MODEL UNIFORM PRODUCT LIABILITY ACT

See "Ford Motor Co. v. Matthews," 291 So.3d 169 (Miss.1974); "Boeing Airplane Co. v. Brown," 291 F.2d 310 (9th Cir.1961); "Comstock v. General Motors Corp.," 358 Mich. 163, 99 N.W.2d 627 (1959). In this instance, the product seller is required to bear responsibility for the defective product it placed on the market.

(B) *Use of a Product With a Known Defective Condition.*

(1) *By a Claimant.* When it is clear that a claimant voluntarily and unreasonably used a product with a known defective condition, the claimant's damages are subject to reduction. Care must be taken not to allow recovery of a claim in a situation where individuals, in effect, have created their own product liability claim. In that regard, it should be noted that consent is a defense even to intentional wrongs. *See* W. Prosser, "Torts" at 101 (4th ed. 1971).

However, there may be cases where an individual voluntarily uses a product with a known defective condition, but the reasonableness of this conduct becomes a matter of dispute. For example, if a person discovers a welt in a tire, should that person be required to stop immediately and call for assistance, or is it reasonable to proceed to a nearby gasoline station to have the tire repaired? The answer depends on the particular fact situation. Many cases arise in this shadowy zone. *See* "Henderson v. Ford Motor Co.," 519 S.W.2d 87 (Tex.1974); "Ford Motor Co. v. Lee," 237 Ga. 554, 229 S.E.2d 379 (1976). Subsection (B)(1) allows the trier of fact to consider the claimant's conduct in the particular fact situation and to reduce damages to the extent that it is appropriate to do so. From both the claimant's and the product seller's perspective, this mitigates the "all-or-nothing" approach that has arisen as a result of some court interpretations of Comment to Section 402A of the "Restatement (Second) of Torts."

(2) *By a Non-claimant Product User.* Subsection (B)(2) is placed in brackets as an optional section. It would apportion responsibility for injuries caused by a defective product between the product seller and a product user who voluntarily and unreasonably exposed the claimant to the product risk. Some case law and, perhaps, proper placement of incentives for loss prevention support this result. *Cf.* "Aetna Ins. Co. v. Loveland Gas & Elec. Co.," 369 F.2d 648 (6th Cir.1966); "Drazen v. Otis Elevator Co.," 96 R.I. 114, 189 A.2d 693 (1963). On the other hand, case law will not shift responsibility where the product was entirely unfit for its intended use,[16] and Subsection (B)(2) may create a situation in which a claimant injured by a defective product cannot bring a successful suit against anyone. This could occur when the Subsection shields the seller of the defective product,

---

16. *See, e.g.,* "Clement v. Crosby & Co.," 148 Mich. 293, 111 N.W. 745 (1907); "Farley v. Edward E. Tower & Co.," 271 Mass. 230, 171 N.E. 639 (1930).

and an immunity (*e.g.,* Worker Compensation) shields the negligent third-party actor. Moreover, as Professor Phillips has observed,

> The third party rarely intends to cause the plaintiff injury. Where there is no such intent, the third party's failure to prevent the injury is attributable to his inadvertence, regardless of whether he actually knew or merely should have known of the danger.

Phillips, supra, 28 "Drake L.Rev." at 372.

In light of the very close balance of equities with regard to this Section, it has been bracketed and should be regarded as optional.

(C) *Misuse of a Product.* Subsection (C) provides for a reduction or apportionment of the liability of the product seller when an injury occurs, in whole or in part, because the product user misused the product in some way that the product seller could not reasonably anticipate. *See* "Netzel v. State Sand & Gravel Co.," 51 Wis.2d 1, 186 N.W.2d 258 (1971); "General Motors Corp. v. Hopkins," 548 S.W.2d 344 (Tex.1977). The definition of "misuse" is based on the Act's concept of "reasonably anticipated conduct." *See* Subsection 102(G) and analysis.

Damages are reduced or apportioned "to the extent" that the misuse caused the harm and, under Subsection (C)(2), the trier of fact may determine that the harm arose *solely* because of product misuse. "Helene Curtis Indus. v. Pruitt," 385 F.2d 841 (5th Cir. 1967).

Subsection (C)(3) indicates that a third party who is not immune under state or federal law and who has misused a product may be subject to liability to the claimant.

(D) *Alteration or Modification of a Product.* Subsection (D) deals with the situation in which a person or entity other than the product seller has altered or modified the product and this has led to the claimant's harm. Alteration or modification (as contrasted with misuse) occurs when a claimant or third-party product user changes the product's design, construction, or formula, or modifies or removes instructions that accompanied or were displayed on the product.

Some courts have imposed liability on the product seller in this situation if the alteration or modification was in some manner "foreseeable." *See, e.g.,* "Blim v. Newbury Indus., Inc.," 443 F.2d 1126 (10th Cir.1971) (machine safety guard removed by co-worker). Courts that have held the original product seller responsible in these instances have bordered on imposing absolute liability. Thus, insurers have a just concern about the broad-scale imposition of liability where intervention by another party was the principal cause of the accident. As the American Insurance Association has noted:

> It is difficult enough to calculate the risk associated with a given product even where there is access to knowledge about its basic inherent characteristics.... The task becomes impossible if the premium calculations must take into account not only the inherent properties of the machine, but also its transformation in the hands of others, and their neglect of repair and maintenance.

AIA, "Product Liability Legislative Package" at 16 (monograph 1977).

Moreover, if the law ignores alterations and modifications of products, it fails to place an incentive for loss prevention on those who might engage in such conduct.

The authors of the "Restatement (Second) of Torts" Section 402A, Subsection 1(b), recognized this fact and subjected the product seller to liability only when the seller's product reached "the user or consumer without substantial change in the condition in which it was sold." Comment g to that Section stated the matter more firmly:

> The seller is not liable when he delivers the product in a safe condition, and subsequent mishandling or other causes make it harmful by the time it is consumed. The burden of proof that the product was in a defective condition at the time that it left the hands of the particular seller is upon the injured plaintiff; and unless evidence can be produced which will support the conclusion that it was then defective, the burden is not sustained.

Recently, a number of state legislatures have enacted the essence of this comment into law. "Ariz.Rev.Stat.Ann." Section 12-683(2) (Supp.1978); "Ind.Code Ann." 33-1-1.5 Section 4(b)(3) (Supp.1978); "Ky.Rev.Stat.Ann." Section 411-320 (1978); "N.H.Rev. Stat.Ann." Section 507-D:3 (Supp. 1978); "R.I.Gen.Laws" Section 9-1-32 (1978); "Tenn.Code Ann." Section 23-3708 (1978); "Utah Code Ann." Section 78-15-5 (1977).

According to the statistics of the Insurance Services Office, product modification only occurs in approximately 13 percent of product liability cases. Of these cases, the largest number of the product modifications (39 percent) result from the conduct of employers. See "ISO Closed Claims Survey" at 140–41. This raises the main problem with rules that limit a product seller's responsibility for subsequent product alterations or modifications—often the injured worker cannot sue the one who is really at fault because of the "exclusive remedy" provisions of Worker Compensation statutes. However, it is fair to state that the destruction of a tort remedy against the employer

> should not of itself create a third-party remedy against the manufacturer or distributor of the product in question. If Worker Compensation is regarded as a proper remedy in other cases of an exclusive employer's wrong, then so too should it be where that wrong involves the product acquired from third-party defendants.

AIA, "Product Liability Legislative Package," *supra* at 15–16.

Nevertheless, Subsection (D) takes account of the hardship that can result from an overly broad liability limitation in cases of product modification or alteration. Thus, the provision is very narrowly drawn.

Subsection (D)(2) ensures that the principles of comparative responsibility are correctly applied by reference to Section 111. If an alteration or modification was made by the claimant, damages are subject to reduction in accordance with the claimant's percentage of responsibility. If a party other than the claimant is responsible for the modification or alteration, damages are to be apportioned in accordance with the parties' percentages of responsibility.

In the case of an employer or co-employee immune from tort liability or a released party under Subsection 113(E), the rules set forth in Subsection 112(B)(2) would apply with regard to reduction of damages.

Under Subsection (D)(2), a product seller may avoid liability to the extent it proves that claimant's harm was proximately caused by the alteration or modification. If the harm arose solely because of the product alteration or modification, the product seller will not be liable at all. On the other hand, the rule adopted ensures that the product seller will remain liable to the extent that it is responsible for the harm. *See* "Fincher v. Surrette," 365 So.2d 860, 863 (La.Ct.App.1979). Subsection (D)(2) applies the comparative responsibility procedural principles set forth in Section 111.

As Subsections (D)(2)(a) and (b) indicate, the product seller cannot avoid responsibility for product alterations or modifications which the seller suggested (per instructions) or to which the seller expressly consented.

Subsection (D)(2)(c) indicates that the product seller may have a duty to warn against modifications or alterations of its product when it may reasonably anticipate that such conduct will occur on the part of persons who are likely to use the product. As Subsection 102(G) (definition of "reasonably anticipated conduct") indicates, this refers to conduct that would be engaged in by an ordinary reasonably prudent person.

Subsection (D)(2)(c) is not intended to encompass every type of act foreseeable by virtue of hindsight or otherwise. If alterations or modifications involve conduct which should have been reasonably anticipated by the product seller, such product seller will be responsible for harms that result if the failure to provide warnings against the type of alteration or modification at issue renders the product defective under Subsection 104(C). A general warning against any alterations or modifications will not suffice.

Subsection (D)(3) indicates that a third party who is not immune under state or federal law and who has negligently altered or modified a product may be subject to liability to the claimant.

* * *

Code

§ 113. Multiple Defendants: Contribution and Implied Indemnity

(A) A right of contribution exists under this Act between or among two or more persons who are jointly and severally liable, whether or not judgment has been recovered against all or any of them. It may be enforced either in the original action or by a separate action brought for that purpose. The basis for contribution is each person's equitable share of the obligation, including the equitable share of a claimant, as determined in accordance with the provisions of Section 111. For the purposes of this Act, contribution and implied indemnity are merged.

(B) If the proportionate responsibility of the parties to a claim for contribution has been established previously by the court, as provided in Section 111, a party paying more than its equitable share of the obligation may, upon motion, recover judgment for contribution.

(C) If the proportionate responsibility of the parties to the claim for contribution has not been established by the court, contribution may be enforced in a separate action, whether or not a judgment has been rendered against either the person seeking contribution or the person from whom contribution is being sought.

(D) Contribution is available to a person who enters into a settlement with a claimant only (1) if the liability of the person against whom contribution is sought has been extinguished by the settlement, and (2) to the extent that the amount paid in settlement was reasonable.

(E) A release, covenant not to sue, or similar agreement entered into by a claimant and a person liable discharges that person from all liability for contribution, but it does not discharge any other persons liable upon the same claim unless it so provides. However, the claim of the releasing claimant against the other parties is reduced by the amount of the released party's equitable share of the obligation, determined in accordance with the provisions of Section 111.

(F) If a judgment has been rendered, the action for contribution must be commenced within one year after the judgment becomes final. If no judgment has been rendered, the person bringing the action for contribution must have (1) discharged by payment the common liability within the period of the statute of limitation or repose applicable to the claimant's right of action against him and commenced the action for contribution within one year after payment, or (2) agreed while action was pending to discharge the common liability and, within one year after the agreement, have paid the liability and brought an action for contribution.

* * *

Analysis

§ 113. Multiple Defendants: Contribution and Implied Indemnity

Section 113 is based on Sections 4, 5, and 6 of the "Uniform Comparative Fault Act" ("UCFA"). Here, however, contribution and implied indemnity are merged in one section. Express indemnity—where one party has agreed to hold the other harmless for damages arising out of product liability actions—is left to commercial and common law. See "Task Force Report" at VII-99-103.

There is clear precedent for the merger of contribution and implied indemnity. See "Safeway Stores, Inc. v. Nest–Kart," 21 Cal.3d 322, 579 P.2d 441, 146 Cal. Rptr. 550 (1978); "Skinner v. Reed–Prentice Division, Etc.," 70 Ill.2d 1, 374 N.E.2d 437 (1977), cert. denied, 436 U.S. 946 (1978); "Busch v. Busch Constr., Inc.," ___ Minn. ___, 262 N.W.2d 377 (1977); "Dole v. Dow Chemical Co.," 30 N.Y.2d 143, 282 N.E.2d 288, 331 N.Y.S.2d 382 (1972); see also "N.Y.Civ.Prac.Law" Section 1402 (1976). This approach avoids the "all-or-nothing" aspect of implied indemnity law. In most situations, fault will be apportioned among product seller defendants. However, a situation could arise where the trier of fact could find that one product seller in the distribution chain was entirely responsible for a product harm. In that regard, this Section should be read in conjunction with Sections 111 and 112.

Subsection (A), which is based on "UCFA" Subsection 4(a), establishes a right of contribution which may be enforced in the original action or in a separate action and provides that contribution will be determined by the proportionate responsibility of the defendants. The Subsection outlines the procedure for the trier of fact to make the appropriate determination.

Subsection (B), which is based on "UCFA" Subsection 5(a), outlines a simplified procedure whereby a party adjudged liable who has paid more than its proportionate share can recover from one who has paid less.

Subsection (C), which is based on "UCFA" Subsection 5(b), provides a mechanism for apportioning responsibility when all potential defendants were not parties to the original action. It indicates that if the court has not determined the proportionate responsibility of all parties in the original action, contribution may be obtained in a separate action.

Subsection (D), which is based on "UCFA" Subsection 4(b), makes it clear that a person who has settled a claim may seek contribution from another person. However, this Subsection limits the right of contribution in such a situation by requiring that the amount paid in settlement be reasonable and that the claimant's right to recover from the other person be extinguished by the settlement.

Subsection (E), which is based on "UCFA" Section 6, deals with the effect of the release of one or more, but not all, tortfeasors. Under this Subsection, a released person is free from liability for contribution, and the liability of other persons to the claimant is reduced by the released person's equitable share of the responsibility as determined in accordance with the provisions of Section 111. Although this provision "may have some tendency to discourage a claimant from entering into a settlement, this solution is fairly based on the proportionate-fault principle." "UCFA Comment" Section 6. Furthermore, the provision that the liability of the nonsettling persons is reduced by the settling person's percentage of the responsibility should discourage claimants from entering into collusive settlements with one defendant at the expense of the other parties.

The Act does not directly address the validity of "Mary Carter agreements." Such agreements are typically entered into between a claimant and one or more, but not all, of the product sellers. They are usually made in secret, and the agreeing product sellers remain as parties to the action. The agreeing product sellers' liability is decreased in direct proportion to the nonagreeing product sellers' increase in liability, and, in return, the agreeing product sellers guarantee the claimant a certain amount of money if the claimant does not obtain a judgment, or if it is less than a specified amount. While such an agreement appears collusive, some state courts currently regard "Mary Carter agreements" as valid. *See, e.g.,* Frier's, Inc. v. Seaboard Coastline Ry.," 355 So.2d 208 (Fla.Dist.Ct.App.1978). However, to the extent that a court chooses to regard a "Mary Carter agreement" as a *settlement,* Subsection (E) is intended to discourage such agreements.

Subsection (F) is based on "UCFA" Section 5 and sets forth the period of time in which an action for contribution may be brought.

* * *

Code

§ 114. Relationship Between Product Liability and Worker Compensation

(A) In the case of any product liability claim brought by or on behalf of an injured person entitled to compensation under a state

Worker Compensation statute, damages shall be reduced by the amount paid as Worker Compensation benefits for the same injury plus the present value of all future Worker Compensation benefits payable for the same injury under the Worker Compensation statute.

(B) Unless the product seller has expressly agreed to indemnify or hold an employer harmless for harm caused to the employer's employee by a product, the employer shall have no right of subrogation, contribution, or indemnity against the product seller when the harm to the employee constitutes a product liability claim under this Act. Also, the employer's Worker Compensation insurance carrier shall have no right of subrogation against the product seller.

(C) When final judgment in an action brought under this Act has been entered prior to the determination of Worker Compensation benefits, the product seller may bring a subsequent action for reduction of the judgment by the amount of the Worker Compensation benefits, or for recoupment from the employee if the product seller has paid a judgment which includes the amount of such benefits.

* * *

Analysis

§ 114. Relationship Between Product Liability and Worker Compensation

The relationship between product liability and Worker Compensation is a major topic covered in depth in the "Task Force Report" at VII–85–113. Under current law in a number of states, the interaction of product liability and Worker Compensation law results in the manufacturer of a workplace product paying the entire out-of-pocket cost of a product-related workplace injury, plus damages for pain and suffering. This result occurs because the product manufacturer is unable to place a portion of the cost of that injury on an employer whose negligence may have helped bring about the claimant's injury. *See* "Seaboard Coast Line R.R. v. Smith," 359 So.2d 427 (Fla.1978); "Task Force Report" at VII–89–99.

After weighing many considerations, the Task Force and the United States Department of Commerce concluded that the development of Worker Compensation as a sole source of recovery in product-related workplace accidents would be the best solution to the problem, but only if the worker received additional benefits in the course of overall Worker Compensation reform. A model product liability law, however, is an inappropriate vehicle for making alterations of that dimension in Worker Compensation law.

The search for the next best solution is not an easy one. One approach is to permit a full contribution claim in all cases in which the employer is at fault. *See* "Dow v. Dole Chem. Co.," 30 N.Y.2d 1, 282 N.E.2d 288, 331 N.Y.S.2d 382 (1972); "Skinner v.

Reed–Prentice Division, Inc.," 70 Ill.2d 1, 374 N.E.2d 437 (1977). This approach is in accordance with the principle of comparative responsibility, and it places strong incentives for loss prevention on the employer.

However, if full contribution or indemnity by the product manufacturer against the employer is permitted, the employer may be forced to pay an employee—through the conduit of the third-party tortfeasor—an amount in excess of the employer's statutory Worker Compensation liability. This thwarts a central concept behind Worker Compensation, *i.e.*, that the employer and employee receive the benefits of a guaranteed, fixed-schedule, no-fault recovery system, which constitutes the *exclusive* liability of the employer. The approach also increases transaction costs.

On the other hand, if contribution or indemnity is not allowed, the product seller might have to bear the burden of a full common law judgment, despite the possibly greater responsibility of the employer. As the Supreme Court of Minnesota recently noted, "[t]his obvious inequity is further exacerbated by the right of the employer to recover directly or indirectly from the third party the amount he has paid in compensation regardless of the employer's own negligence." "Lambertson v. Cincinnati Corp.," ___ Minn. ___, 257 N.W.2d 679, 684 (1977).

Equally troublesome is the fact that the present system dulls employer incentives to keep workplace products safe. The "ISO Closed Claims Survey" suggests that employer negligence is involved in 56 percent of product liability workplace cases. "ISO Closed Claims Survey," Report 10 at 81 (1978).

The purpose of the solution adopted in Section 114 is to sharpen employer incentives to keep workplace products safe without undermining the limited-liability concept that is central to the Worker Compensation system. The approach is based, in substantial part, on a proposal developed by the American Insurance Association (AIA). *See* AIA, "Product Liability Legislative Package" at 75–76 (1977). This approach has also been incorporated in the "National Workers' Compensation Standards Act of 1979," S. 420, 96th Cong., 1st Sess. (1979) and "Standards for State Product Liability Tort Litigation Act," H.R. 1675, 96th Cong., 1st Sess. (1979), and recommended by the "LaFalce Subcommittee Report" at 74.

Subsection (A) reduces the liability of a product seller by the total amount that has been or will be awarded in a state Worker Compensation proceeding. This Subsection operates regardless of whether the employer was, in fact, at fault. *See also* Subsection 112(B)(4) and accompanying analysis.

Subsection (B) abolishes the subrogation lien of the Worker Compensation carrier, or the right of a self-insuring employer to contribution or indemnity, in all workplace harm cases which are covered by this Act, except where the product seller has expressly agreed to indemnify or hold the employer harmless for harm caused by the product. As with Subsection (A), Subsection (B) operates regardless of the employer's fault or lack thereof.

Subsection (C) provides a procedural mechanism for reducing the product seller's liability when final judgment has been entered before the amount of Worker Compensation benefits has been determined.

The principal benefit of the approach adopted in Subsections (A) and (B) is a reduction in litigation transaction costs. Subrogation actions are not allowed. Furthermore, proceedings under this Act will be streamlined because in cases of employer negligence, there will be no three-party litigation as to the relative percentages of fault of employers and manufacturers. *See* AIA, "Legislative Package" at 67–68.

An additional benefit of the approach in Subsections (A) and (B) is that an injured employee will recover the same benefits received under the present system. At the same time, Section 114 cuts off the ability of the Worker Compensation carrier or self-insuring employer to shift its liability to the manufacturer. The employer, therefore, will have a greater incentive to provide a safe workplace than it has under the present system.

A third benefit is that the approach will also, to some degree, eliminate the harshness of the present system as it applies to manufacturers, by allowing product sellers to reduce their liability for workplace injuries. It will do this in all cases, even where the employer was not at fault.

While cases may arise where a product seller may pay more than its fair share under a comparative fault system, they are likely to be few in number under this Act. This is because an employer's misuse, or improper alteration or modification of the product, will in turn reduce the employee's award under Subsection 112(C). As the analysis to that Subsection indicates, this is also fair to employees because they agreed, within the context of their Worker Compensation system, to forego their right to sue when it is based on their employers' or co-employees' fault.

A closely related alternative approach to Section 114 was advanced by the Supreme Court of Minnesota in "Lambertson v. Cincinnati Corp.," *supra*. The court in that case held that the product manufacturer would be allowed limited contribution up to the amount of the Worker Compensation lien. This reduces the inequity against the product manufacturer, but preserves the employer's interest in not paying more than its Worker Compensation liability. The principal disadvantage of the "Lambertson" approach, as compared with Section 114, is that "Lambertson" does not reduce transaction costs.

Finally, it should be noted that any modification of the present tort and Worker Compensation systems, short of a sole source remedy, retains the multiple transaction costs of having two separate proceedings—the Worker Compensation proceeding and then the product liability claim—address a single injury. However, considering all the equities involved, Section 114 appears to offer the soundest solution apart from modifying Worker Compensation law to create a sole source remedy.

* * *

Code

§ 115. Sanctions Against the Bringing of Frivolous Claims and Defenses

(A) After final judgment has been entered under this Act, any party may, by motion, seek reimbursement for reasonable attorneys' fees and other costs that would not have been expended but for the fact that the opposing party pursued a claim or defense that was frivolous. A claim or defense is considered frivolous if the court determines that it was without any reasonable legal or factual basis.

(B) If the court decides in favor of a party seeking redress under this Section, it shall do so on the basis of clear and convincing evidence. In all motions under this Section, the court shall make written findings of fact.

(C) The motion provided for in Subsection (A) may be filed and the claim assessed against a party or a party's attorney or both, depending on which person or persons were responsible for the assertion of the frivolous claim or defense.

(D) Claims for damages under this Section shall be limited to expenses incurred by parties to the action or persons under a legal or contractual duty to bear the expenses of the action.

* * *

Analysis

§ 115. Sanctions Against the Bringing of Frivolous Claims and Defenses

The ISO data indicate that substantial product liability costs are incurred in the defense of product liability claims and lawsuits. "ISO Closed Claims Survey," Report No. 14 (1977) (defense costs equal about 35 percent of claim payments). Some have placed the blame for unnecessary defense costs and needless litigation on the contingent fee system. Nevertheless, as the plaintiffs' bar properly observes, the contingent fee brings no return to a claimant's attorney when the claimant is unsuccessful. On the other hand, some have argued that the contingent fee system has a negative impact on certain product liability cases to the extent that it causes insurers to settle non-meritorious claims because the cost of defending such cases may be greater than the amount of settlement.

Analysis of the countervailing arguments suggests that the best solution to reducing unnecessary litigation costs is to address the heart of the problem by discouraging frivolous claims and defenses.

Section 115 is based, in part, on "Ill.Ann.Stat." ch. 110, Section 41 (Supp.1979). It is also predicated on a proposal of the California Citizens Commission on Tort Reform advocating sanctions against "frivolous" claims or defenses. Report of the California Citizens' Commission on Tort Reform, "Righting the Liability Balance" at 146–47, 153–54 (1977).

The underlying purpose of Section 115 has broad support in existing statutes and court rules. For example, Rule 11 of the Federal Rules of Civil Procedure subjects an attorney to disciplinary action if the attorney knowingly files a pleading or defense where no grounds support it. See "Barnett v. Laborers' Int'l Union of N. Am.," 75 F.R.D. 544 (W.D.Pa. 1977). Similarly, Federal Rule of Appellate Procedure 38 permits a court to award "just damages and single or double costs" to a party who has been subject to a "frivolous" appeal.

Additionally, Federal Rule of Civil Procedure 37(c) provides sanctions for an unreasonable failure to admit averments of fact or the genuineness of documents. In the federal courts, the above rules are supplemented by 28 "U.S.C." Section 1927 (1976) (imposing costs on an attorney who "multiplies the proceedings ... to increase costs ..."). See Annot., 68 "A.L.R.3d" 209 (1976).

The Section is not intended to affect the law relating to malicious prosecution.

Under Subsection (A), the statute may be invoked by either a product liability claimant or a product seller. Recovery is limited to reasonable attorneys' fees and other costs that would not have been expended but for the fact that the opposing party pursued a claim or defense that was frivolous.

In order to make a finding that the claim was frivolous, the court must conclude that the claim was without *any* reasonable legal or factual basis. Thus, this standard allows full room for bringing claims under novel legal theories.

Subsection (B) provides additional assurances that only those who bring frivolous claims will be penalized. First, the court may only impose damages under Section 115 on the basis of clear and convincing evidence, not merely a preponderance of the evidence. See "State of West Virginia v. Charles Pfizer & Co.," 440 F.2d 1079, 1092 (2d Cir.1971) ("clear showing of bad faith"). Second, the court must set forth its findings of fact in writing.

Subsection (C) gives the court latitude to impose costs on either attorney or client. As the "Task Force Report" noted, it is unlikely that many claimants will be financially able to respond to such a claim. "Task Force Report" at VII–62. It must be remembered that the attorney is in the best position to make a judgment about the reasonableness of bringing a claim or raising a defense. See "ABA Code of Professional Responsibility," DR 7–102(A)(1)(2); cf. "Acevedo v. Immigration & Naturalization Serv.," 538 F.2d 918, 921 (2d Cir.1976).

Subsection (D) makes clear that recovery under this Section is limited to expenses incurred by claimant or defendant or persons under a legal or contractual duty to bear the expenses of the action.

* * *

Code

§ 116. Arbitration

(A) *Applicability.*

(1) Any party may by a motion institute a pre-trial arbitration proceeding in any claim brought under this Act, if the court determines that:

(a) It is reasonably probable that the amount in dispute is less than $50,000, exclusive of interest and costs; and

(b) Any non-monetary claims are insubstantial.

(2) Arbitration may not be used if both the claimant and one or more defendants state that they do not want an arbitration proceeding.

(B) *Rules Governing.*

(1) *Substantive Rules.* The substantive rules of an arbitration proceeding under this Section are those contained in this Act as well as those in applicable state law.

(2) *Procedural Rules.* These are the procedural rules of an arbitration proceeding under this Section. If this Section does not provide a rule of procedure, reference may be made to the "Uniform Arbitration Act" or other sources of law. Any reference to other sources of law must conform to the intent and spirit of this Section.

* **Optional Subsection**

[(3) *Additional Rules and Administration.*

(i) The _____ (legislature to specify appropriate state agency or administrative body) is empowered to promulgate additional procedural rules for this Section.

(ii) The _____ (legislature to specify American Arbitration Association or similar organization) shall carry out the day-to-day administration of arbitration under this Section.]

(C) *Arbitrators.*

(1) Unless the parties agree otherwise, the arbitration shall be conducted by three persons: an active member of the state bar or a retired judge of a court of record in the state; an individual who possesses expertise in the subject matter area that is in dispute; and a layperson.

(2) Arbitrators shall be selected in accordance with applicable state law in a manner which will assure fairness and lack of bias.

(D) *Arbitrators' Powers.*

(1) Each arbitrator to whom a claim is referred has the power, within the territorial jurisdiction of the court, to conduct arbitration hearings and make awards consistent with the provisions of this Act.

(2) State laws applicable to subpoenas for attendance of wit-

nesses and the production of documentary evidence apply in proceedings conducted under this Section. Arbitrators shall have the power to administer oaths and affirmations.

(E) *Commencement.* Arbitration hearings shall commence not later than thirty (30) days after the claim is referred to arbitration unless, for good cause shown, the court shall extend the period. Hearings shall be concluded promptly. The court may order the time and place of the arbitration.

(F) *Evidence.*

(1) The Federal Rules of Evidence [or designated state evidence code] may be used as a guide to the admissibility of evidence in an arbitration hearing.

(2) Strict adherence to the rules of evidence, apart from relevant state rules of privilege, is not required.

(G) *Transcript of Proceeding.* A party may have a transcript or recording made of the arbitration hearing at its own expense. A party who has had a transcript or recording made shall furnish a copy of the transcript or recording at cost to any other party upon request.

(H) *Arbitration Decision and Judgment.* The arbitration decision and award, if any, shall be filed with the court promptly after the hearing is concluded. Unless a party demands a trial pursuant to Subsection (I), the decision and award shall be entered as the judgment of the court. The judgment entered shall be subject to the same provisions of law, and shall have the same force and effect as a judgment of the court in a civil action, except that it shall not be subject to appeal.

(I) *Trial Following Arbitration.*

(1) Within twenty (20) days after the filing of an arbitration decision with the court, any party may demand a trial of fact or a hearing on an issue of law in that court.

(2) Upon such a demand, the action shall be placed on the calendar of the court. Except for the provisions of Subsection (3), any right of trial by jury that a party would otherwise have shall be preserved inviolate.

(3) At trial, the court shall admit evidence that there has been an arbitration proceeding, the decision of the arbitration panel, and the nature and amount of the award, if any. The trier of fact shall give such evidence whatever weight it deems appropriate.

(4) A party who has demanded a trial but fails to obtain a judgment in the trial court which is more favorable than the arbitration award, exclusive of interest and costs, shall be assessed the cost of the arbitration proceeding, including the amount of the arbitration fees, and—

(i) If this party is a claimant and the arbitration award is in its favor, the party shall pay the court an amount equivalent to interest on the arbitration award from the time it was filed; or

(ii) If this party is a product seller, it shall pay interest to the claimant on the arbitration award from the time it was filed.

* * *

Analysis

§ 116. Arbitration

The "Task Force Report" suggested that mandatory non-binding arbitration may result in more accurate decisions, reduce overall litigation costs, and expedite the decision process in product liability cases. See "Task Force Report" at VII-229-39.

A synopsis of the basis for these conclusions is that: (1) cases will be decided more accurately because a small group, with a member who is an expert in the field, should be able to comprehend the esoteric details of product liability cases; (2) over time, the process will develop a resource bank of relatively neutral experts less easily misled in technical areas than a jury of laypersons; (3) arbitrators will be less affected by the emotional aspects of the case or by the artistry of counsel; and (4) the privacy of arbitration proceedings (as compared to judicial proceedings) will prompt more complete revelation of special manufacturing designs or processes. This, in turn, will permit more accurate judgments. See "Task Force Report" at VII-235.

The "ISO Closed Claims Survey" suggests further that arbitration will reduce accident reparation transaction costs. Even allowing for the fact that more substantial product liability claims are litigated to a verdict than are handled by arbitration, ISO data indicate that the average expense for attorneys and other allocated loss adjustment costs are considerably lower when the case is handled by arbitration as compared with a court verdict. See "ISO Closed Claims Survey," Report 14 at 120.

On the other hand, costs may increase under arbitration if there are numerous demands for trial following arbitration. This potential problem may not be as serious, however, as was once thought. Data collected by the Department of Justice show that appeal rates at the state level for a trial following arbitration have ranged from 5 to no more than 15 percent of all cases arbitrated. Hearings before the Subcommittee on Improvements in Judicial Machinery of the Senate Committee on the Judiciary, 95th Cong., 2d Sess. 22 (1978) (Statement of Former Attorney General Griffin B. Bell). See also report of the California Citizens' Commission on Tort Reform, "Righting the Liability Balance" at 143 (1977).

Broader use of arbitration should expedite the reparations process. The "Task Force Report" showed that in the medical malpractice area, for example, the arbitration process had achieved a more expeditious resolution of claims than the jury system. See "Task Force Report" at VII-238.

Indeed, the benefits of arbitration have prompted the Department of Justice to recommend that mandatory non-binding arbitration be used in federal courts in all tort and contract cases. The Department of Justice reached this conclusion after its Office of Judicial Improvements made a thorough analysis of the matter in a study conducted wholly independently of the "Task Force Report."

Section 116 draws on portions of the Department of Justice's proposed bill on mandatory non-binding arbitration. See S. 373, 96th Cong., 1st Sess. (1979); H.R. 2699, 96th Cong., 1st Sess. (1979); the Statement of Former Attorney General Griffin B. Bell, *supra;* as well as state legislation on the topic of arbitration.

(A) *Applicability.* The Act provides for arbitration when the amount in dispute is less than $50,000. This figure is to be determined by the court under a standard of reasonable probability. In this context, note that the sanctions imposed by Section 115 will apply to any party who delays the proceedings by making a frivolous assertion that the amount in dispute is above or below $50,000. Also, the proceeding is not mandatory if both the claimant and at least one defendant state that they do not want it.

The $50,000 figure is the same as that in the Department of Justice bill, and it should cover the bulk of product liability claims. In that regard, the ISO closed claims data, trended for severity, show that the average paid claim in bodily injury cases is $26,004. While some have suggested limiting arbitration to smaller claims, it is the larger claims that have been the greater transaction cost items in product liability cases. See "ISO Closed Claims Survey" at 113.

While there has been no state experience with cases at the $50,000 level, Former Attorney General Bell has noted that when Pennsylvania increased the jurisdictional amount for the state's arbitration program from $3,000 to $10,000, there was no increase in the appeal rate. Statement of Former Attorney General Griffin B. Bell, *supra* at 20.

It seems relatively certain that an arbitration procedure will help expedite and reduce costs connected with smaller claims. ISO closed claims data show that the large majority of product liability payments are relatively small (more than two-thirds are under $1,000—even when trended for severity). See "ISO Closed Claims Survey" at 113.

(B) *Rules Governing.* Subsection (B)(1) indicates that arbitrators shall apply the product liability substantive law rules of this Act. Where the Act does not provide a rule of decision, relevant state law should be applied.

Subsection (B)(2) indicates that where a procedure is not provided in Section 116—*e.g.,* when a court can vacate a judgment—the "Uniform Arbitration Act" (enacted in a number of states), or another appropriate source of law, is to be used as a resource.

Subsection (B)(3), an optional section, permits the state to designate a supplemental source of procedural rules and to empower the

§ 116 MODEL UNIFORM PRODUCT LIABILITY ACT

American Arbitration Association or similar organizations to carry out the day-to-day administration of arbitration.

This Subsection leaves a great deal of room for the states to develop their own arbitration systems. The drafters of the Act have chosen to include only the most important procedural points concerning arbitration. The goal of substantive uniformity in product liability law will not be compromised by allowing individual states the freedom to choose the arbitration procedures that they find are the most efficient and workable.

(C) *Arbitrators.* The rules under Subsection (C) provide latitude for the parties to select a single arbitrator. Otherwise, the arbitration is to be conducted by three persons, one who is an active member of the state bar or a retired judge, one who has expertise in the subject matter area that is in dispute, and one who is a layperson. This provision differs slightly from the Department of Justice proposal in light of the needs of product liability. Having an individual who is familiar with the scientific nature of the subject matter involved will help expedite the case and serve as a deterrent to the presentation of biased expert testimony.

In addition, Subsection (C) provides for a layperson to be included to help assure that the consumer perspective regarding product safety is represented. The process of selecting a layperson should not be complicated. It is suggested that either normal jury rolls be utilized or that a list of laypersons be compiled for this purpose.

Aside from general guidelines regarding fairness and lack of bias, the Act does not outline the method of choosing arbitrators, but leaves that matter to the individual states. A state can help implement the general guidelines by requiring each arbitration panel candidate to disclose any personal acquaintance with the parties or their counsel and allow a *voir dire* examination. *See* "Mich. Comp.Laws Ann." Section 600.-5045(1)(2) (Supp.1978). Some of the better procedures include:

(1) Having the American Arbitration Association select a pool of candidates according to its established selection procedures. Each party is allowed to reject certain candidates and rate the remainder in order of preference. Additional provisions take effect if this procedure fails to produce a panel. *See* "Mich.Comp.Laws Ann." Section 600.5044(4)(5) (Supp.1978);

(2) Having the court appoint arbitrators. "Mass.Ann.Laws" ch. 231, Section 60(B) (Supp.1978);

(3) Having an arbitration administrator appoint arbitrators. "Wis.Stat.Ann." Section 655.02 (Supp.1979); and

(4) Having the parties and court combine to appoint arbitrators. "Neb.Rev.Stat." Sections 44–2840, 2841 (Supp.1978); "Ohio Rev.Code Ann." Section 2711.-21(A) (Supp.1979).

(D) *Arbitrators' Powers.* These provisions are taken from the Department of Justice proposal on arbitration. They grant the arbitrators jurisdiction and also give them powers of subpoena.

(E) *Commencement.* This provision is also derived from the Department of Justice proposal. Its purpose is to help expedite the proceeding. The Act contains a slight modification of the Justice proposal in order to allow an extension for "good cause shown." This seems appropriate in light of the fact that some product liability cases are very complex. *Cf.* "Ariz.Rev.Stat.Ann." Section 12-567(C) (Supp.1978) (medical malpractice).

(F) *Evidence.* One method of expediting the process is to use informal means of proof. Nevertheless, some guidelines are needed. The Act follows the Department of Justice proposal in referring to the Federal Rules of Evidence as general guidelines. Strict adherence to rules of evidence is not required. *See* "Ariz. Rev.Stat.Ann." Section 12-567(D) (Supp.1978).

(G) *Transcript of Proceeding.* With respect to the provision of a transcript of proceeding, the Act generally follows the Department of Justice draft.

(H) *Arbitration Decision and Judgment.* The Act follows the Department of Justice proposal's provisions on decisions and judgment. The parties may request a trial on issues of law or fact. If they do not so request in a timely manner, the action is at an end—there is no appeal.

(I) *Trial Following Arbitration.* The Act follows the approach taken by a number of state medical malpractice arbitration statutes. It admits the results of the arbitration proceeding into evidence before the jury. This should act as a deterrent against seeking unnecessary trials. *See, e.g.,* "Ariz.Rev.Stat.Ann." Section 12-567(M) (Supp.1978); "Mass. Ann.Laws" ch. 231, Section 60(B) (Supp.1978). *Cf.* "Wis.Stat.Ann." Section 655.19 (Supp.1979) (excluding findings and order of arbitration panel).

The approach of Section 116 appears to be in accord with the Federal Constitution. *Cf.* "*Ex parte* Peterson," 253 U.S. 300, 309 (1920). Moreover, with the exception of two Ohio lower court decisions, state courts have upheld the constitutionality of provisions that do admit panel findings before the jury. *See* "Eastin v. Broomfield," 116 Ariz. 576, 570 P.2d 744, 750 (1977); "Attorney General v. Johnson," 282 Md. 168, 385 A.2d 57, 67-68 (1978)" "Paro v. Longwood Hosp.," Mass.Adv.Sh. (1977) 2353, 369 N.E.2d 985 (1977); "Prendergast v. Nelson," 199 Neb. 97, 256 N.W.2d 657 (1977); "Strykowski v. Wilkie," 81 Wis.2d 491, 261 N.W.2d 434 (1978), *contra* "Simon v. St. Elizabeth Medical Center," 3 Ohio Op.3d 164, 355 N.E.2d 903, 907-09 (C.P.1976); "Graley v. Satayatham," 74 Ohio Op.2d 316, 343 N.E.2d 832 (C.P.1976). *See generally* Reddish, "Legislative Response to the Medical Malpractice Insurance Crisis: Constitutional

Implications," 55 "Tex.L.Rev." 759, 793 (1977); Lenore, "Mandatory Medical Malpractice Mediation Panels—A Constitutional Examination," 44 "Ins.Counsel J." 416, 422 (1977).

A possible drawback of this Section's approach is that a jury may have difficulty evaluating the conclusions of the panel where the jury is not privy to the prior factfinder's qualifications and method of operation. Also, the jury may get sidetracked from the actual evidence in the case. *See* the observations of Judge Hinton in a classic comment, 27 "Ill.L.Rev." 195 (1932); Annot., 18 "A.L.R.2d" 1287 (1951). *But see* Fed.R.Evid. 803(22) (admitting felony convictions in a cognate civil case). Nevertheless, the benefits to be gained by a reduction in transaction costs outweigh these concerns and support the admission of the results of the arbitration proceeding into evidence at trial.

Subsection (I)(4) provides an additional deterrent against ill-considered appeals for trials following arbitration. If a party fails to obtain a judgment more favorable than the arbitration award, the court will assess the cost of the arbitration proceedings, including the amount of arbitration fees, plus interest, against that party.

In light of the fact that the present product liability system has created serious problems and the fact that mandatory non-binding arbitration has the potential for dealing with some of those problems, this slight incentive for retaining a sound arbitration award should not run afoul of constitutions in most states. *See* "Task Force Report" at VII–233. The Act does not enumerate grounds upon which a court may vacate an arbitration award. Guidance on this issue may be obtained from Section 12 of the "Uniform Arbitration Act."

* * *

Code

§ 117. Expert Testimony

(A) *Appointment of Experts.* The court may, on its own motion or on the motion of any party, enter an order to show cause why expert witnesses should not be appointed, and may request the parties to submit nominations. The court may appoint any expert witness agreed upon by the parties, and may appoint witnesses of its own selection. The court may consult with knowledgeable individuals or with professional, academic, consumer, or business organizations and institutions to assist with the selection process. An expert witness shall not be appointed by the court unless the expert consents to serve. An expert witness appointed by the court shall be informed of his or her duties in writing, a copy of which shall be filed with the clerk, or at a conference in which the parties shall have an opportunity to participate. An expert witness so appointed shall advise the parties of any findings; shall be available for deposition by any party; and may be called to testify by the court or any party. The court-appointed expert witness shall be subject to cross-examination by each party, including the party calling that expert as a witness.

(B) *Compensation.*

(1) Expert witnesses appointed by the court are entitled to reasonable compensation for their services in an amount to be determined by the court. The court, in its discretion, may tax the costs of such expert on one party or apportion them among parties in the same manner as other costs.

(2) In exercising this discretion, the court may consider;

(a) Which party, if any, requested the court appointment of the expert;

(b) Which party had judgment entered in its favor; and

(c) Whether the amount of damages recovered in the action bore a reasonable relationship to the amount sought by the claimant or conceded to be appropriate by the product seller or other defendant.

(C) *Disclosure of Appointment.* In the exercise of its discretion, the court may authorize disclosure to the jury of the fact that the court has appointed the expert witness.

(D) *Parties' Selection of Own Experts.* Nothing in this Section shall limit the parties in calling expert witnesses of their own selection.

(E) *Pre-trial Evaluation of Experts.* The court in its discretion may conduct a hearing to determine the qualifications of all proposed expert witnesses. The court may order a hearing on its own motion or on the motion of any party.

(1) *Need for Pre-trial Evaluation.* In determining whether to grant such a motion, the court shall consider:

(a) The complexity of the issues in the case; and

(b) Whether the hearing would deter the presentation of witnesses who are not qualified as experts on the specific issues.

(2) *Factors in Evaluation.* If the court decides to hold such a hearing, it shall consider;

(a) The background and skills of the proposed witness;

(b) The formal and self-education the proposed witness has undertaken relevant to the case or to similar cases; and

(c) The potential bias of the proposed witness.

(3) *Findings of Fact.* In making a determination as to whether a proposed expert witness is qualified, the court shall state its findings of fact to the parties.

(4) *Determination.* Based upon its findings of fact regarding the qualifications of any proposed expert witness, the court, in its discretion, may limit the scope of the witness' testimony, or may refuse to permit such witness to testify as an expert.

* * *

Analysis

§ 117. Expert Testimony

In General. The Task Force's "Legal Study" demonstrated that product liability cases are often compromised because of the lack of standards with regard to selecting and presenting expert testimony. See Volume IV, "Legal Study" at 153–155. One part of the problem is the biased expert; another is the unqualified expert.

Even if experts are properly qualified and objective, a jury of laypersons is often in a poor position to determine which expert is correct. For this reason, this Act gives the court power to make greater use of pre-trial arbitration where an unbiased, qualified expert will serve on the panel. See Section 116. Where arbitration is not used, however, this Section should promote the goal of presenting objective and sound expert testimony to the jury.

(A) *Appointment of Experts.* Subsection (A) is based on Rule 706 of the Federal Rules of Evidence and similar state rules. It indicates that courts have the power to appoint experts on their own authority. A number of courts have utilized this power even without the benefit of Fed. R.Evid. 706 or a similar state rule. See Annot., 95 "A.L.R.2d" 390 (1964). As the "Task Force Report" noted, the presence of a court-appointed expert "has a cautionary impact on the expert for hire whose theories at trial are subject to dispute not only by an adversary expert, but also by a neutral court-appointed one." "Task Force Report" at VII–43, *citing* Mitchell, "The Proposed Federal Rules of Evidence: How They Affect Product Liability Practice," 12 "Duquesne L.Rev." 551, 557–58 (1974). *See also* 2 J. Wigmore, "Evidence" Section 563, at 648 (3d ed. 1940) ("... this expedient would remove most ... abuses").

Subsection (A) also encourages the court to seek the assistance of various individuals, organizations, or institutions in making the selection of a court-appointed expert. The court may wish to utilize this opportunity to establish a panel of independent experts, recognized as such by their peers, from which selections for individual cases may be made. The court may also seek the assistance of these organizations to evaluate the credentials of expert witnesses nominated by the parties.

One problem with court-appointed experts is that the trier of fact may give them an aura of infallibility which they do not deserve. Under Subsection (A), this possibility is diminished because the experts are subject to cross-examination by *each* party. Also, Subsection (C) allows the court in its discretion to decline to disclose to the jury that the expert witness is, in fact, court-appointed.

(B) *Compensation.* Under Fed.R.Evid. 706 and similar state rules, compensation of experts is left to the judge's discretion. Subsection (B) goes a step farther and provides three guidelines for compensating experts. These guidelines should serve as an added inducement for attorneys to present objective expert testimony. The guidelines suggest that the court may impose the cost of the court-appointed expert on losing parties as well as on parties whom the court finds were substantially inaccurate in their estimation of damages.

(C) *Disclosure of Appointment.* Subsection (C) follows Fed. R.Evid. 706. In most instances, it is important for the trier of fact to appreciate that the witness is court-appointed. However, circumstances may arise in which the court believes disclosure of that fact will give the witness too much credence with the jury. Therefore, the court has the discretion to withhold the information when it is appropriate to do so.

(D) *Parties' Selection of Own Experts.* Subsection (D) also follows Fed.R.Evid. 706. Precluding the parties from introducing their own experts would vest too much power in court-appointed experts.

(E) *Pre-trial Evaluation of Experts.* A rule authorizing a court-appointed expert does not, in and of itself, provide guidance about who is properly qualified to testify in product liability cases. There are many approaches to that issue. One approach, used in some medical malpractice statutes, would require that an expert witness spend a substantial portion of his or her professional time in the actual practice of his or her area of expertise. While this approach may be appropriate in the area of medical malpractice, it was not followed here because a person may be well-versed in technical product liability matters even if he or she does devote substantial time to research or other endeavors other than actual practice. *See* "Task Force Report" at VII-44. Unfortunately, it is impractical to utilize a "standard test" for all experts in product liability cases. *See* Donaher, Piehler, Twerski & Weinstein, "The Technological Expert in Products Liability Litigation," 52 "Tex.L.Rev." 1303, 1325 (1974).

(1) *Need for Pre-trial Evaluation.* This rule gives some guidance to the trial court in deciding whether to conduct a pre-trial hearing on the qualifications of expert witnesses. It is not necessary or cost-efficient to utilize the procedure in *all* cases. It is appropriate to do so in more complex cases and also where the pre-trial hearings would serve as a deterrent to the presentation of witnesses who were not qualified. Such a deterrent should discourage parties from prolonging the litigation needlessly and, thus, encourage the expeditious resolution of claims under this Act. Either party may bring this matter before the court by motion.

(2) *Factors in Evaluation.* The factors in evaluation are drawn from Donaher *et al., supra,* 52 "Tex.L.Rev." 1303.

The court should examine the expert witness' background and skills and determine whether they are appropriate for the purposes of the case. The court should not only review the witness' formal education, but also whether the witness had undertaken specific preparation for the litigation before the court. Finally, the court should examine a witness for bias.

A witness with marginal expert skills and a strong bias should be considered unqualified.

(3) *Findings of Fact.* If it seems clear to the court that the expert's background and experience do not qualify the expert to testify, it should state this conclusion in its findings of fact to the parties.

(4) *Determination.* This provision empowers the court to limit the scope of an expert's testimony to the witness' specific area of expertise. It also allows the court to refuse to permit the witness to testify as an expert when that individual is not qualified to do so.

* * *

Code

§ 118. Non-pecuniary Damages

(A) For the purposes of this Section, "non-pecuniary damages" are those which have no market value and do not represent a monetary loss to claimant.

(B) When sufficient evidence has been introduced, the amount of non-pecuniary damages shall be determined by the trier of fact. However, the court shall have and shall exercise the power to review such damage awards for excessiveness.

* Optional Subsection

[(C) Non-pecuniary damages under this Act shall not exceed $25,000, or twice the amount of the pecuniary damages, whichever is less, unless the claimant proves by a preponderance of the evidence that the product caused claimant to suffer serious and permanent or prolonged (1) disfigurement, (2) impaired of bodily function, (3) pain and discomfort, or (4) mental illness.]

* Optional Subsection

[(D) Every third year following the effective date of this Act as stated in Section 122, the _____ Committee(s) of [each House of] the Legislature of this State shall review the monetary limitations contained in Subsection (C) to determine whether such limitations should be changed in view of the economic conditions existing at that time. Upon a finding that such change is warranted, said Committee(s) shall introduce legislation to amend the monetary limitations contained in Subsection (C).]

* * *

Analysis

§ 118. Non-pecuniary Damages

Claimant's "non-pecuniary damages" include awards for pain and mental suffering. They have no market value and, thus, are to be contrasted with pecuniary damages which compensate victims for lost wages, medical and rehabilitation costs, and other actual expenditures brought about by an unreasonably unsafe product.

According to the "ISO Closed Claims Survey," 70 percent of claims closed with payment include amounts in addition to a claimant's pecuniary loss. *See* "ISO Closed Claims Survey" at 54. Moreover, the average amount of payment above pecuniary loss increases significantly in the higher payment range. *Id.* at 54–55. A most important reason for the difficulty in setting product liability rates is the "open-endedness" of damages for pain and suffering. *See* "Task Force Report" at VII–64–65. These escalating premiums have an inflationary impact on consumer prices as the product seller's insurance costs are passed on to the public. Damages that go beyond the amount necessary to ensure that the claimant receives reasonable compensation for the harm suffered represent an unwarranted cost.

The "Task Force Report" suggested that limits on awards for pain and suffering "would reduce uncertainty and thereby mitigate the 'apprehension factor' that has contributed to the rise in product liability insurance rates." *Id.* at VII–65. Nevertheless, such awards have deep historical roots and should not be limited in a manner that unreasonably curtails the rights of injured parties. Section 118 takes the position that a fixed limit on the amount of non-pecuniary damages is appropriate where claimant's harm is only temporary.

Section 118 is predicated on an examination of the weaknesses in the major rationales offered in support of awards for non-pecuniary damages. The award for non-pecuniary damages arose in early common law cases as a substitute for an injured claimant seeking personal "vengeful retaliation." *See* "Task Force Report," *id.* In those cases, the defendant usually committed an intentional wrong. This rationale has little application to cases arising under product liability. Under this Act, a product seller may be held liable for harm caused by products found to be defective in construction regardless of fault. The same result occurs when an express warranty is not true. In cases of harm caused by products found to be defective in design, or defective because of the absence of adequate warnings, the trier of fact must consider more sophisticated matters than would be applied under a general negligence standard.

A second rationale to support the award of damages for pain and suffering is that they have an important deterrent function. The "Task Force Report" found evidence that the general product liability problem caused manufacturers to devote more attention to product liability loss prevention techniques. *See* "Task Force Report" at VI–50. The approach taken in Section 118 retains this deterrent function while placing some reasonable limits on awards for pain and suffering.

A third rationale, supported by members of the plaintiffs' bar and some economic legal scholars, is that awards for pain and suffering are a reasonable attempt to reduce the serious discomfort endured by a claimant. *See* R. Posner, "Economic Analysis of Law" 82 (1972). On the other hand, studies have questioned whether monetary awards for pain and suffering do anything to alleviate the symptoms they are alleged to address. *See* J. O'Connell & R. Simon, "Payment for Pain & Suffering: Who Wants What, When & Why" (1972); Peck, "Compensation for Pain: A Reappraisal in Light of New Medical Evidence," 72 "Mich.L.Rev." 1355 (1974). This Section adheres to the former assumption to the extent that when a claimant suffers serious and permanent or prolonged (1) disfigurement, (2) impairment of bodily function, (3) pain and discomfort, or (4) serious mental illness, the amount of non-pecuniary damages is left to the sound discretion of the trier of fact with appropriate review by the court in cases of abuse of that discretion.

However, when the claimant has not suffered such serious and permanent or prolonged harms,[17] non-pecuniary damages are limited to $25,000 or twice the amount of pecuniary damages, whichever is less.

An ample body of case law in the area of Worker Compensation and, more recently, automobile injury reparation statutes, provides guidance for the court to determine whether a harm is permanent or prolonged. See, e.g., "Falcone v. Branker," 135 N.J.Super. 137, 342 A.2d 875 (1975) (collecting cases); "Vitale v. Danylak," 74 Mich.App. 615, 254 N.W.2d 593 (1977) (summary judgment under automobile no-fault act); "In re Requests of Governor and Senate, Etc.," 389 Mich. 411, 208 N.W.2d 469, 480 (1973) (term "permanent" supplies basis for legal interpretation).

Courts also have defined and explained the term "mental illness" in a number of contexts. "Carroll v. Cobb," 139 N.J.Super. 439, 354 A.2d 355 (1976) (voter registration requirements); "Sachs v. Commercial Ins. Co.," 119 N.J.Super. 226, 290 A.2d 760 (1972) (insurance policy); "In re Humphrey," 236 N.C. 141, 71 S.E.2d 915 (1952) (incompetency proceedings); "Commonwealth v. Moon," 383 Pa. 18, 117 A.2d 96 (1955) (committal proceedings); "Interstate Life & Accident Ins. Co. v. Houston," 50 Tenn.App. 172, 360 S.W.2d 71 (1962) (insanity exclusion provision).

Objections to limits on awards for non-pecuniary damages take several forms. One is that such limits may violate due process or equal protection clauses of some state constitutions. Cf. "Wright v. Central Du Page Hosp. Ass'n.," 63 Ill.2d 313, 347 N.E.2d 736, 743 (1976) (restriction on amount of general damages in medical malpractice); "Graley v. Satayatham," 74 Ohio Op.2d 316, 343 N.E.2d 832, 836 (C.P.1976) (requiring list of collateral source benefits in medical malpractice). Another objection involves state constitutional prohibitions on damage limitations. E.g., "Ariz.Rev.Stat. Ann.," Const. Art. 18, Section 6 (1956); "Ky.Rev.Stat.Ann.," Const. Section 54 (1891); "Penn.Stat. Ann.," Const. Art. 3, Section 18 (1969). An argument that Section 118 does not violate such prohibitions is that a strict product liability cause of action did not exist at

---

17. The Section does not address the question of whether non-pecuniary damages should be allowed or limited in wrongful death or survival actions.

the time the state constitution was adopted and is therefore exempt from its interdictions. *See* "Rail N Ranch Corp. v. State," 7 Ariz.App. 558, 441 P.2d 786, 788 (1968).

These objections notwithstanding, Section 118 can be supported. First, the common law rule will continue to operate where injuries are serious. *Cf.* "Rybeck v. Rybeck," 141 N.J.Super. 481, 358 A.2d 828, 836 (1976), *appeal dismissed,* 150 N.J.Super. 151, 375 A.2d 269 (1977) (limited court access for pain and suffering in no-fault—"the law is permitted to treat large problems differently from small problems if there is a rational basis for the difference"). Second, some ceiling or limit on damages for pain and suffering will reduce uncertainty in one of the greatest liability insurance ratemaking problem areas. Third, the limit will help assure that there is adequate insurance capacity to provide compensation for pecuniary losses caused by unsafe products.

Subsection (D) provides a mechanism for review and evaluation of the $25,000 limitation contained in Subsection (C). It is anticipated that the legislature may wish periodically to modify this limitation in light of significant changes in economic conditions.

Because of the facts that (1) the topic of pain and suffering goes beyond product liability and is applicable to all of tort law, (2) the limitation as drafted may raise transaction costs in regard to the issue of whether a harm is "serious, permanent, or prolonged," and (3) constitutional problems that may arise in some states, Subsections (C) and (D) are placed in brackets as optional sections.

* * *

Code

§ 119. The Collateral Source Rule

In any claim brought under this Act, the claimant's recovery, or that of any party who may be subrogated to the claimant's rights under this Act, shall be reduced by any compensation from a public source which the claimant has received or will receive for the same damages. For the purposes of this Section, "public source" means a fund more than half of which is derived from general tax revenues.

* * *

Analysis

§ 119. The Collateral Source Rule

The collateral source rule is a principle of tort law under which the defendant is not permitted to take "credit" for any money that an injured claimant received from another (collateral) source. The rule embraces both payments for loss of wages and medical expenditures.

The rule may permit double recovery by the claimant and may increase transaction costs. This Section recognizes these possibilities and provides for a limited modification of the collateral

§ 119

source rule when the claimant has received compensation from a public source for the same damages. Its approach is similar to that followed in medical malpractice by the states of Tennessee and Pennsylvania. *See* Volume V, "Legal Study" at 146.

There are two significant arguments against proposals to modify the existing rule. The first is that the "wrongdoer" should not have the benefit of a windfall. Proponents contend that it is better that the claimant have the benefit of a windfall than the defendant.

This argument can be rebutted in the context of product liability. Under Section 104 of this Act, a manufacturer may be held liable for defects in construction or breach of an express warranty on a strict liability basis. In other cases, a product seller's liability is based on fault, but not on gross negligence or intentionally wrongful conduct. Therefore, a selective modification of the collateral source rule in the context of product liability may be justified. Indeed, some states have upheld such selective abolition or modification where liability was predicated solely on a fault basis. *See* "Eastin v. Broomfield," 116 Ariz. 576, 570 P.2d 744, 751–52 (1977); *But see* "Graley v. Satayatham," 74 Ohio Op.2d 316, 343 N.E.2d 832 (C.P.1976) (holding unconstitutional selective abolition in medical malpractice context).

The second argument against modifying the collateral source rule is that a product seller should not be permitted to "externalize" the cost of an injury caused by its products. This argument is very strong when the injured claimant has purchased health and accident coverage. In that instance, the defendant product seller should not be able to benefit from the claimant's prior prudence. Nevertheless, some proposals have modified the rule in that situation. *See* "Neb.Rev.Stat." Section 44–2819 (Supp.1978); "Prendergast v. Nelson," 199 Neb. 97, 256 N.W.2d 657, 669 (1977); National Product Liability Council, "Proposed Uniform State Product Liability Act" Section 207 (undated). *See also* Comment, "An Analysis of State Legislative Responses to the Medical Malpractice Crisis," 1975 "Duke L.J." 1417, 1447–50. The argument is less persuasive when the claimant has not directly contributed to the insurance fund as is the case with Worker Compensation.

When the claimant has received damages from a public source, the argument loses all of its force. The benefits received were not through the claimant's pre-accident financial planning or made a part of the claimant's remuneration as a condition of employment. Rather, they were derived from public tax funds that accumulated in part by contributions from the product seller. Since the product seller would be able to distribute the cost of a judgment that included this amount among consumers through product pricing, the public may be subjected to excessive, duplicative costs.

Section 119 defines a "public source" as a fund more than half of which is derived from general tax revenues. This would include welfare benefits and other forms of medical, hospitalization, and disability benefits which are funded by state or federal tax funds. It does not include Worker Compensation payments (which are specifically dealt with in Section 114), employee group insurance plans, or other similar sources. It also does not presently include payments received pursuant to the "United States Social Security Act." Although Social Security contributions are withheld from an employee's pay, they are not "general tax revenues." However, if the method of funding the Social Security system is changed, such payments might then come within the operation of this Section. *Compare* the approach taken in Section 119 *with* the various approaches taken in state medical malpractice statutes. *See, e.g.,* "Tenn.Code Ann." Section 23-3418 (Supp.1978) (complete abrogation of collateral source rule expressly includes Social Security benefits); "Neb.Rev.Stat." Section 44-2819 (Supp.1978) (partial abrogation of collateral source rule does not include Social Security benefits).

A probable effect of Section 119 will be to reduce double expenditures for medical costs. The "ISO Closed Claims Survey" suggests that medical costs represent approximately 19.7 percent of product liability claims. "ISO Closed Claims Survey" at 57. Nevertheless, the cost savings generated by this Section will probably be modest. The ISO closed claims data, which were quite limited on this point, show that approximately 6.4 percent of claimants have been reimbursed by public collateral sources. *See* "ISO Closed Claims Survey" at 181. Collateral sources paid for 19.8 percent of the claims in those cases (this closely parallels the general percentage of medical benefits). Nonetheless, this Section should help reduce overall insurance costs. Liability insurers should take this matter into account when they formulate rates and premiums.

Section 119 also takes account of existing legislation that may authorize subrogation by public collateral sources. In order to reduce transaction costs and duplicative distribution costs, this Section prohibits such subrogation.

Finally, Section 119 does not alter existing law that prohibits the defendant from introducing into evidence the fact that the claimant has been indemnified by a collateral source. That alternative approach was rejected because it would leave the trier of fact in the role of balancing the delicate policy elements that surround proposals calling for abolition of the collateral source rule. This should be an issue of law for state legislatures or courts. Also, that approach would reduce the potential benefit of collateral source rule modifications in that it would increase transaction costs and lower predictability and consistency in the allocation of collateral benefits. *See* "Task Force Report" at VII-74-75. *Cf.* Defense Research Institute, "Products Liability Position Paper" at 44-45 (1976) (advocating modification of evidentiary rules to allow trier of fact to consider all collateral benefits).

* * *

Code

§ 120. Punitive Damages

(A) Punitive damages may be awarded to the claimant if the claimant proves by clear and convincing evidence that the harm suffered was the result of the product seller's reckless disregard for the safety of product users, consumers, or others who might be harmed by the product.

(B) If the trier of fact determines that punitive damages should be awarded, the court shall determine the amount of those damages. In making this determination, the court shall consider:

(1) The likelihood at the relevant time that serious harm would arise from the product seller's misconduct;

(2) The degree of the product seller's awareness of that likelihood;

(3) The profitability of the misconduct to the product seller;

(4) The duration of the misconduct and any concealment of it by the product seller;

(5) The attitude and conduct of the product seller upon discovery of the misconduct and whether the conduct has been terminated;

(6) The financial condition of the product seller;

(7) The total effect of other punishment imposed or likely to be imposed upon the product seller as a result of the misconduct, including punitive damage awards to persons similarly situated to the claimant and the severity of criminal penalties to which the product seller has been or may be subjected; and

(8) Whether the harm suffered by the claimant was also the result of the claimant's own reckless disregard for personal safety.

* * *

Analysis

§ 120. Punitive Damages

Some product sellers and others have called for the abolition of punitive damages on the grounds that they serve no proper "tort law" purpose,[18] and at least one court has accepted these arguments in the area of product liability. *See* "Walbrun v. Berkel, Inc.," 433 F.Supp. 384-85 (E.D.Wis.1976); "Roginsky v. Richardson-Merrell, Inc.," 378 F.2d 832 (2d Cir.1967) (dictum).

Nevertheless, as Section 120 acknowledges, punitive damages serve an important function in deterring product sellers from reckless disregard for safety in the production, distribution, or sale of

---

18. *See* "Proposed Uniform State Product Liability Act" Section 206 (National Product Liability Council) (undated); *see generally* Defense Research Institute, "The Case Against Punitive Damages" (monograph 1969) (marshalling arguments).

dangerous products. *See* "Toole v. Richardson–Merrell, Inc.," 251 Cal.App.2d 689, 60 Cal.Rptr. 398 (1967); "Gillham v. Admiral Corp.," 523 F.2d 102 (6th Cir. 1975). At the same time, Section 120 recognizes and addresses punitive damages problems in the specific context of product liability.

While many product sellers have expressed great concern about the economic impact of punitive damages, the "ISO Closed Claims Survey" suggests that the number of cases in which such damages are imposed is insubstantial. "ISO Closed Claims Survey" at 183. Nevertheless, concern about punitive damages has caused some insurers to decline to provide insurance coverage for these damages. Also, a number of states and some insurers have declined to permit such coverage. They contend that a product seller should not be allowed to pass this cost on to an insurer. Transcending all of these concerns is the total lack of legal structure surrounding punitive damages. The approach taken in Section 120 is to provide such a structure, so as to reduce product sellers' reasonable concerns about punitive damages, while at the same time retaining the important deterrent function of punitive damages.

Subsection (A) addresses a basic argument against punitive damages—specifically that they apply a criminal law sanction to a civil law case, even though the defendant does not have the benefit of the constitutional protections that would be available under criminal law. Subsection (A) moves away from the ordinary "preponderance of evidence" test of civil cases and toward the criminal standard, but does not turn completely to a pure criminal standard of proof "beyond a reasonable doubt." Because the defendant is not subject to incarceration, and the "punishment" is more in the nature of a civil fine than a criminal sanction, the Act requires the claimant to prove by "clear and convincing" evidence that punitive damages are justified. *See* Subsections 102(H) and (I) (definitions of "preponderance of evidence" and "clear and convincing evidence").

Subsection (A) also requires that the claimant prove that the product seller's conduct demonstrated reckless disregard for the safety of others. The phrase "reckless disregard"—the traditional barrier that the plaintiff must cross in order to obtain punitive damages—means a conscious indifference to the safety of persons who might be injured by the product. *See* Subsection 102(J) (definition of "reckless disregard"); *cf.* W. Prosser, "Torts" at 9–10 (4th ed. 1971). The "reckless disregard" standard is identified in statutory form to avoid any possible misinterpretation of this basic area of law. Thus, it should be clear that a product seller does not have to pay punitive damages under ordinary strict liability or negligence standards which fall short of reckless disregard.

Subsection (B) follows the current common law system in allowing the trier of fact to determine at its discretion whether punitive damages should be awarded. *See* Prosser, *supra* at 9. On the other hand, this Subsection draws upon a newly enacted Minnesota statute in having the court, rather than the jury, determine the amount of those damages. "Minn. Stat.Ann." Section 549.21 (Supp. 1978). This approach is in accord with the general pattern of criminal law where the jury determines "guilt or innocence" and the court imposes the sentence. This is particularly appropriate in product liability cases where, under current law, product sellers are potentially subject to repeated imposition of punitive damages for harm caused by a particular product.

Subsection (B) provides guidelines for the court in determining the amount of punitive damages. The eight factors are derived from "Minn.Stat.Ann." Section 549.-20(3) (Supp.1978). The drafters of that statute relied on a very thorough analysis of product liability punitive damages. *See* Owen, "Punitive Damages in Products Liability Litigation," 74 "Mich. L.Rev." 1257, 1299–319 (1976).

Factors (1) and (2) are self-evident. If the facts show that the product seller was actually aware of the specific hazard *and* its seriousness, *and* marketed it anyway, a higher award is in order.

Factor (3), profitability, recognizes that punitive damages may be used to attack directly the profit incentive that generated the misconduct.

Factor (4) is important regardless of the basic requirement that the product seller must have reckless disregard for the safety of others. If the product seller consciously concealed its activities, this fact argues for a higher award.

Factor (5) acknowledges that the product seller who was reckless in producing the product, but who acted quickly to remove the product from the market upon discovery of the hazard, should not be subject to as harsh a sanction as one who failed to act. Some have suggested that punitive damages should be awarded only where corporate management has either authorized, participated in, or ratified conduct that shows a conscious or reckless disregard for public safety. *See* "Task Force Report" at VII–79. Section 120 rejects that approach because it could foster legal disputes as to whether an individual stood "high enough" in the corporate structure to bear responsibility for punitive damages. Nevertheless, in circumstances where a non-management employee caused the harm and management acted quickly to mitigate that harm once it was discovered, a lower award is appropriate.

Factor (6) permits the court to consider the impact of the award on the product seller in light of its financial condition. This consideration has deep roots in common law. It is one that has been subject to criticism from product sellers and economists. Nevertheless, in light of the fact that the deterrence of wrongful conduct is the principal rationale for punitive damages, it is appropriate to consider the impact an award will have on a particular product seller.

Factor (7) is more important in product liability cases than in other liability cases because it addresses the problem of multiple exposure to punitive damages. This factor directs the court to consider both criminal and civil liability to which the product seller has been or may be subjected.

Factor (8) recognizes that the injury may also be attributable in part to the claimant's reckless disregard for personal safety. In such instances where the defendant can show such reckless disregard on the part of the claimant, punitive damages may be diminished proportionately according to the comparative responsibility of that claimant. The comparison, therefore, is between the reckless disregard on the part of the product seller and that of the claimant, and *not* between the reckless disregard of the product seller and mere negligence of the claimant. *See also* Section 111.

The Act indicates that the award of punitive damages goes to the claimant and not to the state. While the argument that "since the damages are non-compensatory, they should go to the state" has some merit, the approach was rejected because of constitutional problems and the fact that it might place a claimant's attorney in a potential conflict of interest situation by forcing the attorney to represent both the claimant and the state. *See* "Task Force Report" at VII-79.

When the trier of fact determines that punitive damages should be awarded, one option available to the court is to limit the award to a multiple of the compensatory damages as is done in antitrust actions. While this approach has appeal, it is not appropriate in the case of product liability because this area of the law addresses a multiplicity of different kinds of wrongful acts. Antitrust law, on the other hand, addresses one basic kind of wrongful act: an antitrust violation. Under this Section, the defendant's wrongful conduct could range from that which merely could cause damage to property to conduct which could result in the deaths of many people. Antitrust law violations involve economic injury only, and rarely, if ever, result in serious physical injury or death. Thus, the punitive damages in product liability actions do not lend themselves to quantification in the same manner as do such damages in antitrust cases.

* * *

Code

§ 121. Severance Clause

If any part of this Act shall be adjudged by any court of competent jurisdiction to be invalid, such judgment shall not affect, impair, or invalidate the remainder thereof, but shall be confined in its effect to that part of this Act declared to be invalid.

* * *

Analysis

§ 121. Severance Clause

This Section makes clear that in the event any court of competent jurisdiction declares any part of this Act to be invalid, such action shall be confined to that part alone, and shall not affect the validity of the remainder of the Act. The source of this Section is "1976 N.Y.Laws," ch. 955 (12) (McKinney), which concerns medical malpractice.

* * *

Code

§ 122. Effective Date

This Act shall be effective with regard to all product liability claims filed on or after _____, 19__.

* Alternative Section

[This Act shall be effective with regard to all claims accruing on or after _____, 19__. It shall be prospective in operation, and shall only apply to a product-related harm occurring on or after this date. When the facts giving rise to a claim are discovered or should have been discovered after this date, this Act shall govern the claimant's action. When the facts giving rise to a product-related harm are discovered or should have been discovered prior to the effective date of this Act, the law of this State which was applicable at the time of such discovery shall govern the claimant's action.]

* * *

Analysis

§ 122. Effective Date

The issue of the effective date of a tort-related statute has not been given intense analysis in legal periodicals—perhaps because there have been relatively few legislative initiatives in the tort area. In an attempt to balance fairness to all parties against procedural convenience, the drafters of this Act have chosen to apply the statute to all claims *filed* after the effective date.

The shortcoming of this approach is that it may create a rush to the courthouse—or, conversely, a delay—by claimants' attorneys. Also, the new law will apply to some injuries that occurred *before* the effective date.

On the other hand, since the Act does not create new causes of action, but condenses, clarifies, and balances common law development, the approach taken is a fair one. Also, it allows claimants, product sellers, and insurers to know, with precision, what law will be applied to a claim. *See* "1979 Minn.Laws" ch. 81, Section 3; "Conn.Gen.Stat." Section 52-572 1 (rev. 1979); *cf.* "Peterson v. City of Minneapolis," 285 Minn. 282, 173 N.W.2d 353 (1969); "Godfrey v. State," 84 Wash.2d 959, 530 P.2d 630 (1975); *see also* Annot., 37 "A.L.R.3d" 1438 (1971).

Because state legislatures are likely to differ about the issue of effective date, an alternative approach has been drafted. The alternative provision would have the Act apply only to a harm actually sustained or causes of action discovered, or which should have been discovered (*e.g.*, latent disease) on or after the effective date. This approach makes the Act fully prospective in nature and recognizes that certain illnesses, such as malignancies, only become discoverable some time after the actual contact with the product. In the case of disease or other illness with delayed effects, the Act would apply if the harm or the cause thereof were discovered on or after the effective date. *See* Section 109(C); *see also* 73 "Am. Jur.2d" "Statutes" Sections 385 *et seq.* (1974).

A significant shortcoming of this alternative approach is that for many years it will leave claimants, product sellers, and insurance ratemakers with two potential sources of product liability law—existing common law and this Act. It should be noted that the phrase "the law of this State," as used in the alternative, includes a state's conflict of law rules as well as its substantive product liability law.

* * *

Appendix A—A Bibliography of Major Compendium Sources Reviewed in Connection With the Model Code

Final Report, Interagency Task Force on Product Liability (NTIS, 1977).

Product Liability Legal Study, Interagency Task Force on Product Liability (NTIS, 1977).

Product Liability Industry Study, Interagency Task Force on Product Liability (NTIS, 1977).

Product Liability Insurance Study, Interagency Task Force on Product Liability (NTIS, 1977).

Selected Papers, Interagency Task Force on Product Liability (NTIS, 1978).

Insurance Services Office, Product Liability Closed Claims Survey: A Technical Analysis of Survey Results (ISO, 1977).

Product Liability Insurance, A Report of the Subcommittee on Capital, Investment and Business Opportunities of the Committee on Small Business, H.R.Rep. No. 95–997, 95th Cong., 2d Sess. (1978).

"Impact on Product Liability": Hearings before the Senate Select Committee on Small Business, 94th Cong., 2d Sess., 95th Cong., 1st Sess. (1976–77).

"Product Liability Insurance": Hearings on S. 403 before the Consumer Subcommittee of the Senate Committee on Commerce, Science and Transportation, 95th Cong., 1st Sess. (1977).

Department of Commerce Task Force Report on Product Liability Insurance (State of Michigan, 1978).

Final Report of the Governor's Task Force on Product Liability (Maine, 1978).

Product Liability: An Overview, Wisconsin Legislative Council, Research Bulletin 78 (1978).

Illinois House of Representatives, Judiciary I Subcommittee on

Product Liability, Report and Recommendations (1978).

Report of the Senate Product Liability Study Committee, State Capitol, Georgia (1978).

Report of the Senate Select Committee on Product Liability, Missouri Senate (1977).

American Law Institute, Restatement (Second) of Torts, Section 402A and Appendices (1965).

Defense Research Institute, Inc., Products Liability Position Paper (1976).

The Alliance of American Insurers, Product Liability Tort Reform Proposals (1976).

Proposed Uniform State Product Liability Act (National Product Liability Council).

American Insurance Association, Product Liability Legislative Package (1977).

The California Citizens' Commission on Tort Reform, Righting the Liability Balance (1977).

A review was also conducted of all enacted state product liability laws, all proposed federal product liability laws, and major proposed state product liability laws, as well as all law review and other related literature and major case law reported or published since the completion of the Interagency Task Force's seven-volume Legal Study in December 1976. That study reviewed case law and literature published prior to that date. Consideration was also given to pre-1976 sources that were not reviewed by the Legal Study.

S. 640, PRODUCT LIABILITY FAIRNESS ACT

Calendar No. 653

102D CONGRESS
2D SESSION

S. 640
[Report No. 102-215]

To regulate interstate commerce by providing for a uniform product liability law, and for other purposes.

IN THE SENATE OF THE UNITED STATES

MARCH 13 (legislative day, FEBRUARY 6), 1991

Mr. KASTEN (for himself, Mr. ROCKEFELLER, Mr. DANFORTH, Mr. LIEBERMAN, Mr. GORTON, Mr. RIEGLE, Mr. PRESSLER, Mr. PELL, Mr. MCCAIN, Mr. GLENN, Mr. LOTT, Mr. SANFORD, Mr. BURNS, Mrs. KASSEBAUM, Mr. DOLE, Mr. HELMS, Mr. LUGAR, Mr. COATS, Mr. CHAFEE, Mr. NICKLES, Mr. HATCH, Mr. BOND, Mr. SYMMS, Mr. WALLOP, Mr. MACK, Mr. GRASSLEY, Mr. HEINZ, Mr. GARN, Mr. CRAIG, Mr. MCCONNELL, Mr. BOREN, Mr. BROWN, Mr. SMITH, Mr. DODD, Mr. SEYMOUR, Mr. RUDMAN, Mr. GRAMM, Mr. DOMENICI, Mr. HATFIELD, and Mr. JEFFORDS) introduced the following bill; which was read twice and referred to the Committee on Commerce, Science, and Transportation

NOVEMBER 14 (legislative day, NOVEMBER 13), 1991

Reported by Mr. HOLLINGS, without amendment

JUNE 26 (legislative day, JUNE 16), 1992

Ordered referred to the Committee on the Judiciary for a period not to extend beyond August 12, 1992

AUGUST 12 (legislative day, AUGUST 5), 1992

Committee discharged pursuant to the order of June 26, 1992; placed on the calendar

A BILL

To regulate interstate commerce by providing for a uniform product liability law, and for other purposes.

S. 640, PRODUCT LIABILITY FAIRNESS ACT

Be it enacted by the Senate and House of Representatives of the United States of America in Congress assembled,

TABLE OF CONTENTS

TITLE—I

Sec. 101. Short title.
Sec. 102. Definitions.
Sec. 103. Preemption.
Sec. 104. Jurisdiction of Federal courts.
Sec. 105. Effective date.

TITLE—II

Sec. 201. Expedited product liability settlements.
Sec. 202. Alternative dispute resolution procedures.

TITLE—III

Sec. 301. Civil actions.
Sec. 302. Uniform standards of product seller liability.
Sec. 303. Uniform standards for award of punitive damages.
Sec. 304. Uniform time limitations on liability.
Sec. 305. Uniform standards for offset of workers' compensation benefits.
Sec. 306. Several liability for noneconomic damages.
Sec. 307. Defenses involving intoxicating alcohol or drugs.

TITLE I

SHORT TITLE

SEC. 101. This Act may be cited as the "Product Liability Fairness Act".

DEFINITIONS

SEC. 102. As used in this Act, the term—

(1) "claimant" means any person who brings a civil action pursuant to this Act, and any person on whose behalf such an action is brought; if such an action is brought through or on behalf of an estate, the term includes the claimant's decedent, or if it is brought through or on behalf of a minor or incompetent, the term includes the claimant's parent or guardian;

(2) "clear and convincing evidence" is that measure or degree of proof that will produce in the mind of the trier of fact a firm belief or conviction as to the truth of the allegations sought to be established; the level of proof required to satisfy such standard is more than that required under preponderance of the evidence, but less than that required for proof beyond a reasonable doubt;

(3) "collateral benefits" means all benefits and advantages received or entitled to be received (regardless of any right any other person has or is entitled to assert for recoupment through subrogation, trust agreement, lien, or otherwise) by any claimant harmed by a product or by any other person as reimbursement of loss because of harm to person or property payable or required to be paid to the claimant, under—

(A) any Federal law or the laws of any State (other than through a claim for breach of an obligation or duty); or

(B) any life, health, or accident insurance or plan, wage or salary continuation plan, or disability income or replacement service insurance, or any benefit received or to be received as a result of participation in any pre-paid medical plan or health maintenance organization;

(4) "commerce" means trade, traffic, commerce, or transportation (A) between a place in a State and any place outside of that State; or (B) which affects trade, traffic, commerce, or transportation described in clause (A);

(5) "commercial loss" means economic injury, whether direct, incidental, or consequential, including property damage and damage to the product itself;

(6) "economic loss" means any pecuniary loss resulting from harm which is allowed under State law;

(7) "exercise of reasonable care" means conduct of a person of ordinary prudence and intelligence using the attention, precaution, and judgment that society expects of its members for the protection of their own interests and the interests of others;

(8) "harm" means any harm recognized under the law of the State in which the civil action is maintained, other than loss or damage caused to a product itself, or commercial loss;

(9) "manufacturer" means (A) any person who is engaged in a business to produce, create, make, or construct any product (or component part of a product) and who designs or formulates the product (or component part of the product) or has engaged another person to design or formulate the product (or component part of the product); (B) a product seller with respect to all aspects of a product (or component part of a product) which are created or affected when, before placing the product in the stream of commerce, the product seller produces, creates, makes, or constructs and designs or formulates, or has engaged another person to design or formulate, an aspect of a product (or component part of a product) made by another; or (C) any product seller not described in clause (B) which holds itself out as a manufacturer to the user of a product;

(10) "noneconomic loss" means loss caused by a product other than economic loss or commercial loss;

(11) "person" means any individual, corporation, company, association, firm, partnership, society, joint stock company, or any other entity (including any governmental entity);

(12) "preponderance of the evidence" is that measure or degree of proof which, by the weight, credit, and value of the aggregate evidence on either side, establishes that it is more probable than not that a fact occurred or did not occur;

(13) "product" means any object, substance, mixture, or raw material in a gaseous, liquid, or solid state (A) which is capable of delivery itself or as an assembled whole, in a mixed or combined state, or as a component part or ingredient; (B) which is produced for introduction into trade or commerce; (C) which has intrinsic economic value; and (D) which is intended for sale or lease to persons for commercial or personal use; the term does not include human tissue, blood and blood products, or organs unless specifically recognized as a product pursuant to State law;

(14) "product seller" means a person who, in the course of a business conducted for that purpose, sells, distributes, leases, prepares, blends, packages, labels, or otherwise is involved in placing a product in the stream of commerce, or who installs, repairs, or maintains the harm-causing aspect of a product; the term does not include—

(A) a seller or lessor of real property;

(B) a provider of professional services in any case in which the sale or use of a product is incidental to the transaction and the essence of the transaction is the furnishing of judgment, skill, or services; or

(C) any person who—

(i) acts in only a financial capacity with respect to the sale of a product; and

(ii) leases a product under a lease arrangement in which the selection, possession, maintenance, and operation of the product are controlled by a person other than the lessor; and

(15) "State" means any State of the United States, the District of Columbia, the Commonwealth of Puerto Rico, the Commonwealth of the Northern Mariana Islands, the Virgin Islands, Guam, American Samoa, and any other territory or possession of the United States, or any political subdivision thereof.

S. 640, PRODUCT LIABILITY FAIRNESS ACT

PREEMPTION

SEC. 103. (a) This Act governs any civil action brought against a manufacturer or product seller, on any theory, for harm caused by a product. A civil action brought against a manufacturer or product seller for loss or damage to a product itself or for commercial loss is not subject to this Act and shall be governed by applicable commercial or contract law.

(b) This Act supersedes any State law regarding recovery for harm caused by a product only to the extent that this Act establishes a rule of law applicable to any such recovery. Any issue arising under this Act that is not governed by any such rule of law shall be governed by applicable State or Federal law.

(c) Nothing in this Act shall be construed to—

(1) waive or affect any defense of sovereign immunity asserted by any State under any provision of law;

(2) supersede any Federal law, except the Federal Employees Compensation Act and the Longshoremen's and Harbor Workers' Compensation Act;

(3) waive or affect any defense of sovereign immunity asserted by the United States;

(4) affect the applicability of any provision of chapter 97 of title 28, United States Code;

(5) preempt State choice-of-law rules with respect to claims brought by a foreign nation or a citizen of a foreign nation;

(6) affect the right of any court to transfer venue or to apply the law of a foreign nation or to dismiss a claim of a foreign nation or of a citizen of a foreign nation on the ground of inconvenient forum; or

(7) supersede any statutory or common law, including an action to abate a nuisance, that authorizes a State or person to institute an action for civil damages or civil penalties, cleanup costs, injunctions, restitution, cost recovery, punitive damages, or any other form of relief resulting from contamination or pollution of the environment, or the threat of such contamination or pollution.

(d) As used in this section, "environment" has the meaning given to such term in section 101(8) of the Comprehensive Environmental Response, Compensation, and Liability Act of 1980 (42 U.S.C. 9601(8)).

(e) This Act shall be construed and applied after consideration of its legislative history to promote uniformity of law in the various jurisdictions.

S. 640, PRODUCT LIABILITY FAIRNESS ACT

JURISDICTION OF FEDERAL COURTS

SEC. 104. The district courts of the United States shall not have jurisdiction over any civil action pursuant to this Act, based on section 1331 or 1337 of title 28, United States Code.

EFFECTIVE DATE

SEC. 105. (a) This Act shall take effect on the date of its enactment and shall apply to all civil actions pursuant to this Act commenced on or after such date, including any action in which the harm or the conduct which caused the harm occurred before the effective date of this Act.

(b) If any provision of this Act would shorten the period during which a manufacturer or product seller would otherwise be exposed to liability, the claimant may, notwithstanding the otherwise applicable time period, bring any civil action pursuant to this Act within one year after the effective date of this Act.

TITLE II

EXPEDITED PRODUCT LIABILITY SETTLEMENTS

SEC. 201. (a) Any claimant may bring a civil action for damages against a person for harm caused by a product pursuant to applicable State law, except to the extent such law is superseded by this title.

(b) Any claimant may, in addition to any claim for relief made in accordance with State law, include in such claimant's complaint an offer of settlement for a specific dollar amount.

(c) The defendant may make an offer of settlement for a specific dollar amount within sixty days after service of the claimant's complaint or within the time permitted pursuant to State law for a responsive pleading, whichever is longer, except that if such pleading includes a motion to dismiss in accordance with applicable law, the defendant may tender such relief to the claimant within ten days after the court's determination regarding such motion.

(d) In any case in which an offer of settlement is made pursuant to subsection (b) or (c) of this section, the court may, upon motion made prior to the expiration of the applicable period for response, enter an order extending such period. Any such order shall contain a schedule for discovery of evidence material to the issue of the appropriate amount of relief, and shall not extend such period for more than sixty days. Any such motion shall be accompanied by a supporting affidavit of the moving party setting forth the reasons why such extension is necessary to promote the interests of justice and stating that the information likely to be discovered is material, and is not, after reasonable inquiry, otherwise available to the moving party.

(e) If the defendant, as offeree, does not accept the offer of settlement made by a claimant in accordance with subsection (b) of this section within the time permitted pursuant to State law for a responsive pleading or, if such pleading includes a motion to dismiss in accordance with applicable law, within thirty days after the court's determination regarding such motion, and a verdict is entered in such action equal to or greater than the specific dollar amount of such offer of settlement, the court shall enter judgment against the defendant and shall include in such judgment an amount for the claimant's reasonable attorney's fees and costs. Such fees shall be offset against any fees owed by the claimant to the claimant's attorney by reason of the verdict.

(f) If the claimant, as offeree, does not accept the offer of settlement made by a defendant in accordance with subsection (c) of this section within thirty days after the date on which such offer is made and a verdict is entered in such action equal to or less than the specific dollar amount of such offer of settlement, the court shall reduce the amount of the verdict in such action by an amount equal to the reasonable attorney's fees and costs owed by the defendant to the defendant's attorney by reason of the verdict, except that the amount of such reduction shall not exceed that portion of the verdict which is allocable to noneconomic loss and economic loss for which the claimant has received or will receive collateral benefits.

(g) For purposes of this section, attorney's fees shall be calculated on the basis of an hourly rate which should not exceed that which is considered acceptable in the community in which the attorney practices, considering the attorney's qualifications and experience and the complexity of the case.

ALTERNATIVE DISPUTE RESOLUTION PROCEDURES

SEC. 202. (a) In lieu of or in addition to making an offer of settlement under section 201 of this title, a claimant or defendant may, within the time permitted for the making of such an offer under section 201 of this title, offer to proceed pursuant to any voluntary alternative dispute resolution procedure established or recognized under the law of the State in which the civil action for damages for harm caused by a product is brought or under the rules of the court in which such action is maintained.

(b) If the offeree refuses to proceed pursuant to such alternative dispute resolution procedure and the court determines that such refusal was unreasonable or not in good faith, the court shall assess reasonable attorney's fees and costs against the offeree.

(c) For the purposes of this section, there shall be created a rebuttable presumption that a refusal by an offeree to proceed pursuant to such alternative dispute resolution procedure was unreasonable or not in good faith, if a verdict is rendered in favor of the offeror.

TITLE III

CIVIL ACTIONS

SEC. 301. A person seeking to recover for harm caused by a product may bring a civil action against the product's manufacturer or product seller pursuant to applicable State or Federal law, except to the extent such law is superseded by this Act.

UNIFORM STANDARDS OF PRODUCT SELLER LIABILITY

SEC. 302. (a) Notwithstanding the provisions of section 301 of this title, in any civil action for harm caused by a product, a product seller other than a manufacturer is liable to a claimant, only if the claimant establishes by a preponderance of the evidence that—

(1)(A) the individual product unit which allegedly caused the harm complained of was sold by the defendant;

(B) the product seller failed to exercise reasonable care with respect to the product; and

(C) such failure to exercise reasonable care was a proximate cause of the claimant's harm; or

(2)(A) the product seller made an express warranty, independent of any express warranty made by a manufacturer as to the same product;

(B) the product failed to conform to the warranty; and

(C) the failure of the product to conform to the warranty caused the claimant's harm.

(b)(1) In determining whether a product seller is subject to liability under subsection (a)(1) of this section, the trier of fact may consider the effect of the conduct of the product seller with respect to the construction, inspection, or condition of the product, and any failure of the product seller to pass on adequate warnings or instructions from the product's manufacturer about the dangers and proper use of the product.

(2) A product seller shall not be liable in a civil action subject to this title based upon an alleged failure to provide warnings or instructions unless the claimant establishes that, when the product left the possession and control of the product seller, the product seller failed—

(A) to provide to the person to whom the product seller relinquished possession and control of the product any pamphlets, booklets, labels, inserts, or other written warnings or instructions received while the product was in the product seller's possession and control; or

(B) to make reasonable efforts to provide users with those warnings and instructions which it received after the product left its possession and control.

(3) A product seller shall not be liable in a civil action subject to this title except for breach of express warranty where there was no reasonable opportunity to inspect the product in a manner which would or should, in the exercise of reasonable care, have revealed the aspect of the product which allegedly caused the claimant's harm.

(c) A product seller shall be treated as the manufacturer of a product and shall be liable for harm to the claimant caused by a product as if it were the manufacturer of the product if—

(1) the manufacturer is not subject to service of process under the laws of any State in which the action might have been brought; or

(2) the court determines that the claimant would be unable to enforce a judgment against the manufacturer.

UNIFORM STANDARDS FOR AWARD OF PUNITIVE DAMAGES

SEC. 303. (a) Punitive damages may, if otherwise permitted by applicable law, be awarded in any civil action subject to this title to any claimant who establishes by clear and convincing evidence that the harm suffered was the result of conduct manifesting a manufacturer's or product seller's conscious, flagrant indifference to the safety of those persons who might be harmed by a product. A failure to exercise reasonable care in choosing among alternative product designs, formulations, instructions, or warnings is not of itself such conduct. Except as provided in subsection (b) of this section, punitive damages may not be awarded in the absence of a compensatory award.

(b) In any civil action in which the alleged harm to the claimant is death and the applicable State law provides, or has been construed to provide, for damages only punitive in nature, a defendant may be liable for any such damages regardless of whether a claim is asserted under this section. The recovery of any such damages shall not bar a claim under this section.

(c)(1) Punitive damages shall not be awarded pursuant to this section against a manufacturer or product seller of a drug (as defined in section 201(g)(1) of the Federal Food, Drug, and Cosmetic Act (21 U.S.C. 321(g)(1)) or medical device (as defined under section 201(h) of the Federal Food, Drug, and Cosmetic Act (21 U.S.C. 321(h)) which caused the claimant's harm where—

(A) such drug or device was subject to pre-market approval by the Food and Drug Administration with respect to the safety of the formulation or performance of the aspect of such drug or device which caused the claimant's harm or the adequacy of the packaging or labeling of such drug or device, and such drug was approved by the Food and Drug Administration; or

(B) the drug is generally recognized as safe and effective pursuant to conditions established by the Food and Drug Administration and applicable regulations, including packaging and labeling regulations. The provisions of this paragraph shall not apply (i) in any case in which the defendant withheld from or misrepresented to the Food and Drug Administration or any other agency or official of the Federal Government information that is material and relevant to the performance of such drug or device, or (ii) in any case in which the defendant made an illegal payment to an official of the Food and Drug Administration for the purpose of securing approval of such drug or device.

(2) Punitive damages shall not be awarded pursuant to this section against a manufacturer of an aircraft which caused the claimant's harm where—

(A) such aircraft was subject to pare-market certification by the Federal Aviation Administration with respect to the safety of the design or performance of the aspect of such aircraft which caused the claimant's harm or the adequacy of the warnings regarding the operation or maintenance of such aircraft;

(B) the aircraft was certified by the Federal Aviation Administration under the Federal Aviation Act of 1958 (49 App.U.S.C. 1301 et seq.); and

(C) the manufacturer of the aircraft complied, after delivery of the aircraft to a user, with Federal Aviation Administration requirements and obligations with respect to continuing airworthiness, including the requirement to provide maintenance and service information related to airworthiness whether or not such information is used by the Federal Aviation Administration in the preparation of mandatory maintenance, inspection, or repair directives.

The provisions of this paragraph shall not apply in any case in which the defendant withheld from or misrepresented to the Federal Aviation Administration information that is material and relevant to the performance or the maintenance or operation of such aircraft.

(d) At the request of the manufacturer or product seller, the trier of fact shall consider in a separate proceeding (1) whether punitive damages are to be awarded and the amount of such award, or (2) the amount of punitive damages following a determination of punitive liability. If a separate proceeding is requested, evidence relevant only to the claim of punitive damages, as determined by applicable State law, shall be inadmissible in any proceeding to determine whether compensatory damages are to be awarded.

(e) In determining the amount of punitive damages, the trier of fact shall consider all relevant evidence, including—

(1) the financial condition of the manufacturer or product seller;

(2) the severity of the harm caused by the conduct of the manufacturer or product seller;

(3) the duration of the conduct or any concealment of it by manufacturer or product seller;

(4) the profitability of the conduct to the manufacturer or product seller;

(5) the number of products sold by the manufacturer or product seller of the kind causing the harm complained of by the claimant;

(6) awards of punitive or exemplary damages to persons similarly situated to the claimant;

(7) prospective awards of compensatory damages to persons similarly situated to the claimant;

(8) any criminal penalties imposed on the manufacturer or product seller as a result of the conduct complained of by the claimant; and

(9) the amount of any civil fines assessed against the defendant as a result of the conduct complained of by the claimant.

UNIFORM TIME LIMITATIONS ON LIABILITY

SEC. 304. (a) Any civil action subject to this title shall be barred unless the complaint is filed within two years of the time the claimant discovered or, in the exercise of reasonable care, should have discovered the harm and its cause, except that any such action of a person under legal disability may be filed within two years after the disability ceases. If the commencement of such an action is stayed or enjoined, the running of the statute of limitations under this section shall be suspended for the period of the stay or injunction.

(b)(1) Any civil action subject to this title shall be barred if a product which is a capital good is alleged to have caused harm which is not a toxic harm unless the complaint is served and filed within twenty-five years after the time of delivery of the product. This subsection shall apply only if the court determines that the claimant has received or would be eligible to receive compensation under any State or Federal workers' compensation law for harm caused by the product.

(2) A motor vehicle, vessel, aircraft, or railroad used primarily to transport passengers for hire shall not be subject to the provisions of this subsection.

(3) As used in this section, the term—

(A) "time of delivery" means the time when a product is delivered to its first purchaser or lessee who was not involved in the business of manufacturing or selling such product or using it as a component part of another product to be sold;

(B) "capital good" means any product, or any component of any such product, which is of a character subject to allowance for depreciation under the Internal Revenue Code of 1986, and which was—

(i) used in a trade or business;

(ii) held for the production of income; or

(iii) sold or donated to a governmental or private entity for the production of goods, for training, for demonstration, or for other similar purposes; and

(C) "toxic harm" means harm which is functional impairment, illness, or death of a human being resulting from exposure to an object, substance, mixture, raw material, or physical agent of particular chemical composition.

(c) Nothing in this section shall affect the right of any person who is subject to liability for harm under this Act to seek and obtain contribution or indemnity from any other person who is responsible for such harm.

UNIFORM STANDARDS FOR OFFSET OF WORKERS' COMPENSATION BENEFITS

SEC. 305. (a) In any civil action subject to this title in which damages are sought for harm for which the person injured is or would have been entitled to receive compensation under any State or Federal workers' compensation law, any damages awarded shall be reduced by the sum of the amount paid as workers' compensation benefits for such harm and the present value of all workers' compensation benefits to which the employee is or would be entitled for such harm. The determination of workers' compensation benefits by the trier of fact in a civil action subject to this title shall have no binding effect on and shall not be used as evidence in any other proceeding.

(b) A claimant in a civil action subject to this title who is or may be eligible to receive compensation under any State or Federal workers' compensation law must provide written notice of the filing of the civil action to the claimant's employer within 30 days of the filing. The written notice shall include information regarding the date and court in which the civil action was filed, the names and addresses of all plaintiffs and defendants appearing on the complaint, the court docket number if available, and a copy of the complaint which was filed in the civil action. A copy of such written notice shall be filed with the court and served upon all parties to the action. A claimant's failure to comply with the requirements of this subsection shall suspend the deadlines for filing responsive pleadings and commencing discovery in the civil action, until the claimant complies with the requirements of this subsection.

(c) In any civil action subject to this title in which damages are sought for harm for which the person injured is entitled to receive compensation under any State or Federal workers' compensation law, the action shall, on application of the claimant made at claimant's sole discretion, be stayed until such time as the full amount payable as workers' compensation benefits has been finally determined under such workers' compensation law.

(d)(1) Except as provided in paragraph (2) of this subsection, unless the manufacturer or product seller has expressly agreed to indemnify or hold an employer harmless for harm to an employee caused by a product, neither the employer nor the workers' compensation insurance carrier of the employer shall have a right of subrogation, contribution or implied indemnity against the manufacturer or product seller or a lien against the claimant's recovery from the manufacturer or product seller if the harm is one for which a civil action for harm caused by a product may be brought pursuant to this Act.

(2) Paragraph (1) of this subsection shall not apply if the employer or the workers' compensation insurer of the employer establishes, and the trier of fact determines, that the claimant's harm was not in any way caused by the fault of the claimant's employer or coemployees. In order to establish this fact an employer or the workers' compensation insurer of the employer may intervene in a civil action filed by an employee at any time after the filing of a complaint. In the event that the civil action is resolved prior to obtaining a verdict by the trier of fact, any resolution of the action by settlement or other means shall afford the employer or the workers' compensation insurer of the employer an opportunity to participate and to assert a right of subrogation, contribution, or implied indemnity if the claimant's harm was not in any way caused by the fault of the claimant's employer or coemployees.

(e)(1) Except as provided in subsection (f), in any civil action subject to this title in which damages are sought for harm for which the person injured is or would have been entitled to receive compensation under any State or Federal workers' compensation law, no third-party tortfeasor may maintain any action for implied indemnity or contribution against the employer, any coemployee, or the exclusive representative of the person who was injured.

(2) Nothing in this Act shall be construed to affect any provision of a State or Federal workers' compensation law which prohibits a person who is or would have been entitled to receive compensation under any such law, or any other person whose claim is or would have been

derivative from such a claim, from recovering for harm caused by a product in any action other than a workers' compensation claim against a present or former employer or workers' compensation insurer of the employer, any coemployee, or the exclusive representative of the person who was injured. Any action other than such a workers' compensation claim shall be prohibited, except that nothing in this Act shall be construed to affect any State or Federal workers' compensation law which permits recovery based on a claim of an intentional tort by the employer or coemployee, where the claimant's harm was caused by such an intentional tort.

(f) Subsection (e) shall not apply and applicable State law shall control if the employer or the workers' compensation insurer of the employer, in a civil action subject to this title, asserts or attempts to assert, because of subsection (d), a right of subrogation, contribution, or implied indemnity against the manufacturer or product seller or a lien against the claimant's recovery from the manufacturer or product seller.

SEVERAL LIABILITY FOR NONECONOMIC DAMAGES

SEC. 306. (a) In any product liability action, the liability of each defendant for noneconomic damages shall be several only and shall not be joint. Each defendant shall be liable only for the amount of noneconomic damages allocated to such defendant in direct proportion to such defendant's percentage of responsibility as determined under subsection (b) of this section. A separate judgment shall be rendered against such defendant for that amount.

(b) For purposes of this section, the trier of fact shall determine the proportion of responsibility of each party for the claimant's harm.

(c) As used in this section, the term—

(1) "noneconomic damages" means subjective, nonmonetary losses including, but not limited to, pain, suffering, inconvenience, mental suffering, emotional distress, loss of society and companionship, loss of consortium, injury to reputation and humiliation; the term does not include objectively verifiable monetary losses including, but not limited, medical expenses, loss of earnings, burial costs, loss of use of property, costs of repair or replacement, costs of obtaining substitute domestic services, rehabilitation and training expenses, loss of employment, or loss of business or employment opportunities; and

(2) "product liability action" includes any action involving a claim, third-party claim, cross-claim, counterclaim, or contribution claim in a civil action in which a manufacturer or product seller is found liable for harm caused by a product.

DEFENSES INVOLVING INTOXICATING ALCOHOL OR DRUGS

SEC. 307. (a) In any civil action subject to this Act in which all defendants are manufacturers or product sellers, it shall be a complete defense to such action that the claimant was intoxicated or was under the influence of intoxicating alcohol or any drug and that as a result of such intoxication or the influence of the alcohol or drug the claimant was more than 50 percent responsible for the accident or event which resulted in such claimant's harm.

(b) In any civil action subject to this Act in which not all defendants are manufacturers or product sellers and the trier of fact determines that no liability exists against those defendants who are not manufacturers or product sellers, the court shall enter a judgment notwithstanding the verdict in favor of any defendant which is a manufacturer or product seller if it is proved that the claimant was intoxicated or was under the influence of intoxicating alcohol or any drug and that as a result of such intoxication or the influence of the alcohol or drug the claimant was more than 50 percent responsible for the accident or event which resulted in such claimant's harm.

(c)(1) For purposes of this section, the determination of whether a person was intoxicated or was under the influence of intoxicating alcohol or any drug shall be made pursuant to applicable State law.

(2) As used in this section, the term "drug" means any non-over-the-counter drug which has not been prescribed by a physician for use by the claimant.

COMMITTEE REPORT ON S. 640

Calendar No. 321

102D CONGRESS			REPORT
1st Session	SENATE		102–215

PRODUCT LIABILITY FAIRNESS ACT

Mr. HOLLINGS, from the Committee on Commerce, Science, and Transportation, submitted the following

REPORT

OF THE

SENATE COMMITTEE ON COMMERCE, SCIENCE, AND TRANSPORTATION

TOGETHER WITH

ADDITIONAL AND MINORITY VIEWS

ON

S. 640

NOVEMBER 14 (legislative day, NOVEMBER 13), 1991.—Ordered to be printed

U.S. GOVERNMENT PRINTING OFFICE
WASHINGTON: 1991

59–010

COMMITTEE REPORT ON S. 640

COMMITTEE ON COMMERCE, SCIENCE, AND TRANSPORTATION

ERNEST F. HOLLINGS, South Carolina, *Chairman*

DANIEL K. INOUYE, Hawaii
WENDELL H. FORD, Kentucky
J. JAMES EXON, Nebraska
AL GORE, Tennessee
JOHN D. ROCKEFELLER IV, West Virginia
LLOYD BENTSEN, Texas
JOHN F. KERRY, Massachusetts
JOHN B. BREAUX, Louisiana
RICHARD H. BRYAN, Nevada
CHARLES S. ROBB, Virginia

JOHN C. DANFORTH, Missouri
BOB PACKWOOD, Oregon
LARRY PRESSLER, South Dakota
TED STEVENS, Alaska
ROBERT W. KASTEN, Jr., Wisconsin
JOHN McCAIN, Arizona
CONRAD BURNS, Montana
SLADE GORTON, Washington
TRENT LOTT, Mississippi

KEVIN G. CURTIN, *Chief Counsel and Staff Director*
WALTER B. MCCORMICK, Jr., *Minority Chief Counsel and Staff Director*

Mr. HOLLINGS, from the Committee on Commerce, Science, and Transportation, submitted the following

REPORT

[To accompany S. 640]

together with

ADDITIONAL AND MINORITY VIEWS

The Committee on Commerce, Science, and Transportation, to which was referred the bill (S. 640) to regulate interstate commerce by providing for a uniform product liability law, and for other purposes, having considered the same, reports favorably thereon and recommends that the bill do pass.

PURPOSE OF BILL

The bill, S. 640, as reported, creates certain standards of product liability law that are to be applied uniformly throughout the United States.

The present system in the United States for resolving product liability disputes and compensating those injured by defective products is costly, slow, inequitable, and unpredictable. It does not benefit manufacturers, product sellers, or injured persons. The system's high transaction costs, which exceed the compensation paid to victims, are passed on to consumers; moreover, the unpredictability, uncertainties, inefficiencies, and costs of the present system have stifled innovation and have handicapped American firms as they compete in the global economy.

S. 640, as reported, addresses these problems by making a number of changes in product liability law that are applicable in all product liability actions in State and Federal courts. These balanced, limited changes are intended to reduce transaction costs, provide greater certainty as to the rights and responsibilities of all of those involved in product liability disputes, encourage innovation, and increase the competitiveness of U.S. firms.

COMMITTEE REPORT ON S. 640

BACKGROUND AND NEED[a]

INTRODUCTION

Traditionally, product liability has been a matter left to State law, but today the morass of product liability law is a problem of national concern that requires congressional action. The system of compensating people injured by defective products is costly, slow, inequitable, and unpredictable.

Many consumers who are injured by defective products and deserve compensation are unable to recover damages or must wait years for recovery. They are caught up with manufacturers and product sellers in a product liability litigation system in which identical cases can produce startlingly different results. Moreover, injured victims with the severest injuries tend to receive far less than their actual economic losses, while those with minor injuries are overcompensated.

The inefficiency and unpredictability of the product liability system have made it difficult for manufacturers of products, such as machine tools, medical devices, or vaccines, to buy adequate insurance coverage. This unpredictable patchwork of State laws has had a chilling effect on the introduction of new products to market. Moreover, the current U.S. product liability system has hurt our competitive position in world markets because the excessive costs of the system result in higher prices for American products. Department of Commerce Secretary Mosbacher testified before the Consumer Subcommittee during the 101st and 102d Congresses, stating that enactment of a Federal product liability law will enhance American competitiveness in world markets.

Thus, the present system has an adverse impact on plaintiffs and defendants, manufacturers, product sellers, and consumers. The individual States cannot fully address the problems of the product liability system. Reform at the Federal level is urgently needed.

I. The Present Product Liability System Is Costly, Slow, Inequitable and Unpredictable

The present product liability system does not meet its objective of fairly compensating, in a timely fashion, those who are injured by products. It has been faulted for failing to provide an efficient and equitable means of resolving claims about defective products, but rather pushing parties to pursue costly, time-consuming litigation.

A. Costs of the Product Liability System

The costs of the product liability system have increased substantially in recent years. According to the editors of "The Liability Maze," a 1991 book published by the Brookings Institution, "Regardless of the trends in tort verdicts, most studies in this area have concluded that, after adjusting for inflation and population, liability costs have risen

---

a. The footnotes in this report may be found at the end of the majority views.

dramatically in the last thirty years, and most especially in the last decade."[1] Increases in awards in such cases have been much higher than corresponding increases in wages and inflation.[2] Increased product liability costs are reflected in dramatic increases in liability insurance costs. Over the last 40 years, general liability insurance costs have increased at over 4 times the rate of growth of the national economy.[3] Much of this is attributed to "high stakes" litigation which includes "traditional" forms of product liability.[4] The present product liability system's transaction costs—the costs of litigation, court costs, and attorney's fees—are enormous. Today, plaintiff and defense lawyers collect almost as much from the system as injured persons do; most of the money paid out by manufacturers never reaches the injured persons.[5] A recent survey of the membership of The National Machine Tool Builders Association stated that, for 79 closed claims settled and litigated in 1989, $2,600,000 was paid out, but only $400,000 (17 percent) went directly to claimants and $1.5 million in subrogation paid to employers and/or their workers' compensation carriers, regardless of employer fault or the lack thereof.[6]

The overall magnitude of these costs continues to grow because of what some have described as a "litigation explosion."[7] In 1980, 9,118

1. P.W. Huber and R.E. Litan, eds., *The Liability Maze* at 3, Brookings, 1991. (Hereinafter *The Liability Maze*). The preface of The Liability Maze states:

"The President (of the Brookings Institution) bears final responsibility for the decision to publish a manuscript as a Brookings book. In reaching his judgment on the competence, accuracy, and objectivity of each study, the President is advised by the director of the appropriate research program and weighs the views of a panel of expert outside readers who report to him in confidence on the quality of the work. Publication of a work signifies that it is deemed a competent treatment worthy of public consideration but does not imply endorsement of conclusions or recommendations.

"The Institution maintains its position of neutrality on issues of public policy in order to safeguard the intellectual freedom of the staff. Hence interpretations or conclusions in Brookings publications should be understood to be solely those of the authors and should not be attributed to the Institution, its trustees, officers, or other staff members, or to the organizations that support its research."

2. Enterprise Responsibility for Personal Injury, American Law Institute, Reporters' Study, Vol. I, at 270–71. (Hereinafter ALI Reporters study). This study has not been adopted by the American Law Institute and does not represent the position of the Institute. Nevertheless, ALI's bylaws authorize its publication. The Chief Reporter for the study is Professor Paul Weiler of Harvard Law School. Associate Reporters are: Professor Kenneth Abraham of the University of Virginia Law School; Professor Robert Rabin of Stanford University Law School; Professor David Rosenberg of Harvard Law School; Professor Alan Schwartz of Yale Law School; and W. Kip Viscussi, Professor of Economics at Duke University.

3. Id. at 60.

4. Id.

5. Testimony of the Honorable Robert A. Mosbacher, Secretary, U.S. Department of Commerce, before the Consumer Subcommittee of the Senate Committee on Commerce, Science, and Transportation, on April 5, 1990.

6. Statement of Howard H. Fark, Senior Vice President, Minster Machine Company, before the Consumer Subcommittee of the Senate Committee on Commerce, Science, and Transportation, February 22, 1990 at 3.

7. *See, e.g.,* Speech to the American Law Institute by Chief Justice of the United States Warren E. Burger, May 13, 1986.

product liability suits were pending in Federal district courts.[8] By the end of 1988, the number of pending product liability cases had risen to 32,617, an increase of 257 percent in 8 years.[9]

The inefficiency of the present system has been noted often, and has been recently demonstrated in a General Accounting Office (GAO) report on product liability actions in five States. According to the GAO report, jury awards for all damages combined ranged from $255 to $10 million; the average jury award [10] for compensatory damages alone was $906,000, and the median was $375,000.[11] Punitive damages were awarded in an average amount of $1,300,000, with a median of $400,000.[12] Plaintiffs' attorneys' fees average about 35 percent of the money recovered by the client, with actual figures ranging from a low of $1,000 (for a $3,000 recovery) to a high of $3,400,000 (for a $6 million recovery). The average contingency fee was $115,000. Defendants, who paid their attorneys on an hourly fee basis, paid fees ranging from $1,500 to $400,000, with an average of $41,000 and a median of

---

8. U.S. Department of Commerce, Bureau of the Census, *1990 Statistical Abstract of the U.S.*, Chart No. 314, p. 184 (110th ed. 1990).

9. *Id.* Most commentators agree that 90 to 95 percent of all product liability cases are filed in state courts. Statement of Deborah Hensler, Rand Institute for Civil Justice, before the consumer Subcommittee of the Senate Committee on Commerce, Science, and Transportation, September 12, 1991 at 3 (hereinafter September 12, 1991 hearing). At the September 19, 1991 hearing on S. 640, a witness challenged the contention that product liability filings are increasing. Statement of Professor Marc Galanter before the Senate, September 19, 1991 (hereinafter September 19, 1991 hearing). Mr. Galanter studied product liability filings only in federal courts. He found that product liability filings between 1985 and 1990 increased by 49 percent. He contends, however, that when litigation involving asbestos is removed from the data, case filings in federal court decreased during that time. *Id.* at 2. Based on that conclusion and "scattered evidence" that product liability filings account for two to three percent of tort cases in state courts, he concludes that a "sizeable" portion of product liability cases are filed in federal courts. *Id.* at 5–6. Deborah Hensler testified, however, that there are no useful data from state courts on product liability filings and one cannot infer trends in state courts from federal court data. Statement of Deborah Hensler, *supra,* at 3–4.

Opponents of product liability reform also have cited a recent law review article, which found that courts were ruling in favor of product liability defendants more during the late 1980s than in earlier years. Henderson and Eisenberg, "The Quiet Revolution in Product Liability: An Empirical Study of Legal Change," 37 U.C.L.A. Law Review 479 (1990). One of the authors of this study, professor James Henderson, testified that, based on his examination of relevant data, he supports enactment of a federal product liability law, and specifically, S. 640. September 19, 1991 hearing (transcript at 106). He testified further that, regardless of the recent trends he identified, further reform is necessary to make product liability laws more fair, and it must be done on the national level. *Id.* (transcript at 107). Professor Henderson's views are underscored by Professor George Priest who found no evidence that the expansion of litigation has affected the death or injury rate. "Product Liability Law and the Accident Rate," in *Liability: Perspectives and Policy,* edited by R.E. Litan, and C. Winston, 184–222 at 187–194.

10. U.S. General Accounting Office; Report to the Chairman, Subcommittee on Commerce, Consumer Protection, and Competitiveness; Committee on Energy and Commerce, House of Representatives; *Product Liability: Verdicts and Case Resolution in Five States,* at 25 (Sept. 1989) [hereinafter GAO Report].

11. Id. at 29.

12. Id.

$20,000.[13] The average actual cost of all expenses up to the time a verdict was rendered was $168,000 per case, including attorneys' fees. GAO noted that the costs to defendants were probably underestimated due to the probability that an out-of-state defendant would be more likely to have been represented by multiple legal firms.[14] As this survey shows, the costs directly related to product liability actions are high.

Earlier studies have also pointed out the inefficiency of the present system. A 1986 Rand Institute for Civil Justice study showed that the annual overall transaction costs of the U.S. tort system exceed compensation to plaintiffs. The Rand study found that in 1985, net compensation totaled $13 to $15 billion, but the transaction costs—including plaintiffs' attorneys' fees, defense legal fees, public expenditures, and the time of the litigants—were between $15 billion and $19 billion.[15]

The pattern that the Rand study found in the tort system as a whole is repeated in product liability cases, alone. According to calculations derived from a comprehensive 1977 survey of 24,452 closed claims conducted by the Insurance Service Office (ISO), for every dollar paid to claimants, insurers paid an average of 42 cents in defense costs.[16] Moreover, for every dollar awarded to a claimant, he or she typically paid a contingent fee of 33 cents in legal costs and therefore received about 67 cents. Thus, on this basis (adding the average

13. Id. at 52–53.
14. Id. at 54.
15. Testimony of James S. Kakalik, Ph. D., The Institute for Civil Justice of the Rand Corporation, before the Subcommittee on Trade, Productivity, and Economic Growth of the Joint Economic Committee, July 29, 1986, S.Hrg. 99–1090. The same conclusion was reached in a study done by an actuarial consulting firm for members of the insurance industry. The study found that in 1984, 63 percent of the gross insured costs of the United States tort system consisted of payments to claimants. Robert W. Sturgis, "The Cost of the U.S. Tort System," Tillinghast, Nelson, and Warren, Inc. (November, 1985) at 16. If this is reduced by one-third to account for plaintiffs' attorneys' fees, only 42 percent of the costs remain to compensate the injured. Dr. Kakalik, author of the Rand study, explained in his testimony that Sturgis' estimate of transaction costs "is higher than ours because it includes the cost of insurance premiums that cover claims, lawsuits, and the operation of the insurance system. We only report on compensation and costs directly associated with tort lawsuits."
16. Insurance Services Office Product Liability Closed Claim Survey, A Technical Analysis of Survey Results, 11 (1977). A witness at the September 12, 1991 hearing pointed out that the results of this study are over a decade old. Testimony of Deborah Hensler (transcript 106). Nevertheless, more recent studies cited by the editors of *The Liability Maze* confirm these findings. They state that roughly half of total awards and settlements are paid to lawyers and insurers to administer the claim settlement process. *The Liability Maze* at 2, citing Kakalik and Pace, "Cash and Compensation Paid in Tort Litigation," R–3391–ICJ: The Rand Corporation (1986); Schotter and Ordover, "The Cost of the Tort System," New York University, C.U. Starr Center for Applied Economics (March 1986). Further, a 1989 study cited by the editors of *The Liability Maze* found that while the tort system imposes transaction costs of approximately one-half, transaction costs consume only 30 percent of the costs of the workers compensation system, 15 percent of health insurance, and just one percent of the social security system. *The Liability Maze* study at 2, citing Tillinghast, Perrins–Tower Group. *Tort Cost Trends: An International Perspective* at 16 (Dec. 1989).

defense cost to the contingent fee) one can estimate that the product liability tort litigation system appears to cost more in litigation and transaction costs than the net recovery received by the claimant.

Not only do these transaction costs exceed compensation, but they have risen dramatically in recent years. According to a 1986 study by economists at New York University, the tort system's administrative or transactions cost—the amount spent to adjust and litigate claims made by injured parties—has been rising rapidly since 1983.[17] This study noted:

> These increases portend trouble ahead if they are not checked. If current rates of growth continue we can expect that by 1990 we will be spending between $31 and $38 billion per year simply administering the tort system.[18]

The mounting costs from this inefficient system have exceeded the projections made in the 1986 New York University study. According to a 1989 study conducted by the insurance industry, the U.S. tort system is the most costly tort system in the free world.[19] This study estimates that the current overall cost of the U.S. tort system at a staggering $117 billion,[20] an amount almost triple the figure projected in 1986.

Liability insurance costs rise as transactions costs rise. According to a May 1986 ISO report, "The Rising Costs of General Liability Legal Defense," the total legal defense expenses incurred in 1984 in general liability cases, including product liability cases, were $2.7 billion, and the proportion of general liability costs incurred by insurers that are consumed by legal defense costs almost tripled between 1960 and 1984. A more recent study found that between 1950 and 1988, liability insurance costs increased from $1.7 billion to $75 billion, a 44-fold increase. By contrast the American Gross National Product increased tenfold during that time.[21]

During this period, as State courts expanded the scope of product liability laws and extended the situations in which product manufacturers were held strictly liable, product manufacturers have found themselves faced with enormous increases in liability insurance costs, with increases of as much as 1,500 percent in some cases.[22]

Neither plaintiffs nor defendants benefit from the rapidly increasing and excessive costs of the present system for resolving product liability disputes. S. 640 would take a number of steps to encourage resolution of these disputes in a less costly manner.

---

17. Andrew Schotter and Janusz Ordover, The Cost of the Tort System I, New York University, *supra.*
18. *Id.*
19. Tillinghast, *supra.*
20. *Id.* at A3.
21. ALI Reporters' study, *supra,* at n. 3.
22. Priest, *The Current Insurance Crisis and Modern Tort Law,* 96 Yale L.J. 1521, 1527 (1987).

B. Delay

A second problem with the present product liability system is delay. This is particularly a concern for seriously injured victims, who are often in desperate financial straits and must wait years to be compensated while litigation drags on.

One insurance industry survey has shown that 36 percent of bodily injury losses in product liability cases are not paid until at least 4 years after the first report, and that it takes 5 years to pay the claim with the average dollar amount of loss. This study also found that "larger claims tend to take much longer to close than smaller ones." [23]

Another insurance industry study found that the victims of the severest injuries have to wait the longest. This study found that, in cases in which payment exceeded $100,000 21.6 percent of claimants waited more than 5 years for payment. Only 2.1 percent were paid less than a year after they reported their injury, and 62.6 percent took more than 3 years to be paid.[24]

More recently, the 1989 GAO report found that, in the five States studied, on average, product liability cases took 2½ years to move from filing to trial court verdict.[25] One case studied by GAO took about 9½ years to move through the court system.[26]

Such delays plague even the many product liability cases that are settled before trial. One plaintiff's attorney has explained that, even though most cases are settled, "most settlement negotiations get serious only a week or so before trial is scheduled to begin." The delay has become so ingrained in the system that "each week the [lawyer's] firm projects cash flow by estimating the settlement value of the cases set for trial the following week." [27]

Delay also can result in undercompensation of victims. Because many victims of injury—particularly those with the severest injuries—have inadequate resources to pay for their medical and rehabilitation expenses, they are forced to settle for less than their full losses in order to get some payment because they cannot afford to wait longer without compensation.[28] Studies have shown that, when rehabilitation has to be delayed, victims do not recover as fully as they do when the problem

---

23. Insurance Services Office Product Liability Closed Claim Survey: A Technical Analysis of Survey Results, 79–80 (1977).

24. Alliance of American Insurers Survey of Large–Loss Product Liability Claims 4 (1980).

25. GAO Report, *supra* note 6, at 49.

26. *Id.*

27. Wayne E. Green, *A Lawyer Faces Risks In Deciding to Take On Costly Damage Suits,* Wall St.J., May 23, 1986 at 12.

28. See O'Connell, *A 'Neo No–Fault' Contract in Lieu of Tort: Preaccident Guarantees of Postaccident Settlement Offers,* 73 Calif.L.Rev. 898, 901–902 (1985), citing Corstevet, *The Uncompensated Accident and Its Consequences,* 3 Law & Contemp.Probs. 466, 468 (1936).

is treated promptly.[29]

S. 640 uses two approaches to eliminate delays. These are incentives for parties to participate in Alternative Dispute Resolution (ADR) and negotiated settlements.

C. Inequitable Compensation

Not only does the present product liability system generate excessive costs and delays; it is unable to fairly compensate injured victims in proportion to their losses. Numerous studies have found that the tort system grossly overpays people with small losses, while underpaying people with the most serious losses.

The 1977 ISO product liability study found that injured plaintiffs with losses between $1 and $1,000 receive, on the average, 859 percent of their losses, while those with losses of over $1 million received, on the average, 15 percent of their losses (before paying their attorneys' fees).[30] In general, the study found, compensation exceeded economic loss when losses were below $100,000, and then dropped dramatically below economic loss when the claimant's loss exceeded $100,000.[31]

A 1980 insurance industry study of the largest product liability claims confirmed that the most severely injured victims do not even receive full compensation for their pain and suffering. For every dollar of past and future economic loss, the tort system paid claimants $1.22, but if the standard 33-percent attorney's contingent fee is deducted, these claimants were left with only about 81 cents for every dollar of loss.[32]

Reform of the product liability system is essential to assure that those who are injured by defective products are fairly compensated in proportion to their losses.

D. Unpredictability

Consumers, manufacturers, and product sellers are caught up in a product liability litigation system that has often been characterized as a legal lottery. It is a system in which identical cases can produce startlingly different results.[33]

---

29. Statement of Leonard Bender, M.D., on behalf of the American Congress of Rehabilitation and the American Academy of Physical Medicine and Rehabilitation, in Federal Standards for No–Fault Motor Vehicle Accident Benefits Act: Hearings before the Subcommittee on Consumer Protection and Finance, House Committee on Interstate and Foreign Commerce, 95th Cong., 1st Sess., Serial No. 95–55, 594 (1977).

30. Insurance Services Office Product Liability Closed Claim Survey: A Technical Analysis of Survey Results 49 (1977).

31. *Id.* at 383.

32. Alliance of American Insurers Survey of Large–Loss Product Liability Claims iii (August, 1980). This study almost certainly overestimates the compensation that injured victims are receiving; it only includes cases where payment exceeded $100,000 and thus does not average in cases where the claimant had large economic losses, but received less than $100,000—or nothing at all.

33. Sugarman, *Doing Away with Tort Law,* 73 Cal.L.Rev. 555, 594 (1985).

COMMITTEE REPORT ON S. 640

As Professor Jeffrey O'Connell has explained in 1986 testimony before the Committee:

> If you are badly injured in our society by a product and you go to the highly skilled lawyer in all honesty [the lawyer] cannot tell you what you will be paid, when you will be paid, or indeed if you will be paid.[34]

The present system's uncertainty is a problem for both manufacturers and consumers injured by defective products. Plaintiffs need faster, more certain recovery that fully compensates them for their real losses. Defendants need greater certainty as to the scope of their liability under the law.

The inherent uncertainty of the system has been linked by commentators to the diversity of legal standards applied in different jurisdictions and the doctrinal mixture of contract and tort law applied in product liability cases.[35] In addition, it has been linked to expanding doctrines of liability,[36] the difficulties in establishing causation and fault, as well as the difficulties in translating non-pecuniary loss (pain and suffering) into pecuniary terms.[37]

The uncertainties and unpredictability of the system affect settlements as well as judgments. Settlement negotiations are "sabotaged"[38] by the lack of clear standards. With respect to punitive damage claims, for example, uncertainties about liability standards make it difficult for manufacturers to negotiate sensibly.[39]

Greater predictability and uniformity will benefit all parties in product liability disputes. Warren W. Eginton, a sitting Federal judge who is a product liability expert, testified at the Subcommittee's February 22, 1990 hearing:

> "[T]he more uniformity can be accomplished the more quickly the litigation flow and the lighter the economic burden on all parties involved. Certainly the task of the judge and juries in

---

34. Testimony at Feb. 27, 1986 hearing before Consumer Subcommittee, Senate Committee on Commerce, Science, and Transportation.

35. See, e.g., S.Rcpt. 98 176, pp. 3–4; Guido Calabresi and Alvin K. Klevorick *Four Tests for Liability in Torts*, 14 J.Leg. Stud. 585, 585–6 (1985).

36. See e.g., Priest, *The Invention of Enterprise Liability: A Critical History of the Intellectual Foundations of Modern Tort Law*, 14 J.Leg.Stud. 461, 521–7 (1985); Twerski, *A Moderate and Restrained Product Liability Bill: Targeting the Crisis Areas for Resolution*, 18 U. of Mich.J. of L.Reform 575, 580–599 (1985).

37. See e.g., O'Connell, *Offers That Can't be Refused*, 77 Nw.U.L.Rev. 589, 590–591; McCormick, *Handbook on the Law of Damages*, 318 (1935) p. 11.

38. Twerski, *A Moderate and Restrained Product Liability Bill: Targeting the Crisis Areas for Resolution*, 18 U.Mich.J. of L.Ref. 575, 612 (1985).

39. Statement of Professor Aaron Twerski, September 12, 1991 hearing at 8. See Twerski, *A Moderate and Restrained Federal Product Liability Bill: Targeting the Crisis Areas for Resolution, supra,* at 612.

understanding the problems and the rules of law to be applied to those problems will be greatly simplified by uniformity." [40]

S. 640 would attempt to reduce the unpredictability of the current system by taking steps, such as clarifying the responsibilities of product sellers, establishing uniform standards for punitive damage awards, and establishing uniform time limits for pursuing product liability claims.

II. The Present Product Liability System Places a Burden on Productivity and Commerce

The present product liability system extracts high transaction costs from plaintiffs, defendants, consumers, and manufacturers. Valuable resources are wasted on fueling the product liability machinery that could be used to strengthen our economy. Moreover, those transaction costs are only a small part of the enormous burden this system puts on our economy. It deprives consumers of needed products, limits job opportunities, and weakens our competitive position in world markets. In his testimony before the Consumer Subcommittee, Commerce Secretary Mosbacher cited a Baylor University study, which found that in 1988 the current liability system cost the State of Texas alone over $8 billion and 79,000 jobs.[41]

The effects of our current system on the economy were clearly demonstrated in a 1988 survey of over 2,000 CEOs, which was conducted by the Conference Board. Participating businesses indicated that their actions were affected in the following ways by our current product liability system:

Adverse Impacts Cited Based on Actual Liability Experience [42]

Type of Impact	Percent of firms reporting action
Closed Production Plants	8
Laid Off Workers	15
Discontinued Product Lines	36
Decided Against Introducing New Products	30
Decided Against Acquiring/Merging	17
Discontinued Product Research	21
Moved Production Offshore	4
Lost Market Share	22

Adverse Impacts Cited Based on Anticipated Liability Problems [43]

Closed Production Plants	1

---

40. Statement of the Honorable Warren W. Eginton, U.S. District Judge, District of Connecticut, February 22, 1990 hearing at 5.

41. Statement of the Honorable Robert A. Mosbacher, Secretary, U.S. Department of Commerce, April 5, 1990 hearing at 9.

42. McGuire, The Conference Board, Research Report No. 908, *The Impact of Product Liability* (1988), Table 28, pg. 19 [hereinafter Conference Board Report].

43. Conference Board Report, Table 29, pg. 19.

Type of Impact	Percent of firms reporting action
Laid Off Workers	1
Discontinued Product Lines	11
Decided Against Introducing New Products	9
Decided Against Acquiring/Merging	5
Discontinued Product Research	4
Moved Production Offshore	1
Lost Market Share	

Secretary Mosbacher testified that the Conference Board results show the extent of the indirect costs of the current product liability system. These indirect costs include "useful products being discontinued, decisions not to develop new product lines or not to continue product research, and a fear to innovate."[44] This was underscored by the conclusions of the editors and three contributors to "The Liability Maze".[45] Secretary Mosbacher expressed concern that, "Rational business planning is seriously affected by the uncertainty of the system. Just as alarming, 75 percent of the CEOs expect that the future impact of the product liability system on U.S. competitiveness will grow in significance."[46]

A. Product Innovation

Testimony was received to the effect that the current product liability system inhibits the introduction of new products in a number of ways. The expense of litigating claims diverts resources from productive efforts. Excessive management time is diverted from production to assessment of legal claims. Many U.S. companies devote far more to product liability costs than to research and development efforts. For example, The National Machine Tool Builders Association stated recently that its members spend seven times more on product liability costs than on research and development.[47]

Moreover, the current product liability system is having a "profoundly negative impact on the development of new medical technologies," according to a recent report by the American Medical Association.[48] The report concluded that:

44. Statement of the Honorable Robert A. Mosbacher, Secretary, U.S. Department of Commerce, April 5, 1990 hearing at 5.

45. *The Liability Maze*, Huber and Litan, Overview at 19. Commentators in three of the four industries concluded that product liability deterred innovation. *E.G.* Mackay, *Liability, Safety, and Innovation in the Auto Industry,* at 220–221 (Discussions with executives and engineers point to conclusion that strict liability has had a negative influence on innovation.); Lasagna, *Chilling Effect of Product Liability* at 355 (The magnitude and uncertainties involved in product liability litigation serve to discourage certain kinds of pharmaceutical research, development and marketing);

Robert Martin, *General Aviation Manufacturing: An Industry Under Siege* at 496 (Product liability litigation has had a deterring effect on innovation and product improvement at various levels within the industry).

46. Statement of the Honorable Robert A. Mosbacher, Secretary, U.S. Department of Commerce, April 5, 1990 hearing at 4.

47. Statement of Howard H. Fark, February 22, 1990, at 2.

48. Statement of Richard Kingham, at April 5, 1990 hearing, *citing,* AMA Board of Trustees, "Impact of Product Liability on the Development of New Medical Technologies," at 12 (June 1988) in *Brief of*

Innovative new products are not being developed or are being withheld from the market because of liability concerns or inability to obtain adequate insurance. Certain older technologies have been removed from the market, not because of sound scientific evidence indicating lack of safety or efficacy, but because product liability suits have exposed manufacturers to unacceptable financial risks.[49]

A good example of this problem is the diphtheria-tetanus-pertussis (DTP) vaccine. In 1984, two of the three companies manufacturing this vaccine decided to stop producing it because of product liability costs. Later that year, the Centers for Disease Control recommended that doctors stop vaccinating children over age 1 in order to conserve limited supplies of the DTP vaccine for the most vulnerable infants.[50]

The general aviation industry is another sector of the economy that has been adversely affected by the product liability system. In 1985, insurance premiums averaged $70,000 per airplane, despite the general aviation industry's best safety record in years. At the same time these costs increased, sales of new aircraft and jobs have plummeted. In 1979, more than 17,000 general aviation aircraft were sold by United States manufacturers. In 1989, such sales had dropped by over 90 percent to 1,535 airplanes. As a result, tens of thousands of workers have been laid off, and in 1990, unemployment in the industry was over 50 percent.[51]

In the general aviation industry, manufacturers of key components have decided not to put new products on the market or to discontinue sales of current products. Examples include a "head-up display" of critical flight instruments; an electronic ignition system; and shock absorbing equipment for small aircraft.[52]

Moreover, the uncertainties of the present system deter the development of new products and product improvements. One example of this problem is The Merchants Co., which decided not to sell a state-of-the-art child safety seat because of product liability concerns.[53] Another example is a computer-controlled pump that would dispense medicine for transplant patients. Even though the pump, which was developed at the University of Texas, was approved by the Food and Drug

---

Amici Curiae Pharmaceutical Manufacturer Association and American Medical Association in *Browning Ferris Industries of Vermont, Inc. v. Kelco Disposal, Inc.,* 109 S.Ct. 2909 (1989).

49. *Id.* at 1.

50. *The Liability Maze* at 343.

51. The General Aviation Accident Liability Standards Act of 1989, S. 640, Senate Committee on Commerce, Science, and Transportation, 101st Congress, 1st Session, Rept. No. 101-223, 1-3 (1989). *See also* Statement of Robert Martin, Counsel, Beech Aircraft Corp., Wichita, Kansas, before the Senate Judiciary Committee, March 9, 1990.

52. Robert Martin, "General Aviation Manufacturing: An Industry Under Siege," in *The Liability Maze* at 496.

53. Statement of Secretary Mosbacher, September 12, 1991 hearing at 6.

Administration, no manufacturers chose to exercise a license to market this product.[54]

Actual product development is not the only casualty of the product liability system. As Dr. Malcolm Skolnick testified before the Consumer Subcommittee during the 101st Congress, "Scientific inquiry is stifled. Ideas in areas where litigation has occurred will not receive support for exploration and development. Producers fearful of possible suit will discourage additional investigation which can be used against them in future claims."[55]

His views are consistent with the conclusions of Dr. Louis Lasagna of Tufts University Medical School; Mr. Robert Martin of Martin, Pringle, Oliver, Wallace and Schwartz, a Wichita, KS, law firm and Prof. Murray Mackay of the University of Birmingham, England who contributed to "The Liability Maze." For example, Dr. Lasagna observed that, in the pharmaceutical industry, the magnitude and uncertainties of product liability litigation operate to discourage certain kinds of pharmaceutical research and development.[56] Companies reach the decision not to engage in research and development, he observes, after attempting to balance the future risks of marketing a new product. Such risk may result in financial devastation.[57] Robert Martin observed that, in the general aviation industry, the willingness of courts to use current designs as a yardstick against which to measure an old product or design has discouraged research and development.[58] He states further that the only innovation that the system encourages is for lawyers claiming that a product is defectively designed.[59] Professor Mackay concluded that discussions with executives and engineers point to the conclusion that strict product liability has had a negative effect on innovation.[60] Secretary Mosbacher shared a related concern: "Universities are shying away from licensing patents to small manufac-

54. Statement of Dr. Malcolm Skolnick before the Consumer Subcommittee of the Senate Committee on Commerce, Science, and Transportation, April 5, 1990 at 11. During the 101st Congress, there was considerable discussion about Monsanto Corporation's experience with a biodegradable phosphate fiber. Monsanto asserted that this substance could have been a safe substitute for asbestos. Testimony of Monsanto Company (S.Hrg 101-733) at 633. At the May 10, 1990 hearing, this claim was challenged by a witness testifying in opposition to the bill. *Id.* at 427. The witness submitted documents suggesting that the results of the intrapleural implant study with Monsanto's calcium sodium metaphosphate fiber presented a substantial risk that pleural fibrosarcomas might develop. Monsanto responded to this charge with a document indicating that independent experts concluded that the results could not be used as a basis for judging the effects on humans. *Id.* at 427. Moreover, the witness admitted under cross examination that there was a subsequent test of the Monsanto fiber. *Id.* at 503. This test, a chronic inhalation study, has found no evidence of carcinogenicity.

55. Testimony of Dr. Malcolm Skolnick, *supra.*

56. "The Chilling Effect of Product Liability on New Drug Development," in *The Liability Maze* at 355.

57. *Id.* at 337.

58. Martin, *supra,* at 492.

59. *Id.*

60. Mackey, "Liability, Safety, and Innovation in the Automotive Industry" in *The Liability Maze* at 220-21.

turers because of their fear that, as the originators of the idea upon which a product was manufactured, they will become the 'deep pocket' if there is litigation involving the product."[61] Thus, considerable testimony was received that the uncertainty of the system is a deterrent to the research and scientific investigation necessary to develop ideas that ultimately become innovative products.

B. U.S. Competitiveness

The adverse effects of the system have carried over into international trade. American manufacturers and product sellers generally pay product liability insurance rates which are 20 to 50 times higher than those of foreign competitors.[62] This disparity is attributable in large part to the uncertainties and costs of the American tort litigation system.[63] As a result, American manufacturers and product sellers may be at a competitive disadvantage in both foreign and domestic markets. Insurers generally do not discount premiums where a manufacturer exports its goods, because there is always the possibility that a product-related suit will be brought in the United States. Thus, each U.S. product shipped abroad contains an insurance cost element greater than that of a foreign competitor.[64] With respect to domestic markets, the effect of the current uncertainties in product liability law is similar. For example, according to the National Machine Tool Builders Association, the price of imported products can be lower if imports sell only partially in the United States because product liability insurance rates for those products could be lower.[65]

It should also be noted that changes in conflict of law theory have added to the competitive disadvantage for American firms. A foreigner injured by a U.S. product overseas now may be able to sue the manufacturer in the United States and have a U.S. law applied in the case. In the past, the rule of lex loci would have required foreign law, which is less stringent than U.S. product liability law, to be applied in a given case.[66] The diminished importance of lex loci means that U.S. manufacturers may be held to a higher and more costly product

---

61. Statement of the Honorable Robert A. Mosbacher, April 5, 1990 hearing at 9.

62. The Conference Board Research Report at 4 (citing a 1984 study commissioned by the Department of Commerce).

63. Id.

64. See Orban, *Product Liability and International Trade and Policies*, Product Liability and Tort Law Reform, National Legal Center for the Public Interest, 144 (April 21, 1982).

65. Letter from James A. Gray, President, National Machine Tool Builders Association, to Jim J. Tozzi, Deputy Director of Information and Regulatory Affairs, Office of Management and Budget (June 14, 1982). The letter also points out the effect of the lack of a statute of repose on this industry. NMTBA indicates there are cases in which 50 year old products have been the subject of product liability lawsuits.

66. Testimony of Aaron Twerski, September 12, 1991 hearing (transcript at 134); See *Pray v. Lockheed Aircraft Corp.* 644 F.Supp. 1289 (D.D.C.1986) (Washington, D.C. law applied in lawsuit against U.S. manufacturer for damages arising outside Saigon, Vietnam).

liability standard in both U.S. and foreign markets than their foreign counterparts.

The Consumer Subcommittee received testimony indicating that "uncontrolled damages have serious international implication(s)."[67] The United States has been unable to get foreign countries to enter into treaties to enforce American judgments abroad because of the "contempt for our unregulated judgments."[68] American businesses which are unable to enforce simple money judgments overseas are the loser as a result.[69]

C. Product Liability and Product Safety

Opponents of Federal product liability reform believe that the product liability system promotes safety.[70] They believe that the fear of liability provides incentives for the development of safer products.[71] Based on the evidence in "The Product Liability Maze" the editors disagree. They concluded that other factors, such as safety regulation, are responsible for the promotion of safety.[72] Specific conclusions were reached by individual contributors. For example, Robert Martin found that strict product litigation does not enhance safety in general aviation.[73] Similarly, Professor John Graham of the Harvard University School of Public Health did five case studies on whether there was a relationship between motor vehicle safety and product liability law. He concluded that "The case studies provide little evidence that expanded product liability risk was necessary to achieve the safety improvements that have been made."[74] Instead, Graham concludes that vehicle safety regulation can provide a predictable and technically sound forum in which to resolve safety issues.[75]

One contributing author in "The Liability Maze" concluded that, in the chemical industry, the liability system promotes safety.[76] According to the editor of the overall study, Professor Ashford's findings that product liability promotes both safety and innovation is contrary to the findings of all the other authors contributing to the study.[77] Moreover, the study's editor questioned Professor Ashford's use of an expansive "social costs" concept in his analysis.[78] Professor Ashford responded to

67. Statement of Aaron Twerski, September 12, 1991.

68. Id.

69. Id.

70. Statement of the Association of Trail lawyers of America before the Senate Committee on the Judiciary, July 31, 1990, S.Hrg. 101–1188 at 109; Statement of Gene Kimmelmann, Legislative Director, Consumer Federation of America, S.Hrg. 101–743 at 304.

71. Id.

72. See The Liability Maze at 12–13.

73. "General Aviation Manufacturing: An Industry Under Siege" in The Liability Maze at 492.

74. "Product Liability and Motor Vehicle Safety" in The Liability Maze at 183–184.

75. Id. at 184.

76. Statement of Professor Nicholas Ashford, September 12, 1991 hearing; The Liability Maze at 367.

77. Testimony of Peter Huber, September 19, 1991 hearing (transcript at 94).

78. Id.

this testimony in a letter to Senator Hollings.[79] Further, Professor Ashford assumes that product liability costs can be "internalized" in the price of a product, even though a 50-year-old machine can be the subject of a product liability lawsuit.[80] Finally, Professor Ashford assumes that "responsibility can be reasonably allocated or apportioned among the various parties."[81] This analysis fails to consider the doctrine of joint and several liability which allows a plaintiff to collect 100 percent of a judgment from a single defendant even if that defendant is only minimally at fault.

The present product liability system is "overburdened" with "nonproductive legal costs."[82] Supporters of product liability reform believe that the problems associated with this costly system "must be addressed at the national level in order to bring some commonsense and stability to a highly integrated national economy where products flow freely across State lines."[83] S. 640 takes a "commonsense" approach in meeting these objectives.[84]

III. The Limitations of State Efforts at Reform

In 1978, the Federal Interagency Task Force on Product Liability, after conducting an 18-month study of the problem, issued a report which suggested that a model product liability act be drafted with the idea that reforms of the system would be enacted at the Federal level if the States did not enact the model law.[85] A final version of this model law, known as the Uniform Product Liability Act (UPLA), was published on October 31, 1979.[86]

However, UPLA, which ultimately was offered as a model State law, has not been adopted in full in any State. Over 40 States have enacted specific product liability and general tort reform measures.[87] The States' efforts have been helpful and are to be encouraged; however, those efforts at State law reform have not resolved the overall problems of the product liability tort litigation system. Most State statutes are not comprehensive and fail to address all the key issues that arise in product liability litigation. Even if any individual State adopted a comprehensive product liability statute so that its own law was clear and predictable, the legal rules would still vary from State to State.

---

79. Letter of Professors Nicholas Ashford and Robert Stone to Senator Ernest F. Hollings, October 1, 1991 (in Committee files).

80. Statement of Professor Nicholas Ashford, September 12, 1991 hearing at 2.

81. Ashford and Stone, "Liability, Innovation, and Safety in the Chemical Industry," in *The Liability Maze* at 380.

82. Statement of Aaron Twerski, September 12, 1991 hearing at 13.

83. *Id.* at 2.

84. *Id.* at 13.

85. 43 Fed.Reg. 14612 (April 6, 1978).

86. 44 Fed.Reg. 62714 (October 31, 1979).

87. ALI Reporters' Study (Vol. I) at 97.

COMMITTEE REPORT ON S. 640

The National Governors Association (NGA) presented testimony at the Consumer Subcommittee hearing on September 12, 1991, in support of Federal product liability reform. NGA noted that States generally oppose preemption of their laws, but argued that, in the case of product liability, there are highly compelling reasons to enact a Federal product liability law that will preempt State law.[88] The Nation's Governors recognize that individual States cannot address the problems of the product liability system effectively, because reform within one State does little to resolve the tort litigation problems facing those who deal in an interstate market. Products are manufactured, sold, used, and insured in a nationwide market. Data show that most products manufactured in a given State are consumed or used outside the State.[89] As a result, manufacturers and product sellers may be involved in product liability actions governed by the law of any State in which they do business. An attempt by any one State to reform the system cannot relieve the overall burden imposed on interstate commerce.[90] NGA concluded that a Federal product liability law, with its resulting uniformity, will promote economic growth and aid the welfare and safety of our citizens by reducing unnecessary cost, delay, and confusion in our product liability laws.[91] In New York State, the Governor's Advisory Commission on Liability Insurance recently reached the same conclusion:

> Though we are stout defenders of State prerogatives in any area where the context permits at least minimally efficient State governance, we do not believe that product liability any longer falls into that category. The interpenetration of markets, the speed of movement of goods and money, the increasing demanding test of international competition all militate against a system which subjects product makers and sellers to a patchwork of 50 different sets of liability rules. In today's commercial world, such a system, far from permitting States like New York to impose rigorous and effective standards, simply shifts the balance of governmental influence in the direction of other states with different standards, where the same type of action can often be brought against the

---

88. Statement of the Honorable Jim Edgar, September 12, 1991 hearing at 3–4.

89. Statement of the Honorable Wendell L. Wilkie II, General Counsel, U.S. Department of Commerce, February 22, 1990 hearing, at 10. It has been estimated that 30.5 percent of manufactured goods are consumed in the manufacturing state. *See*, 1977 Census of Transportation, Commodity Transportation Survey, Summary, U.S. Dept. of Commerce, Bureau of the Census, 1–77 (1981); American Bar Assoc. Section of Corporation, Banking and Business Law, Report to the House of Delegates, Attachment B. (1982). *See generally* Statement of Randolph J. Stayin on behalf of the American Textile Machinery Association, Product Liability Act: Hearing before the Subcommittee on Consumer of the Senate Committee on Commerce, Science, and Transportation, 99th Cong., 1st Sess., Rept. No. 99–84, 170 (1985).

90. Several State governors have recognized this in vetoing proposed product liability legislation. *See, e.g.,* Schwartz and Bares, *Federal Reform of Product Liability Law: A Solution That Will Work*, 13 Cap. U.L.Rev. 351, 355 (1984).

91. Statement of the Honorable Jim Edgar, *supra,* at 2.

same defendant with quite a different potential outcome. Though we feel that product liability is unique among areas of tort law in this respect, we do believe that in this single case the case for Federal intervention is compelling.[92]

The enactment of product liability reform is within Congress' power to regulate interstate commerce.[93] There are numerous examples of Federal legislation in areas where diverse State laws are deemed a burden on interstate commerce.[94] The fact that product liability law is traditionally an area of State law does not alter the fact that Federal legislation in this area, under the commerce and Supremacy Clauses, can preempt State law to relieve the enormous burden imposed by the product liability system on American commerce.[95]

The question is not about Congress' power to enact reform, but whether it should exercise this power. The Committee believes a strong case has been made that Congress must exercise its power to reform an inefficient system that is a burden to the national economy and to our global competitiveness. As the Department of Commerce has stated, problems of a national scope with international implications require federal solutions.[96] Much of existing product liability law has been fashioned by the courts.[97] However, it is the responsibility of the Congress to deal with the broad policy implications of inconsistent state product liability laws on manufacturers, product sellers, and consumers.

IV. Federal Leadership on Product Liability Reform

S. 640 is the culmination of 15 years of effort to develop a national approach to this issue.

In the mid–1970's, product liability was first recognized as a serious problem of interstate commerce which, in the view of many businesses and academic observers, had reached "crisis" proportions and required

---

92. New York State Governor's Advisory Commission on Liability Insurance, Insuring Our Future, Vol. II, 113 (July 1, 1986).

93. U.S. Const., Art. I, sec. 8, cl. 3.

94. Congress preempted state tort reform to promote the nuclear power industry. See *Duke Power Co. v. Carolina Environmental Study Group*, 439 U.S. 59 (1978). See also Public Utility Housing Company Act of 1935, 15 U.S.C. sec. 79 et seq. (activities involved "not susceptible of effective control by any State"; United States Cotton Standards Act, 7 U.S.C. sec. 51 et seq. (uniform national classifications necessary to protect and promote commerce); Cigarette Labeling and Advertising Act, 15 U.S.C. sec. 1331 et seq. (national standards essential in order that "commerce and the national economy * * * not (be) impeded by diverse, nonuniform regulations"); Federal Employers' Liability Act, 45 U.S.C. 51 et seq.

95. U.S. Const., Art. VI, cl. 2.

96. Statement of the Honorable Wendell L. Wilkie, II, February 22, 1990 hearing at 10.

97. See Priest, *The Current Insurance Crisis and Modern Tort Law*, 96 Yale L.J. 1521, 1535 (1987); see also *Escola v. Coca Cola Bottling Co.*, 24 Cal.2d 453, 150 P.2d 436 (1944) (en banc) (Traynor, J., concurring); Prosser, *The Assault Upon the Citadel (Strict Liability to the Consumer)*, 69 Yale L.J. 1099 (1960).

a Federal response. This recognition came as a result of an increase in product liability claims and litigation and an increase in product liability insurance premiums.

The Federal Government responded to these concerns in 1976 by creating a Federal Interagency Task Force on Product Liability to examine the product liability problem. The task force, chaired by the Secretary of the Department of Commerce, conducted an 18-month study which culminated in a series of reports confirming the legitimacy of the business community's concerns.[98] There was substantial evidence that the cost of product liability insurance had increased dramatically in the early to mid-1970's and evidence that the number of product liability actions had increased.[99]

In 1978, the Department of Commerce formed a second Task Force on Product Liability and Accident Compensation. This new task force developed an options paper outlining what action, if any, the Federal Government should take. The paper found that "the 'hodge-podge' of rules in each of the 50 States makes it almost impossible to set [insurance] rates with any degree of confidence," and recommended that a model product liability law be drafted for implementation at the Federal or State level.[100]

In October 1985, similar concerns prompted the Attorney General to establish the Tort Policy Working Group, an interagency working group consisting of representatives of 10 agencies and the White House. This group issued the Report of the Tort Policy Working Group on the Causes, Extent and Policy Implications of the Current Crisis in Insurance Availability and Affordability. This report recommended a number of tort law reforms applicable to product liability cases. Subsequently, the administration drafted Federal product liability legislation based on the recommendations contained in this report.

During the 101st Congress, Vice President Quayle, Chairman of the President's Council on Competitiveness, established Federal product liability reform as a top legislative priority. Vice President Quayle describes the problems as a "lawyer's tax" which results in higher prices, reduced consumer choice, lost products and jobs.[101] President Bush expressed his support for such legislation in his January 31, 1990 State of the Union Address.

The administration has subsequently expressed its strong support for the reform package contained in S. 640. Commerce Secretary

---

98. *E.g.*, Final Report of the Task Force on Product Liability, 1 vol. (May 1977); Legal Study, 7 vols. (March 1977); Insurance Study, 1 vol. (March 1977); Industry Study, 2 vols. (April 1977).

99. Final Report of the Task Force on Product Liability at I-26 (May 1977).

100. Options Paper on Product Liability, 43 Fed.Reg. 14612, 14624 (April 6, 1978).

101. Now Is the Time for Product Liability Reform, Vice President Dan Quayle, *Product Safety & Liability Reporter*, The Bureau of National Affairs, Inc., Vol. 18 No. 12, March 23, 1990 at 307.

Mosbacher expanded on the administration's support for S. 640 in his testimony before the Consumer Subcommittee on September 12. He cited the effect of the current product liability system on the development of new products and its detrimental effect on the competitive position of domestic manufacturers. Secretary Mosbacher concluded that product liability reform is an important aspect of an overall program to enhance domestic competitiveness in world markets.[102]

LEGISLATIVE HISTORY

Senator Kasten introduced S. 640 on March 13, 1991. There are 36 cosponsors of the bill, including 7 members of the Committee. On September 12, 1991, the Consumer Subcommittee held a hearing on S. 640 and the full Commerce Committee held a second day of hearings on S. 640 and S. 645, the General Aviation Accident Liability Standards Act of 1991, on September 19, 1991. On October 3, the Committee favorably reported S. 640 by a rollcall vote of 13 to 7.

Prior to this Congress, the Committee already had a long history of involvement with product liability reform and had reported three other bills on the subject, which were introduced by Senator Kasten. S. 2631 was reported by the Committee in the 97th Congress (S.Rept. 97–670), and S. 44 was reported by the Committee in the 98th Congress (S.Rept. 98–476). Congress adjourned without Senate action on either of these measures.

At the beginning of the 99th Congress, on January 3, 1985, Senator Kasten introduced S. 100, the Product Liability Act. This bill preempted State law to impose uniform Federal rules and standards of liability governing the recovery of damages for injuries caused by defective products. This bill was substantially the same as S. 44, which had been reported by the Committee during the 98th Congress.

A Consumer Subcommittee hearing on S. 100 was held on March 21, 1985 (Serial No. 99–84) and the bill was reviewed by the Committee at an executive session on May 16, 1985. At that session, the motion to report the bill was defeated by an 8 to 8 vote.

Prior to the May 16, 1985 executive session, two amendments in the nature of a substitute to S. 100 had been introduced. One of these amendments (S.Amdt. No. 16) was introduced by Senator Dodd on March 19, 1985, and the other (S.Amdt. No. 100) was introduced by Senator Gorton on May 14, 1985. These amendments were complete substitutes for S. 100 that preempted certain aspects of state law and also established alternative expedited claim systems for limited recovery of damages in product liability cases. Hearings on the Dodd and

---

102. Statement of the Honorable Robert A. Mosbacher, September 12, 1991 hearing.

Gorton amendments were held by the Consumer Subcommittee on June 18 and June 25, 1985 (Serial No. 99-177).

After these hearings, the Committee staff was instructed by the then Chairman of the Commerce Committee, Senator Danforth, to draft a proposal that combined elements of all these measures. The first draft was released for public comment on July 15, 1985. After review of the extensive comments received from the public, a second draft was released on November 20, 1985. This draft was formally introduced by Senator Danforth on December 20, 1985, as S. 1999. This bill, which was cosponsored by Senators Dodd and Nancy Kassebaum, was the subject of 2 days of hearings before the Consumer Subcommittee on February 27 and March 11, 1986.

On April 30, 1986, Senator Kasten introduced an amendment in the nature of a substitute for S. 100 (S.Amdt. No. 1814).[103] This amendment embodied recommendations for product liability reform that has been made by the administration's Tort Policy Working Group.[104]

On May 12, 1986, Senator Danforth introduced an amendment in the nature of a substitute for S. 1999 (S.Amdt. No. 1951).[105] This amendment, which was cosponsored by Senator Dodd, replaced the expedited claim system of S. 1999 with an expedited settlement system and made a number of other changes in S. 1999. On May 20, 1986, Senator Gorton introduced an amendment in the nature of a substitute to the Danforth amendment (S.Amdt. No. 1968).[106] On May 19 and 20, 1986, the Consumer Subcommittee held hearings on the Kasten amendment, the Danforth amendment, and the other product liability measures before the Committee.

On June 3, 1986, the Committee began its markup of product liability legislation. The markup draft bill was an original bill that embodied the provisions of the Danforth amendment to S. 1999. On June 12, the Committee adopted an amendment in the nature of a substitute for the original markup draft bill. This amendment contained product liability reform provisions that had been agreed to by Senators Danforth, Gorton, and Kasten as a "core package" of product liability reforms. On June 12, 19, 24, 25 and 26, 1986, the Committee continued its consideration of this core package and added a number of other amendments before reporting S. 2760 as an original bill. S. 2760 came before the full Senate on September 17, 1986. On September 25, the Senate agreed to the motion to proceed to S. 2760 by a vote of 84 to 13. The bill was returned to the Senate Calendar, and no further action was taken.

---

103. 132 Cong.Rec. S5106.

104. Report of the Tort Policy Working Group on the Causes, Extent and Policy Implications of the Current Crisis in Insurance Availability and Affordability (February, 1986).

105. 132 Cong.Rec. S5874.

106. 132 Cong.Rec. S6232.

COMMITTEE REPORT ON S. 640

The primary activity on Federal product liability legislation in the 100th Congress occurred in the House of Representatives. On February 18, 1987, Congressmen Bill Richardson and Thomas A. Luken introduced H.R. 1115, which was referred to the House Energy and Commerce Committee. The Subcommittee on Commerce, Consumer Protection, and Competitiveness held extensive hearings on the need for Federal product liability reform and on specific issues in the bill on May 5, May 20, June 18, July 21, August 6, October 7, and December 17, 1987. The Subcommittee met to mark up the bill on November 18, 19, and 20, and December 3 and 8, 1987. H.R. 1115 was reported by the Subcommittee, as amended, on December 8, 1987, by a vote of 11 to 3. On May 10, 12, 18, 19, and 24, June 1, 2, 8, 9, and 14, 1988, the Energy and Commerce Committee met to markup H.R. 1115, voting on June 14 to report H.R. 1115, as amended, favorably by a recorded vote of 30 to 12. H.R. 1115 then received a sequential referral to the House Committees on the Judiciary and on Education and Labor. The Education and Labor Committee held a hearing on September 27, 1988, on provisions in H.R. 1115 that affected workplace safety. The House Judiciary Committee took no action on the bill in the 100th Congress. The sequential referral ran through the end of the session, so the 100th Congress adjourned without considering H.R. 1115 on the floor of the House.

During the 101st Congress, the Committee held three hearings on S. 1400, the Product Liability Reform Act, introduced by Senator Kasten (S.Hrg. 101–743). On May 22, 1990, the Commerce Committee reported an amendment in the nature of a substitute to S. 1400 by a rollcall vote of 13 to 7 (S.Rept. 101–356). The full Senate took no action before the adjournment of the 101st Congress.

Summary of Major Provisions

A. EXPEDITED SETTLEMENTS OF CLAIMS

Either party may offer to settle after a lawsuit is commenced. If the plaintiff offers to settle but the defendant refuses and then loses subsequent litigation, the defendant would be liable for the plaintiff's attorney's fees, in addition to damages awarded to the plaintiff for his injuries. Likewise, if the defendant offers to settle but the plaintiff refuses and the judgment is for an amount less than the settlement offer, the plaintiff would be liable for the defendant's attorney's fees. The plaintiff will not be liable for the defendant's attorney's fees in excess of the amount the plaintiff receives from collateral sources, such as insurance.

Either party may offer to participate in state ADR procedures. If a party refuses unreasonably to participate in an ADR procedure, the refusing party shall be liable for the offering party's reasonable attorney's fees.

COMMITTEE REPORT ON S. 640

B. RESPONSIBILITY OF PRODUCT SELLERS

In any product liability action, a product seller is liable if the seller's own lack of reasonable care in handling the product or the seller's own breach of an express product warranty was a proximate cause of the claimant's harm. Where, however, the manufacturer is not subject to service of process or is determined to be judgment-proof, the seller may be responsible for harms attributable to the manufacturer.

C. PUNITIVE DAMAGES

Punitive damages may be assessed if the claimant establishes by clear and convincing evidence that the harm suffered was the result of conduct manifesting a conscious, flagrant indifference to the safety of persons who might be harmed by a product.

Punitive damages may not be imposed upon manufacturers or product sellers for harm caused by prescription and over-the-counter drugs, medical devices and aircraft, when the safety of those products has been approved by the appropriate Federal agency prior to the marketing of the product. This defense is not available, however, to any defendant who has withheld or misrepresented relevant information during the approval process. This defense also is not available when the certification was achieved as a result of a bribe or illegal payment.

D. UNIFORM TIME LIMITATIONS ON LIABILITY

A 2–year statute of limitations for filing complaints in all product liability actions is provided, which does not begin to run until the claimant discovers or should have discovered both the claimant's harm and its cause. This "discovery rule" is more favorable to claimants than the "time of injury rule" followed by some States.

If a product is a capital good, no claim may be brought for harm caused by the product more than 25 years after delivery to the first buyer or lessee not engaged in the business of selling or leasing the product. Capital good is defined as a product used in trade or business or held for the production of income. This 25–year statute of repose for capital goods applies only when the claimant is entitled to receive work compensation benefits and if the harm alleged by the claimant is not a toxic harm.

E. WORKERS' COMPENSATION OFFSET

Damages in a product liability action shall be reduced by the amount paid to the claimant under any State or Federal worker's compensation law. An employer's right to recapture worker's compensation benefits from a product liability award is eliminated unless the employer can prove that he and other employees were in no way responsible for the employee's injuries. A manufacturer is prohibited from suing an employer for his contribution to the product liability award, unless the employer attempts to assert his subrogation lien.

F. DEFENSE INVOLVING INTOXICATING ALCOHOL OR DRUGS

No plaintiff may recover for harm caused by a product if the claimant was under the influence of alcohol or any drug and such condition was more than 50 percent responsible for the claimant's harm. Determination of whether a person was under the influence of alcohol shall be made pursuant to applicable State law.

G. SEVERAL LIABILITY FOR NONECONOMIC DAMAGES

In any product liability action with more than one defendant, each defendant's liability for noneconomic damages shall be limited to the defendant's percentage of responsibility as determined by the trier of fact. This provision addresses the so-called deep-pocket problem, which could make even a minimally responsible defendant fully liable, under the doctrine of joint and several liability, for the claimant's entire damage award.

Estimated Costs

The cost impacts of the bill are summarized in the Congressional Budget Office cost estimate below, submitted in accordance with paragraph 11(a) of rule XXVI of the Standing Rules of the Senate and section 403 of the Congressional Budget Act of 1974. The Committee believes that this cost estimate should be viewed in the following context.

Section 305(d) of the bill would prevent, in some instances, an "employer" (or its workers' compensation insurer, if any) from pursuing a subrogation lien against a manufacturer or product seller to recover the workers' compensation benefits paid to the employer's injured worker. The term "employer" would include the Federal Government, because the bill does apply to the Federal Employees Compensation Act (FECA).

As a consequence, the Federal Government's workers' compensation program, established under FECA, would, in some instances, be prohibited from seeking to recover FECA benefits paid to a government employee injured in a product-related workplace accident. The Federal Government could, however, seek recovery of FECA payments in those instances in which it could show a claimant's harm was in no way caused by it or one of the claimant's coworkers. In addition, the Federal Government could continue to seek subrogation recoveries in workplace accidents in which no product was involved. For example, if a postal worker was injured in an automobile accident or bitten by a homeowner's dog in the course of the postal worker's delivery rounds, FECA could seek to recover the benefits paid to the injured worker from the insurer of the non-government vehicle or the homeowner's liability insurer.

Moreover, the loss of such FECA subrogation rights must be considered in the context of the Supreme Court's decision in *Lockheed Aircraft Corp. v. United States*, 460 U.S. 190 (1983). In this case, the Supreme Court rules that FECA's exclusive liability provision did not bar manufacturers' indemnity claims against the Federal Government under the Federal Tort Claims Act; if the applicable State law permits manufacturers to bring indemnity claims against employers, such claims are not barred by FECA.

Section 305(e) of the bill would limit the ability of product manufacturers and sellers who have been forced to pay damages in product liability actions to maintain an action for implied indemnity or contribution from an employer, when the injured person is entitled to workers' compensation benefits under State or Federal law. This provision would bar in those product liability actions the third-party recovery from the Federal Government permitted by the *Lockheed Aircraft* decision where no right of subrogation, contribution or implied indemnity is asserted against the manufacturer or product seller.

The Congressional Budget Office notes that this provision would result in some savings for the Federal Government, but has been unable to assess fully the extent to which such savings would offset the loss of subrogation recoveries. According to Justice Department's Civil Division, approximately 100 suits against the Federal Government by third-party product liability defendants are pending. The amount of recovery being sought has not been estimated, but it is anticipated that the savings produced by section 305(e) could be substantial and that this provision could significantly limit the liability of the Federal Government in future litigation.

In accordance with paragraph 11(a) of rule XXVI of the Standing Rules of the Senate and section 403 of the Congressional Budget Act of 1974, the Committee provides the following cost estimate, prepared by the Congressional Budget Office:

OCTOBER 15, 1991.

Hon. ERNEST F. HOLLINGS,

Chairman, Committee on Commerce, Science, and Transportation, U.S. Senate, Washington, DC.

DEAR MR. CHAIRMAN: The Congressional Budget Office has reviewed S. 640, the Produce Liability Fairness Act, as ordered reported by the Senate Committee on Commerce, Science, and Transportation on October 3, 1991. S. 640 could result in a small cost or savings to the Federal Government. Such costs or savings would be considered direct spending and thus subject to pay-as-you-go scoring as required under section 252 of the Balanced Budget and Emergency Deficit Control Act of 1985.

However, CBO does not have sufficient information to estimate the amount of the budget impact.

S. 640 would establish a federal product liability law. It would define certain responsibilities of manufactures and product sellers and would establish an expedited procedure for settling product liability disputes. In cases where S. 640 would establish a rule of law on an issue, it would preempt state laws on product liability. The bill would set uniform standards of product seller liability and for punitive damage awards and would establish incentives for plaintiffs and defendants to avoid trial. The bill also would keep the workers' compensation system and the tort liability system somewhat separate in cases involving both work injury and product liability by restricting:

> suits by an employer or its insurance carrier against a manufacturer or product seller to recoup funds paid in worker's compensation cases;
>
> employer or insurance carrier liens against claimants' recoveries; and
>
> recoveries by third parties against negligent employers for monies paid in product liability judgments.

S. 640 could increase certain costs to the Federal Government in its role as an employer. This would occur because the bill would restrict suits by an employer or its insurance carrier against a manufacturer or product seller to recoup funds paid in workers' compensation cases, and because it would restrict the employer or insurance carrier liens against claimants' recoveries. A Labor Department review of Federal Employees Compensation Act (FECA) claims over the past five years showed that about $10 million annually was recovered by the Federal Government through actions brought by injured federal workers against third parties. Some portion of this amount would be lost to the Federal Government, because under this bill, the government would be restricted in such recoveries. However, there is no basis for determining how much of this $10 million a year would be lost, since the Federal Government could continue to recoup funds in cases where no product was involved, and in those product liability cases where the Federal Government was not at fault. Because the recovery of such damages directly offsets FECA obligations, their loss would result in an increase in budget authority and outlays in an amount less than $10 million annually.

The bill also could result in some savings to the government, because it would limit the ability of product manufacturers and sellers who have been forced to pay damages to injured federal workers in product liability actions to sue the Federal Government as an employer. Until 1983, the Federal Government successfully argued that FECA's exclusive liability provision protected it from such actions. However, in *Lockheed Aircraft Corporation v. the United States,* 103 S.Ct. 1033

(1983), it was held that FECA's exclusive liability provision did not bar third-party liability defendants from pursuing indemnity actions against the United States as an employer. CBO is not able to estimate the potential savings to the Federal Government that could be realized as a result of this provision of the bill.

The provisions in S. 640 regarding workers' compensation actions would affect the budgets of state and local governments in much the same way as they affect the federal budget. However, CBO does not have sufficient information to estimate any such budget impact.

If you wish further details on this estimate, we will be pleased to provide them. The CBO staff contacts are Mitchell Rosenfeld, who can be reached at 226-2860, and Cory Oltman, who can be reached at 226-2820.

Sincerely,

ROBERT D. REISCHAUER,
Director.

REGULATORY IMPACT STATEMENT

In accordance with paragraph 11(b) of rule XXVI of the Standing Rules of the Senate, the Committee provides the following evaluation of the regulatory impact of the legislation, as reported.

NUMBER OF PERSONS AFFECTED

The purpose of this product liability reform legislation, as reported, is to provide greater certainty as to the rights and responsibilities of all those involved in product liability disputes, to reduce transaction costs, and to relieve the burden imposed on interstate commerce by the present product liability litigation system. It is anticipated that it will affect the conduct of those involved in product liability disputes by making a number of significant changes in the law that are applicable to all product liability actions. This legislation does not change the jurisdiction of State or Federal courts. Thus, the number of persons covered should be consistent with current levels.

ECONOMIC IMPACT

It is anticipated that this legislation will result in substantial cost and paperwork savings to all parties affected by product liability lawsuits. First, the legislation will bring greater predictability to this area of the law, and, thus, save time and money for manufacturers, product sellers and consumers alike, each of whom will be able to determine their rights more readily than under current law. Moreover, the provisions of this legislation will promote early settlement of product liability disputes, thus reducing the enormous costs of product liability litigation, which are ultimately passed on to the consumer. It should also foster product innovation and enhance the competitive position of U.S. product manufacturers in world markets.

PRIVACY

S. 640 will have no adverse impact on the personal privacy of the individuals or businesses affected.

PAPERWORK

S. 640 creates no new regulations and imposes no additional regulatory requirements at either State or the Federal level. Nor will the legislation change the jurisdiction of State or Federal courts.

SECTION-BY-SECTION ANALYSIS

SECTION 101—SHORT TITLE

As reported

Section 101 states the short title of the legislation, providing that the legislation may be cited as the "Product Liability Fairness Act."

SECTION 102—DEFINITIONS

In general

Section 102 defines terms or phrases used in the bill. Whenever a defined term or phrase is used, reference should be made to the definition in section 102.

As reported

Section 102 defines the following terms:

(1) *Claimant.*[107]—As used in the act, a "claimant" is any person who brings a product liability action and any person on whose behalf such an action is brought. If such an action is brought through or on behalf of an estate, the term includes the claimant's decedent. If a product liability action is brought through or on behalf of a minor, a claimant includes the minor's parent or guardian.

(2) *Clear and convincing evidence.*—The bill adopts the generally accepted definition of clear and convincing evidence.[108] This is a degree of proof which produces in the mind of the trier of fact a firm belief or conviction as to the truth of allegations sought to be established. The clear and convincing evidence standard requires more proof than the preponderance of the evidence standard and less proof than the beyond a reasonable doubt standard.

---

[107]. The bill does not alter, modify, change, or preempt State laws governing who may be a "claimant." For example, state statutes stating who may bring a wrongful death or survival action are not affected by the bill. Such persons, if authorized by State law to bring the action, are "claimants" under the bill.

[108]. *See, Hobson v. Eaton,* 399 F.2d 781 (6th Cir.1968), cert. denied 394 U.S. 928 (1969). *See also* 30 Am.Jur.2d Evidence Sec. 1167 (1967).

(3) *Collateral benefits.*—This term includes all benefits and advantages received or entitled to be received by any claimant harmed by a product, under any Federal or State law (other than through a claim for breach of an obligation or duty), or any life, health or accident insurance or salary continuation plan. The term also applies to such other benefits as disability income or replacement services insurance payments, or any benefit received or to be received as a result of participation in any pre-paid medical plan or Health Maintenance Organization.

Collateral benefits include all such benefits regardless of any right any other person has or is entitled to assert for recoupment through subrogation, trust agreement, lien, or otherwise.

(4) *Commerce.*—This definition covers the full extent of the Congress' powers to regulate and promote interstate commerce.[109]

(5) *Commercial loss.*—This term applies to economic injury, whether direct, incidental, or consequential, including property damage and damage to the product itself, incurred by persons regularly engaged in business activities consisting of providing goods and services for compensation. A civil action for commercial loss is not subject to this bill and is to be governed by applicable commercial or contract law.

(6) *Economic loss.*—This term means any pecuniary loss resulting from harm, which is allowed under State law. The essential distinction between economic and noneconomic loss is that the amount of the plaintiff's economic loss is subject to empirical measurement and confirmation. In contrast, there is no objective standard for measuring a plaintiff's pain and suffering.[110]

(7) *Exercise of reasonable care.*—The definition is based directly on section 283 of the Restatement (Second) of Torts and the accompanying comments, which refer to the "reasonable man" standard. The "reasonable man" denotes a "person exercising those qualities of attention, knowledge, intelligence, and judgment which society requires of its members for the protection of their own interests and the interest of others."[111]

(8) *Harm.*—The bill provides that a claimant may bring a civil action for "harm" caused by a product, against the product's manufacturer or product seller. Harm is limited to injury or damage recognized under applicable State law, and does not include loss or damage caused to a product itself or commercial loss. Therefore, damage to the product itself or commercial loss is not a compensable harm under the bill.

---

109. *See, e.g., Wickard v. Filburn,* 317 U.S. 111 (1942); *Perez v. United States,* 402 U.S. 146 (1971).

110. McCormick, Handbook on the Law of Damages 318 (1935).

111. Restatement (Second) of Torts, Sec. 283, comment b (1965).

Damage to the product itself traditionally has been left to commercial or contract law, under which a purchaser has a right of action for out-of-pocket losses relating to the value of a product.[112] In addition, indirect economic losses caused by damage to the product itself, i.e., commercial losses, are not compensable harms under the bill. Indirect economic losses include, for example, loss of profits due to an inability to use the damaged product. Under the majority case law which follows *Seely v. White Motor Company* [113] and the Supreme Court's decision in *East River Steamship Corp. v. Transamerica Delaval, Inc.,* [114] (admiralty case) recovery for such losses is left to commercial law and the Uniform Commercial Code. These losses are, in essence, contract damages and not tort damages.[115] They arise in the course of commercial dealings and can be resolved through contracts and claims based on those contracts.

Such claims for direct or indirect economic loss are not claims for "harm" caused by a product. Under the Uniform Commercial Code and other contract law, recovery is available for economic losses. It is the Committee's intent that where recovery is not allowed because of a State statute of limitations defense or other defenses to contract liability, this bill will not create an independent cause of action. For example, a claim for commercial loss could not be brought under the Product Liability Fairness Act if recovery under State contract or commercial law is barred because of the statute of limitations, contractual disclaimers or limitations of remedies. If the claim is for damage to the product itself or for commercial loss, a civil action cannot be brought under this legislation.[116]

(9) *Manufacturer.*—A manufacturer means any person [117] engaged in a business to produce, create, make, or construct any product [118] (or component part of a product) and who designs or formulates the product (or component part of the product) or has engaged another person to design or formulate the product or component part. The

---

112. *The Baltimore Football Club, Inc. v. Lockheed Corp.,* 525 F.Supp. 1206 (N.D.Ga.1981); *Industrial Uniform Rental Co. v. Int'l Harvester Co.,* 463 A.2d 1085 (Pa.Super.1983); *Noorman Mfg. Co. v. National Tank Co.,* 91 Ill.2d 69, 435 N.E.2d 443 (1982); *Superwood Corp. v. Siempelkamp Corp.,* 311 N.W.2d 159 (Minn.1981).

113. 63 Cal.2d 9, 403 P.2d 145, 45 Cal. Rptr. 17 (1965).

114. 476 U.S. 856 (1980).

115. *See* Note, *Economic Loss in Product Liability Jurisprudence,* 66 Colum.L.Rev. 927 (1966).

116. At the September 12, 1991 hearing before the Consumer Subcommittee, questions were raised about whether this legislation affected lawsuits brought by manufacturers to cover commercial loss. Statement of Senator Ernest F. Hollings, September 12, 1991 hearing, (transcript at 10–11). This legislation is not a broad-ranging reform of the civil justice system. Rather, it preempts only product liability law in areas addressed by the bill. Therefore, it does not affect lawsuits that would address commercial law under the Uniform Commercial Code or contract law, but only product liability law. Cases involving commercial loss would continue to be governed by the Uniform Commercial Code or contract law.

117. "Person" is defined in section 102(11).

118. "Product" is defined in section 102(13).

term does not include a person who only designs or formulates a product—such as an architect or engineer. These persons, although not liable under S. 640, may be liable under traditional tort law for failure to exercise reasonable skill and care in rendering their design services.[119]

A product seller [120] may be a "manufacturer" of the product the product seller sells or otherwise places in the stream of commerce in two situations. First, the product seller is a "manufacturer" of a product with respect to all aspects of the product that are created or affected by this product seller's own conduct in designing, or formulating and producing, creating, making, or constructing an aspect of a product made by another. Where a product seller engaged in such conduct before placing the product in the stream of commerce, the product seller is responsible for the consequences of that conduct as if the product seller were a manufacturer.

For example, a company may manufacture a truck and deliver it to a product seller. Prior to selling that vehicle, the product seller may design and create what becomes a new aspect of the truck by, for example, adding a larger engine or a cabin unit. The product seller is, then, the manufacturer of the end product with respect to all aspects of the product that are affected or created by the addition, thus, the product seller is the manufacturer with respect to defects in the cabin unit itself and with respect to defects created by adding the unit to the original truck, such as lack of a warning back-up buzzer.[121] This rule fairly holds the product seller responsible for the consequences of the product seller's actions in designing and creating a new product from the original product; it is not intended to impose the manufacturer's liability on a product seller who merely cleans, paints, or reconditions the truck with parts that are designed or manufactured by someone else.

Second, a product seller is a manufacturer of a product where the product seller holds himself out as the manufacturer to the user of the product. Where a product seller attaches the product seller's own private label to a product made by another, the product seller's name and reputation become a representation of the product's quality in design and manufacture. The rule holding a product seller responsible for harms caused by products that the product seller "endorses" with

---

119. *E.g., Mechanical Rubber & Supply Co. v. Caterpillar Tractor Co.*, 80 Ill.App.3d 262, 399 N.E.2d 722 (1980). *See also New Mexico v. Gatham–Matotan Architects and Planners, Inc.*, 98 N.M. 740, 653 P.2d 166 (1982).

120. "Product seller" is defined in section 102(14).

121. *See, e.g., Green v. City of Los Angeles*, 40 Cal.App.3d 819, 115 Cal.Rptr. 685 (1974) (seller of crane liable for harm caused by defects in the crane created by the seller's modifications; given the modifications made by the seller, it was "tantamount to a manufacturer").

the product seller's private label is uniformly followed by the States.[122]

(10) *Noneconomic loss.*—This includes loss caused by a product other than economic loss or commercial loss.

(11) *Person.*—The act uses a broad definition of the term "person," which includes individuals, corporations, companies, associations, firms, partnerships, societies, and any other entities.

(12) *Preponderance of the evidence.*—This standard of proof is that used most often in civil litigation. It is a degree of proof which leads the trier of fact to find that a fact is more probably either true or untrue.[123]

(13) *Product.*—As used in the bill, a product is any object, substance, mixture, or raw material in a gaseous, liquid, or solid state (a) which is capable of delivery itself or as an assembled whole, in a mixed or combined state or as a component part or ingredient; (b) which is produced for introduction into trade or commerce; (c) which has intrinsic economic value; and (d) which is intended for sale or lease. The term does not include human tissue, blood and organs unless specifically recognized as a product pursuant to State law.[124]

(14) *Product seller.*—A product seller is any person engaged in business to sell, distribute, lease, prepare, blend, package, label, or otherwise place a product into the stream of commerce, or who installs, repairs, or maintains the harm-causing aspect of a product. The definition includes anyone in the chain of distribution, such as a wholesaler, distributor, or retailer.

A seller of real property is not a product seller under this bill and, therefore, tort suits against a person who sells real property will be governed by State tort or real estate law.[125]

A person who provides professional services is not a product seller where the essence of the transaction is furnishing judgment, skill, or service and the sale or use of a product is only incidental. This follows

---

122. Restatement (Second) of Torts Section 400 (1965). *E.g., Smith v. Regina Mfg. Corp.,* 396 F.2d 826 (4th Cir.1968); *Carter v. Joseph Bancroft & Sons Co.,* 360 F.Supp. 1103 (E.D.Pa.1973); *Moody v. Sears, Roebuck & Co.,* 324 F.Supp. 844 (S.D.Ga.1971).

123. *See* 30 Am.Jr.2d Evidence Section 1164 (1967); Cleary, McCormick on Evidence section 339 (3d ed. 1984).

124. Human tissue, blood, and organs are generally used pursuant to medical treatment. Claims for harms caused by these substances are, in the view of most courts, claims for negligently performed services. In the past, however, a few states have held that the law of product liability is applicable to harms caused by such substances, and this act does not prevent them from doing so. *See, e.g., Cunningham v. MacNeal Memorial Hospital,* 47 Ill.2d 443, 266 N.E.2d 897 (Sup.Ct.1970) (overturned by Ill.Ann.Stat. Ch. 111½, sections 2 and 3). In those states which do not recognize such substances as products, the law with respect to such harms will not be changed. In states that do extend such recognition, suits for harm caused by such substances, which are brought under a theory of product liability would be governed by the provisions of this bill. *See generally Prod. Liab.Rep.* (CCH) Paragraph 1187.

125. *E.g.,* Restatement (Second) of Torts Sections 353, 385 (1965) (providing standards of care for builders, contractors, and sellers of real estate).

the law of the majority of States.[126] Where, for example, an engineer, pharmacist, optician, or physician provides or uses a product in connection with that person's professional services, the person is not a product seller.[127] The majority rule is that a professional is required to exercise reasonable care, prudence, and skill in rendering services. Where failure to do so results in harm, injured persons have remedies under traditional State tort law theories and do not have a claim under this bill.

If, however, a professional engages in a commercial transaction where the essence of the transaction is not the furnishing of professional skill and judgment, the professional may be a product seller. For example, a pharmacist who sells perfume or photographic film may be a product seller within the scope of the bill. In such a case, the sale rather than the exercise of professional skill is the essence of the transaction.

A product lessor is not a product seller if (1) the product lessor acts only in a financial role in the sale or distribution of the product, and (2) the product lessor has no control over the lease arrangement. Such a person, called a "financing lessor," generally has no contact with the product and does not provide advice about the product or its selection. Such a person merely provides the money to transfer the product to the lessee. The cases that have considered the issue uniformly hold that financing lessors are not product sellers.

(15) *State.*—This definition is broad and includes the District of Columbia, all the States, territories, and possessions of the United States, and any political subdivision thereof.

SECTION 103—PREEMPTION

In general

Section 103 provides that the bill governs any civil action brought against a manufacturer or product seller for harm caused by a product and that the bill supersedes State law to the extent that it establishes a rule of law applicable to recovery in such actions. When a rule of law is not established by the bill, the issue is left to applicable State law.

Present law

The law governing the liability of manufacturers of products, who routinely sell products across State lines, is presently governed by State law. The inefficiency and unpredictability of the law as it is presently administered has become a major burden on interstate commerce. The

---

126. W. Prosser and W. Keeton, Torts (5th ed.) 1984 at 719–20.

127. *See., e.g., Carmichael v. Reitz,* 17 Cal.App.3d 958, 95 Cal.Rptr. 381 (1971); *Bichler v. Willing,* 58 App.Div.2d 331, 397 N.Y.S.2d 57 (1977); *Barbee v. Rogers,* 425 S.W.2d 342 (Tex.1968); *Magrine v. Krasnica,* 94 N.J.Super. 228, 227 A.2d 539 (1967), aff'd 100 N.J.Super. 223, 241 A.2d 637 (1968), aff'd 53 N.J. 259, 250 A.2d 129 (1969).

bill seeks to simplify the law and reduce the costs and unpredictability of the system.

Congress has the power under the Commerce Clause of the Constitution to enact a Federal product liability statute that preempts State law. "Any such legislation would offend neither the Tenth Amendment's recognition of state sovereignty * * * nor the Fifth Amendment's traditional notions of due process and equal protection." [128]

As reported

Section 103(a) states that this bill governs any civil action brought against a manufacturer or product seller, on any theory, for harm caused by a product. Consistent with the definition of "harm" set forth in section 102(a)(9), section 103 states that a civil action for loss or damage to the product itself or for commercial loss is not a product liability action subject to this bill, but is governed by applicable commercial or contract law. This follows traditional law, which leaves recovery for purely commercial losses to actions founded on commercial law.

Section 103(b) provides that the bill supersedes State law regarding recovery for harm caused by a product only to the extent that the bill establishes a rule of law applicable to an action for such recovery. Any issue arising in an action governed by this legislation that is not governed by a rule of law established by the legislation shall be governed by applicable State common and statutory law.[129]

As has been noted, the Commerce Clause of the Constitution [130] gives Congress the power to enact a uniform Federal product liability act.[131] The Supremacy Clause of the United States Constitution also gives Congress the power to enact a Federal law that replaces State law in the area of product liability.[132] The fact that tort law is traditionally

---

128. Schmidt & Derman, *The Constitutionality of Federal Products Liability/Toxic Tort Legislation,* 6 J.Prod.Liab. 171, 184 (1983). *See also Duke Power Co. v. Carolina Environmental Study Group,* 438 U.S. 59, 93 (1978), where the Court held that preemption of state tort law in order to promote the nuclear power industry is permissible under the Commerce Clause and does not violate the Fifth Amendment. In reaching this decision, the Court also rejected a challenge under the Equal Protection Clause.

129. The effect of the bill on State law is the same as the effect, for example, of the Federal Employers' Liability Act on the law applied in actions involving injuries to railroad employees. 45 U.S.C. Sections 51 et seq. (1982). *E.g., Urie v. Thompson,* 337 U.S.C. 163, 174 (1949); *Brown v. Cedar Rapids and Iowa City Ry. Co.,* 650 F.2d 159, 161 (8th Cir.1981); *Isgett v. Seaboard Coast Line R. Co.,* 332 F.Supp. 1127 (D.S.C.1971).

130. U.S. Const. art. I, Section 8, cl. 3.

131. The Commerce Clause power extends to interstate and intrastate activities which affect interstate commerce. *See e.g., Federal Energy Regulatory Comm'n v. Mississippi,* 456 U.S. 742 (1982) (discussion of scope of Commerce Clause); *Fry v. United States,* 421 U.S. 542 (1976); *Katzenbach v. McClung,* 379 U.S.C. 294 (1964); *Wickard v. Filburn,* 317 U.S. 111 (1942).

132. U.S. Const. art. VI, cl. 2.

a matter of State law does not alter this rule. Congress has enacted a number of statutes that preempt State tort law.[133]

Section 103(b) is intended to ensure that the rules set forth in the bill are uniformly applied in all product liability actions, regardless of where the harm occurred and which court hears the claim. Under the Supremacy Clause, State courts are bound to apply Federal law,[134] and it is expected that State and Federal courts with jurisdiction over product liability actions will interpret the bill in a manner consistent with the intent of Congress.

However, section 103(b) also makes it clear that where the bill does not establish a rule of law, State law will apply. Recently, a number of State legislatures have considered the question of tort liability, including product liability, and some have adopted measures dealing with this matter. It is not the Committee's intention that this legislation preempt such State legislation—or any other rule of State law—that provides for defenses, places limitations on the amount of damages that may be recovered, or covers other topics that are not addressed by a rule in this bill. For example, the bill establishes certain rules of liability for product sellers. Those rules supersede State law. With respect to other issues regarding the liability of product sellers not covered by the bill, such as contributory versus comparative fault, State law applies.

Section 103(c) lists a number of laws that are not superseded or affected by the bill. The bill does not waive or affect the defense of sovereign immunity of any state or of the United States. The legislation does not affect any provision of the Foreign Sovereign Immunities Act of 1976. Nothing in the bill shall be construed to supersede any Federal law except the Federal Employees Compensation Act.[135] The bill does not preempt State choice-of-law rules with respect to claims brought by a foreign nation or a foreign citizen.

Nor does the bill supersede any statutory or common law, including an action to abate a nuisance, that authorizes a State or person to institute an action for civil damages or civil penalties, clean-up costs, injunctions, restitution, cost recovery, punitive damages, or any other form of relief resulting from contamination or pollution of the environ-

---

133. *E.g.*, Longshoremen's and Harbor Workers's Compensation Act, 33 U.S.C. Sections 901 et seq. (imposing liability without regard to fault); Price–Anderson Act, 42 U.S.C. Section 2210 (limiting liability for nuclear power plant accidents); Federal Employers' Liability Act, 45 U.S.C. Sections 51 et seq. (governing the liability of interstate railway carriers to their employees and altering State tort law on available defenses).

134. *Dice v. Akron, Canton & Youngstown R.R. Co*, 342 U.S.C. 359 (1952) (Federal Employers' Liability Act). In addition when there is a variance between State and Federal law, "Incompatible doctrines of local law must give way to principles of federal ... law"; *Local 174, Teamsters, Chauffeurs, Warehousemen and Helpers of America v. Lucas Flour Co.*, 369 U.S. 95, 102 (1962) (National Labor Relations Act).

135. For example, the provisions of the Federal Tort Claims Act, 28 U.S.C. Sections 1346(b), 2671 et seq. are not affected by the act.

ment, or the threat of such contamination or pollution. Such actions involve separate policy considerations and relate to acts that are different from the acts for which this bill provides rules of law. It is possible that the same event or conduct may give rise to both a product liability action governed by this bill and an action relating to contamination or pollution of the environment. The two types of actions could be alleged as separate counts in a single complaint and may or may not be alleged against the same defendant.

Section 103(d) provides that as used in this section, "environment" shall have the same meaning given to this term in section 101(14) of the Comprehensive Environmental Response, Compensation, and Liability Act of 1980 (42 U.S.C. 9601(14)).[136]

Section 103(e) requires that this bill be construed and applied after consideration of its legislative history to promote uniformity of law in the various jurisdictions.

SECTION 104—JURISDICTION OF FEDERAL COURTS

As reported

Section 104 provides that the bill does not provide any new basis for Federal Court jurisdiction. The resolution of product liability claims is left to State courts or to Federal courts that currently have jurisdiction over those claims.

Specifically, section 104 states: "The district courts of the United States shall not have jurisdiction over any civil action pursuant to this Act, based on section 1331 or 1337 of title 28, United States Code." These sections of the United States Code establish district court jurisdiction with respect to Federal questions and acts of Congress regulating commerce; it is the intent of the Committee that these sections shall not be a basis for bringing a product liability action governed by this bill in Federal court.

Civil actions governed by this bill will continue to be handled by State courts currently open to litigants and only by Federal district courts where there is currently a basis for Federal jurisdiction.[137] The bill does not affect these bases for jurisdiction and, therefore, does not expand the caseload of the federal courts.

---

136. This Act provides: " '[E]nvironment' means (A) the navigable waters, the waters of the contiguous zone, and the ocean waters of which the natural resources are under the exclusive management authority of the United States under the Fishery Conservation and Management Act of 1976, and (B) any other surface water, ground water, drinking water supply, land surface or subsurface strata, or ambient air within the United States or under the jurisdiction of the United States."

137. Section 1332 of title 28, United States Code, establishes Federal district court jurisdiction in cases involving diversity of citizenship.

SECTION 105—EFFECTIVE DATE

As reported

Section 105(a) provides that the bill shall be effective on the date of its enactment and shall apply to all civil actions governed by the bill commenced on or after that date, including any action in which the harm or the conduct which caused the harm occurred before the effective date. Applying the statute to all claims filed after the effective date, regardless of when the harm occurred, allows all parties and courts to know precisely what law applies in a product liability action.

Section 105(b) provides that if any provision of the bill would shorten the period during which a manufacturer or product seller would otherwise be exposed to liability, the claimant may, notwithstanding the otherwise applicable time period, bring an action within 1 year after the effective date of the legislation. This exception is intended to prevent an unfair situation from arising as a result of the application of the time limitations set forth in section 304.

TITLE II

Title II of the bill establishes two schemes for expedited settlement of product liability claims in the initial stages of litigation. These schemes are based on incentives for settlement that will reduce the delays, excessive transaction costs, and uncertainties associated with such claims.

SECTION 201—EXPEDITED PRODUCT LIABILITY SETTLEMENTS

In general

Section 201 sets forth rules governing economic incentives for encouraging settlements based on Rule 68 of the Federal Rules of Civil Procedure. Either party may offer to settle. The claimant may include an offer of settlement with the complaint. The defendant may make an offer of settlement within the time permitted for responsive pleadings or 60 days after the service of the complaint. This provision provides that a party that refuses to accept an offer of settlement would be liable for the other party's reasonable legal fees if the offeree would have fared better by opting to settle. The claimant will not be liable for the defendant's attorney's fees in excess of the portion of the verdict for which a claimant may receive collateral benefits.

The purpose of this provision is to encourage settlements when a reasonable offer is made.[138] By doing this, S. 640 will alleviate some of the delay problems associated with the current product liability system.

---

138. Statement of Professor James Henderson, September 19, 1991 hearing at 3.

COMMITTEE REPORT ON S. 640

As reported

Section 201(a) provides that a claimant may bring a civil action for damages against a person for harm caused by a product pursuant to State law, except to the extent that such law is superseded by this title. This section provides a mechanism for settlements of disputes. It does not create or eliminate causes of action or alter standards of liability under State law.

Section 201(b) provides that a claimant may, in addition to any claim for relief made pursuant to State law, include in the complaint an offer of settlement for a specific dollar amount.

Section 201(c) provides that the defendant may make an offer of settlement within 60 days after service of the claimant's complaint or within the time permitted for a responsive pleading pursuant to State law, whichever is longer. If the defendant's responsive pleading includes a motion to dismiss in accordance with applicable law, the defendant may tender payment in the amount of the settlement offer within 10 days after the court's determination regarding such motion.

Section 201(d) provides that if an offer of settlement is made pursuant to section 201(b) or (c), the court may enter an order extending the applicable period for response upon a motion made prior to the expiration of the applicable response period. Any such motion must be accompanied by a supporting affidavit of the moving party setting forth the reasons why such extension is necessary to promote the interests of justice and recommending a schedule for discovery of evidence material to the amount of relief. The affidavit must state also that the information likely to be discovered is material and would not otherwise be available to the moving party after reasonable inquiry. Any such order granted by the court shall contain a schedule for discovery of evidence material to the issue of the appropriate amount of relief, and should not extend such period for more than 60 days. This section leaves it to the court's discretion to decide whether to grant a motion for an extension.

Section 201(e) provides that if the defendant does not accept the offer of settlement made by a claimant pursuant to Section 201(b) and a verdict is entered for an amount equal to or greater than the specific dollar amount of the offer, the court shall include the reasonable attorney's fees and costs in the judgment entered. For the purposes of this section, reasonable attorney's fees are defined in section 201(g). Such fees shall be offset against any fees owed by the claimant to the claimant's attorney by reason of the verdict. This subsection recognizes that a claimant's attorney may be paid on a contingent basis rather than on an hourly fee basis. The amount of the penalty imposed upon a defendant does not change if the claimant's attorney is paid on a contingent basis. The defendant must pay reasonable attorney's fees, as defined in section 201(g).

Section 201(e) provides that a defendant must accept the offer in a timely fashion. The defendant must respond within the time permitted pursuant to State law for a responsive pleading or, if the defendant's pleadings included a motion to dismiss, within 30 days after the court's determination regarding such motion. Failure to respond to the claimant's offer within these time limits will trigger the imposition of the sanctions described above when the judgment is entered.

Section 201(f) provides that if the claimant does not accept the defendant's offer of settlement in accordance with section 201(c) and a verdict is entered for an amount equal to or less than the specific dollar amount of the settlement offer, the court shall reduce the amount of the verdict by an amount equal to the reasonable attorney's fees, as defined in section 201(g), and costs owed by the defendant to the defendant's attorney by reason of this verdict. The amount of this reduction shall not exceed that portion of the verdict which is allocated to economic and noneconomic losses for which the claimant has received or will receive collateral benefits as defined in section 102(3).

The claimant must respond within 30 days after the date on which the offer is made. If the claimant does not respond during that time and the verdict is not favorable to the claimant as described above, then the claimant will be required to pay attorney's fees and costs pursuant to this section.

Section 201(g) provides that for the purposes of section 201, attorney's fees shall be calculated on the basis of an hourly rate which should not exceed that which is considered acceptable in the community in which the attorney practices, considering the attorney's qualifications and the complexity of the case.

SECTION 202—ALTERNATIVE DISPUTE RESOLUTION PROCEDURES

In general

Section 202 allows either party to settle their dispute pursuant to an approved State alternative dispute resolution (ADR) procedure. This may be initiated by either party and, it may be undertaken in addition to, or in lieu of, the procedures in section 201.

If the offeree party is unwilling to participate in such a procedure, and the court determines that the refusal was unreasonable or not in good faith, the court will assess reasonable attorney's fees and costs against the offeree. A rebuttable presumption is created that the offeree's refusal to participate in the ADR procedure is unreasonable or not in good faith if a verdict is entered that favors the offeror.

A witness at the September 19, 1991 hearing testified that this provision violates an individual's right to a jury trial under the Seventh

Amendment.[139] The Committee received testimony indicating that the creation of incentives to use voluntary ADR programs is a proposal that applies equally to defendants and plaintiffs and cannot be described as an antiplaintiff provision.[140] Twenty-four States have mandatory arbitration or mediation laws.[141] Under these programs, litigants are required to enter into arbitration or mediation and the decision reached in this procedure is subject to a trial de novo at the request of either party.[142] The Federal District Court for the Eastern District of Pennsylvania has held that ADR procedures that are not binding on the parties do not violate the Seventh Amendment.[143] The proposal in this section refers only to voluntary ADR programs, which parties elect to use, and it contains incentives to encourage their use.

Eighteen States with mandatory arbitration or mediation laws have financial incentives to resolve cases before trial in order to conclude the litigation.[144] There is a similar incentive to settle cases before trial in the Federal court system.[145] The use of attorneys fees as an incentive to parties to accept an arbitrator's decision in the Washington State ADR system has been upheld as consistent with the State's constitutional provision on jury trials, which is similar to the Seventh Amendment.[146]

As reported

Section 202(a) provides that either a claimant or a defendant may offer to proceed pursuant to a voluntary ADR procedure. Such procedure must be established or recognized under either the law of the state where the civil action is brought or under the rules of the court in which such action is maintained. The offer to proceed under this section must be made within the time period established in section 201 for making a settlement offer. Except as explicitly provided in this section, it does not in any way preempt State ADR procedures. The determination of whether a party's refusal to enter into an ADR

---

139. Statement of J. Kendall Few, September 19, 1991 hearing.

140. Statement of Professor James Henderson, September 19 at 4–5.

141. McIver and Kerlitz, *Court-Annexed Arbitration*, The Justice System Journal, Volume 14, Number 2 at 123 (1991).

142. *Id.*

143. *Kimbrough v. Holiday Inn,* 478 F.Supp. 566 (1979). *Cf. United Farm Workers National Union v. Babbitt,* 449 F.Supp. 449 (1978) where the court held that a mandatory arbitration program that is binding violates the Seventh Amendment.

144. McIver and Kerlitz, *supra*, at 127, 130.

145. F.R.C.P. 68; See Section 201, *supra*.

146. *Colaruso v. Peterson,* 812 P.2d 862 (Wash.App.1991); *Christian–Lembert Van and Storage Co. v. McLeon,* 693 P.2d 161 (Wash.App.1984).

Article 1, section 21 of the Washington Constitution provides: "The right of a trial by jury shall remain inviolate, but the legislature may provide for a jury of any number less than twelve in courts of record, and for a verdict by nine or more jurors in civil cases in any court of record, and for waiving of the jury in civil cases where the consent of the parties interested is given thereto."

procedure was unreasonable shall occur after a verdict is entered or the proceeding is otherwise concluded (e.g., summary judgment granted, directed verdict entered).

Section 202(b) provides that if the offeree refuses to proceed pursuant to such ADR procedures and the court determines that such refusal was unreasonable or not in good faith, the court shall assess reasonable attorney's fees and costs against the offeree. No sanctions would apply to either party in the event of a settlement.

Section 202(c) provides that a rebuttable presumption is created that a refusal by an offeree to proceed pursuant to such ADR procedure was unreasonable if a verdict is rendered in favor of the offeror.

TITLE III

This title of the bill sets forth uniform standards that govern product liability actions litigated in the courts.

SECTION 301—CIVIL ACTIONS

As reported

Section 301 provides that a person seeking to recover for harm caused by a product may bring a civil action against the product's manufacturer or the product seller pursuant to applicable state or federal law, except to the extent that such law is superseded by this bill. For the purposes of title III, this means that such civil actions will be governed by existing liability standards and rules, except to the extent that they are superseded by Federal standards.

SECTION 302—UNIFORM STANDARDS OF PRODUCT SELLER LIABILITY

In general

Section 302 specifies when a product seller other than a manufacturer [147] is responsible for harm caused by a product. A product seller is liable for harm caused (1) by its own failure to exercise reasonable care with respect to the product, or (2) by a product that fails to conform to an express warranty made by the product seller. In addition, the product seller may be liable as if it were the manufacturer if the manufacturer responsible is not subject to service of process or if the court determines that the claimant would not be able to enforce a judgment against the manufacturer.

Present law

In a majority of States, product sellers are liable for harms caused by a product as if they were manufacturers of the product.[148] Thus,

---

147. Product seller is defined in section 102(14).

148. W. Prosser and W. Keeton, Torts (5th ed.) 1984 at 705. This rule extends

product sellers may be held responsible for product-related harms that they did not cause and over which they had no control.

Two reasons have been advanced for holding product sellers liable as if they were manufacturers. First, it has been argued that the rule promotes safety and reduces the risk of harm, because product sellers will seek to avoid liability by pressuring manufacturers to make safe products.[149] This rationale, however, fails to recognize that manufacturers will feel the same, if not greater, pressure to make safe products if they are sued directly for harms caused by their own product defects.

Second, it has been argued that the rule is fair because a product seller who is held liable for harm caused by a manufacturer's defect can seek indemnity[150] and thereby shift the cost of liability to the manufacturer who actually caused the harm.[151] Data show that, in fact, product sellers account for less than 5 percent of product liability payments[152] because generally they are successful in shifting the cost of liability to the manufacturers.

Although the end result may be fair, the system is inefficient. Product sellers are routinely sued for harms caused by a manufacturer and are forced to incur substantial legal costs both to defend the product liability lawsuit and to seek indemnification from the responsible manufacturer.[153] As courts have recognized, the product seller is not truly "held harmless" through indemnification if the product seller must "expend large sums to defend a products liability action merely because a defective product, the defect of which may be attributable solely to the manufacturer's conduct, passed through [his or her] hands."[154] Further, indemnity does not reimburse product sellers for loss of good will or reputation caused by lawsuits.

Some cases[155] and a number of State statutes[156] have recognized the inequity of the majority rule. Section 302(a)(1) is based on the case

strict liability to product seller: "[A]ll states would accept the proposition that strict liability extends ... to one who vouches for the manufacturer-assembler by selling a product assembled by another as his own." Id. See also P. Sherman, Product Liability at 234.

149. E.g., Vandermark v. Ford Motor Co., 61 Cal.2d 256, 391 P.2d 168, 37 Cal. Rptr. 896 (1964).

150. See, e.g., Ark.Stat.Ann. Section 16-116-107; Ariz.Rev.Stat.Ann. 12-684.

151. See, e.g., Hales v. Monroe, 544 F.2d 331 (8th Cir.1976); Litton Systems Inc. v. Shaw's Sales & Services, Ltd., 119 Ariz. 10, 579 P.2d 48 (1978); Fairburn v. Montgomery Ward & Co., 349 So.2d 1280 (La.App. 1977); Anderson v. Somberg, 158 N.J.Super. 384, 386 A.2d 413 (1978) cert. denied, 77 N.J. 509, 391 A.2d 522 (1978).

152. Insurance Services Office Product Liability Closed Claim Survey, A Technical Analysis of Survey Results, 35 (1977).

153. E.g., Kelly v. Hanscom Bros., Inc., 231 Pa.Super. 357, 331 A.2d 737, 740 (1974). ("It is not unusual for liability to move transactionally up the chain of distribution until the manufacturer ultimately pays ...").

154. Piedmont Equipment Co. v. Eberhard Mfg. Co., 665 P.2d 256, 259 (Nev.1983) (holding that a product seller, absolved of liability in a products case, may seek indemnification from the responsible manufacturer for his legal costs).

155. See, e.g., Sam Shainberg Co. v. Barlow, 258 So.2d 242, 246 (Miss.1972) ("[I]t would not be reasonable, logical or practical to place on every retail merchant the

156. See note 156 on page 673.

law and State statutes which provide that product sellers are responsible only for the harms caused by their own products, and claims should be brought directly against them rather than against product sellers. In the event, however, that the manufacturer responsible for the harm is not subject to service of process by the injured claimant or would be unable to pay the judgment, the product seller should be treated as if the product seller were the manufacturer. Under the circumstances, the claimant would have no recourse unless the product seller is held responsible as the manufacturer.[157]

This approach eliminates unnecessary and burdensome legal costs [158] and provides incentives for product safety without affecting a claimant's ability to recover for harms caused by a product defect.

As reported

Section 302(a) identifies two situations in which a product seller other than a manufacturer is liable for harm caused by a product. Both follow the rule that a product seller is responsible for the consequences of the product seller's own conduct. This concept of individual responsibility, of placing responsibility on the party that actually caused and could have prevented the harm, encourages product safety on the part of product sellers.

First, a claimant will recover from a product seller if: the individual product unit that caused the harm was sold or otherwise placed in the stream of commerce by the product seller; the product seller failed to exercise reasonable care with respect to the product; and the failure to exercise reasonable care was a proximate cause of the claimant's harm. Second, a claimant will recover from a product seller if the product seller made an express warranty about the product, independent of any express warranty made by the manufacturer; the product failed to conform to the warranty; and the failure to conform to the warranty caused the claimant's harm.

Section 302(b) sets forth factors that may be relevant in determining whether the product seller failed to exercise reasonable prudence with respect to the product. The trier of fact may consider, among other factors, the effect of the seller's conduct with respect to the construction, inspection, or condition of the product and any failure of

absolute duty of inspecting for latent defects in every article ... that the retailer might offer for sale. Such a rule of law would make each retail merchant an insurer or guarantor of every one of the thousands of items he handles merely as a sales conduit.")

156. *E.g.,* Colo.Rev.Stat. Section 13–21–402 (Supp.1984); Idaho Code Section 6–1407 (Supp.1985); N.C.Gen.Stat. Section 99B–2 (1985).

157. *See Vandermark v. Ford Motor Co.,* 61 Cal.2d 256, 391 P.2d 168, 171, 37 Cal. Rptr. 896 (1964) ("the retailer may be the only member of that enterprise reasonably available to the insured plaintiff").

158. Statement of Professor Aaron Twerski, September 12, 1991 hearing at 12–13. (It is unfair to keep defendants who are in no way responsible for the harm in a case: it serves only to increase transition costs. *Id.*)

the product seller to pass on adequate warnings or instructions about the dangers and proper use of the product. The product seller is not liable for failure to warn if it provided to the person who took possession and control of the product any written warnings or instructions it had received up to that time, and made reasonable efforts to provide users with those warnings and instructions it received after the product left its possession and control. Nor shall the seller be liable, except for breach of express warranty, if there was no reasonable opportunity to inspect the product in a manner that would have or, in the exercise of reasonable care, should have revealed the product's danger. For example, a seller may not have had a reasonable opportunity to discover a product defect if the product was prepackaged [159] or if the product never passed through the seller's hands (e.g., a person may have held title to a product but may never have had possession of it).[160]

Section 302(c) provides that a product seller shall be treated as the product manufacturer and shall be liable for the claimant's harm as if the product seller were the manufacturer if (1) the manufacturer is not subject to service of process under the laws of any State in which the action might have been brought by the claimant, or (2) the court determines that the claimant would be unable to enforce a judgment against the manufacturer. For example, a judgment would be unenforceable if the court finds that the manufacturer is bankrupt, insolvent, or otherwise unable to pay. A claimant may recover from the product seller for harms that were caused by the manufacturer if one of the two provisions applies, and if the claimant proves that the manufacturer would have been liable under State law. Although section 302(c) departs from the notion of individual responsibility for harms, it ensures that a claimant can recover from the product seller if he or she is unable to recover from the manufacturer responsible for the harms.

Section 302 will encourage safety by placing responsibility on the party who caused and could have prevented the harm. It will reduce the unnecessary costs and inefficiencies associated with the current system.[161] Sellers will no longer be exposed routinely to liability for harms caused by manufacturers. The legal costs of defending product liability claims and seeking indemnification will be substantially reduced. At the same time, section 302 ensures that claimants harmed by defective products may recover from product sellers if the responsible manufacturer cannot be brought into court or is judgment-proof.

---

159. See Ky.Rev.Stat. Section 411.340 (Supp.1984); Tenn.Code Section 29–28–106 (Supp.1985). See also Brady v. Steyr–Daimler–Puch, A.G., 429 So.2d 1348 (Fla.App. 1983) (summary judgment for distributor who shipped product in sealed container to dealer).

160. See, e.g., Kirby v. Rouselle Corp., 108 Misc.2d 291, 437 N.Y.S.2d 512 (1981); Canifax v. Hercules Powder Co., 237 Cal. App.2d 44, 46 Cal.Rptr. 552 (1965).

161. Statement of Professor Twerski, supra.

COMMITTEE REPORT ON S. 640

SECTION 303—UNIFORM STANDARDS FOR AWARD OF PUNITIVE DAMAGES

In general

Section 303 establishes a uniform standard of liability for punitive damages. Such damages may be awarded only if the claimant establishes by clear and convincing evidence that the harm suffered was the result of the manufacturer's or product seller's conscious, flagrant indifference to the safety of those who might be harmed by a product. Except in certain circumstances, punitive damages may not be imposed upon manufacturers or sellers of prescription and over-the-counter drugs, and medical devices, as well as the manufacturers of aircraft, for harm caused by those products, when the safety of those products has been approved by the appropriate Federal agency prior to the marketing of the product. The defense is unavailable to a medical or aviation manufacturer who committed fraud during the reviewing process by withholding or misrepresenting relevant information. The defense is also unavailable to a manufacturer of prescription and over-the-counter drugs and medical devices, if the defendant made an illegal payment to an official involved in the certification process for the purpose of securing approval of such drug or device. Finally, a manufacturer or product seller may request that the trier of fact conduct a separate proceeding on the punitive damages issues.

Present law

The purpose of punitive damages is to punish a defendant for outrageous conduct and deter such conduct in the future by the defendant and by others.[162] Such damages are a quasi-criminal sanction and, thus, go beyond compensating the claimant for the claimant's injuries. Punitive damages may be awarded to a claimant in civil actions in most States. Five states have prohibited punitive damage awards except in those instances where there is explicit statutory authorization for specific cases.[163]

The trier of fact has total discretion over whether punitive damages should be assessed against a defendant. State standards or guidelines for determining whether a defendant should pay punitive damages are not uniform; these standards involve some degree of conscious misconduct and refer variously to "willful," "wanton," "malicious," or

---

162. *See* Restatement (Second) of Torts Section 908(1) (1965).

163. Punitive damages not permitted in Louisiana, *e.g., Ricard v. State,* 390 So.2d 882 (La.1980); Massachusetts, *e.g., Caperci v. Huntoon,* 397 F.2d 799 (1st Cir.) (dictum), cert. denied, 393 U.S. 940 (1968); Nebraska, *e.g., Abel v. Conover,* 104 N.W.2d 684 (Neb.1960); Washington, *e.g., Kammerer v. Western Gear Corp.,* 96 Wash.2d 416, 618 P.2d 1330 (1980); and New Hampshire, *e.g.,* N.H.Rev.Stat.Ann. Section 507:16 (Supp.1988). Other States put some limits on the allowance of punitive damages, for example, in breach of contract or wrongful death actions.

"reckless" disregard for the rights of others.[164]

In most jurisdictions today, the claimant must prove by a preponderance of the evidence that the defendant acted in a manner that warrants punitive damages. However, 22 States have adopted a standard of clear and convincing evidence as the burden of proof for punitive damages. Nineteen States have done so by legislation, and three by judicial decision.[165] To reflect the quasi-criminal nature of such punishment, section 303 of the bill follows this emerging rule: the burden of proof is raised to clear and convincing evidence, a standard of proof closer to the criminal law standard for imposing punishment.

While commentators disagree as to the full extent of this growth, it is clear that punitive damage awards have been increasing both in size and in number in the past ten years. Until 1977, there had been only a small number of punitive damage awards in products liability cases. Since then, the frequency of these awards has increased. Punitive damages are routinely sought [166] and, when awarded, tend to be very large.[167]

---

164. See J. Chiardi & Kircher, "Punitive Damages—Law and Practice," Section 5.01 at 8 (1981); Ellis, "Fairness and Efficiency in the Law of Punitive Damages," 56 S.Cal.L.Rev. 1, 38 (1982); Owen, "Problems In Assessing Punitive Damages Against Manufacturers of Defective Product," 49 U.Chi.L.Rev. 1, 21 (1982).

165. See, e.g., Ala.Code Section 6–11–20(a) (Supp.1989); *Linthizum v. Nationwide Life Ins. Co.*, 150 Ariz. 326, 723 P.2d 675 (1986) (en banc). See also Colo.Rev. Stat. Section 13–25–127(2) (1973) (proof beyond reasonable doubt).

166. American College of Trial Lawyers, *Report on Punitive Damages of the Committee on Special Problems in the Administration of Justice* 16 (March 3, 1989).

167. The Alliance of American Insurers' continuing series of studies of large (over $100,000) product liability claims found that in 1975 punitive damages were sought in only 5 percent of product liability cases; by 1979, they were being sought in 18 percent of cases. AAI Survey of Large–Loss Product Liability Claims (1980) at iii. The Rand Institute for Civil Justice study found that the average punitive damage award in personal injury cases in Cook County, Illinois increased from $40,000 to $1,152,174 in 1980–84. See Peterson, Punitive Damages: Preliminary Empirical Findings, Rand Corp. N–2342–ICJ at 25 (1985), cited in Report of the Tort Policy Working Group on the Causes, Extent and Policy Implications of the Current Crisis in Insurance Availability and Affordability at 39–43 (1986). (These figures were adjusted for inflation and are stated in 1984 dollars.) See generally Schwartz, *Deterrence and Punishment in the Common Law of Punitive Damages: A Comment*, 56 S.Cal. L.Rev. 133 (1982); Owen, *Problems in Assessing Punitive Damages Against Manufacturer of Defective Products*, 49 U.Chi. L.Rev. 1 (1982). Two witnesses at the hearing on S. 640 testified that punitive damages awards are rare, and when awarded, they are not excessive. Statement of Stephen Daniels, the American Bar Foundation, September 12, 1991 hearing; statement of Professor Michael Rustad, September 19, 1991 hearing. Professor Rustad's data indicate that in 1969–70, there were no punitive damage awards in product liability cases, but in 1984, there were over sixty awards. Statement of Professor Michael Rustad at 6. Punitive damage awards in product liability cases, including asbestos cases, continued to increase in number through 1989–90. Between 1960 and 1989, punitive damages were awarded in a total of 355 product liability cases. Punitive damage awards in non-asbestos cases were far more frequent in 1989–90 than in 1969–70. *Id.* According to Professor Rustad, the average punitive damage award in product liability cases is $625,000. *Id.* at 6. It should be noted, however, that median awards are far lower than "mean" awards, indicating that there is a subset of very large awards that account for a large percentage of total punitive awards. ALI study at 234 (Vol. II).

A claimant may include, as a routine matter, a count for punitive damages in a product liability complaint in order to have an opportunity to present evidence to the jury as to the resources of the defendant;[168] moreover, such claims discourage settlement, because of the absence of clear guidelines as to liability. As one legal scholar has noted:

> When the prospect of punitive damages enters the picture, these guidelines disappear. It is close to impossible to negotiate sensibly with a plaintiff who believes that he can shoot for the moon. Furthermore, a defendant who believes that the situation does not call for punitive damages cannot factor their potential into settlement discussions. To do so is to set a pattern for all future settlements in countless cases already in litigation or yet to be brought. In short, unless the situation truly calls for punitive damages, they sabotage settlement negotiations by thrusting a huge "unknown" into the negotiations.[169]

Moreover, punitive damage awards are excessive as most are reduced substantially after trial according to a recent study.[170] Further, as Prof. Kathryn Kelly of Catholic University observed, the deterrence effect of punitive damage awards is diminished when they are routinely overturned.[171] In order to be fair to defendants and to enhance the deterrent effect of punitive damages, juries need clear standards to apply when deciding whether a defendant's conduct merits the assessment of punitive damages.

At present, compliance with Government standards is not a defense against punitive damages.[172] Instead, courts generally are not bound by

---

The problem that this provision attempts to address is the appropriate standards by which punitive damages are awarded. Statement of Professor Aaron Twerski, September 12, 1991 hearing at 6. According to Professor Twerski, "To inject punitive damages blithely, without carefully limiting the occasions in which courts may impose them, threatens the entire structure of product liability litigation." Id. at 6. The ALI Reporters' Study agreed, stating, "defendants always face the risk that ... juries will second-guess decisions that seemed entirely appropriate at the time they were made ... (This is) probably unnecessary when the issue is whether to add ... a punitive component." ALI Reporters' Study (Vol. II) at 247. Section 303 provides the needed standards by creating a "floor" standard so that manufacturers and product sellers will understand what standard of conduct they must meet in order to avoid punitive liability. Testimony of Professor Aaron Twerski, September 12, 1991 hearing (transcript at 127). See also Testimony of Professor Kathryn Kelly, September 19, 1991 hearing (transcript at 120–21) (enactment of S. 640 will enhance uniformity in the awarding of punitive damages by ensuring that those states that allow them do so in a rational and predictable way).

168. American College of Trial Lawyers Report at 6, 16.

169. Twerski, *supra*, 18 U.Mich.J. of L.Ref. 575, 612.

170. Statement of Professor Michael Rustad, *supra*, at 7; GAO Report at 42.

171. September 19, 1991 hearing (transcript at 114–115).

172. Compliance with a federal, state or local government safety standard is not generally a defense of any sort in a product liability action; however, four state statutes do provide for consideration of compliance with government standards as a defense in product liability actions. In Utah,

safety determinations made by regulatory agencies. The results have raised questions about judicial nondeference to agency determinations with respect to industries that are comprehensively regulated.[173] Such was the case, for example, when a Kansas jury decided to assess $8 million in punitive damages against the manufacturer of the Sabin polio vaccine, although this verdict was reversed on appeal.[174] One scholar concluded that the jury "was invited to, and did, impose punitive damages for the purpose of forcing the United States to change its polio vaccination policy."[175]

In a recent Supreme Court decision that addressed the issue of punitive damage awards, *Pacific Mutual Life Insurance Co. v. Haslip,* the Court noted "once again our concern about punitive damages that 'run wild'."[176] According to Professor Kelly, the Court in *Haslip* indicated "that it had in several previous cases expressed a profound uneasiness with some of the common law punitive damage schemes in place in the various States."[177] She went on to say that the Court in *Haslip* has recognized that the due process clause puts limits on the ability of states to impose punitive damages, and has "invited" the legislature to enact punitive damage reform proposals along the lines of the provisions in this section.[178]

As reported

Section 303(a) specifies when punitive damages may be assessed against a manufacturer or product seller in a product liability action. If otherwise permitted by applicable law, punitive damage may be awarded to any claimant who establishes by clear and convincing evidence that the harm suffered was the result of conduct manifesting a manufacturer's or product seller's conscious, flagrant indifference to the safety of those persons who might be harmed by a product. While *Haslip* held that the Due Process Clause does not require that the

---

Colorado, Tennessee, and North Dakota, such compliance establishes a rebuttable presumption as to the safety of the product. In New Hampshire, such compliance is one element of an affirmative defense. See Utah Code Ann. 78–15–6(3); Colo.Rev. Stat. 13–21–403(1)(b); Tenn.Code Ann. 29–28–104; N.D.Century Code 28–01–05(3); N.H.Rev.Stat.Ann. Ch. 507–D:4.

173. *See, e.g.,* Huber, "Safety and the Second Best: The Hazards of Public Risk Management in the Courts," 85 Col.L.Rev. 277 (1985); *The Bhopalization of U.S. Tort Law,* Issues in Science and Technology, Fall 1985.

174. *Johnson v. American Cyanamid Co.,* Eighteenth Judicial District for the District of Sedgwick County, Kansas, June 1984, reversed, Kan.Sup.Ct., No. 57,369. The Kansas Supreme Court reversed by a narrow 4–3 margin, and did not reach the government standards issue.

175. Edmund W. Kitch, *Vaccines and Product Liability: A Case of Contagious Litigation, Regulation,* May/June 1985, at 15.

176. 111 S.Ct. 1032 (1991) at 1043. The Court indicated in this case that the Due Process Clause limits states' ability to impose punitive damages. Statement of Professor Kathryn Kelly, September 19, 1991 hearing at 5.

177. Statement of Professor Kathryn Kelly, *supra,* at 6. The ensuing discussion will reveal that the Court noted agreement with principles concerning punitive damage awards that resemble section 303's provisions.

178. *Id.* at 11.

burden of proof for damages be higher than a preponderance of the evidence, language in the *Haslip* opinion indicated that the Court looks favorably upon a clear and convincing standard.[179] The "clear and convincing evidence" burden of proof was recommended by the American Bar Association in 1987, by the American College of Trial Lawyers in 1989, and the ALI Reporters' Study in 1991.[180] Moreover, one State has adopted an even higher standard. Colorado requires proof beyond a reasonable doubt for the awarding of punitive damages.[181]

The standard of liability for punitive damages in this section requires a "conscious, flagrant indifference" to consumer safety. This is a high standard of culpability, requiring a showing of fault far in excess of mere negligence. The specifications that the misconduct be "conscious" and "flagrant" are designed to assure that punitive damages will not be assessed unless the defendant's conduct was knowingly far in excess of acceptable behavior. The misconduct must be an extreme deviation from ordinary conduct.[182] According to Professor Kelly, this standard "follows the Supreme Court's lead" in *Haslip* by requiring intentional conduct.[183]

It is important to establish the punitive damages threshold far from ordinary negligence in order to assure that manufacturers are not subjected to punitive damages assessment, on top of compensatory damages, for making good faith errors.[184] As one legal scholar has explained:

---

179. *Id.* at 8. *Haslip,* 111 S.Ct. at 1046, n. 11.

180. *See* American Bar Association Action Commission to Improve the Tort Liability System, Report to the House of Delegates: Recommendations to Improve the Tort System (adopted Feb. 1987) [hereinafter ABA Action Commission Report]; American College of Trial Lawyers, *Report on Punitive Damages of the Committee on Special Problems in the Administration of Justice,* 18–19 (March 3, 1989) [hereinafter American College of Trial Lawyers Report] ALI Reporters' Study (Vol. II) at 264.

181. Colo.Rev.Stat. Section 13–25–127(2) (Supp.1979).

182. The ALI Reporters' Study states that the standard should be "reckless disregard for the safety of others." ALI study (Vol. II) at 264; *See* W.P. Keeton, D. Dobbs, R. Keeton, D. Owen, Prosser and Keeton on Torts 214 (5th ed. 1984); Owen, *Punitive Damages in Products Liability Litigation,* 74 Mich.L.Rev. 1257, 1368–69 (1976); Owen, *Problems in Assessing Punitive Damages Against Manufacturers of Defective Products,* 49 U.Chi.L.Rev. 1, 20–28 (1982); Owen, Civil Punishment and the Public Good, 56 So.Cal.L.Rev. 103, 116 (1982) ("Punishment becomes appropriate [only] at an 'extreme' distance from the norm, where the conduct has become clearly flagrant").

183. Statement of Professor Kathryn Kelly, *supra,* at 7.

184. Owen, *supra* note 173, 49 U.Chi. L.Rev. at 27–28. *See Laney v. Coleman Co.,* 758 F.2d 1299 (8th Cir.1985) (reversing punitive damages award); *Roth v. Black & Decker, U.S., Inc.,* 737 F.2d 779 (8th Cir. 1984) (same). *See also* American Motors Corp. v. Ellis, 403 So.2d 459, 469 (Fla.App. 1981) (Cowart, J., dissenting in part) ("Even assuming that the AMC engineers were wrong in these determinations, at most that could only amount to negligence, not the malicious refusal to implement a 'safer' design required to support an award of punitive damages."); *Ford Motor Co. v. Nowak,* 638 S.W.2d 582, 598, 602 (Tex.App. 1982) (Gonzalez, J., dissenting) ("there is no evidence that Ford was consciously indifferent to appellees' rights"); *American Cyanamid Co. v. Roy,* 466 So.2d 1079, 1085 (Fla.App.1984) (Amstead, C.J., dissenting in part on rehearing) ("The facts simply do not reflect the kind of flagrant misconduct that would justify" punitive damages).

> [E]ven if the product is finally found "defective," the case for punitive damages almost always will be quite weak if a plausible case for nondefectiveness was made the other way. Such damages usually will not be appropriate unless the product was very defective, and plainly so, at the time it was sold. A plaintiff usually should be entitled to a directed verdict on defectiveness, or close thereto, before the punitive damages issue is properly before the jury at all.[185]

Finally, to be "conscious" of its flagrant misconduct, a manufacturer or product seller must be aware that its product is legally defective and that its conduct in selling it in such a condition is therefore improper. Mere consciousness that its product is dangerous, that it can or indeed probably will cause substantial harm or even death, is thus insufficient by itself, since manufacturers of many dangerous products—such as cars, power saws, and chemicals—surely are fully conscious of the inherent dangers in their products.[186] It is only when a manufacturer consciously leaves in its product a danger that is unreasonable, and sells the product to the public knowing it to be defective, that its conduct can be said to manifest a "conscious, flagrant indifference" to consumer safety.[187]

Section 303(a) adds that a failure to exercise reasonable care in choosing among alternative designs, formulations, instructions, or warnings is not, in itself, conduct for which the award of punitive damages would be appropriate. This sentence clarifies further the punitive damages standard of liability by drawing a clear distinction between mere negligence and the aggravated misconduct which justifies the imposition of punitive damages. The mere failure to exercise reasonable care as to such a choice does not, in itself, warrant the imposition of punitive damages. In some circumstances, however, failure to exercise reasonable care as to a whole series of choices might constitute aggravated misconduct for which punitive damages are appropriate.

The "clear and convincing evidence" standard of section 303(a) requires more proof than the "preponderance of the evidence" standard of proof traditionally used in civil actions; however, it requires less proof than the "beyond a reasonable doubt" standard that is required for use in criminal actions.[188] Thus, it is a standard of proof between the civil and criminal standards. This standard is appropriate for

---

185. Owen, *supra*, 49 U.Chi.L.Rev. at 38.

186. *Id.* at 16, 24.

187. *See Roth v. Black & Decker, U.S., Inc.*, 737 F.2d 779 (8th Cir.1984) ("the evidence must show that the defendant was aware that its acts were wrongful in some way"); Prosser and Keeton on Torts *supra* note 1, at 214 n. 62 ("a consciousness that the conduct is unlawful or morally wrong"); R. Epstein, *Modern Products Liability Law* 181 ("defendant knew that the conduct was wrongful").

188. "Clear and convincing evidence" is defined in section 102(2). "Preponderance of the evidence" is defined in section 102(12).

determining what is, in effect, a quasi-criminal sanction in a civil case.[189] It is proposed in the Uniform Product Liability Act and has recently been adopted by some States as the sound and fair rule.[190]

The rationale for the higher standard of proof rests on fairness. As one commentator explained:

> [A]n unjustified punitive damages award causes more harm to the defendant than erroneous failure to award punitive damages to the plaintiff. To reflect this imbalance, the burden of proof should favor the defendant more than does the "a preponderance of evidence test." [191]

A higher standard of proof is necessary to ensure that punitive damages are assessed only where appropriate.

Section 303(a) adds, as well, that punitive damages may not be awarded in the absence of a compensatory award, except as provided in subsection (b), which addresses an issue that is unique to the wrongful death law of a few States. Section 303(b) relates to wrongful death product liability actions where applicable State law provides, or has been construed to provide, that only punitive damages are recoverable.[192] In these unique situations, punitive damages are a substitute for compensatory awards. In such situations, a defendant is liable for punitive damages regardless of whether a claim is asserted under section 303. Further, recovery of damages in such an action shall not bar a claim under this section.[193]

Section 303(c) bars an award of punitive damages against manufacturers and sellers of prescription and over-the-counter drugs (including vaccines and other biologicals), and medical devices, as well as against manufacturers of aircraft including aircraft components, for harms caused by those products, when the safety of those products has been reviewed and recognized by the appropriate Federal agency. This defense is consistent with the recommendations of the ALI Reporters' study and the views of Peter Huber and Robert Litan, editors of "The Liability Maze." [194] Five States have enacted similar FDA defenses against punitive damages.[195] The defense in section 303(c) is not, however, available to any defendant who has committed fraud during the approval or review process by withholding or misrepresenting

---

189. See Owen, "Crashworthiness Litigation and Punitive Damages," 4 J.Prod. Liab. 221, 226 (1981).

190. Uniform Product Liability Act Section 120, 44 Fed.Reg. 62714, 62748 (1979).

191. Wheeler, "The Constitutional Case for Reforming Punitive Damage Procedures," 69 Va.L.Rev. 269, 298 (1983).

192. See Ala.Code 6-5-410 (1975).

193. Cf., Federal Tort Claims Act, 28 U.S.C. Section 2674 (1982).

194. ALI Reporters' Study (Vol. II) at 101; The Liability Maze at 21.

195. The five states are Arizona, e.g., Ariz.Stat.Ann. Section 12-701; New Jersey, e.g., N.J.Stat.Ann. Section 2A:58C-5(c); Ohio, e.g., Ohio Rev.Code Ann. Section 2307.80; Oregon, e.g., Or.Rev.Stat. Section 30.927; Utah, e.g., Utah Code Ann. Section 78-18-2.

material and relevant information, with respect to the approval or review of the product in question, from any agency involved in the approval or review process. The defense is also unavailable to any manufacturer or seller of prescription and over-the-counter drugs or medical devices that makes an illegal payment to an FDA official for the purpose of securing approval of such drug or device. This last limitation on the defense is in response to the generic drug approval scandal.[196]

Section 303(c) is intended to deal with the question of imposition of punitive damages in those actions involving drugs, medical devices, and aircraft. It is not intended to preempt state laws that may establish any other defense against liability in product liability actions based on compliance with Government standards or the requirements of statutes or regulations concerning product design, labeling, or warnings.

This defense applies to drugs as defined in section 201(g)(1) of the Federal Food, Drug, and Cosmetic Act (21 U.S.C. 321(g)(1)) or medical devices as defined under section 201(h) of the same Act. Punitive damages shall not be awarded when these products are approved by the Federal Food and Drug Administration (FDA) and are subject to pre-market approval by the agency with respect to the safety of the formulation or performance of the aspect of such drug or device which caused the claimant's harm, or the adequacy of the packaging or labeling of such drug or device.[197] In addition, this provision applies to drugs that are generally recognized as "safe and effective" pursuant to conditions established by the FDA and applicable regulations, including packaging and labeling regulations.

Likewise, this defense applies to aircraft which are subject to premarket certification by the Federal Aviation Administration (FAA) with respect to the safety of the design or performance of the aspect of such aircraft which caused the claimant's harm or the adequacy of the warnings regarding the operation or maintenance of such aircraft. Punitive damages shall not be awarded against the manufacturer of such an aircraft or aircraft components certified by FAA under the Federal Aviation Act of 1958 (49 App. U.S.C. 1301 et seq.), provided the manufacturer complied with FAA requirements and obligations regarding continuing airworthiness after delivery of the aircraft to a user. This includes FAA requirements to provide maintenance and service information related to airworthiness whether or not such information is used by the FAA to prepare mandatory maintenance, inspection or repair directives.

---

196. Testimony of Richard Kingham, May 10, 1990 hearing.

197. This provision does not apply to medical devices that were never subject to pre-market approval by the FDA, such as the intrauterine device known as the Dalkon Shield, which was taken off the market before FDA pre-market regulation of medical devices began in 1976. *See* Report on H.R. 11124, Medical Devices Amendments of 1976, H.Rep. No. 94–853, 94th Cong., 2nd Sess. 8 (1976).

The Federal Government has implemented comprehensive regulatory structures which require that a governmental agency regulate the safety of products such as drugs and aircraft.[198] The Government has delegated to an agency with specific expertise the ability and obligation to establish reasonable and effective safety standards. The Government has established and funded these regulatory systems to assess the safety risks of these products for consumers. Where the Government has carefully assessed these risks and certified that these products meet safety standards established by expert regulatory agencies, manufacturers should not be punished by individual juries or threatened with punitive damages on a case-by-case basis. Moreover, imposing tort liability on top of safety regulation can result in overdeterrence of socially desirable products and activities.[199] According to the ALI Reporters' study, regulatory compliance should be available as a defense.[200]

Section 303(c) contains a provision removing this defense where a defendant has withheld or misrepresented material and relevant information concerning the product's performance, operation, or maintenance. The rationale behind the defense is based on the Federal Government's access to and knowledge of product information. Thus, section 303(c) of the bill shields a defendant from punitive awards only if it has disclosed to the appropriate Federal regulatory agency all required information during and after the licensing process. Where a defendant withholds information or misleads a Federal agency or official, the defense shall not apply.

Section 303(c)(1)(B)(ii) provides further that in any case in which a defendant made an illegal payment to an official from FDA in order to secure approval of a drug or medical device, the defendant is not afforded the protection against punitive damages provided in section 303(c).

In sum, section 303(c) represents a congressional determination that drugs and aircraft are so extensively regulated for society's benefit that punitive damages are not appropriate. In the case of these

---

198. In the case of drugs and medical devices, Section 505 of the Federal Food, Drug and Cosmetics Act provides that a drug must be "safe and effective." Moreover, these products are generally evaluated on a risk-benefit basis. *See* Report Prepared by the Subcommittee on Science, Research, and Technology, "The Food and Drug Administration's Process for Approving New Drugs," 96th Congress 2nd Sess. (Committee Print 1980) at 21; Merrill, *Compensation for Prescription Drug Injuries*, 59 Va.L.Rev. 8–10 (1973). In the case of aircraft, section 601 of the Federal Aviation Act (FAA), directs the Secretary to "promote safety" of civil aircraft and to establish "standards governing the design, materials, workmanship, construction and performance of aircraft ... in the interest of safety." Moreover, section 305 of the FAA Act directs the Secretary "to encourage and foster the development of civil aeronautics and air commerce." In the case of both of these products, the federal government is certifying the safety of these products for consumer use. *See also:* Testimony of Richard Kingham; Statement of Robert Martin, *supra*, note 42.

199. ALI Reporters' Study (Vol. II) at 95.

200. *Id.* (Vol. II) at 110.

products, the Government has conducted a thorough review of the product's safety aspects and risks and has dedicated a great deal of resources to assessing its benefits and risks for society. As a result, the tort system should defer to that regulatory judgment.

Section 303(d) provides that a manufacturer or product seller may request that the trier of fact conduct a separate proceeding to consider (1) whether punitive damages are to be awarded and the amount of such award, or (2) the amount of punitive damages following a determination of punitive liability. In such a proceeding, evidence relevant only to the claim of punitive damages, as determined by state law, shall be inadmissible in any proceeding to determine whether compensatory (economic and noneconomic) damages are to be awarded. The American Bar Association, the American College of Trial Lawyers, and the ALI Reporters' study have recommended bifurcation of punitive damage claims. These groups believe bifurcation can avoid prejudice to defendants by providing that evidence of wealth or financial condition is admissible only on the punitive damage claim.[201]

Section 303(e) provides that when the trier of fact determines the amount of punitive damages to be awarded, all relevant evidence should be considered including the financial condition of the manufacturer or product seller, the severity of harm, the duration of the conduct, any concealment of the conduct, the profitability of the conduct, the number of products sold, other awards of punitive or exemplary damages to persons similarly situated to claimant, and any criminal penalties or civil fines assessed against the manufacturer or product seller as a result of the conduct complained of by the claimant.

Section 303 does not preempt State laws that limit the amount of punitive damage awards nor does it create any rights to punitive damages in those States that do not currently permit recovery of punitive damages.

SECTION 304—UNIFORM TIME LIMITATIONS ON LIABILITY

In general

Section 304 establishes uniform standards of limitation and repose. All civil actions governed by the bill are subject to a uniform statute of limitations that runs for 2 years from the discovery of the harm and its cause. In addition, such actions are subject to a 25-year statute of repose, which establishes the time period during which a manufacturer or product seller may be held responsible for harm allegedly caused by capital goods, except in cases involving toxic harm. The statute of repose applies only in cases where the claimant is entitled to receive worker's compensation benefits.

---

201. *See* ABA Action Commission Report; American College of Trial Lawyers Report at 15–16; ALI Reporters' Study (Vol. II) at 264.

The 2-year statute of limitations for product liability actions begins to run when the claimant discovers or, in the exercise of reasonable prudence, should have discovered the harm and its cause. This provision will ensure that a claim is not barred before the claimant knows or has reason to know about the claimant's harm. A uniform statute of limitations for product liability actions will benefit injured persons whose rights to sue will no longer depend on which state statute happens to apply to their claim.

This section's 25-year limitation on liability for harm allegedly caused by capital goods, referred to as a statute of repose, bars actions seeking recovery for harm caused by such products. This time limitation on liability establishes the period during which a manufacturer or product seller may be held responsible for harm caused by the product. The rationale for this time limitation is that manufacturers and product sellers of capital goods, which usually have a long life, should not be exposed to liability for harms caused by these products for an unlimited period of time.[202]

Present law

All States have statutes of limitations that have been applied to product liability actions.[203] A statute of limitations specifies that time within which the claimant must file his or her action. Failure to file within the specified time bars the claim.

In a number of States, the statute of limitations period begins to run at the "time of injury."[204] When an injury caused by a product is immediate and traumatic, this date is easy to determine. The claimant generally knows of his or her harm and the cause of the harm at the time of the injury. However, where the harm has a latency period or becomes manifest only after repeated exposure to the product, the claimant may not know immediately of the harm or its cause. In these situations, a "time of injury" statute of limitations may expire and bar a claim before the claimant even knows he or she has been harmed.

In response to this problem, some courts and State legislatures have adopted a rule under which the limitations period begins to run

---

202. According to testimony received by the Committee, 30 percent of the lawsuits brought against machine tool manufacturers involve machines that are over 25 years old. As a result of the transaction cost associated with this litigation, this industry spends seven times as much on product liability cases as on research and development. Testimony of Howard H. Fark, February 22, 1990 hearing.

203. Under present law, different statutes of limitations apply in product liability actions depending upon the particular theory of the case. For example, a statute of limitations applicable in tort may be the rule in an action based on negligence while a statute of limitations applicable in contract may be the rule in an action based on breach of warranty. The act will establish one statute of limitations for all product liability actions.

204. *See, e.g., Wojcik v. Almase,* 451 N.E.2d 336 (Ind.App.1983); *New Mexico Electric Service Co. v. Montanez,* 89 N.M. 278, 551 P.2d 634 (1976); *Lange v. Bucyrus–Errie Co.,* 707 F.2d 94 (4th Cir.1983).

when the claimant discovers the harm.[205] Even this rule may be unfair, however, because the claimant may not discover the actual cause of his or her harm until some time after he or she discovers the harm itself. The statute of limitations may expire before the claimant can reasonably discover both his or her harm and its cause.[206]

A growing number of courts and State legislatures have addressed this problem by adopting a statute of limitations that does not expire until the claimant discovers both the claimant's harm and the cause of the harm.[207] The Committee believes that this rule is the better reasoned approach and that it strikes a fair balance between the interests of the parties.

As noted, section 304 also establishes a uniform statute of repose for product liability actions. Sixteen States have adopted such statutes of repose in response to the problems created by open-ended liability for old products—the so-called long tail of liability.[208] Some States have adopted conclusive statutes, which establish an absolute bar to product liability actions for harms caused after a specified period. These time periods range from 8 to 12 years and are applicable to harms caused by all products.[209]

As reported

Section 304(a) provides that in any civil action brought under the bill, the complaint must be filed within 2 years of the time the claimant

---

205. See, e.g., Conn.Gen.Stat. 52–577(a) (1983); *Witherall v. Weimer*, 52 Ill.2d 146, 421 N.E.2d 869 (1985); *Hansen v. A.H. Robins, Co.*, 113 Wis.2d 550, 335 N.W.2d 578 (1983); *Hines v. Tenneco Chemicals, Inc.*, 546 F.Supp. 1229 (S.D.Tex.1982).

206. As one judge said, this follows the logic of "topsy-turvy land" where one can "be divorced before [he] ever ... marr[ies], or harvest a crop never planted, or burn down a house never built, or miss a train running on a non-existent railroad." *Dincher v. Marlin Firearms Co.*, 198 F.2d 821, 823 (2d Cir.1952) (Frank, J., dissenting).

207. See, e.g., *Williams v. Borden, Inc.*, 637 F.2d 731, 734 (10th Cir.1980); *Nelson v. A.H. Robins, Co.*, 515 F.Supp. 623 (N.D.Cal. 1981); *Lundy v. Union Carbide Corp.*, 695 F.2d 394 (9th Cir.1982); *Fidler v. Eastman Kodak Co.*, 555 F.Supp. 87 (D.Mass.1982) aff'd, 728 F.2d 729 (5th Cir.1989); *Mack v. A.H. Robins Co.*, 573 F.Supp. 149 (D.Ariz. 1983) aff'd, 759 F.2d 1482 (9th Cir.1985); *Olsen v. Bell Telephone Laboratories, Inc.*, 388 Mass. 171, 445 N.E.2d 609 (1983); *Elmore v. Owens–Illinois, Inc.*, 673 S.W.2d 434 (Mo.Ct.App.1983); *Sahlie v. Johns–Manville Sales Corp.*, 99 Wash.2d 550, 663 P.2d 473 (1983).

208. "Statutes of repose for products currently exist in some form in at least 16 states. In all but one state, these statutes of repose apply to *all* products, and are not limited to capital goods." Ariz.Rev.Stat. Ann. Section 12–551; Ark.Stat.Ann. Section 34–2804(c); Colo.Rev.Stat. Section 13–80–107; Conn.Gen.Stat. Section 52–577; Ga.Code Ann. Section 51–1–11; Idaho Code Section 6–1403; Ill.Rev.Stat. ch. 110, para. 13–213(b); Ind.Code Section 33–1–1.5–5; Kan.Stat.Ann. Section 60–3303; Ky.Rev. Stat.Ann. Section 511.310; Mich.Comp. Laws Section 600.5805; Minn.Stat. Section 604.03; Neb.Rev.Stat. Section 25–224; Or. Rev.Stat. Section 30.905(1); Tenn.Code Ann. Section 29–28–103; and Wash.Rev. Code Section 7.72.060. None of these statutes of repose is limited to cases where the claimant is eligible to receive workers compensation benefits.

209. See, e.g., Ill.Stat.Ann. Ch. 110, 13–214(b) (1984) (claim is barred if harm occurred more than 12 years after the first sale, lease, or delivery, or ten years after the sale to the initial user, whichever is shorter); Or.Rev.Stat.Ann. 30.905(1) (Supp. 1985) (eight-year statute of repose).

discovers or, in the exercise of reasonable prudence, should have discovered the harm and its cause. Actions filed more than 2 years after the harm and its cause were or should have been discovered are barred.

If a person with a product liability claim has a legal disability—for example, the person is a minor or is insane—the person may file his or her complaint any time until 2 years after the legal disability ceases. If the filing of a product liability complaint is stayed or enjoined by court order, the running of the 2-year period of limitations is suspended until the stay or injunction is lifted or ceases. According to Prof. James Henderson, this is a liberal discovery of harm provision which will improve the lot of injured persons who file a lawsuit in a jurisdiction that does not have such a provision.[210]

Section 304(b) provides that any product liability action alleging harm, which is not toxic harm,[211] caused by a capital good is barred unless the complaint is served and filed within 25 years of the date of delivery of the product to its first purchaser or lessee who has not engaged in a business of selling or leasing the product or using the product as a component part. Peter Huber and Robert Litan, editors of "The Liability Maze," endorsed statutes of repose for nontoxic products, reasoning that it is unfair to impose liability on a product that has been in the market for decades and never found previously to be liable for an injury.[212] Section 304(b) applies only if the claimant has received or is eligible to receive workers' compensation benefits for harm caused by the product. Section 304(b)(3)(B) defines "capital good" as any product or component part of any product, which is both of a character and type depreciable under the Internal Revenue Code of 1954, and (1) used in a trade or business, (2) held for production or income, or (3) sold or donated to a governmental or private entity for the production of goods, for training, for demonstration, or other similar purposes.

Section 304(b)(3) provides that any motor vehicle, vessel, aircraft, or railroad used primarily to transport passengers for hire shall not be subject to the time limitations set forth in subsection (b).

Section 304(c) provides that the time limitations in this section do not affect the right of any person to seek contribution or indemnification from the person who is actually responsible for the harm.[213]

---

210. Statement of Professor James Henderson, September 19, 1991 hearing at 5.

211. As defined in section 304(3)(c), "toxic harm" means harm which is functional impairment, illness, or death of a human being resulting from exposure to an object, substance, mixture, raw material or physical agent of particular chemical composition. Recovery for such harm is not impeded by the 250-year statute of repose for capital goods.

212. *The Liability Maze* at 21.

213. *See* Uniform Product Liability Act, sec. 110(B)(2)(C), 44 Fed.Reg. 62714, 62732-33 (1979).

SECTION 305—UNIFORM STANDARDS FOR OFFSET OF WORKERS' COMPENSATION BENEFITS

In general

According to Prof. Aaron Twerski, a Federal product liability law must address the unjust results that arise from the conflict between tort and workers' compensation systems. The solution proposed in S. 640 addresses this problem in a rational way.[214]

Section 305 clarifies the relationship between the workers' compensation system and the product liability system with rules that keep these systems separate, minimize legal costs, and promote safety. Section 305 eliminates the employer's subrogation lien and strengthens employer immunity from tort liability without affecting the employer's obligation to pay workers' compensation benefits. The exception is when the employer can prove that it or the employee-claimant's coworkers were in no way responsible for the claimant's harm. Further, a manufacturer is prohibited from suing an employer for contribution to a product liability award. If the employer attempts to assert a subrogation lien, the employer loses his or her protection against a suit for contribution. These rules provide economic incentives for the employer to minimize workplace accidents and, by eliminating the subrogation lien in most cases, Section 305 reduces transaction costs. The employee-claimant obtains from the employer the workers' compensation benefits to which he or she is entitled and may obtain tort damages from the responsible manufacturer reduced by the amount of benefits he or she has been paid. Subtracting the amount of workers' compensation benefits from the product liability judgment prevents double recovery by the employee, and, thus, serves the purpose of the subrogation lien without the associated legal costs. The manufacturer pays for the harm caused by the manufacturer's own conduct and the conduct of the employer or coworker less the amount of workers' compensation. Reforms similar to those contained in section 305 are supported by the ALI Reporters' study.[215]

Present law

Workers' compensation statutes are designed to ensure that an employee injured in the course of his or her employment has a fast and inexpensive way to recover for his or her injury, regardless of who, if anyone, is at fault for causing the injury. The employer automatically pays workers' compensation benefits to an employee injured in the course of employment, without regard to fault. As originally conceived, workers' compensation is a tradeoff: While the employer is liable regardless of fault, the employer is immune from tort liability for the

---

214. Statement of Professor Aaron Twerski, September 12, 1991 hearing at 10–11.

215. ALI Reporters' study (Vol. II) at 191. The reforms contained in this section also have been advocated for many years by Professor Arthur Larson, a leading expert on workers compensation law. *See* testimony of Professor Larson, Hearings on S. 44 before the Subcommittee on Consumer of the Senate Committee on Commerce, Science, and Transportation, 98th Cong., 1st Sess., pp. 269–270 (1983) (Serial No. 98–302).

injury. Workers' compensation was, thus, intended to be the employee's exclusive remedy against the employer for work-related injuries.[216] The purpose of the system is to provide swift and certain recovery for injured workers, while maximizing the incentives for employers to maintain a safe workplace.

However, the safety incentive provided by workers' compensation has been undermined by the subrogation lien, which allows an employer to shift the costs of the workers' compensation system to the product liability (tort) system.[217] In most States, an employer can recover the amount of workers' compensation benefits the employer pays to an injured employee through a subrogation lien, if the employee has a successful product liability claim against a manufacturer or product seller. This is done regardless of whether the employer is responsible for the injury.

Some States have gone to the other extreme by permitting employees and manufacturers in product liability actions to recover from the employer. Also, employees have been permitted in some States to bring product liability suits against their employers. In addition, manufacturers have been permitted in a few States to sue employers in contribution and implied indemnity actions on the basis that it was the employer who caused all or a part of the employee-claimant's harm.[218] Other States permit such suits, but limit the amount recoverable to the employer's workers compensation liability.[219] Most jurisdictions, however, respect the employer immunity concept and do not permit a manufacturer to shift the tort judgment to the employer through a contribution or indemnity action.[220]

In sum, the current relationship between the workers' compensation system and the product liability system generates substantial and unnecessary legal costs, leads to unfair cost shifting between the two systems, and may reward unsafe workplace practices.

As reported

Section 305(a) specifies how product liability judgments are calculated in actions involving claimants who are entitled to workers' compensation benefits. Any damages awarded would be reduced by the value of past and future workers' compensation benefits received for

216. A. Larson, 2A "The Law of Workmen's Compensation" Sec. 65.10 (1982). See *Kofron v. Amoco Chem. Corp.*, 441 A.2d 226 (Del.1982).

217. Statement of Victor Schwartz, May 10, 1990 hearing, at 3.

218. E.g., *Skinner v. Reed-Prentice Div.*, 70 Ill.2d 1, 374 N.E.2d 437 (1977), cert. denied, 426 U.S. 946 (1978); *Dole v. Dow Chem. Co.*, 130 N.Y.2d 143, 331 N.Y.S.2d 382, 282 N.E.2d 288 (1972).

219. *Lamberton v. Cincinnati Corp.*, 114, 257 N.W. 679 (1977).

220. E.g., *Hammond v. Kolberg Mfg. Corp.*, 542 F.Supp. 662 (D.Colo.1982); *Glass v. Stahl Specialty Co.*, 97 Wash.2d 880, 652 P.2d 948 (1982); *Union Carbide Corp. v. Dunn Bros. Gen. Contractors*, 294 F.Supp. 704 (M.D.Tenn.1968); *Jack Morgan Constr. Co. v. Larkan*, 254 Ark. 838, 496 S.W.2d 431 (1973).

the same harm. A court or jury determination of workers' compensation benefits shall have no binding effect on and shall not be used as evidence in any other proceeding.

The calculation works as follows. The claimant's total damage for which the defendant would be liable is reduced by the amount of workers' compensation benefits that the claimant is entitled to receive under State or Federal law for the same harm.[221] Judgment is then entered in the amount remaining against the defendant.

Section 305(b) provides that a claimant in a court action subject to this title who is or may be eligible to receive workers' compensation benefits must provide written notice to the employer of the filing of the civil action within 30 days of the filing. Such notice must include the following information: the date of the filing; the court in which the civil action was filed; the names and addresses of all plaintiffs and defendants appearing on the complaint; the court docket number, if available; and a copy of the complaint. This notice must be filed with the court and served on all parties. Failure by the claimant to comply with these requirements will result in the suspension of the deadlines for filing responsive pleadings and commencing discovery proceedings, until the claimant complies with this requirement. The purpose of this requirement is to preserve the rights of an employer to pursue a subrogation lien pursuant to the terms of this section.

Section 305(c) permits a claimant, who has sole discretion to seek a stay, to obtain a stay in the product liability action until the amount payable as workers' compensation benefits has been determined under the workers' compensation law.

Section 305(d)(1) eliminates the employer's subrogation lien—the right of an employer to recover the amount of workers' compensation benefits paid to the injured employee-claimant in a product liability action.

Unless the manufacturer or product seller has expressly agreed to indemnify or hold the employer harmless for harm caused by a product, neither the employer nor the workers' compensation insurance carrier of the employer shall have a right of subrogation, contribution, or implied indemnity against the claimant's recovery from a manufacturer or product seller. This provision will reduce the transaction costs associated with pursuing a subrogation lien.

Section 305(d)(2) provides that a claimant's employer or the workers' compensation insurer of the employer may assert a subrogation lien by providing that the claimant's harm was in no way caused by the

---

221. In a hypothetical case, a claimant is entitled to $50,000 in workers' compensation benefits and sustains total damages of $500,000. The judgment against the defendant would be $450,000, calculated as follows: $500,000 total damages less $50,000 workers' compensation benefits. The claimant still receives a net total of $500,000 in compensation.

fault of the claimant's employer or coworkers. An employer's or the employer's workers' compensation insurer's right to establish this fact is preserved by intervening in a civil action. If the civil action is resolved prior to entry of a verdict by the trier of fact, any resolution of the action by settlement or other means shall afford the employer or the workers' compensation insurer of the employer an opportunity to assert a right of subrogation, contribution or implied indemnity if the employee-claimant's harm was not in any way caused by the fault of the claimant's employer or coworkers. This is a procedural safeguard to preserve the employer's right under this section to assert that he or she and the claimant's coworkers were in no way responsible for the claimant's injuries.

Section 305(e)(1) eliminates contribution and indemnity actions by third-party tortfeasors against the employer or coworker of the claimant, except as provided in section 305(f). A minority of jurisdictions allows a third-party tortfeasor, such as a manufacturer or product seller, to pursue a claim against the employer or coworker alleging that the employer or coworker was at fault and should pay all or part of the product liability judgment. Permitting a manufacturer to sue an employer for an employee accident undermines the workers' compensation principal that the employer or coworker should be immune from tort liability.

Section 305(e)(2) adds that the bill does not affect any other provision of State or Federal workers' compensation law prohibiting a person entitled to workers' compensation benefits from recovering for harm caused by a product in any action except a workers' compensation claim against an employer, coworker, workers' compensation insurer of the employer, or the exclusive representative of the injured person. Section 305(e) also states that the bill is not intended to affect any workers' compensation laws that permit claimants to recover on the basis of a claim of intentional tort by the employer or coworker. These intentional torts include, for example, assault, battery, trespass or false imprisonment.

Section 305(f) provides that section 305(e) shall not apply and applicable State law shall control if the employer or the workers' compensation insurer of the employer, in a civil action subject to this title, asserts or attempts to assert, because of section 305(d), a right of subrogation, contribution or implied indemnity against the manufacturer or product seller or a lien against the claimant's recovery from the manufacturer or product seller.

Section 305 applies only to claims involving workplace injuries that are subject to State or Federal workers' compensation statutes. Therefore, where a product liability action involves a workplace injury covered by other laws, such as the Federal Employers Liability Act, 45 U.S.C. Section 51, section 305 does not apply. Section 305 only affects the rights of subrogation in product liability actions. This provision does not affect nonproduct-related subrogation claims, which frequently arise in such industries as the construction industry.

SECTION 306—SEVERAL LIABILITY FOR NONECONOMIC DAMAGES

In general

Section 306 provides that the liability of each defendant in a product liability action for noneconomic damages shall be several only and shall not be joint. Noneconomic damages, for the purposes of this section, are subjective, nonmonetary losses, including pain and suffering awards. Each defendant shall be liable only for the portion of noneconomic damages allocated to it in accordance with its proportionate share of responsibility. The basic policy underlying this section is to address inequitable application of the doctrine of joint and several liability that makes one defendant pay for the misconduct of another.

Joint and several liability was limited originally to situations where defendants had conspired with one another to harm a plaintiff— so-called concert of action. Today, it has been extended far beyond its original application to situations where defendants' conduct played any role, however minor, in causing a harm. In such circumstances, the full implementation of joint and several liability can have inequitable consequences. When joint and several liability is applied, counsel for a claimant need not pursue a wrongdoer whose conduct played a principal role is causing the harm at issue so long as there is a larger "deep-pocket" defendant available. In those instances where certain defendants are not equipped to pay damages in proportion to their responsibility, the claimant can obtain the entire cost of that harm on the "deep-pocket" defendant even though its participation in the harm was relatively small.

This section takes a balanced approach to the problem by limiting the application of joint and several liability to situations where it is defensible on public policy grounds—where a person's economic loss otherwise would be uncompensated. The ALI Reporters' study also recommends reforming the doctrine of joint and several liability.[222] This distinction between economic and noneconomic loss is consistent with the underlying policy of joint and several liability to make the injured party whole. It does not preclude the claimant from being made whole for actual losses while limiting a defendant's liability for noneconomic losses to that portion for which the defendant is responsible.

---

222. ALI Reporters' study (Vol. II) at 147. The ALI Reporters' study proposes an "allocation" theory. This would require multiple defendants to pay damages in proportion to their fault. The portion of damages attributable to an insolvent defendant would be allocated to the plaintiff and all solvents defendants in proportion to their fault.

COMMITTEE REPORT ON S. 640

Present law

The application of joint and several liability must be understood in the context of legal history. This doctrine holds one person responsible for another's conduct. It arose at common law in connection with procedural joinder of parties. At first, joinder was limited and was usually permitted when two or more defendants had conspired to harm a claimant—when they had engaged in "concert of action" by wrongfully pursuing a common scheme or plan that was likely to result in injury to another. Joint and several liability meant that the persons who acted in concert were equally at fault and jointly responsible for the harm; thus, the injured person could recover damages from any one of them.[223]

A growing number of States have abolished or modified the doctrine of joint and several liability.[224] In June 1986, those voting in a California State referendum approved an initiative measure to abolish joint and several liability with respect to noneconomic damages.[225] Section 306 is modeled on that initiative.

As reported

Section 306(a) and (b) limit each defendant's liability for noneconomic damages to that defendant's percentage of responsibility as determined by the trier of fact. The result is that, in any product liability action, the liability of each defendant for noneconomic damages shall not be joint and several.

In most cases the percentage determination required by this section will not be subject to an exact mathematical computation. Rather, it will be based on the commonsense approximation assigned to it by the jury or by the court.

In determining the percentage of each defendant's liability, the trier of fact should take into consideration the proportionate share of each party's responsibility for the total harm caused, including that portion attributable to the claimant. The focus of the inquiry should be on the defendant's "responsibility." For example, if a defendant's share of responsibility for the harm is found to be 25 percent, that defendant is liable for 25 percent of the noneconomic damages.

Section 306 does not specify who has the burden of proof as to apportionment of noneconomic loss. Based on the evidence presented, the trier of fact should apportion responsibility among all parties.[226] All the parties will have an opportunity to present their case to the trier of fact as to the appropriate apportionment of responsibility, so

---

223. *See* Statement of Alfred Cortese, May 10, 1990 hearing at 9–14, which provides a detailed history of the development of joint and several liability and indicates that the use of this doctrine has expanded well beyond its original intent.

224. *Id.* at notes 37–39 and accompanying text.

225. *Id.* at 16.

226. *See* Prosser and Keeton on Torts, *supra*, section 52 at 348–351.

that liability can be assigned based on that apportionment. The trier of fact shall make a determination as to apportionment without a requirement that any particular party "prove" which apportionment formula should be applied.

Responsibility should be apportioned for the purposes of this section among all persons who are parties to the action at the conclusion of the trial and persons who were parties to the action and have entered into settlement agreements with the claimant.[227] Courts should apply existing law with regard to the effect of settlement on the judgment and the settlor, but, for purposes of apportioning responsibility under subsection (b), the responsibility of the settlors who were parties should be included in the apportionment.

Section 306(c)(1) defines "noneconomic damages" for the purposes of section 308 and includes an illustrative, nonexhaustive list of examples.

Section 306(c)(2) provides that, for the purposes of this section, a product liability action includes "any action involving a claim, third-party claim, cross-claim, counterclaim, or contribution claim in a civil action in which a manufacturer or product seller is found liable for harm caused by a product." This subsection gives nonproduct liability defendants the protection of section 306 whether the product manufacturer or seller is an original party to the suit or brought in through impleader. To make the point explicit, the Committee included the words "third-party claim" in subsection (c)(2).

Section 306 limits the doctrine of joint and several liability as applied to noneconomic damages in product liability actions. This section, however, does not preempt other limitations on joint and several liability with respect to economic damages, which have been imposed by individual jurisdictions. Indeed, a number of jurisdictions have enacted more sweeping reform with respect to joint and several liability.[228] These reforms are in no way affected by the Committee's action.

SECTION 307—DEFENSES INVOLVING INTOXICATING ALCOHOL OR DRUGS

In general

Section 307 establishes a complete defense for manufacturers or product sellers in actions subject to the bill, if the claimant was under the influence of intoxicating alcohol or any drug and such condition was more than 50 percent responsible for the accident or event that resulted in the claimant's harm. Barring liability in such cases is

---

227. *See* Uniform Comparative Fault Act, Section 2, 12 U.L.A. 39 (Supp.1985); V. Schwartz, Comparative Negligence, *supra*, section 16.5 at 263–65.

228. *See* note 222, *supra*.

sound public policy. The use of intoxicating alcohol and drugs for nonmedicinal purposes by a person creates serious risks to the safety of such a person and to the safety of others. For example, drunk driving is a major cause of death on our highways. A person who impairs his or her ability to act safely should not be able to shift the cost of such risks on to the manufacturer or seller of a product used by such person and ultimately on to society itself. This rule will encourage persons to take responsibility for their own safety and the safety of others.

The Committee has chosen the rule that would require that a claimant be more than 50 percent responsible so there would be no question as to the principal cause of the harm—alcohol or drug use. In order to avoid the inequitable shifting of liability on to other codefendants, such as municipalities, the Committee also has made section 307 applicable only in cases where manufacturers or product sellers are subject to liability and no liability exists against those codefendants who are not manufacturers or product sellers.

Present law

The State of Washington has enacted tort legislation that establishes a complete defense to an action for damages for personal injury or wrongful death, if the person injured or killed *was* under the influence of intoxicating liquor or any drug and such condition contributed to more than 50 percent to his or her wrongful death.[229] This provision was included as part of Washington tort reform legislation that was enacted "in order to create a more equitable distribution of the cost and risk of injury and increase the availability and affordability of insurance."[230] A provision of this nature is an important component of federal product liability reform.

The very strong public policy underlying this rule justifies preemption of conflicting State laws—it is a national policy of overriding importance to the American public. Thus, if a State has pure comparative fault as its general rule of tort law, this provision will prevail if claimant was under the influence of alcohol or any drug and such condition was more than 50 percent responsible for the harm. On the other hand, if a State retains the contributory negligence defense and believes that a person's claim should be barred if the person's fault in any way contributed to his or her harm, this bill is not preemptive. It only addresses situations in which, currently, a person could bring a successful claim when such person was more than 50 percent responsible due to drugs or alcohol.

229. Wash.S.B. No. 4630, Sec. 902 (enacted March 10, 1986). The Washington Statute specifies that "If the amount of alcohol in a person's blood is shown by chemical analysis of his or her blood, breath, or other bodily substance to have been 0.10% or more by weight of alcohol in the blood, it is conclusive proof that that person was under the influence of intoxicating liquor."

230. Wash.S.B. No. 4630, Sec. 100.

COMMITTEE REPORT ON S. 640

As reported

Section 307(a) provides that in any civil action subject to this bill in which all defendants are manufacturers or product sellers, such defendants may assert as a complete defense that the claimant was under the influence of intoxicating alcohol or any drug and that such condition was more than 50 percent responsible for the accident or event that resulted in such claimant's harm. This complete defense to liability for manufacturers or product sellers only applies in cases in which all defendants are manufacturers or product sellers, because otherwise the result might be to release manufacturers or product sellers from liability, while leaving other defendants (such as municipalities) liable for the claimant's entire loss. While it is unjust for an intoxicated person who is primarily to blame for his or her own harm to recover in tort for his or her injuries, it would be still more unjust to release some defendants from liability in such a case while leaving others to bear the entire amount of damages.

Section 307(b) provides that in any civil action in which some, but not all, of the defendants are manufacturers or product sellers, and that the trier of fact determines that no liability exists against those defendants who are not manufacturers or product sellers, the court shall enter a judgment notwithstanding the verdict in favor of any defendant manufacturer or product seller, if it is proved that the claimant's intoxicated condition was more than 50 percent responsible for the accident or event which resulted in such claimant's harm. Thus, if a manufacturer or product seller was barred from invoking section 307(a) because of the presence of codefendants who were not manufacturers or product sellers, and those codefendants were not found to be liable, the manufacturer or product seller could still be released from liability pursuant to this provision.

Section 307(c)(1) provides that the determination of whether a person is under the influence of intoxicating alcohol shall be made pursuant to applicable State law. For example, if applicable State law provides that a particular amount of alcohol in a person's blood is evidence that the person was under the influence of intoxicating alcohol, that standard shall apply. Paragraph (2) of subsection (c) defines the term "drug" as any non-over-the-counter drug which has not been prescribed by a physician for use by the claimant.

ROLLCALL VOTES IN COMMITTEE

In accordance with paragraph 7(c) of rule XXVI of the Standing Rules of the Senate, the Committee provides the following description of the record votes during its consideration of S. 640:

Senator Hollings offered an amendment regarding the reporting of insurance data. By a rollcall vote of 10 yeas and 10 nays as follows, the amendment was defeated:

COMMITTEE REPORT ON S. 640

YEAS—10	NAYS—10
Mr. Hollings	Mr. Exon
Mr. Inouye	Mr. Rockefeller
Mr. Ford	Mr. Bentsen [1]
Mr. Gore	Mr. Robb
Mr. Kerry [1]	Mr. Danforth [1]
Mr. Breaux	Mr. Pressler
Mr. Bryan	Mr. Kasten
Mr. Packwood	Mr. McCain
Mr. Stevens	Mr. Burns
Mr. Gorton	Mr. Lott

[1] By proxy.

At the close of debate on S. 640, the Chairman announced a rollcall vote on the bill as amended. On a rollcall vote of 13 yeas and 7 nays as follows, the bill was ordered reported:

YEAS—13	NAYS—7
Mr. Inouye	Mr. Hollings
Mr. Exon [1]	Mr. Ford
Mr. Rockefeller	Mr. Gore
Mr. Bentsen [1]	Mr. Kerry [1]
Mr. Robb [1]	Mr. Breaux
Mr. Danforth [1]	Mr. Bryan
Mr. Pressler	Mr. Packwood
Mr. Stevens	
Mr. Kasten	
Mr. McCain	
Mr. Burns	
Mr. Gorton	
Mr. Lott	

[1] By proxy.

CHANGES IN EXISTING LAW

In compliance with paragraph 12 of rule XXVI of the Standing Rules of the Senate, the Committee states that the bill as reported would make no change to existing law.

ADDITIONAL VIEWS OF SENATORS EXON AND LOTT

We voted to report S. 640 the Product Liability Fairness Act of 1991. However, we have grave concerns about the implications to employers, particularly small business employers, of Section 305 known as the workers' compensation offset provision. Unlike other sections of the bill, this section does not directly involve product liability lawsuits. Rather, Section 305 involves the economic relations between employers and manufacturers in the aftermath of such lawsuits.

As it is still early in the legislative process for S. 640, we urge that Section 305 be given close further scrutiny with the hope that the concerns of employers, can be addressed. If those concerns cannot be addressed, we would urge that Section 305 be deleted from S. 640 in the interests of the overall legislation.

Our concerns are based on the fact that most State and Federal workers' compensation laws give employers the right to recover, through a subrogation lien, their workers' compensation expenses paid to employees injured by defective products, in cases where an injured employee successfully sues the product manufacturer. The benefit to employers of the system of workers' compensation subrogation liens under present laws is obvious. This system reduces the burden on the individual employer's workers' compensation costs, reduces the burden overall workers' compensation system, and thereby reduces the pressure for workers' compensation insurance rate increases. However, this system would change under Section 305 of S. 640, except in those situations where the employer had the financial ability to pursue a lien through the litigation process in the courts.

Not surprisingly then, the business community is not united in support for Section 305. Many business groups have expressed reservations or opposition to this section, including the National Federation of Independent Businesses (NFIB), the Associated General Contractors of America (AGC), the American Subcontractors Association (ASA), the Shipbuilders Council of America, and the National Association of Stevedores (NAS).

We urge that these problems arising from Section 305 be satisfactorily addressed prior to Senate floor consideration of S. 640.

MINORITY VIEWS OF SENATORS HOLLINGS AND GORE

INTRODUCTION

In the past, we have urged our colleagues to reject Federal product liability laws as unwise Federal legislation. Since then, the proponents of this legislation have had many years to make their case, and they have completely failed to do so. After this extended examination of the facts, we believe that, not only is this legislation unwise, but to enact it would amount to a complete distortion of the proper legislative process.

This measure would federalize an area of law that always has been the province of the States. Such an action should never be undertaken lightly. Those who propose such dramatic change through the legislative process should, at a minimum, bear the burden of proving that such change is both warranted and likely to be effective. Unfortunately, the Committee has ordered this bill reported without requiring anything close to a demonstration that either factor is present. On the contrary, the factual record clearly demonstrates that each stated basis for this legislation cannot withstand even minimal scrutiny. What is deeply disturbing about this legislation is the total lack of verifiable, objective data which supports the proponents' claims.

COMMITTEE REPORT ON S. 640

In fact, the stated basis for this legislation is a constantly moving target. A new reason that this bill is necessary is suggested periodically, the facts are examined, and that reason evaporates when exposed to the light of day and to the objective facts.

Contrary to the claims of the bill's supporters, the Committee's work on this issue has demonstrated that (1) there is no litigation explosion, and the number of most kinds of product liability cases is decreasing; (2) the insurance crisis (which has now ended) was not due to product liability; (3) the current system generally works properly to fairly compensate injured victims; (4) the competitive position of U.S. business is affected very little, if at all, by product liability; and (5) products kept off the market by product liability concerns are not necessarily safe, innovative products, but rather are examples of the product liability system deterring unwarranted risks to consumer. Each of the issues discussed above has been the basis, over the years, for the almost frenzied cry for Federal product liability law, but none of them withstands scrutiny.

This year, "competitiveness" is the buzz word on which the legislation is based. We are asked to pass this legislation to make U.S. business more competitive in world markets. However, these are the facts: less than 1 percent of the price of products is attributable to product liability; the Office of Technology Assessment (OTA) does not list product liability as a primary problem for U.S. manufacturers competing in world markets; this bill will not reduce product liability claims or insurance costs; our competitors in the European Community are moving toward a product liability system more like ours, which appropriately reflects the need for consumer protection; and the General Accounting Office (GAO) says that this bill will not reduce transaction costs, but could actually increase them. The facts show that product liability is not the cause of competitive problems, nor is this bill the cure.

This year the President's Council on Competitiveness, headed by Vice President Quayle, has added its voice to the fray. Using political rhetoric instead of objective reality, it has made unsupported or inaccurate claims about the civil justice system and particularly the costs of the tort system. The cost figures cited by the Vice President cite no credible authority and have no explanation for how they were calculated or what is included in the general term "tort costs." Yet those cost figures are the centerpiece of the Vice President's call for a major overhaul of the civil justice system. It is troubling that even the executive branch, like the business advocates of S. 640, would base its arguments for such a major change on unsubstantiated, arbitrary numbers.

The proponents of S. 640 have represented that this bill is not as draconian as earlier Federal product liability measures, and will not impact as drastically on consumers. First, it should be noted that, despite efforts to characterize this as a bill that will impact similarly on plaintiffs and defendants, it is written for the benefit of the business community, and in most areas changes only the laws of the States that currently favor plaintiffs. We should not misunderstand the purpose of this bill.

The current form of this bill gives us little comfort in any event, since the primary effect of this or any such measure would be to begin the federalization of product liability law. Once that process has begun, Congress will never hear the end of the clamor for additional changes in this law, and will be spending an ever-increasing portion of its working time on this issue. Moreover, the form of even this bill is not cast in stone until enactment into law, and the administration and others are already calling for more stringent amendments. In addition, many of the substantive provisions of this bill are unwise or unworkable and the bill is riddled with ambiguity and conflicts for court practice and procedure.

Supporters of this bill are fond of implying that its only enemies are trial lawyers. It is important to note who the opponents of this bill *really* are. It is opposed by every major consumer organization, a wide range of health organizations, the American Bar Association, the National Conference of State Legislatures, and the Conference of State Supreme Court Justices. Over 70 law professors from all over the country have written to the Committee in opposition to this bill, stating that it is "unwise, unfair and ill-conceived." (See letter to Chairman Hollings from Andrew Popper, Deputy Dean, Washington College of Law, dated September 27, 1991, reprinted in record of Consumer Subcommittee hearing on S. 640, September 19, 1991.) These are the experts in health, consumer protection, and legal jurisprudence. They are concerned not with fees, but with product safety, justice and the proper functioning of the legal system. So, it is not just the trial lawyers who are concerned about the bill's effects.

We are being asked to enact legislation when there has been no credible demonstration that there is a problem that will be addressed by that legislation. At the same time, enactment of such a law would alter, in one stroke, the fundamental federalism inherent in this country's tort law, and would add to the difficulties already faced by the victims of defective products.

We yield to no one in our desire to assist American business in every way, and to ensure its viability in ever-changing world markets. However, we urge our colleagues to insist, at a minimum, on some objective demonstration that Federal product liability law is a reasonable means to address the problems of the business community. We have not yet seen such a demonstration, and in our view the legislative process is ill-served by taking such dramatic action in these circumstances. Legislative proposals of this type have been much ado about nothing for over a decade, but the "much ado" has been a considerable drain on the limited resources of the Congress. We have very limited time, and we must insure that it is spent on work that can be most productive for the nation. It is time to recognize where the burden of proof on this issue lies, to recognize that it has not been met despite 10 years of work, and to turn the resources of the Committee and the Senate to work on other more useful matters.

In the discussion below, we will set out in more detail the facts that have been developed on this issue. These facts demonstrate why we should not move forward on this bill.

THERE IS NO FACTUAL BASIS FOR THIS LEGISLATION

I. The Current System Achieves Fair Results, and There Is No "Explosion" of Litigation

Before we make dramatic changes in the product liability law, we should, at the least, have information to demonstrate that the current system needs fixing—that it is not achieving its purpose of fairly and properly compensating victims of defective products, and of deterring the marketing of unsafe products. As each additional piece of objective data becomes available, it becomes more clear that the system is working. The number of nonasbestos product liability cases is actually declining, punitive damages are a rare occurrence, and the compensatory awards are reasonably related to the cost of the injuries involved.

Prof. Marc Galanter of the University of Wisconsin Law School has completed the most recent review of statistics from the Federal courts, and found that, if asbestos cases are excluded, the number of product liability cases in the Federal courts has declined in the last 5 years— from 8,268 cases in 1985 to 4,992 in 1991, a 40–percent decrease.[1] He points out that asbestos filings account for all recent increases in product liability filings, and that asbestos cases are quite distinct in that they involve a product of "unparalleled deadliness to which there was massive exposure that continued long after the dangers of its use were suspected and suppressed."[2]

Moreover, the Rand Corp. this year issued a report reviewing the way in which victims of accidental injuries are compensated and found, contrary to popular belief, that only 10 percent of those injured ever use the tort system at all to seek compensation for their injuries.[3] The

---

1. Testimony of Professor Marc Galanter, Director, Institute of Legal Studies, University of Wisconsin Law School, before the Consumer Subcommittee September 19, 1991, transcript at 86–87. *See also* Galanter and Rogers, "A Transformation of American Business Disputing? Some Preliminary Observations," working paper # DPRP 10–3, Institute for Legal Studies, University of Wisconsin (April 1991).

2. Galanter testimony, *supra*, transcript at 88.

3. Hensler, et al., "Compensation for Accidental Injuries in the United States," Rand Corporation, Institute for Civil Jus-

report further found that only 7 percent of all compensation for accident victims is paid through the tort system. The report concluded that "[m]ost Americans who are injured in accidents do not turn to the liability system for compensation. * * * In this respect, Americans' behavior does not accord with the more extreme characterizations of litigiousness that have been put forward by some." [4]

Similarly, the National Center for State Courts recently published updated statistics from State courts that reviewed civil court filings in 13 general jurisdiction State court systems from 1984–89. The Center concluded that "the most dramatic increases in the civil caseload tended to be for real property rights cases or contract cases, not torts." [5] These statistics showed that tort filings make up less than 1 percent of all cases filed in State courts, and less than 10 percent of most States' civil caseload. Product liability cases, which are a subset of tort cases, would make up an even smaller percentage of the total.[6]

As Professor Galanter also has found, the real increase in litigation in recent years has been business suing business, not consumers seeking compensation through product liability litigation. For example, contract filings in Federal courts increased by 232 percent between 1960–88, and by 1988 were the largest category of civil cases in the Federal courts.[7]

Additionally, GAO last year completed one of the first extensive reviews of data related to State court product liability cases.[8] Since most product liability cases are litigated in State court, and most of the past data has been only from the Federal courts, this report is very significant. GAO found that the size of compensatory awards varied by type and severity of injury in a manner consistent with underlying economic loss, so that compensatory awards were neither erratic nor excessive.[9] It further found that plaintiffs won fewer than 50 percent of the cases litigated, that awards were based on negligence in almost three-quarters of the cases (even in the States that permit recovery based on strict liability without a demonstration of negligence), and that the amount of punitive damages awarded was highly correlated with the size of compensatory damages.[10]

Another significant research effort concludes that, even if product liability cases could be characterized as unfairly favoring plaintiffs in

tice (1991), Executive Summary at 18. *See also* testimony of Dr. Deborah Hensler, Consumer Subcommittee hearing on S. 640, September 12, 1991, statement at 6.

4. *Id.*, Executive Summary at 18, 20.

5. National Center for State Courts, "State Court Caseload Statistics: Annual Report 1989," (February 1991) at 46.

6. State Court Caseload Statistics, *supra* n. 5, at 45–6.

7. Galanter and Rogers, "A Transformation of American Business Disputing?," *supra*, at 1, 5–6.

8. U.S. General Accounting Office, "Product Liability: Verdicts and Case Resolution in Five States," GAO/HRD–89–99 (September 1989). Hereafter referred to as "1989 GAO Report."

9. *Id.* at 27.

10. *Id.* at 29–31.

the past, the current trend is clearly favoring defendants. Prof. James A. Henderson Jr. and Prof. Theodore Eisenberg of Cornell Law School performed an extensive study of all reported product liability decisions and found a "quiet revolution * * * away from extending the boundaries of products liability and toward placing significant limitations on plaintiffs rights to recover in tort for product-related injuries." [11] Specifically, they found that in 1976 and continuing to 1983, defendants benefited in roughly 51 percent of product liability cases. By 1988, the figure had risen by 12.2 percent, so that defendants prevailed in 63.4 percent of product liability cases.

Similarly, GAO [12] and Rand Corp. [13] studies have indicated that, despite increases in absolute numbers of Federal product liability filings during the 1970s and 1980s, the data does not support the suggestion, made in past years, that there is an "explosion" of product liability cases from which business must be protected. Rather, GAO found that one product, asbestos, accounting for approximately 60 percent of the growth in filings between 1976-86. [14] GAO further found that, since 1981, product liability cases have grown at about the same rate as other civil filings and at the same rate as personal expenditures on goods, with growth of product liability cases at 4 percent, personal expenditures on goods at 4 percent, and civil filings at 6 percent. [15] The author of the Rand study has stated that "[m]y feeling is that the available evidence doesn't support the notion that products liability is crippling American business." [16]

Prof. Lawrence Mann from Wayne State University Law School performed a similar study for the Governor of Michigan in 1988-89. He began by noting that "* * * much of the debate surrounding products liability litigation has been based upon anecdote and intuition. Hard data describing the products liability litigation landscape are scarce." He conducted his research by surveying over 2,000 businesses as well as attorneys of record in closed cases for the year 1987. His general conclusion was that "[v]erdicts and settlements in products liability cases are not erratic and appear reasonably related to economic losses sustained and injury severity." [17]

---

11. Henderson and Eisenberg, "The Quiet Revolution in Products Liability: An Empirical Study of Legal Change," 37 U.C.L.A. Law Review 479, 480 (1990).

12. U.S. General Accounting Office, "Product Liability: Extent of 'Litigation Explosion' in Federal Courts Questioned," GAO/HRD-88-36BR (January 1988).

13. Dugworth, "Product Liability and the Business Sector: Litigation Trends in Federal Courts," Rand Corporation, The Institute for Civil Justice, R-3668-ICJ (1988).

14. GAO Report, supra, note 12, at 32, 43.

15. Id. at 32, 43.

16. Wall Street Journal, "Survey Questions Liability Crisis at U.S. Companies," January 18, 1989.

17. Testimony of Professor Lawrence C. Mann, Wayne State University School of Law, Consumer Subcommittee Hearing on S. 1400, February 22, 1990, statement at 1-2.

His research found a "phenomenal concentration of litigation among a handful of defendants who are 'repeat players' in civil litigation." In 1987, four companies accounted for 92 percent of the cases filed. In 1982, four companies accounted for 91 percent of the cases filed, and in 1979, four companies accounted for 83 percent.[18]

Professor Mann concluded that " * * * fewer and fewer litigants are accounting for an increasing share of the litigation pie." He further found that " * * * the distribution of cases filed for the years covered in the * * * survey yield a picture of products litigation that is inconsistent with the conclusion that the business community in general is the victim of a products liability explosion."[19]

Additionally, according to one study by the Insurance Services office approximately 73 percent of the bodily injury claims and 83 percent of the property damage claims are settled without the filing of a lawsuit. Only 3.5 percent of claims go all the way to a court verdict, and in these cases, fewer than 25 percent of defendants are found liable. Thus, according to this study, 96.5 percent of product liability claims are resolved before the verdict.[20]

Much has been made of the unpredictability of results in product liability trials. However, it has been recognized, as it must be, that most of this is due to our jury system.[21] We cannot believe any of our colleagues want to tamper with that system. When a product liability case goes to trial, the jury is not impaneled for the purpose of giving away someone else's money. Rather it is charged with the administration of justice. These juries are composed of our friends and neighbors, who conclude, some of the time, that the defective products involved and the injuries sustained require compensation. And it is our friends and neighbors—who work for a living and know the value of a dollar—who occasionally conclude that punitive damages are justified when the defendant has engaged in outrageous behavior.

In addition, with respect to punitive damages, the extent to which they are awarded has been the subject of outrageous exaggeration. Much new data is available on punitive damages, which shows, among other things, that very few punitive damage awards have been made in all State and Federal product liability cases over the last 25 years. Punitive damages simply are not a factor in any but the rare product

---

18. *Id.*, at Report to the Governor of Michigan 2.

19. *Id.* at Report to Governor 1, 2.

20. See Insurance Services Office Product Liability Closed Claim Survey: A Technical Analysis of Survey Results at 95 (1977); 1986 Hearings on Product Liability, before the Consumer Subcommittee, 99th Cong. 2nd Session (Statement of the Public Citizen's Congress Watch, Consumers Union, U.S. Public Interest Research Group, Consumer Federation of America). Testimony on file at Senate Committee on Commerce, Science, and Transportation.

21. See Testimony of Peter Huber, Consumer Subcommittee Hearing on S. 1400, April 5, 1990, transcript at 119, 141; testimony of Professor Mark Hager, Consumer Subcommittee Hearing on S. 1400, April 5, 1990 transcript at 137.8.

liability case, and have little effect on the business community. Dr. Stephen Daniels of the American Bar Foundation conducted a nationwide study of over 25,000 civil jury awards between 1981 and 1985. He concluded that the debate over punitive damages "changed in the 1980s as a part of an intense, well-organized, and well-financed political campaign by interest groups seeking fundamental reforms in the civil justice system benefiting themselves." He went on to state that this "politicization of the punitive damages debate * * * makes the debate more emotional and manipulative, and less reasoned. The reformers appeal to emotions, fear, and anxiety in this political effort while avoiding reason and rational discourse."[22]

His review of the data on punitive damage awards found that punitive damages were not routinely awarded, were awarded typically in modest amounts, and were awarded more often in financial and property harm cases [business v. business] than in product liability cases.[23] His research also pointed up the errors in the data from Cook County, IL, and San Francisco, CA, which have in the past been used by supporters of bills like S. 640 as indicative of the nationwide pattern on punitive damages. He found that there were flaws in the method of data analysis used, and that it was inappropriate in any event to generalize from data in two counties to a nationwide trend.[24]

Dr. Daniels' findings were similar to those by Professor Michael Rustad of Suffolk University Law School and Prof. Thomas Koening of Northeastern University. They reviewed all product liability awards from 1965–90 in both State and Federal courts. During that time, punitive damages were awarded in only 355 cases—only 355 total punitive awards in 25 years! One-quarter of those awards involved one product—asbestos. Another one-quarter of those cases was reversed or remanded upon appeal. He further found that the amount of punitive damage awards were not skyrocketing, and in 35 percent of the cases in which punitive damages were awarded they were less than the amount of compensatory damages. He concluded that "[t]here is a widespread misperception that punitive damage awards are skyrocketing because of frivolous lawsuits * * *."[25]

By reviewing the data representative of the entire system, as opposed to the few anecdotes of high damage awards often cited by the supporters of this bill, we see that the system is not out of control in terms of numbers of cases filed or amount of compensation awarded. It

22. Daniels and Martin, "Myth and Reality in Punitive Damages," 75 Minn.Law Review 1, 10–12 (Oct.1990). See also testimony of Dr. Stephen Daniels, Consumer Subcommittee Hearing on S. 640, September 12, 1991, transcript at 122.
23. 74 Minn.L.Rev., supra, at 43.
24. Id. at 22–27.

25. Rustad and Koenig, "Demystifying the Functions of Punitive Damages in Products Liability: An Empirical Study of a Quarter Century of Verdicts," Executive Summary at 11–15, 1. See also testimony of Professor Michael Rustad, Consumer Subcommittee Hearing on S. 640, September 19, 1991, transcript at 74–78.

also is important to note the beneficial aspects of the current system that stand to be undermined if this bill is enacted, as discussed below.

II. The Current System Promotes Product Safety

One of the primary effects of the current system is to promote product safety—to make manufacturers more careful in the design and production of their products. We know this because manufacturers themselves have told us. The 1987 Conference Board survey of risk managers of corporations found that "[w]here product liability has had a notable impact—where it has most significantly affected management decisionmaking—has been in the quality of the products themselves. Managers say products have become safer, manufacturing procedures have been improved, and labels and use instructions have become more explicit." [26]

Indeed, according to the Consumer Federation of America (CFA), only a small minority of companies had a product safety management position in the early 1970s. By the end of the 1970s, virtually all companies had a very strong product safety presence in their management structure. CFA further stated that there has been a dramatic change in the rate of accidental injuries and deaths in the United States, so that "approximately 6,000 deaths and millions of injuries have been prevented on an annual basis now because of product liability and other forces toward greater safety in our society." [27]

Moreover, Professor Rustad in his survey of punitive damage awards found that 190 of the 252 nonasbestos defendants who were subject to punitive damage awards between 1969 and 1990 "have taken some safety step in the wake of punitive damages litigation. In 80 percent of these cases, there were steps such as fortified warnings, product withdrawals, and safety features added to products which followed shortly after the [litigation]." [28]

A similar finding was made by Prof. Nicholas Ashford and Prof. Robert Stone of MIT, in work done for inclusion in "The Liability Maze," and a collection of articles on product liability, innovation, and safety. This book is often mischaracterized by proponents of S. 640 as a monolithic study reaching results supportive of their position. Rather, it is a collection of research articles reaching various conclusions on the issue of innovation and safety in assorted industries.

Professors Ashford and Stone researched the effect of product liability on the chemical industry. They found that manufacturers pay "no more than 5 percent, and often less than 0.1 percent, of the

---

26. "Product Liability: The Corporate Response," The Conference Board Report No. 893 (1987) at 2.

27. Testimony of Gene Kimmelman, Legislative Director, Consumer Federation of America, at Consumer Subcommittee Hearing on S. 1400, April 5, 1990, transcript at 77–78.

28. Rustad, *supra*, executive summary at 28.

corresponding social costs" of the chronic injuries caused by chemicals.[29] They concluded that, although the system is not stringent enough on the manufacturers to provide appropriate deterrence to prevent all unsafe products, it still has helped in the development of safer products. They recommend, however, that if the liability system were more, not less, stringent with respect to manufacturers it would be even more effective in promoting safety and innovation.[30]

The editor of "The Liability Maze," Peter Huber, has suggested that the work by Professors Ashford and Stone is somehow unique. However, Professor Ashford has responded that he and other authors of the book found it impossible to separate innovation and safety, and found that "the liability system can both promote safety and innovation of desirable products and discourage unsafe products though they may be innovative." Professor Ashford goes on to state that "we believe most scholars would subscribe to our methodology * * * "[31]

The effect of product liability in promoting product safety relates not only to consumer protection, but to competitiveness. As Prof. Mark Hager of American University testified,

> * * * our products, because of their superior reputation for safety, due in part to the effects of product liability over the last 20 years, have a superior reputation in the international marketplace. * * * [W]e cannot compete at this time with the low labor costs of newly industrializing countries, but we can compete very effectively * * * in safety, and it would be a grave risk to our international competitiveness to toy with the tort system that helps bring about that competitive advantage.[32]

III. The Current System Promotes Important Principles of Federalism

The value of the principles of federalism embodied in our current system of tort law should not be overlooked. As Congressman Mike Box, of the Alabama House of Representatives, has testified:

> [t]he issues of proper compensation for injured persons and suitable protections for businesses are matters of social values and public policy that should be addressed at the state level, in the absence of a national economic crisis. * * * Arguments for uniform laws as a means of promoting competitiveness ignore the advantages of a decentralized and federal system of civil justice. * * * Remember why we developed as a federal nation * * * Our founding fathers

---

29. Ashford and Stone, "Liability, Innovation, and Safety in the Chemical Industry," in *The Liability Maze* (Brookings 1991) at 414.

30. *Id.* at 415–417.

31. Letter from Professor Nicholas Ashford to Senator Ernest Hollings, October 1, 1991, submitted for the record of the Consumer Subcommittee Hearing on S. 640, September 19, 1991.

32. Testimony of Professor Mark Hager, Assistant Professor of Law, Washington College of Law, American University, at Consumer Subcommittee Hearing on S. 1400, April 5, 1990, transcript at 126.

recognized the importance of having governments responsive to the electorate. Broad powers were reserved to the states so they would serve as bulwarks of freedom, an antidote to an overpowering national government. * * * S. 1400 [the identical predecessor to S. 640] is radical because it opens the door to substantially greater federal intrusions.[33]

These concerns were reiterated at this year's Subcommittee hearing by Delegate Bernard Cohen on behalf of the National Conference of State Legislatures. Delegate Cohen pointed out that Federal "preemption should not occur unless it could be proved that the variation in State laws is significantly impeding commerce among the States and unless the specific legislative response is the only way to resolve the conflict. * * * [T]his burden has not been met with respect to product liability laws." Delegate Cohen went on to note that, not only had the burden of proof not been met, but "the basic rationale for this bill, the underlying rationale for it, is fallacious."[34]

Professor Eisenberg from Cornell Law School also has raised these concerns, and pointed out the practical problem with Federal tort law that we believe should provoke serious concern.

> The changing nature of products liability law make me cautious about wishing for Congress to implement a single rule. For the rule Congress adopts had better be a good one, since it may preempt further experimentation and change by the states. I see no basis for believing that the rules embodied in S. 1400 [predecessor to S. 6401] are superior to the collection of rules embodied in various state laws and to the ability of the states to adopt the best rules of their sister states, as those rules evolve over time. The one thing we do know is that state product law does change. I worry that Congress may freeze the law with the wrong set of rules at a time when there is no clear reason to [do so].[35]

We have the same concern. We are constantly surprised that some are willing to take their chances with Congress setting the rules over the long haul. Such an effort would limit flexibility, and could eventually result in rules more oriented toward plaintiffs than those the states would craft. In any event, we only should tinker with the fundamental principles of federalism in the most extreme circumstances—a record such as we have on this issue is insufficient to take such action.

---

33. Testimony of Rep. Mike Box, Alabama House of Representatives, at Consumer Subcommittee Hearing on S. 1400, April 5, 1990, Statement at 1–3.

34. Testimony of Delegate Bernard Cohen, Virginia House of Delegates, Consumer Subcommittee Hearing on S. 640, September 12, 1991, transcript at 85–86; 87.

35. Testimony of Professor Theodore Eisenberg, Professor of Law, Cornell University, in response to post hearing questions of Senator Rockefeller, from Consumer Subcommittee Hearing on S. 1400, April 5, 1990, at 2.

IV. The Current System Did Not Cause The Insurance "Crisis"

In past years, the cry for product liability law has been based on a "crisis" in the availability and price of insurance. That argument has become nonexistent, since virtually everyone agrees that insurance is now generally available and well-priced—we are in a "soft" market.[36] Even before that occurred, however, it was clear that the product liability system was not responsible for insurance availability problems.

The primary allegations concerning the existence and magnitude of this crisis have proved vastly exaggerated. In 1976, the Federal Government created a Federal Interagency Task Force on Product Liability (hereinafter the Task Force) to examine the problem. The Insurance Study commissioned by the Task Force found that, while insurance costs did increase in the mid-1970s, insurance premiums exceeded 1 percent of the total sales for only three industries.[37]

By 1983, evidence indicated that product liability insurance costs had stabilized or decreased, and that the insurance crisis had disappeared. A 1983 Institute for Civil Justice study concluded not only that reports of a product liability crisis in the mid-1970s were greatly exaggerated, but that even the perception of a crisis had receded because it had become evident that product liability claims had not imposed unreasonable costs on most manufacturers.[38] Costs increased and availability decreased again in the mid-1980s.

The increases in product liability insurance costs were a result not of product liability but of the cyclical nature of the insurance industry and the industry's ratemaking practices. The Congressional Research Service (CRS) has described the repeating cycles of high and low premiums as an historical alternation between soft and hard insurance markets, and has discussed the management practices of the companies which contribute to this cycle. In a soft market, rates are adequate, and risk selection careful, and the industry generally performs well. New capital is attracted from a number of sources and capacity increases. Price cutting of premiums results when new sources of capacity begin to generate increased competition for available premium volume. Underwriting standards (the standards for deciding whether to insure a particular manufacturer) for risk selection diminish with increased competition, and insurers take on riskier business endeavors. According to CRS, this practice results in rising claims losses.

---

36. *See* Testimony of J. Robert Hunter, President, National Insurance Consumers Organization, Consumer Subcommittee Hearing on S. 1400, April 5, 1990, transcript at 133-4; testimony of Deborah Ballen, Vice President, American Insurance Association, Consumer Subcommittee Hearing on S. 1400, April 5, 1990.

37. U.S. Department of Commerce, Interagency Task Force on Product Liability, Final Report VI-20 (1977) [hereinafter cited as Task Force Final Report].

38. Rand Corporation, The Institute for Civil Justice, "Designing Safer Products: Corporate Responses to product Liability Law and Regulation 121" (1983) [hereinafter cited as Designing Safer Products].

At the point that competition is severe and that losses are too high, insurers withdraw from the market and the capacity shrinks, resulting in a hard market. Availability and affordability problems ensue as the remaining insurers raise prices and tighten the underwriting standards. Eventually the market stabilizes, a soft market emerges, and the cycle begins again.[39]

Interest rates, which reached historic heights in the late 1970s, aggravated the cycle. Companies engaged in price wars in order to obtain a larger volume of premium income for investment.[40] Basically, companies were willing to accept lower premiums for certain insurance lines in order to encourage sales and obtain funds for investments.[41]

On February 19 and March 4, 1986, the Committee held hearings to conduct a more comprehensive examination of the availability and cost of liability insurance. Testimony was presented at hearings on the reasons for the insurance crisis. Witnesses noted that the insurance crisis has arisen during a period of falling interest rates, prior to which competing insurance companies had been underpricing their product in order to maximize cashflow and enhance investment income. When interest rates began to fall, companies were forced to increase premiums because investment income was no longer compensating for underwriting losses. The Committee report accompanying S. 2129, the Risk Retention Amendments of 1986, states that "[t]his practice of cashflow underwriting was linked directly to the current crisis."[42]

GAO testified in May 1986 before the Consumer Subcommittee that the underwriting cycle turned again and "is now moving in a positive direction." The property/casualty industry will enjoy "an expected net gain before taxes of more than $90 billion over the years 1986–90."

GAO also found a profitable industry over the last 10 years, stating that "the property/casualty companies have used a pricing strategy which sacrificed underwriting profit margins in order to generate cash for investment purposes. As a result of the strategy, the property/casualty industry has made between $52 and $79 billion in net gains over the last 10 years."[43]

---

39. *See* Congressional Research Service, "Property–Casualty Insurance Market Operation", CRS Report No. 85–629E (March 20, 1985).

40. *See* "A Rate War Rips Casualty Insurers," Business Week, December 8, 1980.

41. Hearing on Product Liability before the Consumer Subcommittee, 99th Cong.2d Sess. (1986) (hereafter cited as 1986 Product Liability Hearing). (Statement of Johnny C. Finch, Senior Associate Director, General Government Division General Account Office) (Testimony on file at Senate Committee on Commerce, Science, and Transportation).

42. S.Rep. No. 294, 99th Cong., 2nd Sess. 4 (1986).

43. 1986 Hearing on Product Liability, *supra* note 25 (Statement of Johnny C. Finch, Senior Associate Director, General Government Division General Account Office) (Testimony on file at Senate Committee on Commerce, Science, and Transportation).

The irony of the continuing debate over a Federal product liability bill is that insurance costs were emphasized by the proponents as the reason for passage of a Federal product liability bill in the 96th and 97th Congresses when premiums were high, and were deemphasized as a reason for passage of product liability legislation during the 98th Congress when insurance premiums were reduced. In the 99th Congress, the proponents again pointed to the high premiums as a justification for a Federal bill, but these arguments have disappeared in the 101st and 102nd Congresses.

V. *Product Liability Is Not A Major Factor in The Competitiveness of U.S. Business*

This year's stated reason for this legislation is that product liability inhibits the ability of U.S. business to compete in world markets and to market innovative products. The facts are to the contrary.

OTA has recently completed a study of the competitiveness of U.S. manufacturers.[44] The study concluded that American manufacturing clearly is being challenged by competitors, particularly from Japan, and that there is no single solution. However, the recommended policy options for Government activity to address this challenge did not include Federal product liability law. Rather, OTA listed as the four most important steps that the United States could take to improve competitiveness: (1) lower the cost of capital; (2) improve the quality of human resources through education and quality of workforce; (3) improve the diffusion of manufacturing technology to small- and medium-sized business; and (4) provide Government funding of risky but promising long-term research and development.[45]

Additionally, in 1987, the Conference Board surveyed risk managers of 232 major U.S. manufacturing, trade, and service corporations about the effect of product liability on their companies.[46] Risk managers are the corporate employees that have the greatest corporate responsibility for addressing product liability issues—40 percent, as compared to a 6-percent responsibility by Chief Executive Officers (CEOs).[47] Two-thirds of the risk managers said that product liability contributed 1 percent or less to the final prices of their products. For another 11 percent of the companies, the liability cost was only 2 to 3 percent of the final price.[48] Additionally, most of the companies surveyed said that the area in which product liability had most significant-

---

44. U.S. Congress, Office of Technology Assessment, "Making Things Better: Competing in Manufacturing," OTA–ITE–443 (Washington, D.C.: U.S. Government Printing Office, February 1990).

45. Testimony of Dr. Julie Fox Gorte, Office of Technology Assessment, Consumer Subcommittee Hearing on S. 1400, April 5, 1990 at transcript pp. 61–2.

46. Weber, "Product Liability: The Corporate Response," The Conference Board, Report No. 893 (1987).

47. *Id.* at v.

48. *Id.* at 13.

ly altered management decision-making was in the quality of the products themselves.[49]

GAO made similar findings in a 1988 report on the issue.[50] GAO found that insurance costs represented a relatively small proportion of businesses' annual gross receipts—0.6 percent for large businesses, and about 1 percent for small businesses.[51]

The Institute for Civil Justice of the Rand Corp. concluded in 1983 that product liability costs in most cases were only a minute percentage of costs to business:

> It appears safe to conclude that for most large manufacturing firms, product liability costs—including the cost of defending litigation and certain product liability prevention activities—probably amount to much less than 1 percent of total sales revenue.[52]

Also, the Rand Corp. has found that only a small percentage of U.S. manufacturers are even involved in product liability litigation. In 1986, only 0.9 percent of all manufacturing concerns in the United States were defendants in product liability litigation.[53]

The only claims to the contrary regarding the competitiveness of business are based on self-serving anecdote or unsupported claims. For example, the Vice President's Council on Competitiveness has claimed that the cost of the tort system is crippling U.S. business, using various dollar amounts for the total cost of the system. Upon scrutiny, these dollar amounts are completely without factual basis.

The Vice President asserted that the "direct" costs of the tort system are $80 billion per year, and that indirect costs were considerably higher. The "authority" cited for that figure is Forbes magazine, which in turn cited no authority. The figure can be located in only one other place we have been able to uncover—Peter Huber's book, "Liability: The Legal Revolution and Its Consequences." However, as an analysis of this book for the Stanford Law Review points out, this number was simply lifted from a comment made by Robert Malott, Chairman of the Business Roundtable's product liability task force and CEO of the FMC Corporation, in the 1986 issue of Chief Executive magazine. Mr. Malott was quoted as saying, "insurance liability costs industry about $80 billion per year" with no documentation for that remark.[54] These "authorities" speak for themselves about the extent to

---

49. *Id.* at 2.
50. U.S. General Accounting Office, "Liability Insurance: Effects of Recent 'Crisis' on Businesses and Other Organizations," GAO/HRD–88–64 (July 1988).
51. *Id.* at 5.
52. Designing Safer Products, *supra*, note 22 at 121.
53. Dugworth, "Product Liability and the Business Sector: Litigation Trends in Federal Courts," *supra*, at 53–56.
54. Hager, "Civil Compensation and Its Discontents: A Response to Huber," 42 Stanford L.Rev. 539, 547–550 (January 1990).

COMMITTEE REPORT ON S. 640

which we should rely on these estimates in deciding to overhaul the civil justice system.

The only other discordant note in the general agreement that product liability has a very small impact on business comes from a 1988 Conference Board survey of 500 chief executive officers of corporations, 42 percent of whom stated that product liability had a major impact on them.[55] Some components of the Conference Board apparently were dissatisfied with the results of their 1987 survey, cited above, which did not support their theory of product liability. So, they decided to ask different people, in hopes of a different result. This is virtually the only piece of information cited by the supporters of this legislation for the proposition that product liability affects competitiveness.[56]

However, as Prof. Theodore Eisenberg of Cornell Law School has stated with respect to this survey, " * * * the case for reducing defendant liability seemed rather weak. It depended in large part on a survey of CEOs in which they were asked whether products liability was a problem for their companies. The flaws in such a survey are so substantial and obvious that no self-respecting legislature should act on the basis of the results."[57] We could not have said it better ourselves. We cannot responsibly move forward on this legislation based on a self-serving survey of corporate executives, particularly when it is contrary to all other data. The data demonstrates that the actual impact of product liability on businesses' bottom line is very small.

What is truly troubling about this debate over competitiveness is not the effect of the tort system on business, but the total lack of reliable information on which this competitiveness claim is based. As Dr. Deborah Hensler of the Rand Corp. testified, "[p]roduct liability litigation has been a source of controversy and public policy debate for almost a decade in this institution. I think it is remarkable that we still lack very basic information about the extent and nature of that litigation and the costs of resolving claims."[58]

When the debate on this bill first began in this Congress, the supporters declared that the product liability system must be altered because of the changes taking place in the European Economic Community (EEC). It was argued that the EEC was moving toward a uniform product liability system, and the United States must do the same. It also was argued that other countries in the world had lower product liability costs than the United States, implying that this country should

---

55. McGuire, "The Impact of Product Liability," The Conference Board, Report No. 908 (1988).

56. *See, e.g.,* Testimony of Wendell Wilkie, General Counsel, Department of Commerce, Consumer Subcommittee Hearing on S. 1400, February 22, 1990.

57. Responses of Professor Theodore Eisenberg, Professor of Law, Cornell University, to post-hearing questions of Senator Rockefeller, April 10, 1990, response to question 1.

58. Testimony of Dr. Deborah Hensler, Consumer Subcommittee, September 12, 1991, hearing, transcript at 106.

somehow emulate those other systems. However, like so many arguments on this issue, when the facts were examined, the argument disappeared.

The Council of the European Communities issued a directive in 1985 "concerning liability for defective products."[59] Despite the August 1, 1988, compliance deadline in the directive, only five member states—the United Kingdom, Italy, Greece, Luxembourg, and Denmark—had adopted the Directive as of March 15, 1990.[60] More significantly, the Directive by its terms does *not* preempt existing law in the various countries, but merely provides an additional cause of action in those countries in which remedies for harm already exist, and therefore is not likely to establish a more uniform system. As Prof. Lawrence Mann of Wayne State University School of Law testified, "[the Directive] is not in derogation of each member state's substantive tort law. And so, side by side, they will have a dual system operating."[61] Additionally, while the Directive establishes certain rules of law, it leaves many issues optional with the member states.[62]

Equally interesting, it is apparent that the EEC is moving toward a system of substantive product liability that is more consumer-oriented than that which is currently in place, and more like that in the United States. For example, its directive introduces the concept of strict liability for defective products,[63] expands the scope of potential defendants,[64] and institutes joint and several liability.[65] Since product liability is being expanded, insurance premiums are likely to go up, with an accompanying significant additional cost for producers in the EEC.[66]

Thus, the EEC Directive does not provide an incentive for changing U.S. product liability law. Rather, it is a recognition of the value of current U.S. law in protecting consumers and promoting safe products. As Wendell Wilkie, General Counsel of the Department of Commerce, has testified, " * * * the protection [other countries] afford their consumers is so radically smaller than is the case in this country [that] the disparity in the costs associated between our system and theirs is inordinately great. * * * "[67] We do not believe we should sacrifice the

---

59. 28 O.J.Eur.Comm. (No. L 210) 29 (1985) (hereafter cited as "Directive".).

60. Letter of Robert C. Holland, Committee for Economic Development, to Senator Richard Bryan, Chairman, Consumer Subcommittee, dated March 15, 1990, in response to post-hearing questions at 1.

61. *See* Directive, Article 13; Testimony of Professor Lawrence D. Mann, Wayne State College of Law, Consumer Subcommittee Hearing on S. 1400, February 22, 1990, transcript, p. 167.

62. *See, e.g.* Dielmann, "The European Economic Community's Council Directive on Product Liability," *The International Lawyer,* Vol. 20, No. 4, 1391 at 1400 (1986).

63. Directive, Article 1.

64. Directive, Article 3. *See also* Theiffry, Doorn, and Lowe, "The Single European Market: A Practitioner's Guide to 1992," 7 B.C.Int'l & Comp.L.Rev. 357 at 383.

65. Directive, Article 5. *See also,* Thieffry, Doorn and Lowe, *supra,* at 383.

66. Dielmann, *supra,* at 1399.

67. Testimony of Wendell Wilkie, General Counsel, Department of Commerce, at

greater degree of consumer protection we enjoy for some unsubstantiated hope of greater competitiveness.

It also has been argued that product liability costs are much higher in the United States than in the countries of some of our foreign competitors. However, a direct comparison of the costs of the tort systems in various countries, without more, is not valid because it ignores other types of compensation systems available in other countries. For example, in the Netherlands several social insurance programs are available which may preempt the need for compensation through the litigation process—the ZW/Sick Statute; the ZFW/Sick Fund Law; the WAO/Workers Disability Act of 1967; the AAW/General Act on Disability of Work; and the AWBZ/General Act on Special Medical Costs. The ZW is funded by collecting 5 percent of employers' gross income and 1 percent of employees' gross income. An injured employee may receive up to 70 percent of earned wages for 1 year. AAW and WAO continue funding if further assistance is needed.[68]

Moreover, the tax burden on business in the various countries must be included in any calculus of the relative competitive status of business. Taxes on business are higher in virtually every advanced country than they are in the United States.[69]

Thus, while business' costs related directly to the tort system may be lower in other countries, the relevant comparison is between the overall cost of compensation, which is likely to be similar to that in the United States. The proof of the fact that U.S. laws do not unduly burden companies doing business here is that foreign businesses are increasingly trying to locate here. In fact, foreign direct investment in the United States has increased from $83 billion in 1980 to $530 billion in 1990.[70] They would not do that if the tort system were the crippling burden that has been suggested by the proponents of S. 640.

It is clear that the facts do not support this contention that the current product liability system puts American businesses at a competitive disadvantage. If we are going to legislate to assist American business, we should do it in a way that will be effective, and S. 640 will not be.

VI. S. 640 Will Not Reduce Product Liability Costs for Business

Even if we assume that product liability is a significant barrier to the ability of U.S. firms to compete in world markets, that barrier

---

Consumer Subcommittee Hearing on S. 1400, February 22, 1990, transcript p. 30.

68. Mann and Rodrigues, "The European Directive on Products Liability: The Promise of Progress?" 18 Ga.J.Int'l & Comp.L. 391, 416.

69. Testimony of John G. Wilkins, Director of Tax Policy for Economic Analysis, Coopers and Lybrand, before the House Committee on Ways and Means, hearing on factors affecting U.S. international competitiveness, July 18, 1991.

70. Bureau of Economic Analysis, Department of Commerce (1991).

cannot be reduced by any legislation unless the legislation somehow reduces businesses' costs. The Committee received virtually unequivocal testimony that enactment of bills such as S. 640 will not have any such effect.

First, the insurance industry testified before the Committee about the identical predecessor to S. 640 in no uncertain terms that " * * * the bill is likely to have little or no beneficial impact on the frequency and severity of product liability claims. * * * [I]t is not likely to reduce insurance claim costs or improve the insurance market." [71]

No explanation has been offered, and none could logically be offered, for any way in which a bill could improve competitiveness if it does not reduce product liability claims or costs. As J. Robert Hunter, President of the National Insurance Consumer Organization, testified, "[m]ake no mistake about it, if insurance costs and availability are not improved, competitiveness is not affected." [72]

Indeed, that the bill will not have its purported effects becomes clear when its actual impact is reviewed. For example, it is claimed that the bill will provide additional uniformity in product liability law nationwide. However, the bill only selectively preempts State law, leaving much of State law in place to be interpreted with the new Federal law. Additionally, it provides a Federal rule of law to be interpreted by both the State and the Federal courts, although the State courts are not bound by the decisions of Federal courts other than the Supreme Court.

As Professor Eisenberg testified,

> * * * for a period of time, at least, predictability may be reduced rather than increased. Each state will have to decide the scope of S. 1400's [the identical predecessor to S. 640] preemption and its relation to state tort law. The interaction between state and federal law in tort will be made more rather than less complex. * * * [U]niformity will not be quickly, if ever, achieved. * * *. [W]e are at risk of having not just 55 jurisdictions but an additional dozen federal courts of appeals making products law. At least before enactment of S. 1400 the [federal] courts of appeals should have felt bound by state law. Until the Supreme Court speaks, it is not clear that state supreme courts would or should be bound by federal interpretations of S. 1400 as it interacts with the relevant state law.[73] With respect to punitive damages, S. 640 provides a

---

71. Testimony of Deborah T. Ballen, Vice President for Policy Development and Research, American Insurance Association, at Consumer Subcommittee Hearing on S. 1400, April 5, 1990, transcript p. 110.

72. Testimony of J. Robert Hunter, President, National Insurance Consumer Organization, Consumer Subcommittee hearings on S. 1400, April 5, 1990, at 132.

73. Testimony of Professor Theodore Eisenberg, Cornell Law School, Responses to post-hearing questions of Senator Rockefeller at 3. See also Note, "Authority in State Court of Lower Federal Court Decisions on

standard of proof for punitive damages that is more restrictive than that in many states. However, punitive damages are not a significant factor in product liability cases. As Professor Eisenberg has stated, "[t]here is a widespread perception that punitive damages are awarded frequently and in great amounts. Yet every serious study of the area finds that punitive damage awards are relatively infrequent, that they usually are commensurate with the defendant's wrongdoing and that they bear a substantial relationship to the size of the compensatory awards. * * * [P]unitive damages are awarded in not more than one percent of filed cases. * * *"[74] The 1989 GAO Report also looked at punitive damages, and found that, on the few occasions when they were awarded, their amount had a high correlation with the amount of compensatory damages.[75]

In fact, regardless of the scope of the product liability legislation enacted, the record indicates that it will be ineffective in reducing product liability insurance costs. For example, Florida passed very strong changes in its tort law in 1986, and also required the insurance industry to make rate filings indicating the effect of the changes on its rates. The Florida law eliminated joint and several liability, limited noneconomic damages to $450,000, and limited punitive damages. Nevertheless, when Aetna's rate filing came in, it listed the effect of each change on its rates as "zero."[76] There was no change in insurance costs, despite the dramatic changes in tort law, and we could expect none with enactment of S. 640.

When this is pointed out, the supporters of the bill often fall back on "transaction costs," and suggest that the bill may not reduce damages paid but will reduce transaction costs, or the costs of litigation such as attorneys' fees. Of course, if transaction costs were reduced, they should be reflected in reduced insurance costs, and insurance costs will not be reduced by this bill. In any event, the available evidence demonstrates that the bill will not reduce transaction costs, either.

GAO has stated unequivocally:

> [w]e believe that S. 1400 [the bill in the 101st Congress identical to S. 640] is unlikely to reduce transaction costs in product liability suits. For cases that are litigated, the procedural features of the tort system would not be changed by the bill. It is also not clear that the bill provides strong incentives for alternative dispute resolution, which could cut litigation costs. Moreover, the alternative dispute resolution mechanisms that may be used are left to the

---

National Law," 48 Columbia L.Rev. 943, 954 (1948); Stern and Grossman, *Supreme Court Practice* (5th ed. 1978) at 280; *Testa v. Katt*, 330 U.S. 386 (1947).

74. Testimony of Professor Theodore Eisenberg, Responses to Post-hearing questions of Senator Rockefeller *supra*, at 4-6 and authorities cited therein.

75. 1989 GAO Report, supra, at 27.

76. Testimony of J. Robert Hunter, *supra*, transcript at 135.

discretion of the states. If these mechanisms are not binding, then they may add to rather than substitute for litigation. If this happened, costs could actually increase.

GAO went on to note that transaction costs are largely a function of the length of litigation, and that delays caused by defendants are common. However, if a complete and accurate record is necessary to insure a fair outcome of the case, "lengthy litigation and its attendant costs might be justified." [77]

One justification offered for Federal product liability legislation in that legal fees paid to plaintiffs' attorneys are too high. However, this bill would not have any effect on attorneys fees. In any event, it is important to understand the value of the current system of compensation for plaintiffs' attorneys. Plaintiffs' lawyers who accept product liability cases work on a contingency fee basis. If they win the case they get a percentage of the case (which is usually about 30 percent); if they lose, they get nothing. This system allows injured plaintiffs who are not wealthy to obtain a lawyer. At the same time, the system acts as a deterrent to frivolous cases because attorneys are spending their own time and money in the case.

Figures from the Institute for Civil Justice state that plaintiffs receive approximately one-half of the cost of litigation.[78] Any problem with the cost of the system is not with the cost of the attorney who is "investing" his or her own time and money to win a case. The problem is with the defense attorney who has an incentive to delay the case with dilatory motions, and thereby encourage severely injured plaintiffs to settle for less in order to get an expedited payment of the plaintiff's medical and other costs. Meanwhile, the company is making interest on money that would otherwise be in the hands of the prevailing plaintiff.

Moreover, defendants' attorneys are apparently better paid, on average, than plaintiffs' attorneys. According to calculations derived from a 1977 survey conducted by the Insurance Services Office, for every dollar paid to claimants, insurers paid an average of an additional 42 cents in defense costs, while for every dollar awarded to a plaintiff, the plaintiff pays an average contingent fee of 33 cents out of that dollar.[79] Thus, in cases in which plaintiffs prevail, out of each $1.42 spent on litigation, half of that goes to attorneys' fees, with defendants' attorneys, on average, paid better than plaintiffs' attorneys. Of course, defendants' attorneys are paid regardless of the outcome of

---

77. Testimony of Joseph F. Delfico, Director, Income Security Issues, General Accounting Office, Consumer Subcommittee Hearing on S. 1400, February 22, 1990 in response to post-hearing questions of Senator Bryan at 2.

78. Id. at 2-3.

79. Hearing before the Subcommittee on Trade, Productivity and Economic Growth of the House Joint Economic Committee, 99th Congress 2d Sess. (1986) (Statement of James S. Kakalik).

the case, while plaintiffs' attorneys are paid only if they win their case. Otherwise, they take a loss for the time and expenses they have incurred. Thus, existing transaction costs are not inappropriate, and in any event would not be reduced by this bill.

The facts lead to the conclusion that no reduction in costs will occur through changes in the current tort liability system, and thus that no competitive advantage for American business can result.

VII. The Product Liability System Does Not Stifle Innovation, but Can Encourage Innovations in Safety.

Another theme sounded in support of the bill this year is that the current system deters innovation, and discourages new products from being brought to market. Of course, this effect is, by its nature, somewhat subjective and very difficult to examine. However, witnesses at the Consumer Subcommittee hearing examined the effects of the tort system on the chemical industry. In this case study, they noted that desirable innovation must mean safe innovation, and that if the tort system discourages unsafe innovation, that is valuable. They also found that, even in the chemical industry in which manufacturers pay a minuscule percentage of the costs of the injuries caused by their products, the tort system works to encourage the innovation of safer products.[80]

Business can, and often does, say it is discouraged from bringing innovative products to market, but they do not say what those products were, so the claim cannot be analyzed. However, the actual products that have been cited by witnesses in support of this claim subsequently had legitimate questions raised about their safety. In such cases, until such questions are resolved, we do not think we should presume that the product liability system has not worked properly to keep those products from the market.

Some examples of products cited as unfairly kept from the market by the system are set out below, together with the facts as they developed through the Committee's hearing process.

Monsanto Asbestos Substitute—Calcium sodium metaphosphate was cited by several supporters of S. 640 as a primary example of a safe product kept from the market by the product liability system. However, an Environmental Protection Agency (EPA) Status Report dated August 19, 1986, reviewed studies of this product submitted by Monsanto, and stated that "EPA believes that the evidence obtained from Monsanto's * * * study in rats offers reasonable support for the conclusion that calcium sodium metaphosphate fibers can cause cancer." (Report p. 9). Dr. Philip Landrigan, Chairman, Department of Community Medicine, Mt. Sinai Medical Center, reviewed the EPA and Monsanto documents, and stated: "I am extremely concerned about the

---

[80]. Ashford and Stone, *supra*, at 415, 417.

potential carcinogenicity of sodium calcium metaphosphate."[81] Monsanto's CEO, Richard Mahoney, subsequently wrote to the Committee stating that later tests of the fiber showed no evidence of health problems, that the first test was not done to determine the health risk to humans, and that the product was kept off the market solely because of concerns about "unwarranted litigation".[82] However, this letter does not explain why the first test would have been done if not to examine risks to human health.

Copper 7 IUD—Supporters of S. 640 claim that this product, although safe, was taken off the market because of unwarranted product liability suits. The court in *Kociemba v. Searle*, 707 F.Supp. 1517 (D.Minn.1989), (settled w/out appeal), a Copper 7 case, stated that the plaintiff "presented evidence which would have allowed a reasonable jury to conclude that defendant knowingly placed millions of American women, especially [women who have not had children], at risk of serious infection, loss of fertility, and surgery for removal of internal organs" and that "responsibility for this conduct was shared throughout defendant's corporate hierarchy, and that the conduct continued for over ten years." Michael Ciresi, the lawyer who litigated many Copper 7 cases for plaintiffs, has written to the Committee stating that his firm spent millions of dollars on discovery of documents that Searle resisted through litigation to the Supreme Court. Cases litigated before completion of that discovery were not successful because of the lack of documentation. According to Mr. Ciresi, the documents ultimately obtained demonstrated that the company knew the product was dangerous to women who have never had children, but continued to market the product to those women. That action was the basis for punitive damages against the company.[83]

Sturm Ruger "Old Model" Single Action Revolver—This product was cited as one which was the victim of unreasonable verdicts based on injuries that were really due to plaintiff negligence. However, documents submitted at the Committee's May 10, 1990, hearing demonstrated that since 1962 Ruger had received reports of serious injuries and deaths resulting from accidental discharges of this gun. In 1968, the gun failed a test for accidental discharge performed by the Bureau of Alcohol, Tobacco and Firearms, and it subsequently failed Ruger's own tests. Ruger did not redesign the gun to add a transfer bar safety device until 1973, and estimated that between 1968 and 1973 more than 150,000 "old models" were sold. Bill Ruger, CEO of the company, testified during product liability litigation that no safety device was put

---

81. S. Rep. No. 476, 98th Cong., 2d Sess. 7 (1984) (citing Insurance Services Office, Product Liability Closed Claim Survey: A Technical Analysis of Survey Results at 11 (1977).

82. Letter from Richard Mahoney to Senator Richard H. Bryan dated May 17, 1990, reprinted in record of Consumer Subcommittee Hearing on S. 1400, May 10, 1990.

83. Statement of Michael Ciresi, submitted for record of Consumer Subcommittee hearing on S. 1400, April 5, 1990.

on the gun because a revolver "is supposed to be designed in the traditional way." The Court in *Sturm Ruger v. Day,* 594 P.2d 38 (Alaska 1979) found Ruger liable for punitive damages for failure to add a safety device. According to testimony before the Committee, by 1989 about 230 product liability claims had been filed against Ruger for this defect, but the gun has never been recalled.[84]

Puritan–Bennett Anesthesia Gas Machines—This was cited by some witnesses as a product unjustly removed from the market by the product liability system. The machines were implicated in four deaths in 1983–84 hearings in the House Subcommittee on Oversight and Investigations, September 24, 1984, found that the company failed to notify the Food Drug Administration (FDA) of deaths that were caused by an overdose of anesthesia due to swelling of "O" rings and resultant sticking of a valve. This problem was known in the 1970s, and reflected in an appendix to the 1979 voluntary standard for anesthesia machines. The FDA, testifying before the subcommittee in 1984, stated that the company "appears * * * [to have] failed to conduct adequate design review of certain critical components" including use of certain rubber-like materials in the presence of high concentrations of anesthetic gas. The company instituted a limited recall, and the FDA required the recall extended to all valves distributed through July 1984.[85]

CJ–5 and CJ–7 Jeeps—These vehicles were cited by hearing witnesses as examples of products subjected to unjust litigation. In response to this assertion, other witnesses said that these Jeeps are designed with narrow track width, a high center of gravity, and short length, and consequently have a propensity to roll over, even at low speeds. The Federal Trade Commission (FTC) in 1982 issued a complaint charging AMC with unfair and deceptive advertising because the Jeeps were portrayed as safe for reckless, off-road driving. The Insurance Institute for Highway Safety found these Jeeps to have a rollover risk between 12 and 19 times greater than regular passenger vehicles. Testimony indicated that AMC continually denied any problem, and continued to market the Jeeps until they were subjected to product liability suits. This model Jeep has now been taken off the market.[86]

Ortho Contraceptives—Witnesses at the Committee's hearings claimed these products were unfairly subjected to product liability actions, citing *Wooderson v. Ortho,* 681 P.2d 1038, cert. denied 105 S.Ct. 365 (1984). It was claimed that, in that case, the company was held liable for failure to warn even though the FDA had determined that the

---

84. Supplemental Statement of Linda Lipsen, submitted for record of Consumer Subcommittee Hearing on S. 1400, May 10, 1990.

85. Supplemental statement of Linda Lipsen, *supra,* reprinted in record of Consumer Subcommittee Hearing on S. 1400, May 10, 1990.

86. Supplemental Lipsen statement, *supra,* reprinted in record of Consumer Subcommittee Hearing on S. 1400, May 10, 1990.

warning was not necessary. However, an examination of the Court's decision reveals that the Court held that there was no clear determination by the FDA as to whether such a warning was necessary, so that the defense was not valid. Ortho was held liable by the Court for punitive damages because it ignored substantial evidence that its product caused renal failure.

Taking all the evidence presented on both sides of these issues, we are not prepared to conclude that the current product liability system is not working properly to insure the safety of new products.

S. 640 IS SUBSTANTIVELY FLAWED

Enactment of S. 640 would amount to legislation which dramatically revises our current legal system without any serious factual predicate for such a change. In addition to this flaw as a matter of policy, it has numerous substantive legal problems. A few examples are set out below.

I. Non-uniform Selective Preemption

S. 640 is touted as a move toward a more uniform system of product liability law through Federal preemption of State law. It is important to look carefully at how this preemption would work, because it is not uniform, and, more significantly, it is one-way preemption. It covers only certain areas of State law and, in those areas it addresses, it revises the law only in the States that currently have law favorable to the plaintiffs. It would leave the State law intact if that State law currently favors defendants.

For example, section 303 of the bill purports to establish "Uniform Standards For Award of Punitive Damages." It establishes the burden of proof for punitive damages, and provides a defense to punitive damages for drugs or aircraft that have been approved by Federal authorities. However, by its terms, it applies to punitive damages only "if otherwise permitted by applicable law. * * *" Thus, in States which have, through State law, eliminated or limited punitive damages, this bill would not restore the availability of such damages. In some States, there would be no right to punitive damages; in some States they would be capped at a stated amount; and in others they would be available if the burden of proof in S. 640 is met. We do not call that uniformity in the law of punitive damages. If we truly wanted uniformity we would, at a minimum, restore punitive damages in the States that have limited them so that the law would be consistent nationwide.

Another example of this selective preemption of State law is in the area of joint and several liability for damages. Section 306 states that "the liability of each defendant for noneconomic damages shall be several only and shall not be joint." However, it does not restore the availability of full noneconomic damages in States in which such damages have been capped at a certain amount. It does not restore joint and several liability for economic damages in States in which such liability has been limited by State law. So, again, we will not have uniform nationwide law on joint and several liability. We will have some States that have no joint and several liability, some that have joint and several liability only in certain circumstances, and some that follow the rule of S. 640.

Additionally, the bill provides a Federal rule of law to be interpreted by both the State and the Federal courts, although the State courts are not bound by the decisions of Federal courts other than the Supreme Court.

As Professor Eisenberg testified on the identical predecessor to S. 640,

> * * * for a period of time, at least, predictability may be reduced rather than increased. Each state will have to decide the scope of S. 1400's preemption and its relation to state tort law. The interaction between state and federal law in tort will be made more rather than less complex * * * [U]niformity will not be quickly, if ever, achieved. * * * [We] are at risk of having not just 55 jurisdictions but an additional dozen federal courts of appeals making products law. At least before enactment of S. 1400 the [federal] courts of appeals should have felt bound by state law. Until the Supreme Court speaks, it is not clear that state supreme courts would or should be bound by federal interpretations of S. 1400 as it interacts with the relevant state law.[87]

II. Defense Based On FDA Or FAA Approval

Section 303 creates an absolute defense to the award of punitive damages ("[p]unitive damages shall not be awarded") if a drug or medical device has received pre-market approval by the FDA (so long as that approval was not based on misrepresentations or bribes by the manufacturer to the FDA). Section 303 also creates an absolute defense against punitive damages for aircraft if the aircraft were subject to pre-market certification by the Federal Aviation Administration (FAA). In effect, this section makes the FDA and the FAA the first and last line of defense against manufacturer misconduct that is harmful to consumers. These agencies were never created to function in this manner, and there are numerous examples of their inability to afford this protection to consumers. Federal standards are minimum standards in most cases, and it is inappropriate to establish categorical-

---

87. Testimony of Professor Theodore Eisenberg, Cornell Law School, Responses to post-hearing questions of Senator Rockefeller at 3. See also Note, "authority in State Court of Lower Federal Court Decisions on National Law," 48 Columbia L.Rev. 943, 954 (1948); Stern and Grossman, Supreme Court Practice (5th ed. 1978) at 280; *Testa v. Katt*, 330 U.S. 386 (1947).

ly this level as the only necessary level of safety that must be met in all cases.

A. Food and Drug Administration

The House Subcommittee on Human Resources and Intergovernmental Relations has devoted considerable time and resources, from 1983 to the present, conducting extensive investigations into the FDA's activities with respect to particular drugs. The Chairman of that Subcommittee, Congressman Ted Weiss, has written to the Committee expressing serious concern about section 303 of S. 1400 [the identical predecessor to S. 640] stating: "I believe that any proposal that would deprive parties injured by drugs and devices of punitive damages relief currently provided by State law would diminish manufacturers' incentives to produce safer products, thereby putting consumers at greater risk." [88]

Congressman Weiss' letter contains numerous examples of drugs which were approved by the FDA despite the existence in FDA files of information about harmful effects of the drug. For example:

> The FDA failed to review all significant safety information *in its possession* concerning the new drug *Oraflex* prior to approving the drug for marketing. FDA had received several reports of Oraflex-associated liver and kidney disease during premarket clinical trials of the drug. Nevertheless, the agency approved labeling that * * * mentioned nothing about liver disease and * * * denied altogether any evidence of kidney disease * * *" [89] Only 3 months following FDA approval, the manufacturer withdrew Oraflex from the market after it was implicated in numerous reports of serious and sometimes fatal liver and kidney disease.[90]

Similarly, the FDA approved the new drug Versed, a sedative, in 1985, at doses that were substantially higher than those shown to be effective in published studies dating back to 1982, and without knowing how the drug was regulated in foreign countries. The FDA finally lowered the recommended dose in 1987 to levels that had been in effect in Europe for several years.[91]

The defense established by S. 640 also overlooks the fact that "important evidence regarding drug safety problems sometimes does

---

88. Letter dated May 7, 1990, from Congressman Ted Weiss, Chairman, Subcommittee on Human Resources and Intergovernmental Relations of the Committee on Government Operations, to Senator Ernest F. Hollings, Chairman Committee on Commerce, Science, and Transportation, at 1. Letter available in Consumer Subcommittee files.

89. Weiss letter, *supra*, at 2 (emphasis in original). *See also* H.R.Rep. No. 98–511, "Deficiencies in FDA's Regulation of the New Drug 'Oraflex'," 98th Cong., 1st Sess. (1983), at 4–6.

90. Weiss letter, *supra*, at 2. *See also* H.R.Rep. No. 98–511, *supra*, at 8–13.

91. Weiss letter, *supra*, at 2. *See also*, H.R.Rep. 100–1086, "FDA's Deficient Regulation of the New Drug Versed," 100th Cong., 2d Sess. (1988), at 10–27.

not surface until after FDA approval."[92] Indeed, GAO recently issued a report on this issue which contained some alarming statistics. GAO found that:

> * * * of the 198 drugs approved by FDA between 1976 and 1985 for which data were available, 102 (or 51.5 percent) had serious postapproval risks, as evidenced by labeling changes or withdrawal from the market. * * * The serious postapproval risks are adverse reactions that could lead to hospitalization, increases in the length of hospitalization, severe or permanent disability, or death.[93]

These are only a few of the examples which amply demonstrate why we cannot responsibly rely only on the FDA to protect consumers from all the dangers of drugs. It is argued that S. 640 only protects manufacturers from the award of *punitive* damages, and that this is reasonable once they have achieved FDA approval for their product. It is certainly true that, in many cases in which defective drugs are approved by the FDA, the manufacturer should not be held liable for punitive damages. Indeed, awards of punitive damages in product liability cases are exceedingly rare.[94] However, problems with drugs that have achieved FDA approval are prevalent, and there are documented cases in which the manufacturers' misconduct was a primary factor in the continued marketing of such products.[95]

Given these facts, it is unreasonable to conclude, as S. 640 does, that there could never be circumstances in which punitive damages should not be awarded for pharmaceutical manufacturers' misconduct. The proper course is to leave that decision where it is now—with the jury and the court.

B. FAA

Similarly, it would be inappropriate to eliminate any potential for punitive damages for aircraft based on FAA approval of the aircraft design. The possibility of punitive damages provides an important deterrent which helps insure that manufacturers police themselves, and do not rely on the FAA to uncover any defects. Moreover, the FAA is required to set only minimum safety standards "in the interest of safety". *See* 49 U.S.C. 1423(a)(1). The FAA also has a duty "to promote air commerce." 49 U.S.C. 1346. Thus, the FAA arguably may

---

92. Weiss letter, *supra*, at 2.

93. U.S. General Accounting Office, "FDA Drug Review: Postapproval Risks 1976–85," GAO/PEMD–90–15 (April 1990) at 3.

94. Landes and Posner, "New Light on Punitive Damages," (October 1986). *See also*, Public Citizen's Congress Watch, et al., "The 'FDA Excuse'" (May 1990) at 3; Notes 54 and 55, *supra*.

95. For example, the evidence is strong that the Copper 7 IUD, which was approved by the FDA, was known to the manufacturer to pose dangers for women who had not had children but continued to be marketed by the manufacturer to such women for many years. The Court reviewing this conduct upheld the award of punitive damages. *See, Kociemba v. Searle*, 707 F.Supp. 1517 (D.Minn.1989) (settled without appeal); "The 'FDA Excuse'", *supra*, at 1–2; Letter of Michael Ciresi, *supra*.

balance safety standards against the interests of commerce. Moreover, compliance with FAA standards indicates no more than that the manufacturer performed the minimum required. *See Wilson v. Piper Aircraft Corp.*, 577 P.2d 1322 (D.Or.1978).

Additionally, there are real questions about the effectiveness of the FAA's safety inspection management system. GAO, in a report released on November 13, 1989, is extremely critical of this system, noting that: "[i]nadequate oversight of the inspection program resulted in (1) FAA headquarters management's being upward that its inspection policies were not always followed by local FAA staff and (2) inaccurate reporting to Congress of FAA achievements." [96]

The effect of this inadequate inspection system on the defects in aircraft was recently recognized by the Chairman of Cessna Aircraft who stated that: "[W]ith tougher airworthiness requirements implemented aggressively by the FAA, and with type-specific flight standards, I believe it is realistic to reduce the level of accidents by at least 50 percent." [97] If even the aircraft manufacturers believe there is room for a 50-percent improvement from the FAA, it would not be appropriate to leave the FAA as the only line of defense for the safety of the flying public. We must require continued maximum vigilance from the manufacturers themselves.

III. Statute of Repose

Section 304(b) of the bill would bar liability for any harm caused by a capital good more than 25 years after its original delivery. This would shield from liability a significant number of products in use. Howard Fark, a member of the Board of Directors of the National Machine Tool Builders Association, testified that over 50 percent of the claims filed against machine tool builders involve machines over 25 years old.[98]

It is argued that, if machines are defective, the defects will show up before the expiration of a 25-year period, so that manufacturers typically should not be liable for such products after that time. We have no reason to dispute that, but, by the same token, there has been no demonstration that there could never be a defective 26-year-old product. As long as that possibility exists, it is appropriate to leave the responsibility to decide who should be liable for harm from a product where it now exists in most States—with the jury and the court.

96. U.S. General Accounting Office, "FAA's Inspection Management System," GAO/RCED 90-36 (November 1989) at 8.

97. AOPA (Aircraft Owners and Pilots Association) "Pilot" magazine, "G.A. Manufacturers Propose New Inspections," (June 1989).

98. Testimony of Howard Fark, Vice President, Minster Machine Company, Response to Post-Hearing Questions of Senator Rockefeller at question 2, Consumer Subcommittee Hearing on S. 1400, February 22, 1990.

It is also often suggested that this will be a proplaintiff change in the law, since some States have statutes of repose shorter than 25 years. What those suggestions do not say is that only 17 States, a small minority, has any statute of repose.[99] This is not a proplaintiff change, because it would enact statutes of repose in the vast majority of States that currently have chosen not to have such bars to filing suit.

IV. Worker's Compensation Offset

Section 305 purports to establish uniform standards for offset of worker's compensation. Among other things, it would do away with the traditional lien on awards of damages from third-party manufacturers that is currently available to employers who have paid workers' compensation payments for an injury. This provision is opposed, and understandably so, by the National Association of Stevedores, the Association of General Contractors, and the Shipbuilders Council of America, among others, who point out that it shifts these costs, without justification, from manufacturers to the industry that uses machinery and equipment.[100]

It has been recognized that the workers' compensation insurance systems in many states are having difficulty meeting their financial obligations.[101] The cost-shifting required by S. 640 only will exacerbate that problem for the no-fault workers' compensation system in the vain hope of reducing the costs of the tort system for third-party manufacturers.

This cost-shifting also will affect the federal government in its position as employer, because it will be unable to obtain reimbursement from liable third parties for payments made to workers under the Federal Employees Compensation Act and the Longshoremen and Harbor Workers' Compensation Act.[102] The Congressional Budget Office has stated that, in a 2-year period, the Government recovered $9 million in such situations from liens against liable third parties. At least a sizable portion of that money will be lost to the Government under this bill.

V. Alternative Dispute Resolution

Section 202 purports to encourage parties to use alternative mechanisms of resolving cases prior to going to court. That may sound good,

---

99. Only 17 states currently have valid statutes of repose in effect. In those states, the statutes of repose are typically shorter than 25 years. However, the majority of states have not enacted such statutes and, in some states, the statutes have been struck down as conflicting with state constitutional rights to access to the courts or equal protection. *See, e.g., Danguard v. Baltic Cooperative Building Supply Association*, 349 N.W.2d 419 (S.D.1984); *Heath v. Sears, Roebuck & Co.*, 464 A.2d 288 (N.H. 1983).

100. Testimony of Thomas D. Wilcox, Executive Director and General Counsel, National Association of Stevedores, Consumer Subcommittee Hearing on S. 1400, May 10, 1990, statement at 2.

101. *Id.* at 2–3.

102. *Id.* at 1–2.

but in the heavy-handed way that it is written, this provision really discourages parties from exercising their constitutional right to a trial by jury. It creates a presumption that if a party refuses to pursue alternatives to trial, exercises his or her right to trial by jury, and loses his or her case, that party has not acted in good faith and may be required to pay the litigation costs of the other party.

As Consumer Subcommittee testimony from the South Carolina Jury Trial Foundation pointed out, we must be particularly vigilant about inroads into the constitutional trial by jury.

> From its inception as a safeguard of individual liberty in the Magna Carta, those who would wield the tools of tyranny have tried to undermine or destroy the institution of trial by jury. King John attempted to revoke the Magna Carta. Henry VIII and Elizabeth I would have abolished it if they could. Charles I circumvented jury trials through the Star Chamber. * * * George III denied the right of trial by jury to colonists through expansion of the jurisdiction of admiralty courts and the state of Rhode Island attempted to deny the right altogether in suits under the State Bank Act.[103]

As the representative of the South Carolina Jury Trial Foundation further pointed out, "[c]an I guarantee my intimidated client that if he declines a defendant's offer to arbitrate and exercises his constitutional right to a civil jury trial he will not wind up having to pay the attorney's fees of a small army of Philadelphia lawyers?"[104] Section 202 of S. 640 creates too great a risk that, by exercising the right to a jury trial, an injured party can be punished for acting "unreasonably" or in "bad faith" and thereby required to pay defendants' costs.[105] This same party could run the same risks under section 201 of S. 640, which creates "incentives" for accepting settlement proposals, by requiring the payment of costs if the case is litigated and the claimant receives less than the settlement offer.[106] These provisions create a chilling effect on the exercise of the Seventh Amendment right to trial by jury which is unacceptable in our system of government.[107]

As testimony at the Consumer Subcommittee from the South Carolina Jury Trial Foundation demonstrated, an injured consumer, often without resources, can hardly risk the possibility that he or she may have to pay the legal fees of a corporate defendant in order to allow his or her case to be heard by a jury. By requiring plaintiffs to run that risk or forgo their right to trial, S. 640 runs counter to the

---

103. Testimony of J. Kendell Few at Consumer Subcommittee hearing on S. 640, September 19, 1991, statement at 21–22.
104. Id. at 23–4.
105. Id. at 6.
106. Id. at 5–6.
107. Id. at 1.

Seventh Amendment of the Constitution."[108]

That these provisions have a chilling effect on the exercise of plaintiffs' constitutional rights is made even more clear by sections 102(5) and 103 of S. 640. In those sections, the authors of the bill have excepted from its provisions all commercial cases. Thus, in cases in which businesses will sue other businesses, they will not face these barriers to exercise their Seventh Amendment rights. However, they would require injured consumers to accept burdens that they themselves do not want to bear in their own litigation. Not only is this provision counter to the Constitution, but it creates a double standard— one for consumers as plaintiffs and one for businesses as plaintiffs— and, needless to say, the consumer suffers.

As the South Carolina Jury Trial Foundation testified before the Committee, "[i]t has been an elemental concept of constitutional law * * * that any infringement of the Bill of Rights, however slight, is a violation of the clearly written constitutional rights of every American citizen."[109] As Winston Churchill said in 1956, "[t]he jury system has come to stand for all we mean by English justice. The scrutiny of 12 honest jurors provides defendant and plaintiff alike a safeguard from arbitrary perversion of the law."[110]

The proponents of this bill attempt to justify it as a "national necessity," claiming that manufacturers cannot compete in a world economy without these infringements on the Constitution. As testimony before the Committee pointed out, that was also the primary excuse for the exercise of arbitrary power in the Star Chamber, and was the reason why Germany scrapped its jury system in 1924. As Hudson's Treatise on the Star Chamber put it, "if those of the poorer sort" bring suits, there is a presumption that they are "clamorous", and then the poor must pay the rich man's costs "if they prove not the bill."[111] That attitude is found in S. 640 as well. Surely this type of infringement upon the Seventh Amendment is not necessary in order to allow our industry to compete in world markets. Such a sacrifice on the altar of competitiveness must not be made.

CONCLUSION

A Committee of the United States Senate should not report legislation to federalize product liability tort law without any comprehensive data to demonstrate (1) that such legislation is necessary, and (2) that such legislation will work.

---

108. Testimony of J. Kendell Few, Consumer Subcommittee Hearing on S. 640, September 19, 1991, transcript at 98–99.

109. Few testimony, *supra*, statement at 10.

110. *Id.* at 19.

111. *Id.* at 33, citing Hudson, "A Treatise on the Court of Star Chamber," (1792) reprinted by Legal Classics Library 1986, at 130.

Do we know what we are getting into? Based on the scant evidence provided by the proponents of this legislation, the answer to that question is: "obviously not." We do know that enactment of this legislation would not affect insurance premiums of this legislation would not affect insurance premiums or businesses' product liability costs, S. 640 will not make American businesses more competitive, and may actually undermine current levels of product safety. We are not going to solve the problems of U.S. business with legislation of this type, and in fact, we run the risk of harming the consumer. The bill should be rejected.

MINORITY VIEWS OF SENATOR FORD

S. 640 should be rejected because it would unjustifiably intrude upon settled State laws and significantly burden employers—particularly small businesses. The proponents of S. 640 argue that it is a "procompetitiveness" bill uniformly backed by the business community and opposed only by consumer groups and trial lawyers. However, we have seen significant opposition to the bill within the business community and particularly among small employers.

The premise of the bill is that Congress knows better than the States. The bill selects areas of product liability law for preemption without adequate consideration of the harm and confusion that will be caused by undoing settled law. It is for this reason that the Conference of Chief Justices and the National Conference of State Legislatures oppose the legislation. Many small businesses oppose it because it disturbs settled law that protects their rights under the workers' compensation and tort system.

S. 640 would repeal basic aspects of the workers' compensation systems of a majority of States, including Kentucky. A majority of States have long protected employers—and especially small businesses—from excessive workers' compensation costs by providing rights of subrogation. A worker injured by a defective product is entitled to fixed benefits from his or her employer, regardless of the employer's fault. The injured worker may, however, have a cause of action against a responsible third-party manufacturer. Under majority State law, this right becomes the right of the employer or insurance carrier that has paid the benefits. They can, therefore, recover at least a portion of the workers' compensation they have paid from the manufacturer whose defective product caused the damages to begin with.

These States have made the decision that their employers—particularly small businesses—should not bear the overwhelming burden of product-related workplace accidents. However, by taking away subrogation rights, S. 640 shifts all of these costs back to the employer. Under the bill, the employer cannot recover compensation paid even if that employer is only 1 percent at fault for a workplace injury and a third-party manufacturer is 99 percent at fault. The responsible third party would be liable only for the damages in excess of the workers' compensation award any time an employer fails to hire a lawyer, come into court, and prove that the manufacturer was no less than 100 percent at fault.

For many businesses the assertion of subrogation rights against the manufacturer of a defective product is an important safeguard against excessive workers' compensation costs. This loss of subrogation rights would be especially burdensome for small businesses whose main business is not the manufacturing of products, and self-insurers who cannot easily spread additional workers' compensation costs. Even without the increased burdens of S. 640, these businesses are struggling with the excessive costs of providing workers' compensation coverage.

S. 640 is particularly troubling in Kentucky because of Kentucky's State workers' compensation fund scheme. Kentucky has created a fund that will pay workers' compensation claims when employers are unable to do so. This fund is financed by tax revenues. S. 640 not only clearly takes away the subrogation rights of Kentucky employers and their insurance carriers, but it also appears to eliminate the similar rights of the State financed fund. If this is true, S. 640 would burden the financial strength of this fund and could lead to the prospect of increased taxes to maintain its current viability.

I object to any characteristics of S. 640 being a bill that will make American business more competitive. There is a significant segment of the business community opposed to S. 640 because the bill would result in increased costs on many businesses, especially small employers. In the case of Kentucky, S. 640 might result in further burdens on the State budget and the prospect of increased taxes.

We should not be in such a hurry to enact a law that will unsettle State law and inadvertently and unnecessarily burden our nation's employers, particularly entrepreneurs and small businesses.

MINORITY VIEWS OF SENATOR BREAUX

I oppose S. 640, the so-called Product Liability Fairness Act of 1991. I believe that this bill would be more properly termed the "Big Government Act of 1991" because of the way the bill tramples State law and State rights. The supporters of this bill apparently believe that when it comes to product liability laws, Washington knows better than the States, and Congress should make all the decisions. The reasoning that we, the Congress, know better than the States seems quite misplaced, considering especially that the States have been handling this area of the law for many, many years. I further find it ironic that the very same people who are supporting this intrusion into State rights and this interference with private business are the very same people who, when it comes to issues such as parental leave, are the first to argue that Washington should not interfere with State law or with the private sector.

S. 640 is further ill-advised because there is no evidence that it will accomplish the admirable goal of lowering insurance rates. In fact, many insurance companies have said to us that they cannot guarantee that they will lower their rates if this bill is passed. Some insurance companies, further, have opposed the legislation. We have not even seen credible evidence on the fundamental issue that existing product liability laws have even contributed to increased insurance rates. I find it somehow hard to believe that insurance rates will come down just because Washington takes over the law of product liability.

I am further unconvinced by Secretary Mosbacher's argument that this bill will make America "more competitive." Again, I find it hard to believe that having Washington take over will make America "more competitive." Furthermore, this argument makes no sense even on its own terms since, when an American company sells a product in a foreign country, that American company is governed by the product liability laws of that country. Similarly, when a foreign company sells a product in this country they are governed by our product liability laws. There are simply no competitive advantages of one over the other. Therefore, the so-called competitiveness argument in favor of Washington taking over this area from the States and from the private sector is unpersuasive.

I am also concerned about the precedent that we are setting by this bill. If Congress preempts States and the private sector on product liability, are we next going to preempt all other State tort laws? Are we going to preempt even the criminal laws of the States? Under the McCarran–Ferguson law, insurance is an area handled by the States. Are the supporters of this bill saying that we are going to overturn McCarran–Ferguson and have Congress decide insurance rates and how insurance policies ought to be written in each of the 50 States? Again, we should reject the concept that Washington knows best.

Additionally, and perhaps most egregiously, S. 640 may prove particularly harmful to small business employers. Section 305 of the bill, known as the Workers' Compensation Offset provision, does not seem to directly involve product liability at all. But again, this section involves complete preemption of settled majority State law. In the majority of States, including Louisiana, employers who pay compensation to injured employees are given rights of subrogation so that they may recover the amount of compensation they have paid when a third-party manufacturer is responsible for the injury. Section 305 of S. 640 would, for reasons not ever explained, shift all of these costs back to the employer. Needless to say, this would be burdensome for any employer, but it would be particularly burdensome for small businesses that are less able to spread these additional costs. Employers are already faced with dramatically increasing workers' compensation costs, partly because of the soaring costs of medical care, and to now add another burden on top of those costs seems ill-advised. I believe that the Congress should not do anything to make it more difficult for small businesses to survive, particularly given the difficult economic times that we are in.

We simply do not have enough information on the possible effects of S. 640, or whether any legislation in this area is needed at all. I believe that we should get more information on how this bill might effect insurance rates, and what impact the bill would have on employers, particularly small businesses. It seems that we have not done our homework. While I believe this legislation is ill-advised on its face, there is also little question that we have not taken the time to gather the necessary information before reporting this bill to the full Senate. I urge my colleagues to vote against S. 640.

EEC DIRECTIVE ON LIABILITY FOR DEFECTIVE PRODUCTS

COUNCIL DIRECTIVE
of
25 July 1985
on the approximation of the laws, regulations and administrative provisions of the Member States concerning liability for defective products

(85/374/EEC)

THE COUNCIL OF THE EUROPEAN COMMUNITIES,

Having regard to the Treaty establishing the European Economic Community, and in particular Article 100 thereof,

Having regard to the proposal from the Commission,

Having regard to the opinion of the European Parliament,

Having regard to the opinion of the Economic and Social Committee,

Whereas approximation of the laws of the Member States concerning the liability of the producer for damage caused by the defectiveness of his products is necessary because the existing divergences may distort competition and affect the movement of goods within the common market and entail a differing degree of protection of the consumer against damage caused by a defective product to his health or property;

Whereas liability without fault on the part of the producer is the sole means of adequately solving the problem, peculiar to our age of increasing technicality, of a fair apportionment of the risks inherent in modern technological production;

Whereas liability without fault should apply only to movables which have been industrially produced; whereas, as a result, it is appropriate to exclude liability for agricultural products and game, except where they have undergone a processing of an industrial nature which could cause a defect in these products; whereas the liability provided for in this Directive should also apply to movables which are used in the construction of immovables or are installed in immovables;

Whereas protection of the consumer requires that all producers involved in the production process should be made liable, in so far as their finished product, component part or any raw material supplied by them was defective; whereas, for the same reason, liability should extend to importers of products into the Community and to persons who present themselves as producers by affixing their name, trade mark or other distinguishing feature or who supply a product the producer of which cannot be identified;

Whereas, in situations where several persons are liable for the same damage, the protection of the consumer requires that the injured person should be able to claim full compensation for the damage from any one of them;

Whereas, to protect the physical well-being and property of the consumer, the defectiveness of the product should be determined by reference not to its fitness for use but to the lack of the safety which the public at large is entitled to expect; whereas the safety is assessed by excluding any misuse of the product not reasonable under the circumstances;

Whereas a fair apportionment of risk between the injured person and the producer implies that the producer should be able to free himself from liability if he furnishes proof as to the existence of certain exonerating circumstances;

Whereas the protection of the consumer requires that the liability of the producer remains unaffected by acts or omissions of other persons having contributed to cause the damage; whereas, however, the contributory negligence of the injured person may be taken into account to reduce or disallow such liability;

Whereas the protection of the consumer requires compensation for death and personal injury as well as compensation for damage to property; whereas the latter should nevertheless be limited to goods for private use or consumption and be subject to a deduction of a lower threshold of a fixed amount in order to avoid litigation in an excessive number of cases; whereas this Directive should not prejudice compensation for pain and suffering and other non-material damages payable, where appropriate, under the law applicable to the case;

Whereas a uniform period of limitation for the bringing of action for compensation is in the interests both of the injured person and of the producer;

Whereas products age in the course of time, higher safety standards are developed and the state of science and technology progresses; whereas, therefore, it would not be reasonable to make the producer liable for an unlimited period for the defectiveness of his product; whereas, therefore, liability should expire after a reasonable length of time, without prejudice to claims pending at law;

Whereas, to achieve effective protection of consumers, no contractual derogation should be permitted as regards the liability of the producer in relation to the injured person;

Whereas under the legal systems of the Member States an injured party may have a claim for damages based on grounds of contractual liability or on grounds of non-contractual liability other than that provided for in this Directive; in so far as these provisions also serve to attain the objective of effective protection of consumers, they should remain unaffected by this Directive; whereas, in so far as effective protection of consumers in the sector of pharmaceutical products is already also attained in a Member State under a special liability system, claims based on this system should similarly remain possible;

Whereas, to the extent that liability for nuclear injury or damage is already covered in all Member States by adequate special rules, it has been possible to exclude damage of this type from the scope of this Directive;

Whereas, since the exclusion of primary agricultural products and game from the scope of this Directive may be felt, in certain Member States, in view of what is expected for the protection of consumers, to restrict unduly such protection, it should be possible for a Member State to extend liability to such products;

Whereas, for similar reasons, the possibility offered to a producer to free himself from liability if he proves that the state of scientific and technical knowledge at the time when he put the product into circulation was not such as to enable the existence of a defect to be discovered may be felt in certain Member States to restrict unduly the protection of the consumer; whereas it should therefore be possible for a Member State to maintain in its legislation or to provide by new legislation that this exonerating circumstance is not admitted; whereas, in the case of new legislation, making use of this derogation should, however, be subject to a Community stand-still procedure, in order to raise, if possible, the level of protection in a uniform manner throughout the Community;

Whereas, taking into account the legal traditions in most of the Member States, it is inappropriate to set any financial ceiling on the producer's liability without fault; whereas, in so far as there are, however, differing traditions, it seems possible to admit that a Member State may derogate from the principle of unlimited liability by providing a limit for the total liability of the producer for damage resulting from a death or personal injury and caused by identical items with the same defect, provided that this limit is established at a level sufficiently high to guarantee adequate protection of the consumer and the correct functioning of the common market;

Whereas the harmonization resulting from this cannot be total at the present stage, but opens the way towards greater harmonization; whereas it is therefore necessary that the Council receive at regular intervals, reports from the Commission on the application of this Directive, accompanied, as the case may be, by appropriate proposals;

Whereas it is particularly important in this respect that a re-examination be carried out of those parts of the Directive relating to the derogations open to the Member States, at the expiry of a period of sufficient length to gather practical experience on the effects of these derogations on the protection of consumers and on the functioning of the common market,

HAS ADOPTED THIS DIRECTIVE:

Article 1

The producer shall be liable for damage caused by a defect in his product.

Article 2

For the purpose of this Directive "product" means all movables, with the exception of primary agricultural products and game, even though incorporated into another movable or into an immovable. "Primary agricultural products" means the products of the soil, of stock-farming and of fisheries, excluding products which have undergone initial processing. "Product" includes electricity.

Article 3

1. "Producer" means the manufacturer of a finished product, the producer of any raw material or the manufacturer of a component part and any person who, by putting his name, trade mark or other distinguishing feature on the product presents himself as its producer.

2. Without prejudice to the liability of the producer, any person who imports into the Community a product for sale, hire, leasing or any form of distribution in the course of his business shall be deemed to be a producer within the meaning of this Directive and shall be responsible as a producer.

3. Where the producer of the product cannot be identified, each supplier of the product shall be treated as its producer unless he informs the injured person, within a reasonable time, of the identity of the producer or of the person who supplied him with the product. The same shall apply, in the case of an imported product, if this product does not indicate the identity of the importer referred to in paragraph 2, even if the name of the producer is indicated.

Article 4

The injured person shall be required to prove the damage, the defect and the causal relationship between defect and damage.

Article 5

Where, as a result of the provisions of this Directive, two or more persons are liable for the same damage, they shall be liable jointly and severally, without prejudice to the provisions of national law concerning the rights of contribution or recourse.

EEC DIRECTIVE

Article 6

1. A product is defective when it does not provide the safety which a person is entitled to expect, taking all circumstances into account, including:

(a) the presentation of the product;

(b) the use to which it could reasonably be expected that the product would be put;

(c) the time when the product was put into circulation.

2. A product shall not be considered defective for the sole reason that a better product is subsequently put into circulation.

Article 7

The producer shall not be liable as a result of this Directive if he proves:

(a) that he did not put the product into circulation; or

(b) that, having regard to the circumstances, it is probable that the defect which caused the damage did not exist at the time when the product was put into circulation by him or that this defect came into being afterwards; or

(c) that the product was neither manufactured by him for sale or any form of distribution for economic purpose nor manufactured or distributed by him in the course of his business; or

(d) that the defect is due to compliance of the product with mandatory regulations issued by the public authorities; or

(e) that the state of scientific and technical knowledge at the time when he put the product into circulation was not such as to enable the existence of the defect to be discovered; or

(f) in the case of a manufacturer of a component, that the defect is attributable to the design of the product in which the component has been fitted or to the instructions given by the manufacturer of the product.

Article 8

1. Without prejudice to the provisions of national law concerning the right of contribution or recourse, the liability of the producer shall not be reduced when the damage is caused both by a defect in product and by the act or omission of a third party.

2. The liability of the producer may be reduced or disallowed when, having regard to all the circumstances, the damage is caused both by a defect in the product and by the fault of the injured person or any person for whom the injured person is responsible.

EEC DIRECTIVE

Article 9

For the purpose of Article 1, "damage" means:

(a) damage caused by death or by personal injuries;

(b) damage to, or destruction of, any item of property other than the defective product itself, with a lower threshold of 500 ECU, provided that the item of property:

  (i) is of a type ordinarily intended for private use or consumption, and
  (ii) was used by the injured person mainly for his own private use or consumption.

This Article shall be without prejudice to national provisions relating to non-material damage.

Article 10

1. Member States shall provide in their legislation that a limitation period of three years shall apply to proceedings for the recovery of damages as provided for in this Directive. The limitation period shall begin to run from the day on which the plaintiff became aware, or should reasonably have become aware, of the damage, the defect and the identity of the producer.

2. The laws of Member States regulating suspension or interruption of the limitation period shall not be affected by this Directive.

Article 11

Member States shall provide in their legislation that the rights conferred upon the injured person pursuant to this Directive shall be extinguished upon the expiry of a period of 10 years from the date on which the producer put into circulation the actual product which caused the damage, unless the injured person has in the meantime instituted proceedings against the producer.

Article 12

The liability of the producer arising from this Directive may not, in relation to the injured person, be limited or excluded by a provision limiting his liability or exempting him from liability.

Article 13

This Directive shall not affect any rights which an injured person may have according to the rules of the law of contractual or non-contractual liability or a special liability system existing at the moment when this Directive is notified.

Article 14

This Directive shall not apply to injury or damage arising from nuclear accidents and covered by international conventions ratified by the Member States.

Article 15

1. Each Member State may:

(a) by way of derogation from Article 2, provide in its legislation that within the meaning of Article 1 of this Directive "product" also means primary agricultural products and game;

(b) by way of derogation from Article 7(e), maintain or, subject to the procedure set out in paragraph 2 of this Article, provide in this legislation that the producer shall be liable even if he proves that the state of scientific and technical knowledge at the time when he put the product into circulation was not such as to enable the existence of a defect to be discovered.

2. A Member State wishing to introduce the measure specified in paragraph 1(b) shall communicate the text of the proposed measure to the Commission. The Commission shall inform the other Member States thereof.

The Member State concerned shall hold the proposed measure in abeyance for nine months after the Commission is informed and provided that in the meantime the Commission has not submitted to the Council a proposal amending this Directive on the relevant matter. However, if within three months of receiving the said information, the Commission does not advise the Member State concerned that it intends submitting such a proposal to the Council, the Member State may take the proposed measure immediately.

If the Commission does submit to the Council such a proposal amending this Directive within the aforementioned nine months, the Member State concerned shall hold the proposed measure in abeyance for a further period of 18 months from the date on which the proposal is submitted.

3. Ten years after the date of notification of this Directive, the Commission shall submit to the Council a report on the effect that rulings by the courts as to the application of Article 7(e) and of paragraph 1(b) of this Article have on consumer protection and the functioning of the common market. In the light of this report the Council, acting on a proposal from the Commission and pursuant to the terms of Article 100 of the Treaty, shall decide whether to repeal Article 7(e).

Article 16

1. Any Member State may provide that a producer's total liability for damage resulting from a death or personal injury and caused by identical items with the same defect shall be limited to an amount which may not be less than 70 million ECU.

EEC DIRECTIVE

2. Ten years after the date of notification of this Directive, the Commission shall submit to the Council a report on the effect on consumer protection and the functioning of the common market of the implementation of the financial limit on liability by those Member States which have used the option provided for in paragraph 1. In the light of this report the Council, acting on a proposal from the Commission and pursuant to the terms of Article 100 of the Treaty, shall decide whether to repeal paragraph 1.

Article 17
This Directive shall not apply to products put into circulation before the date on which the provisions referred to in Article 19 enter into force.

Article 18
1. For the purposes of this Directive, the ECU shall be that defined by Regulation (EEC) No 3180/78, as amended by Regulation (EEC) No 2626/84. The equivalent in national currency shall initially be calculated at the rate obtaining on the date of adoption of this Directive.
2. Every five years the Council, acting on a proposal from the Commission, shall examine and, if need be, revise the amounts in this Directive, in the light of economic and monetary trends in the Community.

Article 19
1. Member States shall bring into force, not later than three years from the date of notification of this Directive, the laws, regulations and administrative provisions necessary to comply with this Directive. They shall forthwith inform the Commission thereof.
2. The procedure set out in Article 15(2) shall apply from the date of notification of this Directive.

Article 20
Member States shall communicate to the Commission the texts of the main provisions of national law which they subsequently adopt in the field governed by this Directive.

Article 21
Every five years the Commission shall present a report to the Council on the application of this Directive and, if necessary, shall submit appropriate proposals to it.

Article 22
This Directive is addressed to the Member States.
Done at Brussels, 25 July 1985.

For the Council
The President
J. POOS

†